BOMBARDIER BILLY WELLS

BOMBARDIER BILLY WELLS
The life and times of a boxing hero

Stan Shipley

1993
Bewick Press
Tyne and Wear

First published in Great Britain by
Bewick Press
132 Claremont Road
Whitley Bay
Tyne and Wear
NE26 3TX

ISBN 0-9516056-6-6

Printed and bound in Great Britain by Mayfair Print
Group, William Street, Sunderland, SR1 1UL

For Raph Samuel and Ruskin College

i

CONTENTS

ACKNOWLEDGEMENTS

This work owes a lot to friends who all go back many years. I would first like to thank Pat Thane, of Goldsmiths' College, for her encouragement and invaluable advice on doctoral thesis writing, and Tony Mason, of University of Warwick, for numerous helpful and humorous chats. The earlier editors of *History Workshop Journal* gave me tremendous support as we all served an apprenticeship in people's history, and I thank that splendid collective. Mary Shipley, I thank for almost everything.

More recently, I received aid from Archie Potts of Bewick Press, whose cheerfulness is infectious; Christina Ball, who set text brilliantly, and Bill Shipley, who handled photography professionally. Thank you to all three.

Lastly, I would like to thank the staff at three libraries: Tower Hamlets Bancroft Library, especially Chris Lloyd; the National Army Museum in Chelsea, and British Newspaper Library at Colindale. It is a pleasure to research at such places. Mistakes, I claim them all because they're mine.

Stan Shipley,
Walthamstow. May 1993.

Sources of the illustrations, where not shown, are as follows: 1, Wells, *Modern Boxing*, 1911, this photograph was dropped in later editions; 4, Sims, *Living London*, vol. 3; 5, *Mirror of Life*, 14 Dec. 1912, 30 July 1910; 7, *Ibid.*, 12 Nov. 1910; 8 and 9, Lynch, *Complete*, 1913; 10 and 13, Fleischer, *Jack Dempsey*, 1929; 14, Carpentier, *My Methods*, 1913; 15, by courtesy of Willie Mahoney; 16, *Health & Strength*, 4 July 1914; 17 and 18, *Boxing*, 31 May 1922, 6 Dec. 1913; 21, St John Adcock, *Wonderful London*, vol. 1, 1928; 22, Moir, *Complete*, 1909, *Boxing*, 9 Nov. 1912; 23, Furniss, *By Ways*, 1919; 24 and 28, *Boxing*, 19 May 1920, 24 May 1922; 26, *Encyclopaedia of Sport & Games*, vol. 1, 1912; 27, Hare, *Gladiators*, 1925; 29, Palmer, *Recollections*, 1927; 30-32, Bill Shipley.

ILLUSTRATIONS

1

INTRODUCTION

There's a game some call the fight game
And some the noble art
Blokes who play this game need bags of courage, bags of
heart
It's a rough game, a tough game
Needing guts and skill
And you'll never make a boxer if you haven't got the will

from "The Fight Game", a radio ballad by Ewan MacColl and
Charles Parker, 1967.

Bombardier Billy Wells was British heavyweight boxing
champion from 1911 until 1919, the longest holder of this title until
1966, when Henry Cooper overtook him. Unlike many holders, such
as Bruce Woodcock and Joe Erskine, Wells had not won amateur
championships. When he landed at Southampton in 1910, he was
well known only among sporting enthusiasts in India.

Army boxing fell awkwardly between amateur and
professional. The Services ran competitions at every conceivable
level. They were along the lines of the Amateur Boxing Association,
with some gorgeous Regimental trophies, but they added small
money prizes for individuals. Other ranks never boxed officers for
where would discipline have gone? Officers, anyway, would seldom
have been good enough, for the Forces were well stocked with
pugnacious and athletic young men who had enlisted to get away
from dead-end jobs.

Wells was from Stepney in London's East End, and he would
have stood out anywhere. He was over six feet tall when several
inches less was considered to be a good height for men. With a fine
physique, distinguished face, and wavy fair hair he could have been
a model for Rodin, and those who disliked boxing admired Wells.

People who were paid to report the sport were hardly ever severe with him. In despair in April 1915 *Boxing* wrote:

> ... Never has any man been admired, courted, feted as this... Not on the strength of anything which he has ever done, but always on his *promise* to work all the miracles they need, and to prove himself a deity in very truth. The promise has been broken... and the disciples disappear, but they flock back again at his lightest whistle with their hope and faith as strong and fervent as ever.

The weekly newspaper, which was started in 1909 and is still being published, complained that Wells and his manager, Jim Maloney, took too few contests, and there was some justification in this argument.   After returning from India, Wells fought five contests in as many months.   In 1911, however, he had just four contests, in 1912 only three, but two of these were in New York City.   Promoters could not get the two men from Stepney to sign up for a match cheaply after Corporal Brown was knocked out at Wonderland. The music halls were after Wells, and he immediately went on stage at the Euston Empire and the Canterbury Palace, sparring with partners who included his manager, and audiences warmed to the big fellow even as he walked on.   Unlike Jack Johnson, who toured the music halls in 1911, Wells was not really an entertainer, he simply showed himself and went through his pugilistic paces. Wells earned money freely from this point in his life, lived expansively, married a very young and attractive daughter of a South London publican, raised a family, made a second career in the film industry. When he died at his home in Ealing aged 79 years in 1967, Wells had experienced a range of situations which few people combine. The route march in India; the tournament at Poona; the British title gained; a match made, and fought in the Law Courts; Madison Square Garden; his wedding photographs in a boxing paper;   cheers in the U.S.A., and some jeers for not wearing khaki: these events spanning seven years, would have broadened the outlook of a wizard or sage, yet Wells stayed unassuming. Modesty, a rare quality when most men can find something to boast about, was Wells's stock in trade.

The table of boxing matches which Wells engaged in during his lengthy fighting career forms chapter one of this book. It is at the front rather than an appendage because thoughtful supporters of the sport, and its critics, will analyse this record in a variety of ways. Moreover, a table of contests gives structure to a boxing biography whilst the table of contents suggests a mystery tour until you've read the book. Chapter one shows when he boxed, whom he boxed, in which place, and with what result. The outcome of this arrangement, hopefully, will be less tedium for the reader who will know immediately that Wells was in the U.S.A. in 1912, and that Gunner Moir was the first boxer to stop Wells in his tracks. Given this career outline, the peaks and troughs can be visualized, and the flow of his professional life scouted. Since the reader is expected to do this, my own analysis of this interesting man as a boxer is left until Chapter 15.

Boxers are performing artists, they execute feats at a public show. Boxing at times becomes a fine art with a superlative display, usually by two contrasted masters. The match is a story constructed before the eyes of the spectators, who carry away a tale to tell. Cinematograph recordings have been made since 1894, yet a contest must be witnessed whilst it is taking place or there is no match. Wells drew spectators in extraordinary numbers for three reasons. First, the decade 1910 to 1920 was one of consistent economic growth when most people had more money to spend and the standard of living of a growing majority rose beyond subsistence level. The market for entertainment swelled amongst young and old even as troops were getting killed. Indeed, the inter-allied boxing tournament, held at the Royal Albert Hall in December 1918, made it seem as if the British with their white colonies and the U.S.A. had won the war because the other side did not go in for boxing. Secondly, a black man with superb boxing skills had won the heavyweight championship of the world in December 1908. Jack Johnson won the title in Australia and was hounded from his home in the U.S.A. for his temerity in marrying a white woman. Boxing aroused race hatred not in the arena, but in the press, and gave the sport a marketability until 1915 it had never previously possessed. Thirdly, professional boxing in Britain and France opened its doors to the middle classes, including a minute number of women spectators. The ambience of large boxing shows changed as impresarios moved into the business of promoting, and property speculators invested by building exhibition centres. Wells came into "the game" as these three tendencies converged, and without any one of them the memory of "Beautiful Billy" might be insignificant. He was an exciting boxer to watch, yet the sport itself is a machine for producing the spectacular. For good or ill it remains so.

The problems posed in biography of a boxer are manifold. Few people still living could have seen Wells box in a serious way, though thousands of words were written by scores of boxing correspondents describing his contests, and in between fights words from and about Wells flowed in an almost continuous stream of hot lead. Columns of newspaper commentary overwhelm the researcher, and most contain a shred of information not previously noted. Not all can be read, so mention must be made of the select few which were, and how they were used. Two weekly newspapers entirely devoted to boxing were started in 1909, and these were combed for Wellsiana; *Boxing World* until its incorporation with *Mirror of Life* in 1912, and *Boxing* until 1925. For particular incidents, other newspapers were more informative, *The Times* on the legal action to stop the Wells-Johnson match, and *Mirror of Life* on boxing tournaments in India. *Answers* carried "My Life and Fights by Bombardier Wells" for six issues in 1914; *Thomson's Weekly News* ran his "My Life and My Fights" for five months in 1920 contemporaneously with *Lloyd's Sunday News*'s "How I came back as a Boxer". It is quite possible that Wells gained a greater proportion of space in the British press than any sportsman who has followed. Every periodical with sporting pretensions published in London in the decade from 1910, covered Wells's boxing contests, hence the academic style of referencing has been used in this book. Lengthy quotations from boxing correspondents' accounts of any of his bouts in boxing rings in England, Ireland, Wales, Belgium, France, India and the U.S.A. are left out because everyone sees a fight differently. That Wells was eminently newsworthy was a trial for him, and a headache for any biographer.

The other major difficulty stems from distinguishing how boxing looked in the first quarter of the twentieth century, and how much ability did Wells have compared to his contemporaries. Without question boxing was slower in pace than it became, say, with Muhammad Ali. Yet boxing in 1910 was, in turn, faster than it had been twenty years earlier. Wells's many championship contests were made over 20 rounds, the standard distance at that time, and most champions trained hard, yet without the knowledge which medical science has gained for invalids and athletes subsequently. It is hard to believe that boxers, like people generally, have not improved in physical condition over the last seventy years. Indeed, it may well be that because boxers are now fitter, they are more able to take punishment; longer to stand up to opponents, stronger on their feet, and more susceptible to serious damage in a boxing ring than Wells was. If boxing was then slower, and this is a different point, it was probably more tactical. One of the books Wells strongly commended was Robert Fitzsimmons, *Physical Culture and Self-Defense*, published by Gale and Polden, in 1902. Fitzsimmons had been middle and heavyweight champion of the world in the 1890s, and Wells read the book whilst in India. The feature of this book is the excellent quality of its numerous photographs. Chapter 18 consists simply of 21 full-page posed illustrations of Fitzsimmons and partner purporting to show the famous blows of the champion. These are shown, yet a close study of this series of photographs must result in the conclusion that stopping or slipping your opponent's blows is what is most valuably brought out. The noble art of self defense became a cliché when avoiding punishment became mechanised by always presenting a moving target, thus reducing the need to think. Boxing at the slower pace denied the cumulative power of combinations of punches, and working for an opening took a more prominent place in boxing than it now does. That boxing has changed there is no doubt.

Wells was a delight to watch. Every contemporary observer agreed him to be a fast man with a heavy punch. His record confirms the latter for Wells won damned near three-quarters of his professional matches by knockouts. In order to embed that in fistic lore, contemporary masters, Jimmy Wilde and Jim Driscoll, scored two-thirds and one-half respectively of the same measure. The heavyweight was a terrific puncher.

For speed of footwork Wells should be compared with the men he boxed. Some like Frank Moran and Petty-Officer Curran were notoriously slow, whilst others, Dick Smith for instance, were reckoned to be the epitome of nimbleness. Wells was faster by far than most big men previously seen. In his book, *Modern Boxing*, which was published in 1911, Wells wrote that he believed he was "a more than average speedy boxer", and the knowledgeable editor of *Mirror of Life* enthused about the "agile, graceful and speedy Bombardier". Thus we have a notion of how Wells looked in action, and with the severe limitations of documentary historical research superior signs may not emerge except in the photographs.

Action photographs which could not have been faked appeared in Guy Campbell's *The Vaulting Horse*, which was published in 1906. The technology of printing and shutter speeds was refined at the right time for the white hopes' era in boxing. Science was invading everything; communications, horseless transport, and two machines had actually raced between London and Manchester, above the ground. It was entirely right that at this time a tall slim scientific model replaced the rotund, cast iron one in British heavyweight boxing.

The sport's publicists - journalists, editors, promoters, managers and some boxers - delighted in a change of style heavily imitative of their tribe in the United States. Personal stories of boxers' lives infiltrated the sports' pages. Hague may or may not have had a wife; Moir was the better known for wrestling with Hackenschmidt, Wells was more lovable than both because readers and the handsome young man were close. Wells, then Carpentier, bestrode sporting affairs at times, and their lives were explored under headlines. Such national attention to sportsmen from working-class backgrounds was unprecedented. Column inches multiplied as the subject diversified, spectators grew in numbers, but more significant socially was the increased familiarity of everybody with such figures. Catch phrases enjoy life only if people understand them, and Weldon's joke about Colin Bell in Chapter 10 is testimony to the great spread of press readership.

The boxing career of Billy Wells can be seen as abject failure, but this is incorrect. His fourth round with Goddard provided the climax of a great novel, so far not written, about a magnificent attempt to stretch the boundaries of physical perfection into middle age. Had Wells then died, the tragedy would have been sublime. The individual grappling with the serpent Time, is half of art, literature and life. Wells, as far as we can tell, did this admirably from 1887 until 1967, inside the ring he occasionally failed, but entertainingly.

CHAPTER ONE

THE CONTESTS

(Early record incomplete)

STOP FOR LEFT-HAND BODY BLOW.
Like all stops this requires very accurate timing. Having
foreseen your adversary's intention, hit him full in the face
with your left hand....

Ned Donnelly, *Self-Defence;   or, the Art of Boxing*, n.d.
(1879), p. 61

Date	Opponent *(Place/Promoter)*	Result
1904	William Hazell *Federation of Working Men's* *Social Clubs*	L. pts 3
1908	Serg't Magee *Quetta*	W. pts 3
Sept. 1908	Serg't Bateman *Quetta*	W. pts 3
March 1909	Gunner Turner *Poona*	W. ko 2
March 1909	Private Jarvis *Poona*	W. ko 2
March 1909	Private Tansell *Poona* (won heavyweight championship of All India)	W. pts 3

Date	Opponent *(Place/Promoter)*	Result
Sept. 1909	Corporal Goulburn *Simla*	W. ko 1
Sept. 1909	Staff Sgt Gale *Simla*	W. ko 2
Sept. 1909	Private Clohessy *Simla*	W. pts 3
Feb. 1910	Gunner Blatcher *Lucknow*	W. ko 1
Feb. 1910	Drummer Ness *Lucknow*	W. ko 1
Feb. 1910	Private Clohessy *Lucknow* (retained heavyweight championship of All India)	W. ko 3
1910	Private Cooper *Lahore*	W.
1910	Private James *Lahore*	W.
1910	Corporal Houston *Lahore*	W. ko 2
June 1910	Gunner Joe Mills *Ernest Wells Club London, W.*	Exhibition 6 rounds
22 June 1910	Gunner McMurray *Shoeburyness*	W. ko 1

Date	Opponent *(Place/Promoter)*	Result
23 July 1910	Corporal Brown *Wonderland*	W. ko 3
15 Sept. 1910	Sergeant Sunshine *King's Hall/Hugh McIntosh*	W. ko 6
19 Oct. 1910	Private Dan Voyles *King's Hall/McIntosh*	W. ko 10
16 Nov. 1910	Seaman Parsons *King's Hall/McIntosh* ------------------------------	W. ko 1
11 Jan. 1911	Gunner Moir *Olympia/McIntosh*	L. ko 3
8 March 1911	Porky Flynn (Boston, U.S.A.) *Olympia/McIntosh*	W. pts 20
24 April 1911	Iron Hague *National Sporting Club* (won heavyweight championship of England)	W. ko 6
18 Dec. 1911	Fred Storbeck (South Africa) *National Sporting Club* -----------------------------	W. ko 11
28 June 1912	Al Palzer (Iowa) *Madison Square Garden*	L. ko 3
18 July 1912	Tom Kennedy (U.S.A.) *Madison Square Garden*	W. ko 8
6 Dec. 1912	George Rodel (S. Africa) *King's Hall/Jimmy White*	W. ko 2

Date	Opponent *(Place/Promoter)*	Result
14 March 1913	Gunboat Smith (U.S.A.) *Madison Square Garden*	L. ko 2
1 June 1913	Georges Carpentier (France) *Ghent*	L. ko 4
30 June 1913	Packey Mahoney *National Sporting Club*	W. ko 13
4 August 1913	Pat O'Keefe *Ring/Dick Burge*	W. ko 15
10 Sept. 1913	Gunner Moir *Canterbury Music Hall*	W. ko 5
8 Dec. 1913	Georges Carpentier (France) *National Sporting Club*	L. ko 1
14 Jan. 1914	Gunner Rawles *Theatre Royal, Belfast*	W. rtd 10
24 Jan. 1914	Gaston Pigot (France) *Cardiff*	W. ko 1
2 March 1914	Bandsman Blake *London Palladium*	W. ko 4
2 April 1914	Albert Lurie (France) *Canterbury Music Hall*	W. ko 7
30 April 1914	Bandsman Rice *The Stadium, Liverpool*	W. pts 20
30 June 1914	Colin Bell (Australia) *Olympia/Charles Cochran*	W. ko 2

Date	Opponent *(Place/Promoter)*	Result
12 Feb. 1915	Dan McGoldrick *Cosmopolitan, Plymouth*	W. rtd 7
24 Feb. 1915	Bandsman Rice *Grand Opera House, Belfast*	W. ko 6
29 March 1915	Frank Moran (Pittsburg) *London Opera House*	L. ko 10
31 May 1915	Dick Smith *Ring/Dick Burge*	W. ko 9
27 Dec. 1915	Bandsman Rice *The Stadium, Liverpool*	W. ko 1
21 Feb. 1916	Dick Smith *Golders Green Hippodrome*	W. ko 3
31 March 1916	Petty-Officer Curran *Cosmopolitan, Plymouth*	W. rtd 5
26 Aug. 1916	Dick Smith *St James's Park, Newcastle*	W. rtd 9
18 Dec. 1916	Dan Voyles *National Sporting Club*	W. rsc 2
11 Dec. 1918	Seaman Ivor Powell (Royal Navy) *Royal Albert Hall/I.S.B.A.*	W. pts 3
11 Dec. 1918	Private Eddie McGoorty (U.S.A.) *Royal Albert Hall/I.S.B.A.*	W. pts 3
12 Dec. 1918	Sgt Joe Beckett (Royal Air Force) *Royal Albert Hall/I.S.B.A.*	W. pts 3

Date	Opponent *(Place/Promoter)*	Result
27 Feb. 1919	Joe Beckett *Holborn Stadium/Charles Cochran* (lost British heavyweight championship)	L. ko 5
17 Oct. 1919	Jack Curphey *Holborn Stadium/Cochran*	W. ko 2
2 Nov. 1919	Arthur Townley *Holborn Stadium/Cochran*	W. rsc 9
27 Jan. 1920	Harry Reeve *Canterbury Music Hall*	W. ko 4
17 March 1920	Paul Journée (France) *Royal Albert Hall*	W. ko 13
8 April 1920	Eddie McGoorty (Wisconsin) *Holborn Stadium/Cochran*	W. ko 16
10 May 1920	Joe Beckett *Olympia/Cochran*	L. ko 3
7 Sept. 1920	Paul Journée (France) *Deauville*	W. ko 17
24 April 1922	Albert Lloyd (Australia) *National Sporting Club*	W. rtd 10
27 May 1922	Frank Goddard *Crystal Palace*	L. ko 6
12 Oct. 1922	Jack Bloomfield *Royal Albert Hall/J. Arnold Wilson*	L. ko 6

Date	Opponent *(Place/Promoter)*	Result
24 Nov. 1924	Charles Penwill *Hoxton Baths/Jack Callaghan*	W. ko 2
15 Dec. 1924	Gunner Bennett *Olympia Theatre, Liverpool*	W. rtd 9
30 Jan. 1925	Soldier Horace Jones (Canada) *The Dome, Brighton/Callaghan*	W. disq 6
30 April 1925	Jack Stanley *Royal Albert Hall/Harry Jacobs*	L. ko 3

Summary of professional contests:

Total	48	
Won	37	34 knockouts or stoppages, one disqualification
Lost	11	all by knockouts

Abbreviations: W. - won; L. - Lost; pts - points; ko - knockout; rtd - retired; rsc - referee stopped contest; disq - disqualified; I.S.B.A. - Imperial Services Boxing Association.

CHAPTER TWO

FAMILY, SCHOOL AND BROAD STREET BOYS' CLUB

In the early part of 1897 at the Excelsior Hall, Bethnal Green, I met... the Bantamweight Champion of Australia and, after having all the best of five rounds, I nearly got murdered in the sixth. When I got home my mother said: "Have you been run over as your face looks like a butcher's shop? You never was an oil painting, but, oh dear, you must have got a punch on the nose with a steam roller as your carmine dial looks like an imitation sunset."

Jack Hare, *Gladiators of the Prize Ring*, Nottingham, n.d. (1925), p. 51.

Billy Wells was born 31 August 1887 at 250 Cable Street, a tenement dwelling close to the East London Railway and the Vestry Hall of St George's-in-the-East. The previous census showed five families and 18 people in occupation, whilst the premises were for many years used by a wine merchants called Motion & Co. The address was in Shadwell by the London Docks, and Shadwell New Basin, completed in 1858, could take vessels which were a hundred yards long. The neighbourhood housed dock labourers, warehouse workers, railwaymen and seamen, and some very poor people. Social workers, in the form of University Settlements, had moved in in 1886, and they had a keen nose for deprived areas.

William Thomas Wells, the father of the boxer (who was given the same name) was a musician who had married Emily Rhoda Farrier in 1885. Both came from skilled workers' families. His father was a waterman, and her father was a lighterman. The latter was not on the census in 1881, however, and Emily's mother's occupation was shown as launderess at 250 Cable Street, where she lived with two daughters. William Senior and Emily had both been born locally, her in 1867 and him in 1862. They married and moved into the same building as Emily's mother. Mr Wells taught a fife and drum band which practised in a sail loft and played at musical-drill and swimming displays at the Stepney Meeting Hall and the Betts Street Baths. The band master and his wife had nine children, and Billy was the eldest of five brothers. Alfred Valentine Wells, the second eldest boy, was two years younger than Billy, and an enthusiastic athlete who frequently seconded his brother in the ring until he was killed in action in France in September 1914.

Broad Street School to which the children went was an Elementary School with Girls, Boys and Junior Mixed departments. Broad Street was a continuation of High Street Shadwell until 1937 when both names were replaced by the easier "The Highway". Education in London was progressive, and sometimes energetic. The teaching of swimming was allowed in 1890, and competitive schools' football in East London had started in 1888. Since Broad Street School won the Tower Hamlets fourth division football shield in 1896[1] it seems likely that it was one of many strongly sporting schools under the administration of the School Board for London, a body which was both hated and respected until abolished by Central Government decree in 1904.

Broad Street, which was adjacent to Free Trade Wharf and Stone Stairs, not only contained a vigorous school, but also a boys' club. Frederick Charles Mills was a graduate of Pembroke College, a Yorkshire man and barrister, though he did not practice, and a deeply religious member of the Church. Under the influence of the Rev. Samuel Augustus Barnett, Vicar of St Jude's, Whitechapel, and the Warden of Toynbee Hall from its foundation in 1884, Mills moved into a small house, became a school governor, and started the boys' club in 1886. Broad Street Club, the first of seven "Highway" Clubs for girls as well as boys, flourished until the second World War. The original club was for boys between the ages of 14 and 18. It was open from 7 until 10 every night of the week except Sundays. There were classes for gymnastics on Tuesday and Friday, and for boxing on Thursday. The teacher for these subjects was a man named Chambers, "Late Instructor 1st Surrey Rifle Corps", who must have given Billy Wells his first lessons in boxing, though in autobiographical newspaper articles which were perhaps "ghost-written", Wells suggests that he was largely self-taught until he met Jim Maloney in India. The Club where his father taught music was keenly athletic, and Mills allowed no smoking on the premises. There were twice-weekly trips to the local swimming baths in the summer, and a week's camp in August, whilst rowing, cricket and football matches were contested by Broad Street Club boys under the auspices of the games committee of the Federation of Working Men's Social Clubs. "The Fed.", yet another emanation from the effervescent University Settlement movement, had enroled over a hundred clubs within eight years of its formation in 1889 and though this may have been a slight exaggeration, a great deal of this voluntary association fervour went into sport, particularly boxing.

Broad Street Boys' Club occupied what had been a shop, and it could accommodate only a small membership, probably less than a hundred boys. This was typical of boys' clubs in London, and with a weekly subscription of one penny, expenditure outran income. F.C. Mills had to subsidize his club. Each January he gave a supper for members; the week's camp in 1891 was at Clacton; the famous swimmer, Annie Regan, gave an exhibition at the fourth annual swimming display in 1894, and he must have paid instructors like Mr Chambers and Mr Wells. Mills not only had a private income, he had important friends for the Attorney General presented the swimming prizes at one *Annual Soiree*. Jim Maloney, whom we shall meet later, appears in the surviving records of the club in a swimming programme of 1891 where he was one of the seconds in the "Boxing on Raft" item. Billy and Alf Wells' names appear in a 1901 programme for a gymnastics' display where they were both among 18 boys forming pyramids, and Billy was in goal for item 14 "Hand Ball (First time in London by School Boys)". The club was active and enterprising, and its records, carefully preserved in Tower Hamlets Local History Archives[2], throw some light on the Wells' family.

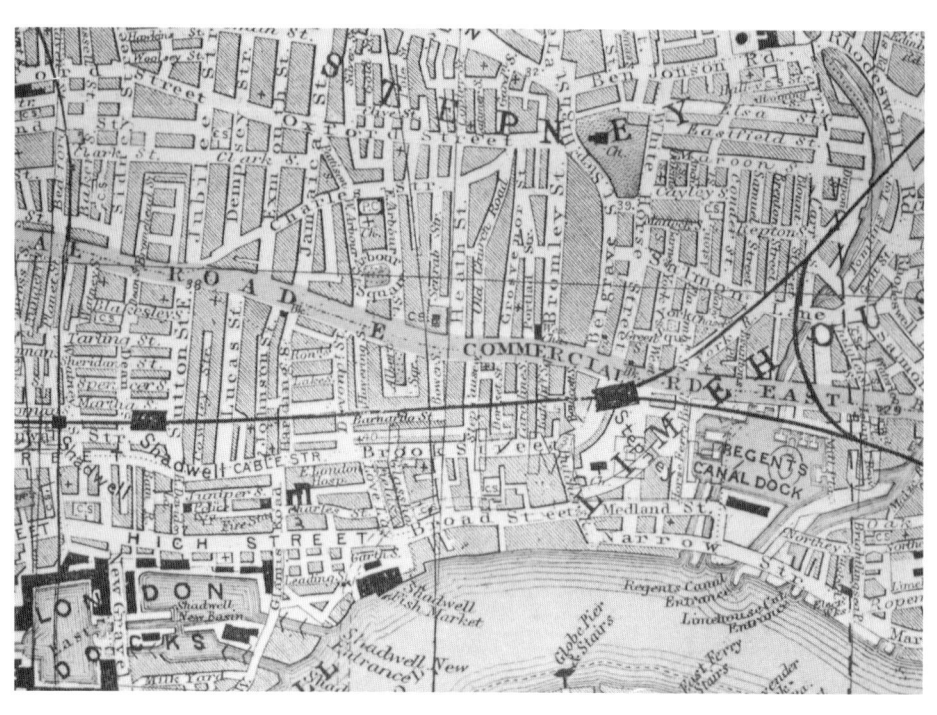

Schoolboy's Playground. *Bacon's Large Scale Atlas of London and Suburbs*, "new, enlarged and improved edition", not dated (1913?)

Mr Wells was band-master until 1892, when the Broad Street band continued to play but his name disappeared. By 1899 a mandoline band had replaced the fifes and drums for a gymnastic display, and we know little about this man with an unusual occupation, except that he was an Eastender with a large family, and he had died by the time his eldest son married. Since William Thomas Wells senior was born in 1862 the most likely source of his musical education was the army, the volunteers, or possibly the Salvation Army, for "General" Booth's Christian Mission had begun in Whitechapel, however, this is speculation. Why he did not follow his father, also William, as a waterman, the most exclusive trade on the river, is a conundrum.

The swimmers of Broad Street called themselves the White Cross Swimming Club, and their annual gala was advertised in beautifully designed and printed programmes as "Costume Entertainment". At the thirteenth such gala, for which in September 1903 the modern Whitechapel Public Baths were booked, there can be found the brothers, Billy and Alf, competing singly, and also against each other. With nearly two years difference in age between them, this suggests that the younger boy was an extremely able swimmer, and this is reinforced by his name entered for the junior five lengths championship, whilst Billy in a senior-boys' club handicap received 22 seconds, the longest time from scratch of the 25 entries. At the swimming pool Alf shone more than Billy. Alf was a keen gymnast. He came fourth of 15 boys in the Club's over-16 competition, when he was only 15 years old. He joined the "Health and Strength League" and when he was killed his younger brother wrote to the magazine *Health and Strength* of Alf as follows:

> He was an ardent Physical Culturist, and an Army gymnast and footballer above the average. *Health and Strength* and Alf were my encyclopaedias on Physical Culture methods, and now half of it is no more.[3]

The young man who wrote this moving tribute to Alf, had enjoyed this brother's influence more than Billy's because Billy had left home to join the army when he, Albert, was eight years of age. The influence of Alf on his older brother could not have been negligible since they grew up together, sharing school and club, and this facet of the boxer's background should be remembered as we turn to Billy Wells after he entered the world of work.

With a good report from his Headmaster, employment was not difficult to find for a school leaver in 1901. The quadrant between Minories, Great Eastern Street and Waterloo was peppered with firms, large and small, who needed errands run and messages taken. At thirteen or fourteen years of age jobs could be found which paid small wages, and which terminated abruptly before a man's rate was due. The trade cycle had commenced an upward turn and the post office, newspaper and insurance offices, banks and brokers, would have been taking on boys straight from school. The Wells' family must have lost all connection with journeyman trades, for an apprenticeship was much preferable, especially for an eldest boy whose claim was strongest to such "property". That he was a member of a Christian youth club would have appealed to many employers, and a word from Mr Mills might have opened doors. The event was recalled by Wells without elaboration:

> My parents were not endowed with too many of this
> world's goods, and directly I became of school-
> leaving age I was hurried into the wage-earning
> world. My first job was as a messenger with the
> Eastern Telegraph Co., and looking back I can see
> that the experiences of this humble job served me
> in very good stead in after life...[4]

It caused him to walk in the open air and, of course, to talk and mix with adults, one being a man who was an ardent reader of *Sandow's Magazine of Physical Culture*. This was a substantial, well-produced monthly paper for men on all fitness subjects which ran from 1898. The boy, who was already a keen footballer and swimmer, would not have needed converting to a majority of Sandow's themes, and he resisted body-building in favour of boxing.

Billy Wells boxed at the club between his last year at school and joining the army. He seems to have had a change of jobs during this period for he mentioned working for a bank, presumably as a messenger. Only the Stock Exchange in the City with its Mincing Lane Boxing Club provided opportunities for sport, though the Business Houses' boxing championships were to become important in the 1920s. In 1904 a member of Broad Street Club had reached the final of the annual Federation of Working Men's Social Clubs' boxing championships, but it was J. Sullivan, at bantamweight, not W. Wells. *Oxford House Chronicle* covered the two evenings of boxing at the University Club in Bethnal Green,[5] and Sullivan lost to the A.B.A. champion, such was the high standard of boxing in boys' clubs. Wells, aged 16, almost certainly boxed and lost on the 14th or 16th of March as an over 10 st. junior, and though he was the best of his age at Broad Street success in "The Feds" eluded him.

The 1905 Federation championships were held at the same place in Victoria Park Square, and the last night was reported in the *Sporting Life* with a member of Eton Mission winning the 10 st. 2 lbs championship with ease.[6] In 1906 the championships went to Southwark Baths, where the heavyweight novices' was won by W. Hazell, of All Saints' Rotherhithe.[7] Wells recalled this in his book, *Modern Boxing*, where he wrote:

> ... as a member of the [Broad Street] Old Boys' Club, I met W. Hazel (sic) of the City Police, in a men's heavy-weight competition, and lost on points after three rounds. I was only 17 at the time, while Hazel was certainly a few years older.[8]

Hazell won the A.B.A. heavyweight championship in 1911, and this was why Wells mentioned him, and though Hazell became a policeman, it is unlikely he already was one in 1906. Wells had lost to a capable boxer.

Notes

1   East London Schools' Athletic Association, *Sports Magazine*, No. 20, May 1932, p. 12.
2   TH/8192/1, Broad Street Clubs Record Book; TH/8192/16, manuscript, F.C. Wright, "The Highway Clubs in East London: a history", 1986; Fred Wright, "F.C. Mills and the Broad Street Boys Club", *East London Record*, No. 13, 1990, pp. 18-22.
3   *Health and Strength*, 31 October 1914, p. 516.
4   *Thomson's Weekly News*, 17 April 1920.
5   *Oxford House Chronicle*, June 1904.
6   *Sporting Life*, 8 April 1905; *Oxford House Chronicle*, May 1905.
7   *Oxford House Chronicle*, May 1906.
8   Bombardier Billy Wells, *Modern Boxing: a practical guide to present-day methods*, n.d. (1911), p. 89.

CHAPTER THREE

"... BRILLIANT IN BRASS AND SCARLET"

Our Indian Letter

Since our last letter, several important tournaments have taken place, amongst them, however, stands out alone, the Civil and Military Tournament at Lahore. There every boxer of note in India fought, including our champion heavyweight Wells... Without a doubt he is the best and most scientific boxer of his weight seen in India for many a long day.

Mirror of Life, 2 July 1910.

Wells enlisted in the summer of 1906 and spent his first months in a depot at Dover where he played centre forward in the football team and boxed in the gymnasium whilst he did his military training. The Royal Garrison Artillery, which Wells joined, had a Mountain Division stationed in North-Western India and to here his company was sent. On the troop ship there were many boxers, and Wells sparred with one, Gunner McMurray, whom he was later to box in England professionally. The army had encouraged boxing as recreation since the early 1890s, and instituted championships in 1896. There were small money prizes in army contests, and the dividing line was drawn between officers and other ranks, not between amateur and professional. Thus a top non-commissioned army boxer could be very good indeed, and the contemporary English heavyweight champion was a former artilleryman, Gunner Moir. This remarkable Lambeth man we shall meet later.

The Mountain Division had eight Batteries, and Wells joined 6th Mountain Battery at Rawalpindi. This was a station in the Punjab, 1700 feet above sea level, and some 80 miles north of Amritsar, in what is now Pakistan. The British Raj ruled India imperiously, and regarded Russian territorial aims suspiciously. Control of the North West frontier with Afghanistan caused considerable difficulty with indigenous peoples. Kipling romanticised the hardness of the British rankers' life in India with poems like "Route Marchin'".

So 'ark an' 'eed, you rookies, which is always
grumblin' sore,
There's worser things than marchin' from Umballa
to Cawnpore;
An' if your 'eels are blistered an' they feels to 'urt
like 'ell,
You drop some tallow in your socks an' that will
make 'em well.

Wells and his Battery marched 200 miles to Quetta (not 700 miles as recounted in *Thomson's Weekly*) and here the slim and fit young gunner began his boxing career.

Sport was hugely important to Europeans in India. Horse racing meetings were relished by tea planters, civil servants, Governors and Viceroy alike. Cricket matches were social occasions, and army officers felt ill-equipped without several polo ponies. Hunting was endemic, hockey was popular, and gentlemen and their wives organised their lives around the sporting calendar. The British serviceman, bottom of the pile in whiteman's India, was encouraged by his officers to play football and shinty, and especially to box. Captain Ambrose Awdry wrote home to his Father from Mhow in 1904:

I have just now got a two night job to judge boxing
of which I know nothing though the place is full of
boxers: however folk seem satisfied, and it is a
great thing to be in all the game and sport events
and get to be known to the soldiers as keen...

Four months later the young officer wrote again:

... They made me judge some boxing again the other night and wouldn't let me off when they brought up a Championship match (9 stone, of India).[1]

Awdry was keen on horses and polo and batting at cricket, yet in India boxing so engaged the men that officers were drawn into the administration of boxing tournaments which were ubiquitous among 80,000 British soldiers.

Wells entered the divisional boxing tournament at Quetta at novices and open level and won both competitions. In both finals he had to beat non-commissioned officers, and his long reach played some part in this. Seasoned army sergeants tended to be bulky men from time spent in the mess, whilst Wells was a tall, slim youngster with no taste for alcoholic refreshment. His experience in London boys' club boxing would have made him no fool in the ring, and he was invariably fit. According to *Thomson's Weekly*, the 14 stones Sergeant Magee went down 27 times in three rounds, and one wonders who kept count. Sergeant Bateman was outboxed in a better contest.[2]

The archives of the National Army Museum contain fascinating material on boxing in India including the programmes of three nights of boxing at the annual tournament of the Third Battalion Royal Fusiliers in March 1914. Wells had long since left India, even so these documents give the best idea of what boxing was like in his time abroad. The tournament went on for nine nights with contestants from 30 companies including Horse, Field and Garrison Artillery, Guards, Hussars, Royal Scots, Seaforths, Camerons, Leinsters, the 1st Welch, in what appears to be a résumé of regiments in the British Army. The hours and hours of contests over three rounds led to finals at six weights for divisional novices, and the same again for the "All India" championships.[3] Each day an up-to-date programme was printed, and these boxing tournaments in India were bigger than any organised by the British Army elsewhere, including those at Aldershot. The 1911 championships were held in Delhi in an arena which could hold

8,000 spectators, and it went on for 16 evenings in the open air.[4] The British Army in India was isolated, and far from home, and it had created a sporting universe of its own.

The 6th Mountain Battery must have been enormously proud of Gunner Wells' winning the Quetta Division heavyweight title. The battery was commanded by Lieutenant-Colonel G.C. Dowell, and from him downwards, every possible favour would come Wells's way to aid training for boxing. In this atmosphere, permission to travel to Poona for the March 1909 tournament could have been taken for granted. At Poona, Wells beat Gunner Turner, Private Jarvis of the Northamptonshire Regiment, and Private Tansell of the Worcestershires, to become heavyweight champion of "All India". Wells, who was a modest young man, was fêted on his return to barracks.[5]

For two seasons of cool weather in the North-West, several Regiments had clubbed together to engage a professional boxer to train their men, and this was Jim Maloney, from Stepney, whom we met briefly at Broad Street Boys' Club. Wells first met Maloney, who was 12 years older than himself, at the gymnasium of the South Wales Borderers, and both were impressed by each other. Maloney had boxed as a lightweight, and in 1902 he had fought a former world champion, Frank Erne. Maloney had lost the fight, but enhanced his reputation. He had coached Wells for the tournament at Poona, and for a month at the start of 1910, Wells was allowed to stay at Maloney's training camp at Umballa, in preparation for the championships in February to be held at Lucknow. Here again Wells fought three contests and won the "All India" heavyweight competition. By this time Wells, though in the army, was boxing and training continuously, and following Maloney's advice he bought himself out of the service for £21.[6]

The heavyweight final at Lucknow was a classical contest between boxer and fighter. So highly regarded was it that it was described in *The Complete Amateur Boxer*, published by Methuen in 1913, for three pages, concluding with the great praise in this

PTE. M. CLOHESSY.

Photo by Wise, Tidworth

Heavy weight Champ'on of all India 1908 and 1910.
Runner up to Bombadier Wells in 1909.
Army Heavy weight Champion in 1912.

Proud illustration from Royal Munster Fusiliers, *Regimental Annual 1912*

studious book: "A most instructive fight".[7] Wells was the boxer,
standing off behind a long left lead, whilst his shorter, heavier
opponent strove to pile-drive gloves through Wells's body. Martin
Clohessey, a private in the Royal Munster Fusiliers, won countless
contests between 1908 and 1912, yet this may have been his best
performance and he lost. Those who enjoy beautiful artefacts may
see the Limerick man's name on a regimental trophy in a room
devoted to silverware of disbanded Irish regiments at Royal Hospital
Road in Chelsea.

Wells spent three years in India. He understated his age in
Thomson's Weekly, and his claim to have had 15 fights, winning all
of them,[8] may be an oversimplification. The opportunity for boxing
contests in India was enormous.   Tournaments were held at
Lucknow, Poona, Secunderabad, Umballa and Simla on an "All
India" scale.[9]   Between these, enthusiastic regiments would stage
open boxing competitions, and compete between themselves for
trophies like the "Sir Robert Seallon Cup".[10] Wells was a novice
boxer when he arrived in India, and to have won the highest
honour twice, in keen boxing territory, seems hardly credible within
a mere 15 contests. Documentary evidence of services' boxing in
India is extremely patchy, yet we can be certain that Wells had
more matches than he recalled ten years later.

Since the foundations of more than one boxing career were
laid in the British Army in India, it is worth questioning why this
happened. First, India was a second home to the British Army, and
every regiment did tours of duty there. A man signing on in
Edwardian Britain would half expect to sail through the Suez Canal
before he traded in his gorgeous uniform for civilian clothes.
Secondly, other-ranks arriving, entered a closed all-male society;
they had no dates with local girls, and scarcely the sight of a
woman in many cantonments. Then the soldier in India had proof
that British were best for they ruled these millions of people, yet
this chauvinism meshed with intense regimental competitiveness.
The Viceroy, the King-Emperor's representative, would present
prizes at the Delhi Durbar boxing tournament, and hundreds of

Wells's comrades dragged him in an unhorsed carriage when he arrived back from Poona. The zest for sporting victory was unchecked in India, where *esprit de corps* was a sinew of imperial rule.

Notes

1 National Army Museum 8307-27. Letters of A.J. Awdry dated 12 August and 1 December 1904. The unfortunate officer contracted an illness and died in hospital at Barrackpur in 1909.
2 *Thomson's Weekly News*, 24 April 1920.
3 National Army Museum 7404-13. The man who saved these programmes and boxed in the tournament was Islington born, Sidney Rogers, a corporal in the 1st Leinster Regiment.
4 Captain C.A. Knapp (ed.), Royal Munster Fusiliers, *Regimental Annual 1911*, pp. 41-43.
5 *Thomson's Weekly News*, 24 April 1920.
6 *Ibid.*, 1 May 1920.
7 J.G. Bohun Lynch, *The Complete Amateur Boxer*, 1913, contained two chapters by J.H.W. Knight-Bruce on army boxing which included this passage pp. 221-3. Both chapters were dropped from the second edition of 1924.
8 *Thomson's Weekly News*, 1 May 1920.
9 *Indian Planters Gazette*, 15 February 1908.
10 National Army Museum 7404-13-2; *Indian Planters Gazette*, 28 March, 12 Sept. 1908.

CHAPTER FOUR

WONDERLAND

Someone of an enquiring turn of mind will one day set himself to the task of discovering why the succulent eel is no longer sold at the lesser boxing halls.

Trevor Wignall, *Thus Gods are Made*, n.d. (1923), p. 25.

Professional boxing in Britain in 1910, when Wells returned from India, was a well established leisure industry. Two competing weekly magazines, *Boxing* and *Boxing World*, had been founded in the previous year, and shows were being staged regularly in cities and towns all over the country. The largest in London was Wonderland, in the Whitechapel Road, and it held over 2,000 people. The outstanding boxer was the Cardiff-Irishman, "Peerless" Jim Driscoll, a featherweight, but the heavyweight division was short of talent.

The champion was a miner from Mexborough called "Iron" Hague, who had looked good winning the title from Gunner Moir in one round, but he steadfastly refused to train and lost his next four non-title contests. These failures by Hague illustrate the breadth of boxing as popular entertainment in this country. He lost to the black American Sam Langford in London; to Petty Officer Curran at Plymouth; to Jewey Smith in Sheffield, and lastly to the curiously named Sergeant Sunshine at the Liverpool Arena. Hague's performances were sad, but boxing supporters needed long memories to recall a credible British heavyweight champion; Jem Smith perhaps, Charlie Mitchell certainly, but they were back in the 1890s.

Wells left India before Maloney, and arrived at Southampton on the troopship "Passy" in April 1910.[1] He had been briefly mentioned in the British press in reports probably sent by Maloney, whose letter of introduction got Wells into the National Sporting

Club to watch Driscoll beat Spike Robson. His first work was at the Lawns Hotel, Hove, as a sparring partner to Gunner Moir, who was preparing for a contest at Mountain Ash with Petty Officer Curran. Wells was in Moir's corner as he knocked the naval man out, unfortunately for them, it was after the bell had sounded to end the second round, and the Gunner was disqualified.

The first two matches Wells engaged in were outside the mainstream of professional boxing. At a gentleman's club in the West End of London he boxed an exhibition with Gunner Joe Mills, and then at the army garrison at Shoeburyness he knocked out the man he had previously met shipboard, Gunner McMurray. With the success of these try-outs, Maloney, now back in London, issued a challenge in *Boxing World* as follows:

> Ex-Bomb. Billy Wells to Heavyweights - With a desire to aid the solution of the problem of the heavy-weight championship of England, Wells can be matched with any of the claimants to the title for any part of £50 a side: date or place no object. Jim Maloney, Wells's manager, is prepared to back him for £50 a side upwards...[2]

Neither Wells nor Maloney expected a 20-rounds match with Hague, Moir or Curran immediately, and they would not have wanted one. Wells had not boxed beyond six rounds, and he was still filling out physically; this challenge was cheekily adding to the publicity Wells was already receiving in two papers, *Boxing World* and *Mirror of Life*. The papers came from the same address on Bread Street Hill, and the highly respected boxing referee, Frank Bradley, had a large part in producing both of them. He was assuming the role of publicity agent for Wells, and in *Mirror of Life*, 13 August 1910, no less than five large posed photographs of Wells appeared. Such hyperbole was an innovation even in the boxing business.

"Wonderland"

Boxers were invariably associated with place, usually where they were brought up, but this was not so with Wells for two reasons. First, he was the Army's boxer, always billed as "Bombardier" even when he was a sergeant-major at the end of the war. Secondly, he seemed to have little sense of local patriotism. In nearly fifty professional contests, he boxed only once in the East End of London. His family had moved to Southend, in Essex whilst he was in India, but his youth club might have expected a visit from the illustrious "Old Boy". Instead, the *Federation Chronicle* belatedly reported in October 1911:

> It may not be generally known to Federation members that Bombardier Billy Wells is (sic) a member of the Broad Street Old Boys' Club... We are sure all members will join with us in wishing him success.

This was not a notice about a member who had kept in touch, and his name is missing from a long list of contributors to the Fed's appeal for funds in the same number. The East End match was at Wonderland, where Jack Woolf paid Wells eight pounds for a ten rounds' contest against Corporal Brown. Woolf had promoted boxing on many Saturday nights, though never with a fuller house, and Brown was knocked out with a right hook to the chin in the third round.

A world heavyweight championship contest in Reno, Nevada, played a part in Wells's next few years. The champion, Jack Johnson, comprehensively defeated the man who had been champion, and who had retired undefeated, the former boilermaker from Ohio, Jim Jeffries. The huge whiteman had been encouraged out of retirement, by the novelist Jack London and others, specifically to beat the blackman, who though born in Galveston, had won the title in Australia in 1908. The match had been made by racialists, and they were dismayed at the result. The repercussions were felt in Britain as the search for a white heavyweight to beat Johnson went on. The term "White Hope" was used in the *New York Evening Journal*, 27 October 1910,[3] and frequently thereafter in the American press, but it was not used venomously in British newspapers. *Boxing World*, 12 January 1911, replied in its "Fistic Enquiry" column:

> Best not mention Jeff and Reno... as they are a painful combination to some folks, especially those that shout loudest about "Hopes of the White Race"

and to another correspondent:

> In our opinion Jack Johnson has never been estimated at his true worth... The black is a splendid boxer, a hard hitter, and one of the finest defensive fighters that ever put on a glove. He does not shine when on the aggressive, but Johnson could hold his own in company with the fistic giants of a decade ago.

There were several black boxers in British rings, indeed one had been boxing on the same night as Wells at Wonderland, racialism did exist, but black people were too few in 1910 to feel the force of it.

The Sydney promoter, who had given Johnson the chance to win the world title, arrived in London just after Wells had beaten Brown.[4] Hugh D. McIntosh was of course a businessman (he had come from New York), yet he knew boxing, and, indeed, he had refereed the Johnson-Tommy Burns match. After winning at Wonderland, Wells and Maloney accepted an offer of a short music hall engagement. Wells sparred four one-minute rounds, twice-nightly, at the Euston Palace and the Canterbury in Westminster Bridge Road.[5] They had also signed for a 20 rounds' contest with Jewey Smith for £100 a side, which was awaiting the best purse offer.[6] This match never came off, for McIntosh outbid metropolitan promoters with a contract for three fights in six months, for which, win, lose or draw, Wells would receive £100.[7]

Music Hall attraction

Before we follow Wells into the matches staged by McIntosh at the King's Hall, near the Elephant and Castle, it is worth looking at boxing turns on London's music halls. They were not new. In 1890 a local middleweight called Toff Wall had topped the bill at the Sebright Music Hall in Hackney.[8] Boxing neighbourhoods loved to watch a local hero. The boxer would be engaged immediately after a great fight (Wall had just beaten Chesterfield Goode), and this practice continued with boxers like Jem Smith and Dick Burge, though they were not necessarily champions. They sparred and skipped (some were brilliant with a skipping rope) and a few, like Jack Johnson, sang. What they did, above everything else, was to show themselves to the audience which had talked and read about their latest fight. An eulogistic account of Wells appearing at the Empress, Brixton, in 1912, makes plain that Wells was not an entertainer in the sense that he played to the audience. The friendly reporter wrote:

> I saw a tall, slim young man, fair, not at all bad-looking, and possessing a smile that must have brought unto him a host of friends... There was no fanfare of cornets, no limes, no chord on; he just stood there, a fine, clean specimen of British manhood, with almost a blush on his face, while the master of ceremonies briefly extolled his abilities...[9]

It was Maloney who did the talking, and Wells sparred with Maloney and Stoker Smith. On the music hall stage Wells was simply the boxer.

Notes

1   *Answers*, 20 June 1914.
2   *Boxing World*, 14 July 1910.
3   *Times Literary Supplement*, 9 October 1987, letter from Leonard Zwilling, University of Wisconsin.
4   *Boxing World*, 11 August 1910.

5   *Apollo's Magazine*, August 1910; *Mirror of Life*, 30 July 1910; *Boxing World*, 28 July 1910.

6   *Mirror of Life*, 6 August 1910; *Boxing World*, 4 August 1910.

7   Eugene Corri, *Refereeing 1,000 Fights*, 1919, p. 57; *Mirror of Life*, 13 August 1910.

8   *Referee*, 16 February 1890.

9   *Mirror of Life*, 28 December 1912. The author of this article was R. Vernon Grey, who described himself as a member of the vaudeville profession.

CHAPTER FIVE

OLYMPIAN ARTILLERY

[Style] is a matter of physique and temperament. Some men are built for out-fighting, like Bombardier Wells, who generally lost his fights when he got in close and indulged in or couldn't avoid in-fighting. He had a long reach, a fine left hand and a good following right, but wasn't built for in-fighting. A stocky man with a terrific hook ... could bore right in and be a terrible danger immediately.

Thomas Inch, *Boxing and Physical Culture*, Aldershot, n.d. (1945), p. 46.

The hall, two minutes' walk from the Elephant and Castle, had been licensed by the L.C.C. in September 1909, and launched with considerable publicity as a boxing stadium. It was described as "a Palace of 2,000 lights", had a capacity for the same number of spectators, and took the dignified name of King's Hall. It was not as cheap to get in as at Wonderland, and prices ranged from one to five shillings.[1] Then McIntosh, promoting on a different evening, raised the price of reserved seats to a guinea, and general admission to 2/6d, for Bombardier Wells *versus* Sergeant Sunshine, in what was headlined on bills as "The Search for a White Champion".

Sunshine, a 33 years old Royal Fusilier, nearly beat Wells. Wells was saved by the bell in round three, and in the following round he went down three times. From his previous efforts, Sunshine was puffing and blowing in the next three minutes, and Wells knocked him down and out in the sixth of the scheduled twenty rounds. Wells looked game, though lacking in ability, and a smarter opponent would have disposed of him in the fourth session.[2] The referee, Eugene Corri, wrote some years afterwards "perhaps Wells was a trifle lucky in winning"[3]. *Mirror of Life* commented:

BOXING WORLD & ATHLETIC CHRONICLE, Sept. 15th, 1910.

LONDON AND MERIDUN.

Vol. 2.—No. 42.

½ D.

BOXING WORLD
AND
ATHLETIC CHRONICLE.

SEPTEMBER 15th, 1910.

ONE HALFPENNY

VOL. 2 — No. 42.

BOMBARDIER WELLS.

The English Heavyweight, who is to meet Seaml. Donalson in a twenty rounds contest at the King's Hall, London Road, on Thursday night. This will be the Bombardier's first serious contest in England, and as both men have trained hard for the encounter, an exciting battle is expected.

THE SEARCH FOR A
WHITE CHAMPION.

(Under the direction of Hugh D. McIntosh.)

KING'S HALL,
"Elephant & Castle."

WEDNESDAY EVENING, NOV. 16th.

THIRD STEP towards pro- ::
ducing a CHAMPION.

20 full 3-minute rounds with Spalding's 6oz.
Championship Gloves.

BOMBARDIER WELLS

(unbeaten) (England's Best) v.

SEAMAN PARSONS

(Winner of Army and Navy Championship
and Conqueror of Private Voyles).

10 full 3-minute rounds.

STEVE SMITH v. HARRY CROXON.
(one of England's Best)   (West Drayton)

6 full 3-minute rounds,

KID SMITH v. GEORGE HEARNE.
(Bermondsey)   (Brixton)

A Full Band in Attendance.

Reserved Seats, 21s, and 10s. 6d., on sale at
Keith Prowse, Alfred Hay's, District Mee-
senger, and all other Booking Agencies.
General Admission, 5s. and 2s. 6d.

It was a great contest as far as excitement went, but
as a scientific display it was very poor.

Wells was to improve in science a great deal, yet his hallmark was
the same over the years, with a Wells contest there was always
likely to be excitement.

The second McIntosh promotion in England featured Wells
against Dan Voyles, who was a private in the Irish Guards. Voyles,
aged 22 years and born in Dublin, made a particularly good pairing
because at six feet tall, and weighing around 13 stones, Wells and
he were almost the same build. Voyles had fought and won at the
National Sporting Club, and was being trained for this contest by
an experienced boxer from Canning Town, Pat O'Keefe. The match
lived up to expectations at the well-filled King's Hall, where Wells,
though down twice in the fifth, knocked Voyles out in the tenth
round.[4]

On the same bill there was a second "Search for a White
Champion" heavyweight contest, and this was won by Seaman
Parsons who beat an Australian. Fred Parsons, formerly of H.M.S.
Black Prince, had left the Royal Navy presumably because of the
prospects in boxing for any big man after Reno. Parsons trained
hard at Portslade, and was considered to be a big puncher (he had
earlier beaten Voyles in two rounds) so that Wells' third contracted
contest for McIntosh was naturally against Parsons. In a
disappointing bout, however, Wells knocked him out in a little over
two minutes.[5] The contract between boxer and promoter for the
three matches must have been profitable, for McIntosh continued
the association at a stadium with twice the capacity of the King's
Hall. We do not know what Wells was paid for his contests with
Gunner Moir and Porky Flynn at Olympia in January and March
1911, but we can look at the style in which he prepared.

Maloney, Wells and sparring partners stayed at the Elms
Hotel, Leigh-on-Sea, which had a gymnasium. Maloney was trainer,
and went with Wells on his roadwork; the gymnasium was used in

the early evening, and after supper they played billiards, and sang songs to the accompaniment of a piano. The training camp probably monopolised the Elms for three weeks before each contest, and their host, a Mr Forman, presided at meals and played the piano.[6] This was not training with a view to saving money, consequently we must assume that Wells was earning handsomely, and that this was in some part due to his manager's astuteness. Wells and Maloney were inseparable, and such a relationship was a little unusual in professional boxing.

Against Gunner Moir, at a packed Olympia, Wells lost in a three rounds' shambles. Moir had boxed around the world, and had been champion, but aged thirty-two he had an "expansive *bread basket*", and he had spent much time on stage as wrestling partner to George Hackenschmidt. He easily lost the first round, then used his weight to lean on Wells, apparently threw him down during the second round, and knocked him out in the third. *Boxing World* called it:

> ... a mixture of wrestling, tumbling, and wild swinging, with very little direction in the blows of either man.[7]

The Referee, in its curiously old-fashioned style, described the second round as follows:

> The gong once again sounded, ...and there was the unhappy Moir; there, too, was Wells, and again he put in his left just as he chose. Suddenly a wild roar ran round the building. Wells was down! Could it be? Yes; there was no doubt about it...[8]

This was, of course, Wells's first defeat as a professional boxer, and he had been an odds-on favourite to beat the rotund Gunner within the distance. Wells was not, in January 1911, strong enough to do that.

The remedy for lack of strength was to engage the services of a physical culturist. There were many practitioners to choose from because fitness had become a marketable commodity from the 1890s when Eugen Sandow, with business acumen, led a host of weight lifters and strong men beyond appearances on the music hall stage. The one chosen was Professor Inch, and he is worth examining as a representative of this new species, muscular men who wrote text-books and conducted correspondence courses.

Thomas Inch had a fifty-inch chest and a gymnasium in Fulham.[9]   Born in 1882 in Yorkshire, his interest in physical culture led him to claim the title of "The Scarborough Hercules", and he was tempted to London by the magazine *Health and Strength* in 1902.[10]   Thereafter, anyone who read that monthly publication, or *Apollo's Magazine of Strength, Skill, and Sport*, would have known of Inch through his advertisements, which included one using 42 quotations from Shakespeare's plays.[11] The physical culture movement was novel and politically progressive. Women were encouraged to take it up, and photographs of their bodies were not used salaciously until the 1930s.   Muscles of strongmen featured Russians, Turks, Jews and Gentiles, for physical culturists were apparently free from chauvinism and racial bias. Subjects like garden cities, camping, rational clothing, sea bathing, jujitsu and cycling, alongside stories and articles by Hannen-Swaffer, William Carpenter and Patrick MacGill were published for Demos, not a sect. This was indubitably popular physical culture.

The negotiations between Maloney and Inch about Wells's course of body building must have been interesting, for both sides stood to gain financially. The National Sporting Club had put up a Lonsdale Belt for heavyweights and were anxious to see their nominal champion, Hague, either win or lose it in a decent contest at their premises in Covent Garden.   Hague had won a contest there in January when he outclassed a contender, Bill Chase, a butcher from Forest Gate, who was little more than a novice. Thus the self-appointed ruling body of British boxing was eager to see

versus Moir and Flynn

Wells, or any other youngster, developing into a genuine heavyweight prospect. If Wells went on to gain the championship, the publicity for Inch would be enormous, and one suspects that Inch worked for expenses only, for he used "Bombardier Wells" in bold print in his advertisements immediately.[12]

Inch had worked on boxers before, indeed, he had trained Moir in 1907 for his unsuccessful attempt against Tommy Burns for the heavyweight championship of the world. Inch's aim with Wells was to retain his speed whilst strengthening his stomach muscles and building up his chest and neck. For this he used 80 lbs bar-bells and a wall machine which was later marketed as "The *Health & Strength* Exerciser" as used by Wells. Inch retained a high opinion of him as a boxer, yet Wells never mentioned Inch in any of his newspaper memoirs.

Dan Flynn was the next opponent chosen by McIntosh for Bombardier Wells. For reasons unknown, he was called "Porky" Flynn, though he was of athletic build. Born in Ireland, he had learned to box in Boston, U.S.A., where he had been in the ring with champions like the ferocious Stanley Ketchel. Flynn had lost four contests, yet in good company. McIntosh was by now staging regular top-flight boxing shows at Olympia, and he brought Flynn over with an outstanding black boxer, Sam Langford, who was in Flynn's corner as Wells outpointed him. The editor of *Boxing* thought that Wells won 19 of the 20 rounds. He boxed cautiously, knocked his opponent down, and satisfied a disappointingly small crowd of 2,000, that here was England's heavyweight hope.[13]

The victory over the Bostonian is worth analysing for its several effects and the question it raises. It allowed Wells to overstep Moir, Curran and others as challenger to "Iron" Hague. Inch received high praise from boxing reporters, and continued working with Wells for many weeks. Maloney was no longer dependent on promoter McIntosh, and he and Wells could ask three-figure sums for a week on the music halls. In the previous history of British boxing no active pugilist had opened such floods of money. Yet the twenty-rounds' points win over Flynn was perhaps not worth the acclaim it received. The referee, Corri, recalled Wells boxing brilliantly, but in his memoirs he referred to Flynn dismissively as Sam Langford's sparring partner[14]; Ketchel,[15] though a middleweight, had knocked Flynn out in only three rounds, and whilst McIntosh billed him as an "American White Heavyweight of Class", Porky lacked a heavy punch. Spectators and scribes desired a great British heavyweight, they willed Wells to be another Charlie Mitchell, and overestimated Dan Flynn.

Wells won the heavyweight championship of England, as it was then called, and wore the first heavyweight Lonsdale Belt, at the National Sporting Club when he knocked out an unusually well-trained Hague in the sixth round.[16] Wells boxed at a distance and was much too fast for the Mexborough man. *Boxing World* commented:

> ... it must be something like a record for a boxer to win an English championship in his first contest at the N.S.C. But then Wells has come to the front so fast... Twelve months ago he was only a name to some of us... through Jim Maloney, who had "mentioned him in despatches" from India...[17]

The N.S.C. had been founded in 1891 as a gentlemen's club with a main purpose of running Monday evening boxing shows for members and male friends. It attained the prestige of a sporting institution by enrolling members of the Amateur Boxing Association (founded 1880); by being exclusive and slightly bohemian; and by having a dictatorial manager, A.F. "Peggy" Bettinson, who knew the sport extremely well. The problem for such a middle-class body arose when boxing at large attracted superior money from the sixpences of the working class. Thus Wonderland or the Cosmopolitan in Plymouth, for example, could pay larger purses than the self-styled "Home of Boxing". The Club died from this class conflict after 1918, but it tried to tackle the disease in 1909 by instituting Lonsdale Belts. Bettinson maintained, and almost everyone agreed, that English boxing titles could be at stake only in the clubhouse at Covent Garden. Boxers delighted in the prestige of being asked to box there, but a few, particularly heavyweights, felt that the purses put up were tiny. Hence, the symbols with the famous member's name, were designed to underline the claim that championship matches were only made by the N.S.C. The Club produced the best of referees, including Angle and Corri, and virtually adopted boxers, particularly Jim Driscoll, yet the appearance of promoters like McIntosh added to Bettinson's problem of attracting major contests to his club.[18]

The winning of the championship had an interesting sequel. The newspapers announced that Wells would meet another opponent at the Club during Derby week (always an occasion for big boxing matches). Bettinson named Fred Storbeck, a South African who had won the 1910 A.B.A. heavyweight championship, as Wells's opponent, without apparently consulting Wells or Maloney. Bettinson was soon corrected, as *Boxing World* paraphrased Maloncy:

> ... he says he saw in half-a-dozen papers that Wells and Storbeck had been matched before he or Wells was (sic) approached about it. Jim felt aggrieved at such treatment, and says the financial end of the deal was not to his liking...[19]

So the match was off.

Notes

1   *Mirror of Life*, 25 September 1909; *Boxing*, 2, 9 October 1909.

2   *Boxing World*, 22 September 1910; *Mirror of Life*, 24 September 1910.

3   Eugene Corri, *Refereeing 1,000 Fights*, 1919, pp. 57-58.

4   *Mirror of Life*, 22 October 1910; *Boxing World*, 27 October 1910.

5   *Boxing World*, 13 October 1910;   *Mirror of Life*, 25 November 1910.

6   *Boxing World*, 12 January 1911.

7   *Ibid.*, 19 January 1911.

8   *Referee*, 15 January 1911.

9   Thomas Inch, *Boxing and Physical Culture*, Aldershot, n.d. (1945), p. 190.

10   *Health and Strength Magazine*, May 1902, p. 271.

11   *Ibid.*, April 1905, p. 440.

12   *Boxing*, 28 January 1911.

13   *Boxing World*, 16 March 1911; *Boxing*, 18 March 1911.

14   Corri, *op. cit.*, pp. 59-60.

15   "I had heard that Ketchel's dynamic onslaught was such it could not readily be withstood, but I figured I could jab his puss off...", Philadelphia Jack O'Brien quoted in A.J. Liebling, *The Sweet Science*, 1958, p.7.

16   *Referee*, 30 April 1911.

17   *Boxing World*, 4 May 1911.

18   A.F. Bettinson and W. Outram Tristram, *The National Sporting Club*, 1902; Guy Deghy, *Noble and Manly*, 1956; Douglas Sutherland, *The Yellow Earl*, 1965, pp. 176-7.

19   *Boxing World*, 11 May 1911.

CHAPTER SIX

JACK JOHNSON

It is generally believed that Johnson did not fight in this country, but [Ben] Taylor met him at the Cosmopolitan Club, Plymouth..... The bout only went eight rounds. Two points about it that stand out in my memory are, firstly, the wonderful courage of Taylor, who was quite outclassed and hit all over the place; and, secondly, the super-human boxing skill of Johnson... to find his equal one would have to resurrect some of the great ones of the past.

Joe Palmer, *Recollections of a Boxing Referee*, 1927, pp. 47-8.

The match for the world's championship between Jack Johnson and Bombardier Wells was announced in July 1911.[1] Johnson had arrived earlier for a music hall tour. He had been to this country previously as we have seen; he had boxed at Plymouth in 1908 before he relieved Tommy Burns of the world title. There was no challenger for his boxing crown in the U.S.A., where racial disturbances had followed his defeat of Jim Jeffries, and Johnson had taken a wife who was a white woman. He would not kowtow to white-american public opinion, but this was not the only reason for his inability to get matches. He demanded too much money, would not meet black opponents who could draw few spectators and little film money; and there appeared to be no white heavyweight good enough to stand a chance of beating him. The two best heavyweight contenders were black Americans who were also in Europe. Sam McVea had just beaten George Rodel in Liverpool, and Sam Langford had won at Olympia topping a McIntosh bill. In Paris in April they had boxed a twenty-rounds draw with each other, and Johnson had beaten both of them before he became champion. The fact that all three were in Europe in 1911, suggests that the boxing market in the U.S.A. had flagged since Reno,

certainly newly formed Law and Order Leagues and Committees of Public Decency had campaigned to get the sport banned.[2] Alternatively, racial tension may have made the U.S.A. an unhappy place for black boxers to be. According to Gerald Astor:

> From 1907 to 1921 more than twice as many bills to bar interracial marriage as statutes to halt lynchings were tossed into the Congressional hopper. In fact, the only force that saved the United States from a total codification of segregation was the inertia of Congress...[3]

Wells had been engaged with the same things in England as Johnson had been doing in the U.S.A. He made his debut as an actor at the Hackney Empire,[4] and boxed exhibitions. One of these was at the camp of the Loyal North Lancashire Regiment at Tidworth where he watched his old opponent, Clohessy, stop a sergeant in the Dragoon Guards, and then boxed "three smart rounds" with Jim Maloney.[5] One can only presume that they were well paid, because Wells's name produced "a large gathering of spectators".

The articles of agreement for the world title contest were signed on the 15th of July. Under these, Johnson was to receive £6,000 one hour before the contest started, and Wells, £2,000 within a month after the fight. Jimmy White, the promoter, was to have the film rights, worth £5,000, and the proceeds of copy to newspapers (supposedly written by Johnson), as well as four/fifths of the admission money to see Johnson train.[6] White was a Lancashire business man, who became a financier, and committed suicide in 1927 when his finances collapsed.[7] At this time he was heading a sure-fire gamble because the match, to be held at Earl's Court on 2 October was a fantastic attraction. A great black champion meeting a hugely popular underdog who was British; had the contest come off White would have been much richer. As it was he earned publicity which probably paved the way for his future career.

The story of how and why the match was called off has been told by Stuart Mews in "Studies in Church History" published in 1972.[8] Unfortunately, an otherwise well-researched, scholarly article, is marred at the start where the author confused Billy Wells with a contemporary boxer, the lightweight champion, Matt Wells, who was also a Londoner. Matt, a Jewish boy, captained Lynn Boxing Club, and won the A.B.A. championship four times in succession, before going on to become a successful professional.[9] The two Wells's must have known each other closely, but there was almost a foot difference in their height.

Britain's non-conformists had gained political influence in the nineteenth century through the Liberal Party. This political "clout" was in decline from the turn of the century, and "Free Church" leaders bewailed their smaller following and their flagging power. Their ills were similar to those felt by white protestants in rural North America. An order in which their values took precedence, appeared to be on its way out with, they said, dire consequences for morality.[10] The campaign to stop the Johnson-Wells "fight" was not an imitation of the agitation in the U.S.A. over Johnson *versus* Jeffries. There was no deep resentment in this country against black people for most people had never seen a black person. James Butler, who became a distinguished boxing correspondent for the *Daily Herald*, related an anecdote which is important in this context. He had to meet Sam Langford in 1907 in Liverpool and bring him to London:

> Langford's arrival in Town... created a mild sensation. Negroes were seldom seen in the streets in those days, and we hadn't walked a hundred yards before we were surrounded by scores of youngsters lustily singing: "I see you've got your old brown hat on!".[11]

It was the black man, not his brown bowler, which caused the sensation. There was prejudice in the abstract for black people, in

practice there was real bias against alien immigrants, who in 1911
were Central-European Jewish people.

Johnson was popular in England.[12] Newspapers thought it
an unhappy match because he would be far too good for Wells.
They worked out separately at Earl's Court, and whilst Wells
trained at Leigh-on-Sea, Johnson took an apartment at the Royal
Forest Hotel in Chingford. Whether he did much roadwork round
Epping Forest is doubtful, but the local paper raved over his music
hall show, and poked fun at "Pastor" Meyer who was trying to stop
the forthcoming contest.[13]   F.B. Meyer's name would have been
unknown to readers who were not Baptists, only three weeks
earlier. He was the secretary of the National Free Church Council
which had asked the licensing authority, the London County
Council, to stop the contest soon to take place at Earl's Court. The
L.C.C., through its Chairman, did warn Earl's Court Ltd. that when
their licence came up for renewal in November, the application
might be jeopardized if the contest went on. The L.C.C., however,
had no power to stop the match said its Chairman. Promoter
White told the press there was nothing to stop the fight, and he
thought Wells would win. The Free Church Council was not
objecting to boxing in general, but to this one contest because,
following Reno, the two men were to:

> ... batter one another, not in self-defence, nor to
> protect the weak, but for high stakes, and to gratify
> that craving for the sensational and brutal which is
> inconsistent with the manhood that makes a great
> nation.[14]

The argument was weak, and Meyer, in his first year as Secretary,
was probably trying to raise the profile of the Free Church Council,
and demonstrate his own administrative energy. The non-
conformists needed to be seen as evangelic, campaigns were
necessary to revive membership, and the fight, with all its publicity,
was a suitable issue at an appropriate time. White and Meyer
continued their controversy through press statements, and many

others joined in. The question of colour was brought into the public domain by a member of the ruling Conservative group on the L.C.C., George Swinton, who had once been extra A.D.C. to the Viceroy of India. He wrote whilst holidaying in Northern France:

> ... it is a question of a fight between a white soldier and a black champion. If it were to be fought at the National Sporting Club, if there was to be no advertisement and no cinematographic reproduction, it would concern nobody... If the fight itself is to be sanctioned at the heart of the Empire... Are we not thereby making quite unnecessary trouble wherever the black and white races are side by side?[15]

The old soldier added that the L.C.C. had no power in the matter, and that the Home Secretary should stop the match taking place, or ban film cameras from Earl's Court. When Winston Churchill, the Home Secretary in a Liberal Government, had been asked in 1910 to ban the films of the contest at Reno, he had said he had no power to do so. The Baptist Union urged him to ban the October 2nd contest in a letter to the *Times*, and added a genetic point to their argument:

> There can be no greater disservice to the negro race than to encourage it to seek a glory in physical force and in beating the white man..... Slowly they are climbing the steep path... It matters not to us if an Englishman is beaten, for we have proved our... courage, endurance, service, art, and learning. But to a race which has not yet achieved glory it is a crime to turn its ambitions to... glory... in the Prize Ring.[16]

The campaign to ban the match had arisen only in September, long after, and because of, the great excitement caused by White's promotion. This was by far the largest amount of money ever to be paid to boxers in this country, and he had raised the cheapest price of admission to half a guinea. The Empress Hall in Earl's Court, since 1887 *the* place for exhibitions, was said to accommodate 20,000 spectators. This was a boxing show on an unprecedented scale outside the U.S.A. where only five times had boxers fought for a larger sum of money.

It is difficult to find in the sporting press an opinion that Wells would beat Johnson. Lord Lonsdale compared the match to a horse race, with a two year-old running against a three-year old.[17] Ben Tillett, the dockers' union leader, took the opposite view, he felt sure that Wells was going to win.[18] The supporters of boxing, however, were unanimous that the match should not be stopped, especially by a "Puritan party which would kill all sport in English life".[19] *Boxing World* objected to Wells having to work out at Earl's Court twice daily (4p.m. and 8p.m.) because he looked stale.[20] The *Times* regretted the match because it was premature in Wells's career, and went on to matters callisthenic:

> .....Wells is not, nor ever will be, the equal of
> Johnson. His drooping chin and swan-like neck and
> unprotected middle storey are weaknesses which no
> amount of physical culture can cure completely...[21]

but the newspaper did believe that he was "the speediest and most skilful of the many *white man's hopes*", and there was some truth in both these judgements. Johnson was perfectly built for heavyweight boxing. He was six feet tall, weighed around 15 stones, with the all-important, short thick neck. In the last ten years he had fought 75 contests, and had lost only four of them, the latest in 1905. He had boxed in Canada, Australia, England, and all over the United States. Wells was an inch or so taller than Johnson, weighed two stones less, and he had had fewer rounds of professional boxing, than Johnson had had contests. With the campaign to stop the contest reaching a crescendo it is impossible to say whether bookmakers were taking bets on the result of the fight; if they were laying wagers, it must have been long odds-on a Johnson victory.

In the week before Wells was due to meet Johnson the campaign to stop the contest was successful. The Home Secretary did not ban the match though he was prepared to try to. On Sunday, 24 September, he wrote to his wife from Balmoral a letter which, towards the end, contained this enigmatic sentence:

> I have made up my mind to try to stop the Wells-Johnson contest. The terms are utterly unsporting and unfair.[22]

Meyer and his supporters had been to the Home Office four days before and, in Churchill's absence, had spoken to officials. They had sought a government veto on the grounds described earlier. Churchill's decision to try to ban the contest followed Lord Lonsdale's argument which had appeared in Thursday's *Times*. This was that if the large slice of the purse was to go to the winner of the contest, and not Johnson, win, lose, or draw, then the terms would have been fair. Lonsdale had refused to add his name to Meyer's memorialists, and as steward of Lanark and Edinburgh he was in Scotland at this time.[23] Churchill was not interested in plebeian sport, he was a Liberal Party Home Secretary under pressure from that Party's natural supporters to ban the fight. Lonsdale did not want the fight banned, but his view of the terms of the contract made by the promoter, was used by Churchill to get the well-organised non-conformist conscience off his back. It was not as Mews claimed a sporting decision on the Home Secretary's part,[24] it was a party political one. He objected to the terms, not the fight.

Three legal actions were started on the Wednesday before the match, and these can be dealt with briefly. The one which stopped the contest taking place was an application by the freeholders of Earl's Court, the Metropolitan District Railway Company, for an injunction against the leaseholders, Earl's Court Ltd, restraining them from allowing the fight to take place. This was granted on the grounds that the L.C.C. would refuse to renew the licence of the hall if the match went through. The second action was initiated by the Director of Public Prosecutions. This was to require White, Wells, Johnson and the boxers' managers to enter into recognizances not to commit a breach of the peace, and it was dropped when the High Court interlocutory injunction in the first case was granted. The third action, by the Variety Theatres Controlling Company, was for an injunction to restrain Johnson from appearing anywhere other than the Birmingham Hippodrome. This was adjourned and Johnson left Chingford, returning to the United States just before Christmas. His next contest, which he won easily, was not until July, in Las Vegas.

The most interesting point brought out in the first-mentioned hearing was that the Railway Company had allowed posters advertising the match to be displayed at their railway stations. White's publicity had been outstanding.[25] The second case was held at Bow Street and hours before it began, crowds gathered outside the Court. Johnson conducted his own defence whilst White, Wells and Maloney were collectively represented by luminaries of the legal profession. Johnson showed most effectively how the Police Superintendent witness knew nothing about boxing. When the five defendants left the Court they were loudly cheered by huge crowds outside.[26] Such evidence is not conclusive, but it does suggest that the general public favoured this contest. Meyer's campaign, however, had found support in the ruling classes. Churchill, coincidentally, left the Home Office three weeks later seeking greater glory as First Lord of the Admiralty.[27]

Wells resumed his acting activity. The sketch was called "Wanted, a Man", a costume drama where he meets beautiful Lady Molly, and wins a bare-knuckle fight with Squire Hazelton. It was written by Walter Macnamara, and had parts for one of Wells's brothers and for Jim Maloney, who played Merrill, a scoundrel. At the Palace, Tottenham, there was huge applause for the hero's line "I'm afraid of no man, white or black".[28] This was melodrama presumably, and the audience in 1911 came to see a boxer from their own background who had been matched with the supremely formidable Johnson, and not Wells the actor. We can safely assume that Maloney extracted appropriate salaries for all three parts, and from poor photographs in newspapers, the costumes appeared excellent. The publicity gained from beating Hague, the announcement of the match with Johnson, Meyer's campaign, Earl's Court training, and the appearance at Bow Street Magistrates' Court had given Wells and Maloney three months of ascending attention by the newspapers. They were headline news and could not fail to make money. There were articles and interviews, "Why I am Fighting Jack Johnson"[29] and "How Bombardier Wells was discovered".[30] The weekly *Boxing* devoted a full page to advertising *Modern Boxing: A practical Guide to present-day Methods*, by Bombardier Billy Wells, which on 29 July was "now in preparation". Throughout September it must have been impossible for Wells to walk anywhere without being recognised, and his whole family must have been minor celebrities in Southend-on-Sea. Referee Corri, a fine teller of stories, revealed how Wells reacted to fame:

> I have seen him in the stalls of a theatre of varieties at Southend... when one of the girl singers ingeniously worked his name into a topical song. He blushed scarlet, [and] covered his face with his hands.....[31]

The National Sporting Club eventually tempted Wells into signing for his next contest. It was the match Maloney had rejected in June, and the terms now would certainly have been better. Fred Storbeck and Wells were to box for a purse of £1,250, with the winner to receive £850, and the loser the remainder. They were allowed £25 each for training expenses. In addition, each side staked itself for £260.[32] The winner would therefore receive a total of £1,135, and Maloney would place large bets privately, though bookmakers would offer Wells to win at long odds-on. This quashed rumours about a rematch with Moir; an offer of $20,000 to go to the United States; and a fight with Johnson in Paris because White had undertaken not to stage the contest in the British Empire. The contest at the National Sporting Club a week before Christmas was disappointing. Wells knocked out the South

African in the tenth round but looked poor in winning.[33]   The
former A.B.A. champion was slow and cumbersome yet held his
own for nearly thirty minutes.   Storbeck, like many boxers, was "a
talker" in the ring, and though he swore strenuously,[34] Wells
remained composed.   Wells had not had a contest for seven months,
and he was in boxing terminology "ring rusty", yet he stopped a
man weighing 14 stones, though some newspapers suggested that
Storbeck had failed to pick up the count of the referee.   Wells's
next contest was to take place in the U.S.A.

Notes

1   *Boxing World*, 20 July 1911.
2   Randy Roberts, *Papa Jack*, New York, 1983, pp. 93-94.
3   Gerald Astor, *Gloves Off: the Joe Louis Story*, 1975, p. 18.
4   *Boxing World*, 29 June 1911; *Boxing*, 22 July 1911.
5   *Ibid.*, 30 March 1911.
6   *The Times*, 28 September 1911.
7   Seymour Hicks, *Between Ourselves*, 1930, pp. 184-8;   R.D.
          Blumenfeld, *R.D.B.'s Procession*, 1935, pp. 233-5;
          Sir Harry Preston, *Leaves from my unwritten Diary*,
          n.d. (1936), pp. 228-37.
8   Stuart Mews, "Puritanicalism, Sport, and Race: a symbolic
          crusade of 1911", in G.J. Cuming and Derek Baker,
          Popular Belief and Practice, Studies in Church
          History, Vol. 8, Cambridge, 1972, pp. 303-31.
9   John Harding, *Ace of Clubs: 100 years of the Lynn A.C.*,
          1992, chapter 2.
10   Mews, *op. cit.*, pp. 305-6, 313-4.
11   James Butler, *Kings of the Ring,* n.d. (1936), p. 30.
12   *The Times*, 12 September 1911.
13   *District Times*, 21, 28 July, 29 September 1911.
14   *The Times*, 16 September 1911.
15   *Ibid.*, 19 September 1911.
16   *Ibid.*
17   *Ibid.*
18   *Boxing*, 5 August 1911.

19   *The Times,* 27 September 1911, reporting statement of the
      Rev. Everard Digby.
20   *Boxing World,* 7 September 1911.
21   *The Times,* 12 September 1911.
22   Randolph Churchill, *Winston S. Churchill,* Vol. 2
      Companion Part 2, p. 1128.
23   *The Times,* 23, 27 September 1911.
24   Mews, *op. cit.,* p. 331. Churchill was keen on big game
      hunting, see his letter to his mother from British
      East Africa in 1907 in Churchill, *op. cit.,* pp. 692-5.
      The letter is not recommended reading for animal
      lovers.
25   "For four weeks every main thoroughfare in London and the
      suburbs has been placarded with the date and place
      of the contest" *Boxing World,* 21 September 1911.
26   *The Times,* 28 September 1911. *Boxing World,* 5 October
      1911, reported: "The police had the utmost difficulty
      in keeping the ... streets [surrounding Bow Street]
      from getting congested, and when Wells made his
      appearance the crowd literally swept down on him
      and he was cheered again and again... An equally
      fine reception was in store for Johnson...".
27   For Churchill sniping at McKenna, the First Lord of the
      Admiralty, with whom he succeeded in changing
      jobs, see especially Churchill's letters to Lloyd
      George, 14 February, 14 September 1911, and
      telegram to Master of Elibank 14 October 1911, in
      Churchill, *op. cit.,* pp. 1041-2, 1124-5, 1129-30.
28   *Boxing,* 22 July 1911; *Boxing World,* 24 August 1911.
29   *Boxing,* 5 August 1911.
30   *Mirror of Life,* 16 September 1911.
31   Eugene Corri, *Refereeing 1,000 Fights,* 1919, p. 45.
32   *Referee,* 5 November 1911.
33   *Ibid.,* 24 December 1911; *Mirror of Life,* 14 December 1912.
34   Joe Palmer, *Recollections of a Boxing Referee,* 1927, pp.
      122-3; *Answers,* 29 May 1915.

Cartoon by Franklyn Turner of Johnny Thwaites, Petty Officer
Curran, and Gunner Moir. Mr Thwaites was Curran's manager.
Note the fowl. From *Boxing*, 29 June 1912.

CHAPTER SEVEN

NEW YORK, NEW YORK

The clever boxing held the attention of the fans all the time, Wells' brilliant work especially enthusing the sports. No roughhouse work ever entered into the skirmish, such as creeps into the usual heavyweight battle, this allowing the go to commence and continue in a smooth, even and scientific glide.

John J. Haas on "Bombardier Wells stops Kennedy", *New York Call*, 19 July 1912.

Public interest in Wells diminished in the early part of 1912. He signed for no matches, and though he was expected to box an exhibition at the National Sporting Club, in Bettinson's annual benefit at the end of January, he did not appear. Gunner Moir took his place to spar with the City of London Policeman, William Hazell, whom Wells had boxed as an amateur.[1] Moir was clamouring for a return contest with Wells, and promoters were not interested for two reasons. Although Moir had previously knocked out Billy at Olympia, it was generally thought that his victory was lucky, and that Wells had developed so much since then that he would win easily next time they met. Secondly, Maloney was asking for too much money for what promised to be a one-sided contest. Moir fell ill in the Spring, went into hospital, and melodramatically came out to sprint after Wells's train as the latter was leaving for the U.S.A. At least, that was how *Boxing* described the events of Saturday, 11 May.

Wells, his brother Sid, and Maloney sailed on the *Mauretania*, a Tyne-built Cunard liner with the speediest service to New York City. No articles for a match had been signed before they left, but the American press was sure that he wanted to meet Al Palzer. Palzer was 22 years of age, of German descent, from a farm in Iowa, and the latest "White Hope". He was a large young man, with little artistry, but great strength and a strong punch, which had won him four of his last five bouts by knockouts.[2] He had fought entirely in New York City, where the Frawley Law ruled boxing from 1911 until 1917. This allowed contests to be a maximum of ten rounds, with no decision to be given in a fight which went the distance, thus a champion could lose his title only if he was knocked out in New York State.[3] Palzer never became a champion, but he entered boxing's side-show history because he was shot dead in 1914 by his father. When Wells arrived, Palzer had never lost a contest, and both men had ambitions to meet and beat Johnson who was now in his mid-thirties and talking of retiring.

Sports' writers in New York found the Bombardier polite and pleasant. Richard Edgren thought he looked more like a student than a boxer, and another suggested to Wells that he should take an easier opponent first, to which the boxer replied that he had travelled this far to meet only the best heavyweights.[4] Wells made a very favourable impression on the American press. He trained at Rye with a minimum of publicity. Truman Harte, who wrote for *Boxing* complained:

> We know next to nothing of him... and scarcely anyone has seen him work out... He has shown... that he is fast both on his feet and with his hands, and... can let go a snappy punch... The only doubts I have heard expressed... are first that he looks a bit weak about the neck and also about the mid-section, that he is too much of a good-looker to be a real fighter, and that he seems to be lacking in stamina...[5]

which was faint praise indeed.

The Americans were not unused to British boxers campaigning on the East Coast. Matt Wells, the lightweight champion, on his latest visit, had disappointed in three contests, and was actually recuperating at Rye. They were, however, unused to heavyweights coming, for not one worth mentioning had been seen since Charlie Mitchell in 1894. Most commentators thought Palzer would win, and Wells was two stones the lighter man.

The contest at Madison Square Garden is worth describing. Wells punished Palzer throughout the first round, and a "dandy right hook" put the blond farmboy down for a short count. This did not stop Palzer coming forward in the second round like an advancing monolith, with Wells fending him off with the traditionally-British straight left. In the third round Palzer got inside this defence and, with punches to the stomach, and with some of the 9,000 spectators standing on their chairs, he dropped Wells twice, and finally knocked him out.[6] Wells later wrote that this was almost a repeat of his contest with Moir,[7] yet that was not accurate because there was no doubt that Palzer, a young boxing prospect, had won well. The important comparison was that both Moir and the Iowan had taken Wells's best punches without being knocked out.

Al Palzer squandered the chances that his victory gave him. He had long been wrangling with his manager Tom O'Rourke, and instead of keeping in training, he left his next match, a minor one, until November, and finally fought seriously on New Year's Day when he was stopped in 18 rounds, in California, by yet another "white hope". Had Wells kept out of harm's way for ten rounds with Palzer, it would have enabled Maloney to command thousands of dollars in his matchmaking. In New York State alone, boxing supporters paid nearly a million dollars for admission in one year.[8] As it was, the Wells' camp stayed in New York for another contest, chose a lesser opponent, and a modest purse from Madison Square Garden Athletic Club. Wells was hugely admired for twice dragging himself up off the canvas in that dreadful round three, and boxing fans of New York City seemed to have loved the tall limey.

Wells's second contest in the U.S.A. was against Tom Kennedy, an experienced professional who, unusually for American heavyweights, had boxed previously as an amateur. He was therefore dubbed by newspapers "the millionaire boxer". He had boxed Palzer twice, going 19 rounds under New York rules, and as he weighed the same as Wells, this was good form. Kennedy was a boxer rather than a mauler, and Wells won every round before knocking the local man out in the eighth round.[9] This match had been taken only three weeks after the defeat by Palzer, and the effect of his quick return to winning, minimized the impact in the U.S. and British press of his defeat. It was now considered that possibly fatigue, rather than Palzer, had knocked Wells out on a hot June evening. Would Wells have knocked big Al out in the first round if Maloney had not shouted to Billy "Stand away"?[10] Wells himself wrote that he never heard his corner's calls to stand off after he had Palzer in trouble in the first round, but he did think, with hindsight, that he should have gone in to stake all on a quick knockout.[11] Thus as the three men sailed home, the contest lost might be excused, and everyone in Britain could easily agree with "Gareth" in the *Referee* that:

> ... According to my judgement Bombardier Wells stands out by himself among the heavies......[12]

meaning, of course, on this side of the Atlantic.

Wells returned from the United States intent on a short holiday, and then more matches, and a further visit to the U.S.A., perhaps in October. In the event he got married in September, and stayed home a little longer. He married a girl from South London, Ellen Kilroy, who was the daughter of a publican. They married at Tooting Parish Church the week after his 25th birthday, and her age was 16 years. Pubs and prize-fighting went together, and had done so for a couple of hundred years, it is reasonable to guess that Billy met Ellen through her father Luke. *Boxing* filled the front page of its next issue with a photograph of the handsome couple and wrote:

THE BOMBARDIER'S FUTUR

BOXING

PUBLISHED EVERY TUESDAY IN LONDON; EVERY WEDNESDAY IN THE PROVINCES. ONE PENNY.

THE ONLY PAPER IN THE WORLD SOLELY DEVOTED TO BOXING.

Vol. VI.—No. 158. SEPTEMBER 14TH, 1912. Registered at the General Post Office as a Newspaper and for Canadian Magazine Post.

THE BOMBARDIER AND HIS BRIDE.

... surely on no previous occasion has any intimate
event in the life of any professional boxer created
such widespread interest...[13]

and this was true. It marked a change in the coverage of sport in
the British press. The sportsman could be written about as a
person, and these columns were written to be read by women as
well as men. The music hall had long recognised that sparring on
stage used the boxer's *charisma*, and drew large audiences. Women
would not attend boxing matches, but they could read and talk
about the sport. Photographs were commonplace in many
newspapers, and to know the face made a subject more interesting.
Wells looked what he was, a nice young man, whilst some previous
heavyweight champions had been roisterers. Wells was an ideal
type boxer who came along at a time when society was loosening
sexual and religious shackles. The press was responding to social
changes wrought by compulsory education (1870); rise of socialism
(1880s); organisation of general workers (1890s); formation of a
Labour Party; agitation for votes for women, and legislation to
soften the impact of old age, unemployment and sickness.
Journalism became different not through any individual, or
overnight: but gradually through decades of cumulative change, in
the economy and technology, in pay and working hours, in the
expectations of the working class, and the heightened consciousness
of the middle class.

Wells went back into training at a gymnasium in
Hampstead.[14] Promoter Jimmy White, undismayed apparently by
the Earl's Court fiasco, booked the King's Hall and halved his
admission prices for Wells against white South African George
Rodel.[15] Rodel had come to this country to box in the A.B.A.
championships in 1911, and was not allowed to enter because he
was regarded as a professional. He had given Storbeck a close
contest in Johannesburg,[16] but he was no match for Wells in South
London where he was knocked out in the second round. The so-
called hall of a thousand lights which had not seen such a grand
show since McIntosh had gone back to Australia, was packed for

this evening of disappointing boxing. Wells looked fine, the chief supporting contest, however, was an undignified scramble between Petty Officer Curran and Gustave Pigot, billed respectively as the heavyweight champions of Ireland and France. The *Mirror of Life* half-humorously reported that "Nutty" was disqualified for hitting the "frogeater" after the bell sounded to end round nine. The pride of Plymouth had a propensity to get disqualified. For the main event, Wells had in his corner the usual four seconds, two of whom were his brothers, Sid and Alf. Newspapers praised his performance, and it was noticed in the New York press.[17]

Wells went back on the halls with exhibitions during the weeks before Christmas. At the Empress, he sparred with Maloney and Stoker Smith at 6.10 and 9 p.m., and did the same at the Oxford at ten o'clock, where also a film of him training for Johnson was shown. Record business was done at the thousand-seater music hall in Oxford Street, where among the supporting artists was George Formby.[18] Wells's huge success in show business was attributable to two factors. First, the upturn of the trade cycle between 1909 and 1913, there was a boom in the economy; and secondly, to Maloney's astute handling of their business. Wells was not a man to sell himself, he was certainly modest, and possibly shy, yet he travelled extensively and caught the public eye in a series of pleasing ways. At Cardiff he gave an exhibition for charity during the great miners' strike, and later ran in a sprint race at the Stadium. When a party of boy scouts from Walworth were drowned whilst boating, Wells sparred at a benefit which raised £150 for their parents.[19] He played football for Variety Stage *versus* the Legitimate, and scored two goals.[20] He sparred at benefits in Leicester and Sheffield in the same week, and since his wife was with him at the Attercliffe Hall, he may well have used a circuit of leisurely exhibitions against local boxers as an extended honeymoon. Everywhere he received an enthusiastic audience, and at the Ring, Blackfriars, they threw their caps in the air.[21]

Willie versus Bombardier Wells, a thousand feet comedy film, was made in France in November 1912. Little Willie, the star of a series of films, was around five years of age, and of course he beat the six footer. M. Faivre directed for the Eclair Company at Epinay, and the lead was played by a boy called Sanders. The Tyler Film Company Ltd. released this "excellent comedy"[22] in Britain in February, and F. Hurdman Lucas, who was the Paris correspondent of *Boxing* wrote of it:

> Without undue exaggeration, this film is about the most detailed and yet most amusing representation of a boxing contest ever put before the public. It is not, as might be supposed, a ridiculous knock-about sort of thing that we see far too much of at picture palaces, but just a cleverly-thought-out little sketch...[23]

It was the start of Wells's film acting career which lasted longer than his time in professional boxing.

Despite his defeat by Al Palzer, 1912 was a remarkably successful year for Wells. He was being compared with Jem Mace. His victory over Tom Kennedy was the first time a European heavyweight had won in the United States in living memory, and plaster casts of Wells's bust were even available in Paris where boxing had only recently displaced savate as a major spectator sport.[24]   Maloney could pick and choose between offers from promoters, in the event, the Wells party, including Billy's wife, took the Mauretania for New York and Madison Square Garden again.

The heavyweight boxing situation had changed a little since Wells's first visit. Johnson had easily beaten another "white hope" and he was more subject to racial discrimination.[25]   He was not to box again in the United States before 1920, yet he was the World's Champion until 1915. Promoters shuffled white contenders. The latest, whom Wells wanted to meet, was Luther McCarty, a twenty-year-old from Nebraska, who had beaten Palzer. This match failed to materialise, however, and McCarty was killed three fights later in Calgary.[26]   Whilst Wells trained at the same quarters in

"Gunboat" Smith

Westchester, Garden Athletic Club secured a suitable opponent for
him who turned out to be a man with a similar boxing background
to his own. They were almost exactly the same age, and Edward
Smith had served in the United States Navy from 1905 until 1909.
Gunboat Smith learned to read and box, and became champion of
the Pacific Fleet. Although he was light for a heavyweight and
could not box scientifically, he would fight anyone and had a
powerful punch. Since leaving the Navy he had fought almost
fortnightly from coast to coast,[27] and briefly had been a sparring
partner to both Ketchel and Johnson.

Smith is one opponent of Wells who speaks to us in later
years. In the early 1970s, a young graduate, Peter Heller,
interviewed former boxers all over the United States for his
wonderful book of oral history, *In This Corner*. Smith, aged 83,
was living with his wife in Brooklyn when he was tape recorded,
and, historically, there is no excuse for not quoting Heller's book at
length:

> .... I made an awful lot of money in those fights for
> that time. There was no taxes, and I spent money
> like a drunken shoemaker. I'd get it today and I'd
> be broke tomorrow. I begin to get into the big class
> in '12 or '13. I was in the height of my glory then.   .
> I'm what they call a top-notcher... Bombardier Billy
> Wells, he come over here to fight Jack Johnson.
> They wanted him for the Heavyweight Champion of
> the World. But they wanted to give him what we
> call a setup, somebody he could knock over. They
> said, "Let's pick up the Gunboat. He's out in San
> Francisco and we'll bring him here to the Madison
> Square Garden and he'll be a pushover for this
> fellow 'cause this guy can box, he can hit, and he's
> a scientific fighter, this Bombardier Wells". Which
> he was.

Smith and his manager travelled to New York, and Smith trained hard:

> Now, when I come to the fight I thought I was in great shape. I didn't think there was a man in the world that could lick me... But I'm about 20 to 1 on the short end.

Wells was an 8 to 5 on favourite according to the *New York Times*:

> The house was packed to the rafters, and when I come out there one fellow was sitting way up in the balcony clapping, and... when that lousy Englishman come out, I thought the building fell in. It made me sore how they... think so little of me and make a big fuss over this bum...[28]

Wells had the better of round one, and Smith knocked him unconscious in round two. Smith said in his interview, and newspapers reported at the time, that he walked through Wells's punches, though he was ten pounds the lighter man.[29] Wells was warmly applauded as he left the ring, yet there was no point in staying in America, for promoters could no longer give him top billing. Smith went on to beat, among others, Jess Willard, George Rodel and Sam Langford, and the next fight he lost was in July 1914 at Olympia, in London, a disputed disqualification against Georges Carpentier.

Notes

1   *Referee*, 14 January, 4 February 1912.
2   *New York Call*, 10 May 1912; Nat Fleischer (ed.), *Ring Record Book*, 1968, New York City, p. 322.
3   *Ibid.*, p. 761.
4   *Boxing*, 8 June 1912.
5   *Ibid.*, 29 June 1912.

6   *New York Herald*, 29 June 1912; *New York Call*, 29 June 1912; *Boxing*, 6 July 1912.
7   *Thomson's Weekly News*, 19 June 1920.
8   *Boxing*, 18 January 1913.
9   *New York Call*, 19 July 1912; *Boxing*, 27 July 1912.
10 *Ibid.*
11 *Boxing*, 10 August 1912; *Thomson's Weekly News*, 19 June 1920.
12 *Referee*, 25 August 1912.
13 *Boxing*, 14 September 1912.
14 *Mirror of Life*, 14 December 1912.
15 *Ibid.*, 7, 14 December 1912.
16 *Boxing World*, 9 March 1911; *Mirror of Life*, 12 November 1910.
17 *Referee*, 8 December 1912; *Mirror of Life*, 14 December 1912; *New York Times*, 7 December 1912.
18 *Mirror of Life*, 14, 28 December 1912.
19 *Boxing*, 3 August, 7 September 1912.
20 *"Boxing's" New Year's Annual 1913*, p.13.
21 *Boxing*, 7, 28 September 1912.
22 *The Bioscope*, 26 December 1912, p. 1003.
23 *Boxing*, 4 January 1913.
24 R.G. Allanson-Winn, *Boxing*, 1897, pp. 346-55;   W.H. Pollock et al., *Fencing, Boxing, Wrestling*, 1904, p. 132; *Boxing*, 26 October 1912, pp. 612, 629.
25 Randy Roberts, *Papa Jack*, New York, 1983, pp. 130-7.
26 Nat Fleischer and Sam Andre, *Boxing*, 1980, p. 89.
27 Fleischer, *Ring Record Book*, 1968, pp. 282-3.
28 Peter Heller, *"In This Corner"*, New York, 1974, pp. 29-44.
29 *New York Call, New York Times, New York Herald*, 15 March 1913; *Thomson's Weekly News*, 3 July 1920.

CHAPTER EIGHT

PACKEY AND PAT

This sport for ruffians is really a refuge for gentlemen.

Eamonn Andrews' introduction to Patrick Myler, *The Fighting Irish*, 1987.

Friday evening in New York City, 14 March, and Sunday afternoon, Ghent, 1 June 1913, were critical times in the life of Billy Wells, and it is interesting to compare and contrast the three boxers, American, French, and British respectively, who were involved. They were, of course, all working class, for the bourgeois boxer appears in fiction,[1] but not in the history of the sport. Edward (Gunboat) Smith was by far the most disadvantaged for he was brought up in an orphanage, whilst Georges Carpentier and Wells had strong family support. Both kept close links with their families, and had brothers in training quarters, and in their corners. Smith and Wells were aged 25 years, and whilst Carpentier was only nineteen, he had had as much professional boxing experience as the two who had been in the armed forces. Smith had a poor opinion of boxing managers, whilst the others were closely attached to, and friends with, their managers throughout their careers, and Maloney and François Descamps were compared in their dedication to their charges. All three were ready to engage in contests with black boxers, though Wells never met one, the others did. The high point of Smith's career was when he outpointed Sam Langford in Boston between his contests with Wells and Carpentier, whilst the latter won and lost to black opponents in the same period, and Carpentier eventually lost his world's light-heavyweight title to Battling Siki from Senegal. Objectively, Wells was less ready than the others to box black men, probably because he had less confidence. None of them had a contest with Jack Johnson. Only one, Carpentier fought for the world's heavyweight championship, when he lost to Jack Dempsey in 1921 in the first ever million-dollar-gate. Smith boxed Dempsey three times before the latter

became champion, and he beat the man who reigned between
Johnson and Dempsey, Jess Willard, again before the huge white
man took the title. The profound difference between Wells and his
first two opponents in 1913, however, was in the frequency of their
matches. In the two preceding years (1911-12), Smith had engaged
in 31 contests; Carpentier had taken 27; and Wells had seven.[2]

Wells returned from his second trip to the United States to
a disheartened British boxing milieu. Not only had he lost, but a
year earlier the British middleweight and bantamweight champions
had lost to Frenchmen. The former victory, in Monte Carlo, had
gone to Carpentier, and he and Wells knew each other. Carpentier
had been Wells's sparring partner when he was training to meet
Johnson. Jimmy White had brought him over for the chief
supporting bout at Earl's Court, and though the main contest was
ruled out, the programme went on, and Carpentier outpointed his
useful British opponent over 15 rounds. When he had sparred with
Wells, Carpentier was aged 17 years, and we need to look briefly at
this youthful prodigy.

Carpentier was brought up in Lens, a small mining town in
Northern France between Arras and Lille. His father was a
labourer, and both his parents were of peasant stock. In his own
story, published in English in 1955, *Carpentier* described his
cramped home and happy childhood in detail. They never went
hungry, perhaps because Carpentier was a younger brother, they
drank beer, and this translation by Edward Fitzgerald is a
wonderful model of sporting autobiography. His future manager,
Descamps, was a gymnastics' teacher in Lens, and they met at
classes at the Maison du Peuple which were outside the jurisdiction
of formal Catholic school. Descamps was a free-lance teacher,
qualified in gymnastics, scratching a living, and part of the
community. His new young pupil soon stood out in class at
tumbling and savate, and when their team entered for a gymnastic
competition at Le Havre, Carpentier did well. After about two
years he went into the adult class at École Descamps, and
Carpentier, now nearly 13 years old, was entered in regional savate

Carpentier

competitions. In Paris, for the national championships, Carpentier lost in the semi-finals, and about this time he gave up his messenger's job to team up with Descamps giving exhibitions of conjuring, acrobatics, savate, boxing and hypnotism in halls and cafes around their home region. The thought-reading act followed discreet inquiries locally, and "the local bumkins were invariably impressed".[3] In the Spring of 1908 the "nipper from Lens" won the national savate championships at the Salle Wagram in Paris; he weighed just over seven stones and now turned seriously to boxing. He had two contests scheduled for 20 rounds before his fifteenth birthday; won the lightweight championship of France in 1909; the welterweight championship of France, then Europe, in 1911; and as he grew through the weights he won frequently. Carpentier was occasionally beaten. One British boxer, Young Snowball of Walworth,[4] had knocked him out in Paris in 1910; two Frenchmen[5] and three Americans[6] had also won contests with him, yet by 1912 he was a hero in France and the middleweight champion of Europe.

Wells was a strong favourite to beat the smaller man. The match had been made to coincide with an international exposition, and special trains from Paris and London helped to fill the great hall. The international aspect of the contest was accentuated, and a band played *The Marsellaise* as Carpentier walked to the ring for a contest which many thought he was ill-advised to have taken.[7] It could be described in very few words. The first round was fought at distance, a right to the chin put Carpentier down and he barely survived the three minutes. From the next bell, the younger man adopted a crab-like stance and attempted to work his way inside the much longer reach of Wells. During round two Carpentier recovered. Once inside, he stayed close using short punches mainly to the body. Both men wrote their own full accounts of this contest, and the following quotations come from Carpentier in 1913, and Wells in 1920. They described the fourth round:

I had previously landed several blows on Wells'
body... they seemed to affect his wind, for his short
gasping breathing told me that much, but he
remained on his feet. Then I bethought me to try
a little higher or nearer the heart, and immediately
I began to feel the weight of his body on mine... my
opponent was floundering ... just about to step away.
That was the instant to let go the right... and Wells
falling forward on to me was sufficient proof that he
was now all in... While being naturally elated at my
victory, I felt a tremendous pang of regret for the
defeat of so excellent a fellow and boxer as
Bombardier Billy Wells.[8]

The excitement was at white heat... Cheer after
cheer greeted Carpentier as he left his corner. I
tried hard to keep him at a distance, but I was
becoming very conscious of my own bodily weakness,
and Carpentier was inconveniencing me by being too
clever to allow me to keep him at a distance for
long. Within a minute my opponent hit me on the
jaw, and, as I went to guard against the blow, [he]
drove home to the stomach. The blow was
surprisingly powerful, and caused me to wince. I
was getting very badly confused, and when he
landed a powerful left to the body I instinctively
dropped my hands to guard my stomach. It was
Carpentier's golden chance, and I give him all credit
for taking it on the instant, and with both hands...
No man could withstand the tattoo, and down I
went to be counted out.[9]

The terms of the Ghent contest are not known, but neither
boxer would have signed articles for less than a guaranteed £2,000
for themself. This was a major promotion, the first for the
heavyweight championship of Europe, and both boxers were already
well-off men. The finances of individuals are notoriously difficult to

determine. Both of them could spend money freely. Carpentier
had had a house built for his parents in Lens, and himself lived in
a large apartment in the centre of Paris.[10] Curiously, we learn of
Carpentier's bank balance from Billy Wells. *Pearson's Magazine* for
December 1913, carried his article "The Boom in Boxing". In it he
praised boxing as healthy exercise, and maintained that the boxer
had to live a clean well-regulated life. Intelligence was most
important in the ring, he argued, and went on to give four
examples of wise boxers who had saved lots of money. Carpentier
"not yet twenty, is worth £15,000"[11] he wrote, and Carpentier had
the least saved-up of Wells's examples. Not surprisingly, Wells did
not tell readers of *Pearson's* what his own bank balance was.

After Ghent, Jim Maloney's bargaining powers were
subdued. In six contests since Wells had won the English title he
had lost three times. There was consolation in that the defeats had
come in away matches, and that win or lose, each had ended in
knockouts, and five had been exciting fights. Additionally, everyone
agreed that Wells needed to box more frequently in order to develop
his potential. For all these reasons, the National Sporting Club,
despite cramped premises and shortage of funds, was back in the
market. Their Lonsdale belts, instituted in 1909, had added spice
to the claim that no match outside their portals could be considered
a national championship, and Wells, having won there twice, could
keep the belt if he won again. The club put up a purse of £400 for
Wells to defend his title against the heavyweight champion of
Ireland, Packey Mahoney, of Cork. Both sides lodged a £200 stake,
and Wells was only a slight favourite at 5-4 on to win.[12]

Mahoney was born in Cardiff, though his father had been
a school-teacher in Cork.[13] The first mention of him as a boxer
comes from July 1912, when he knocked out a member of the Royal
Irish Constabulary in a ten rounds' contest in Dublin. *Boxing's*
Dublin correspondent had heard a great deal of his "prowess in
Cork", and thought he had "considerable possibilities".[14] The *Cork
Evening Echo*, much later, claimed that Pakey (as they spelled it)
had not taken up the sport until he was 24 years of age,[15] and this

Packey
Mahoney

Wells
versus
Colin
Bell

made him about the same age as Wells. He had boxed at the Cork
Opera House, he was a strong, under twelve stones man, though a
trifle slow, and he had come to London as a boxer in the Autumn
of 1912.[16] He was under the management of Jim Sullivan, the
boxer who had lost his European middleweight title to Carpentier
at Monte Carlo, and Mahoney made his English debut at the Ring,
Blackfriars, as a light-heavyweight, with a splendid win over
Gunner Ellis.[17]

As if making up for his late start in professional boxing,
Mahoney boxed anywhere, and he boxed often. His next opponent
was the black American, Young Johnson, whom he beat twice, first
at the Albert School of Arms in East London, and then at the
Opera House in Cork City which was packed from "floor to ceiling"
for this contest.[18] In March 1913, he reached the National Sporting
Club in Covent Garden, where he stopped, in 16 rounds, Wells's
former opponent, Dan Voyles. The Dubliner had recently met the
County Clare-born Petty Officer Curran, and had won on a foul in
the third round, so Mahoney decisively became the heavyweight
champion of Ireland,[19] and he so impressed the members of the
Club that they matched him with the English champion.

Wells knocked Mahoney out in the thirteenth round before
a packed house at the Club in Covent Garden. It was not a close
contest. Mahoney won the first and sixth rounds, but was down in
the eighth, and three rounds later the right side of his jaw was
badly swollen. It had been broken earlier, and the Irishman fought
on with courage and determination. The *Daily Herald* wrote:

> Mahoney took enough punishment for twenty
> champions, but nature could not withstand it all,
> and although out-classed he proved one of the
> gamest boxers who ever pulled off a shirt.[20]

Wells had an eye closed at the end of the fight, and Mahoney went
to hospital. He recovered and continued to box until 1917, when
the citizens of Cork presented him with a silver replica of the

Lonsdale Belt, and when Packey died at the age of 85, this proud trophy adorned the home of his son William.[21] A match with world-class Wells was the high point of more than one boxer's career as we shall see.

Wells kept the real Lonsdale heavyweight belt either by winning three contests for it against Hague, Storbeck and Mahoney, or retaining it for three years, the circumstances are not clear. Wells's next opponent was a London-Irishman, born in Bromley-by-Bow.

Pat O'Keefe had been boxing professionally since 1902, and, aged nearly 30, he was a top-class middleweight. He had boxed all over the globe; at the National Sporting Club eleven times: in Paris thrice, and twice in Sydney Australia, as well as New York City, Philadelphia, Brisbane, Dublin, Glasgow and Liverpool. He was a clean, canny boxer, of whom *Boxing* wrote that he "seems, like old port" to improve with age. He had briefly claimed the national 11 st. 6 lbs championship in 1906, and he was to win it again in 1914. O'Keefe was an accomplished boxer, used to meeting opponents heavier than himself; more experienced than most, he had been Tommy Burns' sparring partner in training for Johnson, and a second in the losing corner at Rushcutter's Bay.[22]

The Ring, Blackfriars, had boxing shows three times a week: on Monday and Saturday evenings, and a matinee on Thursday. The sport in 1913 was highly popular and profitable. The promoter, Dick Burge, who had been a lightweight champion of the 1890s, had converted the 1783 Surrey Chapel, and latterly an engineering workshop, into a boxing hall in 1910. The cyclical building was ideal for the purpose, holding 1,700 persons at area level, and 400 in the balcony.[23] The negotiations between Burge and Jim Maloney to sign this match would have been tough, for Wells was far and away the most famous boxer to appear there since it opened, yet Ring purses were minute generally, and the match was a crowd-puller. The contest was a battle between two clever boxers, and the bigger one won. Wells knocked O'Keefe out in the fifteenth, of a twenty rounds' bout, and the spectators cheered themselves hoarse, as much for O'Keefe's pluck as for Wells's competent win.[24]

The return match with Gunner Moir caused chaos outside the Canterbury Music Hall in Westminster Bridge Road. The Canterbury was one of London's earliest music halls, opened in 1851, it had been rebuilt in 1876 with a patented sliding roof. It held over 1,500, but many more people tried to get inside to see Wells meet the old soldier from Lambeth. Moir had trained hard at Brighton, and although he scored with massive right swings, Wells knocked him out with lefts to the stomach. "The match did not go five full rounds" wrote a reporter, yet "more action and excitement were crowded into those 14 minutes of actual boxing" than is usually seen in much longer contests.[25] Jack Johnson was introduced before the fight started, and the packed spectators were difficult to control. Wells turned in from body punches which, consequently, struck him round the kidneys raising shouts of "foul" from the Bombardier's supporters. *Boxing* blamed Wells for his evasive tactics. In the fourth round, Moir partisans thought he was about to win, as Wells clinched and the referee had to get into the ring to separate the tiring gladiators. Johnson, interviewed after the knockout, said:

> This is the first time I have ever seen Wells fight...
> He can certainly box, and I should say that he can
> hit tremendously hard. He is really very clever, but
> he strikes me as being a terribly nervous man.[26]

and this seems to be a thoughtful commentary on all we know of Wells throughout his boxing career.

Notes

1   For example, Bernard Shaw, *Cashel Byron's Profession*, and
        Conan Doyle, *The Croxley Master*.
2   Fleischer, *Ring Record Book*, 1968, pp. 70-1, 282-3, 332.

3   *Carpentier by himself*, 1955, p. 29.

4   Better known as a successful boxing manager of Tommy Farr and Freddy Mills under his real name, Ted Broadribb. See also his, *Fighting is my Life*, 1951.

5   Fernand Cuny and Henri Piet.

6   Dixie Kid, Frank Klaus and Billy Papke.

7   Fred Dartnell, *"Seconds Out!"*, n.d. (1924), p. 10; *Carpentier by himself*, pp. 68-74.

8   Georges Carpentier, *My Methods: or boxing as a fine Art*, n.d. (1913), translated by F. Hurdman-Lucas, pp. 78-80.

9   *Thomson's Weekly News*, 10 July 1920.

10   *Carpentier by himself*, pp. 66-7.

11   *Pearson's Magazine*, December 1913, p. 706.

12   *Cork Examiner*, 1 July 1913.

13   Willie Mahoney, Packey's son who lives in Cork, very kindly sent me the papers about his father, and we spoke on the telephone. This arose from my letter requesting information in the lively weekly paper, *Irish Post*, 31 October 1987.

14   *Boxing*, 6 July 1912.

15   *Cork Evening Echo*, 16 April 1980, for which reference I thank Willie Mahoney.

16   *Boxing*, 7 September 1912.

17   *Boxing*, 14 September 1912.

18   *Boxing*, 5, 26 October 1912.

19   *Boxing's Book of Records*, 1914, pp. 54-5, 200-1.

20   Quoted in *Cork Examiner*, 1 July 1913.

21   *Cork Evening Echo*, 16 April 1980 and conversation with Willie.

22   *Boxing*, 9 October 1909, 28 January, 11 March 1911, 15 June, 10 August 1912; *Boxing World*, 13 October 1910, 6 April 1911; J.G.B. Lynch, *Prominent Pugilists of Today*, 1914, pp. 40-48; *Boxing's Book of Records*, 1914, pp. 158-9.

23   London County Council, *Boxing... Licenses*, 1935, p. 41; *Boxing World*, 19 May 1910; Leslie Bell, *Bella of*

Blackfriars, 1961, pp. 81-90;   Dartnell, *op. cit.*, pp. 203-4.

24   *Thomson's Weekly News*, 17 July 1920.
25   *Boxing*, 20 September 1913.
26   *Ibid.*

CHAPTER NINE

CARPENTIER AGAIN

...boxing crowds are not exactly slow on the uptake, and quickly noticed that I was the brother of Bill, who was boxing as "Snowball of Walworth". Why Snowball? Just because he had a white patch about the size of a half a crown on the back of his head. So instead of the spectators saying "Come on, Ted", it was "Come on, young Snowball". I did not think it sounded too badly, so Young Snowball it remained...

Ted Broadribb, *Fighting is my Life*, n.d. (1951), p. 10. The author was the only British boxer to beat Carpentier. This was as a featherweight in Paris, in 1910.

Wells was now 26 years of age, and he and Ellen's first child arrived in September. They lived in Mitcham, which was one of London's most open and attractive suburbs, and it was close to her parents' home. One problem, which still confronts many highly paid boxers, is how to balance the grind of two, three or four weeks training, with leisurely stretches after each fight. Work was erratic for Wells, particularly because he was a heavyweight as there were fewer boxers of his size, and because, in a home context, he was too good. He had lost abroad, so Maloney had to lower his sights on purse money, but not too much because the economy was booming. The scenes outside the Canterbury Music Hall were evidence that boxing promotion was awash with money. Wells and Maloney had layed the admonition that they took insufficient matches by having three contests in ten weeks, and although Mahoney, O'Keefe and Moir had all failed to last the distance, Wells had boxed 33 rounds. The Wells' supporters and he, felt that the route to international honours had opened up again. For a heavyweight he was relatively young in age and experience, and improving at his trade. He had reversed his first loss, and people perhaps forgot that the Gunner was 36 years of age, with only two contests, both losses, in the two previous years.

The National Sporting Club offered a return match with Carpentier. The purse, a huge one for Bettinson to offer, was £3,000, for 20 rounds, with each side to stake £500, and the contest to take place on the second Monday in December.[1] The purse would most likely have been split with £1,750 going to the winner, so that the loser would walk away with only £750. For this figure to be meaningful it must be compared, and in 1913 it would have taken an experienced locomotive driver, the most highly skilled railwayman, six years to earn it.[2]

The English camp chose a seaside bungalow at Selsey Bill as quarters for training. In addition to Stoker Smith, Sid and Alf Wells, and Maloney, there were two new faces to help preparation, trainer Mainwaring (about whom we know little), and Pat O'Keefe. The latter told *Boxing* that Wells's work at close quarters had much improved,[3] then took a contest himself in Paris on December 3, and lost in 17 rounds. Wells was possibly better trained and fitter than he had ever been.

Carpentier knocked Wells out in just over a minute of the first round. Wells described the catastrophe in *Answers*, a popular weekly paper, six months later, in the first of a series of articles entitled "My Life and Fights":

> ...... Stepping into the centre of the ring, he [Carpentier] stood there, calmly waiting for me. Then suddenly, how I can never tell, I became overwhelmed with a sense of the wiliness of my adversary, the importance of the fight, and the responsibility...

Wells, of course, had fought at the National Sporting Club three times previously. He was confident enough to bet an extra £100 on himself just before the contest started. Ringside betting was endemic in professional boxing. The article continued:

> I had made up my mind so much about Carpentier
> rushing me that I was absolutely taken aback... He
> landed two crushing punches in my stomach before
> I hardly moved ... several blows in the same spot...
> doubled me up like a half-shut knife. While I was
> in this bent position, I received a punch on the left
> eye which knocked me over...

Wells heard the count, he simply could not get up.[4]

When Wells described the same match in *Thomson's Weekly News* six years later, his emphasis was different. He had not been so confident before the fight:

> It was only natural, I think, that previous to my
> second meeting with Carpentier I should be a little
> nervous as to the outcome. I was desperately
> anxious to repay the public for the fidelity they had
> shown during all my ups and downs.

There had been an argument between Descamps and Maloney about who was entitled to enter the ring second. This honour fell to the champion invariably, but they were both champions of Europe and England respectively. The French eventually left the dressing room first, and accidentally, wrote Wells, they were left standing in the ring for some minutes before the English camp appeared. Wells described the reaction to this:

> National Sporting Club members were growing very
> impatient at my non-appearance. I was very
> annoyed at this and hurried down... Instead of my
> usual warm reception I was greeted in rather a half-
> hearted manner...

He was already tense from the row in the dressing room, and his
lukewarm reception further upset him, the way he froze when
Carpentier refused to come at him was as he wrote in 1914.[5] It
would have been surprising if Wells had not been nervous
immediately before a contest with an opponent who had
comprehensively beaten him six months earlier.   Carpentier
remembered Wells receiving warm applause despite the time-
wasting before the bout started.[6] The French boxer was giving
away a stone in weight, and several inches in height; boxing at this
famous fistic lyceum for the first time, and he had little English
language in 1913. He had been criticised for his performance in his
last two contests, and, in France, he was not regarded as a heavy
puncher,[7] yet he had, what Wells lacked, confidence in himself.
The British boxer exacerbated his humiliation by attempting to
make a speech of apology from the ring. He felt he had let the
audience down.[8] This audience is worth considering for a moment.
It was not the crowd who had milled around Westminster Bridge
Road in September, or those regulars who attended the Ring
Blackfriars and Stepney's Premierland.   It had been a strictly
members-only club in the 1890s, now a few guineas would get you
in, indeed Wells on his return from India had bought a ticket. It
was still, however, overwhelmingly a middle-class place, and a space
to assert masculinity.[9]   This audience was stunned by the short
contest, and their favourite boxer, a Lonsdale belt-holder, called
Wells a coward to his face. This was not the view that Carpentier
took,[10] and the referee, stockbroker Jack Angle, in his splendid *My
Sporting Memories*, published in 1925, wrote:

> Bombardier Billy Wells must certainly take rank as
> the most sensational heavy-weight boxer this country
> has produced. Wells is an enigma... One might
> speculate for a month... and yet be no nearer an
> elucidation of the mystery than one was at the start.
> Wells is not a coward, but undoubtedly there is
> something lacking in his temperament which puts
> him all wrong just when he ought to be all right.[11]

Angle did not refer directly to this contest which he refereed, yet his choice of words is important, for he was a respected authority on prizefighting and boxing from 1890, and had been a useful amateur himself. Angle was right, Wells was brave and he was temperamental, as was proved in later contests. Wells regained his confidence as we shall see, and his public still loved to see him fight. Wells did not box at the National Sporting Club again for three years, yet the memoirs of members make it clear that they recognised that he was an outstanding British heavyweight champion.[12] Carpentier went on to become the bane of that breed. Six weeks later he stopped Pat O'Keefe rapidly in Nice, and after the war he tore up the credentials of three more contenders. Snowball in 1910 was unique, and Carpentier gained his reputation as a devastating puncher against British opponents. Wells wrote of "that terrible night" and his "sorry display" without reference to himself feeling that he had let down his country. He was ashamed for spectators who had paid "opera prices to see a great pugilistic display"[13] and nationalism seems hardly to have entered his thinking. One anecdote from *Answers* is revealing, he wrote:

> Two or three days after the fight I played football at Fulham before a great crowd. It was a charity match, on behalf, I think, of the *Daily Mirror* Christmas Pudding Fund.

He did not really want to play, he was depressed and unsure of the crowd's reaction to him, yet:

> the moment I entered the field they cheered me as if I had done something very remarkable, instead of having failed most miserably in the attempt.[14]

This personal story raises interesting points about the man. He was a good sport to turn out, and he could play for he scored four goals. More importantly, he thrived on support, and had an affection for his supporters. A modest man, he drew confidence from what the public thought of him, and his public was broader than the members of the N.S.C. in Covent Garden.

In 1914 Wells came back by taking two contests in January, another in March, two in April, and one in June. In this time he almost rehabilitated his reputation with his critics, who still cast doubt on his psychology as a boxer. His supporters were soon convinced that he was yet a contender who would beat Johnson, and promoters' appetites for the Bombardier's name on their bills could not be satisfied. A boxing programme with Wells caused anticipation. Before the main contest there was a thrill not quite to be found in other arenas. When his last fight had been a wash-out, as with Pigot, his next one drew a huge crowd. The most highly publicised match, against Bell, was a disappointment, though that was the big Australian's fault. At Liverpool, in the closing stages, Rice's supporters jeered Wells's tired jabs which were almost dabs, but the Stadium was filled when they met there again. When Maloney was persuaded, and Wells had signed, the promoter's minder ordered extra money bags.

The Theatre Royal, Belfast, staged Wells's first come-back contest, and according to *Boxing* it was "packed to suffocation" with "a mighty gathering outside".[15] Had the champion lost this contest his career would have been in great difficulty. His opponent was Gunner Rawles, a genuine heavyweight, born in Dundalk, he had fought mainly in Liverpool, and he was a southpaw. The southpaw stands right foot and hand foremost, and the textbook reply to such an awkward posture, is for the orthodox boxer to concentrate upon throwing right hands. Rawles had had mixed results in less than first-class boxing company, but he was an experienced man who had won well previously in Belfast,[16] so this was a serious test for Wells. Wells won when Rawles's seconds threw in the towel half way through the twenty rounds, but Rawles had raised a "mouse" under his opponent's left eye, and it had been a grand contest.[17] In Cardiff, ten days later, it was no such case. Gaston or Gustave Pigot had boxed in Paris and London, indeed he was second on the bill when Wells beat George Rodel, but he was dreadfully slow, and the Frenchman was stopped in the first round.[18]   Curiously, Cardiff was not a centre for boxing, in South Wales much more took place in mining towns like Tonypandy.   On this Saturday evening, "huge numbers" turned up only to see a mis-match.

It is difficult to judge the sums of money Wells earned from each of these provincial contests.   One can guess that Maloney would accept a figure, win, lose or draw, which would not have been less than £100.   Wells, boxing frequently, would need to spend little on training;   sidestakes would be small and betting opportunities limited.   Yet it is hard to see how an out-of-town promoter could offer more than £100 for Wells to engage in a contest, when ticket prices could not be raised exorbitantly.   The negotiations would turn on the capacity of the hall.   Early in 1914 Maloney had less leverage in bargaining than for three years. Without contests, endorsement of products would drop off, appearance money would dwindle and requests for magazine articles would vanish.   1913 had produced a strong balance sheet, but the prospect of future dividends was bleak unless the Wells' company turned over some quick wins.   They were not, of course, short of money.   This was still coming in presumably, for *Modern Boxing* ran to at least eight editions.[19]   The Wells' camp, however, believed their man was going to be a world champion, and in order to achieve this he needed extra measures of confidence, stamina, and ringcraft, which could only be gained by taking contests. Promoters, who had been shut out since the victory over Sergeant Sunshine, were in with a chance of signing Wells, thanks to the result of Carpentier II.

British boxers also took a new view of Wells.   If a light-heavyweight could knock him out in one round, then they stood a chance of beating him, and they metaphorically queued up to chance their arm.   The next boxer to gain the opportunity was a young man on a winning run.   Born in Great Yarmouth, Bandsman Blake had left the Norfolk Regiment, with whom he had won the middleweight championship of India, and from March 1913 he had had twenty professional contests, mostly in London, and had won

all of them.[20]   When he met Wells he was aged about 22, and
though an 11 st. 6 lbs man, he must have been fancied for the
match was staged at the London Palladium.   This was the third
entertainment-type building on the Argyll Street site, opened at
Christmas in 1910, it had a huge stage and held an audience of
over three thousands.[21]   The best seats cost five guineas, ladies
came, and men wore evening dress. Since this seems to have been
the first time in London that women were recorded as attending a
professional boxing match, the evidence is important, and the report,
in *Boxing* is worth noting.   Monday evening was prime time for
gentlemen to go to see boxing in London, and evening dress was
often worn, especially at the National Sporting Club.   No women
ever attended that place, however, and neither did the bioscope
cameras. A film was made of Wells *versus* Blake, and the arcing
carbons played havoc with spectators' eyes.   The film was being
shown at the Electric Coliseum, Stoke Newington, a fortnight later,
and there you could get in for threepence.   The crowd at the
Palladium seemed strange to *Boxing*'s Paris correspondent:

> There was something particularly cold in this night's
> entertainment. One might have been present at a
> political meeting. True, cheers rent the atmosphere
> as the gladiators made their appearance... [but] the
> whole thing was so severe after our French rings...

Both boxers wore dressing gowns, and the applause on entry, and
after the announcements, was shared by the boxers:

> The fair sex mustered in huge numbers at the rear
> to indulge their passion for hero-worship, Billy
> being the object. All the ladies wanted Billy to
> win.[22]

The last sentence was probably untrue, if Blake was equally
applauded before the fight began, then the very much smaller man
probably gained sympathy as he tore into Wells for the first three
rounds. Wells was 6-4 on favourite, and Davids generally invite

empathy, though this one was knocked out in the fourth round. The most significant fact, however, is that in March 1914, middle-class women had attended a professional boxing show. They had sat behind the ring, on the stage, in seats which may, or may not have been, segregated from men's seats. In 1911 Wonderland advertisements had included the words "Ladies admitted to Stage Only"[23] so women had attended earlier, though there is no direct evidence. These years, nevertheless, of furious suffragette agitation, do show this odd change in relations between the sexes, and women did start going, in small numbers, to watch men perform in previously all-male situations. In Paris this was commonplace, and in France the sport was very young. Certainly Wells was an acceptable player to this new audience, who also watched three minor contests, and applauded. From Hurdman Lucas's comments we cannot infer who these women were. Members of the National Sporting Club, like Bettinson and Lord Lonsdale, were present, and the price of seats in this plush location suggests a carriage audience, which Wells was not averse to. Ellen never watched her husband box, she had, of course, seen him spar in exhibitions.

The film of this fight was shown with supporting features ("Jack the Wolf" a Western drama in two acts at the Coliseum) so many girls and women, and children perhaps, may have seen the ten minutes of mainly in-fighting, ending with right-left-right to the jaw on a flickering one-reel recording.[24]

The Canterbury Music Hall was the scene of Wells's fourth comeback contest. He was opposed to Albert Lurie, who had been the heavyweight champion of France until deposed in his home town of Bordeaux by the ubiquitous Carpentier. Since then he had managed to beat Pigot, but he was no match for Wells who won easily in a dull contest.[25] This match had been preceded by a Royal occasion which is best described by Wells's words in 1920:

> My serious contests were broken... by a pleasant interlude when in the March month I boxed an exhibition with Pat O'Keefe before the King at the

barracks of the 2nd Life Guards, and both Pat and
I enjoyed ourselves immensely.[26]

George V, who was in his late-forties, would have met the sport
during his time with the Royal Navy, and his sons, Edward and
Albert, then teenagers, were later to attend the National Sporting
Club occasionally.[27] The King had at least one thing in common
with Wells, soon after his coronation he had visited India. This was
in December 1910, and there was a strong rumour that he was
going   to   present   the   prizes   at   the   Delhi   Durbar   boxing
championships.[28] He did not, a General did instead; but whilst he
was there George made Delhi the Capital of India instead of
Calcutta, so his trip was not wasted.[29] Wells at this time had been
demobbed and he was working at the King's Hall, and preparing for
Moir.

Whilst training for his fifth comeback contest Wells
discovered his antidote for the problem of inactivity between
contests, he took up golf. Not far from the Elms, at Leigh-on-Sea,
was a golf course, and when a friend persuaded him to try the
game he quickly became an addict.[30] There was a course also, near
his home, on Mitcham Common, and he found one convenient to
Liverpool when he went up for the match with Bandsman Rice.
Over 500 golf clubs had been formed in England since 1890, and in
these years the game bloomed, particularly as a snobbish recreation
for men of the business and professional classes.[31] Wells did not
need to cultivate bank managers or solicitors, his contacts lay in
sporting newspaper offices, and in any case that was Maloney's
domain. There is no evidence that Wells was a snob. He disliked
the accompaniments of being a public figure, like people addressing
him as Billy in the streets,[32] so the golf course was the ideal retreat
for a home loving man who did not drink a lot. In addition, he
soon became good at the game and wrote lovingly of it in *Answers*
in May:

Billy Wells—Golfing.

Training camp in 1913, with Billy, Stoker Smith, Pat O'Keefe, brothers Sid and Alf, and trainer Mainwaring.

I golfed in the neighbourhood of Liverpool on the
morning of the day on which I fought Rice, and I
golfed the day after, though I found a fight of
twenty rounds was not good for the follow through...
I am now fitted out with a brand-new bag and a
brand-new set of clubs. I am not too old to become
a professional golfer yet, and think it would be good
fun to make a world's record by being at one and
the same time a champion boxer and a champion
golfer.[33]

Bandsman Dick Rice hailed from a fighting family in Leeds
and his brother Ernie was to become British lightweight champion
in the 1920s. The Bandsman, who had been in the Rifle Brigade,
had boxed professionally from 1909, but he had engaged in twice as
many matches as Wells, and he had won most of them. He had
beaten Lurie, Voyles, and Rawles twice, drawn with Rodel, and lost
to Carpentier in Paris. On his return from Australia in 1912 he
was ready to challenge almost anybody, and cartoonists portrayed a
confident fellow blowing his own trumpet.[34] His contest with Wells
went the full distance and the decision was a close one.[35] Rice,
being much shorter, continually tried to work inside, and he was
notorious for his chopping blows, often to the neck, though Wells
complained of kidney punches.[36]

"My Life and Fights by Bombardier Wells" was advertised
to appear in *Answers* immediately after the Rice fight, and promised
to tell the truth about his failure against Carpentier, and in later
issues "his Indian experiences and... plans for the future".[37] The
come-back surely was completed. *Answers* was a hugely popular
16-page weekly magazine, and, costing one penny, it had a large
circulation. It had been a success from foundation in 1888, and its
proprietor Lord Northcliffe now owned a stable of newspapers
including the *Daily Mail, Daily Mirror, Evening News* and the
Times. Northcliffe, as Alfred Harmsworth, was the originator in
Britain of tabloid publications for the masses, and Wells could have
gained no greater publicity.[38] It is impossible to guess what fee

Wells received, but it is possible to speculate about the authority of articles under his name which appeared over the next six weeks. They are well-written, highly readable, and usually accurate. Glaring mistakes, like locating Broad Street Board School in Hackney,[39] are rare. My judgement is that Wells talked at length to a journalist, and a sub-editor prepared the copy for the press. Wells would hardly have had the time to wholly write these lengthy articles whilst training, first for Rice, and then at Brighton to meet Colin Bell. Furthermore, he would surely not have allowed his golf to be neglected as the first wave of enthusiasm for the game swept over him; his baby was at time-absorbing early-toddler stage; and Ellen was expecting again. Wells probably wrote well, other Board School scholars did.[40] Between the "highs" of boxing contests, I suggest, it would be difficult to sustain such work. From popular magazines, with their romantic stories and articles by professional cricketers,[41] we turn to the summer of 1914.

Notes

1   Lynch, *Pugilists op. cit.*, p. 49.
2   Norman McKillop, *The Lighted Flame*, pp. 100-1.
3   *Boxing*, 6 December 1913.
4   *Answers*, 23 May 1914.
5   *Thomson's Weekly News*, 24 July 1920.
6   *Carpentier by Himself*, p. 79.
7   *Boxing*, 25 October 1913.
8   *Answers*, 30 May 1914.
9   Guy Deghy, *Noble and Manly*, 1956, is still the best account of the National Sporting Club.
10   *Carpentier by Himself*, p. 81.
11   Bernard John Angle, *My Sporting Memories*, 1925, p. 79.
12   Norman Clark, *All in the Game*, 1935, pp. 301-2; Trevor Wignall, *I knew them All*, n.d. (1938) p. 111; Corri, *Refereeing op. cit.*, Chapter 3.
13   *Answers*, 30 May 1914.
14   *Answers*, 23 May 1914.
15   *Boxing*, 24 January 1914.

16 *Boxing's Book of Records*, 1914, pp. 169-70; *Boxing*, 28 January, 11 March, 18 March 1911, 17 August, 21 September, 12 October 1912, 20 September 1913.
17 *Boxing*, 24 January 1914.
18 *Sunday Chronicle*, 25 January 1914; *Boxing*, 31 January 1914.
19 R.A. Hartley, *Bibliography of Boxing Books*, n.d. (1988), Alton, Hants, pp. 309-10.
20 *Boxing*, 24 August 1912, 6 December 1913; *Boxing's Book of Records, op. cit.*, is inaccurate on Blake whom it shows boxing at Wonderland after the building had been burned down.
21 Diana Howard, *London Theatres and Music Halls 1850-1950*, 1970, pp. 140-1.
22 *Boxing*, 7 March 1914.
23 For example see *Ibid.*, 11 February 1911.
24 *Hackney Gazette*, 20 March 1914.
25 *Carpentier by Himself*, p. 76; *Boxing*, 11 April 1914.
26 *Thomson's Weekly News*, 31 July 1920.
27 *Deghy op. cit.*, p. 175.
28 Royal Munster Fusiliers, *Regimental Annual 1911*, pp. 41-43.
29 W.J. Makin (ed.), *The Story of twenty-five Years*, n.d. (1935), pp. 86-93.
30 *Answers*, 30 May 1914.
31 John Lowerson "Golf" in Tony Mason (ed.), *Sport in Britain: a social history*, Cambridge, 1989, pp. 187-214.
32 *Answers*, 20 June 1914.
33 *Ibid.*, 30 May 1914; Corri, *Refereeing op. cit.*, pp. 65-66.
34 *Boxing*, 23 March 1912.
35 Dartnell, *op. cit.*, p. 207.
36 Jim Driscoll, *Text-Book of Boxing*, n.d. (1921), pp. 50-1; *Answers*, 30 May 1914.
37 *Health and Strength*, 16 May 1914.
38 For the magazine and its proprietor see, R.C.K. Ensor, *England 1870-1914*, Oxford, 1963, pp. 310-315; Viscount Camrose, *British Newspapers and their*

Controllers, 1948, pp. 4, 9-10, 21-25, 125-6; R.D.
Blumenfeld, *R.D.B.'s Procession*, 1935, pp. 205-10.

39 *Answers*, 27 June 1914, the school was in Stepney, and
Wells could not have made that mistake.

40 Examples are numerous, try Frederick Willis, *A Book of
London Yesterdays*, or T.A. Jackson, *Solo Trumpet*.

41 *Answers*, 3 January 1914 et seq. contained line drawings,
but surprisingly no photographs; articles by Jack
Hobbs, the England cricketer; short stories aimed
at women; articles by George R. Sims; articles on
professional football.

CHAPTER TEN

COLLARS AND TIES

"Did you see what I did to Colin Bell?"
Harry Weldon, star of early twentieth-century music hall.

Music hall comedian, Harry Weldon, was enormously popular, and his acts included several sketches with a sporting theme. Charlie Chaplin, who played "feed" in the football routine, wrote of him:

> Weldon's comedy character was of the cretinous
> type, a slow-speaking Lancashire boob...[1]

In his boxing turn, Weldon offered to fight anybody in the house:

> ... any lady ... any lady?

With Weldon on stage was his comic manager (not Chaplin, who had gone to the U.S.A.) and when eventually any man in the audience showed a sign of responding to the challenge, Weldon would implore his manager:

> tell 'em what I did to Colin Bell.[2]

This became a catchphrase which caused smiles for years, but to understand why, it is necessary to look at the enormity of the build-up to this boxing match.

In the same week as Wells outpointed Bandsman Rice, Bell lost on points in the main event at Premierland, the boxing arena in Stepney which had replaced Wonderland, which had been burned down in 1911. Though Colin Bell lost, it was the quality of opposition he had faced which impressed promoters. Joe Jeannette, a black heavyweight from New Jersey, had many times met

Johnson, and had recently outpointed Carpentier in Paris. Wells had watched the Premierland 20-rounder, and he thought Bell had won. Bell's record is something of a mystery. He claimed to have had over thirty contests in his native Australia, and never to have been counted out.[3] When he arrived in Britain he was matched with Petty Officer Curran at Liverpool Stadium and lost on a foul. Eleven days later he was in the ring with Jeannette, and a month after that he was matched with Wells for what was billed as the championship of the British Empire. Wells knocked Bell out in the second round at the huge exhibition hall at Olympia[4] after the first had been even, and it is not entirely fanciful to suggest that Jeannette had carried Bell at Premierland.[5] The black heavyweights who were prepared to campaign anywhere had difficulty in getting matches against white opponents. They received little pay for boxing each other, though they did this frequently, and there was every reason to make white boxers look good in the hope that more would come forward to give men like Langford, McVea and Jeannette better purses to box for. Johnson was in a different position to these three obviously, he was champion of the world, and, for his own reasons, he would not give them a match either. The great contest at Olympia on 30 June was a triumph of boxing promotion, and on the night Wells outclassed Bell, and music hall gained a funny line.

The promoter of Wells *versus* Bell was new to this particular trade, though he had been involved in wrestling, roller skating, freak shows and, in the U.S.A., theatre. Charles Blake Cochran[6] was a supreme publicist, and this country's leading boxing promoter in 1914 and during the economic boom which followed the war. He had used Olympia to stage fun fairs and circus, zoo and pageant, but this was his entry into boxing, and his impact was massive.

Cochran advertised his boxing promotion as "People's Night", with 10,000 seats ranging in price from five guineas to five shillings:

The occasion has been designed [the newspaper
advertisement read] for the public, and the man in
the street will find himself catered for as never
before.[7]

Whom Cochran was trying to attract must be deduced, for the
elements of his "MAMMOTH CROWD" which "everything points to"
were not specified. There are clues however. All seats were
reserved, and they were bookable at the Olympia box office,
Cochran's offices in New Cavendish Street, and at Keith Prouse
agencies in New Bond Street and Cheapside. Forward ticket sales
were to take place largely in the West End of London, and they
could be booked by telephone. Cochran targeted the carriage crowd
who had attended the Palladium, by referring to "boxes and Royal
enclosure", yet he was aware that they were not numerous enough
to fill Olympia, so his advertising was designed to appeal to the
democracy. Women were not mentioned in the advertising I have
seen. Cochran may have concluded that this was counter-
productive, and that some would attend anyway if he could sell this
Tuesday evening out to men. With his selection of this day of the
week, if he had the choice, Cochran needed an audience which
included people new to watching boxing. Regular boxing supporters
would decide whether to go or not, on their own estimate of the
programme of boxing. Low-paid working men, like those who went
to the Ring, may have viewed five shillings as too expensive
whatever the quality of the boxing matches, in which case they
would have gone in order to stand outside. Whether Cochran sold
cheap last-minute tickets to stand inside, as he may have done, was
not mentioned in the advertising, though it may have happened on
the night. With purses of £500 for the chief supporting contest, and
£2,000 advertised for the main bout, Cochran needed paying
spectators desperately, and he got them. Here is the weekly
magazine *Health and Strength* writing about Cochran's customers:

> The crowd itself was an inspiration, so thoroughly
> British, so heterogenous, so obviously bent on seeing
> fair play. They may say what they like about the

> propriety of the attendance at boxing matches of the
> ladies, but... I say "Let 'em all go". They graced that
> brilliant assembly by their charms, and imparted to
> the scene the aspect of a tourney in the days of
> chivalry.

This reporter was probably not a veteran commentator on boxing,
for *Health and Strength* concentrated more upon physical culture.
His report was flowery, though it had a certain freshness and
accuracy:

> Billy Wells is the idol of the British Public once
> again. There is no shadow of a doubt about that.
> The whole-hearted British cheer that well-nigh lifted
> the roof of (sic) Olympia on Tuesday night when he
> won the Imperial championship, proved that the
> country was with him; was waiting, in fact, to take
> him back into its arms again.[8]

Cochran had embarked on a series of major boxing shows at
Olympia. This was the first of them and he must have made a
handsome profit. A week later he staged a match for the
lightweight championship of the world, paid the holder, Willie
Ritchie, $25,000, and still covered expenses using the same
admission prices.[9] Seven days later Olympia was filled to see
Carpentier's rather lucky win over Gunboat Smith, in this case
though, Dick Burge was the promoter.[10]

There are various levels of explanation of this remarkable
craze for boxing. The physical and personal attractiveness of Wells
and Carpentier was seen by some contemporary observers as
leading the way,[11] and it is true that both were embraced by
families of all social classes in Britain as ideal sons or model
husbands. This was not because they were well-built and
handsome, because many of their pugilistic predecessors had been.
It was because they were presented to the public in a way which
would have amazed boxers of the 1890s.

The penny newspaper or magazine had induced a readership undreamt of in the nineteenth century, and daily and Sunday papers had circulations of 200,000. New technology had introduced picture papers, for example, the *Daily Illustrated Mirror*, started in 1904, gave readers photographs on every page.[12] Wells was a well-known face not because people had watched him box or spar or seen him in the street, but through the marvels of the innovatory printing press. The substitution of portraits and action photographs for lines of print was not the only difference, the subject matter and writing style had changed. The measurements of both boxers ankles were recorded, not to mention thighs and fore-arms. Bell's son, aged two and a half years, was given twice that number of paragraphs by The Editor of *Health and Strength*, and *Answers'* boxing representative conversed with a:

> golden-haired, winsome Australian girl, a proud wife
> [of Colin Bell] and a fond mother...

when a few years earlier any boxing correspondent would have feared the sack for writing such ridiculous copy about her son tugging at her skirt.[13]

The many thousands who went to Olympia on three successive Tuesdays can be explained, but first they need to be analysed. There were four strands which can be detected though they overlap. The myth that there were lots of women was exploded by Cochran who wrote:

> ... it has been the custom of every boxing promoter,
> other than myself, to announce before each match
> an enormous demand for seats from women. I have
> never seen at any match more than the "fair
> sprinkling"...[14]

These would have come with gentlemen from the National Sporting Club, and carriage-set men were the second strand at Olympia, which was still a small minority of the crowd. Boxing fans, meaning men who went regularly or occasionally to watch boxing not held at the N.S.C. made up the third and largest set of spectators, and lastly, there came what we can call new faces. The fourth strand would have attended in the company of fans, gentlemen and ladies to the extent of doubling ticket sales, yet the hall was so large, and the shows so quickly upon each others heels, that one suspects that men went, alone or together, who had never been to professional boxing shows before. Given that this was so, who were they? Five shillings was a lot to pay for a boxing show when you could go elsewhere for "a bob", and probably walk both ways. The customers new to boxing were unlikely to be low-paid or unemployed for they would have to forego too many alternative satisfactions such as food. The argument is that people went who were slightly better off than these. My suggestion is that the lodger population of London, shop assistants, barmen, page-boys, and men of any occupation who were living with families not their own, swelled the crowds attracted to out-of-season boxing shows. In addition to these unattached men there would have been an expansion of attached youngsters, going to a boxing show, probably for the first time, with fathers and uncles or relatives of their best friend. Finally, there would have been men at the fringes of collectivities inspired to join with friends to go this time, because it was special, such as, soldiers in barracks or territorials, football club supporters or canteen talkers.

The boom in boxing did not appear suddenly in the summer of 1914, there had been a period of gestation. From around 1910 a weekly boxing paper had been sustainable, and promoters, especially Burge at the Ring, had whittled away at the traditional close season between Derby week and the first in October. Three figure purses had once tended to be put up in Northern cities,[15] now London monopolised matches with a nought added, and a boxing axis between London and Paris was firmly established. Happily for Wells and Maloney this growth in boxing business had coincided with their advance from promising soldier to international contender, and because Wells was a heavyweight, a rare and popular ring species, he had helped to intensify this boxing activity.

For newcomers venturing to their first boxing show, their
perception of what it was like, including whom they might sit
beside, would decide whether or not they went, and boxing had
tried to soften its image. To abbreviate the evidence of this, a
humorous example. For the Wells *versus* Bell show Cochran
persuaded a Church of England vicar to be the Master of
Ceremonies,[16] and press coverage fails to reveal whether Rev.
Everard Digby wore canonical dress. I suspect he wore only the
collar. Such sales policy was not targeted at boiler-makers or
market porters, for they were the image of a boxing crowd that
Cochran was trying to alter, it was partly directed at men who went
to work in collars and ties, and partly at women. It succeeded in
both cases. White-collar workers began to go to boxing shows like
Cochran's, when they never would have had the slightest inclination
to join the supposedly rough crowds at earlier boxing places like the
Goodwin Club in Shoreditch.[17] Salaried workers who went to
Olympia might have been wary of going to the Ring, Blackfriars, or
Premierland in Stepney. Evidence of this is hard to find, but
around 25,000 spectators at three shows in the space of 15 days
makes the hypothesis credible. As Cochran wrote in 1925, women
did not go to boxing shows in any great numbers. The argument
here is that women's disapproval of boxing would have reduced the
chance of their sons and husbands becoming attracted to the sport.
The object of the Reverend M.C. was to mollify claims that it was
a sport for hooligans, a view that was shared by puritans of all
social classes. The majority of working-class women were not
offended by the subject because their fathers, sons and husbands
had been bringing it in to the home conversationally since the
1890s. Thus the women who were most likely to be persuaded that
watching boxing was a respectable recreation for their men-folk
were middle class. Promoters like Cochran studied ticket sales
closely, and retrospectively he admitted when he had failed to sell
an event successfully,[18] it is impossible to believe that with Wells
versus Bell, Cochran was not marketing boxing's respectability, and
consciously using the indirect target which I have tried to describe.
The new faces went to Olympia partly because many women's

disapproval of boxing was diminishing, and Cochran ended an article he wrote for *Answers*:

> I might add that victory over Colin Bell rehabilitates Bombardier Wells as a "drawing" attraction...[19]

but his article "I promote Boxing" came out in the week that war was declared.

Notes

1 Charles Chaplin, *My Autobiography*, 1966, p. 101.
2 Makin, *op. cit*, p. 43.
3 *Answers*, 4 July 1914.
4 *Health and Strength*, 4 July 1914.
5 Sugar Ray Robinson told a Congressional committee in 1960-1 that most professional boxers had carried opponents, that was to say that, for a variety of reasons, often compassionate ones, the superior boxer would allow his weak opponent to last longer in a contest that could have ended earlier. Direct evidence of this happening is, of course, scarce, yet, in my judgement, Wells was never engaged in this practice. He lacked the composure and self-confidence it demanded, and his attitude towards the spectators was unsubtle, he wanted to give them his best performance.
6 Cochran (1872-1951) wrote four books which often covered the same ground. They were *Secrets of a Showman* (1925), *I had almost Forgotten...* (1932), *Cock-a-doodle-do* (1941) and *Showman looks on* (1945).
7 *Health and Strength*, 20, 27 June 1914.
8 *Ibid.*, 4 July 1914, E. Stewart Smith, "A Hero once again", pp. 240-2.
9 *Ibid.*, Cochran, *Secrets*, p. 191. Freddie Welsh won the title on points over 20 rounds, and the attendance was not as large as the week previously for Wells *v.* Bell.

10   Charles Graves, *The Cochran Story*, n.d. (1951), p. 51.
11   Leslie Bell, *Bella of Blackfriars*, 1961, pp. 120-5;   B.
      Bennison, *Giants on Parade*, 1936, pp. 27, 30;
      James and Frank Butler, *The Fight Game*, 1954, pp.
      61-62; Cochran, *Showman*, p. 252.
12   Camrose, *op. cit.*, pp. 57-60.
13   *Health and Strength*, 20 June 1914; *Answers*, 4 July 1914.
14   Cochran, *Secrets*, p. 290.
15   Jack Goodwin, *Myself and my Boxers*, 1924, p. 20. This
      informative book by a successful boxing trainer was
      edited by B.J. Evans.
16   *Health and Strength*, 4 July 1914.
17   For the Goodwin Club see *Sporting Chronicle Annual for
      1898*, p. 174, and contemporary sporting newspapers.
      Disturbances were extremely rare at boxing shows,
      yet to outsiders the image was riotous.
18   For example, Cochran, *Secrets*, p. 292.
19   *Answers*, 1 August 1914.

CHAPTER ELEVEN

WAR

It is not possible to explain to anyone not old enough to have lived through it, just how absolute was the shock of amazement, bewilderment, consternation and horror which overwhelmed us with the realisation that virtually all Europe was involved in actual War.

T.A. Jackson, *Solo Trumpet*, 1953, p. 114.

Billy Wells did not join up until May 1915 and for the first nine months of the war he was subject to criticism for not so doing. Criticism, which was certainly magnified by his taking four lucrative boxing matches, two in February, in Plymouth and Belfast, then two in London. As the champion of his country's most manly sport, and a former professional soldier, Wells showed determination in resisting orchestrated and popular, pressure to volunteer for Kitchener's army. The war made little difference to Wells's career as a boxer for he fought as frequently as before until December 1916, at which time he was aged 29 years, and seemed unlikely to further his chances of international honours. Wells lost only one contest in 1915-16, yet that was vital for his opponent was an American, whilst he continued knocking over English, Irish and Scots. The second half of the war affected him financially because he had no matches whilst professional boxing managed to continue, though substantially reduced from the programme of 1916. Boxing slowed down as entertainment, and we can speculate about the reasons for this. First, there was the introduction of entertainment tax which reduced takings by a quarter;[1] secondly, the 700,000 men killed would have included a percentage who would otherwise have gone boxing; and thirdly, the gravity of the situation, the black-out and excessive overtime, might have made watching sport less important. Finally, and surely most decisively, a form of entertainment which men could not easily share with women would have persuaded lovers to go to music hall or pictures instead. The war caused separation, and as a natural reaction, more pleasures were wanted to be enjoyed together. On the negative implications of the war and boxing, that sector of the population which gained more than most in terms of earnings, girls, were unable to spend their wealth supporting boxing because groups of girls on their own could not go. This was something women did not do. Women gained football during the war, some played and some started watching it,[2] but the social barriers between them and boxing were impregnable.

Alfred Wells was already in the Reserves, and he immediately volunteered for duty with his regiment the Rifle Brigade. They were sent with the British Expeditionary Force to link with the French Army at Amiens equipped for battles of mobility, for which they were trained. The British advanced towards Aisne where they met the German Army well dug into trenches, from which machine-gunners destroyed the B.E.F. Alf was killed, aged 25 ("an ardent Physical Culturist, and an Army gymnast, and footballer above the average")[3] among the first on 23 September.

In that month 750,000 men enlisted. The enlistment atmosphere was created by Kitchener posters, the press, tumultuous public meetings, rumours of German atrocities, and volunteers signed on at the rate of 100,000 a month until the middle of 1915.[4] Although volunteers exceeded the availability of uniforms and every type of weaponry, Kitchener called for men between the ages of 19 and 35, with the age of ex-soldiers raised to 45 years, and married men were encouraged to join with a separation allowance. Physically, men needed to be at least 5 feet 3 inches tall, with a chest measurement of 34 inches or more,[5] and initially many were rejected for reasons such as flat feet, for the army placed great store on ability at marching. *Health and Strength*, which adopted a much less belligerent tone than other weekly and daily papers, led with "Nonsense about Recruiting" in its editorial on 12 September:

> I maintain that our young men... are rolling up very
> well. ... I know of thousands who have tried to enlist
> and been rejected... I never heard of anything so
> ridiculous as that White Feather Brigade which
> some of the papers seem inclined to boom. A party
> of young ladies at Folkestone banded themselves
> together to ask all the fellows they came across to
> join the Service, and if they refused, to make them
> a present of a white feather.

The Editor was past the required age, but had he not been, he
would have been very rude to these women.

> Equally impertinent, in my opinion, are those
> highly-placed ladies who write stupid letters to the
> papers, calling our young men slackers... These
> ladies are comfortably circumstanced. What right
> have they to dictate to young men of limited
> incomes who have wives and families, or, it may be,
> parents, brothers, and sisters dependent on them?[6]

From this liberal editorial it is easy to gather an impression of the
social pressure put upon ordinary young men at the beginning of
the war. Recruiting meetings produced famous orators like Horatio
Bottomley.

> Bottomley had twice been acquitted of fraud, had been
elected Liberal M.P. for South Hackney in 1906, and in the same
year founded his weekly paper *John Bull*. *John Bull* flourished
though Bottomley became bankrupt in 1911 and resigned his
Commons' seat which he won back as an Independent candidate in
1918. Bottomley re-established his reputation with some 20 early
recruiting meetings for which he received no payment, thereafter
his patriotic lectures (over 300 in 1915-17) earned him £22,000.[7] In
1922 he was finally found guilty of fraudulent conversion and sent
to prison. During the war *John Bull* was used as an organ of hate
against the enemy, and his lectures were as prosecuting counsel

with Germany in the dock charged with the wilful murder of civilisation. Bottomley was a thorough-going scoundrel, other hate-mongers simply stirred the chauvinist pot. One of these, Lord Northcliffe, was honoured in 1917, and later made director of propaganda in enemy countries. It is in Northcliffe's *Answers*, curiously, that we find the first evidence that Wells suffered under the pressure on him to volunteer for the fighting. In the issue of 23 January there appeared "Why I am not OUT There" by Bombardier Billy Wells. It was a weak article, in which he argued that it would be easier for him to join up than not to, which was true. After the shelling of Scarborough, Hartlepool and Whitby, he had wanted to go, but his wife had persuaded him to stay until the Germans invaded, and his main claim was that as a married man he should wait. This was probably a commonly held sentiment, that until all the single men had gone to the front, it was unfair that married men should enlist. They had families to support, in his case, a wife and child, his mother and two teenage brothers, and, in view of the money Wells had recently earned, this part of the case made was pathetic. In "Boxing for War Funds", published in the same paper on 13 March, Wells expostulated:

> Married "stay-at-homes", in my position, are not slackers or shirkers. Were I a single man, I should deserve to be hooted in the streets...

which left the question of whether he had been, open. Confirmation that he had been the subject of attack, spoken and written, comes from his third war-time piece in *Answers* dated 24 July. He had just rejoined the army, and "From the Ring to the Trench" was based on an interview, with the reporter using quotes extensively. Wells had said:

> My position was unlike that of many other married men. I was, so to speak, in business for myself, in the precarious capacity of a professional pugilist, whose reputation stood in constant danger of collapse as a money-earning factor. I had no...

employer who would guarantee two-thirds... of my
salary...

This was a slightly better argument than he had previously
employed, then he told the *Answers'* man:

> You cannot imagine how deeply I used to resent the
> insinuations levelled against me by thoughtless
> people during those months...... even when in the
> ring at the Opera House... I could still find time to
> wonder how many people in that audience were
> regarding me as that unutterably contemptible thing
> - a shirker.

whether the words were Billy's or the reporter's, Wells surely felt
that about the posh crowd in Kingsway when he met Frank Moran.

Though the war was seen as the business of men in the
forces, it was accepted that some concessions to it were necessary
in this country. The War Office took over Olympia; Alexandra
Palace became an internment camp for enemy aliens; the Navy
occupied Crystal Palace, and professional sportsmen, footballers
especially, were strongly criticised if they failed to enlist. By
December, London daily papers refused to report football matches,
and gave the score only whilst as many as 600 single men,
professionally involved with football, had not volunteered. The
Football League reduced all players' wages as the clubs' receipts
dropped from lower attendances,[8] yet it seems to have been
generally agreed that sport should continue because it kept up
morale. Recruiting meetings at league matches flopped, though
money for appropriate war charities was raised on most sporting
occasions. Millions of men did enlist before conscription was
introduced for single men in January 1916, though how they felt
about volunteering, and what inspired the so-called slackers who did
not, is difficult to determine. That a tiny minority opposed this war
is unsurprising,[9] the problem lies with assessing levels of support,
from strong to acquiescence, in the majority of people.

The first contest which Wells signed for after the outbreak of war was with Frank Moran in December 1914. He insisted upon £500, win lose or draw, and got it, unfortunately the American fell ill and the match had to be postponed indefinitely.[10] Wells kept busy sparring exhibitions for war funds. Pat O'Keefe had joined up, and must have been stationed near London for the two men sparred at Premierland and Ilford Skating Rink.[11] Bandsman Blake was reported as having been wounded at the front, and he gained a full-length photograph in *Health and Strength*. The magazine seemed disappointed the following week when it told readers that the report was false.[12] Carpentier had been preparing to box at the White City Stadium on 17 August for a purse reputed to be worth £10,000, the match was dropped when he immediately joined the French air force.[13]

Wells's first war-time contest took place in February at the Cosmopolitan in Plymouth, and the Club was filled with around 6,000 spectators. Wells had every physical advantage over his opponent, Dan McGoldrick, a Scotsman, whose seconds retired him at the end of the seventh round. The purse was advertised as £450, though how it was split is not known.[14] Opponents, anxious for a match, might sign for a percentage of the gate or profits, and they could hardly ever call the tune in negotiations. Furthermore, a boxer who liked to bet, and Wells did, could gain more from the bookmakers than he did from the promoter's purse, so the finances of boxing are speculative, and purses were exaggerated to give publicity to the match.

Bandsman Rice had been promoted to sergeant when he met Wells for the second time in "The Greatest Boxing Tournament ever offered to the Belfast Public". Prices at the Grand Opera House were modest for this 20 rounds' match, ranging from a pound ringside to two shillings in the gallery,[15] though the attendance on 24 February was disappointing. Rice thought he had deserved a draw at Liverpool, and his tactics remained the same, to bore in and attack from the word go. He was giving away over a stone, and he knocked Wells down with what the latter described

Cartoon by W.D. Ford from *Boxing*, 8 June 1912; advertisement in *Boxing*, 20 February 1915.

as "a brute of a blow"[16] in the first round, thereafter Wells
recovered behind his long left lead and he knocked Rice out in the
sixth round.   This had been an exciting contest with ferocious
attacks from Rice and eventually a clean unambiguous counting out
of the music man. *Boxing* thought that fear of German submarines
might have kept the attendance down.[17]

In the Spring of 1915, the war was something men had to
volunteer for; to join the Territorials meant going to camp, but
only to defend our shores from invasion whilst the fighting was
taking place in France and Belgium. A majority of the population
simply talked a good war, and on the home front it was business as
usual. The *Western Mail* which was published in Cardiff, upset
many with its cartoon "French versus English Pugilism" showing
Carpentier in the trenches and British boxers still strutting around
the ring.[18] The cartoon did not depict Wells, and may have been
unfair to boxers anyway compared to the generality of men aged
between 19 and 35 years. Opinion leaders considered that the war
could still be ended quickly, perhaps by the British Navy, and
Churchill was planning to attack Gallipoli. The match with Moran
came off as warships shelled the Dardanelles, and for the former we
turn to the next chapter.

Notes

1   For the rates of Entertainment Duty see, *Whitaker's
          Almanack for 1918*, p. 354.
2   "Adventurous Eves", Channel 4 television programme shown
          18 October 1990, directed by Gabrielle Bown, an
          Artemis Production.
3   *Health and Strength*, 31 October 1914.
4   A.J.P. Taylor, *English History 1914-1945*, 1970, p. 48.
5   *Health and Strength*, 12 September 1914, advertisement p.
          429.
6   *Ibid.*, front page.
7   Henry J. Houston, *The real Horatio Bottomley*, n.d. (1923?),
          p. 73.

8   Tony Mason, *Association Football and English Society 1863-1915*, 1981, pp. 251-5.

9   Ken Weller, *"Don't be a Soldier": the radical anti-war movement in North London 1914-1918*, 1985.

10   Frank Moran, "My Life and Fights", *Answers*, 24 April 1915.

11   *Answers*, 13 March 1915.

12   *Health and Strength*, 12, 19 September 1914.

13   *Ibid.*, 15, 22 August 1914; *Carpentier by Himself*, pp. 93-94. There is reason to suspect the size of this purse; it was advertised, but since Horatio Bottomley was heavily involved, had the fight gone on it may not have been forthcoming in its entirety, see Cochran, *Secrets*, pp. 203-7.

14   *Boxing*, 20 February 1915; *Thomson's Weekly News*, 7 August 1920.

15   *Boxing*, 20 February 1915.

16   *Thomson's Weekly News*, 7 August 1920.

17   *Boxing*, 6 March 1915.

18   *Western Mail*, December 1914; *Health and Strength*, 19 December 1914.

CHAPTER TWELVE

"LOOK OUT BILLY"

He will be remembered for his famous right-hand punch - a terrific swing that went by the name of "Mary Ann".

Viscount Knebworth, *Boxing*, n.d. (1931), p. 74.

Wells's two contests, either side of his enlisting, were among the most exciting of his career. Both opponents were slightly unusual, Dick Smith because he had been an amateur champion (A.B.A. heavyweight, 1912 and 1913); and Frank Moran because he had studied dentistry at Pittsburg University. Both were aged 28 years, the same as Wells.

Moran was at great pains to explain to readers of *Answers* that he was not a gentleman in the English sense.[1] He had never gone hungry, both parents had been born in Ireland, but Cleveland and Pittsburg during his childhood had been places where a family could earn money. At seventeen he had enlisted in the United States' Navy, served five years, latterly as quartermaster on *Mayflower*, the President's yacht, and though he started studying after his discharge, he eventually dropped off the course to become a professional boxer in 1910.[2] He first came to Europe in 1911-12 as a minor member of his manager's team (which included Joe Jeannette) and beat five opponents at the Ring, Blackfriars, and another in Paris.[3] He had wanted a match with Wells then, but the new English champion took on Storbeck and made for the United States and his unfortunate encounter with Palzer. Moran, after wins and losses, enhanced his name by knocking Palzer out in New York City [4] before coming to Europe again. In the same week as Wells beat Bell, Moran met Jack Johnson at the Velodrome D'Hiver over 20 rounds for the world's championship and lost on points. This demonstration of his durability before a huge crowd, and Carpentier as referee, gave the American's boxing career a fillip.[5] His publicity centred upon his "Mary Ann", described as "the wildest

and weirdest right-hand cartwheel" punch ever seen. The Johnson
he had met in Paris was 36 years of age, fat, and "quarter-trained";[6]
and he was to lose his title in Havana nine months later. Moran
was tough, slow, smiling and popular, when Dick Burge persuaded
him to sign for the match at the London Opera House in March
1915.

The ticket prices aimed to attract carriage spectators,[7] the
new building held over 2,000, and it was packed. Unusually Burge
had invited a large party in free, and they were convalescent
soldiers, both officers and men. To raise money for the magazine
Boxing's "Glove Fund", which sent boxing gloves to the armed forces,
an auction was held before the main contest, and this produced £63.
The lot, a prize bull-dog, caused protracted bidding whilst Wells and
Moran stood in the ring, and one of Moran's seconds taunted Wells
in a calculated attempt to increase tension.[8] The Opera House in
Kingsway showed an unpleasant face to Wells, quite possibly it was
the first time he had experienced any hostility in an audience before
a fight.

The first round contained a remarkable incident. Moran
caught Wells with a glancing punch high on the head, whereupon
Wells turned and walked rapidly towards his corner. Moran
followed, and Wells finally turned back to face him again. Moran
could not explain why his opponent appeared to turn and run. The
crowd roared, and Wells later claimed that he must have heard a
sound like the signal for time.

During rounds two to nine Wells jabbed Moran endlessly,
at a distance and in the clinches. Moran was too ponderous with
hands and feet to repeat his success of the first three minutes. Yet
Moran became slower without going down, *Boxing* wrote:

> Frank was getting too slow to be believed. For on
> one occasion he gathered himself up for a punch
> with such fearful deliberation and with such
> manifest intent that a voice from the gallery called

out, "Look out, Billy! Look out!" And even then,
after the voice had died away, the blow did not start
for a full second...[9]

everyone, including the boxers, laughed; Moran missed by a mile,
and Wells neglected to counter. Both boxers wrote accounts of this
contest which read quite uninterestingly. It was the period in
which it took place, the novel arena, the atmosphere on the night,
and the course of the fight which made it so thrilling.

The country was eight months into war, and sport, after
faltering in the Autumn, had regrouped. The first big boxing show
of the war had been staged, at the same place, a week before, and
the London Opera House had not previously been used for boxing.
The atmosphere can be grasped accurately by reading what Corri
wrote in *John Bull*. After lamenting the death in action of a
French boxer he went on:

> The youth of Germany, though their kultur be ever
> so high, have never played any games that have for
> their central object the teaching of fairness. Cricket
> is unknown... Rugby football is foreign to their
> tastes... and Germany has never boasted of a boxer
> worth his salt - gymnasts, creatures of cast-iron,
> bloodless militarism, yes - but no athlete with
> bowels...[10]

They were a nation of arrogant bullies he wrote, and his editor
Bottomley was certain that we would thrash them shortly. Corri
was aged about 50 years, with school-age sons.[11] He had done a
great deal of refereeing for war charities, for example, we find him
at Rochdale in a party organised by Jimmy White which included
Wells, Driscoll and the flyweight sensation, Jimmy Wilde.[12] Corri
was a middle-class sportsman, and he wrote in the same article:

> When the war is over, the boys who shouldered
> arms will be allowed to have their fling. Very

properly, the fit and young boxer who has not joined either the Navy or Army is not in high favour, and you may take it from me that when we are free to enjoy peace again there will be sharp discrimination between those who have done their little bit for their King and country and those who have invented excuses for not getting into khaki.

Both Wells and Wilde fell in Corri's latter category, and this could suggest some difference in attitude towards volunteering between men in Kitchener's age range, and those above it. Though Wells soon did enlist, Wilde initially appealed against his conscription in December 1916, then dropped the appeal and went. Certainly the two most famous British boxers were pragmatic rather than excessively patriotic.[13]

In the tenth round an apparently relaxed and confident Wells attacked Moran as if anxious to finish him off, and he lost. One punch, a left hook to the jaw, put him down for a count of nine, and then Moran's swinging right completed the job because Wells was ready to crash forward in utter collapse.

The press left no figure of speech undisturbed. The Editor of *Boxing* quoted Thomas Carlyle and then suggested:

Strive and wriggle as you will, you cannot escape the inevitable conclusion that the Bombardier is the milk-white hind of the ring. He is the Papacy over again. Repeatedly doomed to extinction, he refuses to die...[14]

When Wells lost, observers suspected he could beat the same man if they met in the ring again. This was certainly the case with Moir, Palzer, Carpentier twice and Moran, and Wells seems to have agreed. He recognised mistakes made, and faults to be remedied so readily that one suspects that his flaw was self-doubt. Instead of willing himself to be a world beater, his own commentary was detached, seemingly as if he had been watching himself. He made few excuses after a contest, and may have lacked necessary arrogance before a match. The feeling that he can't hurt me, that I can take all this opponent has to offer, is one part of the make-up of a top-notch boxer which Wells perhaps did not have. Moran, who from his series of articles in *Answers* personified confidence,[15] won three more fights before meeting Jess Willard for the world's heavyweight championship. Since the match was in New York City, Moran had to stop Willard within the distance in order to win the title, and in this he failed. Moran returned to Europe more than once after the war, and he twice boxed Joe Beckett, the British heavyweight champion, but he and Wells never fought again.

Sergeant Dick Smith had joined the army as a physical training instructor when he was matched with Wells at the Ring, Blackfriars, by Dick Burge. The purse was moderate, £700, and the contest was to take place on the last Monday in May.[16] Smith had been a professional just over 18 months, previously he had been in the City of London Police, and his boxing experience was extensive, chiefly amongst amateurs.

The Amateur Boxing Association, founded in London in 1880, held annual championships at four weights (feather, light, middle and heavy) each Spring. Smaller men, bantamweights, had been added in 1884. Police, for the obvious reason of their size, were disproportionately represented compared to other occupations, at heavyweight. These events were the climax of the amateur boxing season, held all on one day, attracting some hundred entrants including a few from overseas, they started at 10.30 a.m. and concluded some 12 hours later. Spectators were plentiful. Thus these amateur championships were good preparation for professional boxing. Smith had lost in the final of 1911 to another policeman, Hazell, and when he won in the following year, of the

The "Ring" Blackfriars: James Moir and Daniel Voyles

nine entrants, three were policemen.[17]   Smith became A.B.A.
champion for a second time in 1913; left the police force, won his
first paid contest at New Cross Baths, and then went to the
National Sporting Club to box for a new title.[18]   The N.S.C. had
recognised a light-heavyweight title, for men up to 12st 7lbs, only
since 1913 when Tipperaryman Denis Haugh had won it.   Smith
boxed the Irishman twice for his British title, losing in January and
winning in March, both times on points, and when Wells met him,
Smith was British light-heavyweight champion, a Plumstead-born,
popular local man.

Boxing and gambling were bedfellows, yet the betting on
Wells *versus* Smith was exceptionally heavy.[19]   The reasons for this
were twofold;   an increase in the circulation of money, and the
character of this match.   Ten months into the war an industrial
effort to equip the armed forces was being made.   A Ministry for
munitions had been created, and unemployment was releasing its
stranglehold on consumption.   As the "boys" marched off, they left
behind job vacancies, and they increased demand for khaki.   The
benefit from a daughter doing overtime in a clothing factory was
shared with the family;   all forms of transport carried more traffic,
and the bookmaker employed another runner.   To the east of
Blackfriars there lived the largest pool of casual labour in Europe,
and collectively it had more money to spend.[20]

In anticipation, the match was a local derby between
Londoners north and south of the river.   The two men may not
have lived where they were born, but pride in neighbourhood was
strong.   The Ring catered for a cloth-capped clientele for Burge
promoted elsewhere for toffs as we have seen.   Boxer-soldiers could
easily get leave for a contest for the authorities believed sport was
good for morale.   Wells trained at Brighton, and re-enlisted in the
army whilst preparing for this contest.[21]   The Ring was a
comedown for a man who had fought three times in Madison
Square Garden, whilst for Smith the match was an opportunity
which he never would have had so early if Wells had won his
contest at the Opera House.   This was, far and away, the most

exciting match ever to have been staged at this arena with its large proportion of regular customers who knew their sport.

For an exceptional promotion, Burge decided to have a renowned referee. George T. Dunning wrote for *The Sportsman* as "Cestus", and he had refereed contests of major importance since the 1890s. Gamblers could exert pressure on referees, and Dunning was immune from this.[22] Referees were split between those who sat outside the ring, and those who preferred to go in with the boxers, and "Tom" (as he was called) was of the old school who sat outside.

Dick Smith adopted the now usual tactics against Wells. Because he was believed to suffer from stage fright, Smith kept him waiting after they had both arrived in the ring. Whilst "gloving-up" he insisted upon extra bandages for his own hands, and, on top of the by now almost obligatory auction for war charities (£31 was raised),[23] the delay hopefully increased the "butterflies" in Wells's stomach. This move was as old as the sport, and it had entered the Wells' lexicon after Carpentier Two. Smith's second tactic was used when the contest started, and it consisted of "going downstairs", in less colloquial language, of punching to the body. Whether the solar plexus was Wells's weak spot had been debated since January 1911, and *Boxing* concluded after the defeat by Moran:

> Wells does not suffer from any weak spot. He is It. The only conclusion one can draw... is that Wells' weak spot is located in any part of his anatomy on which a really heavy blow may happen to land.[24]

The betting money which followed Smith was encouraged by such commentary, yet it was impossible that a majority of those interested in boxing wanted Wells to lose. When he played football for charity at Goodison Park:

> ... several thousand people gathered outside the Everton dressing-rooms and waited for hours for

their golden-haired hero to emerge, when they bore
him off in triumph... [because] he is easily the most
popular man in England.[25]

Everyone liked the man whether he had volunteered for the army
or not.[26] Even those taking the odds against Wells winning would
have been slightly sad had he lost.

The excitement at Blackfriars came in rounds 8 and 9.
Wells outpointed his opponent, who was a stone the lighter, in the
first six rounds, then he appeared to tire and Smith won the
seventh. In the next round both men attacked hard, and suddenly
up went the shout "He's got him". Wells took left and rights to the
jaw, and fell forward, apparently out.[27] In the uproar caused by
this the referee could not be heard, so Dunning had to leave his
seat and climb into the ring. The start of his count over Wells was
delayed by how long this took, and he was an elderly man. Wells
"managed to stagger up at the count of 9" and Dunning told them
to box on, when Smith was left with 20 seconds or so to land a
winning punch in which he failed. Dunning stayed in the ring for
the ninth round, during which the boxers' roles were reversed.
Both attacked and Smith went down from lefts and rights to his
jaw. Dunning wasted no time with the count, and Smith gained his
feet as it reached ten, he was out, and Wells had won.[28] Some
spectators, and Smith, thought Wells was down for longer than ten
seconds in the previous round, and Wells much later referred to "a
lot of controversy" over timekeeping at this contest.[29] Whether he
should have been counted out, or would have been by a more agile
referee, remains in doubt. Dick Burge thought Wells was down for
17 seconds, and when he promoted the return match he took a
theatre with many more seats.

The question of the long count seems far less interesting
than that of Wells's popularity before he donned khaki. Britain's
champion boxer was not seen as a shirker by thousands who hung
around after the football match, or, presumably, those who attended
his sparring for charity. It seems likely that the generality of

people thought that being a married man with two young children (the baby was a boy) was a sound reason for not enlisting. Indeed, men in Wells's family situation may not have been encouraged to go by many wives when dependents' allowances were not only low but ill-organised. Wives with children too young to work suffered severe privation during the war if they were working class and their husbands joined the forces. They faced rising prices without the aid of additional earnings, when children leaving school in older families gained jobs with ease, and mothers, with children off-hand, went back to work. A craftsman or labourer in Wells's situation could be *criticised* for volunteering, and not unjustly. Wells was no longer, of course, a working-class man, and every boxing fan could have guessed how much he had earned in the last six years, yet working-class values may still have been applied to him by people in the street.

The strongest criticism of men who did not volunteer came from the types of people who attended Bottomley's patriotic lectures, and we must speculate who went. Bottomley usually did two shows (matinee and evening) at any place he journeyed to. He expected, and usually got between £40 and £200 for each performance according to his travelling secretary who was estranged from him when he wrote *The real Horatio Bottomley*. In this, Houston wrote of the "best people" of Bournemouth going to the Winter Gardens, and of Bottomley being lionized by local notabilities from Torquay to Blackpool.[30] Ticket prices ranged between one and four shillings, and going to see Bottomley was an alternative entertainment to a concert or a play. In small towns, the owner and editor of *John Bull* would have been, perhaps, the only entertainment that week in an age when oratory was appreciated. The music (*Land of Hope and Glory* type) was not planned to attract patrons of music hall, and they preferred shorter acts than Bottomley in full flow. He spoke of King and Country, God and German losses, to people who responded enthusiastically. The middle classes and the aristocracy quite probably formed a majority of his cheering audiences. In cosmopolitan cities enmity was directed towards enemy aliens as well as shirkers,[31] though at least one well placed observer thought that jingoism was less pronounced than during the Boer War.[32] Several British boxers saw out the war in other countries, Kid Lewis in the U.S.A. for example, and stayed popular when they came back.[33]   Thus condemnation of men who were not in the forces was not universal.[34]   Wells symbolized boxing, and Corri reflected:

> After Wells, every boxer, whether big or little, if he
> is not really doing his bit, must join the ranks.[35]

This passage in *John Bull*, written after Wells had signed on with the recruiting sergeant in Brighton, suggests that there were other ways of serving your country than by wearing khaki. And of course there were.   Cavalrymen on the Western Front were virtually redundant whilst engineers at Coventry worked round the clock.[36] Wells, however, was not any civilian, he was a sporting icon, and a pattern-maker for Kitchener's army.   The signing up of the heavyweight champion made married men more vulnerable, and eased the nation towards conscription as volunteering for the honour of one's country became less modish.

Notes

1.   *Answers*, 8 May 1915.
2.   *Ibid.*, 1 May 1915.
3.   *Boxing World*, 20 July, 5 October 1911.
4.   *"Boxing's" New Year Annual 1914*, p. 19;   *Boxing*, 20
            September 1913.
5.   *Health and Strength*, 4 July 1914.
6.   A.F. Cameron, "The use and abuse of the right hand",
            Boxing, 29 May 1918.
7.   *Boxing*, 17 March 1915.
8.   Harry Preston, *Memories*, 1928, pp. 105-6;   *Boxing*, 31
            March 1915.
9.   *Ibid.*
10.   *John Bull*, 15 May 1915.
11.   Corri, *Refereeing*, pp. 138-40.

12. *Answers*, 23 January 1915.
13. Jim Driscoll, married and aged 34, had joined the army, see *Health and Strength*, 19 December 1914. Wilde, in his early twenties and also married, left it until much later: "Jimmy Wilde has withdrawn his appeal, and joins the Army gymnastic staff at Aldershot to-day", *Daily Mirror*, 26 January 1917.
14. *Boxing*, 7 April 1915.
15. *Answers*, 27 March, 24 April, 1, 8, 15, 22, 29 May, 5, 12 June 1915.
16. *Boxing*, 26 May 1915; *Answers*, 24 July 1915.
17. *Mirror of Life*, 6 April 1912.
18. *Boxing*, 25 October 1913; *"Boxing's" Book of Records*, 1914, pp. 185, 219.
19. Leslie Bell, *Bella of Blackfriars*, 1961, p. 131.
20. Sidney Pollard, *The Development of the British Economy*, 1970, pp. 45-6, 76-7; Stan Shipley, "The East End Family during the 1st World War", *Romford Record*, 1989, pp. 14-24.
21. According to *Answers*, 24 July 1915, Ellen had said to him "Billy, I cannot stand in your way any longer. You have been very considerate in braving all the taunts that have been thrown at you for my sake so long. You can go now, as you have always wanted to go". The pressure was strong for Wells to volunteer at this point; he was preparing to box Smith who had already done so, Burge had joined up as a recruiting sergeant, and the Ring crowd was brutally frank.
22. B.J. Angle, *My Sporting Memories*, 1935, pp. 92-3; Norman Clark, *All in the Game*, 1935, pp. 45-6; Cochran, *Secrets*, p. 122.
23. *Boxing*, 2 June 1915.
24. *Ibid.*, 31 March 1915.
25. *Ibid.*, 12 May 1915.
26. *John Bull*, 8 May 1915, "I wish he had rejoined the Army, why not?" wrote Corri.
27. *Boxing*, 2 June 1915.

28. *Ibid.*; Leslie Belle, *Bella, op. cit.*, pp. 131-3.
29. *Thomson's Weekly News*, 21 August 1920.
30. Henry J. Houston, O.B.E., *The Real Horatio Bottomley*, n.d., pp. 73-82.
31. Rudolf Rocker, *The London Years*, 1956, p. 245.
32. George Lansbury, *My Life*, 1931, pp. 199, 209.
33. Morton Lewis, *Ted Kid Lewis: his Life and Times*, 1990, pp. 62, 137-8. Horatio Bottomley's "John Bull Boxer", Preston-born Young Ahearne, spent the war years in the United States much to his publicist's chagrin.
34. The Kitchener poster, "Your Country Needs You" by Alfred Leete, may have impressed the provincial petty-bourgeoisie more than the proletariat.
35. *John Bull*, 5 June 1915.
36. D.W. Thoms and T. Donnelly, "Coventry's Industrial Economy 1880-1980", Lancaster & Mason (eds), *Life and Labour in a Twentieth Century City: the experience of Coventry*, n.d., pp. 21-4; D. Lloyd George, *War Memoirs*, n.d., Vol. 2, p. 1426.

CHAPTER THIRTEEN

WAR: THE MIDDLE PHASE

And so, abroad, the war went on, whilst in England football matches drew large crowds of able-bodied young men dressed in civilian clothes..... it certainly was a case of "business as usual"...

A.F. Tschiffely, *Bohemia Junction*, 1950, p. 101.

Wells completed his military retraining and was promoted to sergeant in time to take some Christmas leave and fight Dick Rice, for a third time, at Liverpool Stadium on Boxing Day. In the following year Wells enjoyed four contests, winning without difficulty at the Golder's Green Hippodrome; the Cosmopolitan, Plymouth; Newcastle United's football ground, and at the National Sporting Club. In 1917 he went to France and had no more professional boxing matches until the armistice had been granted to Germany, when he took part in a great two-day boxing tournament staged at the Royal Albert Hall by the Imperial Services Boxing Association between teams from the armies of Britain, United States, Australia, Canada, New Zealand and South Africa; the Royal Navy and Marines; the U.S.A. Navy, and the Royal Air Force. By which time Bombardier Billy Wells was a Company Sergeant Major, though always referred to in the press by his old rank.

The armed forces on home duty during the first world war had no difficulty in obtaining special leave if they were prominent professional boxers. Championship contests took place at most weights, when either or both contestants were servicemen. Servicemen home or abroad were encouraged to take up sport, and all authorities believed eventually that the civilian and military war effort was enhanced by sport soldiering on. Thus flyweight, Jimmy Wilde, an army sergeant, had three contests between March and August 1918, though the I.S.B.A. jibbed at the size of the purse

offered when he fought at Stamford Bridge, as too large.[1] Boxing's
continuance was aided by percentages of the gate going to war
charities like the British Sportsman's Ambulance Fund.[2] The
A.B.A. championships, not surprisingly, ceased during the war years
as the age range they especially catered for, the late teens and early
twenties, single men more often than not, volunteered for acti:e
duty, went abroad, quite often to be wounded, gassed or killed.

Professional boxers have written few books which describe
what they did during the first world war. Wells, writing for
Thomson's Weekly News in 1920, skipped from beating Dan Voyles
in December 1916, to the armistice, in a sentence.[3] Many former
boxers volunteered. Dick Burge, aged nearly fifty, joined the army
and wore a uniform as recruiting sergeant, and still managed to
promote boxing until he died of pneumonia in the epidemic of 1918.
His military funeral was followed by 3,000 people, and his wife
received a message of sympathy from the King and Queen.[4] Jim
Maloney joined the Royal Engineers in 1917 and became a corporal,
though aged over 40, it was unlikely that he served abroad.[5] Your
posting in the forces was crucial, even in France a base camp could
be risk-free. We do not know if Wells engaged in armed combat,
it was far more likely that he was teaching boxing and physical
exercises, for that was where his expertise was greatest.[6]

One former boxer, Jack Hare from West Ham, wrote of his
experience in the war in *Gladiators of the Prize Ring*, published in
Nottingham in 1925. It was sub-titled "and my world travels" as he
had been in the merchant navy, and claimed the bantamweight
championship of South Africa in 1899. Hare was steeped in boxing.
He seconded Johnny Summers in the chief supporting contest at
Olympia when Wells beat Bell, and though the book is anecdotal,
it vividly describes the war. Still as a civilian, Hare described what
he did:

> I joined the hospital ship "Rewa" at Southampton
> and left for the River Humber on August 20th

> where we were to be hospital ship for the fleet...
> We lay off Grimsby for two and a half months...

Inactive until December, they anchored in Yarmouth when they were ordered to sea as follows:

> We went on that same night. At seven o'clock the next morning we were pulling alongside of a jetty (you see in those dark days of 1914, everything was secrecy, we did not know any time whether we were coming or going), which we found was Dunkirk. As soon as we tied up, seven hundred wounded started to be carried on board, Algerians, Moors, French, Senegalese, Germans and Belgians. We laid them anywhere, down below, all over the decks...[7]

where 23 died on the first night sailing to Cherbourg. What Hare described cogently was the confusion of war, and the bloodiness of the business. At the same time both his father and brother went down with the "Rohilla" in the North Sea, and the former drowned. In February 1915, Hare (aged about 39 years) joined the Royal Navy at Chatham, and after five months in training, he and 200 others joined the "Lord Clive", newly built in Belfast. When the ship sailed for Plymouth, Hare seconded a London boxer (Johnny Hughes, of Bloomsbury) in a top of the bill contest at the Cosmo. A week later the "Lord Clive" was shelling Zeebrugge.[8] It is the contrast in Hare's book between the ordinariness at home and chaos up front which is most striking. Pat O'Keefe, whom he met at the National Sporting Club, may have been on the Army Gymnastic Staff, but he was also running a pub, and at home it was very much business is business.[9]

The hat-trick over Dick Rice took less than three minutes. Here is how *Boxing* described the culmination:

> Billy stepped back cleanly and neatly before Dick's rushes, stabbing lefts to the face as the ex-

> Bandsman came in. Rice rushed again, swinging his
> right for all it was worth... Wells met him with a
> straight left to mouth which turned his head round,
> and then crossed him with a right to the jaw...[10]

The very strong light-heavyweight, now serving with the Rifle
Brigade, went down with arms outstretched, and his seconds leapt
into the ring to pick him up before the count reached ten. They
had seen enough, their man was "out to the world".

The Hippodrome in Golders Green had been built in 1913
to the design of theatrical architect Bertie Crewe, and it was the
most sumptuous suburban theatre in the country.[11] Dick Burge
wanted to promote two championship contests on the same bill, the
eagerly anticipated return between Wells and Dick Smith, and a
middleweight title match between the holder Pat O'Keefe and the
former champion, Jim Sullivan. Burge lived in Golders Green, and
with the two purses totalling around £700 he needed a large arena
that was not being used by the War Office. The Hippodrome was
staging music hall, and Vesta Tilly,[12] an enormously popular male
impersonator and singer, was topping the bill and filling the house.
To hold his promotion, she had to be asked to relinquish one
evening, which she agreed to do. Dick and Bella Burge knew Vesta
Tilly, and had connections too numerous to mention with music
hall.[13] It was in this way that the biggest professional boxing
promotion during the war took place on 21 February 1916. By a
curious coincidence the battle of Verdun began on the same day.
Boxing's coverage of the show has an incongruous ring, though it
must be noted that the four boxers and promoter had themselves
volunteered and joined the forces, it opened:

> As anticipated, there was a tremendous crowd at
> Golder's Green, and as assured, the public had no
> difficulty in getting home...[14]

The same could not be said for thousands of troops on the Western
Front.

The fight for the middleweight title was mis-named because the champion weighed-in over the limit by half a stone though the contest is still listed as championship in boxing record books.[15] The genial Pat O'Keefe scarcely survived rounds 15 to 20, and some people booed when he got the decision. The Canning Town-Irishman, pictured often in his billy-cock bowler hat,[16] was so popular that a majority were relieved when referee Corri raised his hand. The main bout was over much more quickly. Smith crouched and smothered throughout three rounds, when Wells knocked him out with a "Bob Fitzsimmons"[17] combination of rights to ribs and chin. Wells had fidgeted a little whilst the Unionist M.P. for Mile End had made a short speech before the contest, yet his performance was most impressive in view of the doubts expressed about their first match at the Ring.

Petty Officer Curran had been a well-built heavyweight boxer with one great weakness, he rarely trained. For the boxer who is not fit, to win means to win quickly for his energy will rapidly drain away as the rounds progress. Born in County Clare in 1882, Curran had long sought a match with Wells, and when they met in March 1916 he retired on his stool at the end of round five. Despite often carrying excess weight, "Nutty" Curran was a great favourite with supporters of boxing in Plymouth where he fought most of his contests. His travels away from the Cosmopolitan Club, had taken him to France and Australia, and in 1912 he had met one of the revered figures of international boxing, Charles "Kid" McCoy. To have boxed the inventor of the left-hook was something of an honour, and though McCoy was aged 40 years he outpointed Curran.[18]

Curran was "fatter even than usual"[19] when he boxed Wells, for he had trained at sea, and his ship had docked only a few days before the fight. They had several opponents in common. Curran had beaten Bell, McMurray, Moir and Hague, and had lost to Voyles, Pigot, Rodel, Storbeck and Porky Flynn, though an extraordinary number of Curran's matches had ended in disqualification.[20] Wells later wrote of tremendous interest being

shown in the West country, and of round two when Curran claimed
he had been hit low:

> The claim was preposterous, and the referee had no
> hesitation in ignoring the charge. This claim rather
> annoyed me, and I went all out after my man...[21]

It was, however, a disappointing contest. For Wells it was
experience he should have gained four years earlier in preference to
the stage.

Open air boxing was rare. Prizefighting with bare-knuckles
had largely been an outdoor sport, but it had rapidly disappeared
with the rise of gloved boxing from the 1880s.[22] Thus Wells's next
contest, his fifth since enlisting, was unusual because it was staged
at a first division football club ground.

Newcastle United played at St. James' Park, and league and
cup football had continued into 1915, when it was stopped for the
rest of the war. The third match between Dick Smith and Wells
attracted the largest crowd yet seen at a boxing match in this
country.[23] The contest itself was not sensational, Smith never
appeared to be winning, was down in the fifth round, and retired
at the end of the ninth after taking much punishment.[24] This was
the last contest between this pair, though both remained top-class
professionals for several years. The ground housed the most
successful football club of Edwardian England. Their short passing
game had, since 1905, won them three first division championships
and one cup final. The ground had seen over 40,000 spectators
(*versus* Nottingham Forest in the first round of the F.A. cup in
1908) and a war-time boxing match could not compare with that.[25]
Just under 12,000 people attended, including many soldiers and the
"real Tyneside welcome" for the boxers had much to do with it
being Saturday and a shorter day of labour. Dick Burge, an old
North-East boxing favourite of the 1890s, had agreed to act as
referee but "the military authorities refused him permission to

travel",[26] nevertheless the last weekend of August 1916 was a sporting treat for Geordies.

Wells's last wartime boxing contest took place a week before Christmas, 1916, at "Peggy" Bettinson's benefit at the National Sporting Club. Here was the extreme irony of the war. Two years into heavy fighting, and the Monday evening boxing shows in Covent Garden had continued uninterrupted. Gentlemen in London could have had tea at Fuller's in Regent Street or a snack at the Savoy Grill, hear a concert at the Queen's Hall, and have been in time for the British heavyweight championship match.[27]

The two boxers had met six years previously at the King's Hall. Since then Dan Voyles, the Guardsman had won the Distinguished Conduct Medal, and he was as brave as ever. In the two rounds that the fight lasted he was knocked down seven times when the referee "somewhat belatedly intervened".[28]

In New York City in March 1916 the world heavyweight championship had been contested, it was not again at stake for three years. The champion Jess Willard successfully defended his title in a ten rounds' no-decision match, when Frank Moran failed to knock the huge Kansan out. Willard preferred theatrical activity to boxing, and whilst he became unpopular Wells's international stock rose. There was, however, no opportunity for international heavyweight matches for Wells, between Moran at the Opera House, and the Royal Albert Hall, where he was drawn against Private Eddie McGoorty, of the United States Army, over three rounds. At the end of 1916 Wells had run out of home grown opponents, and none appeared from overseas. Despite the threat from German submarines a few top-class boxers did visit in 1916. Two American flyweights came and were beaten by Jimmy Wilde, and they validated his claim to the world title.[29] Wilde has been almost universally admired by boxing writers, and this is justified, but at this time contemporaries observed that Wells might yet become world champion. He had lost only once in three years, and he should have beaten Moran. His comeback was complete: "Wells has never either looked better or boxed better in his life", when beating Voyles for the second time.[30] The commentators' thinking was simple, Wells was a late developer and he had improved; black boxers were now ruled out by a colour bar,[31] and world heavyweight standards had dropped. It was suggested that Johnson had laid down in Havana, so how good could Willard be?[32]

Notes

1. James Butler, *Kings of the Ring*, n.d. (1936), p. 113; *Boxing*, 11 September 1918.
2. Deghy, *Noble and Manly*, pp. 194-5; *Daily Mirror*, 29 March 1917.
3. *Thomson's Weekly News*, 28 August 1920.
4. Bell, *Bella of Blackfriars*, p. 146.
5. Maloney was stationed at Sandwich in Kent see, *Sporting Life*, 28 December 1917.
6. "I did not get any proper boxing in France until I was sent to St. Pol on a G.H.Q. Physical Training and Bayonet Fighting Course... [where] amongst the leading Sergeant-Major Instructors were... Jim Driscoll, Johnny Basham [and] Billy Wells...", Clark, *All in the Game*, p. 145. Norman Clark was, of course, an officer.
7. Jack Hare, *Gladiators of the Prize Ring*, Nottingham, n.d. (1925), pp. 126-7, 136-40.
8. *Ibid.*, pp. 144-7.
9. *Ibid.*, pp. 154-5.
10. *Boxing*, 29 December 1915.
11. R. Mander and J. Mitchenson, *The Theatres of London*, 1963, pp. 224, 291.
12. "When Vesta Tilley took the stage, dressed, as always, as a man - and beautifully tailored, too - the Royal ladies averted their eyes, and studied their programmes. A woman in trousers was shocking..." see W. MacQueen-Pope, *Carriages at Eleven*, 1948, p. 182.
13. Bell, *Bella of Blackfriars*, pp. 133-5.

14. *Boxing*, 23 February 1916.
15. For example see, *Hugman's British Boxing Yearbook 1991*, p. 273.
16. Charlie Rose, *Life's a Knock-out*, 1953, facing page 81, for one example.
17. *Boxing*, 23 February 1916.
18. An account of McCoy, by one who fought him in his prime, is to be found in W.J. Doherty, *In the days of the Giants*, 1931. This is among the best books written on boxing.
19. *Boxing*, 5 April 1916.
20. Cartoons featuring Curran and fowls appeared in *Boxing*, 28 January 1911, p. 317, and 29 June 1912, p. 199. John Murray, the editor of *Boxing*, thought Curran was promising "if only he would train" see *"Boxing's" New Year's Annual 1914*.
21. *Thomson's Weekly News*, 21 August 1920.
22. Stan Shipley, "The Boxer as Hero", Ph.D. thesis, University of London, 1986.
23. *Lloyd's Sunday News*, 8 February 1920.
24. *Boxing*, 30 August 1916.
25. Tony Mason, *Association Football and English Society 1863-1915*, Brighton, 1981, pp. 143, 215.
26. *Thomson's Weekly News*, 21 August 1920.
27. Vera Brittain, *Testament of Youth*, 1982, pp. 258, 432 et seq.
28. *Boxing*, 20 December 1916.
29. Gilbert Odd, *Great Moments in Sport*, 1974, pp. 185-191.
30. *Boxing*, 20 December 1916.
31. No black heavyweight boxer fought for the world's championship between 5 April 1915 and 22 June 1936 when Joe Louis won it.
32. *Boxing*, 16 January 1918. Willard was underrated as a champion, and he showed extraordinary courage when losing the title to Jack Dempsey at Toledo on 4 July 1919, as the film of the contest amply demonstrates.

CHAPTER FOURTEEN

PEACE AND THE BIG TOURNEY

*It has, however, long been recognised that there is no
arguing about Wells. He may do anything - from boxing
like a world-beater to displaying himself as one of the most
hopeless "Hopes"...*
*But, then, he is so popular. That is his great curse. If the
public would only "boo" him once he might be all the man
we want him to be.*

Boxing, 25 December 1918, reflecting upon the Great
Tournament.

Wells spent 1917 and 1918 between England, with periods
of leave, and in France and Belgium. There were newspaper jokes
about what he was doing in tanks, sitting upright or on all fours
because of his size,[1] which misunderstood the nature of the war.
The greatest army which Britain had ever raised, some two
millions, was located between the channel coast and the front line
stretching roughly from Ypres to St Quentin. Infantry generally
spent only a few days at a time in the firing line, in attack or
defence they might be deployed for a week, but their numbers were
too large to live off the countryside. They had to be relieved to
sleep, wash and eat, thus field kitchens with billets were set up
behind the front line trenches. The consumption of hand grenades,
shells and bullets was enormous, and supply was never enough, so
the traffic in munitions used existing railway lines, roads and
bridges, and huge depots, some of which had to be built, some
rebuilt after shelling. In addition to the weapons of war, the men
needed boots and clothing and blankets, soap and towels, tobacco
and rum, letters from home, and if they were wounded, stretchers,
medicine, doctors and hospitals. The Western Front required horses
and motor vehicles, artillery and Lewis guns, gas masks and
entrenching tools in quantities never before seen, let alone

transported. Barbed wire would have been a major export order had demand occurred in 1913. The logistics of the operations in France and Belgium are impossible to grasp without this preamble on their scale.

The soldiers spent much of their time in the trenches, and even more within range of the "Jack Johnsons",[2] which was what they called the shells exploding from the heavy artillery of the enemy. But more time still had to be spent at a greater distance from the firing. Men went home on leave for ten days or a fortnight; they went on short courses to learn about new weapons; they needed rehabilitation after slight wounds and minor illnesses; they needed some relaxation from stress quite frequently. Behind the lines they played football and organised boxing competitions. An officer in the Leinster Regiment kept a diary in which he wrote:

> A résumé of the ten days in Hazebrouck billets: while we were "fattening up" as we called it... we had several variations from the usual routine of drill..... Daily at 9 a.m. the Battalion formed up... for... open order, slow marching taking place to the time of the drums... Inter-brigade boxing tournaments were the chief events of the evenings... One evening there was a battalion concert..... Another attraction... was the Variety Show given by the 29th Divisional Troupe...[3]

This was at a deserted French village to which the inhabitants were just returning, further back were the base camps adapted to much larger numbers of soldiers, like Etaples.

Etaples was for this officer "a dull place, crammed with troops".[4] It was a base and transit camp by a small town on the coast with port facilities, railway yards, ordnance stores, hospital, prison, bakery, training grounds (known as the "Bull Ring"), and several Infantry Base Depots each containing "whole streets of hutments and tents".[5] This large military and industrial depot was familiar to raw recruits and experienced troops, and men back from the front line trenches were the more difficult to handle. Such base camps at Dunkirk, Le Havre and Rouen, plus deserted villages further forward, would have been the types of stations that C.S.M. Wells visited to organise bayonet training and physical education; to talk to officers and N.C.O.s about recreation for the men; and to referee boxing tournaments, not as grand as those he had known in India, yet along the same lines, and vitally important for morale. *Boxing* was taken to task for hinting that Wells may not have been roughing it in France in a letter from an officer which they quoted lengthily. The Major had written:

> [Wells] is not a boxing instructor. He is on the Physical Training and Bayonet Fighting Staff, and is attached to an Army Headquarters, which is the furthest he ever goes back. There are thousands of men on the lines behind him and at the Bases who get more credit for their work than he does.

This defence of Wells was published in January 1918, and it continued:

> Wells has to tour round various Infantry Brigades who come out for rest just behind the line, and who are in many cases still in the shelled area. Here his personality, position in the sporting world, and his knowledge of his work compel attention from these war-worn men.....[6]

Major Wilson, who became a leading boxing promoter after the war, went on to make the argument that what Wells was doing was more useful to the war effort than if he had been an Infantry N.C.O. in the front line, which was valid. The camp at St. Pol, where we know Wells was,[7] lay 34 and 29 kilometres respectively from Arras and Bethune. This was in Carpentier-land, shell-ravaged, and very much Western Front. Wells was an experienced soldier, much travelled he had mixed with men of all classes, he was an achiever, and one suspects an excellent instructor, an altogether useful man to have around in hard times. The forces were paid in francs, so during his travels it would have been possible to stop at a café and perhaps stay at an hotel. In July 1918 he did have a day in Paris, and since he had written to, and he met, Hurdman-Lucas, a long account of how the day went was published in *Boxing*. "Billy Wells in Paree" was written humorously and not in the author's best style. They met at a club for the British forces where Billy ate a large meal, later Lucas took him to a swimming pool, where, of course, Billy swam well. On they went to some boxing quarters for more talk, then to the Casino de Paris to meet the artists Maurice Chevallier and Mlle Mistinguett. Finally, they went to visit Carpentier's flat, and, whilst he was not at home, his brother entertained them.[8] The account demonstrates admirably what a public figure Billy Wells was. Obviously, having been given notice of Wells's visit, Lucas had organised the day meticulously though he wrote as if invitations happened spontaneously. The modest British and Commonwealth champion might have preferred a quieter day, but what happened made better copy for the writer. This dream day away from war, was written because Wells was the famous boxer, and it is misleading. No soldier of any nation could face the tragedy in France without a break, and the generation which was there has almost gone. The deprivation which the forces on both sides of the Western Front suffered is difficult to overestimate. Trench warfare claimed millions of casualties, yet the style of life it created is probably beyond the 1990s imagination. Vera Brittain, who served from August 1917 until April in Etaples as a nurse, later recalled:

> Whenever I think of the War to-day, it is not as summer but always as winter; always as cold and darkness and discomfort, and an intermittent warmth of exhilarating excitement which made us irrationally exult in all three. Its permanent symbol, for me, is a candle stuck in the neck of a bottle, the tiny flame flickering in an ice-cold draught, yet

creating a miniature illusion of light against an
opaque infinity of blackness.[9]

the same words might have satisfied anyone over there for a long
spell.

Early in 1918 a tremendous offensive by 90 German
divisions drove the British army back some 60 kilometres, but the
offensive failed to split the French and British forces, or to reach
the Channel Ports.   As usual on the Western Front, attackers
suffered heavier casualties, and from the middle of May the armies
of the Allies, just reinforced by divisions from United States, could
anticipate unconditional victory, though horrific fighting continued
until the day of the Armistice.   Pessimism about when the war
would end, and doubt on the Allies' side about winning, were
dispelled in the Summer, relatively suddenly.

The Imperial Services Boxing Association was formed
towards the end of the war.   The Royal Navy and Army Boxing
Championships had been held annually from 1892 until 1914,[10] and
when they resumed, they were extended to include a team from the
very young Royal Air Force.   In the Autumn of 1918, servicemen
from Australia, New Zealand, Canada, South Africa and the United
States were in Europe in abundance, so I.S.B.A. booked the Royal
Albert Hall for two days, the first time it had ever been used for
boxing, and staged their grand tournament with Prince Albert, later
King George VI, to present the prizes.   It was a triumph for the
organising body which looked as if it might eventually control the
whole of professional boxing in Britain, filling the vacuum left by
the decline in prestige of the National Sporting Club.   The
promotion was novel in that though all the boxers were
professionals, contests were limited to three rounds, and decisions
were given by a trio of judges and not the referee. The tournament
attracted huge crowds, 10,000 spectators at each session, and on
Thursday afternoon some gained admission by breaking down a
door.   The boxing itself was of poor quality, not surprisingly
because time for training had been short, and the level of the

contestants varied ridiculously. At light-heavyweight, the U.S.A. Army team fielded the world middleweight champion, Mike O'Dowd, who outclassed Dick Smith, and went on to win the final. The Irish-American from St Paul, Minnesota, was, incidentally, a private. U.S. Seaman, Harry Greb, who was to win a world title, lost in the same preliminaries. The Shield awarded to the team gaining most marks went to the British Army, which won three of the eight finals, at light, welter and heavyweight.

Wells won yet *Boxing* opined that "Beautiful Billy was *the* disappointment of the whole tourney".[11] In his first trial he outpointed Leading Seaman Powell easily. In the semi-final he met Private Eddie McGoorty, a redoubtable American who had once beaten Pat O'Keefe at the N.S.C., and outpointed him similarly. It was the final, however, which gave rise to criticism.

Wells's opponent was Sergeant Joe Beckett who had stopped an American and an Australian to get that far.[12] Since Beckett was to box Wells three times in eighteen months it is worth considering where this 24 years-old R.A.F. man, who came from Southampton, had gained his experience.

Beckett had been just another middleweight in 1914. Born in 1894, his mother had run a travelling boxing booth where he started to box at the age of 12.[13] It was during the war that Beckett gained prominence with six contests in 1917, and then his attempt at the N.S.C. to lift Dick Smith's light-heavyweight title. This failed, but only on points after 20 rounds, so he was the obvious choice for the R.A.F. team nine months later. At the Albert Hall, Beckett seemed to have the best of the first two rounds, whilst Wells won the third and with it the decision, which some thought "somewhat lucky".[14] These seven minutes of boxing enhanced Beckett's reputation, and did little to harm the champion's, for Wells's partisans could truthfully say that he had not boxed seriously for two years, was out of practice, and less match-fit than his 5 feet 10 inch opponent.

Four years had changed boxing since the Cochran-led boom in the Summer of 1914. The standard of British boxing was to be weak throughout the 1920s, and this was unsurprising since a generation of potential boxers had been lost to the war. Among the heavyweights there had been few homegrown challengers since Voyles had been disposed of; two years later there appeared to be several, chief amongst whom was a large confident soldier who had once been Wells's sparring partner.

Frank Goddard had knocked out Joe Beckett at the National Sporting Club in December 1917. Goddard resembled Wells in many ways, they were the same size, both had been in the army twice, both were Londoners, and neither man's contests usually went the distance. Wells was, however, four years older, more experienced, and much more the boxing stylist. Goddard had a strong punch, and he could take a punch, but he never claimed to be a ring artist. When they finally met at the Crystal Palace in 1922, the fourth round was described by an experienced newspaper reporter as "the most stirring I ever watched",[15] but at the end of the war it was argued that Wells had abdicated because of the admiring way he and Jim Maloney referred to the main contender for the British title. "The big boy" as *Boxing* called Goddard, was not popular with the public, he was too cocksure for many people's tastes, and he seemed unstoppable:

> ... when Beckett sent him down with a punch which
> would have sent most heavy-weights to sleep, he
> stared around in wonder. His supreme feeling was
> obviously one of amazement that such a thing could
> happen to *him*. Yet he rose, full of resolve to take
> a full revenge, and even eager to set about taking it
> before he had fully recovered.[16]

It was the contrasts between champion and challenger, in weaknesses and strengths, in attitudes towards opponents, that made the National Sporting Club put up the biggest purse it had ever offered, for a match between them before either man had been demobilized.

Nearly four million servicemen were demobilized by April 1920, and during this period the British economy enjoyed boom time. Men were given one month's leave and a war gratuity, and those with a job to go to were released first, thus boxers with an offer from a promoter were soon wearing civilian clothing. War workers displaced by the armistice received an out-of-work donation from the State. This unemployment benefit was 24 shillings a week for men, four shillings less for women; for ex-servicemen payment continued for 26 weeks, for civilians it lasted a quarter. Thus a contracting labour force had money to spend at the war's end. This money had gone down in buying power since July 1914, for the cost of living had doubled, whilst wage rates had not quite kept up that level of inflation. When unemployment reached one million, as it did in January 1921, the boom in the economy had ceased, and by May, approaching a quarter of workers were out of jobs. Boom then slump followed the signing of peace.[17]

The National Sporting Club had been under siege before the war. The base of professional boxing, the spectators, had broadened enough to make their seating accommodation in Covent Garden inadequate for the numbers of people who wanted to watch, and promoters who recognised the new market, like Cochran, Burge and White, had upstaged the Club. During the last years of hostilities Anglo-American shows on Wednesday evenings, utilizing U.S. servicemen, had been successful, but the idea that British championship contests were only valid if promoted by the N.S.C. could no longer be sustained. The three thousand pounds,[18] reputedly offered for Wells *versus* Goddard, was the last squawk of a middle-class institution which had outlived the Victorian bohemianism it had been born into.

Notes

1.   *Boxing*, 17 July 1918, "The Editor's Ideas".

2.   F.C. Hitchcock, *"Stand To"*, *a diary of the Trenches*, Norwich, 1988, p. 283; Maurice Baring, *Flying Corps Headquarters 1914-18*, 1985, p. 93. See also, J. Huizinga, *The Waning of the Middle Ages*, 1955, p. 229.

3.   Hitchcock, *op. cit.*, pp. 134, 279-80.

4.   *Ibid.*, p. 303.

5.   D. Gill and G. Dallas, *The unknown Army*, 1985, pp. 63-4.

6.   *Boxing*, 16 January 1918.

7.   See chapter 13, note 6.

8.   *Boxing*, 17 July 1918, "Paris Letter".

9.   Vera Brittain, *Testament of Youth*, 1982, p. 372. This book was first published in 1933.

10.   *Royal Navy and Royal Marines Sports Handbook 1934*, p. 102.

11.   *Boxing*, 25 December 1918.

12.   *Ibid.*, 18 December 1918.

13.   *All Sports Illustrated Weekly*, 29 November 1919.

14.   *Boxing*, 18 December 1918.

15.   Trevor C. Wignall, *The Sweet Science*, 1926, p. 213.

16.   *Boxing*, 3 April 1918.

17.   A.C. Pigou, *Aspects of British Economic History 1918-25*, 1971, pp. 22-34, 222.

18.   *Boxing*, 5 February 1919. The same paper, 26 June 1918, had mentioned a purse of £2,500 with a surplus going to charity. Both figures were probably an exaggeration.

CHAPTER FIFTEEN

TRAGEDY AT THE STADIUM

... and, seeing him turn suddenly up Chancery Lane with that quick jerk and impatient stride which distinguish a lover of the FANCY, I said "I'll be hanged if that fellow is not going to the fight..."

Essays of William Hazlitt, n.d., The Scott Library, vol. 39, p. 164.

Bombardier Billy Wells lost the British heavyweight title in February 1919. Maloney and Wells had had talks with Charles Cochran suggesting that he promote a third contest with Carpentier. This Cochran refused to do until he had staged two or three contests with Wells against less formidable opponents. Wells drew the crowds as everyone knew, so the promoter allowed them to choose their own match with any of four credible British heavyweights, and Joe Beckett was their selection. Maloney asked for £1,000 for Wells, and Cochran bargained him down to £600. This was a modest figure, though it was win, lose or draw, and the champion was expected to beat his British competitors and reach the prize of a large share of a big gate against his old French rival. These hard-headed negotiations went wildly wrong for the newly-demobbed Wells and Maloney.[1]

The old theatre at 85 High Holborn had been briefly used for exciting boxing in the 1890s,[2] and later as warehouse and stables for a haulage firm, before falling into disuse. It became the premier place for boxing in London between the wars in a strange way. A Jewish promoter with the unlikely name of Jack Callaghan[3] had wanted, towards the end of 1916, to match Jimmy Wilde for the flyweight championship of the world. He needed a good overseas opponent to give the match substance, and despite the sinking of shipping, to his surprise, one turned up. Young Zulu Kid (Giuseppe di Melfi) a New York-Italian, heard of the challenge and accepted it. The Young Men's Christian Association was running hostels for servicemen, and was seeking to enlarge its accommodation, whilst Callaghan needed a hall for his title match. He obtained permission to use labour and materials, in the depths of the war, to rebuild Holborn Stadium on condition that the Y.M.C.A. had use of it for the rest of hostilities.[4] Callaghan and his backer, Clarence Hatry,[5] got the work done in 18 days. Zulu Kid, who was very short, and unbeaten as a professional boxer, gave Wilde, the strong favourite, a hard contest until he was knocked out in the 11th round, and with this unusual match-making, The Stadium as it was now called, re-entered boxing, and Wilde was recognised as the world champion at eight stones.

The trade paper, *Boxing*, turned against Wells when he turned down the offers to meet Goddard. The underlying argument was that he was not behaving like a British champion should:

> ... if that popular British idol Bombardier Wells may pick and choose the opponents he will deign to box... then may we bid a final farewell to all our age-old conceptions of the meaning of the word champion.[6]

The paper may also have heard of his other business negotiations, for he starred in two films *The Great Game* and *The Silver Lining* produced in Leyton by I.B. Davidson, which received their first screenings in December 1918 and November 1919 respectively.[7] Wells trained in Brighton at quarters he had used before, and *Boxing* published a rumour that he was loafing instead of training.[8] After he had lost to Beckett the paper became sympathetic to Wells again.

The match with Beckett was Cochran's first show at the Holborn Stadium and it was profitable. When the Y.M.C.A. had removed their beds, the gallery seated 320 and the ground floor held over 1,250 spectators.[9] According to Cochran, ticket sales reached £3,344, and the preliminary bouts cost him £30, so his return on total outlay was at least one hundred per cent.[10] The contest which was Billy's first loss to a British boxer since Gunner Moir in 1911, was gruelling. The introductions were lengthy; Carpentier (in uniform), Wilde and Goddard were presented to the audience, and Horatio Bottomley, freshly elected M.P. for South Hackney, made a speech, then the heavyweight championship occupied the ring. In the first few seconds Wells was on the canvas, then later in the opening round he was down again from a right to the jaw, from which he appeared badly dazed. For the next three rounds Beckett bored in whilst Wells tried to keep him off, with the shorter man having marginally the better of the exchanges. In the fifth, the champion, taking a hammering, struggled back to standing twice, before he was finally counted out. The report in *Boxing* was sub-headed "Full Details of the Tragedy" and included:

> Wells may have boxed badly, he may have beaten himself, and may have written finis to his boxing history, but he has at least the consolation that he put up a singularly game fight...[11]

Wells did not take another contest for eight months, and in that time Cochran crushed the lingering pretensions of the National Sporting Club. The N.S.C. still claimed that since British titles could only change hands in Covent Garden, Beckett was not champion, and they matched Frank Goddard against a promising north country heavyweight, Jack Curphey from Salford, for their version of the championship. Cochran had already matched Beckett against Goddard at Olympia, which had been surrendered by the War Office, and this was scheduled for June. The N.S.C. contest, taking place three weeks earlier, could have destroyed Cochran's gate had Curphey won, but he was stopped in ten rounds, and public interest in Beckett *versus* Goddard was heightened. Goddard inclined to the view that no punch could hurt him, but Beckett knocked him out in round two.

Wells lost the title of British Heavyweight Champion when it was highly valuable. For his first defence Beckett received

£2,500, and the loser of the match collected only £500 less, for the post-war boom was gathering momentum, and Cochran, the leading promoter, fed demand with regular shows in Holborn, and occasional "spectaculars" elsewhere. Cochran was to become bankrupt in 1925, but this was due to the slump which ensued from 1922, and theatrical losses, not boxing promotion which he had dropped.[12]

Wells made his comeback with two matches under Cochran's banner at the Holborn Stadium. In October he knocked out Jack Curphey in the first five minutes of a twenty-rounds' contest, and a month later had slightly more trouble with another northern boxer, Arthur Townley, from Birkenhead. The towel was thrown in from the former seaman's corner in round nine after he had been down several times, but in neither contest did Wells impress. One paper complained "the handsome Bombardier revealed all the old indecision" editorialising on the short-lived Curphey contest;[13] another reporting the rather one-sided Townley fight judged that the Birkenhead man had been "quite unkind to Billy in the 4th".[14] It was difficult for the newspapers to find anything original to say about Wells. Boxing writers had exhausted thousands of words on the man as promising newcomer, contender, champion, white hope, international pretender, and now he was meeting men scarcely known without close scrutiny of the sporting pages. Wells was still a public figure. A reporter going to an exhibition in late-summer 1919 recorded that:

> The writer went to Olympia. He saw an extra big and ugly looking rush down Exhibition Road, and joined in it, expecting to see the capture of a "Tealeaf", or at least a good rough and tumble... Nothing of the kind. It was only William Wells, Esq., accompanied by his better half, seeking admittance at the gate...[15]

Townley was to be courageous, Curphey perhaps unlucky, yet they boxed the personification of British sportsmanship. Though

Bombardier Billy Wells was 32 years old, to the general public he was "the boxer". To many people he represented ideal elder brother, and to boxing fans he symbolized the unpredictableness of the sport. The report of him against the Salford man contained this passage which could be his epitaph:

> Greedy people may complain that they rarely get
> their money's worth in length of entertainment...
> but these must belong to the brand who will never
> be satisfied, even with the earth and the fullness
> thereof, but must go out clamouring for the moon
> and stars, not to mention the sun as well. Because
> ten minutes of Billy Wells is always worth a cycle
> of any other boxer.[16]

Wells was to take more matches, five in 1920, yet at the end of 1919 is an appropriate time to assess the man, not as a personality, which lack of evidence makes impossible, but as a boxer. Few boxers improve after they reach the age that Wells was. He had lost two years of his career as others had not, though the war may have been more untimely and finally destructive to the careers of some potential heavyweight champions than it was to our man. An attempt to analyse the ability of a sportsman using the record of his best years would be statistically happier for a cricketer, but no performing art allows certainty.

Wells had 36 professional boxing contests between 1910 and 1919 of which he lost seven. When Wells lost to Moir, Palzer, Gunboat Smith, Carpentier (twice), Moran and Beckett he was knocked out, and, except in the case of Moran, counted out within five rounds. Wells only had two contests which went the full twenty rounds, and he won both. The history of pugilism is littered with opponents who were not trying. This was never so in Wells's case for to beat him was to unlock the door to riches. Wells packed stadiums, no boxer looks for a soft spot on which to lie down when he knows that to win means his earnings will soar. In terms of boxing career prospects, Wells was the man to defeat. In the corner opposite was always a boxer who wanted to beat him, and Maloney did not, at least obviously, pick matches with "no-hope" opponents. Maloney guided Wells to more money than any previous British boxer had ever dreamed of. He brilliantly exploited the burgeoning profits in professional boxing from Johnson's defeat of Jeffries in 1910.

At his peak in the ring, in 1912-13, Wells lost five out of his nine contests, and some attempt must be made to explain why. He was by all accounts an excellent boxer, as fast as many middleweights, with a strong punch. He failed partly because his punch was not strong enough; Palzer took an absolute specimen and got up, the Gunboat steamed through Wells's punches like an ironclad. Coupled with this marginal disadvantage compared with other world-class boxers, Wells had a more serious weakness which was purely physical. He was not able to take the sort of punch which world beaters must occasionally expect to. Opponents of this view will cite Sunshine where Wells took huge blows only to rise and narrowly triumph, but this demonstrates courage and determination, not the weight of the Sergeant's punches. No one questions Billy's pluck. Wells's much discussed problem of nervousness and temperament arose from his awareness that he was not built to absorb a stunning punch.

Wells's lesser faults were sometimes noticed humorously. A tall man, he was weak at close-quarter work, where:

> he seems unable to do thing[s] save lollop over a
> man, like an electric light standard over a lorry
> which has collided with it.

Of Wells's lack of aggression in some fights:

> he was poking out left and right, as though he was
> a fond but shy bachelor uncle tickling the first baby
> he had ever seen.[17]

MORAN.

BOMBARDIER WELLS.

BECKETT.

The Bombardier blocks a fierce onslaught from Beckett.

and there was an element of truth in these comments. The most astute judgement of Wells the boxer, however, came not from journalists or boxing writers, but from an artist. Harry Furniss (1854-1925), who had illustrated complete editions of Dickens and Thackeray, wrote *The By Ways and Queer Ways of Boxing*, which was published in 1919. This elderly man whose career stretched from the 1870s' *Illustrated London News* to post-war cinematography hit upon the fuller truth when he wrote:

> [assuming] the sculptor's subject is a prize fighter...
> no artist... would select the ex-bombardier as his
> model. Wells is a spendidly (sic) made fellow, with
> the head of an Adonis, a model for innumerable
> things - anything, in fact, *but* a prize fighter..... he
> has not a fighter's face, nor has he a fighter's
> stomach.[18]

and Furniss's caricatures, full length of Wells and Beckett and heads of them and Carpentier and Moran, are illustrative of his point. One must doubt lines drawn by an artist to reinforce his words, yet his argument was right. Wells looked, and was, too fine for a fighter, a ruder Wells might have won more contests.

Notes

1.   Cochran, *Secrets*, 1925, pp. 286-7.
2.   *Licensed Victuallers' Gazette*, 3 August 1894; *Morning Advertiser*, 23 November 1894; *Mirror of Life*, 2 February 1895; *Sportsman*, 3, 5, 6 April 1895; *Memoirs of Robert Patrick Watson*, n.d. (1899), p. 100.
3.   For Jack Callaghan see *Boxing World*, 20 October 1910; *Boxing*, 11 March 1911; *Lloyd's Sunday News*, 21 March 1920; *"Boxing's" New Year Annual 1913*, p. 29; Harry Preston, *Memories*, 1928, p. 118. My letter to *Irish Post*, 31 October 1987, seeking

information on Callaghan, not surprisingly, prompted no response.

4. Gilbert Odd, *Boxing: Cruisers to Mighty Atoms*, 1974, pp. 185-191.

5. For Hatry see Seymour Hicks, *Between Ourselves*, 1930, pp. 181-4.

6. A.F. Cameron, "Is Wells afraid of Goddard?", *Boxing*, 5 February 1919.

7. Rachael Low, *History of the British Film 1918-29*, 1971, pp. 136-7, 376, 450.

8. *Boxing*, 26 February 1919.

9. London County Council, *Boxing, Music... Licenses*, 1935, p. 41.

10. Cochran, *Secrets*, pp. 286-7.

11. *Boxing*, 5 March 1919.

12. Cochran, *Secrets*, pp. v, 292-4, 337, 421; Charles Graves, *The Cochran Story*, n.d. (1951), p. 118.

13. *All Sports op. cit.*, 1 November 1919.

14. *Boxing*, 26 November 1919.

15. *Ibid.*, 17 September 1919.

16. *Ibid.*, 22 October 1919.

17. *Ibid.*

18. Harry Furniss's other book *Our Joe, his great Fight*, published in 1903, lampooned Joseph Chamberlain and his tariff reform campaign.

CHAPTER SIXTEEN

THE VIEWS OF SMITH AND ANGLE

*I have seen all the British heavyweights since Gunner Moir,
but I despair of ever seeing one capable of winning the
heavyweight championship of the world.*

W. Barrington Dalby, *Come in Barry!*, 1961, p. 33.

In 1920 the British economy was exploding with
opportunities to make profits and Jack Callaghan booked the
Canterbury Music Hall for a series of boxing matinees. The home
of metropolitan music hall entertainment since 1851 had seen boxing
often before, we remember the return match between Wells and
Moir before the war, it held 1,500 patrons, and was destroyed by
bombing in 1942. Callaghan put up a purse, size unknown, to be
divided 60-40 between winner and loser, in addition Wells and his
opponent each raised a £200 side stake.[1] Wells trained at Enfield
Lock where *Lloyd's Sunday News* noted that he was one of the best
skippers since the late Dick Burge. Harry Reeve of Plaistow, the
boxer matched with him for the Tuesday afternoon show in
Westminster Bridge Road, was notoriously unenthusiastic about
training though he had a long and distinguished boxing record.[2]

Harry Reeve was born in the East End in 1893 and had
been a boy-boxer, growing up through the weights. He had lost on
points to Pat O'Keefe in 1914 for the vacant British middleweight
title, and in 1916 had beaten Dick Smith over 20 rounds to win the
light-heavyweight championship. This title he relinquished to serve
a prison term for his part in the Etaples mutiny.[3] He had boxed
Joe Beckett twice, both times at the Ring, winning in 1914 and
losing on New Year's Day 1919. Reeve was a stylish boxer with an
appetite for a fight, his twenty rounds with Bandsman Blake in
1915 was long remembered by regulars at Blackfriars.[4] As a small
hall boxer he was hugely popular, rivalling the affection gained with
a different audience by his actress and singer Aunt Ada.[5] Though

six years younger than Wells, pugilistically Reeve was the older man by many matches. His upright style suited Wells admirably, Reeve elected to box, and was knocked out with a clean punch in the fourth round. Wells was soon afterwards contributing his memoirs in numbers to two weekly papers, in one he called this an ideal knock-out blow,[6] in the other he wrote of "the finest blow I ever delivered".[7] The monthly *Health and Efficiency* cautioned its readers in verse:

> Our hope he flatters to destroy,
>   Our confidence to kill;
> And yet we'll never fail to love
>   Our own Bombardier Bill.[8]

Boxing, more prosaically, described how:

> Billy's right shot out straight and true to the chin, and the Plaistow man came forward full length on to his face...

and its Editor reproached Reeve for not boring in:

> Oh, unobservant Harry! We will all admit that you are a vastly better boxer than the average run to-day, but in this department Beautiful Billy has long stood alone among the big men.[9]

Reeve continued to box until 1927, and the contrast between him and Wells, as professionals, is worth dwelling upon. Apart from the latter half of the war, Reeve took contests almost fortnightly, and this was how most contemporary boxers, including champions, lived. They accepted small purses and trained very little because their sparring was kept up in real matches without the aid of partners who required to be paid. Wells invariably trained for his much less frequent contests by engaging three or four sparring partners and Maloney would organise the training camp, often at a hotel, where they would all spend two or three weeks. There was a vast difference between the lifestyles of frequent-fight professionals like Reeve, and what can be called "Pot of Gold" boxers like Billy Wells whose career record might even have read better had he started off as a fortnightly boxer in 1910. Financially, of course, Wells' earnings from 48 contests dwarfed Reeve's returns from more than 150 matches, yet, technically, their career records bear comparison. Wells was matched with a world champion, Johnson in 1911, although he never fought Jack or his successors Willard and Dempsey. Reeve, who was not big enough to be a *bona fide* heavyweight, met two men who in their next contests, won the world's light-heavyweight championship. Battling Siki, of Senegal, boxed the Plaistow man four times (in Rotterdam, Amsterdam, Antwerp and Marseilles) before he knocked Georges Carpentier out in six rounds to win the title. Mike McTigue, from County Clare via New York City, boxed Reeve in Liverpool before relieving Siki of the championship on points in Dublin on St. Patrick's Day 1923. The subjective impression one gets of Reeve is that he was used as a "trial horse" and often fought for next week's rent, yet he probably liked a fight more than Billy.[10]

At the Royal Albert Hall, Wells beat a young French heavyweight called Paul Journée, and he was roundly criticized for taking 13 rounds to do it. Wells and Journée topped the bill before "an immense crowd", though the latter may have been partly due to two attractive supporting bouts involving Londoners, Mike Honeyman and Matt Wells.[11] Three weeks later Wells returned to Holborn Stadium to meet a more illustrious opponent.

Wells had met Eddie McGoorty before, outpointing him at the Inter-Allied Services Tournament; the former United States Army private was, nevertheless, one of the most gifted boxers Wells fought. They were the same age though McGoorty had been a prodigy, winning the lightweight championship of Wisconsin as an amateur at the age of 15. Turning professional soon afterwards, and boxing out of Oshkosh, McGoorty never lost a contest for four years. McGoorty engaged in contests regularly, visiting Europe three times, and Australia twice. He boxed in the British style, standing upright, using particularly a beautifully-timed left hook and jab.[12] Wells and he had many opponents in common. In 1911 Pat O'Keefe and he were close to being the best middleweights in the world when McGoorty "gave the fighting Irishman the boxing lesson of his life"[13] according to James Butler, who became the *Daily Herald's* socialist boxing correspondent. McGoorty stayed on after the war, beating Harry Reeve and Bandsman Rice easily before he was beaten twice, by Joe Beckett and Frank Goddard respectively.

The press enthused about Wells's prospects when, after a hard 16 rounds, he knocked Eddie McGoorty out. *Boxing* dropped its peevish tone and wrote:

> Billy... took the longest step upwards and backwards he has yet taken. He showed that he is to-day a vastly better man than anyone of us has really believed, since he lost to Carpentier at Ghent.[14]

Promoter Cochran's heart would have palpitated as the American had Wells staggering, because he already had the Bombardier and Beckett under contract for a second title match, and a McGoorty victory would have been bad for business.[15] *Lloyd's Sunday News*, with a vested interest in increased circulation for it was carrying Billy's own serial story, wrote:

> It was a most exciting match... and McGoorty deserved every cheer that came his way... Wells has never boxed better... Joe Beckett, who sat near the ringside, must know that he has a difficult task on hand when he faces Wells at Olympia next month.[16]

The press was engaging in wishful thinking. Beckett and Goddard were unpopular except with their own small bands of supporters, in contrast, Wells did not have a knot of fans, he was admired by most of the public, perhaps especially by those who had never watched boxing. The McGoorty of 1919-20 was not the boxer he had been. The trio of top British heavyweights had all beaten a boxer who had been great, but now had an alcohol problem,[17] which killed him before he was 40 years of age. McGoorty was the last man with a masters in ringcraft that Wells was to beat.

The return match for the heavyweight title was promoted by Cochran at Olympia on 10th May 1920. In the 14 months since he had lost the championship, Wells had stopped five opponents, whilst Beckett's progress had been less straightforward.

Beckett's defeat of Wells within three months of the Armistice had been unexpected. Ideally, the public and promoter Cochran wished Wells to win and go on to a hugely attractive third match with Carpentier. Whoever won that could proceed triumphantly to a contest for the world championship, possibly in London. In the immediate aftermath of the war, Wells had been two or three steps away from skimming the cream off the sporting boom in Britain and the U.S.A., but Joe Beckett had won. He was widely believed to be inferior to Frank Goddard at that point, but those who thought so were proved to be massively wrong at Olympia in June. Subsequently, whilst waiting for a curiously-hesitant Carpentier to ratify their match, Beckett knocked-out McGoorty after a fine contest, at another Cochran show at Olympia. When the date was belatedly fixed for Carpentier *versus* Beckett the big exhibition hall was unavailable, so Cochran gambled by staging the match at the relatively small Holborn Stadium using extraordinary ticket prices. Sales almost reached £30,000, and cordons of police controlled some ten thousand people outside waiting for news of the fight. Beckett (receiving £3,000 win, lose or draw) was a slight favourite, and Carpentier (£5,000 same terms) knocked him out in the first round.[18] Wells must have heartily approved of the result. He and Georges had become friends and Beckett was surly, more importantly, it would have raised his hopes of winning back the British title. Carpentier got his match with the world champion, though it was promoted by Tex Rickard, and Cochran had no hand in it. They boxed before a crowd of 80,000 spectators who paid over a million and a half dollars to watch, and

Carpentier received a guaranteed $200,000, and Jack Dempsey won by a knockout in the fourth round.[19]

At Olympia Wells threw caution out of the back door and endeavoured to out-fight Beckett. He had some success in the first two rounds, and was counted out towards the end of the third. The best account of this contest was written by the referee, a Manchester man, Jack Smith, who wrote of the last round:

> Wells was bleeding about the face, but he was dead willing, and the pair again banged away vigorously... Wells gave a wobble or two before the round was half-way through, and Beckett, seeing his chance, went in regardless... Even then Wells was not done with, and he shifted nicely across to... Beckett's corner, but Joe was at him like a lion, and in a fusillade of punches, which included four lefts and three rights to the Bombardier's jaw, Wells was sent crashing to the floor, his head bumping hard, to be counted out...

Smith concluded in *Thomson's Weekly News*:

> If that is the end of Wells, he has gone out in a radiant blaze of glory, true to his reputation as one of the most remarkable personalities that ever graced the British ring, for, whatever his faults and failings might have been, he has certainly lent a tone and dignity to the profession which he adopted.[20]

Wells denied even the possibility that he might retire. His view was that the contest could easily have gone either way.[21] This was probably true, yet the two men never met in a fourth contest. Beckett retired from boxing before Wells did, and had a remarkable record. He juggled with promoters in the post-war economic boom and became a wealthy man. His contests between May 1920 and

1923 provided some spectacular surprises. A former world champion came out of retirement, and it was entirely predictable that Beckett would beat him, for Tommy Burns was forty years old and six years out of the ring. Beckett often talked of wanting to box Dempsey, but his reputation receded as he lost to Frank Moran (December 1920), then beat him in a return (October 1922) before Carpentier gave Beckett the same medicine as before, this time knocking him out within a minute of the start in front of a big crowd at Olympia. Against the French champion, both Wells and Beckett appeared inconsequential, yet in each case Carpentier gained credibility as contender for the highest honours mainly by beating the two Britons. Cochran thought that "Beckett's financial rewards during his career were out of all proportion to his ability"[22] but this was the harsh judgement of showman on cantankerous star. Referee Jack Angle, who was sparing with praise for boxers, took a significantly different view. In his only book, he wrote:

> Joe Beckett, our best British heavy-weight prior to 1920, was perhaps a trifle fortunate to beat Wells and ultimately win a Lonsdale Belt, but he proved himself thoroughly game in his last contest with Moran. If not brilliant, Beckett was at least a tryer, and he did well out of the sport financially, which must be some consolation, for he had a pretty strenuous career, all things considered.[23]

Since Angle had been a good amateur boxer, and had refereed professional contests since 1881 his authority was greater than Cochran's, yet his preference for Beckett over Wells among British heavyweights between 1900 and 1925 ought to be questioned. Their best years as boxers were sharply divided by the war, they had a similar number of professional contests, and both lost eleven of them. Wells, however, did box in the United States, while the man from Southampton did not, and Wells almost certainly faced better competition. Angle admired what in prizefighting was called "bottom", the ability to take punishment and shrug it off, to come up for more when all seemed lost. This facet of the sport was important to him, especially because he had taken an active part in the last decades of bare-knuckle stuff, and possibly nostalgia played a part in his judgement. Comparisons can only be made with contemporary boxers which Wells and Beckett, to be fair, were not, they may have met three times but Wells was some years beyond his prime. In the eyes of the public anyway, Wells was hero and Beckett villain.

Notes

1.   *Lloyd's Sunday News*, 4 January 1920.
2.   *Ibid.*, 25 January 1920.
3.   Reeve was a military policeman at the Etaples base camp in September 1917 when bad feeling between the police and infantrymen in large numbers developed into this first mutiny of English speaking troops during the war. It started at a bridge over the railway where the men had to pass to get out of camp into the town. As scuffling broke out Reeve used a gun, killing a Corporal in the Gordon Highlanders and wounding a French woman. For the next two or three days the authorities lost control of the camp until reinforcements arrived see, D. Gill and G. Dallas, "Mutiny at Etaples Base in 1917", *Past and Present*, No. 69, November 1975, pp. 88-112, and the same authors' book, *The Unknown Army*, 1985, especially pp. 63-76, 152.
4.   *Boxing*, 17 March 1915.
5.   "We English had our great actresses: Ellen Terry, Ada Reeve, Irene Vanbrugh, Sybil Thorndike... all of whom I saw...", Charles Chaplin, *My Autobiography*, 1966, p. 257; Bell, *Bella op. cit.*, p. 163.
6.   *Thomson's Weekly News*, 4 September 1920.
7.   *Lloyd's Sunday News,* 18 April 1920.
8.   *Health and Efficiency*, February 1920, p. 32.
9.   *Boxing*, 4 February 1920.

10.   Reeve was still involved with boxing at the age of 55 years, see his application to the British Boxing Board of Control for a trainer's licence dated 9 February 1948. My thanks to John Morris and Simon Block, for allowing me to inspect the B.B.B.C.'s archives in the Spring of 1990.

11.   *Lloyd's Sunday News*, 21 March 1920; *Boxing*, 24 March 1920; Joe Palmer, *Recollections of a Boxing Referee*, 1927, pp. 182-3.   In this excellent book Palmer misremembered Wells's opponent whom he recalled as the Italian, Erminio Spalla, whom Wells never boxed.

12.   Eddie McGoorty, between 1912 and 1918, boxed six world champions, before or after they won the title.   In over 120 contests, McGoorty was beaten only 15 times, and seven of these losses came between 1919 and 1921.   See Fleischer, *Ring Record Book*, 1968, pp. 311-12, and for McGoorty in Britain, see *Boxing's Book of Records*, 1914, pp. 141-2; James Butler, *Kings of the Ring*, pp. 122-8.

13.   *Ibid.*, p. 124.

14.   *Boxing*, 14 April 1920.

15.   *Lloyd's Sunday News*, 21 March 1920; *Boxing*, 24 March 1920.

16.   *Lloyd's Sunday News*, 11 April 1920.

17.   Butler, *Kings op. cit.*, pp. 123, 126-8; Cochran, *Secrets*, pp. 302-3; Charles Graves, *The Cochran Story*, p. 79.

18.   Cochran, *Secrets*, pp. 305, 308-16. *Carpentier by Himself*, pp. 119-20 quotes an interesting account of the contest from the French newspaper *Auto*.

19.   For the finances of this first ever million dollar gate contest see, *Ring Record Book*, 1968, pp. 750-1, and the piquant commentary on them in *Carpentier by Himself*, p. 134.

20.   *Thomson's Weekly News*, 15 May 1920.

21.   *Boxing*, 19 May 1920; Bombardier Billy Wells, "Joe a trifle lucky to Win", *Lloyd's Sunday News*, 16 May 1920.

22. Cochran, *Secrets*, p. 336.
23. Bernard John Angle, *My Sporting Memories*, 1925, p. 79.

EMPRESS THEATRE, EARL'S COURT EXHIBITION.

BOMBARDIER BILLY WELLS

v.

JACK JOHNSON

For the CHAMPIONSHIP *OF THE* WORLD *and a Purse of* £8,000.

Under the Direction of JAMES WHITE.

Twenty Three-Minute Rounds. Monday, 2nd OCTOBER, 1911.

Preceded by Contest for CHAMPIONSHIP *OF* EUROPE—

GEORGES CARPENTIER (France) v. **SID BURNS** (England).

Seats may be Reserved at all the Principal Libraries, Hotels, Earl's Court, and Midland Grand Hotel
Telephone - 2000 North.

PRICES: 10s. 6d., 21s., 42s., 63s. & £5 5s.

BOMBARDIER WELLS will give Public Exhibitions of Training at Princes Hall,
Earl's Court, assisted by GEORGES CARPENTIER, the Idol of France, next
Thursday and Saturday at 4 p.m.

The match that never was.
Advertisement from *Boxing World*, 28 September 1911.

CHAPTER SEVENTEEN

THE GREAT FIGHT

Our efforts may bring us within sight of the goal, but fortune must favour us if we are to reach it.

Jean Jacques Rousseau, *Émile*, Everyman's Library, 1966, p. 6.

The remaining contests in the career of Billy Wells can be seen in two ways. A boxer has always to say that he feels better than ever, particularly a former champion. If Wells believed he was, we have Greek tragedy, a representative of the best slipping inexorably into degradation. If what Wells said was for public relations, as seems more likely, this notion is absurd. He was simply a canny man extending his period of very high earnings. The sport has a sad history of protagonists who carried on too long with health impaired, yet this was not the Bombardier's case for he remained well until he died at his home in Ealing in 1967. From all the evidence we have, Wells's motives during 1920-25, after his challenge at Olympia, were mixed, he was a spender and he could enjoy using money earned. It is difficult, however, to find an example of Wells exploiting either a promoter or the public. Perhaps he was overly optimistic, but until he reached the age of 35, Wells must have believed he could beat young lions like Bloomfield and soon regain titles. Wells was a thoughtful man and memories of glory are difficult to dislodge, until, one suspects, he found himself topping the bill at the Hoxton Baths.

Wells had for years enjoyed the adulation of a large proportion of the British public. Cheers had resounded in his ears in boxing stadiums since India. Through countless newspaper photographs his features were known to those who could not read, and the majority who could. The scarcely-fed and subscribers to *Country Life*[1] shared an awareness of big blond Billy who had been the People's Champion because he was admired throughout the population, in all social classes, and by women and men who had never ever directly glimpsed him. If one had seen the handsome Bombardier on the street or in his car, it would have been an uncontainable topic of conversation as you reached company. Wells was a "Star" who eclipsed his contemporaries in other fields, for no footballer or cricketer was remotely as popular; no playwright, actor or author half so well known; no music hall performer attracted such custom; no musician or singer received anything like his measure of public approbation, or, indeed, his newspaper column inches of criticism after a disappointing performance. Wells preceded film stars by a decade yet he faced the same attention from the public and the press without training or paid aides, except for the capable Jim Maloney. A comparison may usefully be made between Wells and Charles Chaplin, who was two years his junior. Both went to the United States, Chaplin as a member of a 15 strong Karno troupe, an almost unknown entertainer; Wells to fill Madison Square Garden. When Chaplin was living in cheap hotels,[2] Wells was matched with Jack Johnson. Chaplin was earning, spending and saving money by 1914 but he was not famous as was Wells.

The life style of Wells after his marriage is difficult to determine for he never mentioned it except in relation to his training for a contest. Bohun Lynch, the most literary boxing correspondent, was completely wrong when he wrote:

> About many boxers there is little to tell except the story of their fights. Some boxers have enjoyed adventurous and romantic careers quite apart from their battles. Of the latter group, Freddy Welsh is one, whilst Bombardier Wells belongs to the former.[3]

Welsh was simply a better self-publicist than Wells. Here is an extract from Welsh's lengthy communication to *Boxing*, from Canada, dated 25 August 1913:

> I have been seriously thinking of going up into the
> goldfields and staking a claim... Vancouvre (sic) is
> the best starting point for the new gold strike, and
> I have... the idea of making a dash in the stampede,
> stake a claim, and then get out of Alaska before the
> winter... freezes us in that dreary waste.[4]

Welsh realised, as Wells did not, the importance to a contender of keeping in the public's eye, and to this end he espoused vegetarianism and health farms, motor racing or fruit growing in California, in order to promote himself as a personality as well as a boxer. Wells endorsed products ("Guy's Tonic in large shilling bottles - Get One To-Day"[5]) but never sold himself as a character. Apart from his wedding in 1912, and the publicity for that was unique in British sporting press history, Wells retained his privacy in a most determined way. As a boxer, his labour power was up for sale to the highest bidder, in the ring, on the stage, on film, and later on the wrestling mat, but his private life never was. This confused the Oxford University man, who knew boxing as a sport, but less about popular culture. The general public judged Billy Wells not by the written word, and they found him a colourful sporting man from oral testimony, not his talk, of course, just in everyday conversations at work, in the home, on the corner, indeed in all the spots where working folk found a minute to chat. He was colourful to working-class people because he had been like them, brought up in a poor quarter, Board School, boys' club, messenger, soldier, boxer, his story was interchangeable with the history of most poor families, and he had gone on to do great things, "Good luck to him". Bohun Lynch, of "Prep" School, Public School, University and the middle classes, could be taken in by what the individual wrote or said of themselves, the working masses were much more knowledgeable, to them the career of Wells was precisely adventurous and romantic.

Wells did not take another contest after his second defeat by Beckett for four months until September 1920 when he travelled to France to stop Paul Journée again, this time at the exceedingly

fashionable seaside resort of Deauville.[6]   This would have been
Wells combining business with pleasure for he was easily able to
afford the best hotels from the proceeds of his seven post-war
professional matches.   Whether he took the family, which was
growing as fast as the popularity of seaside holidays, is not certain
for they were possibly happier on the beach at Brighton.   The
atmosphere was one of carnival, for it was a four-days boxing
tournament, and for company Wells had Dick Smith who boxed a
French heavyweight on the penultimate day of this Anglo-French
boxing jamboree.   One can imagine the two Londoners enjoying
something like the background in the film "Monsieur Hulot's
Holiday", trying out their foreign phrases, and basking in their
popularity, for Dick had given Carpentier a stiff contest in Paris in
the previous year.

Wells did not box a contest in 1921. He was signed up for
one, however, at the Royal Albert Hall for January 1921. He was
to meet Battling Levinsky from the U.S.A. In his career, between
1910 and 1929, Levinsky recorded nearly 300 contests, and he was
recognised as the World's light-heavyweight champion until knocked
out by Carpentier just before he signed to cross the Atlantic to box
Wells. Their contest was not to top the bill on this promotion, a
new experience for the Britisher, the big fight was between former
World's bantamweight champion, Pete Herman of New Orleans, and
Jimmy Wilde, whose flyweight title was not at stake because of the
weight difference. This was inspired match-making in both cases,
by whom we know not.   Cochran had dropped out of boxing
promotion in disgust at being let down by Beckett, McGoorty and
Herman,[7] and the syndicate which had booked the Albert Hall, may
have contained his first-lieutenant, Major Arnold Wilson who was
now in control of the Holborn Stadium.[8]   Whoever organised the
show, they secured the attendance of Royalty for what became
something of a flop. Levinsky turned up with his arm in a sling,
a last-minute injury in training made the match with Wells
impossible, and Wilde lost, heavily punished and considerably
disadvantaged in point of weight. The two most popular figures in
sport in this country had a disappointing night, and there was

The National Sporting Club. In the group, Dick Smith is the sergeant in the bottom row; Eugene Corri, right middle; Harry Reeve and Billy are the tallest in the back row.

booing and hissing and stamping and yelling from parts of the house which eventually became equable.[9] Wells retired from boxing for more than a twelvemonth.

After 1921 had seen Wells lost to boxing, his three contests in 1922 were interesting, and the May Saturday match, against Frank Goddard at Crystal Palace, was a sizzler where the din scarcely ceased and spectators surged round the ring.[10] The National Sporting Club staged Wells *versus* the Australian, Albert Lloyd, at Covent Garden towards the end of the Club's season, and *Boxing* recorded:

> It was a "Bombardier house", not only inside but outside. The "Club" seated and "stood" more "members and friends" than on any previous night of the season... And yet there was a larger crowd outside than inside. The outsiders waited for hours, patiently and happily, if in suspense. All they wanted... was that they should be the first to learn the result.[11]

The "horny-handed" outsiders were not disappointed for Wells won comfortably when Lloyd's towel was thrown into the ring almost half way through the twenty-rounds' contest. The much smaller man had risen after several knockdowns and had performed bravely, and Wells had made another come-back. This was not a great international match, Lloyd was the second-string to George Cook in a travelling Australian stable, and the N.S.C. had not been in the market for major promotions since the likes of Cochran, had raised the wages of boxers in the top flight. The last Covent Garden fight between international heavyweights had been between Wells and Carpentier in 1913. In 1920 the N.S.C. had refurbished and started larger boxing promotions at what had been the Holland Park Skating Rink whilst continuing Monday night shows at the Club, but this attempt to regain the lost status of the 1890s was a failure. Plebeian boxing fans had a high regard for familiar places like Premierland, the Ring and the Royal Albert Hall, and they were slow to transfer their patronage. In addition to this conservatism, the Holland Park speculation had hardly got underway when the post-war boom collapsed and audiences for most entertainments were drastically reduced, and the secular decline of the National Sporting Club continued. Wells had had six contests under their auspices and won a Lonsdale Belt outright. Each fight had ended by a knockout, with defeats for Iron Hague, Fred Storbeck, Packey Mahoney, Billy Wells, Dan Voyles, and Albert Lloyd. In his professional record both Olympia and Holborn Stadium gathered four bouts, but the Club was where Wells boxed most. He was therefore not averse to its "old boy" atmosphere as, for instance, Joe Beckett was.[12] Yet members of N.S.C. who wrote memoirs never shared social activities with Bombardier Billy Wells as they did, for example, with Jimmy Wilde.[13] This may have been because when they wrote their books they had fonder recollections of Wilde's fights at Covent Garden, and with hindsight the flyweight's achievements were more satisfactory, yet some professional boxers did mix socially with the middle-class set at N.S.C.[14] The most likely explanation is that Wells avoided social invitations which were offered because he was a boxer, and tried to keep a distance between his professional and his private life. Wells must have had middle-class friends for who else would he play golf with?[15] His life style was bourgeois though making friends with neighbours as wealthy as himself may not have been easy. Suburban villas were likely to be peopled by those who had been born into comfortably-off families where servants had always been employed. The tenement in Shadwell which Wells knew as a young man was simply not that sort of dwelling, and in India, other ranks were the lowliest form of human life, except, of course, for Indians. The British class system was not to be by-passed in the first formative years of Billy Wells's life. His closest and longest associate, Jim Maloney, was from the same background almost exactly, and training camp, over many years, housed sparring partners raised in slums. When Wells won riches he had to adapt as would any working-class man in his middle-twenties.

Sources of evidence on the life style of Bombardier Wells are difficult, if not impossible, to uncover. His home life would certainly have included one servant, possibly more. To draw parallels is dangerous, but Carpentier's wife took her maid when the Frenchman's party travelled to New York City in 1920.[16] Until he lost to Beckett, Wells was almost certainly ahead of Carpentier in annual earnings. Some fragments of evidence about how Wells spent his time can be gained from his *Lloyd's Sunday News* article of 9 May 1920, which was sub-headed "Fits of Staleness during Training, But All Warded Off...". Wells was doing his preparation at a famous boathouse at Putney. The Phelps' family was long associated with gentlemen's rowing clubs, the Phelps were professionals and "Bossie" was "the leader of all riverside characters".[17] Wells had trained here before, and this time employed four sparring partners whom he worked hard in the first week between rowing and sculling. At this stage of his career he bossed his own camp, a mistake for any boxer according to some who knew the sport.[18] Wells wrote:

> I was not quite satisfied with my week, and on the Saturday and Sunday I took the family by motor to Brighton and Margate. My object was to have a rest and at the same time keep in the open air. I found ... a touch of staleness coming on. Hence the joy ride.

Wells sparred 12 rounds, skipped and did floor exercises on the following day, and:

> I was feeling fine, so after a row on the Tuesday I toddled off to the races. These little outings serve to relieve the monotony of training, and I enjoyed every minute of the day, particularly as the winner of the Two Thousand [Tetratema] carried my money.

The account was written to amuse readers on their day off, yet they could be forgiven for concluding that it was Bertie Wooster[19] in training not Bombardier Wells.

Billy was not in love with training. The rigours of road work and sparring, the basic ingredients for three weeks' preparation, could be too easily sidelined in favour of "a light scull to Hammersmith" or motoring to Newmarket.[20] And his family life presented enormous problems; where could he and his wife and children take a stroll at the seaside without being recognised? Though it was early in the season, a meander along the front must have been difficult to achieve, and no British boxer had ever faced this domestic problem.

The Crystal Palace had attracted large crowds to F.A. Cup Finals from 1895 until 1914,[21] and spectators were readily prepared to travel to the South East suburbs of London for football, but the site was generally unsuccessful for boxing.[22] The "International Boxing Syndicate" therefore advertised "Frequent trains and buses from all parts"; backed the Wells-Goddard match with a middleweight championship eliminator; and sold tickets from all the "usual Agents" at prices ranging from 5s 9d to £5 16s (29p to £5.80p).[23] They seem to have drawn a large crowd or, at least, the name Bombardier Billy Wells did. The referee, Joe Palmer, devoted 12 pages of his *Recollections*,[24] published in 1927, to this fight, and the chapter was headed "A Needle Fight - Piccalilli - The One and Only Billy - No Poseur...", and this was more space than the cousin of Pedlar Palmer gave to any of the other twenty contests he described in his excellent book. According to Palmer, the fans who made the journey to Sydenham had a wonderful night of sheer excitement:

> Goddard boxed better than he had ever done in his life, perhaps, because Wells had a habit of drawing the best out of a man. The Bombardier himself boxed as skilfully as of old. His left would flash out piston-like, and connect with Goddard's face, and

> often beat a tattoo thereupon, but there was not the
> sting nor electric swiftness behind it I had seen on
> former occasions...

Goddard, it ought to be remembered, was the man so powerful that
at the close of the war it was held that Wells was reluctant to face
him. Referee Palmer continued:

> At the beginning of the second round I thought it
> was all over. There was a flash of white as Billy's
> left did a feint, and the next instant there was a
> dull thud. Wells's right had crashed home to
> Goddard's jaw with precision... Goddard staggered
> and shook his head, the audience watching
> meanwhile, with bated breath... The blow stung
> him into frenzy, and he lashed into Wells with two
> hands whilst he bodily forced him against the
> ropes...

In the third round Goddard bulled his way back into the fight, and
Wells was dropped for a count of nine. The big boy was not over
enamoured with the rules, and he appeared to be poking his
thumbs towards Wells's eyes whilst they worked inside. Wells
complained "Look what he is doing, Mr Palmer"[25] but the referee
thought it was unintentional. In the fourth:

> Wells electrified the crowd... Instead of staggering
> from the first blow, as we all expected he would do,
> he took no notice of Goddard's rush... he did not
> attempt to move around, but waited for his foe and
> swung hard at him with both hands. The crowd
> rose and cheered frantically this amazing revival of
> its hero. Goddard was dumbfounded, and hurt in
> body as well as mind as Billy made him reel from
> two beautiful punches to the jaw..... Wells collected
> every point in that round.

Billy had been on the edge of being knocked out, and bruiser-like, he had grabbed back the initiative, it was a turn of events which happens frequently in boxing, hence the sport's fascination. In no other physical play space are tables turned so rapidly, Palmer wrote:

> Where he got his reserve of strength from, after the punishment he had received in the previous round, to knock that modern Goliath round the ring beat me and, I think, every one present.

Goddard pounded Wells throughout the fifth round and knocked him down and out towards the close. The timekeeper was about to ring the bell before ten seconds expired when someone threw cold water over the prostrate figure, and when the bell rang Wells was dragged to his corner by his seconds. The Goddard team exclaimed foul, but Palmer had not seen the culprit who had tried to revive Wells:

> When Wells went down crowds surged round the ring, and it was impossible to see who was who in the respective corners. The sentiment for Wells was so great that I believe some of his admirers would have forgotten all about sportsmanship and have lifted their idol up if they had dared... I still thought the towel would come fluttering in... but that was not Wells's idea of things... he insisted on coming up for the sixth round, although he knew he was finished...

The referee's carefully worded account of this contest written some five years later contrasts with the lurid report in *Boxing* which appeared immediately. The trade paper had never previously been quite so flamboyant, and here, as a sample, is its description of the final round:

> ... it was obvious that when he came out... for the sixth that the end was very near. Reeling, arm-

weary, with ashy white, blood-smeared face and twitching lips, Billy Wells strode out to meet his doom. It was his finish, and he knew it, but the indomitable soul of him wouldn't let him quit while strength remained to see or stand. With the scent of victory in his nostrils, Goddard flew at his man like a wild cat.

and modern boxing reportage braced itself to out-Pierce Egan:

Billy lurched towards his man and landed a weak right to the body. Goddard grinned a vicious grin and whipped a left to the chin. Wells threw up both arms and toppled over backwards, his head striking the canvas with a thud, while his legs flew high in the air. Flesh and blood couldn't come back from a punch like that... Wells was carted to his corner as inert as a sack of coals...[26]

Referee Palmer put things more succinctly:

There is no need to labour the sixth and last round of this battle. It did not go its full course. As soon as Goddard touched Wells the latter's legs sagged beneath him. Only his spirit kept him in an upright position until Goddard finally put him out for the full count.

Goddard was given a moderate cheer as Palmer indicated the winner. When, a few moments later, Wells rose from his stool the crowd went wild. *Boxing* recorded that "No winner in the history of the ring has received a greater ovation", and Palmer accepted a bouquet of red carnations for Billy from a lady with tears streaming down her face. Boxing can be dramatic every-so-often, and this evening at Crystal Palace was one such occasion.

At the Royal Albert Hall in October the British heavyweight champion, Joe Beckett, stopped Frank Moran in an extremely bloody battle. The American took one more contest in Paris and then left the ring for film acting in Hollywood. He was admired for his ability to take punishment with a smile and this distinguished him chiefly from his old opponent of 1915 who was in the chief supporting contest. Wells met the new British light-heavyweight champion Jack Bloomfield. Bloomfield was a young Jewish Londoner whose boxing skills had been honed during service with the Royal Air Force. Wells and the twenty-two year old were well matched for artistry in this 15 rounds' contest, but in the sixth Bloomfield got through to the body and then with a short right to the jaw knocked Wells out.

Notes

1. *Country Life*, 23 February 1918.
2. Charles Chaplin, *My Autobiography*, 1966, pp. 134-7.
3. J.G. Bohun Lynch, *Prominent Pugilists of Today*, 1914, p. 7.
4. *Boxing*, 20 September 1913.
5. For example see *Health and Strength*, 16 May 1914.
6. *Thomson's Weekly News*, 4 September 1920; *Boxing*, 15 March 1922.
7. Cochran, *Showman Looks on*, 1945, pp. 269-71, see also his *Secrets of a Showman*, 1925, pp. 332-7. The Showman returned to boxing promotion in 1927.
8. Fred Dartnell, *"Seconds Out"*, n.d. (1924), p. 98.
9. *Daily Herald*, 5, 14 January 1921. For the Royal presence see especially Harry Preston, *Memories*, 1928, pp. 141-6, where the Albert Hall was apparently crammed with monarchists.
10. Joe Palmer, *Recollections of a Boxing Referee*, 1927, pp. 125-32.
11. *Boxing*, 26 April 1922.

12. Beckett never had a contest at the N.S.C. after he became British champion, and see Deghy, *Noble and Manly*, p. 194.

13. B. Bennison, *Giants on Parade*, 1936, p. 43; Trevor Wignall *I knew them All*, 1938, p. 304; Preston, *Leaves...*, pp. 256-7.

14. Some examples of these socially confident boxers are Jem Goode (Angle, *My Sporting Memories*, pp. 27-31), Jim Carney (W. MacQueen-Pope, *Ghosts and Greasepaint*, 1951, pp. 84-90), Tom Berry (Preston, *Leaves...*, pp. 260-1), and, of course, Carpentier.

15. "... early players were usually the younger retired, successful professional men and businessmen with a commercial base sufficiently firm to be left to underlings." John Lowerson, "Golf", Mason, *Sport in Britain, op. cit.*, p. 190.

16. *Carpentier by Himself*, 1955, p. 123.

17. Hylton Cleaver, *Sporting Rhapsody*, 1951, p. 44.

18. Palmer, *Recollections*, p. 125.

19. "The Jeeves and Wooster cycle began in 1919, both Jeeves and Wooster having made brief appearances earlier.", George Orwell, "In Defence of P.G. Wodehouse", *Collected Essays,* 1961, p. 253.

20. *Lloyd's Sunday News*, 9 May 1920.

21. Tony Mason, *Association Football and English Society*, 1981, p. 168; Thomas K. Hodder, *Popular Sports*, n.d. (1935), p. 203.

22. "The fact of the matter is that, except for the Cup Final, sporting fixtures at the Crystal Palace always have been failures", *Boxing*, 24 May 1922.

23. *Ibid.*

24. Palmer, *Recollections, op. cit.*, pp. 121-32.

25. *Ibid.*, p.128.

26. *Boxing*, 31 May 1922.

CHAPTER EIGHTEEN

TIME

You haven't the slightest idea what a great boxing match looks like, now that it takes place in a special sort of light in order that it may be photographed for the picture theatres. The ring under its roof of lamps looks partly like a billiard table. It looks still more like the stage just before the ghost in Hamlet appears.

Robert Lynd, *The Sporting Life and other trifles*, 1922, p. 42.

Billy Wells retired from boxing after the defeat by Jack Bloomfield. A year later, however, he was seen by "Sporting Notions" of the *Referee* doing some training in the gymnasium of the National Sporting Club. The weekly paper was in its 38th year of publication and whoever wrote under the redoubtable pen-name was good enough to draw a gentle cartoon of "Bombardier B. Wells" standing in his dressing gown, hand in pocket, hair immaculate:

> Not a few will be interested to learn that the ever-popular Bombardier Wells is getting himself fit in order to try his luck once more in the ring...

He had been sparring with, and giving advice to, a future British heavyweight champion Phil Scott. "Notions" continued:

> he cannot hope to excel in the evening of his boxing life, where he failed in the noontide of his glory, but... his is still a name that counts in a wide circle of boxing-lovers.[1]

Wells returned to his old livelihood with a match against Charlie Penwill. The contest was top of the bill at a Monday matinee. Jack Callaghan had been promoting boxing matinees on this day of the week since at least 1910,[2] and it demonstrates the tenacity with which some working-class men failed to go to work if they had money left in their pockets after the weekend.   Penwill, formerly Guardsman Penwill, had won the Imperial Services' championships in 1921 and 1922, and turning professional had kept busy in the boxing boom.   He had been a sparring partner to Wells and Carpentier, who both thought highly of him;   had lost a contest or two, but in February 1922 he had upset the applecart by beating Frank Goddard at Premierland.[3]   By the end of 1924 big profits had deserted boxing promotion and most other entertainments.   This particular sport, which achieved high peaks of profit-taking for single occasions, was probably affected by economic depression more than its chief sporting competitor football.   Regular boxing and football supporters continued to go to their weekly shows, some way from   ringside   and   standing   on   the   terraces,   yet   Cup   and International football matches were probably more attractive to hard-up sportsmen than Albert Hall-type boxing shows in the penurious 1920s.[4]   This was the decade when football conquered London   as   the   inner-city   sport   with   lads   deserting   sweaty gymnasium for places like Hackney Marshes, and emulating Dixie Dean rather than a boxing hero.[5]

At the same time that pocket money was short, the standard of professional boxing was low.   Wells was now aged 37 years, and other able professionals who had boxed pre-war, such as Jimmy Wilde and Joe Beckett, had retired.   A hundred thousand or so potential boxers may have been killed or seriously wounded in the four years of ultimate national rivalry, and mostly, one supposes, they were English speaking.   The effect of war on boxing, however, was not entirely destructive for suburban and country youth would have been introduced to the sport during their time in the forces.   The lacuna of world title contenders from outside the United States is obvious from record books, and contemporaries thought that British professional boxing had never been of such poor quality.[6]   If this was so it shows a perverse relationship between boxing and market forces for the high purses of 1919-22 should have drawn participants, including some with talent, into the sport. Instead, boys collectively devoted more time to football which offered comparatively puny financial rewards.[7]

Wells knocked out his former sparring partner in round two and Hoxton Baths was filled to capacity to witness another Wells' comeback.[8] The Hoxton Baths had been opened by Shoreditch Borough Council in 1899, it had two pools, and the larger (100 x 40 feet) was boarded over each winter to facilitate additional use. The economics of this show can be determined with some accuracy without using the promoter's figures. It cost around £15 to hire the hall which was used often for amateur and professional boxing. Admission prices in 1925 ranged from 1/6d in the balcony (7½p) to 5/- ringside (25p) and numbers admitted were restricted to about 900. The capacity of the Baths was colloquially described by a boxing promoter as £80, though Hackney Schools Swimming Association could take almost this sum at their annual swimming gala when winter seating was not available.[9] Since we know that Wells was a huge attraction, we can safely assume that a thousand spectators got in with most of them paying. With a simple calculation Callaghan must have taken £155 in ticket sales. Rent would have been his largest outlay, and Palmer would hardly have refereed for less than a fiver.[10] Winners and losers of five supporting contests would have cost Callaghan about £12-50, and incidentals, like new gloves for the premier bout, would have required the spending of another £7-50, thus before Callaghan paid Wells and Penwill he would have been about £115 in pocket. This was a great deal of money to make in one afternoon in this part of London, but whatever Wells was paid out of it he must have felt that the rewards for boxing had become pathetic. He was just another boxer. In terms of purse size Wells had travelled back to where he had been in the summer of 1910.

Two weeks later Wells arrived in Liverpool for a contest at the Olympia Theatre. This was a hastily arranged match because the contest which had been top of the bill had fallen through.[11] The *Liverpool Sporting Echo* sent a reporter to greet Wells, who was accompanied by his wife, and Billy was keen to play golf at

Hoylake. He was fit, and had been sparring in London with Harry Mallin the Metropolitan policeman who had just won his second Olympic gold medal.[12] Underlying the *Echo*'s enthusiasm for this substitute match there lurks a doubt for this reader that the Merseyside sporting public would turn out for Bombardier Billy Wells. He had been a spectacular national favourite, but at this late stage his dwindling supporters would have been nourished by memories of exciting evenings at King's Hall, Olympia, and the Canterbury Music Hall. They were more likely to be Londoners than Liverpudlians for Wells was very much a Metropolitan man, not an East Ender (as a boxer he had never been that). Wells epitomized the urbane Londoner, sleekly groomed, comfortably-off, holding moderate views, successful in business, an achiever yet a very private man. There was no mention of Jim Maloney, who was presumably no longer receiving a percentage of the purse.

Wells's opponent was Gunner Bennett, of Redbourne, who had won a heavyweight competition held at Crystal Palace in tearaway fashion. He had also beaten Charlie Penwill, and though only a twelve stones' man, Bennett showed promise. Tickets, however, could not have been selling because Friday's *Echo* carried the following:

> The prospects of Carpentier appearing at Olympia, Liverpool, on Monday night as referee in the heavyweight contest... has added interest to the proceedings, and the programme promises to attract an audience which will tax the accommodation of the building. The appearance of Carpentier is practically certain...[13]

The newsworthy former European champion may have received a telegram, but he did not appear, and the astute promoter seems to have filled the theatre. The boxers weighed-in at 2 p.m. and the public were invited to attend "this interesting preliminary". Wells, who "towered over his opponent", was on top throughout the contest; Bennett was nearly counted out in the early stages, and

Cards presented with boys' magazines. *The Champion* issued Wells (15 April) and Beckett (22 April) in 1922. *Boys Friend* issued Penwill (17 May), Soldier Jones (1 July), Dick Smith (22 July) and Goddard (5 August) in the same year.

his seconds threw in the towel half-way through the twenty rounds. Wells was "cheered wildly" upon his entrance, though "Stork" of the *Echo* was critical of his performance.[14]

Soldier Horace Jones, a tough and crude boxer from Canada, who had been campaigning in Britain for about three years, was Wells's penultimate opponent. The press made him out to be Neanderthal man incarnate,[15] yet Joe Palmer found him to be a "humorous, happy-go-lucky fellow". He had lost to Gene Tunney on the record-breaking Dempsey-Carpentier programme, and since coming to England had done well. He had been disqualified against Albert Lloyd, but it was a moral victory, for the Australian was beaten and down when Jones punched him for the last time.[16] The Dome, Brighton, had been booked by promoter Callaghan who lived locally, for Friday evening, and tickets were on sale at the Royal York Hotel and the County Club, which suggests that they may have been priced rather highly. The Wells-Jones match was to be over 15 rounds, and there was a strong supporting bill including Brighton boxers. The *Daily Herald*, previewing the fight, fancied Wells to win, and "Pollux" concluded:

> ... Wells has always given value in the matter of thrills... I shall always maintain that his contests with Joe Beckett and Frank Goddard were the most thrilling of heavy-weight fights in this country, and whether he wins or loses this evening, the Bombardier is certain to have his friends either shouting for joy or full of trepidation.

and in a long column about the contest, Jones was scarcely mentioned. Jones was disqualified in the sixth round for throwing Wells down in a pulling and hauling mill, and the *Brighton and Hove Herald* reported "It must at once be said that Wells was no match for the Canadian".[18] The fight was untidy with Wells laying-on his shorter opponent and going down twice in the first round and twice again in the fourth. Jones was knocked down in the second round, and once they were simultaneously on the canvas.

Sporting Life thought it a thrilling contest with Jones "unlucky so to lose".[19]

The old champion's last serious boxing contest was an anticlimax. It was one of four supporting bouts to a match made at just over the flyweight limit between Elky Clark and Young Johnny Brown, which the former won. Glasgow beat London in this gloriously competitive event staged by Harry Jacobs, of Premierland and Wonderland promotions, at the Royal Albert Hall. Wells was matched with Jack Stanley, of Deptford, a former policeman, over 15 rounds, who knocked him out in round three. *Boxing* lamented:

> No one... could have expected or desired to see that old favourite Bombardier Billy Wells, collapse in such inglorious fashion...[20]

and the *Sporting Life* seems to have deplored the lack of blood.[21] Stanley boxed throughout the 1920s without achieving distinction except through being the first opponent of the gigantic Primo Carnera when the latter arrived in London in 1929. Stanley lost easily. The Italian who became world's heavyweight champion, by coincidence, was introduced to the sport by Wells's old adversary, Paul Journée.[22] Ironically, the outstandingly gifted Wells never climbed in the ring to do serious business with a past, present or future heavyweight champion of the world.

Notes

1. *Referee*, 21 September 1924. The cartoon is inscribed "J.P.".
2. *Boxing World*, 20 October 1910.
3. Prudential Assurance Company, *Sports Records*, n.d. (1929?), p. 43; *Boxing*, 15 February, 15 March 1922.
4. In 1921-22 the Football League expanded from two to four divisions, and the storming of Wembley in 1923 to see Bolton Wanderers beat West Ham United in

the F.A. Cup Final is good evidence of rising public interest.

5. Hackney Marshes contained enormous space devoted to amateur football. *East End News*, 31 December 1937, reporting the provision by the L.C.C. of new changing rooms, recorded the number of football pitches as 140, and 3,000 players taking part each Saturday.

6. "It is a melancholy confession to have to make, but the standard of boxing in this country to-day is at about the lowest ebb it has ever reached" *Boxing*, 19 April 1922. In fact it dropped lower in 1923 when Jimmy Wilde lost his world flyweight title to Pancho Villa in New York.

7. Professional footballers playing for Football League clubs were paid a maximum wage of £8 a week in the winter and £6 in the summer as late as 1939. Top players could augment this with appearances in representative matches and by endorsing advertising, yet this was small financial reward for a whole year compared with what a boxer could earn for one contest.

8. *Liverpool Sporting Echo*, 25 November 1924; *Referee*, 30 November 1924.

9. Shoreditch Borough Council, *Official Guide 1921*, p. 110; *Hackney Gazette*, 23 September 1921, 10 March 1926; *Sporting Life*, 31 January 1925; British Boxing Board of Control, Applications for Promoter's Licence, Leslie Rich, 9 November 1933; Hackney Schools Swimming Association, Report of Finance Sub-committee meeting on 14 December [1936], Hackney Archives D/S20/4. For boxing matinees at Hoxton Baths see for example, *Boxing World and Mirror of Life*, 20 March 1920; *Club Life*, 20 November, 4 December 1920.

10. Joe Palmer, *Recollections of a Boxing Referee*, 1927, p. 211. Palmer never mentions how much he was paid.

11. *Liverpool Sporting Echo*, 4 December 1924. The chief bout was to have been Kid Lewis *versus* Billy Mack, a local boxer, but Lewis had not recovered from his contest with Tommy Milligan in Edinburgh where he had lost his welterweight titles on points over 20 rounds. Mack did feature on the re-arranged programme. He boxed a 15 rounds' draw with Johnny Sullivan, of Covent Garden, in a "contest long remembered in and around Liverpool".

12. *Liverpool Sporting Echo*, 9 December 1924.

13. *Ibid.*, 12 December 1924.

14. *Ibid.*, 13, 16 December 1924.

15. B. Bennison, *Giants on Parade*, 1936, p. 66.

16. Palmer, *Recollections*, pp. 104-7. Soldier Jones, incidentally, had lasted seven rounds against the future world heavyweight champion at Jersey City.

17. *Daily Herald*, 30 January 1925.

18. *Brighton and Hove Herald*, 31 January 1925.

19. *Sporting Life*, 31 January 1925.

20. *Boxing*, 6 May 1925.

21. "Wells did not win; he was scarcely expected to win, but he was expected to produce several thrills. In this he was a distinct disappointment, he went out as tamely as could be imagined..." *Sporting Life*, 1 May 1925.

22. Bennison, *Giants, op. cit.*, pp. 63-5.

CONCLUSION

*I have known the time when a pugilistic encounter between
two noted champions was almost considered in the light of
a national affair; when tens of thousands of individuals,
high and low, meditated and brooded upon it, the first thing
in the morning and the last at night, until the great event
was decided.*

George Borrow, *Lavengro*, 3 vols, 1851, Vol. 1, p. 327.

Bombardier Billy Wells was not the first boxer to catch the
public imagination;   Tom Sayers had done it before, and two
examples, Henry Cooper and Frank Bruno were to do it again. The
secrets of such men's hold on the collective mind is hard to explain.
The sport, of course, claims most explanatory power.   They
ventured where others feared to go, and most people could form a
mental image of how it felt to stand in their boots. The lack of
encumbrances in boxing, like team-mates, horses, sticks or balls,
simplified the mind's eye;   the boxer stood upright and unprotected,
he was alone, the thing all dread most.

These heroes, however, transcended the sport momentarily,
in 1860, 1911, 1963 and 1989 respectively when they were matched
with foreigners.   Their opponents, John Heenan, Jack Johnson,
Muhammad Ali and Frank Tyson were necessarily American
because it was that nation which needed to be taken down a peg or
two.   Race was absent in this context as I hope to have shown in
chapter six.   Thus national pride or international jealousy, not
always the same thing, went into the creation of boxing celebrity.

Wells boxed professionally, as we have seen, from 1910 to
1916, in 1919 and 1920, in 1922, and then came out of retirement
for another six months. His reputation was gained in a period of
sustained economic growth and legendary names in this sport seem
to grow out of boom times followed by decline on all fronts. The

intensely popular boxer it seems, has to be soon followed by mediocrity and the collective memory can say "those were the days".

Boxing legends, paradoxically, do not have to be great boxers. Jim Driscoll, a near contemporary of Wells, was "Peerless", literally by all accounts, but the heavyweight was the public's favourite. As a boxer, the flyweight Jimmy Wilde's record was better than that of Wells, yet the scenes outside the Canterbury Music Hall happened with the Bombardier topping the bill, and delirium crept into many halls where Wells was boxing. This double feature has always been the main attraction of the sport; anticipation with the match; and the contest, at some point, setting the audience figuratively on fire. As an example of the latter we can take any number of Wells's performances. For instance, against Sunshine at the King's Hall; who having seen that match could overlook the fact. Attenders at boxing store memories of moments, often one only, and their general impression of a contest fades, though it can usually be talked about, especially if another witness can be found. Supporting bouts can unexpectedly provide these moments without the flavour of anticipation. Wells was an arch-provider of both.

A name in boxing is often created by one's opponent. Tommy Farr would probably be forgotten but for Joe Louis and their close contest in 1937 which is remembered by so many. Wells made Carpentier into a major boxing figure. Packey Mahoney was revered in Cork for his heroic 13 rounds for many a long year. To get into the ring with the champion was grand, to fight him with a fractured jaw was legendary.

Memorable contests require incident and two styles which do not clash. Wells was never outboxed, often outfoxed. The match which was proscribed may well have been a dull one for Johnson was the superior boxer. Wells shone against slow moving opponents (Hague, Rodel, Clohessy) and looked well when smaller men tried to match him for skill (O'Keefe, Reeve, Dick Smith): he looked poor against big men with a clever defence (Moran) and those able to take his best punch (Palzer). For six years, no British challenger could beat Wells, and Beckett then Goddard won when he was past his prime. Exciting contests happened almost everywhere Wells went; Poona, Simla, Elephant and Castle, Hammersmith, Covent Garden, New York City, Ghent, Holborn and Crystal Palace "went wild" on at least one occasion when the Bombardier travelled to those places. The frequency of high drama in Wells's fights was enhanced by his fragility in the ring. Moir and Palzer both raised questions of his physical development being robust enough against outstandingly powerful men; Gunboat Smith and Carpentier gave the impression that his long left was simply not strong enough to keep them out, and Moran underlined both questions yet the British public still loved to see, read and talk about Billy. His right-hand punch following one or two left leads won contests spectacularly, as in the third match with Rice, and spectators were aware that Wells might win as rapidly as Pommern had run the St Leger at Newmarket, and they were equally pleased. A contest which involved Wells could turn when you averted your eyes from the ring. Boxing delights in surprises, and from that second Wednesday in 1911, it could always happen. The crowd wanted Billy to win, but there always lurked a doubt.

The age of Bombardier Billy Wells was when men appeared to be the phenomenon of sport. In the years between the end of a war which shocked, in South Africa, and the suspension of European civilisation in 1914, general attention to athletic games achieved a new plane. Communications and literacy were the twin engines of this, and it was fuelled by family economic self-sufficiency. Leisure was plannable in more comfortable homes, and young people went out with somewhere to go. Spare time and more money allowed pleasure-consciousness to peck at the work-ethic, especially in middle-class environs. Popular hedonism was mainly masculine until the rise of the dance hall in the 1930s, but that is another chapter of social history.

Other sports had heroes, such as Danny Maher the jockey, or the young batsman from Surrey, Jack Hobbs. Football was slightly different in that teams involved a more shared responsibility for public worship, more locally, and in our period Newcastle United and Celtic are prime examples of that. The four great spectator sports varied again in their sparking of national pride. Race horse owners from any country would be cheered, as was Jack Joel, the most successful, whose three-year olds' won nine of the classic races between 1907 and 1914. At cricket, honour was only seriously at stake against the Australians' touring because scores from "down under" were published abruptly and late. Spectators at the Oval in 1909 had reason to be depressed. Inexplicably, M.C.C. had used 25 players in the series and at Kennington lacked a fast bowler. They lost the series after winning easily at Edgbaston, and the consolation might only have been watching Victor Trumper driving and cutting. Football international matches with foreign teams, such as Germany, Austria, and South Africa, had happened infrequently, however, keen rivalry was reserved for the annual England *versus* Scotland match. Crowds of around 50,000 paid a shilling or more to see these hard fought, usually low scoring, games, which roused the excitement of an F.A. cup tie or local derby on a wider scale.

The followers of sport, meaning those who talked and read about it without often or ever paying to watch, differed considerably. Betting subsumed horse racing, and its large fields and high odds kept the street bookmaker busy. The odds at cricket may have been offered occasionally; and football pools were in their infancy. Bookmakers made a great deal of noise in every boxing stadium and betting was endemic, but outside the stadium the short odds were not attractive. Thus those who enthused about Steve Donoghue often had a vested interest in so doing. His popularity was entirely justified (successive Derby winners 1921-3) yet Wells *versus* Goddard made superior conversation. Reports in print of a fight *read* better: football matches had too many characters as did cricket, and in the sport of Kings the result, the price, and next day's tips were more important than descriptive columns.

Boxing looks set to expire in the next century, and excites one today as a slightly shameful interest. Its hey-day can already be seen to have been from Johnson to Joe Louis, considered that is as a spectacle of vast concern to the general public. In these terms spectator sports have all decayed, and approximately in the same period. The F.A. Cup Final is one of many so-called cup finals, and less memorable for that. Cricket competitions mimic bingo, and who can say it is cricket they play? As traditional sports go grey, the commonalty loses something. A shared enthusiasm, a mutual interest, a talking point, our man was these for a decade, and by this criterion Wells was an enormous success. The results of his fights cannot explain his long term popularity. What can be said is that before the first world war professional boxing was ready to wax fat, and Wells, a heavyweight of impeccable background and demeanour, and Olympian in appearance, grasped the opportunity. Only in his sport's own terms did the "Bombardier" fail.

SELECT BIBLIOGRAPHY

Place of publication is London except where otherwise stated.

BOOKS BY WELLS

How a Boxer should Train, 8 pp., Athletic Appliances Co., is listed
    in the catalogue at the British Library as "destroyed",
    presumably by bombing during the blitz. I have not seen
    a copy.
Modern Boxing: a Practical guide to present-day Methods, n.d.
    Ewart, Seymour & Co. Ltd., was first published in 1911,
    with card covers and 93 pages, including 31 photographs.

The price was one shilling. A note appended to the seventh
edition (78pp., n.d., probably 1923) reads: "Bombardier Wells
wrote this book shortly after his victory over Iron Hague...
He was then at his best and it may be said that the
subsequent variegations of his career have been largely due
to his departures from the precepts set forth herein."

*Physical Energy: showing how physical and mental energy may be
developed by means of the practice of Boxing*, Werner Laurie,
n.d. (1923?), has 153 pages and eight photographs, with a
yellow cloth cover, and was surprisingly expensive at six
shillings.

SERIAL ARTICLES BY WELLS IN WEEKLY MAGAZINES

Answers, 23 May 1914 - 27 June 1914. At this period *Answers*
carried drawings but no photographs. It was 16 pages in
orange-coloured covers, priced one penny.
Lloyd's Sunday News, 18 April 1920 - 16 May 1920. This series,
with many good photographs of Wells in training, was over-
shadowed by the next entry.
Thomson's Weekly News, 17 April 1920 - 11 September 1920
(excepting issue 26 June). "My Life and my Fights" in 21
numbers, ran to some 50,000 words. The early numbers are
profusely illustrated, and the paper claimed a circulation of
623,984 copies weekly.

SINGLE ARTICLES BY WELLS IN CHRONOLOGICAL ORDER

"Why I am fighting Jack Johnson", *Boxing*, 5 August 1911, pp. 329-
31.
"A Prophet is not without Honour", *Boxing New Year's Annual
1913*, pp. 12-13.
"The Boom in Boxing", *Pearson's Magazine*, December 1913, pp.
702-7.
"Why I am not OUT there", *Answers*, 23 January 1915.

"Boxing for War Funds", *Answers*, 13 March 1915.
"Why Tommy Burns failed", *Lloyd's Sunday News*, 18 July 1920.

WEEKLY PAPERS AND MAGAZINES, WITH THE YEARS CONSULTED

All Sports Illustrated Weekly (1919-20)
Boxing (1909-25)
Boxing World and Athletic Chronicle (1909-12)
Health and Strength (1909-14)
John Bull (1915)
Mirror of Life and Sport (1909-12 and 1922)
The Referee (1911-12 and 1924-25)

ARCHIVAL MATERIAL

National Army Museum
Royal Hospital Road, Chelsea, London SW3 4HT.

Accession number 7404-13 (folio). Sport/boxing 1913-15, Corporal Sidney Rogers, 1st Leinster Regiment, annotated programmes of his boxing in India, where he reached the second flights of the "All India" lightweights in 1914.

8307-27 (manuscript). Letters of A.J. Awdry, 2nd Lieut., Royal Artillery, written to his father from 1899 until his death in 1909.

Royal Munster Fusiliers, *Regimental Annual 1911*, (ed. Captain C.A. Knapp), Tralee, 1911, and two further volumes of 1912 and 1913.

Tower Hamlets Local History Library,
277 Bancroft Road, London E1 4DQ.

TH/8192/1   (bound volume).   Broad Street Clubs: Record Book,
1887-1904.
TH/8192/5   (photographs).   1896-1967.
TH/8192/16   (Manuscript).   "History of Highway Clubs in East
London" by Mr F.C. Wright, 113 pp. with many photographs.

Fred Wright, "F.C. Mills and the Broad Street Boys Club", *East London Record*, No. 13, 1990, pp. 18-22.

INSTRUCTIONAL BOOKS COSTING ONE SHILLING (5p.)
PUBLISHED BETWEEN 1895 AND 1908

R.G. Allanson-Winn, *Boxing*, George Bell, 1895, 91 pp., with posed
photographs and line drawings, cloth covered, first edition
1889. This was in the "All-England Series", and the first
boxing book published in London to use photographs.

J.C. Trotter, *Boxing*, Routledge, 1896, 128 pp., with photographs,
drawings, and a limp cloth cover. This was in the "Oval
Series" and a first edition.

A.J. Newton, *Boxing: with a section on single-stick*, Pearson, 1904,
124 pp., with drawings only and a cloth cover. In the series
"Pearson's Popular 1/- Handbooks", a first edition, by the
A.B.A. lightweight champion of 1888 and 1890.

Young Corbett (W.H. Rothwell), *How to Punch the Bag*, British
Sports Publishing Company, 1906, 80 pp., with photographs,
and a paper cover.   In the series "Spalding's Athletic
Library", it was also published in New York by the American
Sports Publishing Co. in the same year.   Corbett, from
Denver, Colorado, was World Featherweight Champion 1901-
4.

"Gunner" James Moir, *The Complete Boxer*, Health and Strength
Ltd., 1907, 107 pp., with one photograph and numerous
drawings, a first edition. Copy in the British Library
"destroyed", but they have it on microfilm.

Wells would have read these along with the following, which cost
five shillings.

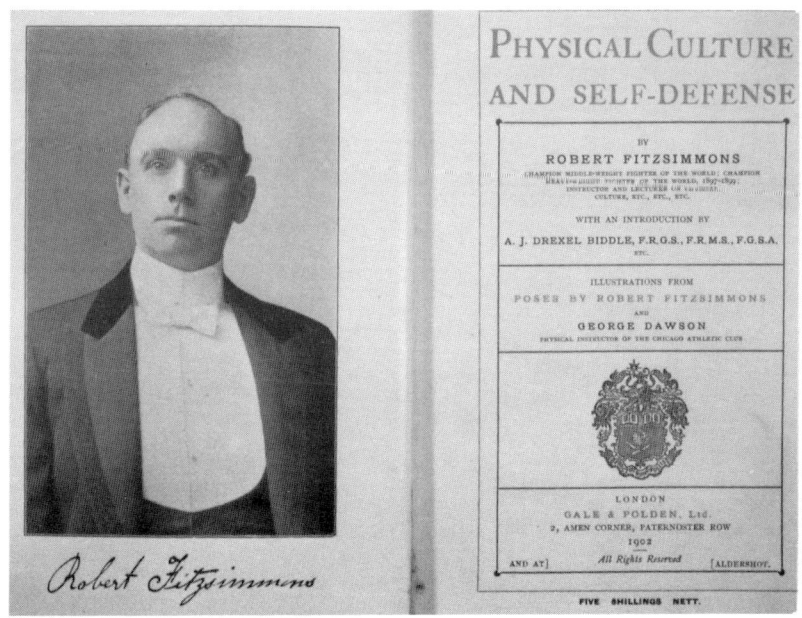

AUTOBIOGRAPHY

Carpentier by Himself, translated by Edward Fitzgerald, 1955.
Charles B. Cochran, *The Secrets of a Showman*, 1925.
Eugene Corri, *Refereeing 1,000 Fights*, 1919.
Jack Hare, *Gladiators of the Prize Ring*, Nottingham, n.d. (1925).
Jack Johnson, *In the Ring and Out*, 1977.
Joe Palmer, *Recollections of a Boxing Referee*, 1927.

BIBLIOGRAPHY

R.A. Hartley, *History and Bibliography of Boxing Books*, Nimrod
    Press, Alton, Hants, n.d. (1988). 349 pages containing over
    2,000 titles compiled by a scholarly, former professional
    boxer.

REFERENCE WORKS

"Boxing's" Book of Records up to 30 June 1914, 231 pp.
Hugman's British Boxing Yearbook 1991, Ickleford, Herts, 1990, 496
    pp.
The 1968 Ring Boxing Encyclopedia and Record Book, compiled by
    Nat Fleischer, New York City, 1967, 832 pp.
The 1984 Ring Record Book and Boxing Encyclopedia, edited by
    Herbert G. Goldman, U.S.A., 1067 pp.

BOOKS ABOUT BOXING

Leslie Bell, *Bella of Blackfriars*, 1961.
James Butler, *Kings of the Ring*, n.d. (1936).
Fred Dartnell, *"Seconds Out!"*, n.d. (1924).
Guy Deghy, *Noble and Manly*, 1956.
Peter Heller, *"In this Corner..."*, New York, 1974.
Thomas Inch, *Boxing and Physical Culture*, Aldershot, n.d. (1945).

Viscount Knebworth, *Boxing*, n.d. (1931)
J.G. Bohun Lynch, *The Complete Amateur Boxer*, 1913.
J.G. Bohun Lynch, *Prominent Pugilists of Today*, 1914.
Randy Roberts, *Papa Jack*, New York, 1983.
Fred G. Shaw, *The Science of Self-Defence*, 1919.
O.F. Snelling, *A Bedside Book of Boxing*, 1972.
Trevor Wignall, *The Sweet Science*, 1926.

GENERAL BOOKS

Charles Allen, *Raj: a scrapbook of British India 1877-1947*, 1977.
Vera Brittain, *Testament of Youth: an autobiographical study of the years 1900-1925*, 1982.
Captain F.C. Hitchcock, *"Stand To" a diary of the Trenches*, Norwich, 1988.
John M. Knapp (ed.), *The Universities and the Social Problem: an account of the University Settlements in East London*, 1895.
Tony Mason (ed.), *Sport in Britain*, Cambridge, 1989, especially chapter 3.
Raphael Samuel, *East End Underworld: chapters in the Life of Arthur Harding*, 1981. Arthur H. was a year older than Wells, and born in neighbouring Shoreditch.
George R. Sims (ed.), *Living London: its work and its play; its humour and its pathos; its sights and its scenes*, 3 volumes, 1902-3.
A.F. Tschiffely, *Bohemia Junction*, 1950. Autobiographical book which has glimpses of the lodger in London from 1912 by a perceptive outsider, who boxed professionally now and again, see chapter 4.
Frederick Willis, *101 Jubilee Road: a book of London yesterdays*, 1948. The first of Willis's books, and it throws an inside light on upper working-class culture.

ARTICLES

Elliott J. Gorn, "The Manassa Mauler and the Fighting Marine", *Journal of American Studies*, vol. 19, no. 1, April 1985, pp. 26-47.

Stuart Mews, "Puritanicalism, Sport, and Race: a symbolic crusade of 1911", G.J. Cuming and D. Baker (eds.), *Popular Belief and Practice*, Studies in Church History, vol. 8, Cambridge, 1972, pp. 303-31.

Ron Olver, "The Professionals: Bombardier Billy Wells", *Boxing News*, 23 August 1991.

Stan Shipley, "Tom Causer of Bermondsey: a Boxer Hero of the 1890s", *History Workshop*, issue 15, Spring 1983, pp. 28-59.

Stan Shipley, "The East End Family during the 1st world war", *Romford Record*, issue 21, 1989, pp. 14-24.

BOMBADIER. B. WELLS

206

INDEX

The alphabetical arrangement is word by word.

Added to the page number, n denotes a note, i an illustration.

Citation references are not indexed.

Construction Delays

Also available from Taylor & Francis

The Presentation and Settlement of Contractors' Claims, 2nd edn
Hb: ISBN 9780419205005
M. Hackett et al.

Construction Contracts Q&A
Pb: ISBN 9780415375979
D. Chappell

Understanding JCT Standard Building Contracts, 8th edn
Pb: ISBN 9780415413855
D. Chappell

Construction Contracts, 4th edn
Hb: ISBN 9780415393683
Pb: ISBN 9780415393690
J. Murdoch and W. Hughes

Risk and Insurance in Construction, 2nd edn
Hb: ISBN 9780419213802
N. Bunni

Professional Negligence in Construction
Hb: ISBN 9780415290661
B. Patten

Development and the Law
Hb: ISBN 9780415290210
G. Bruce-Radcliffe

Information and ordering details
For price, availability and ordering visit our website
www.tandfbuiltenvironment.com/
Alternatively our books are available from all good bookshops.

Construction Delays

Extensions of time and prolongation claims

Roger Gibson

Routledge
Taylor & Francis Group

LONDON AND NEW YORK

First published 2008
by Taylor & Francis
2 Park Square, Milton Park, Abingdon, Oxon OX14 4RN

Simultaneously published in the USA and Canada
by Taylor & Francis
270 Madison Ave, New York, NY 10016, USA

Taylor & Francis is an imprint of the Taylor & Francis Group, an informa business

Typeset in Sabon by
Wearset Ltd, Boldon, Tyne and Wear
Printed and bound in Great Britain by
Antony Rowe Ltd, Chippenham, Wiltshire

British Library Cataloguing in Publication Data
A catalogue record for this book is available from the British Library

Library of Congress Cataloging-in-Publication Data

Gibson, Roger, 1944–
Construction delays: extensions of time and prolongation
claims/Roger Gibson.
p. cm.
ISBN 978–0–415–34586–6 (hardcover: alk. paper) 1.
Building–Superintendence. 2. Production scheduling. 3. Tardiness. 4.
Construction contracts. I. Title.

TH438.4.G53 2007
692–dc22   2007040347

ISBN10: 0–415–34586–3 (hbk)

ISBN13: 978–0–415–34586–6 (hbk)

Contents

Preface

I have been involved in the construction industry in the UK and overseas for over 45 years, both at project level in planning and project positions and in head office organisations in managerial roles. During this time, and in particular during the last 20 years, which I have primarily spent involved in time-related disputes and claims, I have become increasingly aware of the lack of a comprehensive, easy-to-understand, practical and 'down-to-earth' reference book for those involved in the preparation and assessment of extensions of time and prolongation claims.

The views expressed by me in this book represent many years' experience of looking at projects that have gone wrong and resulted in a dispute or disputes between the parties. In practice many projects are completed without major claims and, where these do occur, they are settled promptly and professionally without escalating into a formal dispute. Unfortunately, a claim that evolves into a formal dispute often stretches the resources of the parties and their consultants, and this added financial pressure does not facilitate resolution of the dispute.

Many construction firms, large and small alike, lack staff with the skills required to produce well-presented extension of time submissions and time-related delay claims. Similarly, the receiving party, architect, engineer or employer, often lacks the in-house skills to review such submissions and claims thoroughly, and delays making a proper decision or resorts to external consultants for assistance.

A criticism I have with many books dealing with time-related claims is that they answer all the simple questions, but often avoid the thorny issues of 'who owns the float' and 'concurrency'. This book deals with these issues in detail and offers pragmatic advice.

Finally, this book aims to provide guidance and practical help in preparing extension of time submissions and time-related delay claims.

Roger Gibson
Summer 2007

Acknowledgements

I would like to thank the following for their kind permission to reproduce their material in this book:

The Society of Contract Law;
The Planning Engineers Organisation;
Sweet and Maxwell Publishing: Joint Contracts Tribunal – JCT 2005;
Thomas Telford Publishing – NEC3.

I would also like to thank Primavera Systems, Inc., whose software was used to create the tables in appendices 4 and 5.

I am indebted to my family and Anne-Mette for their encouragement and support during the writing of this book. Thanks are also due to my past and present colleagues who have offered numerous helpful suggestions.

Finally, the views expressed in this work are my own and I take full responsibility for them.

Part I
Introduction

1 The aims of this book

There are a number of excellent books on construction claims; and many other construction books that devote sections and chapters to construction claims. However, the majority of these works give very little guidance on the preparation of time-related delay claims, and even less guidance on the preparation of extension of time submissions.

Throughout this book the term 'delay analysis' is used, being a generalisation to cover both extension of time submissions and the time-related aspects of delay claims. Although there are various sophisticated delay analysis techniques around today, in its essence delay analysis is a fact-based process.

The aim here is to provide this guidance, particularly in relation to extension of time submissions. The contents of this volume are intended to outline the information and practical details to be considered when formulating extension of time submissions and time-related delay claims.

One of the recurring themes is good record keeping on projects. While a lack of progress-related records may not be fatal to a claim, it does make reaching a reasonable settlement an uphill battle. Readers will observe my continuing advice on good record keeping.

The book has been arranged in six parts, or sections:

Part I, 'Introduction', details general principles relating to extensions of time, delay claims and the SCL protocol.

Part II, 'Programmes and record keeping', deals with the fundamental matter of the project programme, together with the associated matter of record keeping during the project.

Part III, 'Contracts and case law', looks at the relevant time-related clauses in the JCT and NEC contracts, plus case law concerning time-related issues.

Part IV, 'The "thorny issues"', deals with the 'thorny issues' that appear in many extension of time submissions, namely, (i) float, (ii) concurrency, (iii) acceleration and (iv) time at large.

Part V, 'Extensions of time', gives details of the various extension of time/delay analysis techniques together with some worked examples.

Part VI, 'Prolongation claims (and time-related costs)', gives details of the claim heads for a prolongation claim together with some worked examples.

A brief synopsis of the contents of each section

Part I: 'Introduction'

The chapters on 'Extensions of time' and 'Prolongation claims' give brief overviews of these important subjects, while the final chapter in the section, 'The SCL protocol', highlights the core principles of the protocol together with the author's views and opinion on these and the other sections of the protocol.

Part II: 'Programmes and record keeping'

Although this section primarily considers the project programme and record keeping, it begins with a chapter covering the background and history of planning. Following this are four chapters concerning programming and programmes. The final chapter gives advice on record keeping during the project.

Part III: 'Contracts and case law'

The second chapter in this section reviews the time-related clauses of the two most popular forms of contract in the UK, namely the *Joint Contracts Tribunal's 2005 edition* (JCT) and *The New Engineering Contract 3rd edition* (NEC).

The remaining chapters, under the headings of 'case law' refer to cases from 1952 to 2005 held initially in the Official Referees Court, and then the Technology and Construction Court. This review of some 15 cases highlights the time-related issues of each dispute followed by a commentary reviewing the important issues such as concurrency, float and delay analysis methodology.

Part IV: 'The "thorny issues"'

There are many 'thorny issues' in the construction dispute arena which could have been included in this section. However, the four issues selected are considered to be the thorniest, if that is the correct phrase, and a chapter is dedicated to each one.

They are float, concurrency, mitigation and acceleration, and time at large.

Part V: 'Extensions of time'

This section reviews and discusses the various types of Delay Analysis methods and techniques. The final chapters give worked examples of prospective analysis and retrospective methods; the techniques chosen are 'time impact' and 'windows' methods of analyses.

Part VI: 'Prolongation claims (and time-related costs)'

This final section looks first at the contractual requirements and conditions for monetary compensation for time-related delays. This is followed by a chapter detailing the various 'heads' of a prolongation claim, followed by worked examples.

The author hopes that this book will provide useful guidance for those responsible for preparing extension of time submissions and time-related delay claims as well as for those dealing with them, the aim being that they can be resolved amicably, professionally and without either party being seriously disadvantaged.

2 Extensions of time

Just when you thought you knew all there is to know about how to prepare or analyse extension of time (EOT) claims, identify critical paths in programmes, and support your conclusions with well-reasoned arguments supported by the facts, something new comes along. Over the past 20 years extension of time methodologies have grown more sophisticated.

Delay analysis has evolved from crude hand-drawn charts in the early years of CPM to sophisticated modelling of impacts and delays using computers and state-of-the-art software. However, more recently, that very software has received criticism for allowing shrewd manipulation of the programme and analysis to favour a particular party.

Awarding extensions of time under a construction contract ought to be easy.

If the form is JCT 2005, the contractor notifies of a delay and the reason for it. The contract administrator reviews the application and, if they believe it to be the result of a 'relevant event', they award a fair and reasonable extension of time and fix a later date for completion of the project. The NEC contract has a more structured compensation event procedure and is specific about the programme information that has to be provided, so should achieve an answer more easily.

Most of the time these processes are applied fairly well, although there are often difficulties when contract administrators do not comply with the time scales for making the awards set out in the standard contracts: 12 weeks for the JCT, usually two weeks with the NEC. Unfortunately, the majority of EOT disputes concern the contract administrator's assessment technique or lack thereof. Most contractors have had experience of their EOT submissions being assessed through a 'wet finger in the air' and/or a quick guess at what 'they can get away with' technique, rather than the application of a logical and analytical method involving the programme and a critical path analysis-based technique.

EOT submissions are common sources of construction disputes. Submissions/claims for extensions of time on construction projects are made by a contractor to:

1   avoid/reduce liquidated damages that could otherwise arise; and/or
2   establish an entitlement to monetary compensation during the extended period.

Extension of time clauses should be drafted so as to include for all delays which may be the responsibility of the employer. Then, if the employer, either personally or through his architect or professional team, hinders the contractor in a way which will delay the date for completion, the architect will have the power to fix a new completion date and thus preserve the employer's right to deduct liquidated damages.

If the employer intends that liquidated damages are to be payable if the contractor fails to complete the works, then a date for completion must be stipulated in the contract. That is because there must be a definite date from which to calculate liquidated damages. There is an implied term in every contract that the employer will do all that is reasonably necessary to co-operate with the contractor and that he will not prevent him from performing. In this respect, the employer also has a duty to ensure that the architect and other professional team members employed by him carry out their duties properly. Alongside the implied term of co-operation, there is an implied term that neither party, employer or contractor, will do anything to hinder or delay performance by the other.

The meaning and purpose of liquidated damages

Construction contracts usually have a time or date by which the contractor must complete the work. The importance of a prescribed time or date for completion is that it facilitates a claim by the employer for damages for delay by the contractor in finishing the work. If there is no prescribed time, the law implies a term that the contractor must complete within a reasonable time. Therefore, the existence of an agreed time is very important for the employer. On the other hand, contractors prefer a reasonable time.

Linked to the problem of proving when the contractor is in breach for delay in achieving the date for completion is the problem of proving what damage was caused to the employer by the contractor's breach. To overcome this, most forms of contract have a provision for the parties to agree upon a daily, weekly or monthly amount as damages for delay by the contractor. This amount is called liquidated and ascertained damages (LADs).

The main purpose of LADs is to stipulate the employer's entitlement to damages for the contractor's breach of the obligation to complete by the agreed date. Even if the employer's actual damages exceed the LADs, the employer cannot recover more by way of damages. Similarly, if the employer's actual damages amount to less than the LADs, the employer can still recover LADs.

3   Prolongation claims

It is generally accepted that failure to give notice of delay for extensions of time purposes is not usually fatal to an extension of time claim. However, failure to give notice in accordance with the contract in respect of additional payment, e.g. prolongation, or loss and expense, claims, may bar or severely prejudice a claim.

Damages act as a means of compensating an innocent party for loss or harm suffered as a result of another party's breach of contract. The generally accepted rule is that contractual damages should be sufficient to compensate for such losses as may fairly and reasonably be considered as arising from the breach of contract.

In order to justify entitlement to damages for breach of contract, the injured party will have to prove that:

- the breach actually causes loss;
- the particular loss is recognised as giving an entitlement to compensation;
- the loss is not too remote;
- the quantification of compensatory damages is fair and reasonable under the circumstances.

The burden of proving that the breach has actually caused loss rests with the claimant, and he will need to produce contemporary records in support of the claim. The quantification of damages must be based upon factual records and not upon theoretical calculations.

There is a mistaken belief in the construction industry that after an extension of time has been granted there is an automatic entitlement to the recovery of loss and expense.

Under the JCT 2005 form of contract extensions of time and recovery of loss and expense are dealt with under separate clauses. For example, in the *JCT 2005 Standard Building Contract with Quantities*, section 2, clauses 2.26 to 2.29 inclusive, deal with extensions of time; while loss and expense is dealt with under section 4, clauses 4.23 to 4.26.

Under the NEC form of contract the situation is somewhat different.

This contract includes core clause 6 entitled 'Compensation events', and under this clause a contractor is entitled to the resultant time and money.

It is common practice for decisions and awards on extensions of time to be made and issued before considering prolongation claims. Once an extension of time has been awarded, the intention of most construction contracts is for the contractor to be reimbursed for the additional costs which have resulted from the employer-responsible delays. Basically, this involves a comparison between the contractor's actual costs incurred and what the contractor's costs would have been had no delay occurred.

When should the delay costs be evaluated?

If, for example, a critical delay occurs to the external envelope works, awaiting details for the external windows, and the contractor is awarded a six-week extension of time, for what period should the delay or prolongation costs be evaluated? Should it be the contractor's costs associated with the six weeks on site following the original contract completion date, or would a more accurate evaluation be achieved by assessing the costs incurred during the six-week period when the information was late in arriving?

The Society of Construction Law's 'Delay and Disruption Protocol' offers good advice on this matter in paragraphs 1.11.2 and 1.11.3,

> *Arguments commonly arise as to the time when recoverable prolongation compensation is to be assessed: is it to be assessed by reference to the period when the Employer Delay occurred (when the daily or weekly amount of expenditure and therefore compensation may be high) or by reference to the extended period at the end of the contract (when the amount of compensation may be much lower)?*
>
> *The answer to this question is that the period to be evaluated is that in which the effect of the Employer Risk Event was felt.*

This is a sensible solution, and it is recommended that it is followed.

Finance charges

A contractor's prolongation, or loss and expense, claim will invariably include a sum in respect of finance charges, the argument being that they have been 'underpaid' for considerable periods of time, which has necessitated borrowing to make up the shortfall or, if money has been taken off the deposit, there has been a subsequent loss of interest.

It is clear from established case law that contractors are entitled to finance charges as part of their prolongation, or loss and expense, claims. However, the contractor will still need to show that the loss was actually suffered.

The 'heads' of a prolongation, or loss and expense, claim

Time-related claims are, as the phrase implies, derived from the time analysis, which has identified: (i) prolongation to the contract period, and (ii) other non-critical delays to work activities.

Both of these elements should be included in a prolongation claim, which under the JCT form of contract is referred to as a 'loss and expense' claim.

4 The SCL protocol

In October 2002, the Society of Construction Law (SCL) published its 'Delay and Disruption Protocol'. This protocol provides guidance to people dealing with submissions for extension of time and delay claims, both during a contract and after completion of the works. The protocol runs to some 82 pages and was drafted by a group of experts from all sections of the construction industry.

The protocol envisages that decision-takers (e.g. contract administrators, adjudicators, dispute review boards, arbitrators, judges) may find it helpful in dealing with time-related issues.

There are 21 'core statements of principle' in the protocol. These are:

1 _Programme and records;_ to reduce the number of disputes relating to delay, the Contractor should prepare and the Contract Administrator (CA) should accept a properly prepared programme showing the manner and sequence in which the Contractor plans to carry out the works. The programme should be updated to record actual progress and any extensions of time (EOTs) granted. If this is done, then the programme can be used as a tool for managing change, determining EOTs and periods of time for which compensation may be due. Contracting parties should also reach a clear agreement on the type of records that should be kept.

2 _Purpose of extension of time;_ the benefit to the Contractor of EOT is only to relieve the Contractor of liability for damages for delay (usually liquidated damages (LDs)) for any period prior to the extended contract completion date. The benefit of an EOT for the Employer is that it establishes a new contract completion date, and prevents time for completion of the works becoming 'at large'.

3 _Entitlement to extension of time;_ applications for EOT should be made and dealt with as close in time as possible to the delay event that gives rise to the application. The Contractor will potentially be entitled to an EOT only for those events or causes of delay in respect of which the Employer has assumed risk and responsibility (called in the Protocol 'Employer Risk Events'). The parties should attempt so far as

possible to deal with the impact of 'Employer Risk Events' as the work proceeds, both in terms of EOT and compensation.

4 *Procedure for granting extension of time; the EOT should be granted to the extent that the Employer Risk Event is reasonably predicted to prevent the works being completed by the then prevailing contract completion date. The goal of the EOT procedure is the ascertainment of the appropriate contractual entitlement to an EOT; the procedure is not to be based on whether or not the Contractor needs an EOT in order not to be liable for liquidated damages.*

5 *Effect of delay; for an EOT to be granted, it is not necessary for the Employer Risk Event already to have begun to affect the Contractor's progress with the works, or for the effect of the Employer Risk Event to have ended.*

6 *Incremental review of extension of time; where the full effect of an Employer Risk Event cannot be predicted with certainty at the time of initial assessment by the CA, the CA should grant an EOT for the then predictable effect. The EOT should be considered by the CA at intervals as the actual impact of the Employer Risk Event unfolds and the EOT increased (but not decreased, unless there are express contract terms permitting this) if appropriate.*

7 *Float, as it relates to time; unless there is express provision to the contrary in the contract, where there is remaining float in the programme at the time of an Employer Risk Event, an EOT should only be granted to the extent that the Employer Delay is predicted to reduce to below zero the total float on the activity paths affected by the Employer Delay.*

8 *Float, as it relates to compensation; if as a result of an Employer Delay, the Contractor is prevented from completing the works by the Contractor's planned completion date (being a date earlier than the contract completion date), the Contractor should in principle be entitled to be paid the costs directly caused by the Employer Delay, notwithstanding that there is no delay to the contract completion date (and therefore no entitlement to an EOT), provided also that at the time they enter into the contract, the Employer is aware of the Contractor's intention to complete the works prior to the contract completion date, and that intention is realistic and achievable.*

9 *Concurrent delay – its effect on entitlement to extension of time; where Contractor Delay to Completion occurs or has effect concurrently with Employer Delay to Completion, the Contractor's concurrent delay should not reduce any EOT due.*

10 *Concurrent delay – its effect on entitlement to compensation for prolongation; if the Contractor incurs additional costs that are caused both by Employer Delay and concurrent Contractor Delay, then the Contractor should only recover compensation to the extent it is able to separately identify the additional costs caused by the Employer*

Delay from those caused by the Contractor Delay. If it would have incurred the additional costs in any event as a result of Contractor Delays, the Contractor will not be entitled to recover those additional costs.

11 *Identification of float and concurrency;* accurate identification of float and concurrency is only possible with the benefit of a proper programme, properly updated.

12 *After the event delay analysis;* the Protocol recommends that, in deciding entitlement to EOT, the adjudicator, judge or arbitrator should so far as is practicable put him/herself in the position of the CA at the time the Employer Risk Event occurred.

13 *Mitigation of delay and mitigation of loss;* the Contractor has a general duty to mitigate the effect on its works of Employer Risk Events. Subject to express contract wording or agreement to the contrary, the duty to mitigate does not extend to requiring the Contractor to add extra resources or to work outside its planned working hours. The Contractor's duty to mitigate its loss has two aspects – first, the Contractor must take reasonable steps to minimise its loss; and second, the Contractor must not take unreasonable steps that increase its loss.

14 *Link between extension of time and compensation;* entitlement to an EOT does not automatically lead to entitlement to compensation (and vice versa).

15 *Valuation of variations;* where practicable, the total likely effect of variations should be pre-agreed between the Employer/CA and the Contractor, to arrive if possible at a fixed price of a variation, to include not only the direct costs (labour, plant and materials) but also the time-related costs, an agreed EOT and the necessary revisions to the programme.

16 *Basis of calculation of compensation for prolongation;* unless expressly provided for otherwise (e.g. by evaluation based on contract rates), compensation for prolongation should not be paid for anything other than work actually done, time actually taken up or loss and/or expense actually suffered. In other words, the compensation for prolongation caused other than by variations is based on the actual additional cost incurred by the Contractor. The objective is to put the Contractor in the same financial position it would have been if the Employer Risk Event had not occurred.

17 *Relevance of tender allowances;* the tender allowances have limited relevance for the evaluation of the costs of prolongation and disruption caused by breach of contract or any other cause that requires the evaluation of additional costs.

18 *Period of evaluation of compensation;* once it is established that compensation for prolongation is due, the evaluation of the sum due is made by reference to the period when the effect of the Employer Risk

Event was felt, not by reference to the extended period at the end of the contract.

19 *Global claims; the not uncommon practice of contractors making composite or global claims without substantiating cause and effect is discouraged by the Protocol and rarely accepted by the courts.*

20 *Acceleration; where the contract provides for acceleration, payment for the acceleration should be based on the terms of the contract. Where the contract does not provide for acceleration but the Contractor and the Employer agree that accelerative measures should be undertaken, the basis of payment should be agreed before the acceleration is commenced. It is not recommended that a claim for so-called constructive acceleration be made. Instead, prior to any acceleration measures, steps should be taken by either party to have the dispute or difference about entitlement to EOT resolved in accordance with the dispute resolution procedures applicable to the contract.*

21 *Disruption; disruption (as distinct from delay) is disturbance, hindrance or interruption to a Contractor's normal working methods, resulting in lower efficiency. If caused by the Employer, it may give rise to a right to compensation either under the contract or as a breach of contract.*

Further background and guidance on each of the 21 core principles is contained in the four 'guidance sections', which are:

i   Section 1: Guidelines on the protocol's position on core principles and on other matters relating to delay and compensation.
ii   Section 2: Guidelines on preparing and maintaining programmes and records.
iii Section 3: Guidelines on dealing with extensions of time during the course of the project.
iv   Section 4: Guidelines on dealing with disputed extension of time issues after completion of the project – retrospective delay analysis.

Observations

First, I present some observations on the core principles,

1 Core principles 2 to 6: Extensions of time
   The position on extensions of time is generally good and the advice is sound, although fairly general in nature.
2 Core principle 7: Float, as it relates to time
   One of the more controversial principles in the protocol, the nub of this principle is,

i   Should the contractor be awarded an extension of time and so preserve the float period for its own use; or

ii Should no extension of time be awarded on the basis that the
employer's delay is simply absorbing float and not impacting the
contractual completion date?

The protocol's recommendation is that float is available to the project.
In other words, it is available to whichever party uses it first; contactor
or employer.

3 Core principle 8: <u>Float, as it relates to compensation</u>
Where a contractor plans to complete before the contract date for
completion, the protocol recommends that he is entitled to compensation, but not an extension of time, if he is prevented from completing
to his own planned date, but finishes before the contract date for completion. This is a complicated topic. However, the basic recommendation must be rejected. The position is that in deciding this question all
the circumstances must be taken into account.

4 Core principle 9: <u>Concurrent delay – its effect on entitlement to extension of time</u>
The protocol's approach seems to be to take a particular position on
the subject of concurrency on the basis that it is a complex topic and a
compromise situation is necessary. A basic principle is that no concurrent cause of delay which is the result of any fault of the contractor
should reduce the extension of time to which he would otherwise be
entitled. This approach basically follows the 'prevention principle' of
English law where an employer cannot take advantage of its own
breach of contract, by imposing liquidated damages on the contractor.

5 Core principle 13: <u>Mitigation of delay and mitigation of loss</u>
A clear exposition of the situation. More could have been said in the
protocol about the contractor's rights, or otherwise, to claim reasonable costs of mitigation.

6 Core principle 15: <u>Valuation of variations</u>
The protocol recommends a mechanism similar to the current JCT
price statement for dealing with the valuation of variations and associated extension of time and loss and expense.

7 Core principle 16: <u>Basis of calculation of compensation for prolonga-
tion</u>
It is rightly stressed that ascertainment must be based on actual additional costs incurred by the contractor. However, there appears to be
some confusion between a contractor's claims for loss and expense
under the contract machinery and claims for damages for breaches of
contract. The former are reimbursable under most standard forms of
contracts while the latter, being a claim outside the contract, are not
so reimbursable.

8 Core principle 17: <u>Relevance of tender allowances</u>

It is refreshing to see that the protocol considers that tender allowances have little or no relevance to the evaluation of the costs of prolongation or disruption.

9   Core principle 19: <u>Global claims</u>
It is good to see that global claims are discouraged.

10   Core principle 20: <u>Acceleration</u>
This is a broadly correct interpretation of the position, but the reference to the possibility of accelerating by instructions about hours of working and sequence of working is to be doubted.

11   Core principle 21: <u>Disruption</u>
The definition of disruption does not adequately explain that disruption can also refer to a delay to an individual activity not on the critical path where there is no resultant delay to the date for completion. The protocol also states that most standard forms do not expressly deal with disruption; that, of course, is true. However, the JCT forms refer to regular progress being materially affected. That appears to be broad enough to encompass both disruption and prolongation.

The protocol's 'Guidance section 2' deals with guidelines on preparing and maintaining programmes and records. However, there is not a great deal of guidance on maintaining records generally.

Stress is placed on obtaining an 'accepted programme'; that is a programme agreed by all parties. There are several problems with this. Perhaps the foremost is that the architect will be unlikely to have the requisite skills and/or experience or indeed the information required to accept the contractor's programme. He is probably capable of questioning parts of it, but highly unlikely to be possessed of sufficient information to be able to satisfy himself that the programme is workable. The protocol, rightly, accepts that the contractor is entitled to construct the building in whatever manner and sequence he pleases, subject to any sectional completion or other constraints. The protocol states,

> *Acceptance by the CA merely constitutes an acknowledgement by the CA that the Accepted Programme represents a contractually compliant, realistic and achievable depiction of the Contractor's intended sequence and timing of construction of the works.*

This is placing a responsibility on the architect (or CA as the protocol prefers) which he is not required to carry. There appears to be no need for a programme to be accepted. It is sufficient if the contractor puts one forward as the programme to which he intends to work. The architect is entitled to question any part which appears to be clearly wrong or unworkable. But, in the light of the contractor's insistence that he can and will carry out the works in accordance with the submitted programme, it is difficult to refuse a programme unless firm objections can be raised.

The protocol also recommends that the 'accepted programme' be updated with progress at intervals of one month, and more frequently on complex projects.

The protocol describes the updating process as follows:

> *Using the agreed project planning software, the Contractor should enter the actual progress on the Accepted Programme as it proceeds with the works, to create the Updated Programme. Actual progress should be recorded by means of actual start and actual finish dates for activities, together with percentage completion of currently incomplete activities and/or the extent of remaining activity durations. Any periods of suspension of an activity should be noted in the Updated Programme. The monthly updates should be archived as separate electronic files and the saved monthly versions of the Updated Programme should be copied electronically to the CA, along with a report describing all modifications made to activity durations or logic of the programme. The purpose of saving monthly versions of the programme is to provide good contemporaneous evidence of what happened on the project, in case of dispute.*

All of this is good and sensible advice.

'Guidance section 3' gives guidelines for dealing with extensions of time during the course of the project. It provides much good practical advice including the importance of calculating extensions of time by means of various programming techniques. Although every architect should be familiar with such techniques, careful consideration should be given to the aptness of any particular technique in a given situation.

The protocol suggests that extensions of time should be made as close in time to the delaying event, and that these are dealt with promptly by the CA. The protocol recommends that 'the "Updated Programme" should be the primary tool used to guide the CA in determining the amount of the EOT'.

Again sound advice, with one proviso; the facts surrounding the alleged delay event(s). As Mr Justice Dyson noted in his judgment on the Henry Boot Construction v. Malmaison Hotel case, 'It seems to me that it is a question of fact in any case, as to whether a relevant event has caused, or is likely to cause, delay to the works beyond the completion date.'

'Guidance section 4' deals with disputed extensions of time after completion of the project, and spends some time examining the different types of analysis that can be employed.

Conclusion

The protocol sets out ways of dealing with delays and disruption. Most of it is in line with what is generally understood to be the law on these matters. However, in some instances, the protocol steps outside this boundary in order to suggest what it clearly considers to be a simpler or fairer way of dealing with the practicalities. All parties involved in construction contracts must be aware that the protocol does not take precedence over the particular contract in use unless it is expressly so stated in the contract itself. Therefore, the protocol's recommendations should be viewed with caution.

It will be of no avail for the architect, contract administrator or employer to argue that he has acted strictly in accordance with the protocol if the contract prescribes action of a different sort.

Part II

Programmes and record keeping

5   Background and history of planning

From earliest recorded times groups of people have been organised to work together towards planned goals and planners co-ordinated and controlled their efforts to achieve desired outcomes.

The early days

Considerable planning skills were required by, for example, the ancient Egyptians to build their pyramids, the ancient Chinese to build the Great Wall of China, and the Romans when building their roads, aqueducts and Hadrian's Wall.

These time-enduring construction projects required large amounts of human effort with planning, organisation and co-ordination; and all with no computers, faxes or combustion engine!

After the fall of the Roman Empire, the great Dark Ages descended, and it was not until the mechanical clock and Guttenberg's moveable typefaces were invented, that any further major development in 'planning' was forthcoming. The clock, invented by Heinrich von Wych in Paris in 1370, permitted accurate work measurement. The printing press enabled communication by the printed word; and it was while at an early version of the Octoberfest that Guttenberg visualised the technique of combining the small dies used for coin-punching with the mechanics of a wine press. This produced a printed page, made up of moveable individual letters, rather than a single engraved block.

Developments in planning and production management then began. In 1436 a Spanish visitor to the Arsenal of Venice reported:

> And as one enters the gate there is a great street on either hand with the sea in the middle. On one side are windows opening out of the house of the arsenal, and the same on the other side, and out came a galley towed by a boat, and in the windows they handed out to them, from one the cordage, from another the ballistics and mortars, and so from all sides everything which was required. When the galley had reached the end of the street all the men required were on board,

together with the complement of oars, and she was equipped from end to end.

This was an example of the planning of a production line, half a millennium before Henry Ford!

It was not until the First World War that simple barcharts were used by the British army for planning military exercises. Then some 15 years later, in 1930, construction began on the Empire State Building, which on completion was the tallest building in the world and remained so for over 40 years. However, during its construction it was a marvel of programming excellence, the works being elaborately planned and programmed by Andrew Eken, the chief engineer of the contractor. The site in downtown Manhattan was very congested with virtually no lay-down areas. Material deliveries were carefully planned to coincide precisely with the installation works. Another impressive fact about this project is that the building's 56,000 tons of structural steel were erected in six months at the remarkable rate of 4.5 floors per week, again without the aid of a CPM programme or a computer!

Modern times

Mention 'planning' to the average person nowadays, and he or she will think of a barchart, which is the most common form of visually representing a project. The barchart is strictly speaking a Gantt Chart, named after its inventor, Henry Laurence Gantt, an American engineer. He is the first known person to publish a plan in a barchart format – and probably the first to be told off for a project not going to plan!

The Gantt Chart, for which Henry will be remembered, is a visual display chart used to present a schedule or programme of activities. It is based on time, rather than quantity, volume or weight. In other words, a Gantt Chart is a horizontal barchart that graphically displays time relationships. In effect, it is a 'scale' model of time because the bars are different lengths depending upon the amount of time they represent. Gantt Charts have been around since the early 1900s and provide a method of determining the sequence of events and time required to achieve a given objective.

The critical path method (CPM)

The next major development in 'planning' was the advent of PERT and the emergence of critical path method (CPM) programmes.

PERT is an acronym of 'Project Evaluation and Review Technique', and is a variation on CPM programmes that takes a more sceptical view of activity durations. To follow this technique, for each activity you estimate: (i) the shortest possible time the activity will take; (ii) the most likely length of time for the activity; and (iii) the longest time that might be taken if the activity takes longer than expected. Using the following formula, the duration for each activity is calculated thus:

Shortest time (i) + 4 × most likely time (ii) + longest time (iii)\6

Using the PERT technique helps to bias activity durations away from the unrealistically short time scales sometimes assumed.

CPM programming has been around since the 1950s. The first known use appears to be in North America by E.I. DuPont Nemours Co., which developed a CPM programme in 1956 for construction of its $10 million chemical plant in Kentucky. The CPM was run on a large mainframe computer, called a UNIVAC, some 25 feet high and 50 feet in length containing 5,000 tubes and 18,000 crystal diodes.

The type of CPM used in those days was the Activity Diagram Method (ADM) form of network.

However, the first high-profile application of a CPM was the Polaris project in 1957. The team on this huge project had to understand the development process for the most complex machine ever devised by man. Seeking a technique that would get the missile developed and into action, management consultants Booz, Allen and Hamilton used the Critical Path Method to draw their maps of time. Polaris went on to hit the target of 'time'. Everyone celebrated the new behemoth, and the modern version of 'planning' was truly born.

The use of computers and planning software

CPM, preceded by its reputation, spread to other industries and to other environments. In the early 1970s, CPMs were run on mainframe computer systems, which few people owned. The rest of us rented time at a now extinct breed of companies known as 'computer bureaux'. The procedure was that, after hiring time at a computer bureau that was running a critical path software programme, such as Projacs, we worked alongside a data entry person (and it was always a woman in those days). From our data entry sheets, she would type an incomprehensible series of characters and numbers into on-screen forms to create a series of punch cards. These were fed into the mainframe computer and processed. The result was a printout of our project plan, often containing thousands of tasks or activities, and requiring long corridor walls for the huge printouts of green-and-white striped paper containing the network diagram. Computer people in the 1970s all had white coats, little white hats and a supercilious smile. Nowadays, only the white coats and hats have gone.

In the 1980s, a great advance in computing took place in a garage in California; Steve Jobs was astounding the techie world with his Apple II. The Apple II, a small computer that sat on a desktop, changed many people's lives. A huge push was given to the personal computer industry when IBM developed the PC. PCs sprouted everywhere and computer packages and planning software, such as MicroPert, were specially written for the new PCs. Critical path diagrams increasingly took a backseat as far simpler barcharts were quickly and easily drawn by the new software.

The advent and development of personal computers and planning software packages specially written for them allowed the planning of a large construction project to be done on site. The other effect was that these affordable, small computers and planning systems spread into other industries and onto smaller projects. Critical path diagrams and barcharts appeared on walls in offices throughout the world.

Precedence Diagram Method Networks (PDMs)

At the turn of the millennium, the Precedence Diagram Method (PDM) supplanted the Arrow Diagram Method (ADM) form of network as the preferred planning method for CPMs.

The Precedence Diagram Method was developed in the early 1960s by an American company, H.B. Zachary, in conjunction with IBM. It was common in the 1970s and 1980s for planning software programmes to accept and perform calculations for either ADM or PDM networks. However, from the 1990s new software was written only for PDM networks. For example, when Primavera software writers created a Windows version, they opted to use PDM as the platform for the programme.

6 Planning and programming

Time is money, so the old adage says. However, poor planning/programming still ranks in most surveys within the top three problem areas that lead to project failure.

Therefore the 'planning' of a project is a necessity for success; and one would expect that, in this day and age, with computers and planning software available to assist project managers and planners, delays would have been significantly reduced. However, results reveal that the opposite is true.

Time is money; therefore planning shouldn't be ignored. Sadly, the statement that 'if you fail to plan, then you plan to fail' is often true, and sadly too many planners nowadays rely solely on a bit of computer software for 'planning'. The manner in which computers and planning software deal with activity logic and relationships through an interactive screen is an improvement from the days of creating a network programme through punch cards. However, it also encourages planners to generate programmes with illogical activity relationship links; and often this ill-conceived planning is a hindrance in time-related disputes.

Planning and programming are two separate functions, but are often linked together under the general term of 'planning'. However, before you prepare a programme, you must have a plan.

Planning

To plan a project means to identify the tasks or work activities to be performed and logically interrelate them. The question of time for performance and resources required are answered as part of the programming function.

The first stage is a broadbrush approach, and it is best to start with a blank piece of paper – not a computer.

Take a six-storey concrete-framed commercial building for example. First assess how long it will take for the main elements, i.e. (i) substructure works before starting superstructure work, (ii) superstructure work, (iii) envelope and cladding, (iv) services works, (v) internal finishes.

For example, let's say the three main tasks in the substructure work are bulk excavation, piling, and concrete works being pile caps, ground beams and ground floor slab. Taking a broadbrush approach, these are assessed as two weeks, four weeks and six weeks respectively. However, the planner, using his experience, allows for overlapping between these main stages and his conclusion is that work to the concrete frame superstructure can begin ten weeks after starting the bulk excavation.

The next key element, superstructure, is approached in a similar fashion. However, for this element, the key is the cycle time for a typical floor of 400m^2. Now the planner has to go into more detail, to assess how long to follow for fixing the formwork and reinforcement for this area of concrete slab. He also has to take into consideration crane hook-time; that means how many lifts the single tower crane positioned in the central core area must perform. For the example we are using it is probably the crane hook-time that is the governing factor in assessing the cycle time for a typical floor.

On a construction project, 'planning' covers all aspects from overall planning, such as, building 'A' must be completed before building 'B' can start, down to detailed planning, such as the activity 'excavate for foundations' has to be completed before its successor, 'pour concrete in foundations' can start.

By planning the works in detail, and linking activities in a logical manner, a contractor creates a network of activities and their dependencies or interrelationships as shown above. If this is done in a proper manner encompassing all works and all restraints on the project, then this is the basis for a critical path network.

The next stage is to calculate the time each activity will take. This phase is the start of preparing the programme for the project. For example, for 'excavate for foundations', the contractor will know he has 1,000 cubic metres of soil to dig out, and at a productivity rate of 100 cubic metres per day this activity will take ten days. This is known as the activity's 'duration'.

After completing this exercise for all activities, he then has a 'time frame' for the project. For example, 'excavate for foundations' will start on day 1 and, because it has a duration of ten days, it will finish on day 10. Its successor, 'pour concrete in foundations', will start on day 11 and, as it has a duration of, let's say 15 days, will finish on day 26. The contractor now has a programme.

Programming

In its simplest terms, programming (or 'scheduling' as it's sometimes called) is a method whereby the work activities necessary in order to achieve project completion are arranged in a logical order.

A properly developed programme will not only show the sequence in which the activities are intended to be carried out, but will also enable the participants of the project to monitor progress. In addition, the programme will be able to project future work while providing historical data that could be useful in analysing the past. This most common type of programme is a barchart; either hand-drawn or, more likely nowadays, computer-generated using commercially available project planning software.

CPM programmes

A critical path method (CPM) programme refers to the development of a logic-linked network that enables the identification of a critical path. The critical path is the longest activity path from the start of the project to its completion.

Activities on the critical path have no float; conversely, an activity not on the critical path will have float. Float is the amount of time an activity can be delayed without it becoming a critical path activity. Any activity on the critical path that experiences a delay will consequently delay the project completion date.

The calculations necessary to determine activity start and finish dates, together with float and the identification of the critical path, are very simple arithmetic. These CPM calculations can be performed manually, but with computers and project-planning software the thousands of calculations representative of a typical construction project can be effectively compiled and organised into an intelligible format in a matter of seconds.

A network programme, or CPM, provides the ability to analyse the effect of every activity on the project completion date, and far outstrips other methods for progress monitoring, reprogramming or evaluating new factors. At any time, you can determine if an activity is or is not on the critical path, and whether there is any float associated with that activity. If there is float, you will know precisely how much that activity can be delayed without it impacting the project completion date. This knowledge enables the project team to track and control progress, and to mitigate delay to the project completion date should critical activities be delayed.

However, a word of warning. The level of detail that will exist in a CPM programme is largely a matter of judgement on the part of the planner. Too much detail could conceal significant factors, while too little detail may result in a programme that is not very meaningful.

What is the use or benefit of a CPM programme?

By preparing a CPM, a contractor reassures himself that he can complete all the works and achieve completion of the project by the contract completion date. He knows when he has to have available key resources or equipment. Using the earlier simple example, he knows that he is going to 'pour concrete in foundations' starting on day 11, therefore he will have to have his concrete-producing equipment up and running by this date.

The benefit of a CPM programme for the employer or contract administrator is that they are also reassured that the contractor can complete the project on time, and that he has planned the works in a reasonable and logical manner. Again using the earlier example, the employer knows at an early date that the contractor intends to start to 'pour concrete in foundations' on day 11 and that he has to provide the drawings for this work before this date.

Pitfalls in the use of CPM

Although the above paragraphs extol the virtues of CPM, one should be aware of the associated inherent dangers. Detailed below are four of the most common pitfalls.

1 Quality of the CPM programme

Readily available, user-friendly project-planning software makes it possible for almost any computer-literate person to create a CPM programme that appears to be reasonable. It is very easy to input the various activities comprising a project into the software and string them together in such a way that, when looking at a barchart printout, the work seems to flow in a way that seems entirely sensible. Unfortunately, there is no way to tell simply by looking at the printed barchart whether this is a true CPM programme, or simply an 'attractive barchart'. Very often, no network logic, or activity relationship links, are issued with the programme, and therefore the barchart printout on its own is essentially useless.

Flawed programme logic can be hidden from all project participants unless someone works directly with the project-planning software on the computer. Without this direct examination of the electronic file, the programme may, either intentionally or unintentionally:

i   contain flawed logic;
ii   include activity constraints that interrupt the calculation of the critical path and/or float;
iii   show only those activities that the contractor wishes the employer or contract administrator to see;
iv   misrepresent project status at a progress update.

Therefore, the only way to avoid these circumstances is to require electronic copies of the baseline, or as-planned programme and all subsequent updates to be submitted with the barchart printout and paper reports.

2 What is critical today may not be critical tomorrow

The critical path identified in the original baseline, or as-planned programme, will only remain the critical path if everything goes according to plan. As everyone knows, this is almost never the case, as the calculated project completion date is directly dependent upon the completion of every activity on the critical path taking no longer than originally estimated.

Furthermore, if an activity not on the original critical path is delayed by more than its available float, then it will become critical and in effect the project's critical path has changed.

3 Unrealistic activity durations

For many programme activities that are delayed the as-planned duration may have been entirely appropriate, but this is not always the case. All too often the duration of activities in a CPM programme are wild guesses that are unrealistically short, or in some cases excessively long. All activities on the critical path and those that are near critical should have supporting data as to how their durations have been calculated.

4 Managing the programme and regular updates

Unfortunately, many contractors view a programme as nothing more than a requirement of the contract, and do not take it seriously enough to properly develop a CPM programme and maintain this as a management tool. Without proper attention the CPM will become nothing more than a list of activities and a convenient way to record actual start and finish dates.

One of the principles to be followed in maintaining a CPM programme is the regular monitoring of the work by periodically reviewing the programme. Programme updates should be performed on a regular basis for the purpose of gathering progress information and revising programme logic as appropriate. The project-planning software takes this contemporaneous information and recalculates the critical path so that management knows which activities are now driving the project completion date. The update also records project history, as well as projecting start and finish dates for future activities. Unless the CPM programme is updated on a regular basis, it will quickly become inaccurate and consequently useless.

This update information must be collected, inputted and analysed relatively quickly so that the update reports can be distributed to the project's participants while there is still time to react. A CPM programme is dynamic in nature and the critical path is continually evolving over time. Failure to disseminate the update information in a timely fashion may render the information useless from the standpoint of being able to proactively manage the project.

Types of 'programmes'

The construction industry uses a number of different types of programmes to manage projects. The two most common types are the 'barchart' and the 'network'.

The most frequently used of these two types is the barchart, which comprises a list of activities involved in the project. The planned start and planned finish of each activity is shown in a time grid and connected in a bar. The bar therefore represents the duration of the activity. The assumption usually made is that the bar represents a continuous uninterrupted activity, but this may not be the case. It is usual to include a tabular listing of the activities on the left-hand side of the barchart, which may include calendar start and finish dates together with overall durations for each activity.

An example of a simple barchart is given in Figure 6.1, showing the construction of a garage.

The barchart is easily prepared and can be used to show estimated timing and duration of activities, and to record actual progress. It does not require special software or computers and can easily be drawn by hand. The types of activities are not limited in any way, since the barchart is simply a diagrammatic representation of the time characteristics of an activity.

The barchart does not model the interrelationship between activities, and does not model the consequences on the project completion date, if the actual timing or duration of an activity is not met. So, for example, if an activity is started later than shown on the programme, the barchart does not allow the effect on completion to be analysed, without additional information. The barchart simply shows that an activity started later than planned. Similarly if an activity takes longer than its duration as shown on the programme, the barchart only reflects this fact. The barchart therefore simply provides a model of the time characteristics of the activity, and does not model the relationship of the activity with the time characteristics of the project and in particular with the project completion date.

The absence of logic links between activities means that the use of barcharts is limited to monitoring progress rather than forward-planning of the project. It is often used in the initial stages of delay analysis to compare planned and actual progress so as to identify problem activities. Care is required, since the implicit assumption that the planned durations were an accurate and still valid estimate, may not be correct.

The second type of programme, the network, is a model not only of the activities and their durations, but of their interdependence and association with the completion of the project.

The most common network programme is the critical path method (CPM), which models the construction logic links between the activities. The construction logic represents those factors which define the construction sequence of the project and include:

- the method of working – showing how the project is to be carried out and the sequence of activities;
- the construction constraints – which may be access dates for parts of

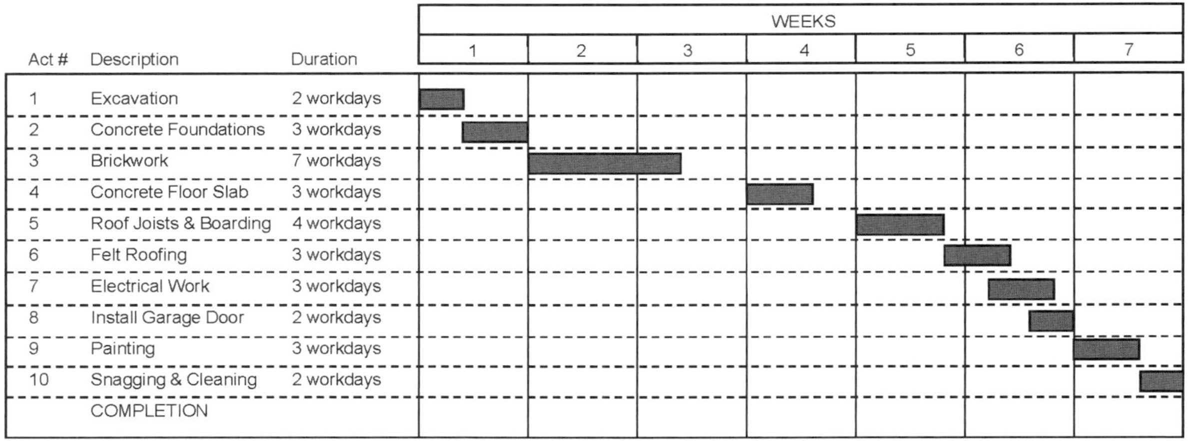

Act #	Description	Duration							
			WEEKS						
			1	2	3	4	5	6	7
1	Excavation	2 workdays							
2	Concrete Foundations	3 workdays							
3	Brickwork	7 workdays							
4	Concrete Floor Slab	3 workdays							
5	Roof Joists & Boarding	4 workdays							
6	Felt Roofing	3 workdays							
7	Electrical Work	3 workdays							
8	Install Garage Door	2 workdays							
9	Painting	3 workdays							
10	Snagging & Cleaning	2 workdays							
	COMPLETION								

Figure 6.1 Example of a simple barchart.

the site or release dates for information or delivery dates for work by others.

There are two types of CPM programmes: Activity-on-Arrow and Activity-on-Node.

The Activity-on-Arrow programme produces an arrow network in which each node represents either the beginning or end of a discrete activity and the arrow linking the nodes is the activity. The nodes are numbered and the activity is identified by the numbers of the nodes at the start and the finish. The example below shows the activities for the construction of a garage (as used in the barchart programme example in Figure 6.1 above). Activity 'Excavation' is identified as Activity 21–22. Node 21 represents the beginning of Activity 21–22 and node 22 the end of Activity 21–22. Node 22 is also the start of Activity 22–23. This demonstrates the logic inherent in the Activity-on-Arrow, which is *finish-to-start*. The arrow activity is not drawn to a time scale but the duration is annotated as shown in the example In Figure 6.2. The Activity-on-Arrow network is helpful in representing the flow of work, but its use has declined in construction.

In the Activity-on-Node programme each node is an activity with a duration and the arrows represent the logic link between the activities. The programme uses *finish-to-start* relationships or links which are the same as used in the Activity-on-Arrow programme. In the example in Figure 6.3 for the construction of a garage, Activity 36 is 'felt roofing' and is linked to Activities 37 and 38. Activity 38 can start once Activity 36 is completed, while Activity 37 can start two days after Activity 36 has started and can only finish one day after the finish of Activity 36. The Precedence Network Method is now the most common form of Activity-on-Node programme and exploits the possibility of defining the links between activities by relationships other than *finish-to-start*. This method permits not only *start–finish* links, but *start–start* and *finish–finish*, as well as allowing a time dimension to be added to the link in the form of a *lag* or *lead*. The choice of logic link depends on which link accurately models the particular restraint.

The facility to define the relationship of activities both in terms of the type of logic as well as with a time dimension, makes the Precedence Network Method a most powerful and flexible method of programming. The assumptions made must be carefully examined when carrying out any delay analysis or management through programming analysis. If for instance the initial design of the equipment in the above example is delayed, then the lag in the above *start-to-start* link will need to be adjusted to take account of the delay. In any analysis, the time dimension of links which are not based on real-time factors needs to be examined carefully to establish that it still accurately models the relationship between activities.

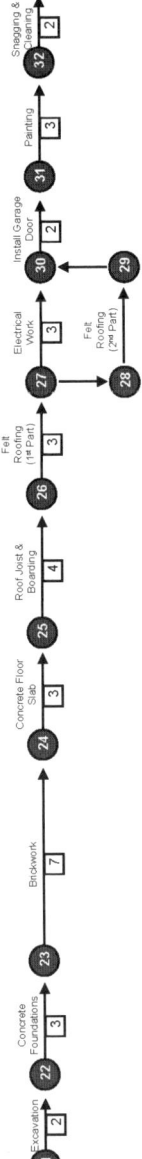

Figure 6.2 Activity-on-Arrow network.

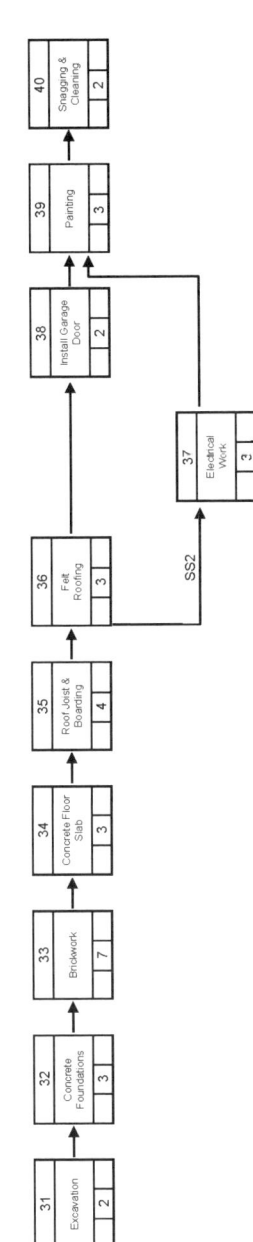

Figure 6.3 Activity-on-Node network.

Nowadays, it is common for the network to be presented as a time-scaled logic-linked programme, as shown in Figure 6.4.

In order to make management decisions and to establish the priority of actions, it is necessary to interrogate the network.

One important attribute relevant to the obligation to complete by a specified date is the critical path. Those activities which can be least delayed without affecting the date for completion are said to be on the critical path. The line, or path, through those activities is the critical path to completion and is usually generated by modern software.

This is shown in Figure 6.5 for the garage construction project, with the activities on the critical path shown.

The activities which are not on the critical path will have 'float'. This is usually shown as the difference between the earliest and latest start dates. There are various types of float, all of which are an expression of the relationship of an activity to other activities and milestones. The term float used here represents the period by which an activity on a programme may be delayed before the programme shows an effect on the date for completion. The activities with the least float are on the critical path to completion.

The emphasis on the programme is important because float is a function of the model represented by the programme, but may not accurately represent the consequences of starting an activity later than it could have been started. The construction logic on many programmes is kept simple in order to produce a workable programme so that management decisions can be taken.

Two other types of programmes are 'line of balance' and 'time chainage'.

Line of balance

The main concept of the line of balance technique is the work continuity of labour gangs, which work with rhythmic production and with no wastes willingly planned into the programme. This planning method fits much more closely to modern construction philosophy.

The line of balance technique is very suitable for repetitive projects like residential buildings; however, it may be adapted for non-repetitive projects as well. Unlike a barchart, which shows the duration of a particular activity, the line of balance chart shows the rate at which the work activity or group of activities have to be undertaken to stay on programme, and it shows the relationship of one activity or group of activities to the subsequent group. More importantly, it shows that, if one group is running behind programme, it will impact on the following group.

The main advantages of this technique are its graphical presentation and the fact that it is easy to understand.

Figure 6.6 is a sample line of balance chart for a residential development of 20 houses. In the above chart, the 'x' axis is the 'time', in this

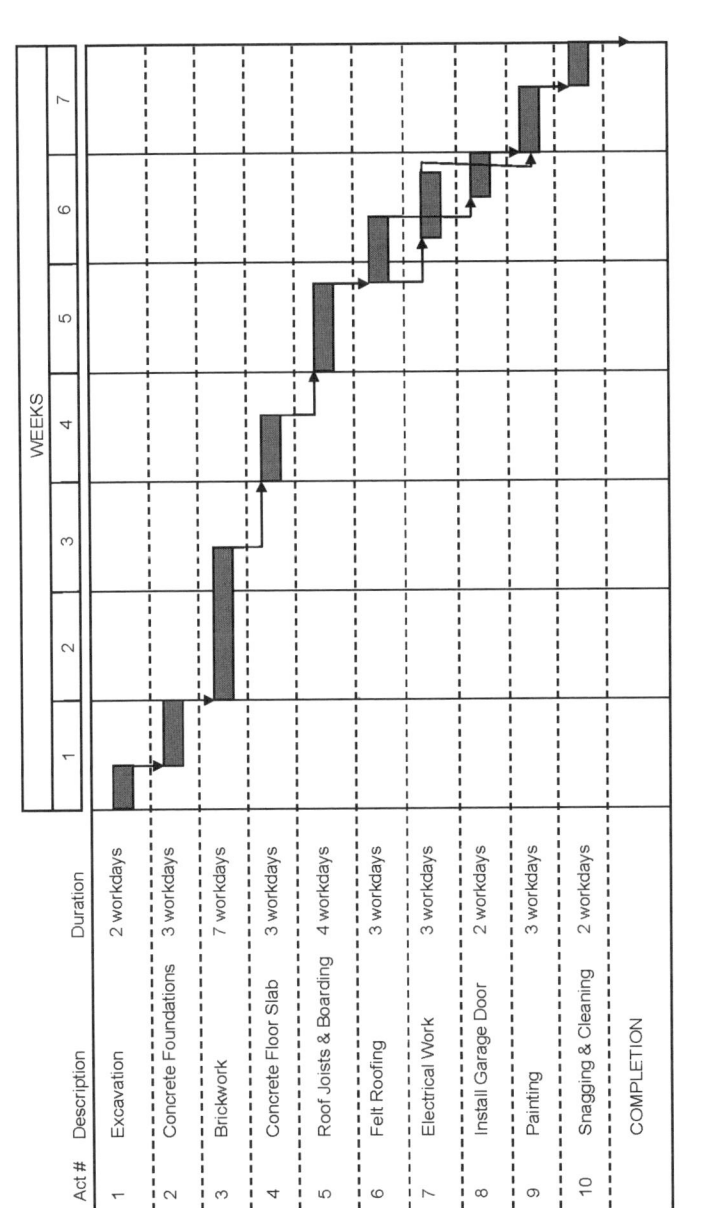

Act #	Description	Duration
1	Excavation	2 workdays
2	Concrete Foundations	3 workdays
3	Brickwork	7 workdays
4	Concrete Floor Slab	3 workdays
5	Roof Joists & Boarding	4 workdays
6	Felt Roofing	3 workdays
7	Electrical Work	3 workdays
8	Install Garage Door	2 workdays
9	Painting	3 workdays
10	Snagging & Cleaning	2 workdays
	COMPLETION	

WEEKS

1 2 3 4 5 6 7

Figure 6.4 Time-scaled logic-linked programme.

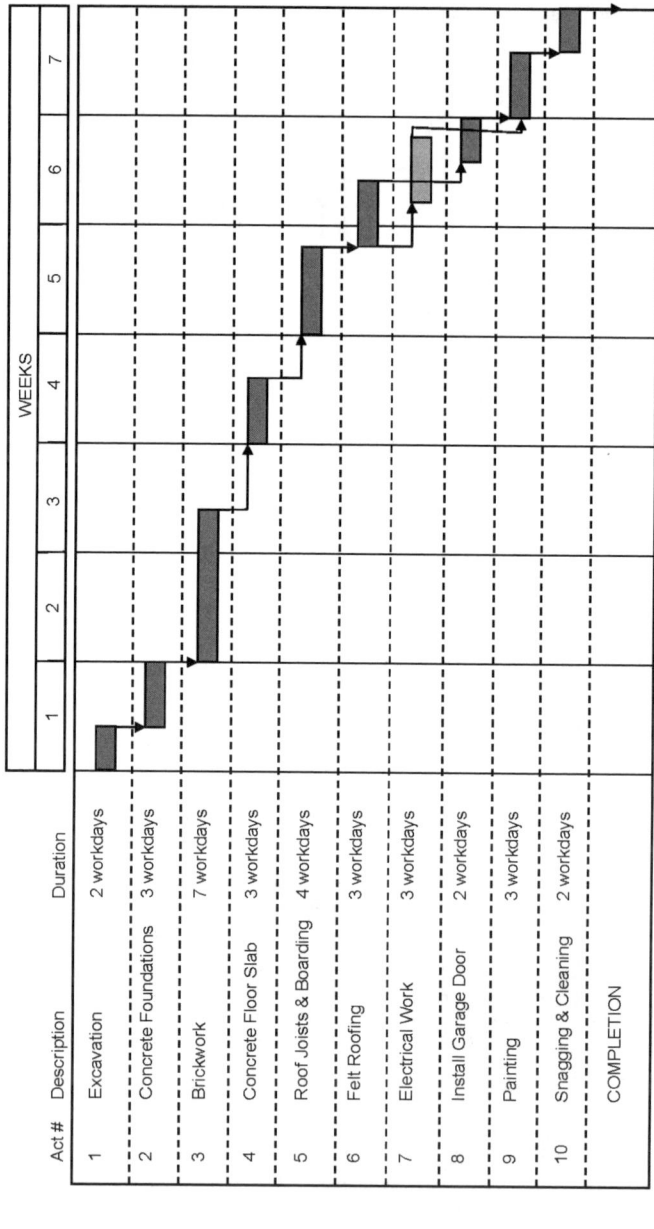

Act #	Description	Duration
1	Excavation	2 workdays
2	Concrete Foundations	3 workdays
3	Brickwork	7 workdays
4	Concrete Floor Slab	3 workdays
5	Roof Joists & Boarding	4 workdays
6	Felt Roofing	3 workdays
7	Electrical Work	3 workdays
8	Install Garage Door	2 workdays
9	Painting	3 workdays
10	Snagging & Cleaning	2 workdays
	COMPLETION	

Figure 6.5 Activities on the critical path.

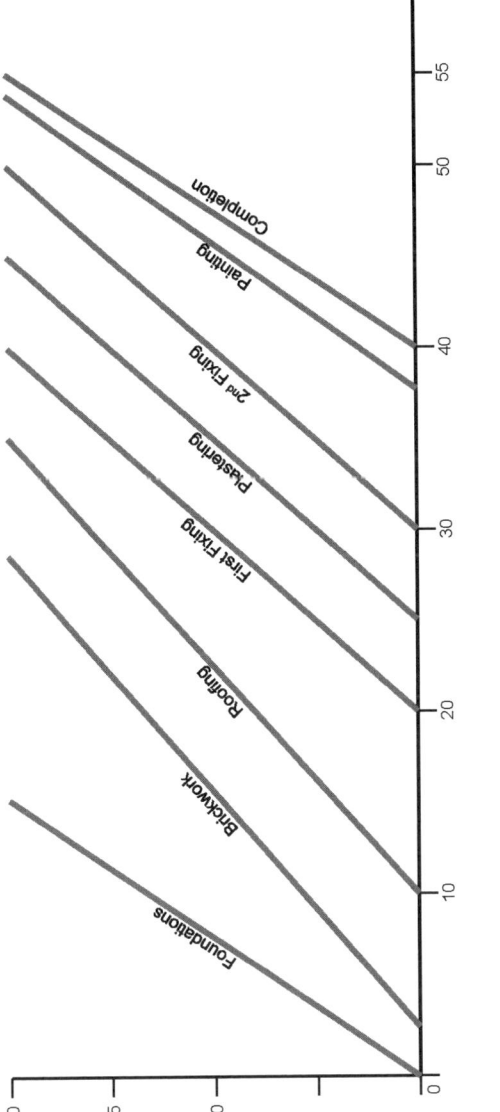

Figure 6.6 A line of balance chart.

example expressed as working weeks, while the 'y' axis is the number of houses.

Time chainage

For certain types of projects the time chainage technique can supply a clearer, more easily understood picture of the plan than the traditional barchart because it has a more graphical structure. The types of project that lend themselves to the time chainage programming technique are:

- roads;
- railways;
- pipelines;
- tunnels;
- transmission lines.

Time is displayed on the 'x' axis and distance is displayed on the 'y' axis. The chart shows the planned start and finish of a work activity against the actual location, or chainage, it is operating within the site as a diagonal line. The chart will also show fixed structures, such as bridges and culverts, as block sections for a fixed period of time (see Figure 6.7).

Levels of programmes

Planners often describe the various types of programmes/schedules that they produce as being of different levels. Each individual person or organisation would set up and use their own system for describing these various levels of programmes, with this inconsistency resulting in confusion.

It is time that the system for describing this hierarchy is standardised in order that some consistency is achieved, so that people can understand what is being referred to by, say, a level 2 programme. Therefore, the Planning Engineers Organisation recently produced a paper to set out standards of description for all planners and schedulers. The purpose was not to determine or set out what programmes/schedules should be produced by whom at which stage. Its use was to be limited to the standardisation of the terminology given to each level of programme/schedule. It is hoped that the recommendations of the Planning Engineers Organisation will be adopted by planners and schedulers as the reference standard against which, in future, programmes/schedules can be described.

The Planning Engineers Organisation has kindly given permission for this paper to be reproduced and included in this book, and it appears as Appendix 2 towards the end of the book.

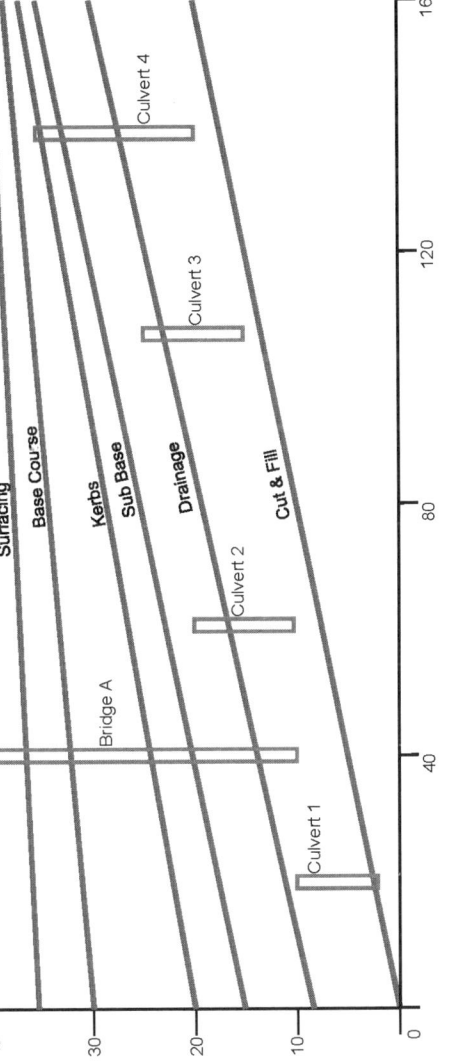

Figure 6.7 A time chainage chart.

7 The importance of a programme

Differences in opinion occur between employers and contractors on many issues. However, both will agree that completing the project as quickly as possible is a common goal, albeit for different reasons. The employer generally wants to have a project completed quickly so that the facility can be put to use as soon as possible. There are circumstances in which an employer may not want to have a project completed earlier than planned for financial or other business reasons; in such a case the employer simply wants the project delivered on time. The contractor, on the other hand, wants to complete the project as quickly as is economical because every day spent on site costs money. Furthermore, cash flow is the lifeblood of the contractor; without it he will not survive. Achieving the scheduled monthly progress helps the contractor to meet his cash flow requirements.

While employers and contractors have similar goals, they have differing needs and expectations from the schedule. Contractors will (or at least should) use the programme primarily as a planning and management tool. The process of planning and programming the project includes determining the overall approach to the job, organising and planning the labour and equipment resources, procuring subcontractors and materials.

However, as well as being used to plan and monitor project performance, a contractor's programme has another key function; that is as a reference and measurement tool for a contractor's entitlement to an extension of time and additional payment for delay and/or disruption.

The programme; as a plan for the works

First, let's look briefly at the programme's role as a plan to manage and monitor the project. Most forms of contract stipulate that the contractor has to submit a programme to the contract administrator. However, many contract forms do not stipulate that the contractor's programme is to be approved or accepted. This, in most cases, leads to distrust of the programme if it is later used by the contractor as a reference and measuring tool for additional time or compensation. It is advisable that the contract administrator should at the very least accept the programme albeit with comments. The programme should then be used by all parties to the project as the means for monitoring and measuring progress and performance.

The degree of detail, form and complexity of the detailed base programme will depend upon the size and nature of the project in question. Except for the simplest minor projects, simple barcharts are not recommended since they do not show the interrelationship between the various activities and in particular the activities' criticality; as a consequence of this it is not possible to demonstrate the effect of events upon the programme without first agreeing an underlying critical path network. In the case of a moderately simple project, it is possible to show links between the activities on a barchart. However, it is strongly recommended that, for any reasonably sized or complex project, whatever its nature, a critical path network programme should be developed from the outset; and indeed this is often a contract requirement. Such programmes are almost invariably produced using proprietary planning software and for presentation purposes, summarised barcharts can easily be produced giving a summary view of the construction sequence.

The level of detail included in a critical path network programme will to some extent depend upon the complexity of a project. In general, as much detail as is reasonably possible should be included in such a programme in order to facilitate the demonstration of the effects of subsequent events upon the programme. It is recommended that all activities in the programme should be coded preferably with a unique activity number and that all other documentation (e.g. correspondence, labour and plant allocations) should be cross-referenced to the programme activities. The actual copy of the programme issued to the other party need not show the wealth of detail underlying the base programme: it is, however, essential for that information to be available in the event of a dispute arising.

The usefulness of a programme can be enhanced by the addition of resource and cost information. This can have considerable benefits in the administration and monitoring of a project. In particular, if these principles are followed through into other documentation it becomes a much easier task to demonstrate the link between cause and effect relative to any single event.

The importance of a comprehensive 'baseline' programme cannot be over-emphasised.

Of the three most common types of construction programmes, i.e. barchart (or Gantt Chart), network, line of balance and time chainage, it is the network format that has become the most popular type for measuring the impact on a project in time-based disputes. Barcharts, although an extremely helpful, visual and graphical medium, are less effective than network programmes in examining time-based construction disputes.

The programme; in a claim situation

Now let's look at the use of the programme in a time-related claim situation. The programme is an essential document in determining the extent of any extension of time and/or compensation for delay. It is the benchmark or measuring tool in these situations. However, to be effective, the programme needs to represent an accurate prediction of future events and model the characteristics of the project with activity relationships, or logic links. This allows the criticality of activities and float cushions to be taken into account when assessing extensions of time or delays.

The roles of a programme as a reference and measuring tool for both contractors and employers in delay situations are:

1   for a *contractor's* entitlement to additional time for completion of the works or for sections of the works, in accordance with the contract;
2   for a *contractor's* entitlement to additional payment for delay and/or disruption, in accordance with the contract;
3   for a *contractor's* entitlement to additional payment for instructed acceleration, in accordance with the contract or on the terms agreed;
4   for the *employer's* right to deduct liquidated damages for the contractor's failure to complete the works on time;
5   for the *employer's* right to terminate the contractor for his failure to comply with the obligation to progress the works.

To establish items 1, 2 and 3 it is recommended that a network, or critical path analysis be carried out. The recommendations and guidelines of the Society of Construction Law's 'Delay and Disruption' Protocol are most useful for this exercise.

For item 4, the employer's right to deduct liquidated damages, it is necessary for the contract administrator to satisfy himself that the contractor is not entitled to an adjustment of the completion date, i.e. an extension of time, due to the occurrence of a relevant or delay event as described in the contract conditions. It is advisable that the contract administrator carries out a critical path analysis to satisfy this condition, otherwise an employer may receive a constructive acceleration claim from a contractor who considers himself entitled to, but did not receive, an extension of time during the project.

In the case of failure to comply with the obligation to progress the works (item 5); this is more difficult to monitor and analyse. Ideally, this requires the actual progress measured in both time and resources to be compared against the standard of progress specified in the contract. However, under most forms of contract the standard required is specified in general terms.

Programme float

A construction or engineering project consists of a series of individual activities which are detailed on a programme and executed over a period of time. If all goes well, the project will be completed on time, but if some activities are delayed will the project be finished late?

Some activities must be completed by their planned date if they are not to delay later activities and the completion of the project. These activities are said to be on the critical path. However, for other activities, the start, or completion, can be delayed to some extent without affecting later activities and completion of the project. This allowable period of delay is called 'float' and, provided that the delay does not exceed it, the project should still be completed on time.

Do all programmes have float? The short answer is yes, but float is only properly identifiable and quantifiable in a programme which is a logic network, more commonly known as a CPM (critical path method). A barchart, unless it is generated from a CPM, will not properly define the extent of float and may not even show any.

Float is an essential and inevitable part of every programme and is used by contractors in the efficient management of manpower and equipment resources. It is also vital in quantifying impact and delay in extension of time submissions and delay claims, where a contractor or subcontractor alleges a particular event caused delay and the effect of the delay may entitle them to an extension of time and ultimately a loss and expense claim.

8 Programme submission, review and acceptance

There is a clear need for a 'baseline' programme to be developed after the award of contract, reflecting the intentions of the contractor.

Contract administrators need front-line skills to review a contractor's baseline programme. Accordingly, contract administrators increasingly have to decide if, and to what extent, they are going to trust, approve or accept a contractor's programme submissions. In today's planning software paradise, CA's should be able to detect common techniques or mistakes when reviewing programmes that attempt to or increase the likelihood of extension of time awards. These techniques mean that a programme will not function as a proper predictive tool for measuring progress or quantifying the impact of delays and changes.

Contract requirements: JCT 2005

The *Joint Contracts Tribunal Standard Building Contract, with Quantities, 2005*, includes in Section 2 Clause 2.9, the following:

Construction information and Contractor's master programme

2.9 .1 *As soon as possible after the execution of this Contract, if not previously provided:*

.1 *the Architect/Contract Administrator, without charge to the Contractor, shall provide him with 2 copies of any descriptive schedules or similar documents necessary for use for carrying out the Works (excluding any CDP Works); and*

.2 *the Contractor shall without charge provide the Architect/ Contract Administrator with 2 copies of his master programme for the execution of the Works and, within 14 days of any decision by the Architect/Contract Administrator under clause 28.1 or of any agreement of any Pre-agreed Adjustment, with 2 copies of an amendment or revision of that programme to take account of that decision or agreement.*

But nothing in the descriptive schedules or similar documents (or in that master programme or in any amendment or revision of it) shall impose any obligation beyond those imposed by the Contract Documents.

Commentary on the JCT 2005 requirements

JCT 2005 has a very basic requirement for submittal of the contractor's programme, the only requirement being a 'master programme for the execution of the Works'. Unlike the NEC3 contract, there are no requirements on the content of the programme and supporting information.

Contract requirements: NEC3

The Engineering and Construction Contract, 'NEC3', includes in core clause 3, 'Time', the following clauses:

The programme 31

31.1   *If a programme is not identified in the Contract Data, the Contractor submits a first programme to the Project Manager for acceptance within the period stated in the Contract Data.*

31.2   *The Contractor shows on each programme he submits for acceptance*
- *the starting date, access dates, Key Dates and Completion Date,*
- *planned Completion,*
- *the order and timing of the operations which the Contractor plans to do in order to Provide the Works,*
- *the order and timing of the work of the Employer and Others as last agreed with them by the Contractor or, if not so agreed, as stated in the Works Information,*
- *the dates when the Contractor plans to meet each Condition stated for the Key Dates and to complete other work needed to allow the Employer and Others to do their work,*
- *provisions for*
  - *float,*
  - *time risk allowances,*
  - *health and safety requirements and*
  - *the procedures set out in this contract,*
- *the dates when, in order to Provide the Works in accordance with the programme, the Contractor will need*
  - *access to a part of the Site if later than the access date,*
  - *acceptances,*
  - *Plant and Materials and other things to be provided by the Employer and*
  - *information from Others,*

- *for each operation, a statement of how the Contractor plans to do the work identifying the principal Equipment and other resources which he plans to use and*
- *other information which the Works Information requires the Contractor to show on a programme submitted for acceptance.*

The next sub-clause, 31.3, concerns acceptance of the contractor's programme by the project manager, while clause 32 is titled 'Revising the programme'. Both clause 31.3 and 32 are referred to in chapter 9 of this book.

Commentary on the NEC3 requirements

The NEC3 contract recognises that the programme is an important tool for use by both the contractor and project manager. The programme is valuable not only as a scheduling tool but also as a project management and change control tool.

NEC3 has distinctive features on the content of the contractor's programme. Indeed, the programme is the contractor's programme and he owns the terminal float. The programme is not only used to portray how the contractor intends to carry out the works, but can also be used for forensic analysis to determine the effect of compensation events for both time and money.

One of the key features of the programme under NEC3 is that upon its acceptance the contractor's programme becomes the 'accepted programme'. Any subsequent programmes submitted by the contractor and accepted by the project manager in turn become the 'accepted programme', superseding the previous programme.

With regard to the required content of the contractor's programme, here are some matters to be aware of:

1 *'planned Completion'* is the date when the contractor plans to complete the works. The requirement is to show on the submitted programme both the 'planned Completion' and the 'Completion Date'. At the start of the contract the contractor's 'planned Completion' may be a date earlier than the contractual 'Completion Date'.

2 *'the order and timing of the operations which the Contractor plans to do in order to Provide the Works'.* This should be clear from the programme, i.e. network logic and listing of activities with start and finish dates. However, incompatibility in this document and with other contractor documents is sufficient reason for the project manager not to accept a programme. The requested information will also facilitate the assessment of compensation events. This item can also include off-site manufacturing of components such as bathroom pods and the like. It is advisable that the procurement chain of these items, e.g. design, approvals, manufacture, etc., be included.

3 *'a statement of how the Contractor intends to do the work'*. In effect this is a resource statement, a list of resources that are intended to be used for each activity. Clearly this list will be based on the scope of the work at the time of submittal of the programme. The resource statement will also facilitate the assessment of compensation events.

4 *'the order and timing of the work of the Employer and Other'*. The employer and project manager need to ensure that any constraints on how the contractor is to 'provide the works' are stated in the 'works information'. The contractor needs to show these constraints in his planning and programme submittal. To introduce constraints at a later date, after commencement of the works, would be a change to the 'works information' and probably a compensation event.

5 *'provisions for float'*. This is an important aspect of NEC3, in that it recognises float in a programme. There are three types of float that should be addressed here:

 i *terminal float, which is the period of time between the planned Completion and the Completion Date;*

 ii *total float, the amount of time a programme activity can be delayed without affecting the planned Completion and reducing the terminal float;*

 iii *free float, the amount of time a programme activity can be delayed before affecting a successor programme activity and thereby possibly reducing the total float.*

6 *'provisions for time risk allowances'*. Another important aspect of NEC3, an example is the amount of down-time allowed for an earthworks activity being carried out during winter. Time risk allowances are owned by the contractor and will be included in the accepted programme.

7 *'acceptances'*. An example here is where the contractor is designing part of the works. If so, he should show on his programme the date(s) by which he requires acceptance of his design.

8 *'Plant and Materials and other things to be provided by the Employer'*. The contractor's programme should show the dates by which he requires plant and materials supplied by the employer.

What to look for in a programme review

When the programme is submitted, the CA should ask the following questions:

1 Does it comply with contractual obligations, milestones or restraints on working hours or methods?

2 Is the entire scope of the work represented?

3 Are any activity durations questionably too long, or too short for the scope of work they represent?

4   Are there any obvious errors in the programme related to the sequence or timing of the works?

5   Are any requirements of the employer's professional team too onerous, e.g. early completion programmes, unrealistic time allowances for approvals or supply of information, which constitute employer's risks?

Review of a CPM programme submittal

A very dangerous misunderstanding exists with a CPM programme submittal; many contract administrators and other professionals are still of the mistaken opinion that a CPM submittal should consist of several pages of activity listings and/or a barchart plot or two. A CPM submission for review should in fact comprise a full copy of the computer files necessary to recreate the programme; everything else is just frills.

A CPM submission, both for the baseline for review and subsequent updates, should consist of three discrete items:

1   The activity details, including description, original and remaining durations, and percentage complete. In conjunction with this, you should see, for each activity, other computed information such as early and late start and finish times, and total float.

2   The logical relationships that connect the various activities together to form a network which makes the CPM work. Full details of any lags and leads, i.e. imposed time durations between activities, is a must in the submittal.

3   Lastly and certainly not least is 'constraints'. The true logic of a network can be overridden by the programme containing various time constraints on an activity or activities. These will artificially reduce total float and could create an invisible delay, or even lead to the activity just expanding to take all the available time. This will never show up on a barchart plot and is only found in a 'constraint' listing and/or a copy of the computer files.

Having been satisfied that the information in the contractor's submittal is sufficient for a proper review, here are five basic checks or tests that should be carried out using the computer files provided by the contractor:

Test 1: Does the 'longest path' filter identify a reasonable critical path for the project?

Make sure the longest path is reasonable, and then check the reasonableness of near critical paths.

Test 2: Are there any open-ended activities in the programme?

In general, there should be only two open-ended activities in the entire network: one beginning activity with no predecessors, and one completion activity with no successors. Every other activity should be logically tied into the network. Furthermore, every activity should have its finish constrained with at least one FS (finish-to-start) or FF (finish-to-finish) successor relationship to another activity. Likewise, every activity should have at least one SS (start-to-start) or FS (finish-to-start) predecessor relationship to another activity.

Test 3: Do any of the activities have too much float?

Activities with too much float may indicate missing logic links, or logic links that have been overridden in a subsequent progress update. Identify any such activities.

Test 4: Are there any unnecessarily long gaps in workflow when grouping activities by work area and sorting by early start dates?

In most cases once work begins in a particular area or phase of the project then the programme should allow work to continue uninterrupted in that area or phase. Long calendar gaps in a work area or phase may indicate less than ideal workflow and suggest an adjustment of preferential logic links to create a better plan.

Test 5: Are there activities with unnecessary contractor-assigned constraints?

As constraints override the network logic in calculating activity start/finish dates and total float they should be used sparingly, if at all. A better approach is to use activity durations and network logic to model the project, and thereby eliminate constraints.

Acceptance of the programme

If the contract administrator fails to comment, it may be implied as acceptance that the contractor's programme is contract-compliant/satisfactory. When 'accepting' a programme, the contract administrator could be merely acknowledging receipt of the contractor's intentions. In 'approving' the programme, the contract administrator is more often seen to have performed some level of due diligence on the programme, such as asking the questions above, and is therefore acknowledging that the submission complies with the terms of the contract. However, it is important that a realistic baseline is established for the management of the works and the assessment of potential and actual effects of changes, unforeseen events or other circumstances that could delay the works.

Programmes are key documents in extension of time and delay claims disputes; therefore their significance in potential dispute resolution forums cannot be underestimated. At the same time, the perspective must be maintained that the programme is a management tool to assist in managing the work. A balance should be struck between keeping the contractor on an accurate progress path and the emphasis on the programme as a claims document. If approval is granted, this should not in any way relieve the contractor from complying with the contract, or in any way increase the employer's liability.

9 Programme updates and revisions

Notwithstanding the acceptance and popularity of detailed programmes, progress updates and their analyses in the dispute resolution arena, they are not held in the same esteem by many of the personnel on the project actually executing the work.

Criticisms that one hears on a construction project regarding programmes are either founded on the detailed use of the tool or the very output. Some typical criticisms of programmes and progress updates by site-based personnel include:

- programme activities and CPM network is too detailed or too condensed;
- no feedback/dialogue between planner and site;
- programme difficult for users to read or understand;
- activity durations haphazard and often changed in subsequent progress updates without rationale;
- programme updated schedules out of date by the time issued.

Contract requirements: JCT 2005

The *Joint Contracts Tribunal Standard Building Contract, with Quantities, 2005*, contains no specific requirements for programme revisions, other than the following reference in Section 2 Clause 2.9:

2.9 *.1.2 the Contractor shall without charge provide the Architect/Contract Administrator with 2 copies of his master programme for the execution of the Works and, within 14 days of any decision by the Architect/Contract Administrator under clause 2.28.1 or of any agreement of any Pre-agreed Adjustment, with 2 copies of an amendment or revision of that programme to take account of that decision or agreement.*

Commentary on the JCT 2005 requirements

JCT 2005 only has a reference in clause 2.9, stipulating that the contractor submit a revised programme after a clause 2.28.1 decision or agreement of a 'Pre-agreed Adjustment'. Clause 2.28 is titled 'Fixing Completion Date', and sub-clause .1 concerns the granting of an extension of time for a delay caused by a relevant event which is likely to cause delay in completion of the works or a section.

Contract requirements: NEC3

The Engineering and Construction Contract 'NEC3', includes in core clause 3, 'Time', the clauses concerning the content, submission and acceptance of the contractor's programme. Sub-clauses 31.1 and .2 refer to the submission and content of the programme, while sub-clause 31.3 concerns approval of the programme as follows:

The programme 31

31.3   *Within two weeks of the Contractor submitting a programme to him for acceptance, the Project Manager either accepts the programme or notifies the Contractor of his reasons for not accepting it. A reason for not accepting a programme is that*
- *the Contractor's plans which it shows are not practicable,*
- *it does not show the information which this contract requires,*
- *it does not represent the Contractor's plans realistically or*
- *it does not comply with the Works Information.*

Clause 32 concerns revising the programme, and reads as follows:

Revising the programme 32

32.1   *The Contractor shows on each revised programme*
- *the actual progress achieved on each operation and its effect upon the timing of the remaining work,*
- *the effects of implemented compensation events,*
- *how the Contractor plans to deal with any delays and to correct notified Defects and*
- *any other changes which the Contractor proposes to make to the Accepted Programme.*
32.2   *The Contractor submits a revised programme to the Project Manager for acceptance*
- *within the period for reply after the Project Manager has instructed him to,*
- *when the Contractor chooses to, and in any case,*
- *at no longer interval than the interval stated in the Contract Data from the starting date until Completion of the whole of the works.*

Commentary on the NEC3 requirements

The contractor submits his programme and upon acceptance of the programme by the project manager it becomes the accepted programme. Subsequent programme submissions by the contractor become the accepted programme when accepted by the project manager.

The first programme is submitted with the tender or within a stipulated time, e.g. four weeks, after contract award. If the contractor does not submit his first programme within the time required, the project manager retains 25 per cent of the value of the work done to date by the contractor until the first programme is submitted. This emphasises the importance placed on the programme by NEC3.

The contract gives only four reasons for which the project manager can refuse acceptance of the contractor's programme:

1 *'the Contractor's plans which it shows are not practicable'*. This refers to the contractor's plans alone. As an example, the contractor's original plan and programme for plasterwork shows an output of 100 sq.m. per gang per day, and his subsequent programme and plan shows 180 sq.m. per gang per day; while his actual production is currently showing 70 sq.m. per gang per day. His plans are therefore not realistic or *practicable*.

2 *'it does not show the information which this contract requires'*. This reason refers to the contract, and it should be remembered that this also includes the works information and whatever else has been incorporated into the contract. An example of this condition not being fulfilled is where the contractor's programme does not show key dates or access dates.

3 *'it does not represent the Contractor's plans realistically'*. For example, the contractor's programme is based on bored piles being used, whereas the project manager knows that driven piles have been procured by the contractor to be used.

4 *'it does not comply with the Works Information'*. An example may be that the contractor's programme has not taken into account a design constraint as shown on the works information.

If the project manager does not accept the programme then the contractor is obliged to resubmit the programme within the period allowed for reply.

The contract gives the following reasons for which the contractor is to submit a revised programme to the project manager for acceptance:

1 *'within the period for reply after the Project Manager has instructed him to'*. If the project manager instructs the contractor to provide a revised programme for his acceptance then the contractor must do so.

2 *'when the Contractor chooses to'*. The contractor may choose to

submit a revised programme to the project manager for acceptance. An example of this may be after deciding to change the sequence or method of working as stated on his then current accepted programme.

3   *'at no longer interval than the interval stated in the Contract Data from the starting date until Completion of the whole of the works'*. The contract data state the time period within which the programme has to be revised by the contractor. This may be every four weeks, two months or even longer, and is usually dependent on the complexity and overall duration of the project.

However, there is a fourth reason for a contractor to submit a revised programme for acceptance, namely,

> *'if a compensation event has affected the Accepted Programme'*. The contractual procedure is that where a compensation event has, or will have, the effect of changing the accepted programme, then the contractor has to submit a revised programme with his quotation for the compensation event, showing the effect of the event on the planned completion and completion date. However, if the contractor does not submit a revised programme with his compensation event quotation, then the project manager will make his own assessment of the effect on the accepted programme of the said event. It is suggested that upon a compensation event being implemented, then the contractor should submit a revised programme, based on the assessment of the event, to the project manager for acceptance as the accepted programme.

Progress updating

Lack of a formal progress updating procedure can cause failure because, without it, problems and delays may not be recognised until too late.

Even a 'perfect' programme becomes outdated unless it is updated on a regular basis. On most projects, programmes are updated monthly, but it is not uncommon to update weekly or even daily.

Some of the most significant purposes to update a project programme are to:

- record progress;
- provide a plan for remaining work to be completed;
- provide a forecast for completion of the project and contract milestones;
- provide progress status for the project team;
- comply with contract requirements.

Maintaining accurate project records through a project control system is an important aspect of updating the programme. Information for the 'update' can come from recording progress data while walking the job-site, site diaries and the like kept by project supervisory staff, and status reports from subcontractors.

An important part of a progress update submission is a narrative. As well as saying what delayed progress during the reporting period, a good narrative should also explain any revisions that have been made to the programme. If a contractor states the revisions contemporaneously then the contract administrator cannot complain at a later date that he was not aware of changes to the contractor's plan.

From a contract administrator's perspective, it is important to obtain a copy of the updated planning software files on disk. Important because, not only are you saving a tree, but how do you know the contractor hasn't made a mistake and accidentally forgot to include in the 'paper' reports some of the critical or embarrassing activities? Or, for that matter, are you really going to spot a change in a logic link to an activity in a paper report? If you were an auditor, would you accept handwritten summaries of the month's transactions or would you want to see the real books?

Programme revisions

Regular revisions of a programme are important because the initial baseline programme is merely a plan with regards to what needs to be accomplished in order to achieve completion of the project on time. How the project actually reaches completion will most likely vary greatly from the original baseline programme, which is why regular programme revisions are crucial.

A revised programme not only records progress at the time of the revision, but should also review and introduce, if necessary, activity logic revisions to reflect current intent. These logic revisions may result in changes to the original baseline critical path.

Detailed review of a progress update or revised programme

A progress update or revised programme submission for review should consist of a full copy of the computer files necessary to recreate the programme, and not just the paper printouts and listings.

In addition to the five basic tests for a programme submittal listed in chapter 8, the following checks should also be carried out on a progress update or revised programme submittal:

Check 1: *System checks*. Most of the recognised planning software packages allow the user to determine the CPM calculation rules. For example, total float in Primavera software can be set to be computed using one of three different formulae; and mismatched dual-activity predecessor links can automatically stretch out activity durations and the project completion date.

Check 2: *Activity checks*. This involves four sub-checks,

i Missing 'status' information. Most planning software packages allow you to status an activity without supplying actual start and finish dates. While the lack of actual dates will not affect the progress update calculations as long as the percentage progress achieved is correctly recorded against the activity, actual start and finish dates provide a good record of work already accomplished.

ii Deleted activities. In progress update submissions, activities that are finished should not be deleted as they form a record of when the work was achieved. However, in a revised programme submission it is acceptable that the programme include only works, and their detailed programme activities, still to be carried out on the project.

One last word on deleted activities. You should never re-use the activity ID from the deleted activity as an activity ID for a new, added activity. This not only confuses the 'checker' software, it makes statistic keeping and forensic investigation of the project very difficult. When you delete activities, also retire the activity ID.

iii Added activities. Adding activities is to be encouraged if done in a way to communicate the change in the work plan. It does no good for the contract administrator or employer to insist on 'sticking to the baseline programme', i.e. updating or statusing the activities as they are completed even though the work is no longer being pack-aged in the manner that was originally planned.

Very little useful information can be obtained from actual start and finish dates if the activity did not describe the way the work was accomplished. Activities by their nature imply that work was being pursued continuously. If the work no longer proceeds in the manner envisioned, the starts and stops of work within an ill-defined work activity will make that activity no more informative than a hammock activity.

iv Modified activities. If an activity was neither deleted nor added, it still may have been modified. It is not 'wrong' that activities are modified. After all, the employer expects progress to be made and that involves modification of activities. The key for the reviewer of the programme is to note those modifications to activities that are other than expected progress. After spotting these types of modifi-cations, the next step is to analyse the modifications.

Check 3: *Actual dates*. Any modification to an existing actual date should be accompanied by an explanation for the change. The obvious reason for this is that there should be only one 'correct' date. The con-tractor earlier reported that the first actual date was correct. Now he or she is revising that certification. Or are they?

If you fail to unambiguously affirm which is the 'correct' date, the original one or the new one, then in the event of a delay or extension of time submission, the contractor can claim that either of the dates is the correct one. Was the first date correct and a new one inadvertently changed? In other words, which of the two dates works best in the contractor's favour?

In addition to modified actual dates, you should also look for newly added actual dates that do not fall within the update period. You should not accept new dates that just happen to fall in the future. You would think that the planning software programme would prevent this from occurring, but it occurs surprisingly often. Much more subtle are newly added actual dates that fall before the start of the last progress update period. The previously reviewed progress update showed this activity as incomplete. Now you are looking at a progress update that says that you reviewed the wrong programme the previous time. Has the critical path for previous progress update moved?

Check 4: *Network logic and activity links.*

i   Where the predecessor and successor activities still exist in both the current update and previous progress update but the activity link is new, it is assumed that the contractor intended to add this relationship. These will have to be reviewed and traced individually.

ii   Similarly, for deleted logic links, where the predecessor and successor activities still exist in both the current update and previous progress update, it is assumed that the contractor intended to delete this relationship. These will have to be reviewed and traced individually.

iii   Modified logic links: for extensively modified activity links, the ramifications of changing an existing logic relationship from one type to another type is very difficult to predict without looking at each change on a case-by-case basis.

Where activity link 'lags' have been modified, this usually results in the programme being 'stretched' or 'shortened' in a way that is very difficult to notice. This is especially true if a lot of small changes have been made to several activity link 'lags'. Many small changes can add up to one large change. You will only note this trend if you list all of these changes together in one list.

Check 5: *Activity constraints.* These are invisible on a plotted network, and unless you check the activity database you will not see them at all. They are very powerful and override the logic of the CPM network. Quite simply put, one constraint can completely revise an entire CRM programme.

Constraints are usually start or finish dates imposed on an activity such as 'start no earlier than' or 'start no later than'. These are more acceptable than other date constraints such as 'mandatory start'.

A careful check has to be made of the data associated with each activity to identify the constraints and a more detailed review carried out to identify their purpose.

Remember, good programme reviews don't just happen, they take a lot of work.

10 Progress records and other record keeping

Comparing the health of the project to that of a vehicle reveals some striking similarities. People who neglect the routine maintenance of a vehicle typically experience premature breakdowns and exorbitant repair costs that could be traced directly back to that neglect. Similarly, if a contractor fails to carry out routine maintenance on a project, instead taking the easy approach of updating schedules, the outcome is very likely to be an expensive 'repair' in the form of a claims battle and often a claims loss, or even missed opportunities.

Most construction professionals do not enjoy reporting progress. This task rivals in unpopularity the other bane of keeping minutes of meetings. The fact that the progress-reporting duty is taken on not with relish, but usually because no-one else will touch it with a barge pole, is evident in the tosh that often passes for the monthly client progress report.

These reports concern more than just progress, of course. The usual sections are there – safety, risk, commercial, etc. – but this chapter concerns the programme/progress section. Quite often the programme and/or progress sections fall into one of two approaches:

1 The 'I'm going to prove to everyone, especially my boss, how clever I am, with lots of technical jargon and long words' approach; or
2 The 'Let's take last month's report and just change the figures' approach.

The first approach will be almost impenetrable and unfathomable to anyone reading it, including the boss. The second approach is plain boring and is effectively saying to the client that you can't be bothered and that the monthly report is unimportant.

On most projects, the client is looking for simplicity in the monthly report, and he is primarily interested in one key thing: when will the project be complete. The information in the programme/progress section of the report to the client should be easy to understand and well annotated/explained.

The format of progress reporting should be agreed with the client at the outset of the project. The programme, which will normally be maintained as a critical path network in proprietary planning software, should be capable of being summarised to level 1 barchart format.

The most readily understood graphic is that of the 'staggered-line'. Graphics of the original baseline programme and the current revised or working programme should have a vertical line showing the progress cut-off date. Progress may be indicated either by colouring along the bar or by the vertical line diverting to the actual progress position for each bar. This is a very simplistic 'progress indicator' chart. See the example in Figure 10.1.

Unfortunately, the client is generally left to interpret the chart for himself, and often he will not have the information to do this meaningfully and may easily jump to the wrong conclusion. Therefore, both the chart and the accompanying narrative should contain an explanation of why activities are shown in delay, what the implications are for completion of the project, and how you intend to redress the situation and by when.

The simple 'progress indicator' chart and an accompanying narrative may be enough for many projects, but each project is unique and many will necessitate auxiliary methods, which may even be required under the contract. Details of three such methods are given below.

The first of these is the 'planned progress' chart. This addresses the volume of work, and simply measures the volume of progress in terms of activity weeks, giving no allowance for weighting of activities. Planned progress can be shown in terms of a cumulative S-curve of activity weeks achieved if the early dates are met. Another curve can be generated from the late dates. When plotted on the same chart, the area between the curves represents the zone within which the actual achievement line should lie. See the example in Figure 10.2.

Figures are calculated after each progress update and the actual line plotted. The closer this line is to the early (lefthand) line, then the more comfortable all parties should feel. A drift towards the late (righthand) line means that float is being used up and more activities are becoming critical.

Even though there is no weighting factor, the fact that every programme activity is taken into account means that the law of averages comes into play, and the outcome is virtually identical to one where complex weightings based on earned value or work content have been laboriously applied.

A second method is the 'Progress Tracking' chart. This is a simple but effective way of showing progress in terms of quantity or value of work done at any point. It is basically two charts in one. The 'x' axis is a common time scale. The lefthand 'y' axis shows unit per time unit (week or month) shown in histogram form; whereas the righthand side relates to the cumulative figure and is shown as a simple line. The actual performance is input on a regular basis and compared to the plan. See the example in Figure 10.3.

Because this method relies on the work being measured in the same units throughout, this approach is well suited for package works or

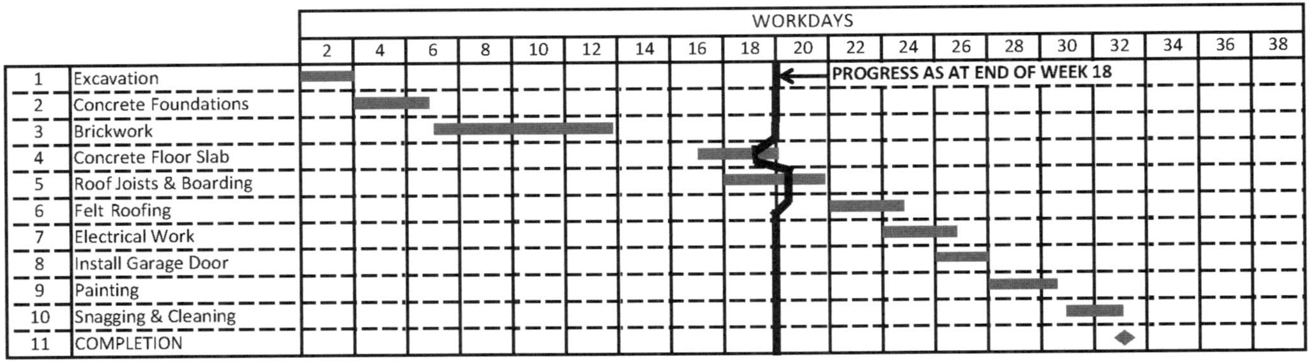

Figure 10.1 A progress indicator chart.

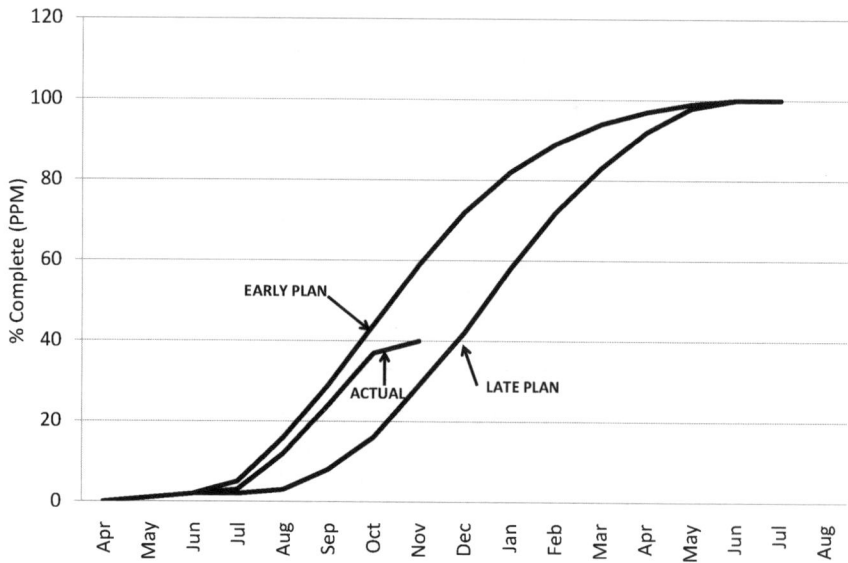

Figure 10.2 A planned progress chart.

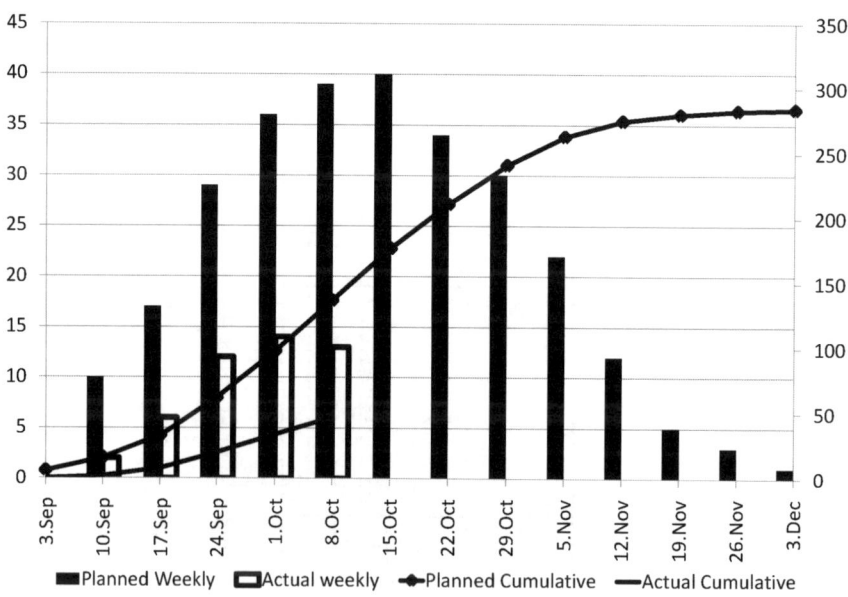

Figure 10.3 A progress tracking chart.

individual operations or trades. It would usually be introduced to show close control of a particular critical or near-critical activity. As the planned figures are likely to be based on early dates, it is important to stress that the plan is target-based and that moderate slippage does not necessarily mean that the programme has been compromised.

The third method is a 'line of balance' chart. This approach comprises a series of cumulative line graphs set against a common time scale. This approach is somewhat specialist in nature and is ideal for situations of repetition, such as housing and high-rise. See the example in Figure 10.4.

The angle of each line represents the rate of output, and the gap between the lines shows the working float between operations or trades. In a situation where the lines represent recorded progress on site, it is easy to see who is delaying whom. This method also allows simple 'what-if' scenarios to be explored.

A further method of recording progress which should be encouraged is that of colouring in drawings as work proceeds. However, the colouring in of drawings is not particularly useful in comparing progress to a plan. But it is an accessible way of showing how the site is proceeding and should not be dismissed on the grounds of crudity. Often it is exactly what is needed to convey a sense of momentum; and this method of recording progress is particularly useful in a claim situation.

However, for progress reports, this method should only cover one or two activities at a time, and one should avoid confusing the message

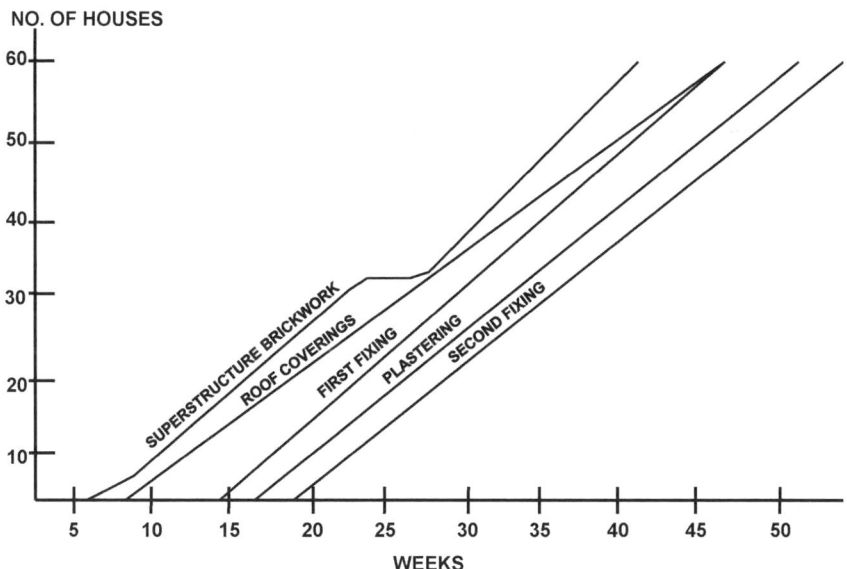

Figure 10.4 A line of balance chart.

through overkill. Types of activities that are particularly suited to this method include piling, pipe caps, slabs, roof coverings and ceilings.

To summarise, simplicity is the watchword. First, the contractor should state when the project is forecast to be complete. Second, give the client a programme with a staggered line and explain the main features; including what is to be done to recoup lost time. Finally, use any of the auxiliary methods, as appropriate, to focus on critical areas or to get key points across.

Progress reporting should not be a complicated progress. Clients do not scrutinise boring or complicated documents to find the hidden message. It is in everyone's interest to present information in as simple a format as possible. The client will never complain of condescension if the message is clear and, if he wants something a little more sophisticated, he will ask for it.

It may be necessary in claim situations to develop a daily, specific, as-built programme to justify a delay claim. An as-built record of the accepted project programme will usually only record the actual start and finish dates for each activity. However, to support a delay and/or disruption claim, it is beneficial to identify and record multiple starts and stops of affected activities.

Site diaries maintained by job-site supervisory staff are important source documents used to develop a daily, specific, as-built programme. The site diaries should record the following information on a daily basis:

- weather;
- manpower by number, trade and subcontractor;
- specific work performed, with reference to the corresponding programme activity number;
- delays/interruptions/issues encountered;
- work stoppages;
- variation, or change in the order work performed;
- repair or rework performed;
- RFIs (requests for information) submitted;
- CVIs (confirmation of verbal instructions) received.

A quality as-built programme can be generated from well-kept site diaries. The as-built data can be maintained in an electronic database, and nowadays can be collected using handheld devices during job-site walkthroughs. Photographs are also a very helpful way of documenting site progress. However, to be useful they should be labelled with the date of the photo and specific description of the subject.

Records in a claim situation

Obtaining a correct extension of time and time-related costs is all to do with the strength of a case, and whether it can be proved with factual records. It is a truism to say that there is no substitute for good record keeping.

For example, can you prove that an entitlement to an extension of time resulted from information being received late? The key element in most cases lies in the contemporaneous project records. Success in a claim is all about keeping them; and then using them to demonstrate cause, effect and entitlement.

First, let's deal with the programme; for if you don't keep details of what was built and when, then there is very little chance of proving cause and effect. Earlier chapters in this section explain the importance of planning and programming.

Now let's consider the contemporaneous project records, and particularly those that relate to the work activities on the programme. Frequently, these records are just a list of percentages for the programme activities as at the date of the site meeting.

Ideally, for each activity the following progress information should be maintained on a fortnightly or monthly basis as a minimum:

1   In addition to recording the percentage of work achieved, record the actual start and finish dates, together with any periods of inactivity or stoppages.
2   Where possible, subdivide the programme activity into smaller elements, e.g. for brickwork and blockwork subdivide into elevations; for suspended ceilings subdivide into floor areas or groups of rooms.
3   Maintain allocation sheets of who did what, where and when.
4   The weather conditions.
5   Any problems encountered together with any steps taken to overcome them including resources used.

In addition all operational supervisory staff should keep meaningful site diaries, supplemented with photographs as these often prove very useful later if a dispute materialises. Photographs must be properly identified and the following information should be recorded on the reverse:

1   the date and time taken;
2   position from where the photograph was taken;
3   full details of the subject matter;
4   a reference number for the photograph;
5   name of the photographer.

Disruption and loss of productivity are difficult to prove as generally very little contemporaneous data are available from site showing the levels of productivity attained before and after the disruptive event. Any data kept that can establish disruption and productivity loss, particularly in respect of subcontractors who carry out the majority of the work, will be invaluable.

Part III
Contracts and case law

11 Introduction

This section of the book deals with two subjects, namely, 'contracts' and 'case law'. Chapter 12 concerns the two most popular forms of contract used in the UK, which are the JCT and NEC. The chapter reviews the clauses relating to time issues, while those clauses dealing with programmes are reviewed in chapters 8 and 9 of this book.

The remaining four chapters in this section review case law regarding disputes and judgments concerning extensions of time and delay claims.

Contracts

All of the standard forms of contract, and subcontract, include clauses for dealing with delays to the project. Most of these standard forms require the contract administrator (architect or engineer) to deal with a contractor's claim for extension of time when actual delay has occurred to the works or when a likely delay is notified.

For example, JCT 2005 contains the following in clause 2.27:

> *If and whenever it becomes reasonably apparent that the progress of the Works or any Section is being or is likely to be delayed the Contractor shall forthwith give written notice to the Architect/Contract Administrator of the material circumstances, including the cause or causes of delay, and shall identify in the notice any event which in his opinion is a Relevant Event.*

The underlying objective is for extension of time applications to be dealt with as close as possible to the occurrence of events giving rise to the delay. In this way the contractor will be working towards a realistic completion date.

If extensions of time are largely ignored until the completion stages of the project, the contractor may have been forced to plan the works against an unrealistic early completion date. This may give rise to unnecessary acceleration claims.

Furthermore, in the latter stages or post-handover of a project, delay events can be assessed with the benefit of hindsight. In this type of scenario, a 'retrospective analysis' method is likely to be adopted. The analysis results may show that an employer-responsible event that was likely to cause delay according to the evidence that was available at the time when it 'it becomes reasonably apparent', with hindsight did not in fact delay the completion of the project. In such circumstances, a contractor will argue that according to the contract he was entitled to an extension of time at the 'time' of the event. However, as there was no actual delay, he probably has no claim for prolongation costs or loss and expense resulting from the event. On the other hand, the employer will contend that, as no actual delay occurred, there is no entitlement to an extension of time; and an analysis at the 'time' of the event can be construed as an overly theoretical prediction of delay.

In such circumstances there is no 'one-size-fits-all' solution. Many factors have to be taken into account, not least:

1   the contract and wording of the extension of time clause;
2   the facts appertaining at the 'time' of the event;
3   if the parties were aware of a 'likely' delay at the time, and if the contractor provided necessary particulars of the event;
4   the circumstances that resulted in a likely delay becoming no actual delay.

Case law

The four chapters covering 'case law' review 15 disputes that were referred to the Court, initially the Official Referee's Court and now the Technology and Construction Court.

The disputes selected are considered to be the most important concerning extensions of time and delays, primarily due to the Court's comments and advice on the approach and methodology used.

The cases include the 'landmark' ones, such as *Fairweather, Glenlion, McAlpine Humberoak, Chestermount, John Barker, Ascon, Malmaison, Royal Brompton, Balfour Beatty, Skanska* and *Great Eastern Hotel.*

For each dispute, details are given of (i) the project concerned; (ii) the dispute itself; (iii) the judgment; and finally (iv) a commentary on the important comments and advice given by the Court.

The delay analysis subjects that are covered by the judgments included in this section are:

1   Extensions of time awarded retrospectively: *Amalgamated Contractors, Balfour Beatty (v. Chestermount).*
2   Time at large: *Peak Construction, Balfour Beatty (v. Chestermount).*
3   Inclement weather: *Walter Lawrence.*
4   Dominant cause of delay: *Fairweather.*

5 Programmed early completion: *Glenlion.*
6 Presentation and methodology of delay analysis: *McAlpine Humberoak, John Barker, Royal Brompton, Skanska, Great Eastern Hotel.*
7 Programme float: *Ascon, Royal Brompton, Motherwell Bridge, Balfour Beatty (v. LB Lambeth).*
8 Concurrency: *Henry Boot, Royal Brompton.*

12 Contracts
JCT and NEC

In 2005, the Joint Contracts Tribunal (JCT) brought out a new suite of contracts, with the Standard Building Contract replacing the 1998 version. The 2005 publication has three main versions, *Standard Building Contract with Quantities*, *Standard Building Contract with Approximate Quantities* and *Standard Building Contract without Quantities*.

The clauses relating to time issues, delays and extensions of time in JCT 2005 are similar, but not identical, to those in JCT 1998. In JCT 2005 the clauses are contained in a section titled 'Adjustment of Completion Date', which contains the following four clauses:

Clause 2.26, '*Related definitions and interpretation*';
Clause 2.27, '*Notice by Contractor of delay to progress*';
Clause 2.28, '*Fixing Completion Date*';
Clause 2.29, '*Relevant Events*'.

Clause 2.26, '*Related definitions and interpretation*', states:

.1   *Any reference to delay or extension of time includes any further delay or further extension of time.*
.2   *'Pre-agreed Adjustment' means the fixing of a revised Completion Date for the Works or a Section in respect of a Variation or other work referred to in clause 5.2.1 by the Confirmed Acceptance of a Schedule 2 Quotation;*
.3   *'Relevant Omission' means the omission of any work or obligation through an instruction for a Variation under clause 3.14 or through an instruction under clause 3.16 in regard to a Provisional Sum for defined work.*

Clause 2.27, '*Notice by Contractor of delay to progress*', states:

.1   *If and when it becomes reasonably apparent that the progress of the Works or any Section is being or is likely to be delayed the Contractor shall forthwith give written notice to the Architect/Contract Administrator of the material circumstances, including the cause or causes of the delay, and shall identify in the notice any event which in his opinion is a Relevant Event.*

.2 *In respect of each event identified in the notice the Contractor shall, if practicable in such notice or otherwise in writing as soon as possible thereafter, give particulars of its expected effects, including an estimate of any expected delay in the completion of the Works or any Section beyond the relevant Completion Date.*

.3 *The Contractor shall forthwith notify the Architect/Contract Administrator in writing of any material change in the estimated delay or in any other particulars and supply such further information as the Architect/Contract Administrator may at any time reasonably require.*

Clause 2.28, '*Fixing Completion Date*', states:

.1 *If, in the opinion of the Architect/Contract Administrator, on receiving a notice and particulars under clause 22.7:*
  .1 *any of the events which are stated to be a cause of delay is a Relevant Event; and*
  .2 *completion of the Works or of any Section is likely to be delayed thereby beyond the relevant Completion Date,*
  then, save where these Conditions expressly provide otherwise, the Architect/Contract Administrator shall give an extension of time by fixing such later date as the Completion Date for the Works or Section as he then estimates to be fair and reasonable.

.2 *Whether or not an extension is given, the Architect/Contract Administrator shall notify the Contractor in writing of his decision in respect of any notice under clause 2.27 as soon as it is reasonably practicable and in any event within 12 weeks of receipt of the required particulars. Where the period from receipt to the Completion Date is less than 12 weeks, he shall endeavour to do so prior to the Completion Date.*

.3 *The Architect/Contract Administrator shall in his decision state:*
  .1 *the extension of time that he has attributed to each Relevant Event; and*
  .2 *(in the case of a decision under clause 2.28.4 or 2.28.5) the reduction in time that he has attributed to each Relevant Omission.*

.4 *After the first fixing of a later Completion Date in respect of the Works or a Section, either under clause 2.28.1 or by a Pre-agreed Adjustment, but subject to clauses 2.28.6.3 and 2.28.6.4, the Architect/Contract Administrator may by notice in writing to the Contractor, giving the details referred to in clause 2.28.3, fix a Completion Date for the Works or that Section earlier than that previously so fixed if in his opinion the fixing of such earlier Completion Date is fair and reasonable, having regard to any Relevant Omissions for which instructions have been issued after the last occasion on which a new Completion Date was fixed for the Works or for that Section.*

.5   *After the Completion Date for the Works or for a Section, if this occurs before the date of practical completion, the Architect/Contract Administrator may, and not later than the expiry of 12 weeks after the date of practical completion shall, by notice in writing to the Contractor, giving the details referred to in clause 2.29.3:*

    .1   *fix a Completion Date for the Works or for the Section later than that previously fixed if in his opinion that is fair and reasonable having regard to any Relevant Events, whether on reviewing a previous decision or otherwise and whether or not the Relevant Event has been specifically notified by the Contractor under clause 2.27.1; or*

    .2   *subject to clauses 2.28.6.3 and 2.28.6.4, fix a Completion Date earlier than that previously fixed if in his opinion that is fair and reasonable having regard to any instructions for Relevant Events issued after the last occasion on which a new Completion Date was fixed for the Works or Section; or*

    .3   *confirm the Completion Date previously fixed.*

.6   *Provided always that:*

    .1   *the Contractor shall constantly use his best endeavours to prevent delay in the progress of the Works or any Section, however caused, and to prevent the completion of the Works or Section being delayed or further delayed beyond the relevant Completion Date.*

    .2   *in the event of any delay the Contractor shall do all that may reasonably be required to the satisfaction of the Architect/Contract Administrator to proceed with the Works or Section.*

    .3   *no decision of the Architect/Contract Administrator under clause 2.28.4 or 2.28.5.2 shall fix a Completion Date for the Works or any Section earlier than the relevant Date for Completion; and*

    .4   *no decision under clause 2.28.4 or 2.28.5.2 shall alter the length of any Pre-agreed Adjustment unless the relevant Variation or other work referred to in clause 5.2.1 is itself the subject of a Relevant Omission.*

Clause 2.29, '*Relevant Events*', states:

The following are the Relevant Events referred to in clauses 2.27 and 2.28:

.1   *Variations and any other matters or instructions which under these Conditions are to be treated as, or as requiring, a Variation;*

.2   *Instructions of the Architect/Contract Administrator:*

    .1   *under any of clauses 2.15, 3.15, 3.16 (excluding an instruction for expenditure of a Provisional Sum for defined work), 3.23 or 5.3.2; or*

    .2   *for the opening up for inspection or testing of any work, materials or goods under clause 3.17 or 3.18.4 (including making good), unless the inspection or test shows that the work, materials or goods are not in accordance with this Contract;*

.3 *deferment of the giving of possession of the site or any Section under clause 2.5;*

.4 *the execution of work for which an Approximate Quotation is not a reasonably accurate forecast of the quantity of work required;*

.5 *suspension by the Contractor under clause 4.14 of the performance of his obligations under this Contract;*

.6 *any impediment, prevention or default, whether by act or omission, by the Employer, the Architect/Contract Administrator, the Quantity Surveyor or any of the Employer's Persons, except to the extent caused or contributed to by any default, whether by act or omission, of the Contractor or any of the Contractor's Persons;*

.7 *the carrying out by a Statutory Undertaker of work in the pursuance of its statutory obligations in relation to the Works, or the failure to carry out such work;*

.8 *exceptionally adverse weather conditions;*

.9 *loss or damage occasioned by any of the Specified Perils;*

.10 *civil commotion or the use or threat of terrorism and/or the activities of the relevant authorities in dealing with such event or threat;*

.11 *strike, lock-out or local combination of workmen affecting any of the trades employed upon the Works or any of the trades engaged in the preparation, manufacture or transportation of any of the goods or materials required for the Works or any persons engaged in the preparation of the design for the Contractor's Design Portion;*

.12 *the exercise after the Base Date by the United Kingdom Government of any statutory power which directly affects the execution of the Works;*

.13 *force majeure.*

The main changes in JCT 2005 affecting EOT submissions

The main difference in the wording between the two forms is that JCT 2005 does not include any reference to 'nominated subcontractors'; and introduces two new terms, 'Pre-agreed Adjustment' and 'Relevant Omission'.

The approach taken by the 1998 and 2005 contracts is generally the same; the contractor has to notify the contract administrator of the cause or causes of delay, 'whenever it becomes reasonably apparent that the progress of the Works or any Section is being or is likely to be delayed'. The contract administrator then has 12 weeks to give an extension of time and fix a new completion date with adjustments for relevant events, which are listed in clause 2.29.

The 12-week period was introduced in the 1980 version of the JCT contracts in order to set a limit to the amount of time the contract administrator, or architect, could take for an extension of time decision. Many observers were of the opinion that one of the principal reasons for the slow take-up of the 1980 contract was that it was considered unreasonable to set a time limit on the architect's decision-making process. However, there has always existed a 'get-out' condition in that the contract administrator had only to deal with EOT submissions once 'reasonably sufficient particulars' had been received.

JCT 2005 has tightened the rules on how contractors and contract administrators must approach extensions of time. For example, the qualification that the contract administrator has to have 'reasonably sufficient information' in order to be able to make a decision has been deleted. This appears to mean that the contract administrator must make a decision even on insufficient information. However, the contract administrator needs to make his decision, and fix a new date which he considers fair and reasonable, based on the information received.

Another example is that the contractor has to give a wider picture of all the delays and the reasons for them, and the contract administrator has to respond to all of the events and say in detail why extra time is being given.

Other changes affecting extensions of time are:

1   The contractor has to give notice of a relevant event and estimate 'the expected delay in the completion of the works'. JCT 1998 went on to say 'whether or not concurrently with delay resulting from any other relevant event'. This has been omitted from JCT 2005. However, although that wording has been left out, the contractor's obligation is still to provide an estimate of the delay in relation to any relevant event, regardless of whether they are concurrent with other events.

2   The contract administrator has to 'decide' on extensions of time, rather than, as under JCT 1998, where he had to 'in writing to the contractor give an extension of time'. This change in words indicates a more active approach.

3   The contract administrator's decision has to state the extension that has been attributed to each relevant event. Previously, in JCT 1998, the decision was only obliged to state which of the relevant events had been taken into account.

4   If the contract administrator's decision is that no extension of time is due, then there is an obligation to notify the contractor of this, in writing. In JCT 1998 there appeared to be no obligation for the contract administrator to respond to the contractor if an extension of time had not been granted.

5   Clause 25.4.10 in JCT 1998; concerning the unavailability of labour and materials has been deleted from JCT 2005. As this was invariably deleted in the previous version, the omission may not make much difference.

6   Where the period of time between the particulars being received and

the completion date is less than 12 weeks, then the contract administrator has only to 'endeavour' to provide its decision prior to the completion date. Previously, in JCT 1998, the obligation was to make a decision 'if reasonably practicable'.

The New Engineering and Construction Contract, 'NEC3'

In June 2005, the third edition of the New Engineering and Construction Contract, NEC3, was published. This contract is endorsed by the Office of Government Commerce (OGC) as complying fully with the principles of the *Achieving Excellence in Construction* report, and the OGC recommends the use of NEC3 by public-sector construction procurers on their construction projects. Furthermore, in 2006 the Olympic Delivery Authority indicated that NEC3 was likely to be the contract of choice for the design and construction elements of the 2012 London Olympics projects.

Despite these auspicious endorsements, together with the NEC team's efforts to promote the use of the contract, the take-up in the industry has not been as widespread as hoped; the private sector in particular remains to be convinced. However, a point in its favour is that the NEC has been remarkably litigation-free since it was introduced.

One of the key aspects of the NEC is the early warning of matters that are likely to impede progress and cause delay, and the contract requires the parties to notify each other as soon as they become aware of any matter which could delay completion.

The NEC also takes a distinctive approach to delay by way of compensation events in that it requires ascertainment of additional time and cost in advance and the present provisions are deliberately worded to avoid uncertainty on these issues.

The notification period of compensation events is one of the most controversial changes in NEC3. Most of the other forms of contract require 'events' which are causing or likely to cause delay to be notified within a reasonable time of their becoming apparent to the contractor. Under NEC3, clause 61, the contractor must notify the project manager within eight weeks of 'becoming aware of the event' which he believes to be a compensation event 'which has happened or which he expects to happen'. Should the contractor not give notice within this period of time, he is not entitled to a change in the completion date or key dates unless the project manager should have notified the event to him but did not.

Clause 63.3 of NEC3 deals with the assessment of compensation events and stipulates the following:

> *A delay to the Completion Date is assessed as the length of time that, due to the compensation event, planned Completion is later than planned Completion shown on the Accepted Programme.*

This in effect protects a period of float built into the programme by the contractor. In other words, if the contractor plans to complete the project earlier than the completion date and this is shown in the accepted programme, then the period of time between the planned completion and the completion date is the contractor's float, or risk allowance. This period of float is sometimes called 'terminal float', though this phrase is not used specifically in NEC3. Therefore, if a compensation event assessment is a delay of, say four weeks to the planned completion then the 'terminal float' period in the accepted programme is maintained and the completion date is extended by the same four weeks.

However, a few words of warning on 'terminal float'. The fact that the contractor's programme shows a period of 'terminal float', or apparently unused time, at the end gives some doubt as to the credibility of the activity durations he has assessed for the project's scope of work.

In my view it is better to distribute the contractor's risk allowance by adding a specific activity, or activities, after a risky activity in the programme. For example, if the contractor considers that, due to the current market situation, the delivery of external façade-cladding materials may be late, then it would be more prudent to add an activity, for contractor's risk allowance, after the external façade-cladding activity.

In summation, NEC3 requires that the programme is:

- a critical path network;
- updated monthly with progress achieved;
- used in determining the actions following a compensation event.

Furthermore, the content of the contractor's programme is clearly defined in NEC3. Further details and observations on programmes, acceptance, updating and revisions can be found in chapters 8 and 9.

13 Case law
Pre-1993

The cases reviewed in this chapter are:

- *Amalgamated Contractors* v. *Waltham Holy Cross UDC* (1952);
- *Peak Construction (Liverpool) Ltd* v. *McKinney Foundation Ltd* (1970);
- *Walter Lawrence & Sons Ltd* v. *Commercial Union Properties Ltd* (1984);
- *H. Fairweather & Co. Ltd* v. *London Borough of Wandsworth* (1987);
- *Glenlion Construction Ltd* v. *The Guinness Trust* (1987);
- *McAlpine Humberoak* v. *McDermott International* (1992).

Amalgamated Contractors v. *Waltham Holy Cross UDC* (1952)

The facts

Waltham Holy Cross UDC employed Amalgamated Contractors to construct 202 houses in Princesfield, Essex. The form of contract was the Royal Institute of British Architects (RIBA)/National Federation of Building Trades Employers (NFBTE) standard. The commencement date was 7 November 1946 and completion was fixed for 7 February 1949. However, the last house was not handed over until 28 August 1950.

The contractor requested an extension of time due to difficulties in obtaining labour and materials and the architect granted an extension of time in December 1950, some four months after completion, revising the completion date to 23 May 1949. The employer deducted liquidated damages for 66 weeks, being the balance of the overrun.

The dispute

Clause 18 of the RIBA/NFBTE contract stated:

> *If in the opinion of the architect the works be delayed....*
> *(ix) by reason of labour or material not being available as required...*
> *Then in any such case the architect shall make a fair and reasonable*
> *extension of time for completion of the works.*

The contractor's argument was that the extension of time was invalid as it was issued some four months after the project was completed, whereas in their view the purpose of clause 18 was to grant extensions of time as and when a delay event occurred to enable a contractor to re-plan for a future date and organise its works accordingly.

The Court decided that the extension of time awarded by the architect was valid. The contractor, Amalgamated Contractors, appealed.

The judgment on appeal

The Court of Appeal agreed that the extension of time awarded was valid.

Lord Denning, one of the appeal judges, did not agree that an architect could not give an extension of time to a date that had passed. He noted that, in this case where a delay was continuous until the works were complete, then the architect was only in a position to grant a fair and reasonable extension of time on completion. In other words, an architect could grant an extension of time retrospectively.

Commentary

In the judgment, Lord Denning gave a hypothetical situation where a contractor was in delay for which he was responsible, which was followed by a labour strike for which he was entitled to an extension of time under the contract. In that situation, according to Lord Denning, the delay period caused by the strike should be added to the contract completion date to give a new completion date; and one that had already passed. The hypothetical situation given by Lord Denning is similar to the situation in *Balfour Beatty Building Ltd* v. *Chestermount Properties Ltd*, which came before the Court some 40 years later.

Peak Construction (Liverpool) Ltd v. *McKinney Foundation Ltd* (1970)

The facts

Peak Construction Ltd was contracted to Liverpool Corporation to construct a 14-storey block of apartments on the East Lancashire Road in

Liverpool. Under this contract McKinney Foundation Ltd was the nominated subcontractor for the design and construction of piling works. The piling works were started in May 1964 and completed within six weeks. Subsequently, in October 1964, it was discovered that some piling works were defective and all works on site were stopped until a full inspection of all piling works was carried out. However, the inspection was not carried out until May 1965; remedial works were carried out and construction works recommenced on site in November 1965. Effectively, the problem with the piling works had caused a 58-week delay to the project.

The dispute

The employer, Liverpool Corporation, deducted liquidated damages from the contractor, Peak Construction, who in turn passed this on to McKinney Foundation. McKinney disputed the deduction of liquidated damages, and the case came before the Official Referee, who upheld the deduction. McKinney took the dispute to the Court of Appeal.

The judgment on appeal

The Court of Appeal overturned the Official Referee's judgment on the basis that the 58 weeks' delay did not flow naturally and in the ordinary course of things from McKinney's breach and that the deduction of liquidated damages was 'beyond all reason'. The Court of Appeal decided that part of the 58-week delay was the fault of the employer, Liverpool Corporation, in that it was dilatory in agreeing to the investigation and remedial works.

Commentary

An issue in this case concerned 'time at large', and it was held that, as delays on the part of the employer in approving remedial works to the piling were not catered for in the extension of time provisions, the right to liquidated and ascertained damages was lost and time became at large. Therefore, the employer was left with an entitlement to claim such common law damages as a result of the contractor failing to complete within a reasonable time as it was able to prove.

Walter Lawrence & Sons Ltd v. Commercial Union Properties Ltd (1984)

The facts

In 1982 Commercial Union Properties Ltd contracted with Walter Lawrence & Sons Ltd for certain construction works. The contract between the parties was the JCT Standard Form of Contract, 1963 edition.

During the course of the work, severe weather conditions were encountered and the project was delayed. Clause 23 of the contract concerned extensions of time and sub-clause b gave entitlement to an extension of time if the weather was 'exceptionally inclement'.

The dispute

The contractor, Walter Lawrence applied for an extension of time under clause 23 (b); and upon receipt of the contractor's claim, the architect obtained the relevant weather records from the Meteorological Office to assist him in his assessment.

In assessing the claim, the architect compared the weather records with the contractor's planned programme and his conclusion was that the contractor was entitled to an extension of time of two weeks. His reasoning was that he compared the weather conditions current when the works were planned to be done not when they were actually carried out.

The dispute was referred to the Official Referee's Court.

The judgment

In the Official Referee's Court, Judge Lewis Hawser decided in favour of the contractor, Walter Lawrence.

In his judgment, he held that the correct test was whether the weather was 'exceptionally inclement' so as to delay the works actually being carried out at the time; and not whether the amount of time lost was exceptional.

Commentary

It is common for extension of time submission to include the impact of inclement weather on the progress of the works. This case provided some useful guidance on the correct approach to this issue.

H. Fairweather & Co. Ltd v. London Borough of Wandsworth (1987)

The facts

H. Fairweather & Co. Ltd was contracted by the London Borough of Wandsworth to build 478 dwellings. The contract between the parties was the JCT *Standard Form, Local Authorities with Quantities*, 1963 edition. The contract commencement date was 15 December 1975 and the completion date was 5 August 1979.

Major delays occurred, including general strikes in 1978–1979. As a result, the architect awarded an extension of time of 81 weeks, under clause 23 (d), by reason of strikes and combination of workmen. The quantum of the extension of time was not challenged by Fairweather, but the allocation of the award under clause 23 (d) was. The parties could not agree and the dispute was referred to arbitration.

The dispute

Fairweather contended, before the arbitrator, that 18 of the 81 weeks should be reallocated under sub-clauses (e) or (f) of clause 23; the reasoning being that only if there was reallocation could Fairweather recover direct loss and expense.

The arbitrator rejected Fairweather's reasoning, agreeing with the architect and in sections 6.11, 6.12 and 6.14 of his interim award stated:

> *It is possible to envisage circumstances where an event occurs on site which causes delay to the completion of the works and which could be ascribed to more than one of the eleven specified reasons but there is no mechanism in the conditions for allocating an extension between different heads so the extension must be granted in respect of the dominant reason.*
>
> *I accept the respondent's contention that, faced with events of this contract, nobody would say that the delays which occurred in 1978 and 1979 were caused by reasons of the Architect's instructions given in 1975 to 1997. I hold that the dominant cause of the delay was the strikes and combination of workmen and accordingly the Architect was correct in granting his extension under condition 23 (d).*
>
> *For the sake of clarity I declare that this extension does not carry with it any right to claim direct loss and/or expense.*

The arbitrator's award was the subject of an appeal by Fairweather. Judge Fox-Andrews heard the appeal in the Official Referee's Court.

The judgment

The judge in the case disagreed with the arbitrator's ruling that the extension of time should relate to the dominant cause of delay, and said in his judgment:

> *'Dominant' has a number of meanings: 'ruling, prevailing, most influential'. On the assumption that condition 23 is not solely concerned with liquidated or ascertained damages but also triggers and conditions a right for a contractor to recover direct loss and expense where applicable under condition 24 then an architect and in his turn an arbitrator has the task of allocating, when the facts require it, the extension of time to the various heads. I do not consider that the dominant test is correct.*

Judge Fox-Andrews also made it clear that there was no connection, explicit or implied, between clause 23, 'Extension of Time, and clause 24, 'Loss and Expense'. His judgment said, 'An extension of time under clause 23 (e) is neither expressly nor I find impliedly made a condition precedent to a right to payment.'

Commentary

In this case the dominant cause of delay theory was rejected by the court.

Glenlion Construction Ltd v. The Guinness Trust (1987)

The facts

The project concerned was a residential development in Bromley, Kent. Glenlion, the contractor, entered into a contract with the Guinness Trust under a JCT 1963 *Standard Form of Contract with Quantities*. The date for possession was 29 June 1981 and the period for completion was 114 weeks.

One of the contract obligations was for the contractor to provide 'a programme or chart for the whole of the works', showing a completion date within the 114-week period for completion. Glenlion duly obliged. However, the programme showed completion only 101 weeks after the date for possession.

The dispute

The project was delayed and the contractor alleged the delay was due to the employer's professional team not providing information to allow the contractor to complete by the early completion date shown on their programme. The dispute was referred to arbitration.

The arbitrator issued an award in favour of the employer, the Guinness Trust.

The contractor, Glenlion Construction Ltd, referred the dispute to the Official Referee's Court.

The judgment

In the Official Referee's Court, before Judge Fox-Andrews, the Court was asked

> *Whether there was an implied term of the Contract between the applicant and the respondent that, if and so far as the programme showed a completion date before the date for completion the Employer by himself, his servants or agents should so perform the said agreement as*

to enable the Contractor to carry out the Works in accordance with the Programme and to complete the Works on the said completion date.

The Judge's conclusion was:

The answer to the question must be 'no'. It is not suggested by Glenlion that they were entitled and obliged to finish by the earlier completion date. If there is such an implied term, it imposed an obligation on the Trust but none on Glenlion.

   It is not immediately apparent why it is reasonable or equitable that a unilateral absolute obligation should be placed on an employer.

Judge Fox-Andrews also said, 'The unilateral imposition [by a contractor] of a different completion date would result in the whole balance of the contract being lost.'

Commentary

This case concerned a contractor programming the works to complete earlier than the contract completion date; and if there was an obligation on the employer and his professional team to provide information to allow the contractor to complete the works in accordance with his 'shortened programme'.

   The Court's ruling was that a contractor is entitled to complete the works earlier than the contract completion date and has a right to do so. However, there is no corresponding duty on the part of the employer to permit him to do so, and in particular to provide him with information or otherwise positively co-operate so as to enable him to do so. The contractor is merely free from any contractual restraint and may complete earlier. The employer must not prevent him from doing so, but this does not mean that the employer is bound to facilitate in a positive way the implementation of the contractor's privilege or liberty.

McAlpine Humberoak v. McDermott International (1992)

The facts

In June 1981 Conoco contracted with McDermott for the construction of the deck structure for a tension leg platform for use in the Hutton oil field. The design of the tension leg platform was a prototype. The deck structure was a complex steel frame comprising nine pallets which had to be fabricated to within small dimensional tolerances to ensure an accurate fit when all nine were bolted together.

In October 1981 McAlpine was invited to tender for the construction of seven of the nine pallets which when joined together would form the weather deck. The pallets were to be fabricated and assembled in McAlpine's yard in Great Yarmouth and delivered by barge to McDermott's base in the Moray of Firth, Scotland. On 18 November 1981, McDermott issued a letter of intent to McAlpine for construction of four of the nine pallets; based on 22 number drawings and a period of completion of 18 weeks.

In early December 1981, new drawings and revised drawings were issued to McAlpine and, by the end of the work, McDermott had issued 191 number additional drawings to McAlpine. In addition, 45 number technical queries (TQs) were issued by McAlpine, and McDermott changed the delivery dates for two of the four pallets.

On 24 March 1982, the parties formally entered into a contract which was expressed as being effective from 18 November 1981. Also on 24 March 1981, McDermott omitted two of the pallets from the contract, citing as the reasons 'serious failure without good cause to make reasonable progress and serious substantial failure by McAlpine to properly perform its obligations under the contract'.

The two pallets remaining in the contract were finally delivered on 15 July 1982 and 7 September 1982. These were delivered some 21 weeks and 31 weeks later respectively than the contract completion dates.

The dispute

McAlpine sued, claiming £2.849 million for delay caused by the large number of revised drawings, technical queries and variation. McDermott counterclaimed for the additional cost it incurred through alleged delay and defective fabrication by McAlpine.

Following a trial lasting some 92 working days between November 1987 and June 1989 and deliberating for a further year, Judge Davies gave his judgment in July 1990.

The judgment

Judge Davies described the defendant's delay claim format as a 'retrospective and dissectional re-creation' of the project. He further stated that this method was unhelpful, artificial and of no particular use in deciding how delays had actually been caused.

Judge Davies found for McAlpine, and ruled that McAlpine was entitled to an additional £1.839 million.

However, in finding that the contract was frustrated, the judge held that, since the contract was agreed to take effect from 18 November 1981, it must be construed in the light of circumstances then existing and what the parties then knew. The judge's decision that the contract had been frustrated surprised both parties since frustration had neither been pleaded nor argued.

McDermott appealed.

The judgment on appeal

The Court of Appeal found for McDermott. In giving judgment the Court of Appeal found that

> *The revised drawings did not transform the contract into a different contract or distort its identity. It remained a contract for the construction of four pallets until 24 March 1982 when W5 and W6 were withdrawn. Thereafter it was a contract for the construction of two pallets.*

The Court went on to say:

> *If we were to uphold the Judge's finding of frustration this would be the first contract to have been frustrated by reason of matters well known to the parties which had not only occurred before the contract was signed, but has also been expressly provided for in the contract itself.*

Having found that the contract had not been frustrated, the Court then turned to the assessment of indirect costs claimed by, and previously awarded to, McAlpine. The Court of Appeal held that the effect of the changes on the overall performance of the contract was just what the defendant had attempted to assess. Judge Davies's findings, 'hardly did justice to the painstaking analyses by the defendant's experts of what actually happened'.

The Court of Appeal held that McAlpine's approach was simply theoretical and unsupportable. Several important points can be extracted from the Court of Appeal's judgment.

First, the claim for an extension of time was presented by considering each variation, identifying how long it would take to do that variation and then simply adding up the number of days to produce an overall delay. The Court of Appeal said that this approach was insufficient. The major defect was that it was assumed that, for each day spent working on a variation, the completion date of the contract was also delayed for that particular day. This was entirely incorrect.

Second, in respect of additional costs, the claimant calculated the additional labour costs by reference to the tender. The claimant calculated the number of man-hours allowed for in the tender. They then divided that by the number of days for each activity as originally planned. The claimant next identified the number of man-hours per day for the whole of the delayed period. The Court of Appeal did not accept this approach, which assumed that the workforce for any planned activity was continuously engaged in that activity from the commencement of the activity until it was complete. It considered this approach entirely unrealistic.

The Court of Appeal stated that a retrospective and dissectional reconstruction of what actually happened on site was the only real acceptable approach to the proof of delay. The Court of Appeal stated: 'No attempt was made by the parties to assess the effect of the changes on the overall performance of the contract by way of delay, disruption and interruption.'

While the original planned intent was important, it was the blow-by-blow deconstruction of the actual sequence of works on site that was required in order to identify actual periods of delay that could then be assigned to the liability of each of the parties.

Finally, the Court of Appeal considered late instructions. This is sometimes referred to as the 'colour of the front door' argument. In other words, if the building was completed very late by the contractor (with this delay being the contractor's fault), but then the employer asked for the colour of the front door to be changed, then in that scenario is the contractor entitled to an extension of time up to the point where the work is finished? The Court of Appeal dismissed the approach by stating:

> *If a contractor is already a year late through his culpable fault, it would be absurd that the Employer should lose his claim for unliquidated damages just because, at the last moment, he orders an extra coat of paint.*

Commentary

In reviewing the facts the Court of Appeal reverted to the maxim 'he who asserts must prove', and quickly concluded that McAlpine had not proven their case.

What appears surprising about this judgment is that, after sitting for only three and a half weeks out of an allotted nine weeks and without hearing evidence firsthand from witnesses, the Court of Appeal came to an opposite conclusion on virtually every finding on matters of fact and law from Judge Davies, who had listened to the evidence firsthand over a period of 92 days and had deliberated for a further year.

The Court of Appeal made two important observations on the standard of proof required for contractors' delay and disruption claims:

1   The claim must be particularised addressing the crucial issue of causation in respect of individual disrupting events and their impact on the programme. It is not proven by generalities concerning impact on the programme such as 'vast amount of disruption', 'utter confusion', 'impossible situation'. The allegations of fact must be sustainable.
2   Proof of the claim is achieved through expert evidence by reconstruct-

ing events so as to show the delaying and disrupting effects of the causal events, e.g. late information, revised drawings, instructions, etc.

This case demonstrates that on complex disputes there is no fast and simple method of defending claims. It is not unusual for those on the receiving end of complex and substantial claims to baulk at committing the resources, whether in terms of finance, staff or time or a combination of all three, to carry out the detailed work necessary to mount an adequate defence. More often than not there is no real alternative. For McDermott such an approach eventually paid handsome dividends.

A final observation is that this case supports the use of retrospective analysis as a technique for demonstrating delay claims. The procedure in this case, involving the comparison of planned and as-built programmes, and thereby tracing the actual critical path through the project from what was planned to what it actually became. This technique allows the effect on the project completion date to be shown and demonstrated for each delaying event.

14 Case law
1993 to 1999

The cases reviewed in this chapter are:

- *Balfour Beatty Building Ltd* v. *Chestermount Properties Ltd* (1993);
- *John Barker Construction Ltd* v. *London Portland Hotel Ltd* (1996);
- *Ascon Contracting Ltd* v. *Alfred McAlpine Construction* (1999);
- *Henry Boot Construction Ltd* v. *Malmaison Hotel (Manchester) Ltd* (1999).

Balfour Beatty Building Ltd v. Chestermount Properties Ltd (1993)

The facts

Chestermount employed Balfour Beatty to construct an office building in the City; and the works concerned the shell, core and certain elements of the fit-out works. The form of contract between the parties was JCT 1980. By clause 2.2 of the contract, Chestermount could elect by a stated date to confine the contract to the shell and core works only. This option was duly exercised but the fit-out works were reinstated into the contract by variation order.

The contract commencement date was 18 September 1987 and the contract completion date was 17 April 1989. In March 1998 Chestermount confined the works to shell and core only. In October 1988, the architect granted an extension of time which made the completion date 9 May 1989. The project was not completed by this date and a Certificate of Non-Completion was issued by the architect under clause 24.1 of the contract. By February 1990, some nine months later, the project had still not been completed.

Between 12 February 1990 and 12 July 1990, the architect issued instructions to the contractor for the carrying out of fit-out works, as a variation to the contract. The instructions and variation for the fit-out works were issued after the revised contract completion date but before practical completion.

Practical completion of the shell and core work was achieved on 12 October 1990, some 22 weeks later than the revised contract completion date; while practical completion of the fit-out work was achieved on 25 February 1991, some 19 weeks later.

The dispute

The contractor's argument was that the effect of variations issued after the contract completion date in a period of contractor-culpable delay was to cause time to be at large, meaning that the contractor had to complete within a reasonable time; and that the employer would lose his rights to levy LADs. The contractor's alternative argument was that, in the circumstances, the architect should have fixed as a new completion date the date upon which the works could fairly and reasonably have been expected to be completed having regard to the date when the variation was ordered. The architect should, they said, have ignored the previous completion date and start his assessment from the date when the variation instruction occurred and then cast the appropriate extension of time forward. On this basis the contractor, although in culpable delay, would get an automatic extension of time for the period between the completion date previously fixed and the date the variation was ordered.

The employer's argument was that any extension of time for the fit-out works should be on a 'net' basis. That is to say, adding to the revised completion date of 9 May 1989 the period that the architect considered to be fair and reasonable for the fit-out works, which was 18 weeks.

The judgment

This case was heard before Mr Justice Coleman in the Commercial Court, and arose from an appeal against an arbitration award of Mr Christopher Willis.

The following preliminary question was put before the Court,

> *In granting an extension of time in respect of the Relevant Event occurring during a period of culpable delay, ought the Architect to award a 'gross' extension (that is one that re-fixes the Completion Date at the calendar date upon which the work would reasonably be expected to be completed, having regard to the calendar date upon which it is instructed), ought it to be a 'net' extension (that is one which calculates the revised Completion Date by taking the date currently fixed and adding the number of days which the Architect regards as fair and reasonable).*

The Court confirmed that the correct approach was that the architect should start with the existing completion date and extend it to the date that he considers 'fair and reasonable', having regard to the delay caused by the requirement to execute the variation instructions. The Court confirmed that it was the 'net' method that was appropriate.

Mr Justice Coleman found in favour of the employer for the following reasons:

1   The objective of clause 25.3.1 is for the architect to assess whether any of the relevant events have caused delay to completion, and if so by how much. He then applies the result of his assessment to give a revised completion date.

2   With regard to the architect's review of extensions of time under clause 25.3.3.2 following practical completion, Mr Justice Coleman said:

> *he* (the architect) *looks back after the most recently-fixed completion date and under clause 25.3.3, perhaps even after practical completion, and assesses the extent to which the period of contract time available for completion ought to be extended or reduced having regard to the incidence of relevant events.*

3   Mr Justice Coleman also gave his yardstick on criticality and concurrency:

> *His yardstick is what is fair and reasonable. For this purpose he ought to take into account, amongst other factors the effect that the relevant event had on the progress of the works. Did it bring the progress of the works to a standstill? Or did it merely slow down the progress of the works?*

With the objective being, 'to assess whether any of the relevant events has caused delay to the progress of the works as a whole and, if so, how much'. And:

> *If the variation works can reasonably be conducted simultaneously with the original works without interfering with their progress and are unlikely to prolong practical completion, the architect might properly conclude that no extension of time was justified.*

Mr Justice Coleman examined the purposes of the completion date, extension of time and liquidated damages regime and stated:

> *At the foundation of this code is the obligation of the contractor within the contractual period terminating with the completion date and on failure to do so pay liquidated damages for the period of time by which practical completion exceeds the completion date.*

If events occur which are non-contractor's risk events and cause the works to be delayed, the contract provides for the completion date to be adjusted in order to reflect the delay caused.

In essence the architect is concerned to arrive at an aggregate period for completion of the contractual works, having regard to the occurrence of non-contractor's risk events and to calculate the extent to which the completion of the works has exceeded that period.

Obviously there is nothing to stop the architect in an appropriate case from re-fixing the completion date at a point of time which is not only before the date on which he exercises the power but is also before the date on which he issued the instruction.

He further said:

The remarkable consequences of the application of the principle could therefore be that if, as in the present case, the contractor fell well behind the clock and overshot the completion date and was unlikely to achieve practical completion until far into the future, if the architect then gave an instruction for the most trivial variation, representing perhaps only a day's extra work, the employer would thereby lose all right to liquidated damages for the entire period of culpable delay up to the practical completion or, at best, on the respondents' submission, the employer's right to liquidated damages would be confined to the period up to the act of prevention. For the rest of the delay he would have to establish unliquidated damages. What might be a trivial variation instruction would on this argument destroy the whole liquidated damages regime for all subsequent purposes. Such extreme a consequence ... could hardly reflect the common intention.

The means by which that period is adjusted is by advancing or postponing the completion date, which can be done prospectively or retrospectively. If it is advanced by reason of an omission instruction, the consequence may well be that the adjustment required by way of reduction of time for completion is sufficiently substantial to justify re-fixing the completion date before the issue of the instruction... (In) the case of a variation which increases the works, the fair and reasonable adjustment required to be made to the period for completion may involve movement of this completion date to a point in time which may fall before the issue of the variation instruction.

The completion date as adjusted retrospectively is thus not the date by which the contractor ought to have achieved, or ought in future to achieve, practical completion but the date which marks the end of the total number of working days starting from the Date of Possession within which the contractor ought fairly and reasonably to have completed the works.

The judge considered the 'gross' method of assessing extensions of time, and stated:

> *if the architect were to assess the length of time to carry out the variation works and to re-fix the completion date at the end of such period starting from the date of the variation instruction, he would produce a result that would be unfair to the employer.*

His conclusion was:

> *The underlying objective is to arrive at the aggregate period of time within which the contract works as ultimately defined ought to have been completed having regard to the incidence of main contractor's risk events and to calculate the excess time, if any, over that period which the contractor took to complete the works. In essence the architect is concerned to arrive at an aggregate period for completion.*
>
> *The completion date as adjusted was not a date which the contractor ought to have achieved practical completion but the end of the total number of working days starting from the date of possession within which the contractor ought fairly and reasonably to have completed the works.*

Commentary

Of special interest in this case were two matters concerning extensions of time:

1   Was the issue of a variation after the extended completion date but before practical completion, and, therefore, can an extension of time be granted or will LADs become unenforceable, and was 'time at large'?
2   If an extension of time could be granted to the contractor, should a 'gross' extension of time be awarded, or simply a 'net' extension of time?

The 'net' basis is simply the amount of delay occasioned by the relevant event added onto the last revised completion date. This is often referred to as the 'dot-on' principle.

The 'gross' approach is the amount of delay occasioned by the relevant event but calculated from the calendar date on which the variation is instructed. This is, of course, the interpretation contended for by contractors because they could then get an extension of time for the period between the completion date previously fixed and the date on which the variation is instructed; and they are often in culpable delay for this period.

To summarise, where a contract administrator, architect/engineer, issues an instruction or variation after the contract completion date but before practical completion, it is appropriate where resultant delays occur for an extension of time to be granted. The starting point for consideration is the completion date currently fixed and such extension of time will be calculated by extending the completion date by the 'net' period of delay caused to completion. The 'gross' method is, as both judge and arbitrator found, 'wholly inconsistent with the distribution of risk'.

Moreover, if the varied works can reasonably be carried out simultaneously with the original works without interfering with their progress and are unlikely to prolong practical completion, the architect might properly conclude that no extension of time is justified.

Furthermore, it is now clear that the issue of a variation in a period of culpable delay and after the current completion date does not set time at large. The chances of establishing such a claim are now very slim indeed because of case law development.

John Barker Construction Ltd v. *London Portland Hotel Ltd* (1996)

The facts

The project concerned alterations and refurbishment of the London Portman Hotel, the contractor being John Barker Construction Ltd. The contract between the parties was JCT 1980 *Standard Form of Contract with Quantities*, incorporating the sectional completion supplement. The works were to be completed by 14 August 1994.

The contractor commenced in April 1994 and practical completion was certified on 23 September 1994.

The dispute

On 1 December 2004, Barker applied for an extension of time for the full period of delay which was six weeks. An extension was awarded by the architect, but not for the full period of delay.

The judgment

The dispute was referred to the Official Referee's Court, and was heard before Mr Justice Toulmin.

The judge was not persuaded that the architect's assessment of a fair and reasonable extension of time was methodical and logical. His conclusion was that the architect's assessment was irrational, illogical and fundamentally flawed, and he mentioned in his judgment that the architect *did not carry out a logical analysis in a methodical way of the impact which the relevant matters had or were likely to have on the planned programme. He made an impressionistic, rather than a calculated, assessment of the time which he thought was reasonable for the various items individually and overall.*

Commentary

Two important observations in this case are:

1   Mr Recorder Toulson QC held that a fair extension of time called for a logical analysis of the impact of relevant matters in a methodical way.
2   An analysis using CPM techniques was held to be a fair way of assessing a reasonable extension of time. However, it was not suggested that such techniques constituted the only way of assessment.

Ascon Contracting Ltd v. Alfred McAlpine Construction (1999)

The facts

Alfred McAlpine was the main contractor for the construction of a five-storey building, known as the Villiers Building along the seafront in Douglas, Isle of Man, and Ascon was appointed as subcontractor for the concrete works. The subcontract period was 27 weeks, commencing on 28 August 1996, with completion by 5 March 1997. Completion of Ascon's works was not achieved until 16 May 1997, some ten weeks late.

Ascon submitted claims for extension of time for 39 days for delays caused by water percolating into the foundations of the building prior to tanking, and the fact that the lift pit was not available. Ascon also claimed loss and expense for both causes of delay and acceleration costs to overcome the delay.

The dispute

McAlpine denied Ascon's claims, arguing that the delays were Ascon's responsibility, caused by Ascon's failure to work in accordance with the detail of the main contract programme. McAlpine also counterclaimed for liquidated damages imposed on it by the employer under the main contract, and for its own loss and expense.

Ascon denied that it was obliged to follow in detail the main contract programme or that it was liable for liquidated damages imposed on McAlpine. McAlpine's argument was that, had all subcontractors started and finished on time and McAlpine executed its own work on time, practical completion of the project would have been five weeks earlier than the contract completion date. McAlpine argued that the five weeks' float was for its benefit in order to absorb its own delays. As the five weeks' float had been used by Ascon and other subcontractors, McAlpine claimed it was entitled to recover its lost benefit.

As the parties were unable to resolve their differences, the dispute was heard in the Technology and Construction Court before Judge Hicks.

The judgment

The first part of Ascon's claim was for an extension of time of 22 days for water percolating into the foundations of the building prior to tanking. Ascon's case was that it was McAlpine's responsibility to keep the works free from water ingress; McAlpine's position was that Ascon's failure to provide sufficient steel fixers was the real cause of this delay.

While Judge Hicks was persuaded that there were insufficient steel fixers, but that Ascon was probably disrupted by the water-percolating matter, he was not persuaded that the water-percolating matter caused the 22-day delay, and only allowed a six-day extension of time for this matter.

The second part of Ascon's claim was for an extension of time of 17 days for the lift pit not working.

On this matter, the judge ruled that Ascon could and should have made more progress on the lift pit, and therefore only allowed an extension time of eight days for this matter. Judge Hicks's view was that Ascon did not do enough to mitigate the effects of the delay and was therefore partly culpable.

On the matter of Ascon's acceleration claim to overcome the delays, Judge Hicks said:

> 'Acceleration' tends to be bandied about as if it were a term of art with a precise technical meaning, but I have found nothing to persuade me that this is the case. The root concept behind the metaphor is no doubt that of increasing speed and therefore, in the context of a construction contract, of finishing earlier.

The judge, in wholeheartedly rejecting Ascon's approach on acceleration, observed:

> It is difficult to see how there can be any room for the doctrine of mitigation in relation to damage suffered by reason of the employer's culpable delay in the face of express contractual machinery for dealing with the situation by extensions of time and reimbursement of loss and expense. However that may be as a matter of principle, what is plain is that there cannot be both an extension of time to the full extent of the employer's culpable delay, with damages on that basis,

*and also damages in the form of expense incurred by way of mitiga-
tion, unless it is alleged and established that the attempt at mitigation,
although reasonable, was wholly ineffective.*

McAlpine had argued in support of its counterclaim that float in the main
contract programme belonged to it. The judge rejected this argument; he
considered the float to be of value in the sense that delays could be accom-
modated in the float time. This would avoid an overrun to the contract
period and hence any liability to pay liquidated damages to the employer.
The judge went on to say that McAlpine, while accepting the benefit
against the employer, could not claim against the subcontractors. The
judgment included the following:

> *The float is certainly of value to the main contractor in the sense that
> delays of up to that total amount, however caused, can be accommo-
> dated without involving him in liability for liquidated damages to the
> employer or, if he calculates his own prolongation costs from the con-
> tractual completion date rather than from the earlier date which might
> have been achieved, in any such costs. He cannot, however, while
> accepting that benefit as against the employer, claim against sub-con-
> tractors as if it did not exist. That is self-evident if total delays against
> sub programmes do not exceed the float. The main contractor, not
> having suffered any loss of the above kinds, cannot recover from sub-
> contractors the hypothetical loss he would have suffered had the float
> not existed, and that will be so whether the delay is wholly the fault of
> one subcontractor, or wholly that of the main contractor himself, or
> spread in varying degrees between several subcontractors and the main
> contractor. No doubt those different situations can be described, in a
> sense, as ones in which the 'benefit' of the float has accrued to the
> defaulting party or parties, but one could suppose that the main con-
> tractor has, or should have, any power to alter the result so as to shift
> the 'benefit'. The issues in any claim against a subcontractor remain
> simply breach, loss and causation.*

Judge Hicks's decision on whether Ascon caused delay to the main contract works was:

> *The date of practical completion will also govern liability for liqui-
> dated damages. Here no subcontract liquidated damages clause is
> relied upon and Ascon was not a finishing trade; the question whether
> a delay on its part caused loss of the kind claimed by McAlpine turns
> not on any nice question of how practical completion is to be under-
> stood or its date identified but on the factual issue whether, and if so
> by how much, delayed working affected the progress of the following
> trades and thereby completion of the main contract.*

This brings me back to the factual issues of causation. The first is whether it is proper, in the absence of other evidence, to infer that the causes of delay at one stage have a continuing effect so as to produce the same delay at a later stage. I believe that in principle it is a proper inference, but that the probability that it will be drawn, or drawn to its full extent, is likely to diminish with the passage of time and the complexity of intervening events. My reasons for regarding it as proper, with those qualifications, are first that such an inference, at least over short periods, is tacitly assumed in all negotiation, arbitration and litigation of delay claims, and secondly that it represents the 'neutral' position, in the sense that if all other activities proceeded according to programme ... that would be the result.

Commentary

With regard to float, although he did not expressly state so, the judge seems to have favoured the argument that the float belongs to the first person to use it, be they employers, contractors or subcontractors. The main contractor has no power to shift the benefit which would effectively result in him having his cake and eating it.

It is noteworthy that the expert appointed by Ascon's to give opinion on the extent of delays claimed was a 'quantity surveying expert', and it is surprising that the judge did not query the relevance of the witness's expertise in planning and programming matters. Litigants should be careful to ensure that evidence is given by independent experts on matters within their expertise.

Henry Boot Construction Ltd v. Malmaison Hotel (Manchester) Ltd (1999)

The facts

Malmaison engaged Henry Boot to construct a new hotel in Piccadilly, Manchester. Completion was fixed for 21 November 1997 but was not achieved until 13 March 1998. However, extensions of time were issued by the architect revising the date for completion to 6 January 1998. The employer, Malmaison, deducted liquidated damages from the contractor. Henry Boot claimed further extensions of time in respect of a number of alleged relevant events; no further extensions of time were awarded.

The dispute

Henry Boot gave notice of arbitration in respect of only two relevant events, which it used to claim extensions of time through to practical completion. If it succeeded in the arbitration, the liquidated damages would be repaid and it would also be in the position to claim time-related costs for the overrun.

Malmaison denied that the two alleged relevant events caused delay and further pleaded many other matters which if proved would demonstrate that the contractor was the cause of the overrun.

Henry Boot argued before the arbitrator that Malmaison should not be permitted to introduce into the arbitration their positive case as this was outside matters defined by its original notice. The arbitrator rejected Henry Boot's argument; Boot appealed, and the matter came before Mr Justice Dyson for his decision.

The judgment

In his judgment, His Honour Judge (HHJ) Dyson confirmed that, when an architect was considering awarding an extension of time in respect of a relevant event, then he should consider the impact of 'other events' in order to see the interaction of those events and in particular whether the delay for a particular relevant event was on the critical path. The architect could then determine whether the contractor was entitled to an extension of time in respect of any particular relevant event. Judge Dyson described the certifier's duty under clause 25 in the following terms:

> *But in both cases his objective must be the same: to assess whether any of the relevant events has caused delay to the progress of the works and, if so, how much. He must then apply the result of his assessment to the amount of delay caused by the relevant event by extending the contract period for completion of the works by a like amount and this he does by postponing the completion date.*

This case also concerned concurrent delays. In his judgment, HHJ Dyson considers how two concurrent causes of delay should be determined; one being a relevant event such that a contractor was entitled to an EOT and the other having no entitlement to an EOT. He clarified this as follows:

> *It is agreed that if there are two concurrent causes of delay, one of which is a relevant event and the other is not, then the contractor is entitled to an extension of time for the period of delay caused by the relevant event, notwithstanding the concurrent effect of the other event. Thus to take a simple example, if no work is possible on site for a week, not only because of exceptionally inclement weather (a relevant event), but also because the contractor has a shortage of labour (not a relevant event), and if the failure to work during that week is likely to delay the works beyond the completion date by one week, then if he considers it fair and reasonable to do so, the architect is required to grant an extension of time of one week.*

HHJ Dyson went on to say that an architect is not precluded from considering the effect of other events when determining whether a relevant event is likely to cause delay to the works beyond completion.

Commentary

The central issue in this case was clause 25, its construction and use. The judge considered the key words in clause 25 were:

> *If, in the opinion of the architect, upon receipt of any notice ... the completion of the works is likely to be delayed thereby beyond the completion date.... The architect shall in writing to the contractor give an extension of time.*

HHJ Dyson acknowledged that while the decision in *Balfour Beatty* v. *Chestermount* was of some assistance, that case involved the retrospective use of clause 25, whereas in this case an opinion had to be formed before practical completion.

This case is also relevant to the function of granting extensions. Should the investigation be limited to looking only at the impact of the 'relevant event' in respect of which the contractor is seeking an extension of time? Or should the certifier also consider the impact of other events? At stake, from the employer's aspect the proper exercise of this function will dictate the extent to which the contractor can be charged liquidated damages. For the contractor, there is the question of its entitlement to recover time-related costs.

This case is also important with regard to concurrency. If it can be shown that there are two equal concurrent causes of delay, for which the employer and contractor were respectively responsible, then the contractor is still entitled to an extension of time.

Judge Dyson illustrated his views on concurrency with an example of the start of a project being held up for one week by exceptionally inclement weather, a 'relevant event', and at the same time the contractor suffered a shortage of labour, not a 'relevant event'. In effect the two delays and causes were concurrent. In this situation, Judge Dyson said that the contractor should be awarded an extension of time of one week, and an architect should not deny the contractor an extension on the grounds that the project would have been delayed by the labour shortage.

Judge Dyson's approach to concurrency is considered to be fair and reasonable, the implications being that the employer cannot levy liquidated damages against the contractor for delay, while the contractor should not be allowed to recover its prolongation costs for the delay.

15 Case law
2000 to 2003

The cases reviewed in this chapter are:

- *Royal Brompton Hospital NHS Trust* v. *Frederick Alexander Hammond and Others* (2000);
- *Motherwell Bridge Construction Ltd* v. *Micafil Vakuumtechnik* (2002);
- *Balfour Beatty Construction Ltd* v. *The Mayor and Burgesses of the London Borough of Lambeth* (2002).

Royal Brompton Hospital NHS Trust v. *Frederick Alexander Hammond and Others* (2000)

The facts

The project concerned the construction of a six-storey hospital, known as the National Heart and Chest Centre Phase 1, in Chelsea, London for the Royal Brompton Hospital (RBH) NHS Trust. Taylor Woodrow was the main contractor, and practical completion was certified as being achieved on 23 May 1990, some 43 weeks and two days later than the original completion date for the project. In total, the architect awarded an extension of time of 43 weeks and two days, thereby revising the date for completion to 23 May 1990.

The contractor claimed loss and expense from the hospital for delays. Some money was paid by the hospital, and in 1992 the contractor commenced arbitration proceedings against the RBH Trust for the remainder of its claim.

In 1995, prior to a hearing, the arbitration was settled with the employer making a payment of £6 million to the contractor.

The dispute

In 1997 the RBH Trust served a statement of claim with allegations of negligence against members of the professional team involved with the project, i.e. architect, project manager, etc. seeking to recover the settlement amount paid to the contractor plus their own arbitration costs.

The action resulted in a series of trials taking place in the Technology and Construction Court between 1999 and 2002.

The judgment

The hospital's main case against the architect was that the contractor was responsible for the delays but the breaches and negligence of the architect had so weakened the hand of the hospital in the arbitration that, instead of recovering from the contractor liquidated and ascertained damages and the loss and expense already paid to the contractor, it paid out further sums to the contractor plus costs of £15 million.

One of the key points in the Trust's case was that, in determining a fair and reasonable extension of time, the architect failed to determine the actual critical path of the contractor's works and that extension of time awards had been given for non-critical path works.

Further, the Trust alleged that the architect had failed to determine the contractor's actual progress against its programme and had not examined the reasons for delay against that programme and the actual progress of the works in assessing the applications for extensions of time.

A key issue in this case was 'concurrency'. On this issue, Judge Seymour distinguished between sequential causes of delay and true concurrency, stating:

> *However, it is, I think, necessary to be clear what one means by events operating concurrently. It does not mean, in my judgment, a situation in which, work already being delayed, let it be supposed, because the contractor has had difficulty in obtaining sufficient labour, an event occurs which is a Relevant Event and which, had the contractor not been delayed, would have caused him to be delayed, but which in fact, by reason of the existing delay, made no difference. In such a situation although there is a Relevant Event, 'the completion of the Works is [not] likely to be delayed thereby beyond the Completion Date'. The Relevant Event simply has no effect on the completion date. This situation obviously needs to be distinguished from a situation in which, as it were, the works are proceeding in a regular fashion and on programme, when two things happen, either of which had it happened on its own would have caused delay, and one is a Relevant Event, while the other is not. In such circumstances there is real concurrency of causes of delay.*

Judge Seymour also gave his view on the analysis that is required to demonstrate delay and the available float:

All activities have potential or theoretical float (even if the period is negative). What is required is to track the actual execution of the works. On a factual basis this case requires no further discussion. In addition clause 25 refers to 'expected delay in the completion of the Works' and for the need for the Architect to form an opinion as to whether because of a Relevant Event 'the completion of the Works is likely to be delayed thereby beyond the Completion Date'. Under the JCT conditions, as used here, there can be no doubt that if an architect is required to form an opinion then, if there is unused float for the benefit of the contractor (and not for another reason such as to deal with p.c. or provisional sums or items), then the architect is bound to take it into account since an extension is only to be granted if completion would otherwise be delayed beyond the then current completion date.

Commentary

The important matters that are gleaned from this case and judgment are:

1   In determining a fair and reasonable extension of time as a consequence of a delay event, an examination of the actual critical path of the contractor's works should be carried out to establish that the delay event affected, or was likely to affect, the completion of the works. Furthermore, the work activities that were critical to the forward progress of the works at the time the delay event occurred should be taken into account.
2   The matter of concurrency should be looked at closely to determine those events that are sequential and those that are truly concurrent.

Judge Seymour also noted that, in order to make an assessment of whether a particular delay event affected the completion of the works and not just a work activity, he considered it correct to take into account what work activities were critical to the forward progress of the works, at the time the delay event occurred.

Motherwell Bridge Construction Ltd v. Micafil Vakuumtechnik (2002)

The facts

Micafil was engaged by BICC as main contractor for the construction of an autoclave, which is a large steel vessel with an internal volume of some $650\,m^3$. The vessel was to be used in the manufacture of high-quality power cables. Micafil undertook the responsibility for the design work and subcontracted its construction to Motherwell Bridge. During construction

Motherwell Bridge raised many technical queries and a number of significant design changes were issued by Micafil. There were two formal amendments to the contract.

The dispute

Delays occurred and Micafil deducted liquidated damages. Motherwell Bridge in turn claimed extensions of time to extinguish the claim for liquidated damages.

The judgment

His Honour Judge Toulmin first dealt with the matter of concurrent causes of delay. He was satisfied that his approach must be outlined from the judgment in the *Henry Boot* case. He said in his judgment:

> *Crucial questions are, (a) is the delay in the critical path? and, if so, (b) is it caused by Motherwell Bridge? If the answer to the first question is yes and the second question is no, then I must assess how many additional working days should be included.*

HHJ Toulmin then departed slightly from the guidance in *Henry Boot*, by going on to comment:

> *other delays caused by Motherwell Bridge (if proved) are not relevant, since the overall time allowed for under the contract may well include the need to carry out remedial works or other contingencies. These are not relevant events, since the court is concerned with considering extensions of time within which the contract must be completed.*

Judge Toulmin went on to add that the approach must always be tested against an overall requirement that the result accords with commonsense and fairness. With regard to the questions raised in the *Balfour Beatty* case, Judge Toulmin concluded that an extension of time for completion of the works may be granted in respect of a relevant event occurring during the period of culpable delay. However, he refused to follow precisely the guidance in *Balfour Beatty* to determine the 'net' effect of delays occurring after the date for completion. By fixing the extended period of time available for completion of the work, having regard to the incidences of the causes of delay and measured by the standard of what is fair and reasonable, Motherwell Bridge became entitled to an extension of time for the full period of delay.

Commentary

The judgment in this case emphasised that a delay must be on the critical path, confirming again what was stated in the *Henry Boot* and *Royal Brompton* judgments.

Judge Toulmin also concluded that an extension of time for completion of the works may be granted in respect of a relevant event occurring during the period of culpable delay; an endorsement of the approach in *Balfour Beatty*.

Balfour Beatty Construction Ltd v. The Mayor and Burgesses of the London Borough of Lambeth (2002)

The facts

The project involved the refurbishment of Falmouth House, Kennington Park Road in London. The project value was £3.8 million and the contract between the parties was JCT 1988 *Local Authorities Edition without Quantities*. The works commenced on 1 November 1999.

As a consequence of delays to the project, the contractor was awarded extensions of time which revised the date for completion to 23 October 2000. However, practical completion was not achieved until 24 May 2001, some 41 weeks and three days later than the revised date for completion. As a result, liquidated damages for this delay of £355,831.00 were deducted from the contractor.

The dispute

Balfour Beatty maintained that it was entitled to further extensions of time and referred the dispute to adjudication. The adjudicator's decision was that Balfour Beatty was entitled to an extension of time of 35 weeks and one day, thereby reducing the liquidated damages levied to some £80,600.

The employer, the London Borough of Lambeth, challenged the decision on the grounds that the adjudicator did not act impartially and that the decision was reached in breach of contract and without jurisdiction.

The judgment

The case was heard before Judge Humphrey Lloyd, who found in favour of the defendant, Lambeth, and Balfour Beatty's application for enforcement was dismissed. Judge Lloyd was persuaded that the adjudicator 'had not acted impartially and that he failed to comply with the rules of natural justice in significant respects'.

Judge Lloyd made the following comments on the importance of establishing a critical path and on extension of time presentations:

> *This is yet another case in which adjudication has been launched after completion of the works and in which the dispute attracts a simple description but comprises a highly complex set of facts and issues relating to the performance of a contract carried out over many months. It may well be doubted whether adjudication was intended for such a situation. If it is to be utilised effectively it is essential that the referring party gives the adjudicator all that is needed in a highly manageable form. From the material available to me it is clear that BB did little or nothing to present its case in a logical or methodical way. Despite the fact that the dispute concerned a multi-million pound refurbishment contract no attempt was made to provide any critical path. The work itself was no more complex than many other projects where a CPN is routinely established and maintained. It seems that BB had not prepared or maintained a proper programme during the execution of the works. By now one would have thought that it was well understood that, on a contract of this kind, in order to attack, on the facts, a clause 24 certificate for non-completion (or an extension of time determined under clause 25), the foundation must be the original programme (if capable of justification and substantiation to show its validity and reliability as a contractual starting point) and its success will similarly depend on the soundness of its revisions on the occurrence of every event, so as to be able to provide a satisfactory and convincing demonstration of cause and effect. A valid critical path (or paths) has to be established both initially and at every later material point since it (or they) will almost certainly change. Some means has also to be established for demonstrating the effect of concurrent or parallel delays or other matters for which the employer will not be responsible under the contract. BB and its claims consultants, whilst recognising that the critical path would constantly fluctuate (see the referral notice), nevertheless decided that not only was it not practicable but that it was unnecessary to determine a constantly changing critical path.*

The judge also made the following observations regarding progress recording and the presentation delay to areas of the works:

> *BB programmed the works on a flat type basis (albeit without identifying the critical path for same) and at the very least BB should have measured progress against these same flat types. That way it would have been possible to compare the planned progress with the actual progress in a meaningful way. Instead all that BB have provided is an aggregate of all the planned time and compared with all the actual*

time on a trade by trade basis. No attempt has even been made by BB to demonstrate any link between the trades.

Commentary

There are some important issues to be taken out of this judgment, such as:

1   A proper programme should be maintained during the execution of the works.
2   In determining an extension of time, the 'foundation' should be the original programme, subject to justification and substantiation of its validity and reliability.
3   A valid critical path, or paths, should be established as it, or they, will almost certainly change.
4   Concurrent, or parallel, delays should be demonstrated where necessary.

Another key aspect in which the Court gave its opinion was that, in granting an extension of time, the purpose was to fix the period of time by which the period available for completion was to be extended. In other words, the date for completion, as adjusted, was not the revised or new date by which the contractor was to have achieved practical completion, but the end of the total number of days.

16 Case law
2004 to 2005

The cases reviewed in this chapter are:

- *Skanska Construction UK Ltd* v. *Egger (Barony) Ltd* (2004);
- *Great Eastern Hotel Company Ltd* v. *John Laing Construction Ltd &*
  Anor. (2005).

Skanska Construction UK Ltd v. *Egger (Barony) Ltd* (2004)

The facts

The project was the design and construction by Skanska of a timber-process-ing facility in Scotland for Egger, an Austrian company, on a former colliery site in Ayrshire. The contract price for Skanska's work was £12 million, under a guaranteed maximum price agreement. Overall, in a period of less than a year, a redundant colliery site with varying levels was transformed into a state-of-the-art, fully automated factory where virgin timber was fed in at one end and a sophisticated chipboard product emerged at the other.

However, during the course of Skanska's works there were delays and disruption; a major issue being the warehouse floor slab which cracked and broke up.

The dispute

Skanska valued the final account as £24.5 million; while Egger's value was £13 million, from which there was a deduction of £4.1 million for defec-tive work and liquidated damages.

The matter was referred to the Technology and Construction Court and was heard before Judge Wilcox.

The judgment

The quantum issues of this case concerned the much greater part of the trial and the subsequent judgment. However, one of the issues was that of loss and expense and, in considering this, the Court was presented with expert evidence relating to delays suffered by several of Skanska's subcontractors.

This judgment considers a technique of delay analysis, which HHJ Wilcox describes as an 'impact analysis'. In this case, the original planned construction programme in barchart form was converted into a network form, i.e. a logically linked critical path analysis.

The judge observed that, if an original programme was converted into a network, then it was essential that the reconstruction was accurate and supported by the evidence; otherwise the Court might decide that the critical path analysis is 'not reliable as a base line'.

During the project there was agreement of the master programme; however, a further three sub-zone programmes were issued by Skanska. Their relevance was stated in the judgment as follows:

> *in order to carry out its impact analysis the master programme prepared by Skanska on 23rd May which for reasons extensively set out in the liability judgment became virtually redundant, almost from the outset because of the late provision of vital information relating to design and layout and changes made on the instructions of Egger. I am satisfied that the sub-zone programmes dealing with each zone separated in planning and programme terms provide a more accurate basis for detailed delay analysis rather than the flawed planned programme....*

Judge Wilcox also commented that 'The reliability of (a) sophisticated impact analysis is only as good as the data put in.'

Commentary

This case emphasises the reliability of a programme used as a baseline for analysis. In establishing a reliable baseline for analysis, the objective is to remove flaws in the original master programme. Furthermore, if more detailed sub-programmes are available, they should be considered in any reconstruction of the master programme, in order to provide a reliable baseline programme for the assessment of delays.

Observations in this judgment were made with regard to the approach of the experts.

1   It is not advisable to overpower the Court with information and numerous delay charts which are difficult to understand. While planning software nowadays is capable of producing a wide variety of reports and charts, careful consideration should be given in selecting the outputs to be incorporated in a report. In his judgment HHJ Wilcox was not impressed with the complexity of a report running to

'some hundreds of pages supported by 240 charts'. There is a lot to recommend the 'keep-it-simple' philosophy. Ensuring the accessibility of a report will always be a problem with delay analysis on large and complex projects as criticism could also be levelled if the report lacks the detailed supporting programmes, hammocks, sub-nets and analysis of alternative critical paths that could be required.

2   Another observation in the judgment is that it is fundamental that the delay analyst is 'objective, meticulous as to detail, and not hide bound by theory as when demonstrable facts collide with computer programme logic'. This applies to all methods and techniques of delay analysis, time impact analysis or other methods. For example, the conversion of the master programme from barchart to network format; if evidence contradicts or conflicts with the output of the computer programme, then adjustment of the input is required to ensure consistency with the facts, i.e. follow the facts, not the computer output. Further, if there are more detailed programmes available, then these should be considered in the development of the reconstructed baseline programme. It will, however, be for the delay analyst to adopt 'intellectual independence and objectivity' in applying his judgment to the weight he attaches to such programmes.

Finally, if a report is to be presented to Court or a tribunal, the expert should be fully conversant with his report. While this may seem self-evident, it is common practice on large and complex projects for an expert to engage assistants to carry out aspects of the investigation. However, an expert's opinion becomes less compelling if he gives the impression that he is not entirely familiar with the details of his own report.

Great Eastern Hotel Company Ltd v. *John Laing Construction Ltd & Anor.* (2005)

The facts

The Great Eastern Hotel (GEH) appointed John Laing as construction manager for the extension and refurbishment of the existing Great Eastern Hotel next to Liverpool Street Station in London. The works included a complete refurbishment and extension of the existing buildings to produce a first-class hotel. This included major demolition work and then re-building, to create a large central atrium and two and a half additional floors within a newly created mansard roof. GEH's budget for the project was £34.8 million; and Laing was appointed under a Construction Management Agreement (CMA). The employer's Indicative Design and Construction Programme for the works was for a period of 113 weeks, but Laing proposed and issued a programme showing a 109-week overall period.

A Letter of Intent was issued to Laing on 19 June 1997, and the works commenced on 30 June 1997, which gave a planned completion date of 2 August 1999. Delays occurred and practical completion was not achieved until 13 July 2000, some 346 days later than the planned completion date. The final cost of the project was £61 million which was some £26 million more than the employer's original budget.

The dispute

The employer, the Great Eastern Hotel Company, sought to recover losses of £17 million from the construction manager, Laing, by way of damages in respect of Laing's various breaches of contract. The matter came before Judge Wilcox in the Technology and Construction Court.

The judgment

The major issue that the Court had to decide was responsibility for the delay. Both the claimant and defendants accepted that there was significant delay. The defendants denied liability, pointing the finger at both other parties and other concurrent causes of delay.

The procurement and erection of the temporary roof was one of the first items on Laing's programme. The judgment describes this situation as follows:

> *Unhappily both the procurement of the Temporary Roof Trade Package and erection of the roof itself went badly wrong. The procurement took three weeks longer than the time programmed by Laing. In consequence the scaffold and Temporary roof contractors TRAD commenced on site on 11th September 1997, three weeks later than programmed. There was thus an immediate three-week delay caused to the Project. The erection of the roof itself took 35 weeks rather than the 10 weeks programmed by Laing. It was completed on 1st May 1998 instead of late October of 1997 as planned. That was a delay in excess of six months. The reasons for these delays had been canvassed a great deal in the evidence.*
>
> *The parties accept that the temporary roof was critical to the whole Project and agree that the delays to the procurement and erection of the temporary roof caused a substantial delay to the project. GEH say that the critical delay caused was 19 weeks and Laing's expert accepts that the critical delay was even more substantial, 26.9 weeks. In either case, the effect on the project was significant. It never recovered from this first fundamental setback, and the delays sadly became worse.*

Judge Wilcox's conclusion on this issue was:

> *In my judgment, in relation to this phase of the project, the defendants are clearly in breach of clauses 2.8, 2.9, 3.1 3.2 (D) and 3.4 of the*

CMA and in consequence by their acts and omissions are proved to have significantly caused the delay during these periods.

The Judge was looking for an objective evaluation from the experts. The two experts approached their analyses of project delay in two different ways.

Both experts approached their analyses for the principal part of the project differently. Mr xxx for the main part proceeding retrospectively from an as built programme to determine the critical path and respective periods of delay and causes. Mr yyy used an impacted as planned programme analysis by which the project is analysed on a monthly basis to measure the impact of events as the project proceeded. The principal critical path determined by each expert was broadly similar. The total extent of delay periods found by each expert broadly coincided. Mr xxx's assessment was several weeks longer than Mr yyy, but I am satisfied that by applying an adjustment for public holidays and not taken account of by Mr xxx, there is no significant overall difference. It was 49.5 weeks. The vital differences relate to some differences as to the route of the critical path and the causes of delay advanced by each expert.

However, there was some agreement between the experts before the matter reached the trial stage:

The experts in their joint statement that Court agreed as built dates for construction activities up to April of 1999. Thereafter, due to lack of information, Mr yyy was unable to confirm the dates relied upon by Mr xxx in his as-built programme. They both agreed that MP/1 demonstrated Laing's programme intentions at the time it was drawn in August of 1997 and at the time the periods allocated to the activities were reasonable. Mr yyy made certain improvement and refinements to MP/1. Not all of these were agreed by Mr xxx but none are particularly significant.

The experts dealt with the delay issues with reference to identified periods of time. In reviewing the evidence I would do so relating to each of these periods.

I accept Mr yyy's careful evidence as to the impact of the flow of design information throughout the Project. It was based on thorough research and objective analysis.

Furthermore, Mr xxx in his report compares the timing of the actual design releases against an original programme which was superseded by later versions of the procurement programme on which Laing showed later dates for the provision of the information required.

Mr yyy took account of the actual events in his researches and exhibited in his researches and conclusions the clear-sighted objectivity that informs the whole of his report.

One of the issues that came up during the trial was progress monitoring and reporting. On this issue Judge Wilcox said:

It is evident in my judgment that Laing consistently underplayed mention of the true causes of critical delay and assert other reasons for delay that would not reflect upon them. They consistently misreported the delays actually occurring and manipulating the data in the programme update to obscure the accurate position.

Another issue that received comment in the judgment was that of alterations to the programme logic. An example of this issue in the judgment was:

The deletion of the logic link between the demolition of the Mansard and demolition of the Infill Block obscured from GEH and the design team that the Infill Block was as critical as it was. Had Laing's manipulation not taken place the criticality of the Infill Block from the delays it was causing would have become more readily apparent to everyone. In that event is it more likely than not that under inevitable pressure from the hotel and design team Laing would have taken steps to commence demolition of the Infill Block after protecting the Rail Track services at a much earlier stage. The misreporting of progress had further serious effects on the following Trade Contractors. Because of the misreporting of progress, some of the following Trade Contractors commenced work on site before the works were ready for them, and this led to claims for extensive extensions of time together with prolongation and disruption costs. Had the true state of progress been declared, whilst it would have been necessary for Laing to have renegotiated with Trade Contractors in order to postpone their commencement on site, the cost consequences of such renegotiation would have been relatively minor, and it would have avoided the subsequent claims for extensions of time and loss and expense.

Commentary

The two party-appointed experts approached their task with different approaches. One expert used a retrospective analysis approach from an as-built programme to determine both the critical path, the periods of critical delay and their causes. This was based on the 'collapsed as-built' technique. The other expert analysed the project on a monthly basis in order to measure the impact of events as the project proceeded. This was based on the 'windows' technique.

Despite the different approaches used by the experts, their results showed that the principal critical path and the extent of the critical delay periods were broadly the same.

The judge had some comments about the potential difficulties with the 'collapsed as-built delay analysis'. His view was that, unless this takes account of the actual events which occurred on the project, it can only give rise to hypothetical answers. One of the key issues in this dispute involved the timing of design release. The judge commented that it was necessary to do more than compare actual release against the original construction pro-gramme, stating that if you only do this, the analysis will not take account of the fact that the design team would have been aware of the significance of any delays which may have occurred to the original master programme. In other words, the design team may have been able to prioritise design and construction to fit actual progress.

The judge preferred the 'as-planned impacted delay analysis'; which is a form of 'windows' analysis in that the delays are determined and assessed by analysing the updated planned programme on a monthly basis to measure the impact of events as they occurred.

In summation, the judge preferred the forward-looking 'impacted as-planned' to the retrospective 'collapsed as-built' approach. In particular he considered it very important that it had been based on a careful analysis of what had actually happened.

Furthermore, while ensuring that his own delay analysis could be sup-ported, the expert had dealt with the question of concurrency by consider-ing all other activities which might have caused delay to the completion date of the project, if the identified critical activities had been completed within the originally programmed period. The expert's conclusion was that none were in fact critical thereby demonstrating to the Court that the case in relation to the alleged concurrent causes to the delay could not be established.

Part IV
The 'thorny issues'

17 Introduction

This section of the book looks at four of the 'thorny issues' which are prevalent in many extension of time submissions:

1 float; ownership and utilisation;
2 concurrency;
3 mitigation and acceleration;
4 time at large.

The first of these issues to be reviewed is 'float'; this is the amount by which individual construction activities can be delayed without affecting completion of the project.

In most standard forms of contract, it is unclear whether it is the employer or contractor who owns the programme float. The view of the Society of Construction Law in their 'Delay and Disruption Protocol' is that the project owns the float, which means that either party can use it. Chapter 18 reviews the issue in detail, discussing the concept of float, the importance of it, and who owns it. Simple diagrams are used to illustrate these aspects of 'float'.

The next issue, 'concurrency', is probably the most prevalent of the four issues. This issue is reviewed in chapter 19, looking first at the usual methods of assessment, such as the 'Devlin approach', the 'Dominant Cause Approach' and the 'Burden of Proof Approach'. This is followed by a sub-section titled, 'A practical approach to concurrency', which discusses how to establish whether delays are truly concurrent, with the help of worked examples. The final part of the chapter presents various scenarios of delays involving concurrency portrayed with some helpful graphics.

The third issue is 'mitigation and acceleration'. Strictly speaking, these are two separate issues, but they are being considered in the book as one. Most forms of contract contain an obligation for the contractor to mitigate delays. However, none of the standard forms define the difference between mitigation and acceleration; the difference is usually from the standpoint of an employer or a contractor.

In the chapter on mitigation and acceleration, the reasons for acceleration are discussed, and in particular the concept of constructive acceleration. On this matter, the American doctrine on constructive acceleration is explained.

The final thorny issue being reviewed is 'time at large'. This argument is often put forward by contractors to defeat the application of liquidated damages. The expression 'time at large' is used to indicate that the contractor believes that there is no enforceable date for completion of the works. Therefore, as there is then no date from which they can be calculated, the employer's right to liquidated damages is defeated. If the contractor's argument succeeds, then his obligation is to complete within a reasonable time.

The chapter on 'time at large' also reviews 'what is a reasonable time to complete', and 'determining a reasonable time to complete'.

18 Float; ownership and utilisation

'Float' is the amount by which individual construction activities can be delayed without affecting completion of the project; it should be properly defined if this vital ingredient is to play its part in both the construction process and the resolution of disputes.

Do all programmes have float?

The short answer is yes. Float is a function of the programme network, and the amount and position of float within a programme is dependent upon the manner in which the network has been constructed. Float provides a contingency or buffer which may be used to absorb the effects of delays to activities not on the critical path. For example, float is used by contractors in the optimisation of manpower and equipment resources, or to absorb the effects of contractor-responsible delays to activities not on the critical path.

In most standard forms of contract, it is unclear whether it is the employer or contractor who owns the programme float. However, the view of the Society of Construction Law in their 'Delay and Disruption Protocol' is that the project owns the float; this means that either party can use the float. In effect, whichever party, employer or contractor, gets to it first can use it.

What is 'float?'

In project-planning terms there are a number of different types of 'float', such as free float, independent float and interfering float, but the most important type, particularly in terms of the project completion date, is 'total float'.

The British Standard BS 4335:1987, defines total float as

The time by which an activity may be delayed or extended without affecting the total project duration.

Take for example a programme for construction of a new garage. If the programme activity 'ground floor slab' has a total float ('TF') of '12', then this activity can be delayed by 12 workdays before completion of the project will be delayed. See Figure 18.1 below.

In the above example, the programme activity 'ground floor slab' has a total float ('TF') of '4', which means that this activity can be delayed by up to four workdays before completion of the project will be delayed.

So where does 'float' come from? It is often talked about as though it is an entity or object that exists, whereas it is a product of the time analysis process of a logic-linked network. In other words, a logically linked programme, or CPM network. Therefore, float is the difference between the earliest and latest start, or finish, dates for each activity.

The time analysis process consists of three parts:

1   a forward pass, which calculates the early start and finish dates based on predecessor activity restraints and activity durations;
2   a backward pass, which calculates the latest start and finish dates based on successor activity restraints and activity durations;
3   a float calculation, which establishes the difference between the earliest and latest dates for each activity.

Figure 18.2 below shows the programme for construction of a garage portrayed in network format.

The above chart shows for each activity:

From the 'forward pass':

i   its earliest start date;
ii   its earliest finish date.

From the 'backward pass':

i   its latest start date;
ii   its latest finish date.

The float calculation; the difference between an activity's early and late dates:

•   its total float.

Effectively, float is the spare time available for an activity and the amount of float is the number of working days the activity can be prolonged or delayed without impacting on the project completion date.

In a path of activities where the float is '0', or the lowest in the programme, the chain of activities is referred to as the critical path. Therefore, the critical path through a project is the sequence of activities that represents the shortest possible time to complete the project (see Figure 18.3).

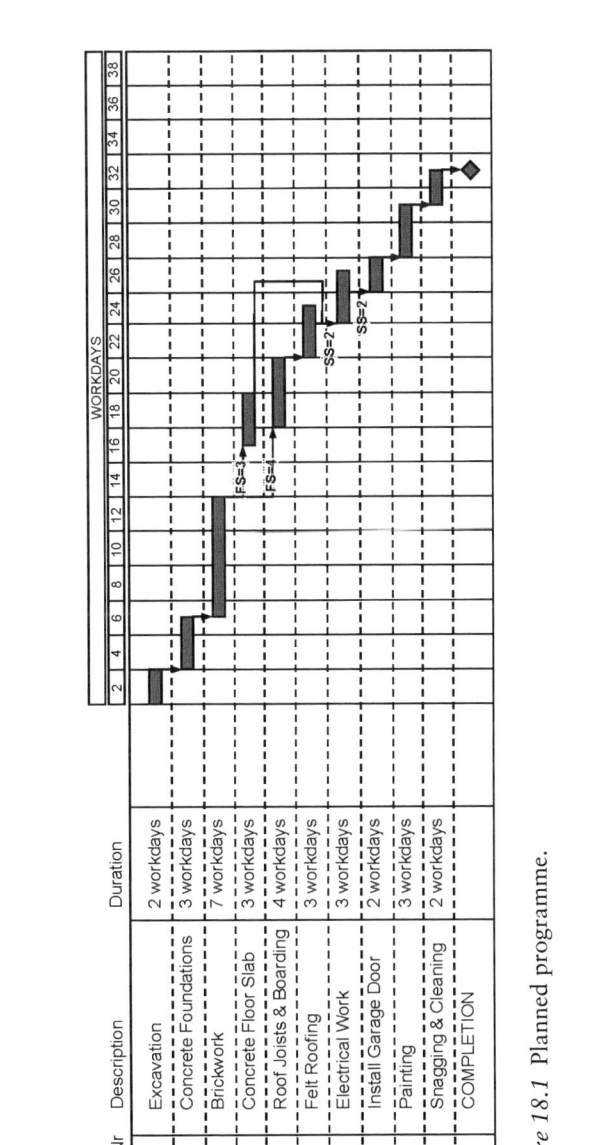

Figure 18.1 Planned programme.

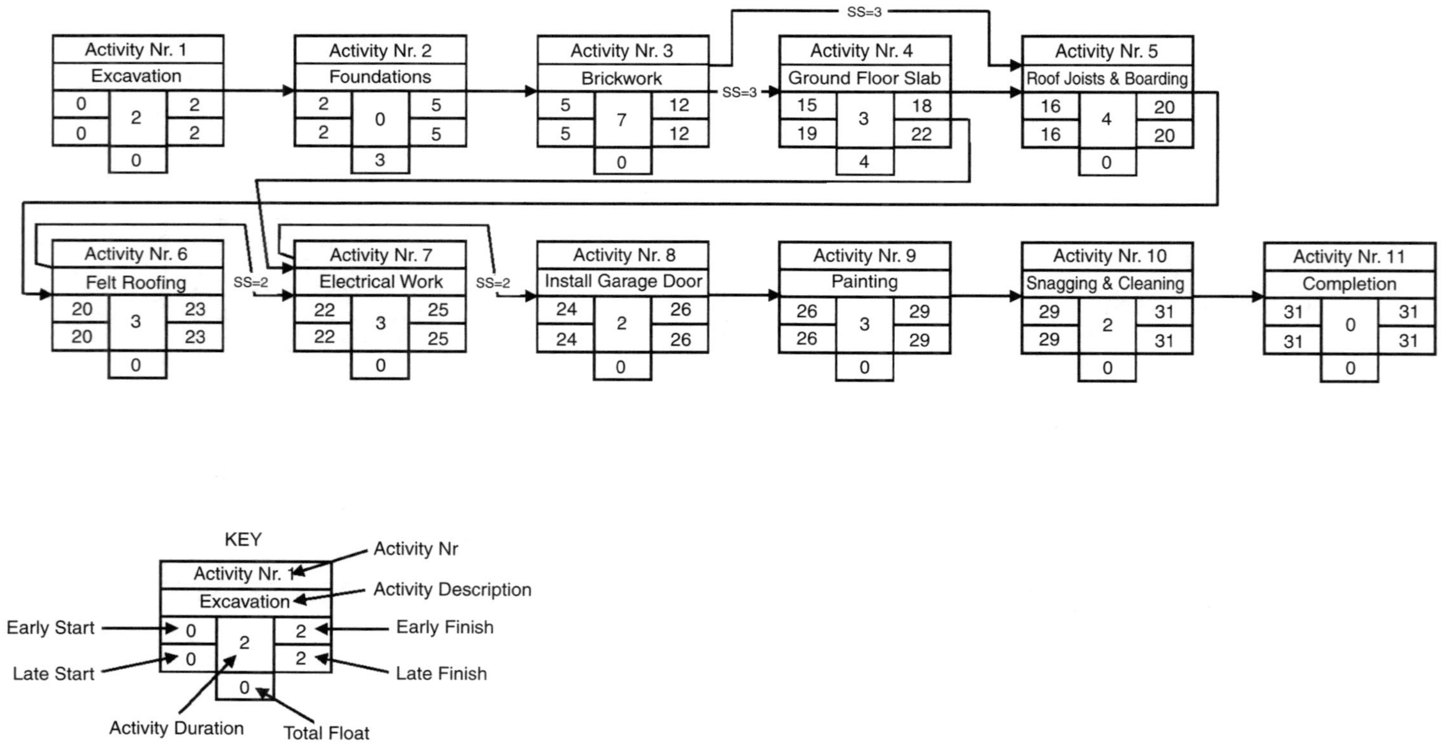

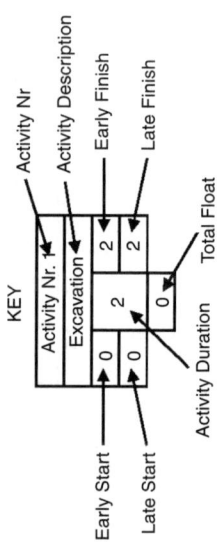

Figure 18.2 Network diagram.

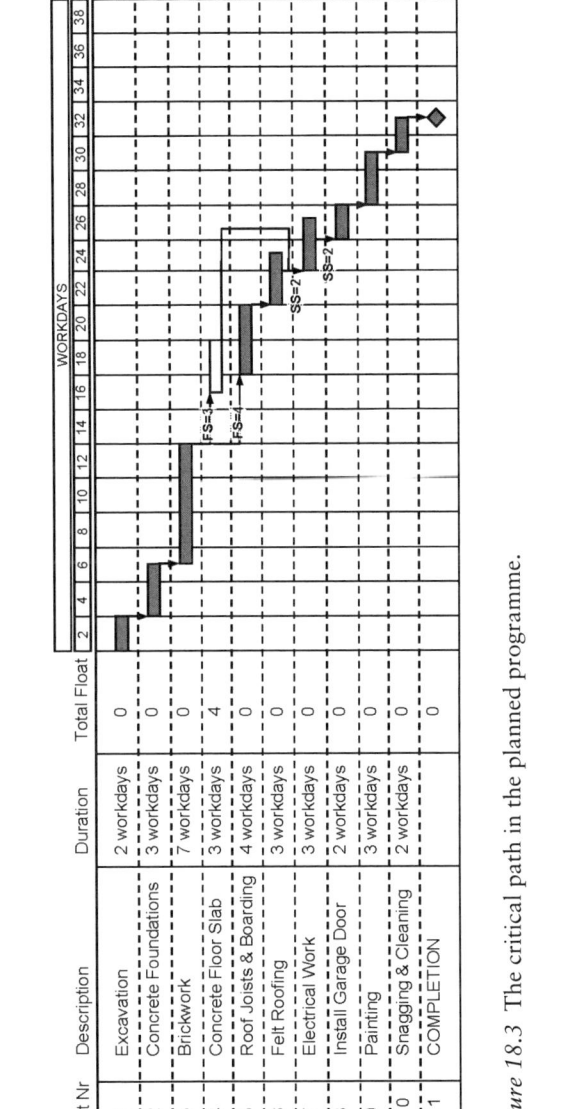

Act Nr	Description	Duration	Total Float
1	Excavation	2 workdays	0
2	Concrete Foundations	3 workdays	0
3	Brickwork	7 workdays	0
4	Concrete Floor Slab	3 workdays	4
5	Roof Joists & Boarding	4 workdays	0
6	Felt Roofing	3 workdays	0
7	Electrical Work	3 workdays	0
8	Install Garage Door	2 workdays	0
9	Painting	3 workdays	0
10	Snagging & Cleaning	2 workdays	0
11	COMPLETION		0

Figure 18.3 The critical path in the planned programme.

The importance of 'float'

If an activity containing float is delayed, then the amount of float will be reduced. When the delayed activity's float has been reduced to zero, then that activity will be critical to the completion date of the project. If the delay to that activity continues, then the activity's float will become negative, and there will be a critical delay to the completion of the project. Using the programme for construction of a garage, and updating it based on actual progress as at workday 26, the updated programme and new forecast now look like this, see Figure 18.4 below.

As can be seen, almost all the remaining work activities are critical, i.e. TF = 0; the only activity that is not on the critical path is 'ground floor slab'. Furthermore, as a consequence of delay to the 'ground floor slab' activity, there has been a critical delay to the project and completion of the project is now forecast to be six workdays late.

Who owns the 'float'?

There are different approaches to the 'ownership' of float, i.e. whether the contractor or employer is entitled to make use of programme float. Propositions and arguments that have been advanced for the 'ownership' of float follow,

Scenario one: the contractor owns the float

The reasoning is that as the contractor created the work programme, he is entitled to use the float to re-programme the work. Float is included in the programme for the contractor's own benefit and helps to plan works and allows the contractor a contingency for any unforeseeable events that occur during the project.

Float enables the contractor to complete on time and, if all goes well and delaying events do not occur, he may complete the works early.

The amount of float that the contractor includes in the programme does not include any allowance for employer-caused delays. The float is in the programme solely as one of the contractor's management tools. As a result, if employer-caused events affect this float, then it is only fair that the contractor should be given an extension of time to maintain that level of contingency.

Scenario two: float belongs to the project

Employers argue that the float is contingency time programmed by the contractor into the programme as insurance against delaying, caused by either party.

If such events do occur, and their only effect is to reduce the float time,

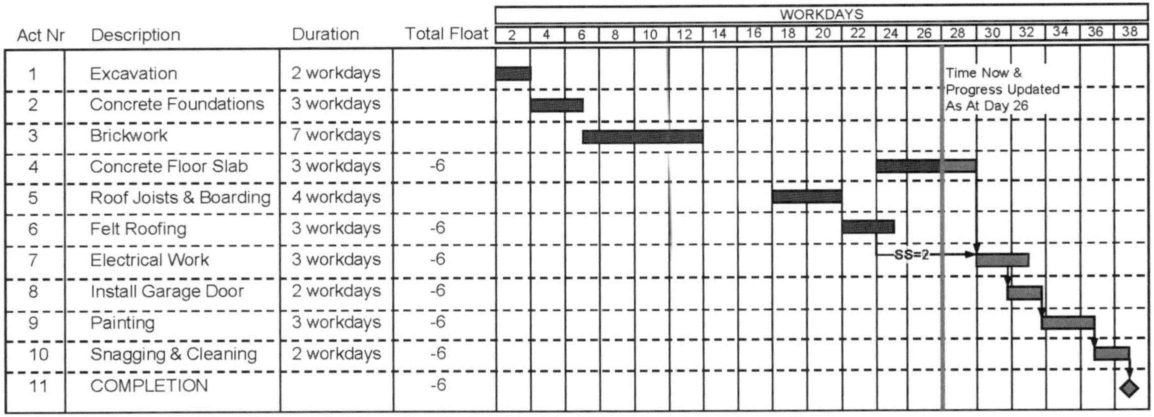

Figure 18.4 The updated planned programme.

the contractor should not be entitled to an extension of time. Employers further argue that this is because the completion date of the project has not been delayed by the event at all.

For example, if only part of the float was used up by delaying events and the contractor was entitled to an extension of time because of these events, then the contractor would still be able to complete the works early, because all of the float had not been used up by the delaying events; but at the same time be entitled to an extension of time beyond the contract completion date.

So employers argue that they own the float, or alternatively that the float 'belongs to the project'.

Disputed liability: an example

On an office-block refurbishment project, because of restricted craneage facilities, the new ventilation equipment has to be hoisted up to the flat roof and then winched across it to the plant room. In order not to damage the new roof waterproofing, the roofing is left off until all equipment is in position.

The contractor's plan is to start internal finishes immediately after the roofing is completed and the building is weather-tight. The contractor's programme shows three weeks' float on the series of activities linking the 'ventilation equipment', 'roofing' and 'internal finishes', i.e. the start of the 'internal finishes' activity can be delayed by up to three weeks without delay to the project completion date. The extract from the contractor's programme is shown in Figure 18.5.

Four weeks before the equipment is due to be delivered the services consultant decides to make an important change to the ventilation equipment which requires a modification in the factory and results in a three-week delay to delivery of some of the equipment. The final installation of the ventilation equipment and the start and finish of roofing will be delayed by three weeks and, as a consequence, the float is used up.

No problem, you might say: the contractor reschedules the works and the project should still finish on time. See Figure 18.6.

In that situation the contractor would not be entitled to an extension of time, as it was not anticipated, or likely, to be 'any expected delay in the completion of the Works or any Section beyond the relevant Completion Date'.

After the start of internal finishes, however, the suspended ceiling sub-contractor sets out his work incorrectly and has to redo much of his ceiling grid work. As a consequence, the whole of the internal finishes takes longer than programmed and the project finishes two weeks late. The as-built programme would look like Figure 18.7.

The question is likely to arise as to who pays for the consequences of the delay in completion of the project.

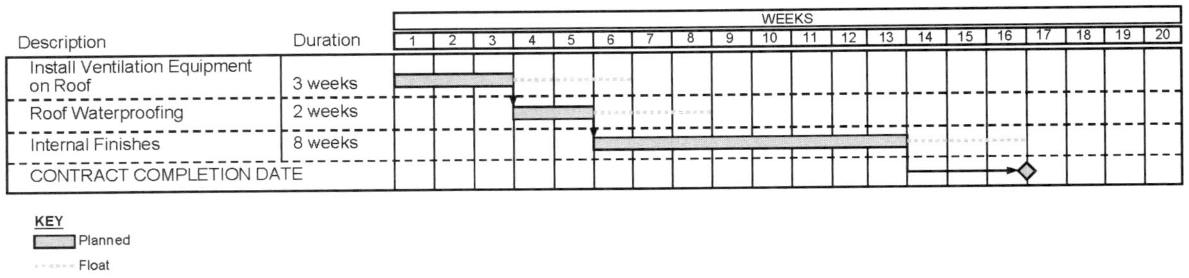

Figure 18.5 Extracts from the contractor's planned programme.

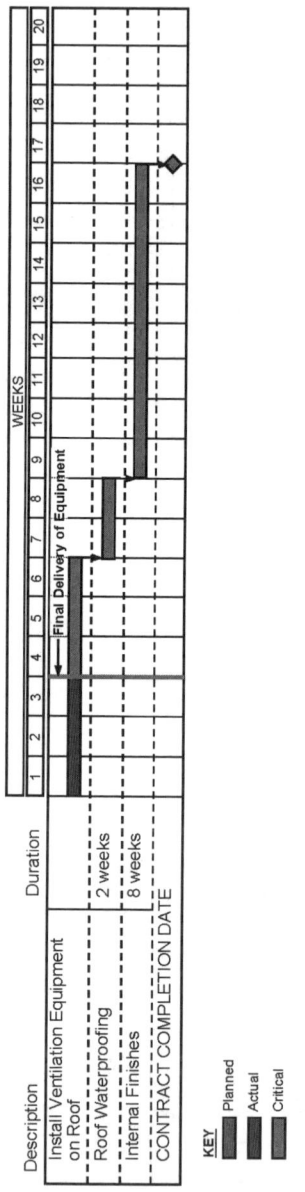

Figure 18.6 As-built programme – after delivery of equipment.

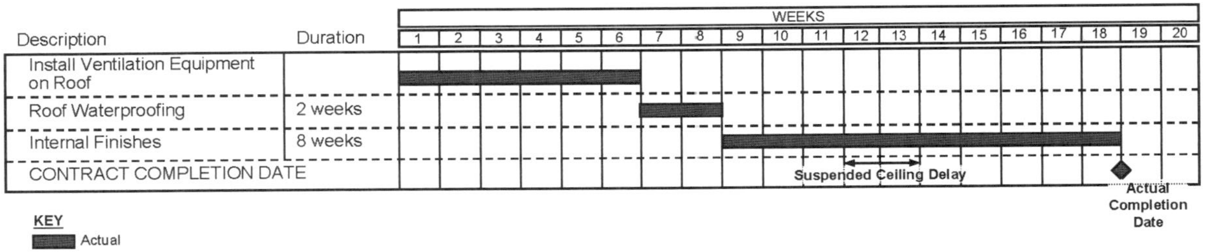

Figure 18.7 Final as-built programme.

The contractor will probably argue that he built float into his programme to cater for his own delays, e.g. the delay in internal finishes, and the cause of the delay in completion was the modification to the ventilation equipment. The architect may argue that the delay in completion was caused by the suspended ceiling subcontractor's default and as such the contractor is not entitled to an extension of time.

Who is right? Most contracts, including the JCT contract, do not address the subject of float and consequently it is a constant source of dispute in time-related claims. Float means flexibility; and both contractor's and employer's representatives argue their need to be able to adjust their programmes as they respond to events that unfold as the project progresses.

The above illustration is a simplified example of problems which can, and do, occur on construction projects. As stated earlier, the standard forms of contract do not address the issue of float. In view of the importance of float, it is essential for employers and contractors alike that it is properly identified in a structured programme, i.e. a critical path network, with any necessary adjustments made to that programme.

Conclusion

Finally, there are five basic tenets that need to be understood regarding delay, disruption and extension of time entitlement. Namely:

1   The programme is dynamic.
2   Float, also being dynamic, is best evaluated, measured and considered at the time of the delay.
3   A critical path analysis is essential to determine the cause and effect nexus required for extension of time entitlement.
4   Contractor-responsible concurrent delays do not reduce the contractor's entitlement to an extension of time.
5   However, contractor-responsible concurrent delays do reduce the contractor's entitlement to prolongation costs.

19 Concurrency

A question that frequently arises is the method of dealing with extensions of time which may be due to either or both of two causes, i.e. concurrency. The more complex the project the more likely that this issue will arise.

Concurrent delays refer to delay situations when two or more delays, regardless of the type, occur at the same time or overlap to some degree – either of which occurring alone would have affected the project completion date.

It is important to differentiate between the delaying event or cause and the delay itself. It is generally recognised that there are times when there are delays which may result from different causes, but that sometimes the causes will run at the same time or overlap. This makes it difficult to decide how to treat the delay, particularly if the causes originate from different parties or the delays are of different kinds. For example, under most forms of contract, some causes may give the contractor entitlement to an extension of time; some causes may give the contractor entitlement to an extension of time and also loss and expense, while other causes may not entitle the contractor to any extension of time or loss and expense whatsoever.

In analysing concurrent delays, each delay should be assessed separately and its impact on other activities and the project date for completion calculated. Much will turn on the quality of planning and programming, and record keeping. Not only will there often be several delay events running in parallel, but there may be parallel critical paths to contend with and periods of acceleration and/or mitigation to take into account. The contract conditions will also have to be taken into account on the analysis technique used.

Methods of assessment

Keating on Building Contracts looks at a number of propositions as follows:

1 *The Devlin Approach.* This contends that if there are two causes operating together and one is a breach of contract, then the party responsible for the breach will be liable for the loss.

2   *The Dominant Cause Approach.* This contends that if there are two causes, the effective, dominant cause is to be the deciding factor.
3   *The Burden of Proof Approach.* This contends that if there are two causes and the claimant is in breach of contract, it is for the claimant to show that the loss was caused otherwise than by his breach.

A further method to consider is the *Malmaison* approach, which is often considered to be the leading modern decision on concurrent delay. Disputes occurred on a hotel project in Manchester which culminated in arbitration and subsequently ended in Court before Mr Justice Dyson.

An agreement on concurrency was reached between the parties and this was ratified in Court by Judge Dyson thus:

> *It is agreed that if there are two concurrent causes of delay, one of which is a relevant event and the other is not, then the contractor is entitled to an extension of time for the period of delay caused by the relevant event, notwithstanding the concurrent effect of the other event. Thus to take a simple example, if no work is possible on site for a week, not only because of exceptionally inclement weather (a relevant event), but also because the contractor has a shortage of labour (not a relevant event), and if the failure to work during that week is likely to delay the works beyond the completion date by one week, then if he considers it fair and reasonable to do so, the architect is required to grant an extension of time of one week.*

Therefore, by using a simple example, Judge Dyson demonstrated that, if a contractor suffered a delay of one week due to exceptionally inclement weather, a relevant event, and in the same period there was a delay due to the contractor's shortage of labour, not a relevant event, then, if the architect considers it fair and reasonable to do so, he should grant an extension of time of one week; and he cannot refuse to grant one on the grounds that the delay would have occurred anyway because of the contractor's shortage of labour.

A simplistic approach sometimes adopted is the 'first-past-the-post' method. This is based on the logic that, where delays are running in parallel, the cause of delay that occurs first in terms of time will be used first to evaluate the impact on delay to the date for completion.

A practical approach to concurrency

When faced with the problem of concurrent delays, it is always worthwhile pausing and asking whether the delays really are concurrent as most delays are in fact consecutive. The test is to look at the project's critical path. Delays will generally be consecutive unless there are two or more critical paths. On some projects, several critical paths running in parallel is not uncommon, but even in such cases, true concurrency is rare. Usually, after investigation it can be established that one delay occurred after the other. Or, for example, only one delay was affecting the critical path and the other delay was using up only available float, so that the non-critical delay is not delaying completion of the project.

Therefore, before the question of concurrency arises at all, it must be established that there are two competing causes of delay operating at the same time and affecting the critical path or paths of the project.

Complications are introduced when, for example, one delaying event is soon followed by another during the delay caused by the first event itself, and it may be unclear as to whether the second event was triggered by the first; or if the contractor's obligation to mitigate delays has to be reassessed.

Worked examples

The project is a new school, consisting of two blocks, a classroom block and a science block. Figure 19.1 shows the planned programme for the project.

Assuming that the criteria for concurrency have been satisfied and assuming further that there are the same two causes in each case; one the fault of the contractor, i.e. equipment breakdown; the other the fault of the employer, i.e. an architect's instruction, then there are three likely scenarios.

Scenario one

This scenario looks at entitlement to an extension of time as a consequence of a relevant event, followed shortly by a contractor-responsible delay; the effect of both delays acting independently but concurrently.

Ten weeks after commencement of the project, the following event occurs (see Figure 19.2):

> *The contractor is due to start facing brickwork to the classroom block on Monday morning (start of week 11) when on the Friday before he receives an Architect's Instruction to change the colour of the facing bricks from red to blue. He orders the new blue facing bricks immediately, but they are on 4 weeks delivery and will not arrive until the end of week 14, which means that the start of facing brickwork will be delayed until the beginning of week 15. This will cause a delay of 4 weeks to the progress of the works and this delay will cause a likely delay of 4 weeks to the date for Completion.*

Shortly afterwards a further event occurs.

> *The contractor is due to start erecting precast floor units to the science block at the start of week 13. Therefore, he carries out preparatory work and organises his labour and lifting crane ready to commence*

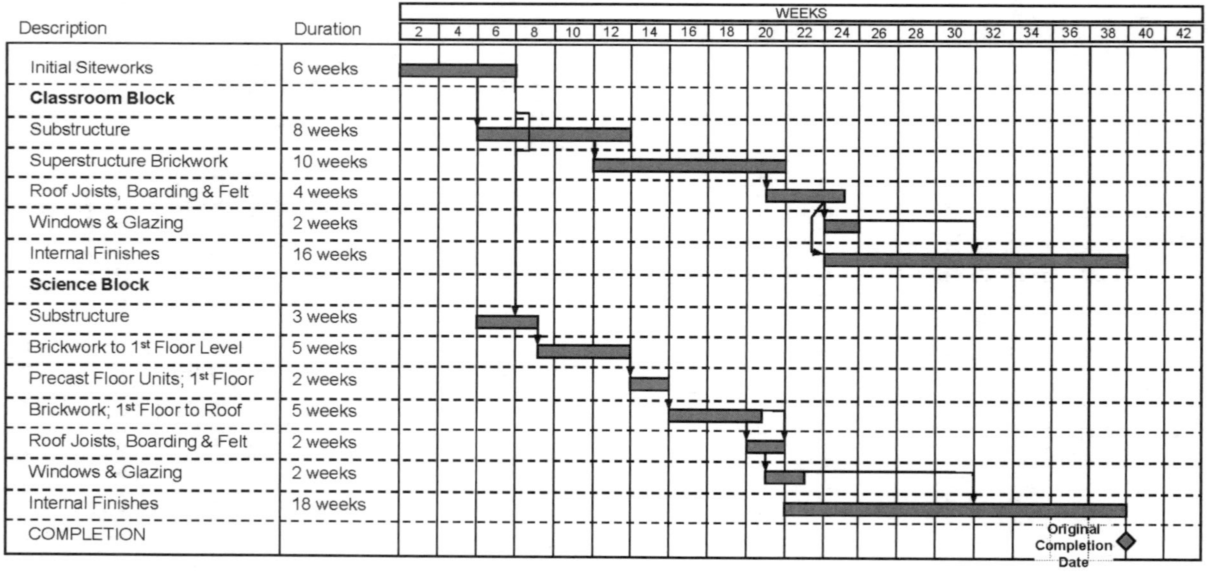

Figure 19.1 Planned programme.

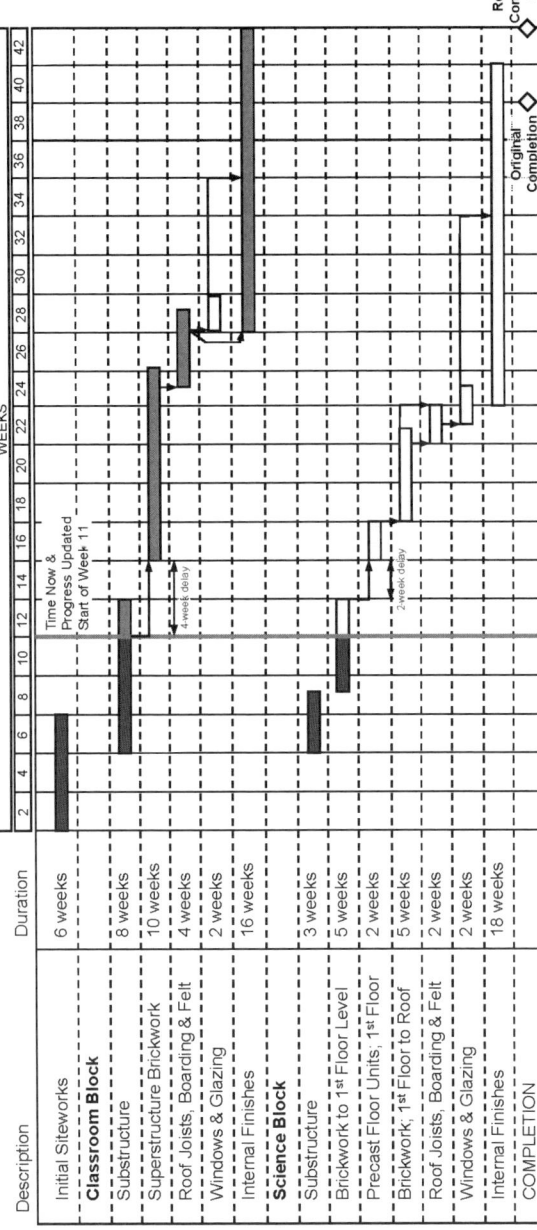

Figure 19.2 As-built situation: as at start of week 11.

Notes

1 4-week delay to progress due to late delivery of changed facing bricks
2 2-week delay to progress due to contractor's craneage breakdown
Extension of Time Entitlement: 4 weeks

lifting the precast units at the start of week 13. On the Monday morning of week 13, his crane breaks down at the start of this operation and it will take 2 weeks to obtain the necessary replacement parts and carry out the repairs. He therefore re-schedules the installation of the precast floor units to start at the beginning of week 15. This will cause a delay of 2 weeks to the progress of the works and this delay will cause a likely delay of 2 weeks to the original date for completion.

However, while the crane breakdown was delaying progress on the science block it had no effect on the forecast date for completion, because this was already being delayed by the architect's instruction revising the facing bricks for the classroom block.

Therefore, in scenario one, the contractor is entitled to a four-week extension of time to the date for completion as a consequence of the instruction to change the facing bricks, which should not be reduced because of his own culpable delay of mechanical breakdown.

However, for prolongation costs/loss and expense, the contractor's two-week concurrent culpable delay should be taken into account.

Scenario two

This scenario looks at entitlement to an extension of time as a consequence of a relevant event, when a contractor-responsible delay occurs at the same time; the effect of both delays acting independently but concurrently.

Using the same events as for scenario one, except that in the early part of week 11 the facing brick manufacturer receives an order cancellation from another contractor and is able to deliver the new blue facing bricks at the end of week 11. We now have the following situation:

1   The new blue facing bricks are delivered to site at the end of week 11 and facing brickwork to the classroom block starts at the beginning of week 12. This causes a delay of one week to the progress of the works and this delay will cause a likely delay of one week to the date for completion.

2   The situation on the new science block is still the same as for scenario one. At the beginning of week 13, the contractor was due to start erecting precast floor units to the science block. His crane breaks down at the start of this operation and it will take two weeks to obtain the necessary replacement parts and carry out the repairs. He therefore reschedules the installation of the precast floor units to start at the beginning of week 15. This will cause a delay of two weeks to the progress of the works and as the science block is on the second critical path, this delay will cause a likely delay of two weeks to the date for completion.

Figure 19.3 below shows the situation for scenario two.

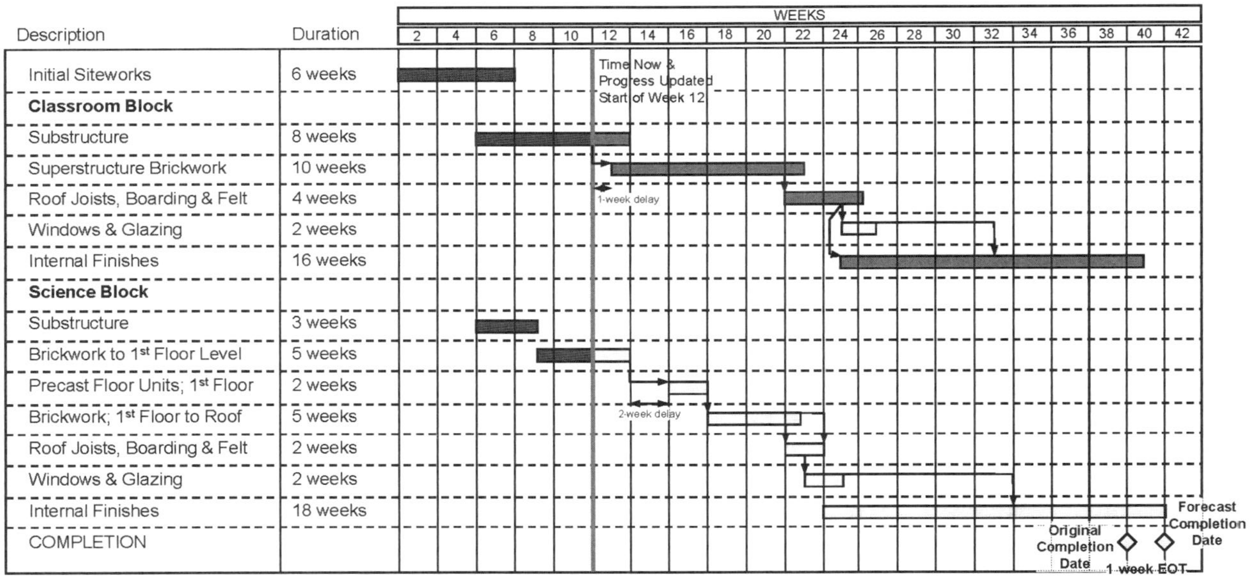

Figure 19.3 As-built situation: as at start of week 12.

Notes
1 1-week delay to progress due to late delivery of changed facing bricks
2 2-week delay to progress due to contractor's craneage breakdown
Extension of Time Entitlement: 1 week

Therefore, in scenario two, the contractor is entitled to a one-week extension of time to the date for completion as a consequence of the instruction to change the facing bricks, which should not be negated because of his own culpable delay of mechanical breakdown.

However, for prolongation costs/loss and expense, the contractor's two-week concurrent culpable delay should be taken into account.

Scenario three

This scenario looks at entitlement to an extension of time as a consequence of a relevant event, when a contractor-responsible delay has occurred just prior to the relevant event; and the effect of both delays are acting independently but concurrently.

Using the same events as for scenario one, except that the facing brick manufacturer can commence delivery immediately of the new blue facing bricks and brickwork to the classroom block commenced on programme at the start of week 11. However, shortly afterwards, the following situation develops.

1 In the early part of week 16 the facing brick manufacturer has a problem with the quality of the changed blue facing bricks which results in a two-week period where no blue facing bricks are delivered to site. This results in completion of the classroom block brickwork being delayed by two weeks until the end of week 22.

2 Meanwhile, the situation on the new science block is still the same as for scenario one. At the beginning of week 13, the contractor was due to start erecting precast floor units to the science block. His crane breaks down at the start of this operation and it will take two weeks to obtain the necessary replacement parts and carry out the repairs. He therefore reschedules the installation of the precast floor units to start at the beginning of week 15. This will cause a delay of two weeks to the progress of the works and, as the science block is on the second critical path, this delay will cause a likely delay of two weeks to the date for completion.

Figure 19.4 shows the situation for scenario three.

Therefore, in scenario three, at week 13 there is a delay to 'the progress of the works' as a consequence of the contractor's equipment breakdown on the science block. At the time, this is likely to cause a two-week delay to the current date completion.

A few weeks later, there is a separate delay on the classroom block, as a consequence of a relevant event. As a result there is a delay to the progress of the works on the classroom block only but no likely delay to the date for completion, as the current forecast completion date has not been delayed further.

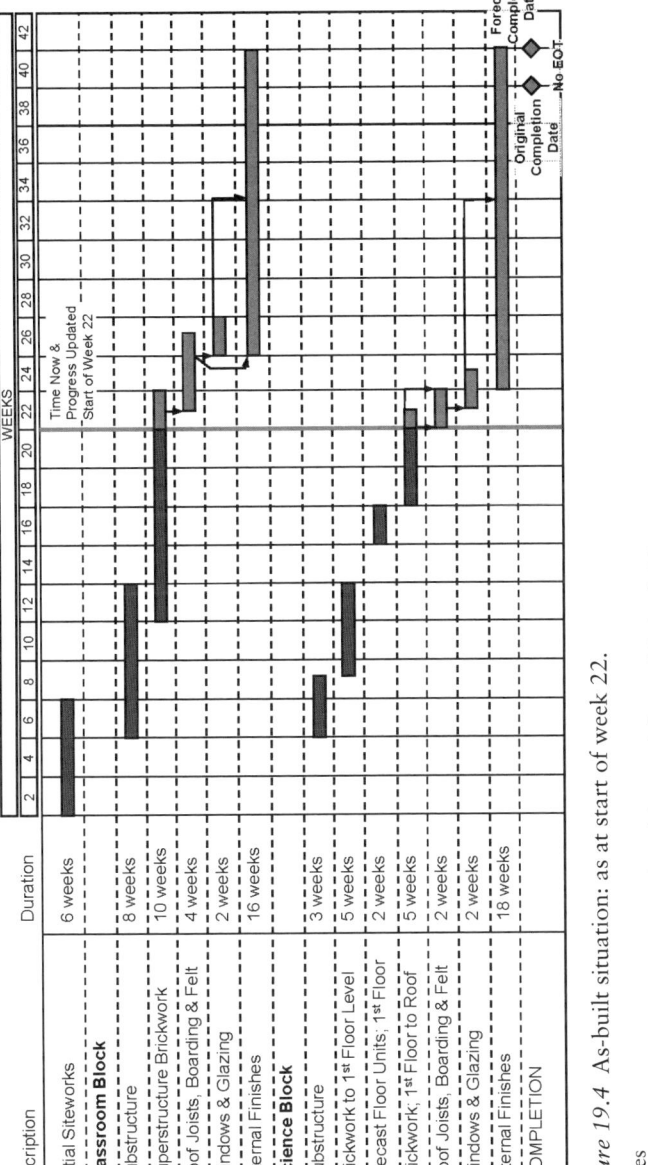

Figure 19.4 As-built situation: as at start of week 22.

Notes

1 2-week delay to progress due to late delivery of changed facing bricks
2 2-week delay to progress due to contractor's craneage breakdown

Extension of Time Entitlement: nil

Therefore, the contractor is not entitled to an extension of time to the date for completion as a consequence of the instruction to change the facing bricks and the resulting delay in delivery of the bricks.

However, an important issue here is that the situation on the science block should be kept under close review for, if the contractor subsequently mitigates his own two-week delay caused by his equipment breakdown, then he will probably be entitled to a two-week extension of time for the relevant event of the changed facing bricks.

For prolongation and time-related costs, unless the circumstances change, as explained above, it is unlikely that the contractor will be reimbursed.

Useful guidelines

Where there are overlapping or concurrent delays, the most popular guidelines are:

1   No extension of time is granted when an employer-responsible delay event is within a non-critical path while a contractor-responsible delay (e.g. poor progress through lack of resources) is on a critical path.
2   An extension of time is awarded when both an employer-responsible delay event and a contractor-responsible delay event occur concurrently on parallel critical paths, on the basis that either delay by itself could have prolonged the project by the same period.

However, where the delays are unequal, or where an employer-responsible delay is followed by a contractor-responsible delay (or vice versa) on the same or parallel critical paths, and it is unclear as to whether the second was triggered by the first, the 'dominant cause' approach could help to allocate liabilities.

Clearly, more explicit guidelines are needed based on sound principles to improve fairness, consistency and certainty in practice, which would in turn lead to better planning and control of potential project risks and less resource wastage on acrimonious disputes where these risks materialise.

20 Mitigation and acceleration

Most forms of contract contain reference to a contractor's obligation to mitigate delays, including the effects of employer-responsible delays.

JCT 2005 contains the following at clause 2.28.6.1:

> *the Contractor shall constantly use his best endeavours to prevent delay in the progress of the Works or any Section, however caused, and to prevent the completion of the Works or Section being delayed or further delayed beyond the relevant Completion Date.*

However, in many instances this leads to conflicting interpretations, for example, as to what extent of 'best endeavours', or mitigation, is required. Beyond a certain level, e.g. if substantially more resources are mobilised, it could be interpreted as 'acceleration' to catch up for delays by others, rather than mere 'mitigation', which could lead to further claims for compensation.

'Acceleration' tends to be bandied about as if it were a term of art with a precise meaning, but this is not the case.

The reasons for acceleration usually fall into one of the following categories:

1 *By agreement or instruction.* By agreement between the parties or, if the contract so provides, on the instruction of the architect.
2 *Unilateral acceleration.* Unilaterally on the initiative of the contractor, often categorised as 'mitigation' by the contractor or as 'using best endeavours' by the employer.
3 *Constructive acceleration.* Constructive acceleration is where the contractor argues that he has no real alternative in the circumstances.

By agreement or instruction

There should be no difficulty in obtaining payment where the architect, in exercise of his powers under a contract, orders acceleration of the work or the employer and the contractor agree acceleration and a claim under the direct loss and expense clause is unnecessary.

However, few standard forms of contract give the architect the power to order the contractor to accelerate.

Unilateral acceleration

This is the situation where a contractor accelerates without any agreement with the employer or instruction from the architect. No pressure has been placed on him by the refusal of an extension of time; indeed in this situation it may be that the contractor is reasonably confident of getting an extension of time. The reason for doing so may be in order to find work for operatives from another site where construction is drawing to a close. The result may be that some time is recovered and an extension of time is not required. In most such cases, the contractor will find it difficult to contend that he was doing other than 'using his best endeavours' to reduce delay.

Constructive acceleration

This is an argument advanced by a contractor and is based on the architect's failure to give an extension of time to which the contractor believes he is entitled. A contractor will put more resources into a project than originally envisaged and then attempt to recover the value on the basis that he was obliged to do so in order to complete on time, because the architect failed to make an extension of time of the contract period. The problem faced by the contractor is that, in the absence of an extension of time, he may have liquidated damages being levied against him. He has a stark choice: he can continue to work as planned and efficiently in the hope that he can later successfully demonstrate that he is entitled to an extension of time and that this will be granted. Alternatively, he can accept, temporarily at least, that he is in default and take steps to mitigate the consequences of this temporary default by putting more resources into the project, and/or reorganising the works, so as to finish by the date for completion.

An important question to be asked before this kind of argument can be entertained is the extent to which pressure is put on the contractor; the contractor's problem is one of causation. Where the architect fails to make an extension of time, either at all or of sufficient length, the contractor's route under the contract is adjudication or arbitration. If, as a matter of fact and law, the contractor is entitled to an extension of time, it may be said that he can confidently continue the work, without increasing resources, secure in the knowledge that he will be able to recover his prolongation loss and/or expense and any liquidated damages wrongfully deducted, at adjudication or arbitration. If he increases his resources, that is not a direct result of the architect's breach, but of the contractor's decision.

In practice, it must be acknowledged that a contractor in this position may not be entirely confident; the facts may be complex and the liquidated damages high. Faith in the wisdom of an adjudicator or arbitrator may not be total. It may be cheaper, even without recovering acceleration costs, for the contractor to accelerate rather than face liquidated damages with no guarantee that an extension of time will ultimately be made. As a matter of plain commercial realism, the contractor may have no other sensible choice than to accelerate and take a chance as to recovery. Unless the contractor can show that the architect has given him no real expectation that the contract period will ever be extended and in those circumstances the amount of liquidated damages would effectively bring about insolvency, this kind of claim has little chance of success.

However, under the Housing Grants, Construction and Regeneration Act, a contractor now has the option to address the uncertainty at an early stage and not wait until after completion of the project. He can refer the architect's/contract administrator's refusal of his extension of time claim to an adjudicator during the course of the contract, rather than to arbitration or litigation after completion.

In the United States, a 'constructive acceleration' doctrine has been established to permit a contractor to claim his acceleration costs. The US doctrine, modified for the British construction scene, comprises a six-stage test:

1   Is there a delay, resulting from a relevant event, that would entitle the contractor to an extension of time?
2   Has the architect/contract administrator been given notice of the delay in accordance with the contract?
3   Has the architect/contract administrator refused or failed to grant an extension of time?
4   Has the architect/contract administrator or employer acted in some manner that can be construed as an instruction to complete by the original or revised date for completion?
5   Has the contractor accelerated its performance?
6   Has the contractor incurred additional costs as a result?

Recovery of acceleration costs

Usually, if it can be shown that the acceleration has been caused by an event for which there should have been compensation, then there is no reason why the costs should not be recoverable as loss and expense and valued in the usual way under the contract. However, if they cannot be so valued, then it is possible that the claim can proceed on a quantum merit basis of the reasonable costs of the accelerated works.

21 Time at large

In the absence of any contractual mechanism for fixing a new date for completion, then no such date can be fixed and the contractor's duty then will be to complete the works within a reasonable time. Provided the contractor has not acted unreasonably or negligently, he will complete within a reasonable time despite a protracted delay due to causes outside his control. In such circumstances, time is said to be 'at large'.

The expression 'time at large' is used to indicate that the contractor believes that there is no enforceable date for completion of the works. Therefore, as there is then no date from which they can be calculated, the employer's right to liquidated damages is annulled. If the contractor's argument succeeds, then his obligation is to complete within a reasonable time. If the argument does not succeed, then the employer may recover his losses as general damages at common law.

Whether time has become at large is a matter for the contract, and the facts and circumstances that are alleged to defeat the application of liquidated damages.

The most common allegation supporting a claim for 'time at large' is that the contract administrator has either failed to grant an extension of time at all, or that the extension of time that has been awarded is very unreasonable.

However, in most standard forms of contract a refusal or unappealing extension of time award by the architect/contract administrator will not set 'time at large'. Under the Housing Grants, Construction and Regeneration Act, a contractor now has the option to refer the architect's/contract administrator's unappealing response to his extension of time claim to an adjudicator during the course of the contract.

All standard forms of contract have clauses permitting an extension of time thereby enabling the architect or contract administrator to fix a new completion date where the employer is responsible for delay to the progress of the works. However, even where a contract contains terms providing for an extension to the contract period, time may yet become 'at large', either because the terms do not properly provide for the delaying event or because the architect/contract administrator has not correctly operated the terms. For example, the JCT 2005 series of contracts list, under clause 28, events giving grounds for extension of time. Because the power of the architect/contract administrator to award an extension of time is restricted to the listed events, there is a danger that the employer may delay the works in a way which does not fall under one of the listed events. In such a case, time would be 'at large'.

Again, with reference to the JCT suite of contracts, where the architect/contract administrator operates the extension of time clause incorrectly, time may become 'at large'. An example would be where the architect was late in issuing drawings or information to the contractor, a fact causing or likely to cause delay to completion of the works, but he failed to give any extension of time.

It is common to find the allegation in a contractor's claim that the employer is not entitled to any liquidated damages and that 'time is at large'. The contractor's position is usually that, for reasons within the employer's control, the contractor was prevented from completing by the date for completion and the date was not properly extended by the contract administrator. The employer can no longer insist upon the completion date, original or revised, and therefore there is no firm date from which liquidated damages can be calculated. Time is then said to be 'at large', as a result of the effect of the 'prevention principle'; a rule of law that 'a man should not be allowed to recover damages for what he himself has caused'.

Determining a reasonable time to complete once time is 'at large'

This is dependent upon the circumstances that led to time becoming at large and, based upon the date when time became at large, the information available from which such a calculation can be made.

There is some case law support for the view that, provided that the contract contained a completion date, or a completion date could be construed from the conduct of the parties, then that is the position from which to commence identifying a reasonable time to complete.

In the case of *Astea* v. *Time Group*, HHJ Seymour considers that the contractor's contract period was the appropriate starting point, by saying that consideration of a reasonable time for performance 'is likely to include taking into account any estimate given by the performing party of how long it would take him to perform...'.

In a further case, *J & J Fee* v. *Express Lift*, there had been correspondence between the parties on the dates of commencement and completion. The last correspondence from the contractor stated that it could see little possibility of improvement on the dates previously given, but suggested that it would try to improve upon it. HHJ Bowsher gave a provisional view (without deciding) that it would be impossible for the contractor to contend that a reasonable time for completion of the works would be any later than the date consistently put forward in contract negotiations.

Determining a reasonable time to complete

Where a contract period is established, it should be possible to take as a baseline the contractor's planned programme for the contract scope and add to this the effect of the employer's delay events or breach. This approach and methodology is known 'as planned impacted'.

Provided the necessary materials are available, a reasonable time to complete can also be calculated by the 'time impact' method. This method is recommended by the Society of Construction Law in their 'Delay and Disruption Protocol'. By taking into account the contractor's culpable delay, if any, and identifying the net effect of the employer-responsible delay events on the contractor's programme, the contractor does not benefit from additional time other than that caused by the employer's delay events or breach.

A further technique, and one that is often used in the absence of a contract period from which to start, is the 'collapsed as-built' method. Provided the materials are available from which to establish an as-built programme, this method uses as the baseline the programme of work that was actually carried out, i.e. the as-built programme for the project. From this programme, the actual periods of time for which the contractor is liable are subtracted from the actual critical path. This shortens the actual critical path and the resultant completion date can be said to be the completion date that reasonably could have been achieved, save for the contractor's culpable delay.

Summary

It is common to see in a contractor's claim the contention that 'time is at large'.

Time being 'at large' does not mean that the contractor has no obligation to complete the work. He has to complete in a 'reasonable time'. What is reasonable depends on the facts and circumstances at the time.

Part V

Extensions of time

22 Introduction

The standard forms of contract set out a number of possible contingencies, the risk of which is to be borne not by the contractor but by the employer. For example, the JCT form, under clause 25, details relevant events which are beyond the control of the contractor. If the occurrence of any of those contingencies occur so as to cause the works to take longer to complete then, because those contingencies are not at the contractor's risk, that much more time must be added to the contract period. Without provisions for more time to be granted, for example for the effect on the contract period for late issue of information, time would become at large. This means that the contractor would have to complete not within the contract period but within a reasonable time, whatever that was determined to be. Furthermore, the employer would not be able to recover liquidated damages for any overrun of the contract period. This is why there are provisions for time to be extended in the event that the contract period is adversely affected by those risks that are borne by the employer.

The amount of time to be added to the contract period for employer-responsible delaying events which have caused delay to the completion date should be calculated logically and methodically by the contract administrator, or architect, and he must form his judgement impartially and objectively. This means that, if it comes to a dispute as to whether a fair and reasonable extension of time has been granted and the contract administrator has determined the period of that extension of time instinctively, intuitively or under the instructions of one of the parties, his decision is likely to be overturned.

Unfortunately, none of the standard forms provide any indication of the sort of information or technique upon which such a logical and methodical appreciation of the factual matrix upon which an extension of time should be calculated.

For example, JCT 1980 requires the contractor to identify any cause of delay or likely delay to progress, and requires the contractor to estimate the effect on the date for completion for each delay event and to provide all the necessary particulars demonstrating how such an effect has been calculated. However, it does not say how, i.e. which EOT assessment technique should be used to demonstrate any such delay to the date for completion.

It is important to recognise that, generally, it is only a delay or likely delay to the progress of the works that the contractor has to notify, but it is the extent, or knock-on effect of such event to the date for completion that the contract administrator has to certify. One of the major difficulties is that the delay in the planned timing of an activity alone gives no clue as to whether it is likely to have an effect on the date for completion. Neither is it of any importance that an activity took longer to achieve than that shown on the contractor's as-planned programme. In the end, the deciding factor to the contract administrator is whether the employer-responsible delay event has adversely affected the date for completion.

Except in the most obvious of circumstances, proving a chain of causation in an environment in which many ongoing activities are being carried out concurrently is by no means a simple exercise. Therefore, even if the contractor provides what is required under the contract, the contract administrator will necessarily have to do an awful amount of work to sort out the wheat from the chaff.

Arising out of its role as an aid to the planning of a project and as a monitor of current performance, it was a short step to the programme being used to provide a quick and simple means for appraising delays and showing entitlement for extensions of time. By the early 1970s the use of computers and project-planning software meant that the critical path method (CPM) was developed as a tool for assessing responsibility in delay and disruption construction disputes.

Since then there has been a proliferation of techniques, which have evolved with increasing sophistication and ingenuity, but most of these suffer from weaknesses in adequately addressing a number of issues relating to the use of CPM for extension of time submissions and delay claims, such as programme float and concurrency.

Delay analysis

'Delay analysis' in respect of a construction dispute is the process in a claim or claim defence that the contractor or employer has to practise in order to be able to:

- establish lines of research and investigation;
- demonstrate the contractor's (or employer's) entitlement to claim (or to reject a claim against it or to counterclaim);
- present the claim (or claim defence) effectively.

The initial research and review stage will help to ascertain whether the delay claim to be pursued involves 'critical' delays or 'non-critical' delays. Critical delays are those that delay the project completion date, whereas non-critical delays are those which affect progress at any given time but which have no ultimate effect upon the completion date of the project.

The next stage is that of investigation, when all the factors relating to the areas of claim made known during the initial research and review stage are analysed. The aim is to establish the specific causes of the delay, in which area or section of the work it took place, and when it began to affect the rate of progress. It is often helpful at this stage to use specific databases to record this information.

Once recorded in a database, these records would then have to be analysed and put into a format that can be used to demonstrate how the particular events led to the delays. After compiling the databases regarding the delay claims, the results may be shown in the form of charts, graphs, histograms, etc.; basically adopting the best format to make the most presentable and convincing argument when presenting the claim.

EOT assessment techniques

Due to the dynamic and often complex nature of a construction project, the simple 'short-cut' method of delay analysis has proved to be inappropriate for anything other than providing a relatively informed feel for what happened. However, this can be useful for the purpose of providing an element of support for positions adopted in the context of normal final account negotiation, but it falls considerably short of the burden of proof in the context of legal proceedings.

Previous experiences of various authors and observations by other investigators indicate the wide spectrum of EOT assessment and analysis approaches/techniques adopted or adapted by various contractors and consultants at different times; but also the lack of consensus on any suitable approach.

A closer examination of the various techniques widely employed for EOT submissions shows that none of the commonly recognised methods allows for the assessment of three important issues at the same time, namely:

1   the progress of the project at the time the event occurred;
2   the changing nature of the critical path at the time the delay occurred;
3   the effects of action taken, or that should have been taken, to minimise likely delays.

It is thus not surprising that the consequential inconsistencies and clashes have fuelled many prolonged disputes on EOT analysis and assessments.

Problems often arise in unravelling 'cause' and 'effect' patterns, given that many EOT causes and entitlement are interrelated and may also be concurrent. Concurrent delays are said to arise when two or more delays occur at the same time or overlap to some degree. Examples of scenarios needing careful consideration and evaluation include those where:

1   a contractor-responsible event on a non-critical path makes a sub-sequent activity critical and this activity is then subjected to an employer-responsible event;
2   an employer-responsible event is followed by a contractor-responsible event;
3   an employer-responsible event and a contractor-responsible event are concurrent and on parallel critical paths.

The following chapter describes most of the recognised EOT assessment techniques, categorised into the following groups:

A   *Impressionistic.* Visually impressive, these are only suitable for simple projects.
B   *Simplistic.* These are static models and do not provide the insights into impacts and relationships afforded by critical path analysis methods.
C   *Prospective analysis.* These techniques use as-planned programmes and essentially project the likely delay an event will cause.
D   *Retrospective analysis.* These techniques use as-built programmes and establish the actual delay an event caused.

However, the critical importance of reliable documentation and records in establishing EOT entitlements cannot be over-emphasised, whichever technique is ultimately adopted.

Extension of time submissions

Major obstacles to prompt settlement of submissions for extensions of time include:

1   The erroneous assumption that an extension of time automatically grants entitlement to monetary compensation.
2   Late, insufficient or total lack of notice of delay or likely delay on the part of the contractor.
3   Failure to maintain contemporary records.
4   Failure to regularly update the programme so that the effects of delay can be monitored.
5   Poor presentation of the claim to show how the progress of the work has been, or is likely to be, impacted.
6   The probability that the cause of delay will reflect on the performance, or lack of it, on the part of the employer's professional team.
7   Pressure, on the part of the employer, to complete the project by the original completion date, irrespective of delays which occur.

The first obstacle, (1) which assumes that delay means money, is understandable. Nevertheless, it should not be a consideration when reviewing and resolving extensions of time. It should be clearly understood that an extension of time merely gives the contractor more time to complete the works and allows the employer to preserve his rights to liquidated damages. An extension of time awarded for a cause of delay which appears to have financial implications does not necessarily lead to additional payment. If the contractor is himself also in delay, then the financial compensation arising out of the extended period to execute the works may, in total or in part, have to be borne by the contractor.

The next three obstacles, (2) notice, (3) contemporary records and (4) programme, are all practical matters which can only be addressed by ensuring that adequate contract administration procedures are followed from the start of the project.

The fifth obstacle concerns presentation of the claim. While the contract administrator must do his best to estimate the length of any extension of time which may be due, irrespective of lack of notice and particulars given by the contractor, contractors cannot complain if the extension made on the basis of inadequate information does not live up to their expectations.

Good practice

It is recommended that for an EOT submission, the contractor should state:

1 the material circumstances giving rise to an extension of time;
2 the event or cause of entitlement;
3 whether the cause is a relevant event under the contract;
4 the delay, or likely delay, to the progress of the works;
5 the likely effect of the event on the completion date of the contract and any contractual sectional completion dates.

Which technique to use sometimes depends on the reason for preparing the delay analysis. For example, a contractor who makes a submission to the employer, or his representative, for an extension of time as part of the final account settlement, may not have the time for an extensive delay analysis and so will lean towards one of the simplistic techniques. Going to the other extreme, if the dispute is in arbitration or litigation, one of the prospective analysis or retrospective analysis techniques should be exploited as the level of sophistication required in these arenas excludes the impressionistic and simplistic techniques.

The claimant is free to choose any format he wishes to present his delay claim but should be aware that the courts have rejected some formats. It may be, however, that the claimant has other reasons for selecting a particular format (e.g. as a negotiating tool or because their client has requested a particular type of presentation). Should the claimant proceed with a claim in a particular format for, say, negotiation purposes and then find that negotiations break down and a dispute ensues, then the claimant may be put to the task (and cost) of reworking the delay claim into a format more acceptable to the court.

Now that the Civil Procedure Rules (CPR) are in place, their objectives and principles should be considered, which basically means that issues of fairness, time and cost effectiveness are important. The Statement of Case (which replaced Pleadings) should clearly set out the case to be answered.

The most detailed claims-programming method is time impact analysis and although not specifically mentioned in the above cases, it requires the application of retrospective analysis techniques (accepted in *McAlpine* v. *McDermott*). However, like other programming methods, its application is dependent on the records available. The purpose and intended use of a delay claim is relevant here in that time impact analysis is not necessarily needed if there is little likelihood that the claim will proceed to litigation/arbitration. Time impact analysis is very detailed and time-consuming and the claimant may wish to proceed with a different technique in appropriate circumstances. As stated in the cases above, the claimant can proceed as he sees fit (subject in legal proceedings to ensuring that the other party knows the case against it).

23 EOT assessment techniques

In the English and Commonwealth jurisdictions there are very few cases setting out guidelines for methodology or techniques that should be adopted when preparing or considering an extension of time submission or claim.

The previous chapter outlined four groups categorising most of the recognised extension of time (EOT) assessment techniques:

A   impressionistic;
B   simplistic;
C   prospective analysis;
D   retrospective analysis.

Only the latter two groups, prospective and retrospective analysis, are considered to be dynamic analysis techniques.

To demonstrate and compare the presentations of the various EOT assessment techniques, a standard project has been adopted, namely the construction of a garage. For this project, the as-planned programme consists of ten number activities and is displayed in network format as shown in Figure 23.1.

When presented in the more usual barchart format, the as-planned programme appears as shown in Figure 23.2.

As can be seen, construction of the garage was planned to take 32 working days. However, during the course of construction there were delays, and the final as-built barchart is shown in Figure 23.3. A side-by-side comparison of the as-planned and as-built barcharts can be seen in Figure 23.4.

The planned duration for construction of the garage was 32 days, but the actual duration was 40 days, representing an overrun of eight days. As stated earlier, delays on the project directly caused this overrun.

An initial review shows that delays occurred to the work activities detailed in Figure 23.5.

Taking the garage-construction project as an example, the EOT assessment techniques within each group are described below.

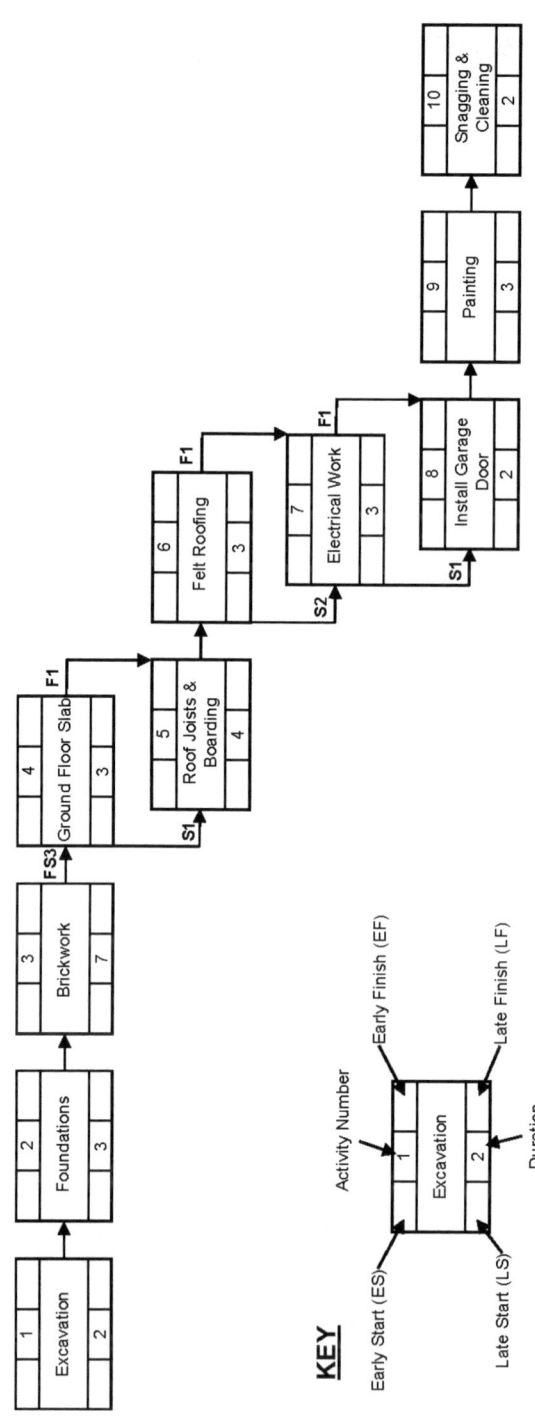

Figure 23.1 As-planned – network format.

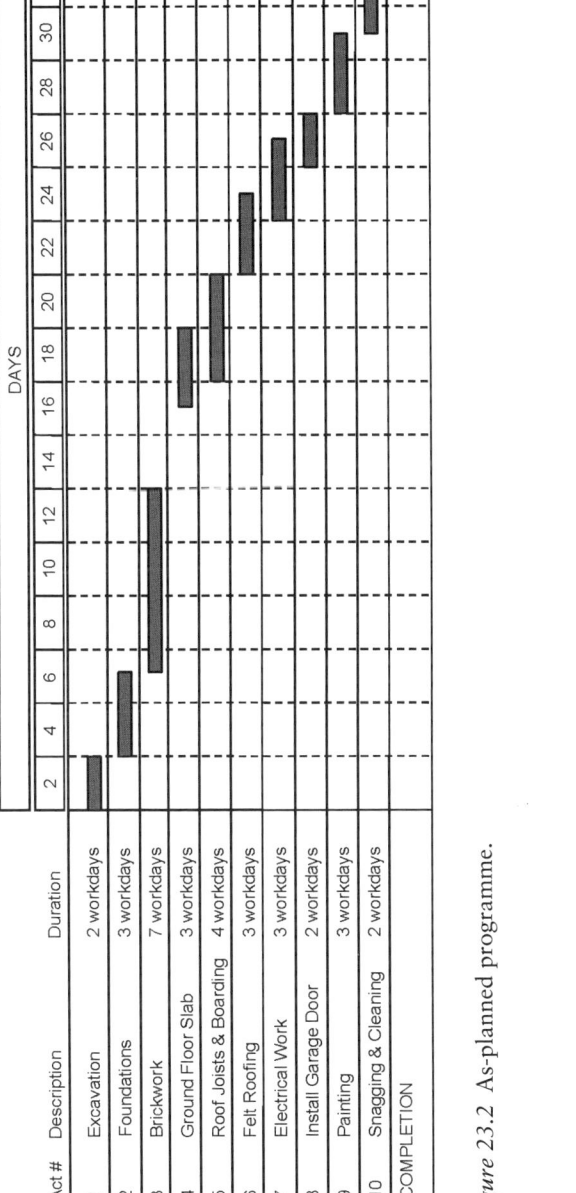

Figure 23.2 As-planned programme.

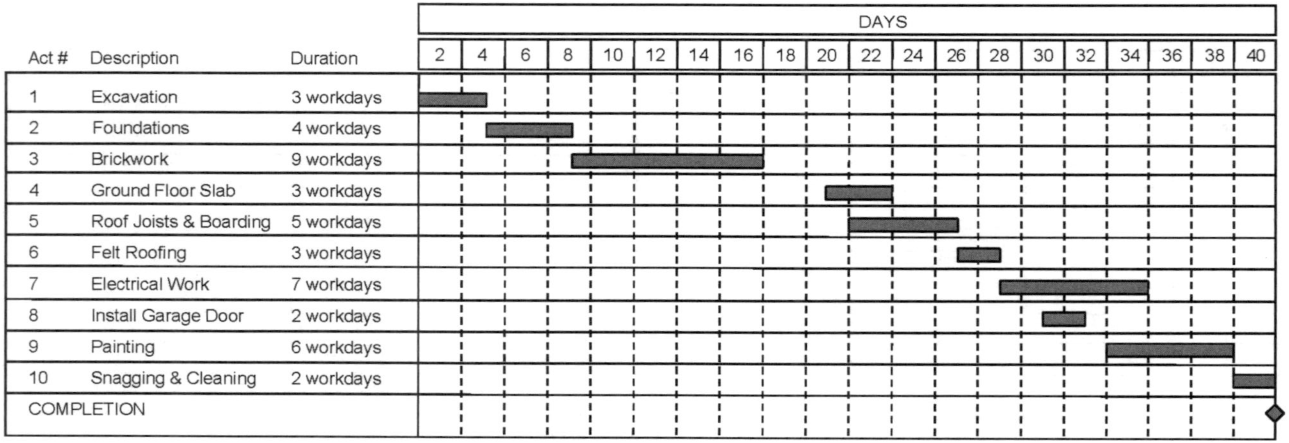
DAYS
2
4
6
8
10
12
14
16
18
20
22
24
26
28
30
32
34
36
38
40
Act #
Description
Duration
1 Excavation 3 workdays
2 Foundations 4 workdays
3 Brickwork 9 workdays
4 Ground Floor Slab 3 workdays
5 Roof Joists & Boarding 5 workdays
6 Felt Roofing 3 workdays
7 Electrical Work 7 workdays
8 Install Garage Door 2 workdays
9 Painting 6 workdays
10 Snagging & Cleaning 2 workdays
COMPLETION

Figure 23.3 As-built programme.

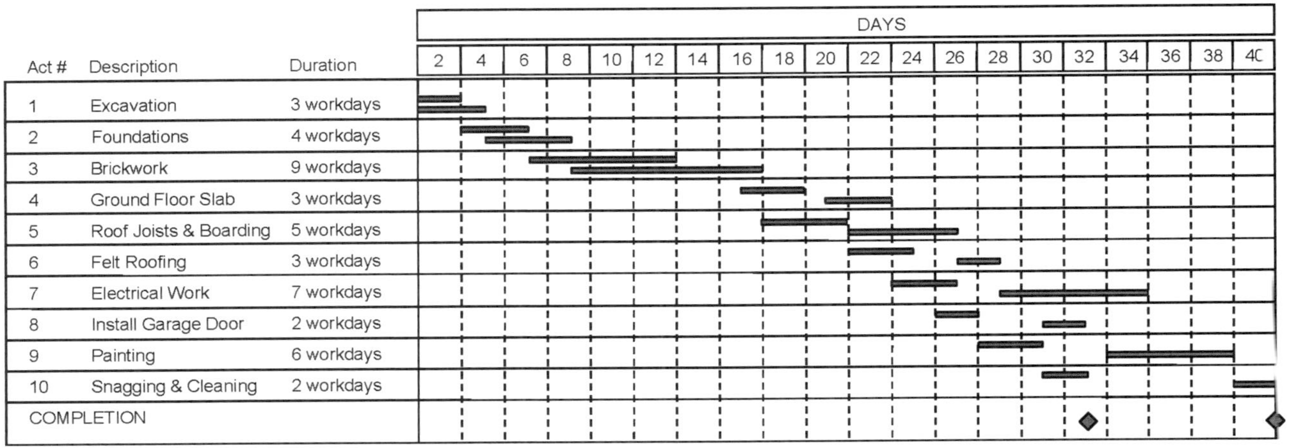

Figure 23.4 As-planned/as-built comparison.

Act.nr.	Description	Duration		Delay responsibility	
		Planned	Actual	Employer	Contractor
1	Excavation	2 workdays	3 workdays		1 workday
2	Foundations	3 workdays	4 workdays	1 workday	
3	Brickwork	7 workdays	9 workdays	2 workdays	
4	Ground Floor Slab	3 workdays	3 workdays		
5	Roof Joists & Boarding	4 workdays	5 workdays	1 workday	
6	Felt Roofing	3 workdays	3 workdays		
7	Electrical Work	3 workdays	7 workdays	4 workdays	
8	Install Garage Door	2 workdays	2 workdays		
9	Painting	3 workdays	6 workdays	3 workdays	
10	Snagging & Cleaning	2 workdays	2 workdays		
			Total	11 workdays	1 workday

Figure 23.5 Initial review showing delays.

A Impressonistic

This group includes the following techniques.

A1 Global impact

The global impact technique is a simplistic way to show the impact of employer-responsible events. All such delays are plotted on a barchart. The delay start and finish dates are determined for each event. The total delay to the project is calculated to be the sum total of all durations of all the individual delaying events. An example of this technique, based on the sample project is shown in Figure 23.6.

In the garage construction project, the planned duration was 32 days and the actual construction was 40 days, an overrun of eight days. The contractor claimed a total of 11 days' extension of time as a consequence of delays which were the responsibility of the employer (see Figure 23.5).

The 'global impact' technique in Figure 23.6 shows on a barchart the as-planned and as-built programmes in summary format, with an additional summary bar representing the total of the delay for which the employer is responsible. The contractor will probably argue that the difference between the 11days' entitlement to an extension of time and the actual project overrun of only eight days was due to his acceleration.

Observations

The 'global impact' technique uses the as-planned programme and therefore assumes the critical path(s) on this programme were constant throughout the project. This leads to delays potentially being deemed as critical when in fact they were not.

There are many other problems with this technique, but the main issues that this technique ignores or disregards, are that

1   it assumes every delay has an impact on the project's date for completion;
2   it does not take into account the effect of concurrent delays.

The above shortcomings can and do lead to a gross overstatement of entitlement due to employer-responsible delays. As in the example, in many cases the entitlement due can exceed the project's actual completion date; the rationale being that the difference between the entitlement completion date and the actual completion date is the amount of time saved by the contractor through his acceleration measures.

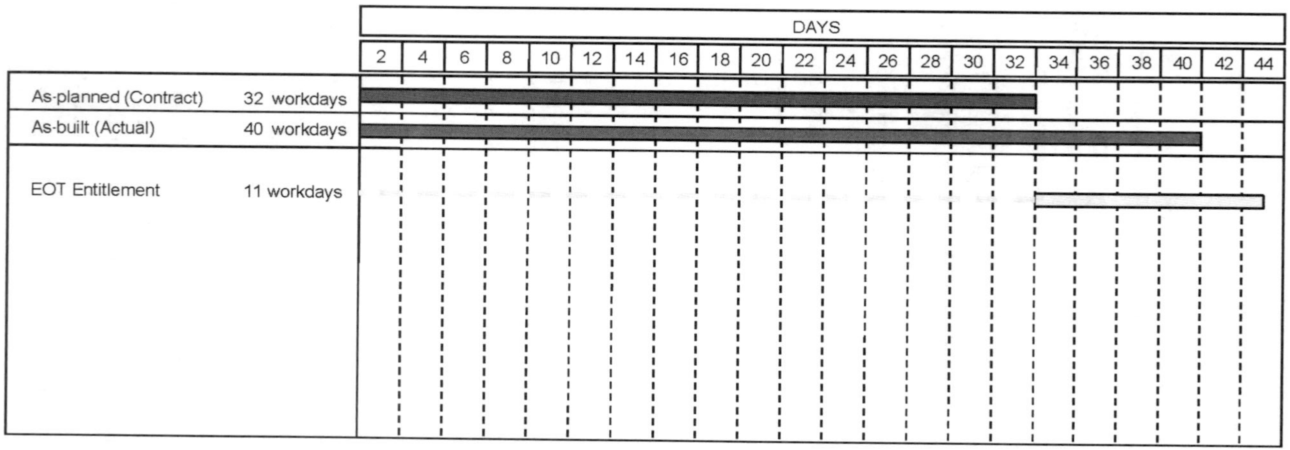

Figure 23.6 Contractor's EOT claim.

A2 *Net impact*

This technique only depicts the net effect of all employer-responsible delays by plotting these on a barchart. The net effect of all delays is calculated and the overall time extension is taken to be the difference between the contract completion date and the 'net impact' programme completion date.

In the example in Figure 23.7 below, all delaying activities were considered but only the net effect, taking into account the concurrency of the delays, was used. The as-planned and as-built programmes appear in summary format as a single bar, and the 'net impact' bar of all the employer-responsible delays is shown.

The difference between the as-planned and as-built completion dates was eight days; and the 'net impact' bar is showing an extension of time entitlement of nine days.

Observations

As with the 'global impact' method, the 'net impact' technique uses the as-planned programme and therefore assumes the critical path(s) on this programme were constant throughout the project. This leads to delays potentially being deemed as critical when in fact they were not.

Although this method attempts to deal with the issue of concurrent delays, it does not show how concurrency has been established and scrutinised. As a result, the amount of delays having an effect on the project's completion date can be overstated. The 'net impact' technique is neither accurate nor realistic in apportioning liability for critical delays, but may be suitable for quick approximate estimates, perhaps at the outset. The absence of a CPM-based analysis camouflages the true effect of a delay on the overall project completion date.

A3 *Scatter diagram*

This technique indicates the timing of employer-responsible delaying events during the project. The basis of the diagram is the as-planned barchart, which is annotated with the incidence of employer-responsible events affecting the project, such as variations, instructions and information issues, etc. By supporting the scatter diagram with a narrative and detailed breakdown for each of the events notified, the contractor is able to supply comprehensive information on each event and argue its impact on the progress of the works and the date for completion. Figure 23.8 represents a 'scatter diagram' chart for the garage-construction project.

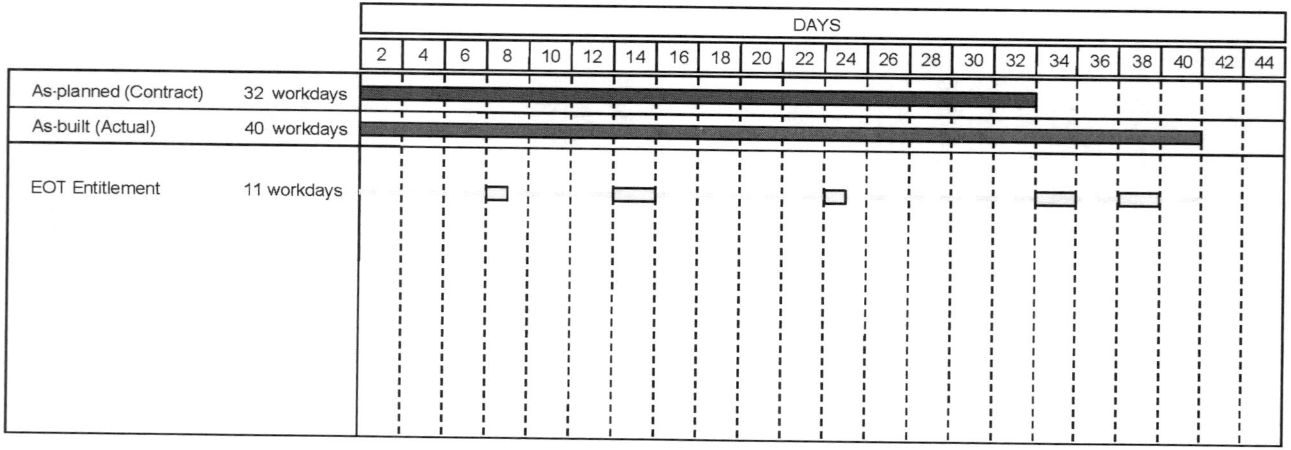

Figure 23.7 Net effect of delays.

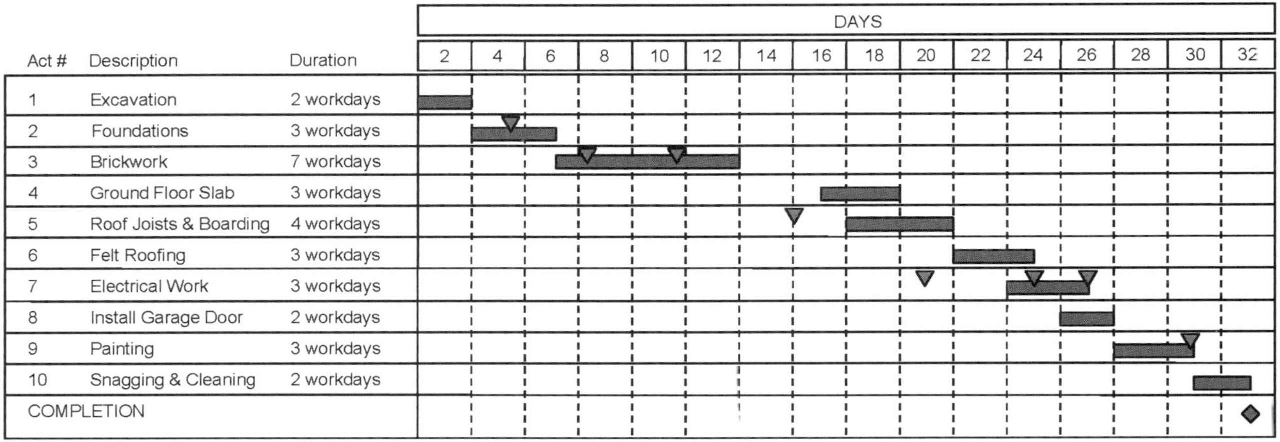
DAYS
2
4
6
8
10
12
14
16
18
20
22
24
26
28
30
32
Act #
Description
Duration
1 Excavation 2 workdays
2 Foundations 3 workdays
3 Brickwork 7 workdays
4 Ground Floor Slab 3 workdays
5 Roof Joists & Boarding 4 workdays
6 Felt Roofing 3 workdays
7 Electrical Work 3 workdays
8 Install Garage Door 2 workdays
9 Painting 3 workdays
10 Snagging & Cleaning 2 workdays
COMPLETION

Figure 23.8 Scatter diagram.

Observations

Although a scatter diagram has little evidential value, it has a powerful visual impact in negotiations.

However, with this technique it is impossible to investigate the impact of a single event or combination of events within the overall period of the project.

B Simplistic

This group includes the following techniques.

B1 *As-planned impacted (aka baseline adding impacts)*

This technique requires the identification and insertion of employer-responsible delays into the original as-planned programme. A schedule of employer-responsible delaying events is produced and each of these is added to the as-planned programme. The resultant scheme is the 'as-planned impacted' programme.

Both programmes should be in network format, i.e. a 'CPM', with the same logic links between activities. A programme time analysis is performed on the 'as-planned impacted' programme and the 'new' date for completion is established.

The difference between the as-planned completion date and the 'new' completion date as shown on the 'as-planned impacted' programme is said to be the EOT entitlement as a result of the employer-responsible delays.

Good practice

The methodology of this technique is as follows:

1   Make a copy of the as-planned programme, and name this the 'as-planned impacted' programme.
2   For each of the employer-responsible delay events, identify the period of time which they would be expected to take on site to carry out, e.g. the addition of suspended ceilings is estimated to take two weeks.
3   Add the new work activity or activities to the 'as-planned impacted' programme, allowing for any off-site time constraints, e.g. procurement of suspended ceilings at four weeks.
4   Make the appropriate relationship logic links from the new activity or activities to the other programme activities, e.g. suspended ceilings to start four weeks after wall plastering commences.
5   Perform a time analysis (recalculate) on the 'as-planned impacted' programme to establish the 'new' date for completion.

Figure 23.9 shows the as-planned programme as at the start of the project. The employer-responsible delay events are then added to the as-planned programme, the CPM re-analysed and the resulting 'as planned impacted' programme constructed as in Figure 23.10.

Observations

The 'as-planned impacted' technique has limited applications. It uses a programme prepared by the contractor as at the commencement of the project, i.e. his original intent. The technique is not based on current progress and the contractor's planned intent as at the time of the employer-responsible event(s). This is an important issue as this technique is not based on the actual progress of the works when the events occurred.

Another important issue here is that whereas the 'prospective analysis' and 'retrospective analysis' methods are based on actual progress information, the 'as-planned impacted' technique does not use or require this information. This means that the impact which is said to have been caused by the delay events analysed may bear scant resemblance to reality.

Furthermore, this technique takes no account of any acceleration or delay on the part of the contractor in calculating the 'new' date for completion. Instead it merely looks at the hypothetical effect of the employer-responsible delay events on the contractor's original planned intent.

Because the results of an 'as-planned impacted' analysis rarely bear any relationship to reality, it cannot be used to demonstrate a period of time for which loss and expense might be assessed. The assessment of loss and expense in a period in which delay occurred cannot be properly identified without good evidence of what actually occurred and when it occurred.

On the plus side, the 'as-planned impacted' technique is a cheap means of analysis. It tends to work well on smaller projects, and on larger projects where the delay events in question have occurred over limited periods of time.

This method is often misapplied; for example, if the as-planned programme contains invalid logic then the results of the 'as-planned impacted' analysis will be meaningless. However, when performed properly, the 'as-planned impacted' technique is a valid delay analysis method.

B2 As-built barchart

A barchart is produced showing the actual start, finish and duration of the work activities for the project. It is common for the chart to be an overlay of the as-planned barchart as at the start of the project. In this way it is easy to identify which work activities deviated from the original plan.

Although the 'as-built barchart' technique provides a simple visual statement of the difference between what was expected to happen and what actually occurred, it suffers from the absence of explicit logic. In

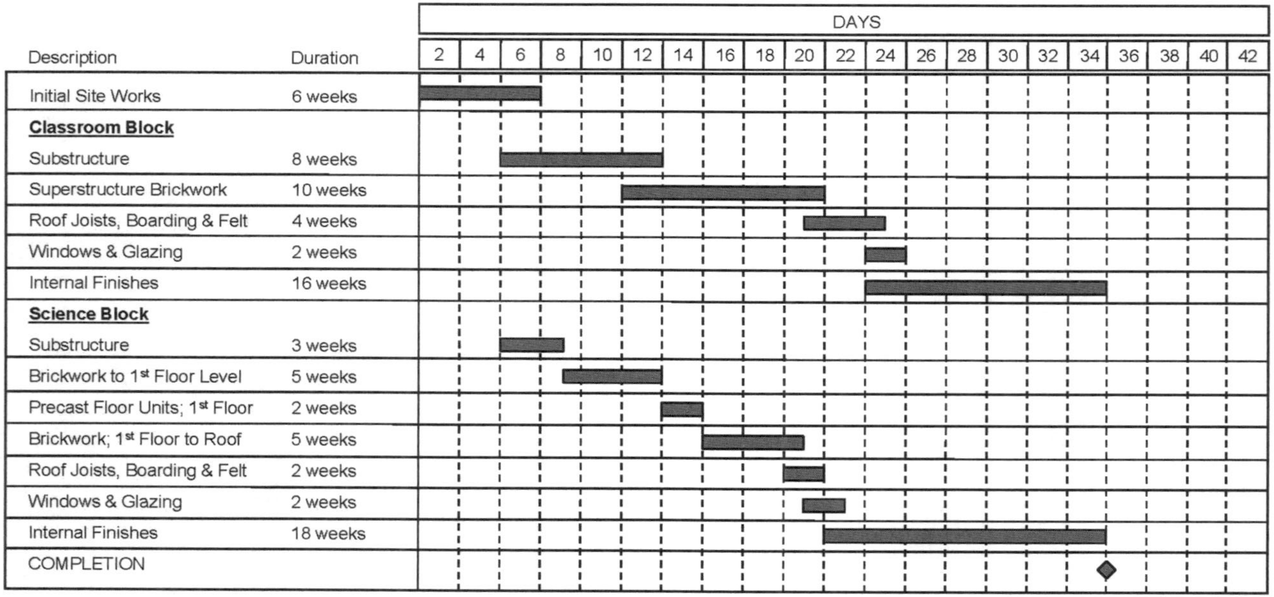
DAYS
Description
Duration
2
4
6
8
10
12
14
16
18
20
22
24
26
28
30
32
34
36
38
40
42
Initial Site Works
6 weeks
Classroom Block
Substructure
8 weeks
Superstructure Brickwork
10 weeks
Roof Joists, Boarding & Felt
4 weeks
Windows & Glazing
2 weeks
Internal Finishes
16 weeks
Science Block
Substructure
3 weeks
Brickwork to 1st Floor Level
5 weeks
Precast Floor Units; 1st Floor
2 weeks
Brickwork; 1st Floor to Roof
5 weeks
Roof Joists, Boarding & Felt
2 weeks
Windows & Glazing
2 weeks
Internal Finishes
18 weeks
COMPLETION

Figure 23.9 As-planned programme.

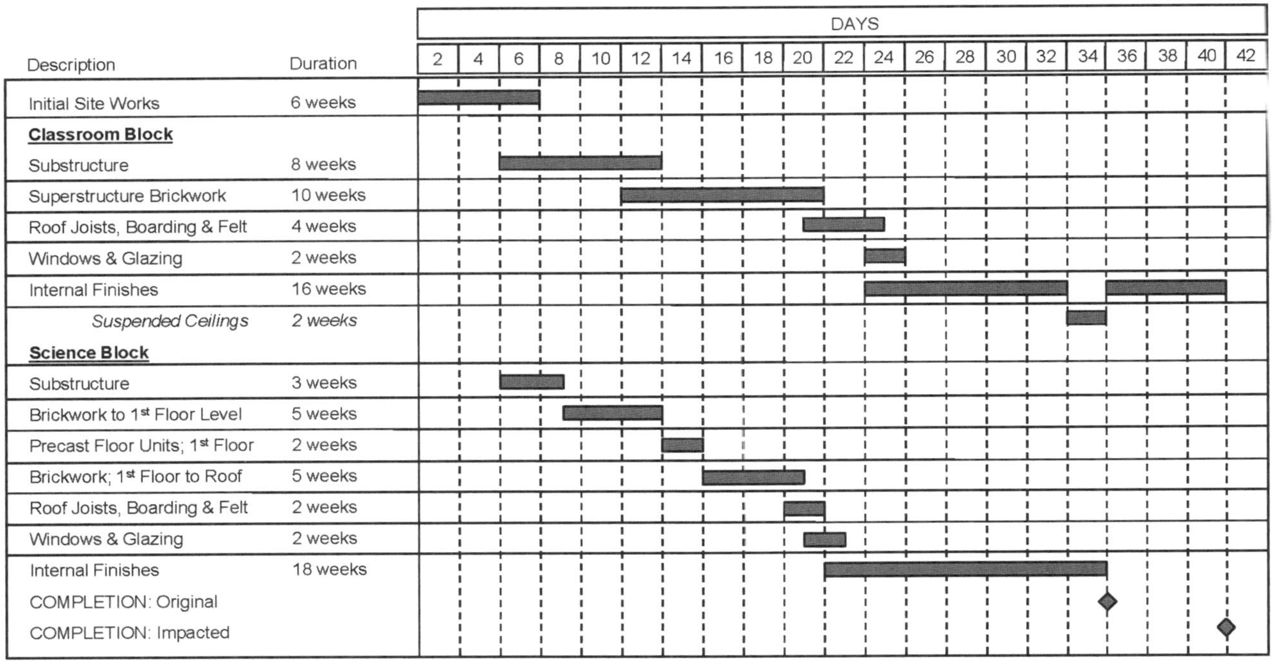

Description	Duration
Initial Site Works	6 weeks
Classroom Block	
Substructure	8 weeks
Superstructure Brickwork	10 weeks
Roof Joists, Boarding & Felt	4 weeks
Windows & Glazing	2 weeks
Internal Finishes	16 weeks
Suspended Ceilings	*2 weeks*
Science Block	
Substructure	3 weeks
Brickwork to 1st Floor Level	5 weeks
Precast Floor Units; 1st Floor	2 weeks
Brickwork; 1st Floor to Roof	5 weeks
Roof Joists, Boarding & Felt	2 weeks
Windows & Glazing	2 weeks
Internal Finishes	18 weeks
COMPLETION: Original	
COMPLETION: Impacted	

DAYS: 2 4 6 8 10 12 14 16 18 20 22 24 26 28 30 32 34 36 38 40 42

Figure 23.10 As-planned impacted programme.

addition, it does not identify actual events that took place and the delays to the programme and date for completion that resulted. See the example in Figure 23.11.

Observations

The 'as-built barchart' method can be carried out without the need for computerised planning software, although such software is often used to present the results.

The method assumes that the as-built situation arises by reason of changes, late information, etc. for which the contractor is entitled to an extension of time; and not due to its own culpability.

This method also assumes that the planned programme was realistic and that the work was appropriately resourced to enable the plan to be achieved. However, this method is well suited for relatively simple projects where the main delays can be easily identified.

B3 As-built adjusted

This technique uses the CPM format to develop an as-built schedule. Employer-responsible delaying events are included as activities and linked to specific work activities on the 'as-built adjusted' programme. The difference in time between the contract completion date and that shown on the 'as-built adjusted' programme is the extension of time the contractor contends it is entitled to.

Linking all the delay activities to their respective work activities, the programme is then updated. The adjusted completion date and project duration was found to be 36 days. As the original contract period for the project was 32 days, the difference between the contract completion date and the 'as-built adjusted' programme completion date of 36 days is the extension of time claimed by the contractor. See the example in Figure 23.12.

Observations

The main problem with the 'as-built adjusted' technique is that, although it utilises the CPM format, which affords an insight into the interrelationships between activities and delay events, it gives very little supporting detail or analysis. It is not much better than the 'net impact' technique, except that the CPM format creates a more sophisticated impression of an analysis.

Another problem is that contractors invariably tie the employer-responsible delaying events to the critical path. Conversely, contractor-responsible delaying events may be shown, but are more likely to be linked to work activities not on the critical path.

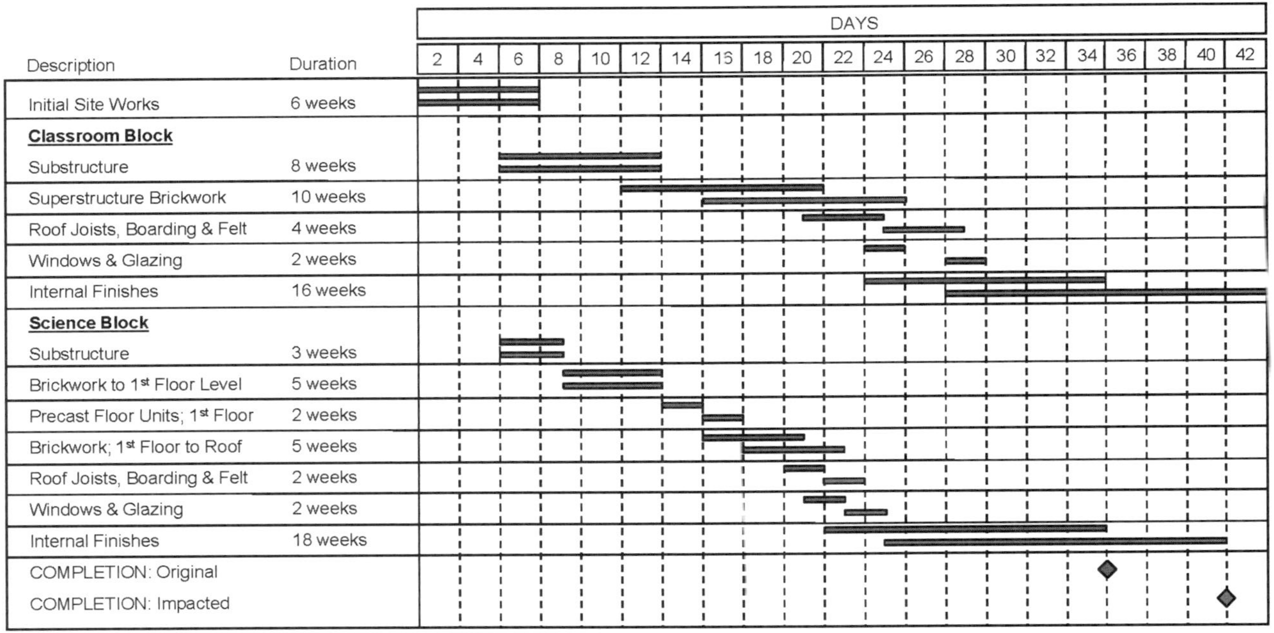

Figure 23.11 As-built programme (also showing the original as-planned programme).

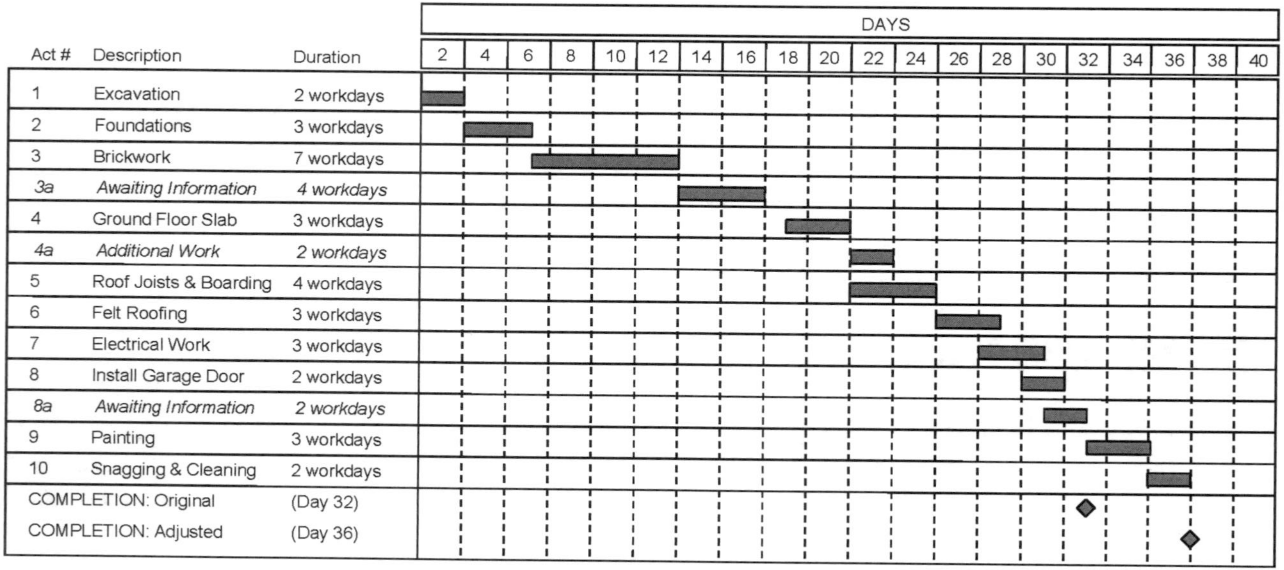

Act #	Description	Duration																			DAYS		
			2	4	6	8	10	12	14	16	18	20	22	24	26	28	30	32	34	36	38	40
1	Excavation	2 workdays																				
2	Foundations	3 workdays																				
3	Brickwork	7 workdays																				
3a	Awaiting Information	4 workdays																				
4	Ground Floor Slab	3 workdays																				
4a	Additional Work	2 workdays																				
5	Roof Joists & Boarding	4 workdays																				
6	Felt Roofing	3 workdays																				
7	Electrical Work	3 workdays																				
8	Install Garage Door	2 workdays																				
8a	Awaiting Information	2 workdays																				
9	Painting	3 workdays																				
10	Snagging & Cleaning	2 workdays																				
COMPLETION: Original		(Day 32)																				
COMPLETION: Adjusted		(Day 36)																				

Figure 23.12 As-built adjusted programme.

C Prospective analysis

This group includes the following techniques.

C1 Time impact

This technique examines employer-responsible delaying events and their effects at different times during the progress of the project, i.e. events are analysed contemporaneously with each event being judged on its own merits and information available at that time.

This method takes the contractor's planned programme as the starting point for the analysis. The likely impact of each specific delaying event on the programme is determined at different construction stages, the intention being to obtain a 'stop action picture' of the project before a delay impact. The expected impact of the delay event is then inserted into the programme. The difference between the two project completion dates, i.e. the 'stop action picture' before the delay event is inserted and the one after it has been inserted, is the likely delay to the project and the EOT entitlement as a consequence of the delay event alone. Each delay event is analysed chronologically.

Good practice

The methodology of this technique is that, for each employer-responsible delay event, the following should be done:

1 Update the as-planned programme to show what had actually been achieved by the time of the employer-responsible delay event.
2 Analyse the updated programme that represents the position of the project at the time of the event. The analysed updated programme will forecast whether the project is likely to be completed ahead of, on or behind schedule.
3 Create an impacted programme demonstrating, with supporting descriptions, the duration of new activities flowing from the 'delay event', and their logical interface with the remaining contract works. It is recommended that a subnet be created for this.
4 Add the subnet into the impacted programme and link this to the existing programme activities. Re-analyse the impacted programme.
5 If the project completion date is later than the project completion date on the current updated programme, then there is entitlement to an extension of time.
6 The extent of the EOT is the slippage between either the contract completion date or the completion date shown on the current updated programme and that shown on the impacted programme.

Observations

This prospective method analyses the expected, or likely, effect of the delay event on the completion of the project, and therefore shows a contractor's entitlement to an extension of time.

The main criteria for this technique are a good as-planned programme and reliable progress and as-built data. However, care must be taken to ensure that the planned programme to complete is reasonable and any apparent errors in activity durations and logic are corrected.

A worked example and methodology of time impact analysis is included in chapter 24.

D Retrospective analysis

This group includes the following techniques:

D1 *Collapsed as-built (aka 'as-built but for')*

This technique applies the 'but for' logic. In simple terms the approach of the 'collapsed as-built' method is to establish the as-built programme, incorporating the planned activities together with activities representing the delaying events by the relevant party, e.g. variations, instructions, issue of information. The consequence of the delaying events is shown by additional work activities.

The activity duration will be the actual duration and the logic links will be so constructed, if technically correct, as to produce the actual start and finish dates for the activities.

The delaying events are then removed, i.e. the programme is collapsed, to produce a programme which in theory shows when the project would have been completed 'but for' the identified delaying events. The difference in project completion dates between that stipulated in the contract and that in the 'collapsed as-built' programme, is the time for which that party is eligible to claim/grant an extension of time from/to the other party. The conclusion thus drawn is that the difference between these dates is the result of delays that were the employer's responsibility.

An example of the 'collapsed as-built' technique is given below. The first chart, Figure 23.13, shows the as-built programme including the discrete delays.

After collapsing the programme, i.e. removing the employer-responsible delays (activity numbers 3a, 4b and 8a) but leaving the contractor-responsible delays (activity numbers 4a and 7a), the collapsed as-built completion date is day 34. As the original contract completion date for the project was day 30 and the actual completion date was day 40, the contractor is entitled to an extension of time of six days as a consequence of employer-responsible delays. See Figure 23.14.

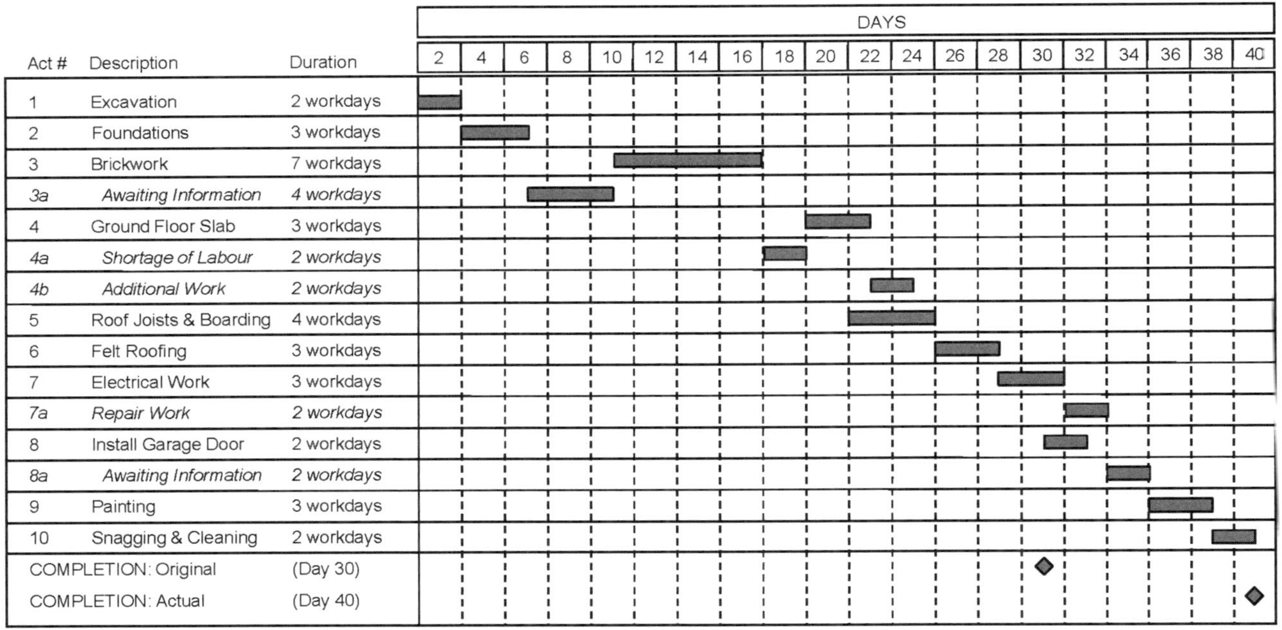

Act #	Description	Duration	DAYS
1	Excavation	2 workdays	
2	Foundations	3 workdays	
3	Brickwork	7 workdays	
3a	*Awaiting Information*	*4 workdays*	
4	Ground Floor Slab	3 workdays	
4a	*Shortage of Labour*	*2 workdays*	
4b	*Additional Work*	*2 workdays*	
5	Roof Joists & Boarding	4 workdays	
6	Felt Roofing	3 workdays	
7	Electrical Work	3 workdays	
7a	*Repair Work*	*2 workdays*	
8	Install Garage Door	2 workdays	
8a	*Awaiting Information*	*2 workdays*	
9	Painting	3 workdays	
10	Snagging & Cleaning	2 workdays	
COMPLETION: Original		(Day 30)	
COMPLETION: Actual		(Day 40)	

Figure 23.13 As-built programme showing discrete delays.

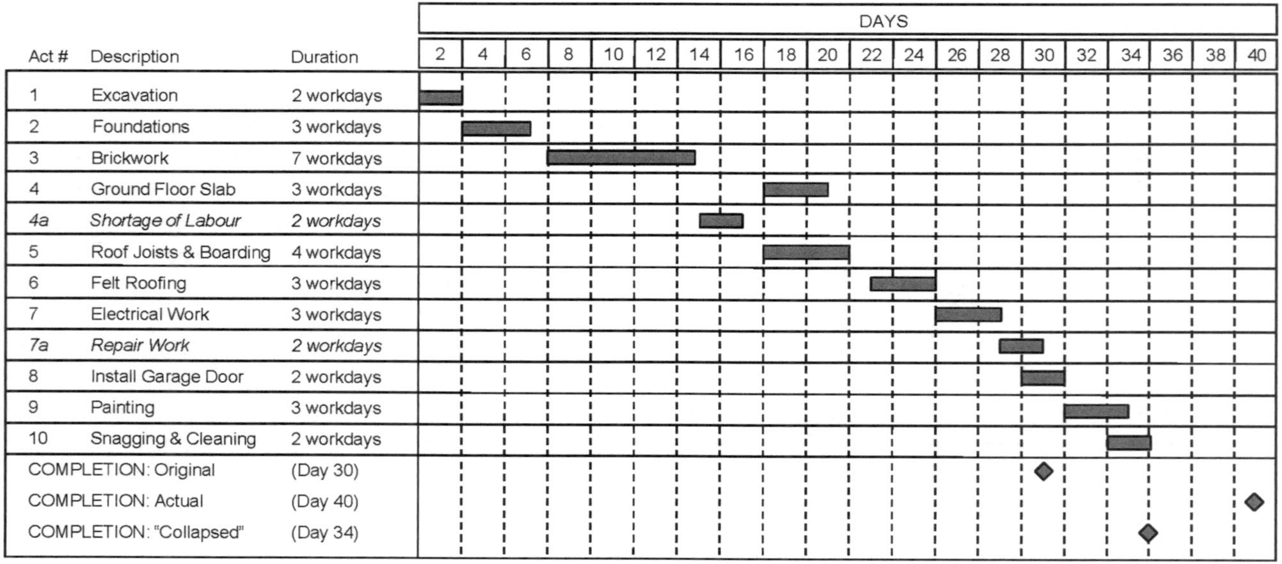

Figure 23.14 Collapsed as-built programme.

Observations

On the face of it the 'collapsed as-built' technique appears accurate and difficult to refute. It uses as-built information and is easy to understand. The production of an as-built network demands considerable time and effort to show a model where both the durations and the logic reflect what actually occurred.

However, supporters of the 'collapsed as-built' technique would argue that the data used is factual and that the analyst interprets the data impartially. This is simply not possible; as with the formulation of the as-built programme, the other stages of the 'collapsed as-built' technique require the analyst to make decisions and form opinions. For example, the analyst must decide matters such as the effect upon productivity of having to move resources more frequently from one activity to another, and that of using inappropriate plant and labour teams on an activity because of resource constraints. These decisions are necessarily subjective and, due to the retrospective nature of the technique, are both theoretical and speculative.

A further important matter is the linking, or relationship, between activities in formulating the as-built programme. These relationships are vitally important because in many cases they will determine the criticality and length of delays. This calls for technical knowledge and experience of the construction process.

A major drawback with this technique is that of 'pacing'. It is not uncommon for a contractor, knowing that he is being delayed by the employer, to take longer on a non-critical activity than he would have done had the delay not occurred. In such a situation, when the employer's delay is collapsed out of the programme, it appears as if the contractor is in default for his late and slow completion of the non-critical activity.

Above all, the 'collapsed as-built' technique requires good and detailed as-built records and contemporaneous information.

Good practice

The following guidelines are recommended:

1 An audit trail should be maintained as to how as-built progress information was determined in formulating the as-built programme.
2 All significant delays should be identified regardless of fault or liability.
3 Where possible, the analyst should identify and model delay activities as discretely identifiable delay periods during the as-built modelling process.
4 The matter of 'pacing' must be addressed by the analyst, by dint of background information and reasoned opinion.

5   For all subjective decisions and opinions, the analyst should record his source information and detail his reasoning.

D2   *Windows (aka 'time slice', or 'snapshot') analysis*

This technique functions to determine the amount of delay that has occurred on a project and when the delay(s) occurred. By identifying the activities that were critically delayed, a more focused investigation as to the causes and responsibility for the delays can take place. The technique is based on as-planned, as-built and revised programmes that have been used during the execution of the project. The basis of the 'windows' technique is that the total life of the project is divided into a number of consecutive time periods, or windows. It is based on the analysis of the effects of delays within each window sequentially. Normally, this is the method adopted in the process of an update of the as-planned programme at monthly project meetings.

The project is updated at the end of each window, i.e. the current progress is recorded against each activity and a time analysis carried out. The 'new' forecast completion date for the project is compared with the forecast completion date for the project as at the start of the window and any slippage between the dates is the delay to the project as a result of delaying events during the window. This procedure is repeated for all windows.

The amount of total delay represents the total extended duration of the project, which should then be investigated for responsibility apportionment between the employer and the contractor.

The 'windows' technique is a systematic and objective method of quantifying the amount of delay incurred in a project on a progressive basis. The accuracy of this technique is a function of the size and number of windows used. It takes into account concurrent delays and considers the effect of delays in the context of time.

Observations

An important aspect of this technique is that it recognises that the critical path of the as-planned programme may, and often does, change during the life of a project. The 'windows' method tracks the actual critical path and the impact on the date for completion. This technique also identifies any contractor mitigation and/or acceleration during the construction of the project.

Only events that affect activities on or near the actual critical path will have an effect on the project completion date. The effect of events is assessed against the critical path of the project at the time the event occurred. This technique also recognises and identifies concurrent delays.

With the project being divided into manageable parts for analysis, i.e.

consecutive 'windows' usually of one-month duration, then the causes and responsibility for the delays highlighted can be reviewed and researched more purposefully.

A worked example and methodology of 'windows analysis' is included in chapter 25.

Good practice

The following guidelines are recommended:

1   The windows should be consecutive commencing at the project start date and ending at date of practical completion of the project.
2   The windows can be weekly, fortnightly or monthly and will generally be defined by the frequency of reports of actual site progress. For example, if progress on a project was recorded monthly as of the last day of each month, then a 'window' would cover the period between 1 January and 31 January, and the next window would cover the period between 1 February and 28 February, and so on up to project completion.
3   It is recommended that the 'baseline programme' established at the start of the project be used for analysis of the first window. However, the programme should be subject to a rigorous 'reliability exercise', and any necessary modifications made, before being used for analysis.
4   If the 'baseline' programme underwent a complete revision, was issued to the contract administrator, and subsequent progress reports were related to the 'revised programme', then this revised programme should replace the original baseline programme for the windows analysis, as and when it became the working programme.
5   If further revised programmes were issued during the life of the project, and became the working programme, then these also should be incorporated into the analysis, replacing the previous programme, again, as and when they became the working programmes.
6   It is recommended that the project's contemporaneous progress reports should be used, where possible, as the basis for the 'progress data' for the analysis.
7   Progress data consist of actual start and finish dates and, where an activity's actual duration spans more than a single window, the percentage progress achieved as at the end of a window.
8   The collected progress data should be reviewed for apparent anomalies, e.g. an activity's reported actual progress achieved reduces in the subsequent window(s); an activity's actual start and finish dates are not consistent with the progress being reported.

24 Prospective analysis
Methodology and worked example

This chapter describes in detail, as a worked example, the 'time impact' method of analysis, as used to demonstrate a contractor's extension of time entitlement.

Project details for the worked example

This technique is applied to the construction of a new science block on a university campus. The contract value was £32 million, the contract start date was 6 August 2002 and the contract period was 87 weeks.

The contractor prepared a detailed programme in CPM format, which was submitted to the employer's project manager at the start of the project. Unfortunately, delays occurred on the project, and practical completion was achieved some 75 weeks late on 8 October 2005.

Detailed methodology used by the contractor for his analysis

The contractor's detailed methodology specifically for the mixed-use development project was as follows:

A: Method of analysis used for this project
The Contract, in respect of Extensions of Time (clause 25), refers to 'the progress of the Works is being or is likely to be delayed', and 'estimate the extent, if any, of the expected delay in the completion of the Works beyond the Completion Date'. Both these statements clearly show that a 'prospective' method of analysis is to be used for the quantification of Extension of Time entitlement for an Employer Risk Event.

We consider that the appropriate methodology for a 'prospective' Extension of Time entitlement analysis is the 'Time Impact Analysis' technique, as recommended in the Society of Construction Law's 'Delay and Disruption Protocol'.

Furthermore, the Architect in his reviews for Extensions of Time has followed the SCL's 'Time Impact Analysis' methodology. In his letter of 'xxx', he states, 'As discussed previously, we have followed the approach of sequentially assessing both "employer risk events" and actual progress, as recommended by the Protocol published by the Construction Law Society.'

Therefore, both the Architect and ourselves are of the same opinion; that for assessment of Extension of Time entitlement, the correct approach is a 'prospective' analysis using the SCL's 'Time Impact Analysis' methodology.

(i) Baseline programme
The starting point is to establish a 'baseline' programme. This should be the Contractor's first meaningful overall programme for the project, and used during the life of the project for monitoring purposes.

The programme should be prepared as a critical path network (more commonly referred to as a 'CPM') using commercially available project planning software. For the programme to be suitable for use as a tool for the analysis and management of change, it must be properly prepared so that when a change occurs, it can accurately predict the affects of that change.

(ii) Events and Subnets
The Employer Risk Events are to be analysed independently and sequentially as they occur chronologically.

A subnet representing the likely consequences of the Employer Risk Event is created. The subnet should be prepared by the Contractor in the same manner and using the same software as used for the 'baseline' programme. It should comprise the activities and durations resulting from the Employer Risk Event.

For example, the subnet for a variation would comprise the instruction for the variation, the activities required to carry out that variation and its linkage to the updated 'baseline' programme.

(iii) Analysis
Immediately prior to the date of the Employer Risk Event, the 'baseline' programme should be updated to reflect the current progress of the project at that time. The updated programme should be 'time-analysed', and the forecast completion date for the project noted.

The subnet representing the Employer Risk Event should be entered into the updated programme. This programme is then time-analysed, and the 'new' forecast completion date for the project is noted.

(iv) EOT Entitlement
The Extension of Time entitlement as a consequence of the Employer

Risk Event is the difference, if any, between the completion dates for the project on (a) the updated programme without the subnet, and (b) the updated programme with the subnet.

B: What information was available and used for the 'Time Impact' analysis

'xxx' submitted their overall programme for the project to the Architect in 'xxx'. This programme is tiled 'Construction Activities', 'Prog. MP01'. The programme is known as 'MP01'.

An important aspect of 'MP01' is the time periods, or 'lead-in', which 'xxx' used for the important work packages in preparing the programme. For example, Windows (activity number 98) has a lead-in period of 18 weeks.

The 'lead-in' period is from placement of order to start on site, and encompasses the subcontractor's off-site work, being detailed design & working drawings, approval, manufacture/fabrication and delivery to site.

A schedule of the subcontractor lead-in periods, as shown in the MP01 programme, is included in appendix 'xxx'.

C: Application of the methodology for this submission
<u>a Outline of the Approach</u>
To follow the methodology of the Society of Construction Law's 'Delay and Disruption Protocol' for Time Impact Analysis, requires the following approach:

i   *Establish a 'Baseline' programme.*
ii *Establish the As-Built data for all activities on the baseline programme.*
iii *Investigate and schedule chronologically the 'Events' considered to potentially give an entitlement to an Extension of Time.*
iv *Create a subnet for each Event.*
v   *Analyse the impact, or likely impact, of the Event on the progress of the works and determine if any delay to progress is likely to cause delay to the Completion Date of the Project.*

Practical completion of the project was achieved on 8 October some 26 months after project commencement on 6 August 2002. For presentation purposes, we have divided the overall time period of the project into 4 number tranches.

The start/finish of each tranche being a key landmark in the project, as follows,

i   *Tranche 1: from start of Project (6 August 2002) to start of Superstructure Work on 24 January 2003.*

ii Tranche 2: from start of Superstructure Work (24 January 2003) to start of Steel Structural Work on 2 July 2003.

iii Tranche 3: from start of Steel Structural Work (2 July 2003) to Building Substantially Watertight on 3 February 2004.

iv Tranche 4: from Building Substantially Watertight (3 February 2004) to start of Practical Completion on 8 October 2005.

b As-Built Data

As the Time Impact Analysis methodology requires a progress update of the 'baseline' programme at the time of each Event, an important aspect is the as-built data for each activity on the MP01 programme.

During the course of the project 'xxx' made various EOT submissions to the Architect. Included in these submissions were as-built data, i.e. actual start & finish dates, for activities on their MP01 programme. We have used this data in establishing an 'As-Built Schedule'.

However, the data shown on the EOT submissions, does not show interim percentage completions for activities that spanned several months. For this information we have relied upon 'xxx's' progress updates which were carried out at approximately monthly intervals, and in most cases presented at the regular monthly site meetings.

A schedule of the As-Built data we have established, and used in the extension of time analysis, is included in appendix xx.

c The 'Events'

A thorough technical investigation of the project's contemporaneous records has been carried out to identify those events which possibly give entitlement to an extension of time.

The results of this exercise are contained within 5 number ring binders accompanying this submission, which include supporting information for each of these possible events.

Following this initial exercise, a subsequent exercise was carried out which involved a review of the possible events by those closely involved with the project to ascertain which of the 'possible events' should now be considered as potential 'Events' for the extension of time analysis.

This rationalisation exercise required the input of those closely involved during the construction of the project to avoid the inclusion of spurious events which may have no factual or likely impact basis.

After this second exercise, the list of 'Events' is now some 762 number; and these are the potential events that were analysed individually for delay, or likely delay, to progress.

The 'Schedule of 762 Events' is included in appendix xx.

A brief explanation of the columns and their 'headings' on this schedule is given below,

i   Col. 1, 'Event ref.nr.'; this is the unique reference number of the Event.

ii   Col. 2, 'Event date'; the date of the Event, i.e. the date of occurrence of the Employer's Risk Event.

iii   Col. 3, 'xxx ref.'; the unique reference number of the supporting factual and technical information contained in the technical files.

iv   Col. 4, 'Description'; a brief description of the Event.

v   Col. 5, 'Document reference'; a note of the technical reference document for the Event, e.g. RFI, drawing number, etc.

vi   Col. 6, 'Programme act.nr. Affected: MP01'; the programme activity number on programme 'MP01', which was directly affected by the Event.

vii   Cols. 7 & 8, 'Clause 25 sub-clause ref.'; an indication of the specific sub-clause(s) of clause 25 for the specific Event.

d The Subnets for each Event

For each Event we have created a subnet. The subnet illustrates the work flowing from the Event.

For example, on receipt of a revised drawing it may be necessary to procure some materials, such as ventilation ductwork. There will be an activity shown on the subnet 'Procurement of ductwork (xx weeks)'. This will then be linked to the MP01 programme activity(s) that the materials are required for.

Similarly, where Events necessitate the design/approval/manufacture of materials, then the 'lead-in' periods for the major sub-contract packages as defined in 'xxx's' original MP01 programme are used.

Full details for each subnet for each Category 1 Event are included in appendix xx.

e 'Time Impact Analysis' Methodology as detailed in the SCL Protocol

The SCL Protocol's guidance and methodology for Time Impact Analysis is set down in three steps in section 3.2.7.

First, 'the Programme should be brought fully up to date (as to progress and the effect of all delays that have occurred up to that date, whether Employer Delays or Contractor Delays) to the point immediately before the occurrence of the Employer Risk Event'.

Second, 'the programme should then be modified to reflect the Contractor's realistic and achievable plans to recover any delays that have occurred, including any changes to the logic of the Programme proposed for that purpose (subject to CA review and acceptance as provided in Guidance Section 2.2.3)'.

Third, 'the sub-network representing the Employer Risk Event should then be entered into the programme and the impact on the contract completion dates should be noted'.

f Performing the Extension of Time Analysis

To adhere to this methodology, for each Event we carried out a progress update (of programme MP01) as of the date of the Event. The project was then time-analysed, i.e. statused to determine the new forecast completion date for the project based on the progress achieved to date.

We then inserted the subnet for the Event into the updated progress update of Ren.01. The programme is then time-analysed, or statused, again, and the new forecast completion date for the project determined.

Any slippage in the forecast completion date for the project from the progress update without the subnet and the progress update with the subnet is a consequence of the subnet, i.e. the Event.

The amount of slippage is the Extension of Time entitlement for that Employer Risk Event.

At this point in the submission, the contractor referred to his baseline programme 'MP01' and informed the reviewer that copies of these were included in appendix 'xxx' to the submission.

A copy of the contractor's programme 'MP01', is included in appendix 4A of this book. Appendix 4A contains two charts as follows:

i   Chart 4A a shows all the programme activities, sorted by work area.
ii   Chart 4A b shows the planned critical path for the project.

As referred to under item 'b' above, 'As-Built Data', the 'time impact analysis' relies on the project's progress to be recorded at the time of each event. Where progress has been reported contemporaneously, e.g. in the contractor's monthly reports, this information should be used, subject to checking for errors. For this submission, the contractor used his contemporaneous progress reports, and these were presented in tabular format in his submission. A copy is given in appendix 4B at the end of this book.

D: Results of the analysis
a Introduction

As explained earlier, our first exercise for this submission was to identify possible events which may on further investigation give entitlement to an extension of time.

Our second exercise, in essence a rationalisation exercise of our first exercise, identified those Events which were to be analyses for entitlement to an Extension of Time under the terms of the Contract; particularly clause 25 which states that, 'If and whenever it becomes reasonably apparent that the progress of the Works is being or is likely to be delayed...'

We also explained, in section A, that 'It is our position that to be awarded an extension of time under the Contract, there are "four steps" in the process for reviewing each potential event.' The 'four steps' are,

Step 1; Is the potential event, an Event which under the terms of the Contract between the parties gives entitlement to an extension of time.

Step 2; If so, is the progress of the Works being, or likely to be delayed as a result of the Event.

Step 3; If so, is the 'progress delay' caused by the Event expected to cause delay to the completion of the Works beyond the Completion Date.

Step 4; If so, to what extent is the Event likely to cause delay to the completion of the Works beyond the Completion Date.

In our second exercise; the rationalisation exercise, we satisfied ourselves that the events as listed on the 'Schedule of Events' comply with 'step 1' and do give entitlement to an Extension of Time, subject to the results of steps 2, 3 & 4.

Therefore, to comply with steps 2, 3 & 4, we have carried out an Extension of Time Analysis for each of the 762 events. The approach and methodology of the analysis has been fully explained earlier in this submission.

Our main reasons for selecting the Time Impact Analysis methodology are:

i   Time Impact Analysis follows the requirements of clause 25 of the Contract.
ii Time Impact Analysis is recommended to be used to determine extension of time entitlement by a recognised organisation, The Society of Construction Law, and they have published guidelines for its use in their 'Delay and Disruption Protocol'.
iii Time Impact Analysis has already been used by the Architect to determine and quantify extension of time entitlements during the project.

As stated earlier, we have analysed all 762 Events in accordance with the Time Impact Analysis methodology. To assist the Architect, and others, we have classified the results for each Event into one of five categories, to allow those Events which show the greater period of entitlement to be at the heart of this submission.

This will, we hope, considerably assist the Architect, and the Parties, to reach a speedy resolution on this matter.

This also allows us to demonstrate that this is not a global claim. We are not saying, 'all of these 762 events delayed the works to the extent that the project was not complete until 8 October 2005'; we have researched, investigated and analysed each Event individually.

The categories we have used to classify each Event are as follows:

- *Category 5; minimal delay to the progress of the works, but no likely delay to Completion of the Works beyond the Completion Date.*
- *Category 4; delay to work/activities in progress, but no likely delay to Completion of the Works beyond the Completion Date.*
- *Category 3; likely delay to future work/activities, but no likely delay to Completion of the Works beyond the Completion Date.*
- *Category 2; delay or likely delay to the progress of the works, and likely delay to Completion of the Works beyond the Completion Date.*
- *Category 1; delay or likely delay to the progress of the works, and likely delay to Completion of the Works beyond the Completion Date. Furthermore, the likely delay to Completion of the Works provides a revised Completion Date later than the previous extended Completion Date.*

As stated earlier, whilst category 1 and 2 Events are at the heart of this submission, Events classified as categories 3 to 5 are being further investigated and we reserve the right to re-classify these Events if necessary. Similarly, our initial exercise identified other possible Events which may give entitlement to extensions of time; but these are not being pursued in this submission. However, again, we reserve the right to submit these Events if, after further investigation, we consider they give entitlement to extensions of time.

We now give a synopsis of the Extension of Time Analysis for each Tranche.

b Synopsis of EOT Analysis: Tranche 1
Tranche 1 covers the time period from the Start of the Project to Start of Superstructure Work on 24 January 2003.

For Tranche 1 we have analysed some 110 number Events. The analysis results show the following:

a 11 number category 1 Events.
b 42 number category 2 Events.
c 57 number category 3, 4 or 5 Events.

The 11 number category 1 Events in chronological order, are:

1 *Event T1–008 Internal Works: Internal Walls (clause 25.4.5 & 25.4.6). 4 workdays EOT entitlement, revising the Date for Completion to 8 May 2004.*
2 *Event T1–011 Internal Works: Internal Walls (clause 25.4.5 & 25.4.6). An additional 5 workdays EOT entitlement, further revising the Date for Completion to 15 May 2004.*

3   Event T1–017 Internal Works: Internal Walls *(clause 25.4.5 &*
    25.4.6). An additional 4 workdays EOT entitlement, further revis-
    ing the Date for Completion to 21 May 2004.
4   Event T1–031 Internal Works: Internal Walls *(clause 25.4.5 &*
    25.4.6). An additional 2 workdays EOT entitlement, further revis-
    ing the Date for Completion to 23 May 2004.
5   Event T1–038 Internal Works: Internal Walls *(clause 25.4.5 &*
    25.4.6). An additional 2 workdays EOT entitlement, further revis-
    ing the Date for Completion to 28 May 2004.
6   Event T1–040 Internal Works: Internal Walls *(clause 25.4.5 &*
    25.4.6). An additional 3 workdays EOT entitlement, further revis-
    ing the Date for Completion to 2 June 2004.
7   Event T1–042 Internal Works: Internal Walls *(clause 25.4.5 &*
    25.4.6). An additional 4 workdays EOT entitlement, further revis-
    ing the Date for Completion to 6 June 2004.
8   Event T1–109 Substructure: Basement *(clause 25.4.6). An addi-*
    tional 11 workdays EOT entitlement, further revising the Date for
    Completion to 23 June 2004.
9   Event T1–127 Envelope: Stonework *(clause 25.4.6). An additional*
    2 workdays EOT entitlement, further revising the Date for Com-
    pletion to 25 June 2004.
10 Event T1–129 Envelope: Stonework *(clause 25.4.5 & 25.4.6). An*
    additional 1 workday EOT entitlement, further revising the Date
    for Completion to 26 June 2004.
11 Event T1–142 Envelope: Stonework *(clause 25.4.5 & 25.4.6). An*
    additional 3 workdays EOT entitlement, further revising the Date
    for Completion to 1 July 2004.

The 42 number category 2 Events, also arranged by programme
work area, are:

Substructure (18 number in total)
i   *'Piling' 1 number*
ii *'Substructure' 8 number*
iii *'Basement' 7 number*
iv *'RC Retaining Walls' 2 number*

Frame/Upper Floors (6 number in total)
i   *'Level 0–1' 3 number*
ii *'Level 1–2' 2 number*
iii *'Level 2–3' 1 number*

Envelope (15 number in total)
i   *'Roof' 3 number*
ii *'Windposts' 2 number*

iii '*Glazing/Louvres*' 1 *number*
iv '*Brick/Blockwork*' 2 *number*
v '*Stonework*' 7 *number*

<u>*Internal Works*</u> *(2 number in total)*
i '*Internal Walls*' 2 *number*

In summary, at the end of Tranche 1, there is an overall Extension of Time entitlement of 41 workdays, or 8 weeks and 3 calendar days; which revises the Date for Completion to 1 July 2003.

It is noted that the last progress update for this Tranche, on 24 January 2003, shows the project to be 19 workdays in critical delay with the forecast Date for Completion being 30 May 2004.

<u>*c Synopsis of EOT Analysis: Tranche 2*</u>
Tranche 2 covers the time period from the Start of Superstructure Work (24 January 2003) to Start of Steel Structural Work on 2 July 2003.

For Tranche 2 we have analysed some 182 number Events. The analysis results show the following:

a 14 *number category 1 Events.*
b 62 *number category 2 Events.*
c 106 *number category 3, 4 or 5 Events.*

The 14 number category 1 Events in chronological order, are:

1 *Event T2–025 Envelope: Stonework (clause 25.4.5 & 25.4.6). An additional 3 workdays EOT entitlement, revising the Date for Completion to 4 July 2004.*
2 *Event T2–029 Envelope: Stonework (clause 25.4.5 & 25.4.6). An additional 1 workday EOT entitlement, further revising the Date for Completion to 7 July 2004.*
3 *Event T2–031 Envelope: Stonework (clause 25.4.5 & 25.4.6). An additional 1 workday EOT entitlement, further revising the Date for Completion to 8 July 2004.*

And so on, down to the last category 1 Event in Tranche 2,

14 *Event T2–276 Envelope: Stonework (clause 25.4.6). An additional 7 workdays EOT entitlement, further revising the Date for Completion to 16 October 2004.*

The 62 number category 2 Events, also arranged by programme work area, are,

Substructure (6 number in total)
i *'Substructure'* 1 number
ii *'Basement'* 2 number
iii *'RC Retaining Walls'* 3 number

Frame/Upper Floors (16 number in total)
i *'Level 0–1'* 3 number
ii *'Level 1–2'* 5 number
iii *'Level 2–3'* 4 number
iv *'Level 3–4'* 4 number

Envelope (32 number in total)
i *'Roof'* 8 number
ii *'Windposts'* 9 number
iii *'Brick/Blockwork'* 2 number
iv *'Stonework'* 10 number
v *'Glazing/Louvres'* 3 number

Internal Works (5 number in total)
i *'Internal Walls'* 2 number
ii *'Ceilings'* 3 number

M & E Services (3 number in total)
i *'Mechanical'* 2 number
ii *'Electrical'* 1 number

In summary, at the end of Tranche 2, there is an additional 75 workdays, or 15 weeks and 2 calendar days, Extension of Time entitlement. This brings the overall Extension of Time entitlement to 116 workdays, or 23 weeks and 5 calendar days; which revises the Date for Completion to 16 October 2004.

It is noted that the last progress update for this Tranche, on 2 July 2002, shows the project to be 44 workdays in critical delay with the forecast Date for Completion being 4 July 2004.

d Synopsis of EOT Analysis: Tranche 3
Tranche 3 covers the time period from the Start of Steel Structural Work (2 July 2003) to Building Substantially Watertight on 3 February 2004.

For Tranche 3 we have analysed some 156 number Events. The analysis results show the following:

a 7 number category 1 Events.
b 63 number category 2 Events.
c 86 number category 3, 4 or 5 Events.

The 7 number category 1 Events in chronological order, are:

1 *Event T3–076 Envelope: Windposts (clause 25.4.6). An additional 1 workday EOT entitlement, revising the Date for Completion to 17 October 2004.*
2 *Event T3–146 Envelope: Steel Roof Works (clause 25.4.6). An additional 13 workdays EOT entitlement, revising the Date for Completion to 5 November 2004.*
3 *Event T3–155 Internal Works: Laboratory Fit-out (clause 25.4.6). An additional 66 workdays EOT entitlement, revising the Date for Completion to 13 February 2005.*

And so on, down to the last category 1 Event in Tranche 3,

7 *Event T3–181 Internal Works: Laboratory Fit-out (clause 25.4.6). An additional 3 workdays EOT entitlement, further revising the Date for Completion to 27 February 2004.*

The 63 number category 2 Events, also arranged by programme work area, are,

Envelope (35 number in total)
i *'Roof' 12 number*
ii *'Windposts' 10 number*
iii *'Brick/Blockwork' 4 number*
iv *'Stonework' 6 number*
v *'Glazing/Louvres' 3 number*

Internal Works (22 number in total)
i *'Internal Walls' 3 number*
ii *'Ceilings' 9 number*
iii *'Laboratory Fit-out' 10 number*

M & E Services (6 number in total)
i *'Mechanical' 4 number*
ii *'Electrical' 2 number*

In summary, at the end of Tranche 3, there is an additional 90 workdays, 19 weeks and 1 calendar day, Extension of Time entitlement. This brings the overall Extension of Time entitlement to 206 workdays, or 42 weeks and 6 calendar days; which revises the Date for Completion to 27 February 2005.
It is noted that the last progress update for this Tranche, on 26 January 2004, shows the project to be 140 workdays in critical delay with the forecast Date for Completion being 18 November 2004.

e Synopsis of EOT Analysis: Tranche 4
Tranche 4 covers the time period from Building Substantially Water-tight (3 February 2004) to the date of Practical Completion on 8 October 2005.

For Tranche 4 we have analysed some 213 number Events. The analysis results show the following:

a 33 number category 1 Events.
b 72 number category 2 Events.
c 108 number category 3, 4 or 5 Events.

The 33 number category 1 Events in chronological order, are:

1 *Event T4–102 Internal Works: Laboratory Fit-out (clause 25.4.6). An additional 1 workday EOT entitlement, further revising the Date for Completion to 1 March 2005.*
2 *Event T4–132 Internal Works: Laboratory Fit-out (clause 25.4.6). An additional 8 workdays EOT entitlement, further revising the Date for Completion to 11 March 2005.*
3 *Event T4–165 Internal Works: Ceilings (clause 25.4.5 & 25.4.6). An additional 4 workdays EOT entitlement, further revising the Date for Completion to 17 March 2005.*

And so on, down to the last category 1 Event in Tranche 4,

33 *Event T6–091B M & E Services (clause 25.4.5 & 25.4.6). An additional 28 workdays EOT entitlement, revising the Date for Completion to 14 November 2005.*

The 72 number category 2 Events, also arranged by programme work area, are:

Internal Works (50 number in total)
i 'Internal Walls' 2 number
ii 'Wall Finishes' 1 number
iii 'Ceilings' 1 number
iv 'Laboratory Fit-out' 46 number

M & E Services (22 number in total)
i 'Mechanical' 12 number
ii 'Electrical' 10 number

In summary, at the end of Tranche 4, there is an additional 186 workdays, or 2 weeks and 5 calendar days, Extension of Time entitlement. This brings the overall Extension of Time entitlement to 392 workdays, or 80 weeks; which revises the Date for Completion to 14 November 2005.

Practical Completion was achieved on 8 October 2005, a delay of 372 workdays, or 74 weeks and 5 calendar days, to the original Contract Completion Date.

f Summary

A total of 762 Events have been analysed for Extension of Time entitlement. These have been analysed individually against the current progress of the project at the time of the Event.

Only those Events that were likely to delay the then current forecast Completion Date for the project are considered to give entitlement to an Extension of Time. These Events are some 304 number in total; and classified in our analysis as either category 1 or 2.

A full schedule of 'Time Impact Analysis Results' is included in appendix xx.

A brief explanation of the columns and their 'headings' on this schedule is given below:

i   *Column 1, 'Event ref.nr.'; this is the unique reference number of the Event.*

ii   *Col. 2, 'Event date'; the date of the Event, i.e. the date of occurrence of the Employer Risk Event.*

iii   *Col. 3, 'Description'; a brief description of the Event.*

iv   *Col. 4, 'Programme MP01 act.nr. Affected'; the programme activity number on programme 'MP01', which was directly affected by the Event.*

v   *Col. 5, 'Forecast completion date Prior to subnet'; this is the forecast completion date of the Project from the progress update as at the date of the Event.*

vi   *Col. 6, 'Forecast completion date After subnet'; after inserting the subnet for the Event into the progress update, this is the forecast completion date of the Project. Any slippage in the Project's completion date from that in column 5 is the likely effect of the Event.*

vii   *Col. 7, 'Extension of Time Entitlement'; the EOT entitlement as a consequence of the Event. The difference between the dates in columns 5 & 6.*

viii   *Col. 8, 'Adjusted Completion Date'; the adjusted, or revised, Completion Date for the Project, taking into account all EOT entitlement to date.*

ix   *Col. 9 to 13, The Event is classified into one of the '5 categories', as explained earlier.*

Appendix xx contains details of the analysis for each of the 65 number category 1 Events.

Included in this appendix for each Event are:

a *Chart A; Progress update at the time of the Event.*
b *Chart B; the progress update with the subnet inserted showing the likely consequences on the progress of the works and the likely delay to the Completion Date of the project.*

As stated earlier, the progress records for the project are an important part of a 'time impact analysis'. For this submission, the contractor used his contemporaneous progress reports which had been presented to the employer and the architect at each monthly site meeting. A tabular report of these progress records was presented in the submission, and a copy of the first few pages is included in appendix 4B at the end of this book.

Appendix 4C contains pages 1 to 5 of the 'full schedule of "Time Impact Analysis Results"', as included in the contractor's submission and referred to earlier in this chapter.

The factual circumstances of four of the category 1 Events for Tranche 1 are explained below, together with the results of their individual analyses.

T1–008   *Revisions to stairs 1, 2 and 3*

This event is an example of additional works being instructed which did not delay current ongoing progress but did lead to future delay to the works. The work activities affected by the additional works are on the critical path as at the time of the event and there is a likely delay to the completion of the project.

On 27 August 2002, the contractor received revised drawings for three of the four internal stairs. These drawings showed considerable additional works involving reinforced concrete, facing brickwork and blockwork, and stud partitions and joinery works.

An estimate of the additional works was produced and the durations of the work activities on the programme were increased to reflect the new scope of works.

The overall programme was updated with the progress on the project as at 27 August 2002, and the result showed a forecast completion date of 23 April 2004. See chart 4D a, which shows the project's critical path based on progress achieved as at 27 August 2002.

The subnet for this event (T1–008) is then inserted into the progress updated programme and the impact of the event on the progress of the works and any likely delay to completion of the project is calculated. For this event the result showed a new forecast completion date of 4 May 2004; which represents a critical delay of six workdays caused exclusively by this event. See chart 4D b, which shows the project's new critical path based on progress achieved as at 27 August 2002, plus the likely impact from the subnet for Event T1–008.

T1–011   Riser 6 shaftwall changes

This event is another example of additional works being instructed which did not delay current ongoing progress but led to future delay to the works. The significance of this event is that the works affected were not due to be carried out for some ten months, but a close examination of the work activities affected by the additional works shows that they are on the critical path as at the time of the event and that there is a likely delay to the completion of the project.

On 30 August 2002, the contractor received revised drawings showing considerable additional internal stud partitions.

An estimate of the additional work was produced and the duration of the 'stud partition' work activity on the programme was increased to reflect the new scope of works.

The overall programme was updated with the progress on the project as at 30 August 2002, and the result showed a forecast completion date of 27 April 2004. See chart 4D c, which shows the project's critical path based on progress achieved as at 30 August 2002.

The subnet for this event (T1–011) is then inserted into the progress updated programme and the impact of the event on the progress of the works and any likely delay to completion of the project is calculated. For this event the result showed a new forecast completion date of 12 May 2004; which is a critical delay of ten workdays caused exclusively by this event. See chart 4D d, which shows the project's new critical path based on progress achieved as at 30 August 2002, plus the likely impact from the subnet for Event T1–011.

T1–102   Information on foul sump chamber

This event is an example of late information impacting ongoing progress which is on the current critical path and will cause a likely delay to completion of the project.

On 27 November 2002, the contractor received information concerning the ongoing underslab drainage. The information meant that additional materials were required particularly for the deep foul sump chamber. The necessary materials were on three weeks' delivery, and the contractor assessed that 'underslab drainage' works could not be completed until ten workdays after the materials were delivered to site.

The overall programme was updated with the progress on the project as at 27 November 2002, and the result showed a forecast completion date of 19 May 2004. See chart 4D e, which shows the project's critical path based on progress achieved as at 27 November 2002.

The subnet for this event (T1–102) is then inserted into the progress updated programme and the impact of the event on the progress of the works and any likely delay to completion of the project is calculated. For this event the result showed a new forecast completion date of 14 June 2004; which is a critical delay of 17 workdays caused exclusively by this event. See chart 4D f, which shows the project's new critical path based on progress achieved as at 27 November 2002, plus the likely impact from the subnet for Event T1–102.

T1–108   Reconstituted stone changes

This event is an example of changes to the external façade material, i.e. reconstituted stone cladding, which has a long procurement period.

On 4 December 2002, the contractor received revised drawings for the external reconstituted stone cladding. The changes were significant and meant that the supplier would have to carry out new design work and obtain approval, fabricate moulds, cast and cure the stone elements. The overall procurement period for the off-site work being 24 weeks; the supplier re-confirmed this procurement period. Furthermore, the changes resulted in more stone elements to be fixed and the affected activity durations were increased accordingly.

The overall programme was updated with the progress on the project as at 4 December 2002, and the result showed a forecast completion date of 26 May 2004. See chart 4D g, which shows the project's critical path based on progress achieved as at 4 December 2002.

The subnet for this event (T1–108) is then inserted into the progress updated programme and the impact of the event on the progress of the works and any likely delay to completion of the project is calculated. For this event the result showed a new forecast completion date of 18 June 2004; which is a critical delay of 16 workdays caused exclusively by this event. See chart 4D h, which shows the project's new critical path based on progress achieved as at 4 December 2002, plus the likely impact from the subnet for Event T1–108.

Appendix 4D contains the supporting charts for the four category 1 Events in Tranche 1, as explained above.

The next section in the submission document should be a narrative on the delaying events. For each event, there should be:

1   An introductory narrative explaining the 'event' and its importance in the construction process.
2   The contemporaneous factual information related to the event, e.g. requests for information, letters, AIs or other instructions, drawing issues, procurement of materials, labour records. Copies of any documents referred to should be included in the submission.
3   The results of the time impact analysis, essentially in tabular format but with specific graphics if necessary. The extension of time claimed as a consequence of the event should be clearly stated.
4   The contract clause under which the extension of time is claimed.

A fully detailed submission, as described above, will demonstrate the cause and effect, i.e. 'causation', of the extension of time claimed.

25 Retrospective analysis

Methodology and worked example

The 'windows' method of analysis is considered to be the most reliable of the various retrospective analysis techniques. Therefore, this chapter uses a worked example of the 'windows' method to demonstrate a contractor's extension of time entitlement and his subsequent entitlement to time-related costs.

Project details for the worked example

The project chosen for applying this technique to is a mixed-use development, comprising 84 apartments, shops, offices, an arts centre with a theatre and studios. The contract value was £72 million, with a start date of 5 November 2002 and a contract period of 110 weeks.

The contractor prepared a detailed programme in CPM format, which was submitted to the employer's project manager at the start of the project. Subsequently, just prior to completing the structural works and before commencing internal finishing works, a more detailed programme for the remaining works was issued by the contractor.

Unfortunately, delays occurred on the project, and practical completion was achieved some 82 weeks late.

Detailed methodology used by the contractor for his analysis

The contractor based his 'windows' methodology on the 'model specification' (included in appendix 3 of the book).

However, his detailed methodology specifically for the mixed-use development project was as follows.

A: Method of analysis used for this project
The analysis technique we have used for this delay analysis is an adaptation of the as-planned – v – as-built technique.

The technique we have used is called the 'windows' method of analysis; and is a recognised and accepted method of analysis for analysing delays on construction and engineering projects.

Using the project's progress records, we carried out comparisons at numerous intervals during the project. By these comparisons, we identified the actual critical path of the project as the work progressed, and established the chain, or chains, of work activities that caused the completion date of the project to be delayed.

B: Detailed methodology of a 'windows' analysis

The 'windows' method is based on analysis of affects of delays over the life of a project. The project is divided into a series of 'windows'. A 'window' is the period of time between progress updates. For example, if progress on a project was recorded monthly as of the 1st of each month, then a 'window' would cover the period between 1st January & 31st January, and the next window would cover the period between 1st February & 28th February, and so on up to project completion.

Because each 'window' is only a segment of the contract period, the results of each 'window' analysis must be summarised and carried forward to the next window.

For a 'windows' method analysis, the key information necessary is:

i   the contractor's baseline programme. That is, the sequence of work activities and their durations based on his knowledge at the start of the project in order to achieve the contractual completion date for the project; and,

ii progress updates at intervals during the period of the project. Ideally these progress updates should be related directly to the contractor's 'baseline' programme.

C: What information was available and used for the 'windows' analysis

As of end of February 2005, there have been two overall programmes for the project prepared by xxx (the contractor) and issued to the Employer's project manager. These are:

i   '01', prepared at the start of the project, and
ii '02', prepared at the onset of internal finishing works.

The contractor recorded progress against these programmes, both internally and in their 'Contractor's Report' submitted monthly to the project manager. Progress was recorded as follows:

i   Against programme '01', from start of the project until 2 November 2003.

ii Against programme '02', from 3 November 2003 until end of February 2004 (and still being reported against).

The 'windows' analysis for this project is therefore divided into two consecutive time periods as follows:

1 *Time Period One: from start of the project until 2 November 2003.*
2 *Time Period Two: from 3 November 2003 to 28 February 2005.*

At the start of each time period, i.e. window, we will explain the information we have used and the preparation steps we took before commencing each analysis. We also list the date span of the 'windows' based on the progress updates.

For each 'window' within each time period, we identify the period of critical delay; give the new forecast project completion date; and identify the work activity that was driving the critical delay.

Our investigation of the analysis results for each 'window' also identifies all the work activities that were delayed and we highlight those activities, as Critical Delay Events, causing critical delay to completion of the Works. We also identify areas of mitigation or acceleration achieved by xxx (the contractor).

As stated earlier, any of the Critical Delay Events identified by the 'Windows' analysis will give entitlement to an extension of time, if the cause or causes are a Relevant Event as described in the Contract.

D: Time Period 'One': information used and preparation for the analysis

As the 'baseline' programme for the 'Windows' analysis for this time period we have used the programme noted as '01'. This programme was prepared by xxx (the contractor) *and issued to the project manager.*

Using the contractor's progress updates, Time Period One was divided into 10 'windows' as follows:

1 *Start of project to 5 January 2003,*
2 *6 January to 2 February 2003,*
3 *3 February to 2 March 2003,*
4 *3 March to 30 March 2003,*
5 *31 March to 4 May 2003,*
6 *5 May to 8 June 2003.*
7 *9 June to 29 June 2003,*
8 *30 June to 3 August 2003,*
9 *4 August to 5 October 2003,*
10 *6 October to 2 November 2003.*

E: Time Period 'Two': information used and preparation for the analysis

As the 'baseline' programme for the 'Windows' analysis for this time period we have used the programme noted as '02'. This programme was prepared by the contractor and issued to the project manager.

Using the contractor's progress updates, Time Period Two was divided into a further 16 'windows' as follows:

11   *3 November to 30 November 2003,*
12   *1 December to 21 December 2003,*
13   *22 December 2003 to 30 January 2004,*
14   *31 January to 1 March 2004,*
15   *2 March to 29 March 2004,*
16   *30 March to 3 May 2004,*
17   *4 May to 31 May 2004,*
18   *1 June to 4 July 2004,*
19   *5 July to 1 August 2004,*
20   *2 August to 30 August 2004,*
21   *31 August to 3 October 2004,*
22   *4 October to 31 October 2004,*
23   *1 November to 29 November 2004,*
24   *30 November 2004 to 12 January 2005,*
25   *13 January to 30 January 2005,*
26   *31 January to 27 February 2005.*

At this point in the submission, the contractor referred to his baseline programmes '01' and '02' and informed the reviewer that copies of these were included in appendix 'xxx' to the submission.

A copy of the contractor's programme '01' for time period one, is included in appendix 5A of this book. Appendix 5A contains two charts:

1   Chart 5A a which shows all the programme activities, sorted by work area;
2   Chart 5A b which shows the planned critical path for the project.

As referred to under item 'B' above, 'Detailed methodology of a "windows" analysis', such an analysis requires the project's progress to be recorded at regular intervals, usually monthly. Where progress has been reported contemporaneously, e.g. in the contractor's monthly reports, this information should be used, subject to checking for errors. For this submission, the contractor used his contemporaneous progress reports, and these were presented in tabular format in his submission. A copy is given in appendix 5B at the end of this book. This records the progress for windows 1 to 10 against the activities shown on the contractor's programme '01', being the programme that was current for 'time period one'.

The contractor then presented the results of the 'windows' analysis in his submission. Detailed below are the results for the first five (of 26) windows.

G: Results of the analysis

Introduction

For each of the 26 number windows that constitute the 'Windows Analysis', we give details and a commentary under the following sub-headings:

i *'Works planned to be carried out and actual progress achieved': In this sub-section we give a brief commentary on the works that were planned to be carried out in the window; followed by a brief commentary on the work actually carried out or in progress as at the end of the window.*

ii *'Analysis results at closing of 'Window': In this sub-section we give the new forecast completion date for section, based on the progress achieved as at the end of the window. The period of critical delay, if any, to the project completion, and the slippage, in workdays, within the particular window.*

iii *'Delayed activities in this window: Critical & sub-critical': The tables in this section show the programme activity(s) that are 'driving' any critical delay to the project completion date. That is to say, the activity identified under the sub-heading 'Delayed activity: critical', is the activity as at the end of the window that is dictating or controlling the new forecast completion date for the project. In other words, it is the work activity on the actual critical path as at the end of the window.*

Under the sub-heading 'Delayed activities: near-critical', we list those activities that are on parallel paths to the date for completion of the project, and whereas they are in some critical delay, they will not delay completion of the project to the same extent as the 'driving' activity on the actual critical path. These activities have been classified as near-critical. The criteria for selecting these activities is that they will cause delay to completion of the project between 1 and 20 workdays less than the critical delay being caused by the 'driving' activity. For example, if the 'driving' activity is on a path that is forecast to cause 38 workdays delay to completion of the project, then a near-critical activity must be on a parallel path that is forecast to cause between 18 and 37 workdays delay.

We give an explanation of the data contained in the tables in this sub-section.

The results for each window are complemented by two charts, which are included in appendix xxx in this submission.

The first chart is titled 'Progress Comparison Chart', and shows the following:

i *All activities which were actually completed in the current window,*

ii   All activities which are currently in progress as at the closing of the current window,
iii Based upon the current progress position, within the next 3 windows.
iv   The current forecast completion dates for the contractual section completion milestones.

The second chart is titled 'The Critical Path', and shows the current critical path from the current activity that is driving this path to the final activity of the project with its completion of 'Section 8'.

Results for the Individual Windows
Window 1: from project start to 5 January 2003; end of week 5
Work planned to be done during this Window
Only 'Preliminary Works' were planned to be carried out during this first window. Whilst this included completion of 'General Site Mobilisation' (act.nr. 0030) and 'Site Establishment' (act.nr. 0050); 'Pile Probing' (act.nr. 0060) was to be completed by 21 December 2001. Similarly, 'Guide Walls' (act.nr. 0070) and 'Install Secant Piles' (act.nr. 0080), were to be progressing and be 67% and 22% complete by the end of this window.

'Analysis' results: at closing of Window

Window 1: from project start to 5 January 2003;				end of week 5	
A	New forecast completion date	12 January 2005			
			T.F.	Delay to project completion	
B	Critical delay to project:-		-7	7 workdays	23 cal. days
C	Time lost in this window			7 workdays	23 cal. days
D	Critical (driving) activity at closing of window				
	Preliminary Works: "Pile Probing" act.no. '0060'	-7		7 workdays	23 cal. days
E	Other 'near-critical' activities at closing of window -none-				

Figure 25.1 Analysis results at closing of window.

'Analysis' results: impact on sectional completion dates

Position at closing of window	Forecast completion	Slippage in window	Total slippage
Section 1: Show Flat (floor 03)	18-Feb-04	5 days	5 days
Section 2: Arts Complex (partial)	17-Mar-04	5 days	5 days
Section 3: Residential Floors 04 to 07 (incl.)	13-May-04	9 days	9 days
Section 4: Shops	13-May-04	9 days	9 days
Section 7: Remaining Residential	29-Sep-04	9 days	9 days
Section 8: All Other Areas	12-Jan-05	23 days	23 days

Figure 25.2 Analysis results: impact on sectional completion dates.

<u>*Commentary on work carried out in this Window*</u>
<u>*Preliminary Works*</u>
1 *'General Site Mobilisation' (act.nr. 0030) was completed on 4 December 2002; some 2 workdays later than its late finish date, thereby causing a potential critical delay to the project completion date. However, this delay was mitigated (out-of-sequence working) by its successor activity.*
2 *'Site Establishment' (act.nr. 0050) commenced on 6 November and was completed on 29 November 2002. There was no critical delay to this activity.*
3 *'Pile Probing' (act.nr 0060) commenced on 13 November 2002, and was 70% complete at the end of this window, as opposed to being 95% complete as was planned at the start of the window. This progress delay is causing a 7 workday critical delay, or 23 calendar days delay, to the project completion date.*
4 *'Guide Walls' (act.nr. 0070) commenced on 5 December 2002 and was 50% complete at the end of this window, as opposed to being 67% complete as planned at the start of this window. The activity is shown as being in critical delay of 7 workdays; however, completion of this activity is being controlled by completion of its predecessor activity 'Pile Probing'; which itself is in critical delay of 7 workdays.*
5 *'Install Secant Piles' (act.nr. 0080) commenced on 11 December 2002 and was 14% complete at the end of this window, as opposed to being 17% complete as planned at the start of this window. The activity is shown as being in critical delay of 7 workdays; however, completion of this activity is being controlled by completion of the activity 'Pile Probing'; which itself is in critical delay of 7 workdays.*
6 *'Cut Down Piles' (act.nr 0090) commenced on 16 December 2002 and was 10% complete at the end of this window, and the activity is shown as being in critical delay of 7 workdays. However, completion of this activity is being controlled by completion of the activity 'Pile Probing'; which itself is in critical delay of 7 workdays.*

<u>*Summary of critically delayed activities in this Window*</u>
Window 2: from 6 January to 2 February 2003; end of week 9
<u>*Work planned to be done during this Window*</u>
'Preliminary Works' were planned to continue during this window period. This included completion of 'Pile Probing' (act.nr. 0060), and 'Guide Walls' (act.nr. 0070). 'Install Secant Piles' (act.nr. 0080) and 'Cut Down Piles' (act.nr. 0090), were to be progressing and be 44% and 15% complete respectively by the end of this window.
'Apartment Block; Substructure' works were due to commence this

SECTION: Element; Activity of Work	Act.Nr.	Nature of delay	Workdays	Calendar days	CDA Ref.
PRELIM.WKS: Piling; Pile Probing	0060	Delayed progress	7 wkdays	23 cal.days	Ref.01 (part 1 of 2)

Figure 25.3 Summary of critically delayed activities in window.

window, with 'FRC Capping Beam' (act.nr. 0110) being 5% complete at the end of the window.

'Time Analysis' results: at closing of Window

Window 2: from 6 January to 2 February 2003;		end of week 9		
A New forecast completion date	02 February 2005			
		T.F. Delay to project completion		
B Critical delay to project:-		-22	22 workdays	44 cal. days
C Time lost in this window			15 workdays	21 cal. days
D Critical (driving) activity at closing of window				
Preliminary Works: "Pile Probing"	act.no. '0060'	-23	23 workdays	44 cal. days
E Other 'near-critical' activities at closing of window				
-none-				

Figure 25.4 Time analysis results at closing of window.

'Time Analysis' results: impact on sectional completion dates

Position at closing of window	Forecast completion	Slippage in window	Total slippage
Section 1: Show Flat (floor 03)	10-Mar-04	21 days	26 days
Section 2: Arts Complex (partial)	07-Apr-04	21 days	26 days
Section 3: Residential Floors 04 to 07 (incl.)	04-Jun-04	22 days	31 days
Section 4: Shops	04-Jun-04	22 days	31 days
Section 7: Remaining Residential	20-Oct-04	21 days	30 days
Section 8: All Other Areas	02-Feb-05	21 days	44 days

Figure 25.5 Time analysis results: impact on sectional completion dates.

Commentary on work carried out in this Window
Preliminary Works

1 'Pile Probing' (act.nr 0060) was 90% complete at the end of this window, as opposed to being 100% complete as planned at the start of the window. The activity is showing as being in critical delay of 23 workdays, and which in turn is causing a 22 workday critical delay to completion of the project. The progress delay in this window caused an additional 15 workday critical delay, or 21 calendar days delay, to the project completion date.

2 'Guide Walls' (act.nr. 0070) was 90% complete at the end of this window, as opposed to being 100% complete as planned at the start of this window. The activity is shown as being in critical delay of 23 workdays; however, completion of this activity is being controlled by completion of its predecessor 'Pile Probing', which itself is in critical delay of 23 workdays.

3 'Install Secant Piles' (act.nr. 0080) was 60% complete at the end of

this window, as opposed to being 44% complete as planned at the start of this window. The activity is shown as being in critical delay of 23 workdays; however, completion of this activity is being controlled by completion of 'Pile Probing', which itself is in critical delay of 23 workdays.

4 *'Cut Down Piles' (act.nr 0090) was 18% complete at the end of this window, as opposed to being 14% complete as planned at the start of this window. The activity is shown as being in critical delay of 23 workdays. However, completion of this activity is being controlled by completion of 'Pile Probing', which itself is in critical delay of 25 workdays.*

Summary of critically delayed activities in this Window

SECTION: Element; Activity of Work	Act./W	Nature of delay	Workdays	Calendar days	CDA Ref.	
PRELIM.WKS: Piling; Pile Probing	0060	Delayed progress	15 wkdays	21 days	Ref.01	(part 2 of 2)

Figure 25.6 Summary of critically delayed activities in window.

Window 3: from 3 February to 2 March 2003; end of week 13
Work planned to be done during this Window

'Preliminary Works' were planned to continue during this window period. This included completion of 'Pile Probing' (act.nr. 0060), and 'Guide Walls' (act.nr. 0070). 'Install Secant Piles' (act.nr. 0080) and 'Cut Down Piles' (act.nr. 0090), were to be progressing and be 60% and 30% complete respectively by the end of this window.

'Apartment Block; Substructure' works were planned to commence in this window. 'Frc Capping Beam' (act.nr. 0110) to commence on 20 February 2002, and 'Bulk Dig Leaving Supporting Berms' (act.nr. 0120) on 24 February 2002. These activities were to be 20% and 6% complete respectively at the end of the window.

'Time Analysis' results: at closing of Window

Window 3: from 3 February to 2 March 2003;		end of week 13		
A New forecast completion date	31 January 2005			
		T.F. Delay to project completion		
B Critical delay to project:-		-20	20 workdays	42 cal. days
C Time lost in this window			0 workdays	0 cal. days
D Critical (driving) activity at closing of window 'Bulk Dig Leaving Support Berms'	act.no. '0120'	-20	20 workdays	42 cal. days
E Other 'near-critical' activities at closing of window -none-				

Figure 25.7 Time analysis results at closing of window.

'Time Analysis' results: impact on sectional completion dates

Position at closing of window	Forecast completion	Slippage in window	Total slippage
Section 1: Show Flat (floor 03)	08-Mar-04	none	24 days
Section 2: Arts Complex (partial)	05-Apr-04	none	24 days
Section 3: Residential Floors 04 to 07 (incl.)	02-Jun-04	none	29 days
Section 4: Shops	02-Jun-04	none	29 days
Section 7: Remaining Residential	18-Oct-04	none	28 days
Section 8: All Other Areas	31-Jan-05	none	42 days

Figure 25.8 TA results: impact on sectional completion dates.

Commentary on work carried out in this Window
Preliminary Works

1 *'Pile Probing' (act.nr 0060) was completed on 14 February 2003, some 7 workdays later than its planned finish date at the start of this window. There was no critical delay to this activity in this window.*

2 *'Guide Walls' (act.nr. 0070) was completed on 1 March 2002, some 7 workdays later than its planned finish date at the start of this window. There was no critical delay to this activity in this window.*

3 *'Install Secant Piles' (act.nr. 0080) was 85% complete at the end of this window. The activity is shown as being in critical delay of 8 workdays; however, completion of this activity is being controlled by completion of its predecessor 'Guide Walls' (act.nr. 0070).*

4 *'Cut Down Piles' (act.nr 0090) was 25% complete at the end of this window. The activity is shown as being in critical delay of 8 workdays; however, completion of this activity is being controlled by completion of its predecessor 'Install Secant Piles' (act.nr. 0080).*

Apartment Block

5 *'Frc Capping Beam' (act.nr. 0110) commenced on 18 February 2003, was 18% complete and showing a critical delay of 8 workdays at the end of this window. The actual start date was ahead of the planned start date; and although progress is slightly behind that planned at the start of the window, this activity's completion is being controlled by completion of 'Cut Down Piles', which itself is in 8 workdays critical delay.*

6 *'Bulk Dig Leaving Supporting Berms' (act. nr. 0120) commenced on 20 February 2003 and was 20% complete at the end of this window. An earlier than planned commencement and achieving better than planned progress for this activity resulted in the overall critical delay to the project completion date being reduced by 2 workdays. This is an example of mitigation by the contractor.*

Summary of critically delayed activities in this Window

SECTION: Element; Activity of Work	Act.Nr.	Nature of delay	Workdays	Calendar days	CDA Ref.
NO CRITICAL DELAYS IN THIS WINDOW	---	---	---	---	---

Figure 25.9 Summary of critically delayed activities in window.

Window 4: from 3 March to 30 March 2003; end of week 17
Work planned to be done during this Window

'Preliminary Works' were planned to continue during this window period. 'Install Secant Piles' (act.nr. 0080) and 'Cut Down Piles' (act.nr. 0090), were to be progressing and be 90% and 70% complete respectively by the end of this window.

'Apartment Block; Substructure' works were planned to progress in this window, with 'Frc Capping Beam' (act.nr. 0110) and 'Bulk Dig Leaving Supporting Berms' (act.nr. 0120) to be 60% and 37% complete respectively at the end of the window.

'Time Analysis' results: at closing of Window

Window 4: from 3 March to 30 March 2003;			end of week 17		
A	New forecast completion date	11 February 2005			
			T.F.	Delay to project completion	
B	Critical delay to project:-		-29	29 workdays	53 cal. days
C	Time lost in this window			6 workdays	9 cal. days
D	Critical (driving) activity at closing of window				
	'Bulk Dig Leaving Support Berms'	act.no. '0120'	-29	29 workdays	53 cal. days
E	Other 'near-critical' activities at closing of window				
	-none-				

Figure 25.10 TA results at closing of window.

'Time Analysis' results: impact on sectional completion dates

Position at closing of window	Forecast completion	Slippage in window	Total slippage
Section 1: Show Flat (floor 03)	19-Mar-04	9 days	35 days
Section 2: Arts Complex (partial)	26-Apr-04	19 days	45 days
Section 3: Residential Floors 04 to 07 (incl.)	15-Jun-04	11 days	42 days
Section 4: Shops	15-Jun-04	8 days	39 days
Section 7: Remaining Residential	29-Oct-04	18 days	39 days
Section 8: All Other Areas	11-Feb-05	9 days	53 days

Figure 25.11 TA results: impact on sectional completion dates.

Commentary on work carried out in this Window
Preliminary Works

1 'Install Secant Piles' (act.nr 0080) was completed on 20 March 2003, some 11 workdays earlier than its planned finish date at the start of this window.

2 *'Cut Down Piles' (act.nr 0090) was 70% complete at the end of this window. The activity is shown as being in critical delay of 9 workdays; however, this is not causing any critical delay to any of its successor activities.*

Apartment Block

3 *'Frc Capping Beam' (act.nr. 0110) was 40% complete and showing a critical delay of 14 workdays at the end of this window. This was somewhat less than the 60% progress planned to be achieved as at the start of this window; however, this is not causing any critical delay to any of its successor activities.*

4 *'Bulk Dig Leaving Supporting Berms' (act.nr. 0120) was 25% complete at the end of this window. This was somewhat less than the 37% progress planned to be achieved as at the start of this window. This delayed progress is causing a 29 workday critical delay to the project completion; which is a slippage of a further 6 workdays in this window.*

5 *'Frc Section of Area 3 Slab for Tower Crane 1' (act.nr. 0130) was 85% complete at the end of the window. At the start of this window no work was planned to be carried out on this activity.*

Summary of critically delayed activities in this Window

SECTION: Element; Activity of Work	Act.Nr.	Nature of delay	Workdays	Calendar days	CDA Ref.
APARTM.BLK.: Substruc.; Bulk Dig Leav. Supp Bms	0120	Delayed progress	6 w'kdays	9 days	Ref.02

Figure 25.12 Summary of critically delayed activities in window.

Window 5: from 31 March to 4 May 2003; end of week 22

Work planned to be done during this Window

'Preliminary Works' were planned to continue during this window period. 'Install Secant Piles' (act.nr. 0080) and 'Cut Down Piles' (act.nr. 0090), were to be progressing and be 90% and 70% complete respectively by the end of this window.

'Apartment Block; Substructure' works were planned to progress in this window, with 'Frc Capping Beam' (act.nr. 0110) and 'Bulk Dig Leaving Supporting Berms' (act.nr. 0120) to be 95% and 45% complete respectively at the end of the window. 'Frc Section of Area 3 Slab for Tower Crane 1' (act.nr. 0130) and 'Erect Tower Crane' (act.nr. 0140) were planned to be completed by the end of the window. 'Frc Basement Slab Area 1' (act.nr. 0150) was planned to commence and be 55% complete by the end of the window.

'Time Analysis' results: at closing of Window

Window 5: from 31 March to 4 May 2003;   **end of week 22**

A	*Now forecast completion date*	17 February 2005			
			T.F.	Delay to project completion	
B	*Critical delay to project:-*		-33	33 workdays	59 cal. days
C	*Time lost in this window*			4 workdays	6 cal. days
D	*Critical (driving) activity at closing of window*				
	'Frc Capping Beam'	act.no. '0110'	-33	33 workdays	59 cal. days
E	*Other 'near-critical' activities at closing of window*				
	-none-				

Figure 25.13 TA results at close of window.

'Time Analysis' results: impact on sectional completion dates

Position at closing of window	Forecast completion	Slippage in window	Total slippage
Section 1: Show Flat (floor 03)	25-May-04	6 days	41 days
Section 2: Arts Complex (partial)	30-Apr-04	4 days	49 days
Section 3: Residential Floors 04 to 07 (incl.)	21-Jun-04	6 days	48 days
Section 4: Shops	21-Jun-04	6 days	45 days
Section 7: Remaining Residential	04-Nov-04	6 days	45 days
Section 8: All Other Areas	17-Feb-05	6 days	50 days

Figure 25.14 TA results' impact on dates.

Commentary on work carried out in this Window
Preliminary Works
1 'Cut Down Piles' *(act.nr. 0090) was 88% complete at the end of this window. The activity is shown as being in critical delay of 21 workdays; however, this is not causing any critical delay to any of its successor activities.*

Apartment Block; Substructure
2 'Frc Capping Beam' *(act.nr. 0110) was 40% complete and showing a critical delay of 33 workdays at the end of this window. There was no progress on this activity in the window, and this activity is now in critical delay by 33 workdays.*
3 'Bulk Dig Leaving Supporting Berms' *(act.nr. 0120) was 70% complete at the end of this window. This activity is 33 workdays in critical delay, which is being caused by its predecessor activity* 'Frc Capping Beam' *(act.nr. 0110)*
4 'Frc Section of Area 3 Slab for Tower Crane 1' *(act.nr. 0130) was completed on 5 April 2003. No delay was caused to its successor activity.*
5 'Erect Tower Crane' *(act.nr. 0140) was completed on 15 April 2003. No delay was caused to its successor activity.*
6 'Frc Basement Slab Area 1' *(act.nr. 0150). This activity was*

commenced on 10 April 2003 and completed on 29 April 2003. No delay was caused to its successor activity.

7 'Install Temporary Works Jigs 1 and 2' (act.nr. 0160). This activity was commenced on 8 April 2003 and completed on 1 May 2003. No delay was caused to its successor activity.

8 'Frc Basement Slab Area 2' (act.nr. 0220). This activity was commenced on 3 April 2003 and completed on 3 May 2003. No critical delay was caused to its successor activity.

9 'Frc Walls and Columns, Lower – Upper Basement' (act.nr. 0190). This activity commenced on 1 May 2003 and was 10% at the end of the window. The activity was in critical delay of 17 workdays.

Apartment Block; Substructure

10 'Frc Basement Slab Area 3' (act.nr. 0660). This activity commenced on 28 April 2003 and was 60% at the end of the window. The activity was in critical delay of 29 workdays; this critical delay is being caused by its predecessor activity 'Frc Capping Beam' (act.nr. 0110).

11 'Relocate Temporary Works Jigs 1 and 2' (act.nr. 0670). This activity commenced on 2 May 2003 and was 70% at the end of the window. The activity was not in critical delay.

12 'Frc Basement Slab Area 4' (act.nr. 0660). This activity commenced on 2 May 2003 and was 40% at the end of the window. The activity was in critical delay of 28 workdays; this critical delay is being caused by its predecessor activity 'Frc Capping Beam' (act.nr. 0110).

Summary of critically delayed activities in this Window

SECTION: Element; Activity of Work	Act.Nr.	Nature of delay	Workdays	Calendar days	CDA Ref.
APARTM.BLK.: Substruc.; Frc Capping Beam	0110	Delayed progress	4 w'kdays	6 days	Ref.03

Figure 25.15 Summary of critically delayed activities.

The submission reviewed and presented the results of the remaining 'windows analysis' in a similar manner, up to the final window, number 26.

As can be seen from the results of the first five number windows above, there were three actual delaying events to the project causing critical delay to the project completion. These are shown in Figure 25.16.

CDA Ref.	SECTION: Element; Activity of Work	Act.Nr.	Nature of delay	Workdays	Calendar days
Ref.01	PRELIM.WKS: Piling; Pile Probing	0060	Delayed progress	22 w'kdays	44 days
Ref.02	APARTM.BLK.: Substruc.; Bulk Dig Leav. Supp Bms	0120	Delayed progress	6 w'kdays	9 days
Ref.03	APARTM.BLK.: Substruc.; Frc Capping Beam	0110	Delayed progress	4 w'kdays	6 days

Figure 25.16 The actual delaying events.

At the end of window 10, on 2 November, the progress update shows the forecast completion date for the project to be 15 April 2005, which is some 75 workdays or 117 calendar days in delay.

However, taking into account the 'windows analysis' results from the first ten windows, the table of critical delaying events at the end of window 10 is shown in Figure 25.17.

CDA Ref	SECTION: Element; Activity of Work	Act. Nr.	Nature of delay	Workdays	Calendar days	
Ref. 01	PRELIM.WKS: Piling; Pile Probing	0060	Delayed progress	22 wkdays	44 days	
Ref. 02	APARTM.BLK.: Substruc.; Bulk Dig Leav. Supp Bms	0120	Delayed progress	6 wkdays	9 days	
Ref. 03	APARTM.BLK.: Substruc.; Frc Capping Beam	0110	Delayed progress	4 wkdays	6 days	
Ref. 04	APARTM.BLK.: Substruc.; Inst.Temp.Supp.Props	0420	Delayed start	9 wkdays	12 days	
Ref. 05	APARTM.BLK.: Substruc.; Frc Basem.Sl. gl.l.1/M-R	0490	Delayed start	10 wkdays	14 days	These critical delays are concurrent
Ref. 06	ARTS CENTRE: Substruc.;Frc Walls/Cols, Area 5	0930	Delayed start	13 wkdays	17 days	
Ref. 07	APARTM.BLK.: Substruc.; Upp Basem.Sl. gl.l.1/A-J	0410	Delayed progress	4 wkdays	6 days	These critical delays are concurrent
Ref. 08	ARTS CENTRE: Substruc.;Frc Basem.Sl. Area 7	0980	Delayed start	7 wkdays	9 days	
Ref. 09	ARTS CENTRE: Superstr.;Frc GF Slab, gl.9-11/A-K	2260	Delayed start	5 wkdays	7 days	
Ref. 10	APARTM.BLK.: Superstr.; 2nd Floor Slab gl.1-7/A-F	1340	Delayed progress	6 wkdays	8 days	These critical delays are concurrent
Ref. 11	ARTS CENTRE: Superstr.;Walls/Cols, Ground to 2nd	2360	Delayed start	9 wkdays	13 days	

Figure 25.17 Updated table of critical events.

The next section in the submission document should be a narrative on the critical delaying events. For each event, there should be:

1 An introductory narrative explaining the 'event' and its importance in the construction process.
2 The contemporaneous factual information related to the event, e.g. requests for information, letters, AIs or other instructions, drawing issues, procurement of materials, labour records. Copies of any documents referred to should be included in the submission.
3 The results of the 'windows analysis' focusing on the critical delay caused by the event, with specific graphics if necessary. The extension of time claimed as a consequence of the event should be clearly stated; this may be the full critical delay caused or only part of the delay.
4 The contract clause under which the extension of time is claimed.

A fully detailed submission, as described above, will demonstrate the cause and effect, i.e. 'causation', of the extension of time claimed.

Part VI

Prolongation claims (and time-related costs)

26 Introduction

Claims are an inevitable feature of many projects that have to be dealt with on the majority of contracts and subcontracts let. Most claims result from the project designer's inability to fully provide for all eventualities, which means that changes will be made to the contract as it proceeds and, where these involve additional work, adjusted payments will be necessary. Disagreements on the level of these payments will be a typical source of claims. As well as changes to the payments made, these variations may also result in delays to the works and where these delays have a knock-on effect on the project as a whole, they may give rise to extra costs. These costs result from the contractor's additional presence on site, generating additional overhead costs for the extended period.

By no means will all changes to a contract delay the project. Some will involve changes in detail that merely affect the nature of the work to be done without increasing its difficulty, requirement for resources or duration. Other changes will actually reduce the work to be carried out. There will, however, typically be changes that do delay, increase the duration of or force a change in sequence in the activities making up the contractor's programme.

The expression 'delay claim' is generally used to describe a monetary claim which follows on from a delay to the project completion. Similarly, the expression 'disruption claim' is generally used to describe a monetary claim in circumstances where part of the works has been disrupted, without affecting the completion date of the project; this typically equates with a delay which is not on the critical path.

There is no such thing as the ideal format for a delay claim; each claim is dependent upon the individual facts of its own project or case. There are, however, some simple guidelines or good practice which are applicable to almost all claim submissions. These are detailed in chapter 28, followed by worked examples in chapter 29.

The starting point for the assessment of a prolongation claim should be 'in respect of what period is the contractor entitled to further payment?'. What is equally important not only concerns how many weeks the contractor is entitled to be paid for, but which weeks. This is because the amount of his entitlement will depend on his actual costs, particularly his time-related preliminary costs which will vary throughout the project.

Classification of 'delays'

Delays can first be classified as either 'excusable' or 'non-excusable'.

Excusable delays are those for which the contractor can be excused due to an act or omission by the employer or his agents. For example, late issue of design information by the architect to the contractor.

Non-excusable delays are those arising from the contractor's own actions or inactions. For example, when a contractor fails to provide sufficient manpower to complete the project on time.

Excusable delays are in turn divided into 'compensable' and 'non-compensable' categories. The former entitles the delayed party, usually the contractor, to monetary compensation for the period of delay through acts or omissions by the employer or his agents. Non-compensable delays on the other hand arise from neutral events (such as exceptionally inclement weather), third parties, etc.; indeed any event for which under the contract between the parties there is no recompense for loss and expense.

Overheads

Overheads can constitute an important element of any claim and are often controversial. It is therefore essential to demonstrate that the overheads being claimed are additional and/or that they could have been deployed elsewhere to commercial advantage but for the problems encountered. It is therefore advisable to allocate additional resources to individual events or only rely on formula methods of overhead recovery, such as Hudson's or Emden's, for those elements which cannot be allocated to individual events.

Overheads are considered under the following broad headings.

1 Site overheads and establishment

Although site overheads are generally dedicated to a particular project, it does not follow that if a project is delayed due to an event on a critical activity then the whole of the site overhead is extended by a period corresponding to that delay. The identification is best achieved through site diaries or daily reports. Associated items such as vehicles and office space usually follow on if the individuals involved can be identified.

Many items will not have a critical delaying effect but will still involve additional supervisory hours being expended; again these should be identifiable through site diaries or daily reports.

Very often it can be demonstrated that such events result in an increase in supervisory staff and associated items. Many other site resources are common items and may be claimable depending upon the circumstances.

2 Head office overheads

Specific head office overheads are those which can be allocated to a project either on a full-time or part-time basis. In the case of certain costs (e.g. drawing office and planning resources) it should be possible to relate the use of such resources to individual events. For example, the necessity to produce a revised drawing may originate from instructions received, while planning work may result from delays and the necessity to revise the programme. It will be more difficult to directly link other resources (e.g. a contracts manager) to specific events although it may be possible to show that, for instance, time was spent attending meetings dealing with problems associated with an event. Similarly, it may be possible to show that additional site visits were required. As a general rule where overheads are claimed, these should be specifically identified and allocated as far as possible to individual events. The head office on-costs (e.g. office space and furniture) of such resources should also be treated as specific head office overheads. Formulae should only be used for calculating the cost of those resources that are not specific to a project and could not therefore be allocated on any other basis.

3 Financing and other charges

General head office overheads can only be allocated to projects on an apportioned basis and for this reason are the most contentious area of overheads when attempting to recover additional costs. In order to have the best chance of being successful in the recovery of such costs, it is necessary to show that there was sufficient work available to one in the general marketplace and that opportunities were turned down because of continuing commitments to a project attributable to claimable events. Comprehensive records should therefore be kept of tender invitations and bids.

Chapter 28 contains more details on the 'heads of claim' for prolongation claims, and chapter 29 contains a worked example of a prolongation, or loss and expense, claim.

27 Contract requirements

The two most commonly used forms of contract in the UK stipulate the following requirements and conditions regarding monetary compensation for time-related delays and changes.

The contractual requirements: JCT

Section 4 of the *JCT 2005 Standard Building Contract with Quantities*, deals with 'Payment', and clauses 4.23 to 4.26 under the sub-heading 'Loss and Expense' state:

> *Matters materially affecting regular progress*
> *4.23 If in the execution of this Contract the Contractor incurs or is likely to incur direct loss and/or expense for which he would not be reimbursed by a payment under any other provision in these Conditions due to a deferment of giving possession of the site or relevant part of it under clause 2.5 or because the regular progress of the Works or of any part of them has been or is likely to be materially affected by any part of the Relevant Matters, the Contractor may make written application to the Architect/Contract Administrator. If the Contractor makes such application, save where these Conditions provide that there shall be no addition to the Contract Sum or otherwise exclude the operation of this clause, then, if and as soon as the Architect/Contract Administrator is of the opinion that the regular progress has been or is likely to be materially affected as stated in the application or that direct loss and/or expense has been or is likely to be incurred due to such deferment, the Architect/Contract Administrator shall from time to time thereafter ascertain, or instruct the Quantity Surveyor to ascertain, the amount of the loss and/or expense which has been or is being incurred; provided always that the Contractor shall:*
>
> *.1 make his application as soon as it has become, or should reasonably have become, apparent to him that the regular progress has been or is likely to be affected;*

.2 in support of his application submit to the Architect/Contract Administrator upon request such information as should reasonably enable the Architect/Contract Administrator to form an opinion; and

.3 upon request submit to the Architect/Contract Administrator or to the Quantity Surveyor such details of the loss and/or expense as are reasonably necessary for such ascertainment.

Relevant Matters
4.24 *The following are the Relevant Matters:*

.1 Variations (excluding any loss and/or expense relating to a Confirmed Acceptance of a Schedule 2 Quotation but including any other matters or instructions which under theses Conditions are to be treated as, or as requiring, a Variation);

.2 instructions of the Architect/Contract Administrator:

    .1 under clause 3.15 or 3.16 (excluding an instruction for expenditure of a Provisional Sum for defined work);

    .2 for the opening up for inspection or testing of any work, materials or goods under clause 3.17 (including making good), unless the cost is provided for in the Contract Bills or unless the inspection or test shows that the work, materials or goods are not in accordance with this Contract; or

    .3 in relation to any discrepancy in or divergence between the Contract Drawings, the Contract Bills and/or other documents referred to in clause 2.15;

.3 suspension by the Contractor under clause 4.14 of the performance of his obligations under this Contract, providing the suspension was not frivolous or vexatious;

.4 the execution of work for which an Approximate Quantity is not a reasonably accurate forecast of the quantity of work required;

.5 any impediment, prevention or default, whether by act or omission, by the Employer, the Architect/Contract Administrator, the Quantity Surveyor or any of the Employer's Persons, except to the extent caused or contributed to by any default, whether by act or omission, of the Contractor or of any of the Contractor's Persons.

Amounts ascertained – addition to Contract Sum
4.25 *Any amounts from time to time ascertained under clause 4.23 shall be added to the Contract Sum.*

Reservation of Contractor's rights and remedies
4.26 *The provisions of clauses 4.23 to 4.25 are without prejudice to any other rights and remedies which the Contractor may possess.*

The contractual requirements: NEC

The New Engineering and Construction Contract is somewhat different to the JCT Contract. Within the NEC is core clause 6, which is titled 'Compensation Events'. Under this clause a contractor is entitled to both time and money, with sub-clauses 62 to 65 inclusive relevant to the money aspect of compensation events. These sub-clauses state:

62   *Quotations for compensation events*

62.1   After discussing with the Contractor different ways of dealing with the compensation event which are practicable, the Project Manager may instruct the Contractor to submit alternative quotations. The Contractor submits the required quotations to the Project Manager and may submit quotations for other methods of dealing with the compensation event which he considers practicable.

62.2   Quotations for compensation events comprise proposed changes to the Prices and any delay to the Completion Date and Key Dates assessed by the Contractor. The Contractor submits details of his assessment with each quotation. If the programme for remaining work is altered by the compensation event, the Contractor includes the alterations to the Accepted Programme in his quotation.

62.3   The Contractor submits quotations within three weeks of being instructed to do so by the Project Manager. The Project Manager replies within two weeks of the submission. His reply is

- *an instruction to submit a revised quotation,*
- *an acceptance of a quotation,*
- *a notification that a proposed instruction will not be given or a proposed changed decision will not be made or*
- *a notification that he will be making his own assessment.*

62.4   The Project Manager instructs the Contractor to submit a revised quotation only after explaining his reasons for doing so to the Contractor. The Contractor submits the revised quotation within three weeks of being instructed to do so.

62.5   The Project Manager extends the time allowed for

- *the Contractor to submit quotations for a compensation event and*
- *the Project Manager to reply to a quotation*

if the Project Manager and the Contractor agree to the extension before the submission or reply is due. The Project Manager notifies the extension that has been agreed to the Contractor.

62.6 *If the Project Manager does not reply to a quotation within the time allowed, the Contractor may notify the Project Manager to this effect. If the Contractor submitted more than one quotation for the compensation event, he states in his notification which quotation he proposes is to be accepted. If the Project Manager does not reply to the notification within two weeks, and unless the quotation is for a proposed instruction or a proposed changed decision, the Contractor's notification is treated as acceptance of the quotation by the Project Manager.*

63 Assessing compensation events

63.1 *The changes to the Prices are assessed as the effect of the compensation event upon*

- *the actual Defined Cost of the works already done,*
- *the forecast Defined Cost of the work not yet done and*
- *the resulting Fee.*

The date when the Project Manager instructed or should have instructed the Contractor to submit quotations divides the work already done from the work not yet done.

63.2 *If the effect of a compensation event is to reduce the total Defined Cost, the Prices are not reduced except as stated in this contract.*

63.3 *A delay to the Completion Date is assessed as the length of time that, due to the compensation event, planned Completion is later than planned Completion as shown on the Accepted Programme. A delay to a Key Date is assessed as the length of time that, due to the compensation event, the planned date when the Condition stated for a Key Date will be met is later than the date shown on the Accepted Programme.*

63.4 *The rights of the Employer and Contractor to changes to the Prices, the Completion Date and the Key Dates are their only rights in respect of a compensation event.*

63.5 *If the Project Manager has notified the Contractor of his decision that the Contractor did not give an early warning of a compensation event which an experienced contractor could have given, the event is assessed as if the Contractor had given early warning.*

63.6 *Assessment of the effect of a compensation event includes risk allowances for cost and time for matters which have a significant chance of occurring and are at the Contractor's risk under this contract.*

63.7 *Assessments are based upon the assumptions that the Contractor reacts competently and promptly to the compensation event, that any Defined Cost and time due to the event are reasonably incurred and that the Accepted Programme can be changed.*

63.8 A compensation event which is an instruction to change the Works Information in order to resolve an ambiguity or inconsistency is assessed as if the Prices, the Completion Date and the Key Dates were for the interpretation most favourable to the Party which did not provide the Works Information.

63.9 If a change to the Works Information makes the description of the Condition for a Key Date incorrect, the Project Manager corrects the description. This correction is taken into account in assessing the compensation event for the change to the Works Information.

64 The Project Manager's assessments

64.1 The Project Manager assesses a compensation event

- *if the Contractor has not submitted a quotation and details of his assessment within the time allowed,*
- *if the Project Manager decides that the Contractor has not assessed the compensation event correctly in a quotation and he does not instruct the Contractor to submit a revised quotation,*
- *if, when the Contractor submits quotations for a compensation event, he has not submitted a programme or alterations to a programme which this contract requires him to submit or*
- *if, when the Contractor submits quotations for a compensation event, the Project Manager has not accepted the Contractor's latest programme for one of the reasons stated in this contract.*

64.2 The Project Manager assesses a compensation event using his own assessment of the programme for the remaining work if

- *there is no Accepted Programme or*
- *the Contractor has not submitted a programme or alterations to a programme for acceptance as required by this contract.*

64.3 The Project Manager notifies the Contractor of his assessment of a compensation event and gives him details of it within the period allowed for the Contractor's submission of his quotation for the same event. This period starts when the need for the Project Manager's assessment becomes apparent.

64.4 If the Project Manager does not assess a compensation event within the time allowed, the Contractor may notify the Project Manager to this effect. If the Contractor submitted more than one quotation for the compensation event, he states in his notification which quotation he proposes to be accepted. If the Project

Manager does not reply within two weeks of this notification the notification is treated as acceptance of the Contractor's quotation by the Project Manager.

65 Implementing compensation events

65.1 A compensation event is implemented when

- *the Project Manager notifies his acceptance of the Contractor's quotation,*
- *the Project Manager notifies the Contractor of his own assessment, or*
- *a Contractor's quotation is treated as having been accepted by the Project Manager.*

65.2 The assessment of a compensation event is not revised if a forecast upon which it was based is shown by later recorded information to have been wrong.

28 Prolongation claims

It is good practice for the detailed prolongation, or loss and expense, claim to be set out in three sections, namely:

1 site overheads and establishment;
2 head office overheads;
3 other costs and charges.

1 Site overheads and establishment

This section can be subdivided as necessary into the following heads of claim:

A Staff

Under this head, the site staff actually based on the project, or directly associated with the project on a part-time basis, for the specific delay period or periods, should be listed together with their actual cost per week. For example:

Delay period one: 4 weeks (weeks 26 to 29 inclusive)

Project Manager	Mr 'aaa'	4 weeks @ £1,200.00 per week
General Foreman	Mr 'bbb'	4 weeks @ £950.00 per week
Assistant Foreman	Mr 'ccc'	4 weeks @ £800.00 per week
Quantity Surveyor	Mr 'ddd'	4 weeks @ £900.00 per week
Area Manager (part)	Mr 'eee'	4 weeks @ £600.00 per week
Buyer (part)	Mr 'fff'	4 weeks @ £250.00 per week

B Site establishment

Under this head, the site establishment costs actually spent on the project for the specific delay period or periods should be listed. For example,

Delay period one: 4 weeks (weeks 26 to 29 inclusive)

Hire of Offices	4 weeks @ £800.00 per week
Office Equipment	4 weeks @ £250.00 per week
Plant & Equipment	4 weeks @ £550.00 per week
Small Tools	4 weeks @ £200.00 per week
Scaffolding	4 weeks @ £500.00 per week
Electricity charges	£1,800.00 ? 4/13 weeks
Telephone charges	£360.00 ? 4/13 weeks
Security	4 weeks @ £400.00 per week
Welfare	4 weeks @ £450.00 per week

C Other project-related costs

Preliminary thickening

This relates to additional staff being employed on the project during the contract period, as a consequence of the number of instructions, revisions to drawings and dealing with a flow of information that was above that anticipated at tender stage.

A narrative will be necessary explaining the circumstances in detail. For example, an assistant QS may have been employed to action an excessive number of architects' instructions and other information flow items; an additional general foreman employed on site to review the many drawing revisions and instructions; an agency engineer to assist the general foreman. Additional to their basic costs are their associated site establishment costs.

Head office-related costs; general

One aspect of a loss and expense claim which is commonly misunderstood is the loss of contribution to head office overheads and profit. In fact many contractors forget the impact of a delayed project on their head office costs. It is, after all, the head office that provides the support and guidance to the on-site project team. Head office costs are paid for by the money received for carrying out work on the company's projects, and head office staff and support facilities are allocated to each project accordingly. Therefore, if a project is delayed and extended in time, then the support provided by the head office must also be extended for the same duration.

Typically, claims for loss of overheads and profit are combined as one head of loss. While this is not necessarily inappropriate, it is important to consider the characteristics of head office overheads and thus to recognise when they can be distinguished as a separate head of claim from loss of profits. Head office costs, sometimes referred to as home-office costs, are typically associated with the overall management of the business. They will usually include property costs, rent, rates, heat and light together with other central services and utilities. They also include the cost of head office staff, the directors and other senior management and support staff, their salaries and other benefits including cars and pension payments; the cost of information systems, finance and accounting departments, perhaps the in-house legal team and secretariat; and, often, the cost of a central QS/design team as well as related selling and marketing costs.

2 Head office overheads

This head of claim is for recovery of, or contribution to, the contractor's overheads and profit. While strictly speaking these are two heads, namely lost overheads and loss of profits, as stated earlier, they are usually combined and treated as one 'head of claim'. In essence, the logic behind a 'contribution claim' is that, as a result of delay or disruption to a given contract, head office resources inevitably become involved in dealing with the problems that arise in managing and providing support services to the contract in such circumstances. This will divert management resources from other duties, including the efficient and profitable running of other contracts, and perhaps, more importantly, looking for and winning new work.

Both of these diversions can lead to a reduction in the claimant's profit, through inefficiencies on other contracts or through failure to obtain contributions towards the overheads and profit of the business from new work.

The concept of lost contribution to overheads and profit is fairly straightforward to argue. But it is often a different matter producing sufficient robust evidence in a particular case to prove loss, even on the balance of probabilities. Again much will depend on the extent and quality of the contractor's records; and this means not just its accounting records. It can be equally important to be able to furnish contemporaneous records demonstrating the impact of the contract disruption on other parts of the business. The records could also include a schedule of tender opportunities not taken up or perhaps an analysis showing a reduction in tender success rate.

Calculation of the loss

Where the evidence justifies a claim for lost contribution to head office overheads and profit, how should it be calculated? By its very nature as a hypothetical loss there is no single right figure for any given claim.

The fact that damages cannot be assessed with certainty does not relieve the wrongdoer of paying damages. Where the precise evidence is obtainable the certifier, contract administrator, arbitrator, adjudicator or court naturally expects to have it; but where it is not, the certifier or court must do the best it can.

As much certainty and particularity must be given, both in submissions and pleadings, as proof of damages. However, damages can be received for future or projected loss – if reasonably anticipated – as a result of the defendant's wrong, whether such future damage is certain or contingent.

Very few companies are prepared to open up their accounting records to demonstrate their head office costs, so this is resolved by applying formulae based on the contract price and the duration of the extended contract period. The three most common formulae for calculating head office overheads are,

1   the Hudson formula;
2   Emden's formula;
3   Eichleay formula.

The Hudson formula

This formula was put forward in *Hudson's Building and Engineering Contracts*, tenth edition (1970). It uses the percentage allowance made by the contractor in his original contract sum for head office overheads and profit as the basis for the loss of contribution to overheads. The following formula is then applied.

$$\frac{\text{HO overheads/profit \%}}{100} \times \frac{\text{Contract price}}{\text{Contract period (weeks)}} \times$$

$$\text{Period of delay (weeks)} = \text{weekly rate recoverable}$$

The Hudson formula is a very broadbrush approach to dealing with claims for head office overheads. However, it may not be appropriate to claim for loss of profit unless there is a clear indication that the contractor would have been able to earn profits on other contracts but for the overrun. Also it takes as its base overhead and profit percentages from the original contract price and these may not properly reflect the contractor's true overhead cost and profitability.

Emden's formula

This formula can be found in *Emden's Building Contracts and Practice*, eighth edition. It involves a two-stage calculation that applies the percentage that the contractor's total overheads and profit bear to the total revenue of the company. The second stage applies this percentage to the contract price, contract period and the period of delay to determine the weekly cost recoverable.

The advantage of this formula is that it uses a head office overhead percentage based on the contractor's total business rather than on the specific contract in dispute. Again this formula does not necessarily reflect the real effect on overhead costs arising from the delay, but it may provide a reasonable approximation particularly if some simplistic approach is looked for to assist in negotiating an out-of-court settlement. See below.

Stage 1

$$\frac{\text{Company overhead cost/profit}}{\text{Company revenue}} = Z\%$$

Stage 2

$$\frac{Z\%}{100} \times \frac{\text{Contract price}}{\text{Contract period (weeks)}} \times \text{Period of delay (weeks)} = \text{weekly rate recoverable}$$

The Eichleay formula

This formula originated in the United States, and seeks to establish the proportion of a contractor's head office overhead attributable to the project in question. It uses this proportion to compute an amount of overhead cost per week or per month and applies this to the period of delay. The Eichleay formula is a three-stage calculation shown below:

Stage 1

$$\frac{\text{Total value of project (incl. variations)}}{\text{Company revenue for contract period}} \times \text{Company overhead cost/profit} = \text{Allocable overhead for the project}$$

Stage 2

$$\frac{\text{The allocable overhead for the project}}{\text{Actual project period, incl. delay (weeks)}} = \text{weekly rate recoverable}$$

Stage 3

$$\text{Weekly rate recoverable} \times \text{Period of delay (weeks)} = \text{Head office's overhead costs}$$

Worked examples of the three formulae are included in chapter 29.

Which formula should be used?

The selection of a formula for head office overheads will depend on the circumstance of each case.

However, a word of caution about the Hudson formula. This relies on the accuracy and reliability of the contractor's tender. Also, the contract sum used for the calculation may contain an element of head office overheads and profit, so there could be double counting.

A further word of caution concerning the Eichleay formula. If a significant proportion of the total value of the project, say 10 per cent, is the value of variations, then an adjustment should be made to the input value into the formula to take account of the fact that the variations themselves may contain an element of head office overheads and profit.

Finally, it is suggested that the certifier, contract administrator, arbitrator, adjudicator or court should not be bound by the results of a particular formula, and that the use of one formula be compared with the results of another formula.

3 Other costs and charges

It is clear from established case law that contractors are entitled to finance charges as part of their prolongation, or loss and expense, claims.

When evaluating the cost of financing, the following important issues should be taken into account:

1   The appropriate rate of interest is that actually paid by the contractor provided that it is not unreasonable.
2   The financing cost shall be calculated on the basis that it is charged by the contractor's bank, i.e. the same rates and compounding interest at the same intervals.
3   However, where the contractor is self-financed or financed from within its own corporate group, the appropriate rate of interest is that earned by the contractor, or its corporate group, on monies it has placed on deposit.

Setting a date for interest payments to start

The Society of Construction Law's 'Delay and Disruption Protocol' offers good advice on this matter in paragraphs 1.15.6 and 1.15.7:

> There are often arguments as to the date on which interest on a Contractor's claim should start to run. Contractors will argue that it should be the date on which they incurred expenditure for which they are entitled to compensation. Employers will say that interest should run only from the date that the Contractor has provided all information needed to satisfy them that the expenditure has been incurred.
>
> The appropriate starting date will not be the same in all circumstances, but generally the starting date for the payment of interest should be the earliest date on which the principal sum could have become payable, which will be the date for payment of the certificate issued immediately after the date the Contractor applied for payment of the loss and/or expense. This will be subject to any notice requirements in the contract. In contracts where there are no certificates, the

Protocol recommends that interest should start to run 30 days after the date the Contractor suffered the loss and/or expense.

These are sensible suggestions, and it is recommended that they are followed.

Prolongation of individual activities

For delays not on the actual critical path, there will be no general prolongation costs. However, there may be some time-related costs attributable to a particular activity, and its associated activities.

For example, an activity, not on the project's actual critical path, such as the fixing of specialist roof fascia and soffit panels may have required scaffolding to be in place for its entire duration together with craneage for part of its duration. If this work was delayed as a consequence of late information for which the employer was responsible then the cost of the scaffolding and craneage required solely for the activity should be recoverable.

Preceding the detailed section of the prolongation claim, it is good practice for the opening sections of the claim to contain the following information:

1   Introduction
2   The parties: formal details of the employer, contractor, architect and others in the professional team.
3   The contract: the form and specific type of contract, the contract sum, and then details of the clauses in the contract that the claim is made under.
4   The works: a brief description of the project.
5   Summary of facts: factual details of major events during the project together with dates of notices issued to the architect, engineer or contract administrator regarding additional costs or loss and expense incurred. Copies of the documents referred to should be included in an appendix.
6   Basis of the claim, referring in detail to the provisions (clauses) in the contract under which the claim is made.
7   Prolongation, the period of prolongation to be stated together with other relevant details such as extension of time and delay analyses submissions.

29 Worked example

Project details for the worked example

The project chosen for the worked example is a new mixed-use development, comprising 22 apartments, shops and offices. The contract value was £22 million, the contract start date was 3 October 2005 and the contract period was 56 weeks. The contract between the parties was the *Joint Contracts Tribunal Standard Building Contract with Quantities*, 2005 edition.

Unfortunately, delays occurred on the project, and practical completion was achieved some 22 weeks late. The contractor submitted several extension of time submissions based on the 'windows' technique, which is a retrospective delay analysis methodology. After reviewing the contractor's extension of time submissions, the contract administrator awarded extensions of time of 18 weeks in total.

After receiving the extension of time award, the contractor submitted the following prolongation claim.

1 *Introduction*
2 *The Parties*
   Details of the employer, contractor, architect, structural engineer, services engineer and Quantity Surveyor are given.
3 *The Contract*
   The Contract between the parties was the *Joint Contracts Tribunal Standard Building Contract with Quantities*, 2005 edition. The Contract Sum is stated, together with the contract start date and Date for Completion of the Works.
   This submission provides the necessary detail to allow the sum of loss and expense that we, the contractor, have incurred under clauses 4.23 to 4.25, 'Loss and Expense', of the Contract.
4 *The Works*
   The nature and location of the intended works are detailed in the first Recital of the Contract, namely,
   'A new mixed-use development, comprising 22 apartments, shops and offices, located at "*xxx*".'

5   *Summary of Facts*
  i   *On 15 September 2005, the Contract Administrator gave written notice to the Contractor to take possession of the site and commence the works on 3 October 2005.*
  ii   *The Contractor took possession of the site and commenced the works on 3 October 2005.*
  iii   *The Contractor gave the following notices of delay in accordance with clause 2.27 of the Contract.*
    i   *Letter dated 12 December 2005, as a result of architect's instruction 007.*
    ii   *Letter dated 17 January 2006, as a result of architect's instruction 022.*
    iii   *Letter dated 22 February 2006, as a result of architect's instruction 043.*
    iv   *Letter dated 16 March 2006, as a result of architect's instruction 062.*
    v   *Letter dated 6 April 2006, as a result of architect's instruction 070.*
    vi   *Letter dated 6 May 2006, as a result of architect's instruction 083.*
    vii   *Letter dated 22 July 2006, as a result of architect's instruction 108.*
    viii   *Letter dated 19 August 2006, as a result of architect's instruction 122.*
    ix   *Letter dated 24 September 2006, as a result of architect's instruction 145.*
    x   *Letter dated 7 October 2006, as a result of architect's instruction 161.*
    xi   *Letter dated 19 October 2006, as a result of architect's instruction 176.*
    xii   *Letter dated 7 November 2006, as a result of architect's instruction 183.*
    xiii   *Letter dated 17 December 2006, as a result of architect's instruction 201.*
    xiv   *Letter dated 7 January 2007, as a result of architect's instruction 211.*
    xv   *Letter dated 22 February 2007, as a result of architect's instruction 222.*
  iv   *The Contractor provided further particulars, as requested by the Contract Administrator.*
  v   *Before the date of Practical Completion the Contract Administrator made 5 number Awards of extension of time totalling 16 weeks, thereby revising the Date for Completion of the Works to 20 February 2007.*
  vi   *Practical Completion of the project was achieved on 3 April 2007, some 22 weeks later than the original Date for Completion of the*

Works and 6 weeks later than the latest revised Date for Completion of the Works.

vii On 4 May 2007, the Contractor submitted a further submission, supported by a detailed Delay Analysis, requesting an extension of time until 3 April 2007.

viii After consideration of the Contractor's latest extension of time, and after reviewing his previous decisions, the Contract Administrator awarded a further extension of time of 2 weeks (making a total of 18 weeks), thereby revising the Date for Completion of the Works to 6 March 2007.

ix Copies of the documents referred to above are included in appendix 'xx'.

5 Basis of this Loss and Expense Claim
The Contract contains the following provisions.
(Note: clauses 4.23 to 4.25 of the Contract are repeated in full)

6 Evaluation of Loss and Expense
For the reasons given in 5 above, the contractor is entitled to direct loss and/or expense as follows:

Prolongation Costs
Site Overheads & Establishment
The period of prolongation is 18 weeks. The contractor is entitled to reimbursement of direct loss and/or expense for 18 weeks which occurred in the following time periods.

a 2005; 4th quarter   3 weeks
b 2006; 1st quarter   4 weeks
c 2006; 3rd quarter   4 weeks
d 2006; 4th quarter   5 weeks
e 2007; 1st quarter   2 weeks

a Direct loss and expense incurred for the 3-week delay in 4th quarter of 2005.

2005, 4TH QUARTER; 3-WEEK DELAY

		Rate per week	% allocated	Number of weeks	Actual cost
1	**Staff**				
1a	Project Manager	£1,100.00	100%	3 weeks	£3,300.00
1b	General Foreman	£950.00	100%	3 weeks	£2,850.00
1c	Site Engineer	£800.00	100%	3 weeks	£2,400.00
1d	Quantity Surveyor	£900.00	100%	3 weeks	£2,700.00
1e	Area Manager (part-time)	£1,500.00	33%	3 weeks	£1,500.00
1f	Buyer (part-time)	£850.00	20%	3 weeks	£2,550.00
2	**Site Establishment**				
2a	Hire of Offices	£800.00	100%	3 weeks	£2,400.00
2b	Office Equipment	£250.00	100%	3 weeks	£750.00
2c	Plant & Equipment	£550.00	100%	3 weeks	£1,650.00
2d	Small Tools	£200.00	100%	3 weeks	£600.00
2e	Scaffolding	£500.00	100%	3 weeks	£1,500.00
2d	Electricity charges	£100.00	100%	3 weeks	£300.00
2e	Telephone charges	£70.00	100%	3 weeks	£210.00
2f	Security	£400.00	100%	3 weeks	£1,200.00
2g	Welfare	£450.00	100%	3 weeks	£1,350.00
				Total	£25,260.00

b　*Direct loss and expense incurred for the 4-week delay in 1st quarter of 2006.*

2006, 1ST QUARTER; 4-WEEK DELAY

		Rate per week	% allocated	Number of weeks		Actual cost
1	**Staff**					
1a	Project Manager	£1,100.00	100%	4	weeks	£4,400.00
1b	General Foreman	£950.00	100%	4	weeks	£3,800.00
1c	Site Engineer	£800.00	50%	4	weeks	£3,200.00
1d	Quantity Surveyor	£900.00	100%	4	weeks	£3,600.00
1e	Area Manager (part-time)	£1,500.00	33%	4	weeks	£1,500.00
1f	Buyer (part-time)	£850.00	20%	4	weeks	£3,400.00
2	**Site Establishment**					
2a	Hire of Offices	£800.00	100%	4	weeks	£3,200.00
2b	Office Equipment	£300.00	100%	4	weeks	£1,200.00
2c	Plant & Equipment	£600.00	100%	4	weeks	£2,400.00
2d	Small Tools	£230.00	100%	4	weeks	£920.00
2e	Scaffolding	£600.00	100%	4	weeks	£2,400.00
2d	Electricity charges	£150.00	100%	4	weeks	£600.00
2e	Telephone charges	£100.00	100%	4	weeks	£400.00
2f	Security	£450.00	100%	4	weeks	£1,800.00
2g	Welfare	£500.00	100%	4	weeks	£2,000.00
					Total	£34,820.00

c　*Direct loss and expense incurred for the 4-week delay in 3rd quarter of 2006.*

2006, 3RD QUARTER; 4-WEEK DELAY

		Rate per week	% allocated	Number of weeks	Actual cost
1	**Staff**				
1a	Project Manager	£1,200.00	100%	4 weeks	£4,800.00
1b	General Foreman	£1,000.00	100%	4 weeks	£4,000.00
1c	Site Engineer	£850.00	25%	4 weeks	£3,400.00
1d	Quantity Surveyor	£950.00	50%	4 weeks	£3,800.00
1e	Area Manager (part-time)	£1,600.00	33%	4 weeks	£1,500.00
1f	Buyer (part-time)	£900.00	20%	4 weeks	£3,600.00
1g	Finishing Foreman	£800.00	100%	4 weeks	£3,200.00
2	**Site Establishment**				
2a	Hire of Offices	£800.00	100%	4 weeks	£3,200.00
2b	Office Equipment	£300.00	100%	4 weeks	£1,200.00
2c	Plant & Equipment	£600.00	100%	4 weeks	£2,400.00
2d	Small Tools	£230.00	100%	4 weeks	£920.00
2e	Scaffolding	£600.00	100%	4 weeks	£2,400.00
2d	Electricity charges	£150.00	100%	4 weeks	£600.00
2e	Telephone charges	£100.00	100%	4 weeks	£400.00
2f	Security	£450.00	100%	4 weeks	£1,800.00
2g	Welfare	£500.00	100%	4 weeks	£2,000.00

d   *Direct loss and expense incurred for the 5-week delay in 4th quarter of 2006.*

2006, 4TH QUARTER; 5-WEEK DELAY

		Rate per week	% allocated	Number of weeks	Actual cost
1	**Staff**				
1a	Project Manager	£1,200.00	100%	5 weeks	£6,000.00
1b	General Foreman	£1,000.00	100%	5 weeks	£5,000.00
1c	Site Engineer	£850.00	10%	5 weeks	£4,250.00
1d	Quantity Surveyor	£950.00	50%	5 weeks	£4,750.00
1e	Area Manager (part-time)	£1,600.00	33%	5 weeks	£1,500.00
1f	Buyer (part-time)	£900.00	10%	5 weeks	£4,500.00
1g	Finishing Foreman	£850.00	100%	5 weeks	£4,250.00
2	**Site Establishment**				
2a	Hire of Offices	£700.00	100%	5 weeks	£3,500.00
2b	Office Equipment	£250.00	100%	5 weeks	£1,250.00
2c	Plant & Equipment	£450.00	100%	5 weeks	£2,250.00
2d	Small Tools	£180.00	100%	5 weeks	£900.00
2e	Scaffolding	£350.00	100%	5 weeks	£1,750.00
2d	Electricity charges	£170.00	100%	5 weeks	£850.00
2e	Telephone charges	£90.00	100%	5 weeks	£450.00
2f	Security	£350.00	100%	5 weeks	£1,750.00
2g	Welfare	£400.00	100%	5 weeks	£2,000.00
				Total	£44,950.00

e   *Direct loss and expense incurred for the 2-week delay in 1st quarter of 2007.*

2007, 1ST QUARTER; 2-WEEK DELAY

		Rate per week	% allocated	Number of weeks	Actual cost
1	**Staff**				
1a	Project Manager	£1,200.00	100%	2 weeks	£2,400.00
1b	General Foreman	£1,000.00	50%	2 weeks	£2,000.00
1d	Quantity Surveyor	£950.00	100%	2 weeks	£1,900.00
1e	Area Manager (part-time)	£1,600.00	15%	2 weeks	£1,500.00
1f	Buyer (part-time)	£900.00	10%	2 weeks	£1,800.00
1g	Finishing Foreman	£850.00	100%	2 weeks	£1,700.00
2	**Site Establishment**				
2a	Hire of Offices	£600.00	100%	2 weeks	£1,200.00
2b	Office Equipment	£200.00	100%	2 weeks	£400.00
2c	Plant & Equipment	£350.00	100%	2 weeks	£700.00
2d	Small Tools	£150.00	100%	2 weeks	£300.00
2e	Scaffolding	£250.00	100%	2 weeks	£500.00
2d	Electricity charges	£150.00	100%	2 weeks	£300.00
2e	Telephone charges	£90.00	100%	2 weeks	£180.00
2f	Security	£300.00	100%	2 weeks	£600.00
2g	Welfare	£250.00	100%	2 weeks	£500.00
				Total	£15,980.00

Total Site Overheads and Establishment   £160,230.00

Head Office Overheads

As a consequence of the 18 weeks' delay to the project, the Contractor was required to retain key staff and resources on site for an additional period of 18 weeks and was deprived of making a contribution to the company's head office overheads and profit. Furthermore, head office support staff and services were involved with the project for a period of 18 weeks. The Contractor is therefore entitled to recover this loss pursuant to the provisions mentioned in '5' above.

Using the Eichleay formula,

Stage 1

$$\frac{£21,000,000}{£56,000,000} \quad X \quad £2,800,000.00 \quad = \quad £1,050,000.00$$

Stage 2

$$\frac{£1,050,000.00}{74} \quad = \quad £13,461.54$$

Stage 3

£13,461.54   X   18 weeks   =   £242,307.72

Total Head Office Overheads   £242,307.72

Note: the Eichleay formula was presented in the submission, but for comparison purposes, the results using the Hudson and Emden formulae are given below.

$$\frac{6\%}{100} \quad X \quad \frac{£22,000,000.00}{56} \quad X \quad 18 \quad = \quad £388,928.57$$

Stage 1

$$\frac{£3,080,000.00}{£56,000,000.00} \quad 5.50\%$$

Stage 2

$$\frac{5.50\%}{100} \quad X \quad \frac{£22,000,000.00}{56} \quad X \quad 18 \quad = \quad £392,464.29$$

Total Loss and Expense claim for 18 weeks' Prolongation   £402,527.72

Appendices

Appendix 1
Definitions and glossary

This appendix provides definitions and explanations for words and expressions commonly used in extension of time and delay situations.

The appendix includes information in the 'Glossary of Terms' as produced by the Planning Engineers Organisation, which has kindly given its permission for this inclusion.

Acceleration Taking or planning active measures to complete work ahead of the project programme and/or to recover delays. Such action usually increases the overall cost of the project. See also **Mitigation**.

Accepted programme A programme submitted by a contractor, or subcontractor, for the whole of the works for acceptance by the CA (or similar). Once so accepted, it becomes known as the 'accepted programme'.

Activity An operation or process in a project that consumes time and also usually consumes or uses other resources, e.g. people, materials, equipment. An activity is a measurable element of the total project programme, but depending on the hierarchy or level of detail of the programme, may be divisible into smaller or more detailed activities.

Activity duration The time calculated or estimated to carry out an activity, generally taking into account a specific level of resource.

Activity ID A unique code, usually alpha-numeric that identifies each activity in a project.

Activity-on-arrow network A network technique that uses arrows to represent activities. Preceding and succeeding activities join at nodes or events.

Activity-on-node network A network technique that uses nodes (generally symbolised by 'boxes') to represent activities. Also known as a precedence diagram.

Activity-orientated scheduling The method of developing a programme that determines the sequence and timing of activities based on the logical work process only and does not take account of any potential limitations of resources.

Actual dates The dates relating to when an activity started and/or finished.

Actual duration The length of time an activity took to complete.

Actual finish The date when an activity finished.

Actual progress The amount of work that has been completed at a given point in time.

Actual start The date when an activity started.

As-built dates The actual start and finish dates for an activity.

As-built network A network such that the activity durations, sequence and start and finish dates reflect the actual durations, actual start and actual finish dates. Dependencies and other constraints in the as-built network should be carefully considered to represent the actual dependencies and constraints encountered in the project and as such they result in the actual durations, actual start and actual finish dates of the activities.

As-built programme A programme that represents the history of the project showing the actual start, actual finish and actual duration of the activities. The as-built programme does not necessarily have any logic links. It is usually in barchart format.

As-late-as-possible Timing or positioning of an activity in a programme at its latest start/latest finish dates such that there is no free float on the activity and the timing of other activities in the programme and overall duration of the programme is not affected.

Backward pass The procedure whereby the latest dates of activities in a network are calculated.

Barchart A graphical chart on which activities are represented as bars drawn to a common time scale. Typically, a date scale is drawn across the top of the page and a list of activities down the lefthand side of the page. Activity timing and durations are represented by horizontal bars. Additional information, such as resources, costs and dependencies are also often shown on the chart.

Baseline programme A fixed or record programme against which current or future activity is referenced. Often taken to mean the first or original plan, but can be reset (for instance following a change to the project scope) at which point the reset programme becomes the baseline programme.

Branch A discrete part of a programme generally represented by a single activity that is broken down by a project hierarchy and comprises further detail at sub-activity level.

Buffer activity An activity in a programme that acts as a contingency or to artificially absorb float.

Calculate schedule The mathematical analysis of a network, generally using a computer and project management software, to determine the earliest and latest starts and finishes and float of the activities and the overall project duration. Often carried out following the addition of actual progress to determine the effect of progress on the network, primarily the completion date of the project.

Calendar A list of the time intervals during which activities can be worked and/or resources used. Typical data includes working days/non-working days, start and finish times for shifts, weekends, holiday periods and extra workdays. Each activity and/or resource will have a calendar attached to it. A project can contain many calendars, each with different working and non-working periods.

Change or **variation** Any difference between the circumstances and/or content of the contract works as carried out, compared with the circumstances and/or content under which the works are described in the contract documents as required to be or intended to have been carried out. A change or variation may or may not carry with it a right to an extension of time and/or additional payment.

Collapsed as-built A method of delay analysis where the effects of events are 'subtracted' from the as-built programme to determine what would have occurred but for those events.

Compensable event Expression sometimes used to describe an employer risk event in respect of which the contractor is entitled to compensation.

Compensation The recovery or payment of money for work done or time taken up whether by way of valuation, loss and/or expense or damages.

Concurrency True concurrent delay is the occurrence of two or more delay events at the same time, one an employer risk event, the other a contractor risk event, the effects of which are also felt at the same time. The term 'concurrent delay' is often used to describe the situation where two or more delay events arise at different times, but the effects of them are felt (in whole or in part) at the same time. To avoid confusion, this is more correctly termed the 'concurrent effect' of sequential delay events.

Constraints Restrictions that affect the sequence or timing of an activity. These include predecessor dependencies but more often refer to imposed dates.

Constructive acceleration Acceleration following failure by the employer to recognise that the contractor has encountered employer delay for which it is entitled to an EOT and which failure required the contractor to accelerate its progress in order to complete the works by the prevailing contract completion date. This situation may be brought about by the employer's denial of a valid request for an EOT.

Contract administrator (CA) The person responsible for administration of the contract, including certifying what extensions of time are due, or what additional costs or loss and expense should be allowed. Depending on the form of contract, the person may be referred to by such terms as employer's agent, employer's representative, contract administrator, project manager or supervising officer or be specified as a particular professional, such as the architect or the engineer. The contract administrator may be one of the employer's employees.

Contract completion date The date by which the contractor is contractually obliged to complete the works. As well as being an overall date for completion, the contract completion date may be the date for completion of a section of the works or a milestone date. The expression 'completion date' is sometimes used by contractors to describe the date when they plan to complete the works (which may be earlier than the contract completion date).

Contractor risk event An event or cause of delay which under the contract is at the risk and responsibility of the contractor.

Critical activity An activity with zero float. If a critical activity is delayed or extended, it will delay or extend the completion of the project and, generally, if a critical activity is advanced or reduced it will advance or reduce the completion of a project.

Critical delay A delay to progress of any activity on the critical path will, without acceleration or re-sequencing, cause the overall project duration to be extended, and is therefore referred to as a 'critical delay'.

Critical path The sequence of activities through a project network from start to finish, the sum of whose durations determines the overall project duration. There may be more than one critical path depending on workflow logic.

Critical path analysis (CPA) and **Critical path method (CPM)** The critical path analysis or method is the process of deducing the critical activities in a programme by tracing the logical sequence of tasks that directly affect the date of project completion. It is a methodology or management technique that determines a project's critical path. The resulting programme may be depicted in a number of different forms, including a Gantt or barchart, line-of-balance diagram, pure logic diagram, time-scaled logic diagram or as a time-chainage diagram, depending on the nature of the works represented in the programme.

Culpable delay An expression sometimes used to describe a contractor delay.

Delay analysis The methodological investigation of the causes and effects of activities, or sequences of activities, completing later than planned.

Delay event An event or cause of delay, which may be either an employer risk event or a contractor risk event.

Delay to completion This expression may mean either delay to the date when the contractor planned to complete its works, or a delay to the contract completion date.

Delay to progress A delay which will merely cause delay to the contractor's progress without affecting the contract completion date. It is either an Employer Delay to Progress or a Contractor Delay to Progress.

Dependency Logical interrelationships between activities. In a network there can be one or more dependency between any two activities. There are four types of dependency: 'finish to finish', 'finish to start', 'start to finish' and 'start to start'. The dependencies dictate the sequence in which activities can be carried out.

Disruption Disturbance, hindrance or interruption of a contractor's normal work progress, resulting in lower efficiency or lower productivity than would otherwise be achieved. Disruption does not necessarily result in a delay to progress or delay to completion.

Driving Where there are a number of dependencies to an activity the driving dependency is the dependency, or dependencies, that result in the timing of the start and/or finish of that activity. The implication is that there is free float on non-driving dependencies.

Drop line A method of indicating progress of activities on a barchart. A vertical line starting at Time Now links the ends of the bars at the point representing the progress achieved for that activity. Where the drop line deviates to the left the activity is behind programme, where the drop line is vertical the activity is on programme and where the drop line deviates to the right the activity is ahead of programme.

Duration The length of time needed to complete an activity. The time period can be determined inductively, by determining the start and finish date of an activity or deductively by calculation from the time necessary to expend the resources applied to the activity.

Early finish This is the earliest programmed calendar date on which an activity can be finished before any of its succeeding float is consumed.

Early start This is the earliest programmed calendar date on which an activity can be started before any of its preceding float has been consumed.

Employer delay An expression commonly used to describe any delay caused by an employer risk event.

Employer delay to completion A delay which will cause a contract completion date not to be met.

Employer delay to progress A delay which will merely cause delay to the contractor's progress without causing a contract completion date not to be met.

Employer risk event An event or cause of delay which under the contract is at the risk and responsibility of the employer.

Excusable delay Sometimes used to describe an employer delay in respect of which the contractor is entitled to an extension of time.

Extension of time (EOT) Additional time granted to the contractor to provide an extended contractual time period or date by which work is to be, or should be completed and to relieve it from liability for damages for delay (usually liquidated damages).

Float or Slack The amount of time between the early start date and the late start date, or the early finish date and the late finish date of any of the activities in a programme.

Free float The amount of time an activity can be delayed beyond its early start/early finish dates without delaying the early start or early finish of any immediately following activity.

Gantt Chart Barchart named after its originator, Henry Gantt.

Global claim A global claim is one in which the contractor seeks compensation for a group of employer risk events but does not or cannot demonstrate a direct link between the loss incurred and the individual employer risk events.

Hammock An activity representing the period from the start of an activity to the completion of another. Sometimes used as a way of summarising the duration of a number of activities in a programme as one single duration.

Hanging activity An activity not linked to any preceding or successor activities. Sometimes called a 'dangling activity'.

Head office overheads Head office overheads are the incidental costs of running the contractor's business as a whole and include indirect costs, which cannot be directly allocated to production, as opposed to direct costs, which are the costs of production. Among other things, these overheads may include such things as rent, rates, directors' salaries, pension fund contributions and auditors' fees.

Impact The effect that a change has on an activity or the effect that a change to one activity has on another activity.

Key date Expression sometimes used to describe a date by which an identifiable accomplishment must be started or finished. Examples include 'power on', 'weathertight' or the start or completion of phases of construction or of phases or sections of the contract, or completion of the works.

Lag Lag in a network diagram is the minimum necessary lapse of time between the finish of one activity and the finish of another overlapping activity.

Lead The opposite of lag, but in practice having the same meaning. A preceding activity may have a lag to a successor activity – from the perspective of the successor activity, that is a lead.

Liquidated and ascertained damages (LADs) or **Liquidated damages (LDs)** A fixed sum, usually per week or per day, written into the contract as being payable by the contractor in the event that the works are not completed by the contract completion date, original or extended.

Logic links The normal links are as follows:

- finish-to-start (FS);
- lagged finish-to-start (FS+/–);
- start-to-start (SS);
- lagged start-to-start (SS+/–);
- finish-to-finish (FF);
- lagged finish-to-finish (FF+/–);
- lagged start and finish (SF+/–).

See Appendix 2 for further details and examples of logic links.

Method statement A written description of the contractor's proposed manner of carrying out the works or parts thereof, setting out the assumptions underlying the programme, the reasoning behind the approach to the various phases of construction and listing all the work encapsulated in the programme activities. It may also contain the activity duration calculations and details of key resources and gang strengths.

Milestone A key event selected for its importance in the project. Commonly used in relation to progress, a milestone often serves to signify a key date.

Mitigation To mitigate means to make less severe or less serious. In connection with delay to progress or delay to completion, it means minimising the impact of the risk event. In relation to disruption or inefficient working, it means minimising the disruption or inefficiency. Failure to mitigate is commonly pleaded as a defence or partial defence to a claim.

Must start/Must finish Most project management software allows the user to specify that an activity must start or must finish on a specific date. Using the software in this way restricts the ability of the programme to react dynamically to change on the project.

Negative lag See **Logic links** above.

Negative total float Expression sometimes used to describe the time by which the duration of an activity or path has to be reduced in order to permit a limiting imposed date to be achieved. Negative float only occurs when an activity on the critical path is behind programme. It is a programming concept, the manifestation of which is, of course, delay.

Non-compensable event Expression sometimes used to describe what the protocol calls a contractor risk event.

Non-excusable delay Sometimes used to describe what the protocol calls contractor delay.

Path An activity or an unbroken sequence of activities in a project network.

PERT 'Programme Evaluation and Review Technique': a programming technique, similar to critical path analysis, but whereby the probability of completing by the contract completion date is determined and monitored by way of a quantified risk assessment based on optimistic, pessimistic and most likely activity durations.

Planned completion date See **Contract completion date**.

Practical completion The completion of all the construction work, subject only to very minor items left incomplete. It is generally the date when the obligation to insure passes from the contractor to the employer and the date from which the defects liability period runs. This is the term used under the Joint Contracts Tribunal family of contracts. Under the Institution of Civil Engineers forms and in the International Federation of Consulting Engineers forms it is referred to as substantial completion.

Precedence diagram A multiple dependency, activity-on-node network in which a sequence arrow represents one of four forms of precedence relationship, depending on the positioning of the head and the tail of the sequence arrow. See also **Logic links**.

Programme The programme illustrates the major sequencing and phasing requirements of the project. Otherwise known as the schedule.

Prolongation The extended duration of the works during which costs are incurred as a result of a delay.

Resource Expression to describe any variable capable of definition that is required for the completion of an activity and may constrain the project. This may be a person, item of equipment, service or material that is used in accomplishing a project task.

Resource levelling Expression used to describe the process of amending a schedule to reduce the variation between maximum and minimum values of resource requirements. The process removes peaks, troughs and conflicts in resource demands by moving activities within their early and late dates and taking up float. Most project-planning software offers an automated resource-levelling routine that will defer the performance of a task within the imposed logical constraints until the resources assigned to the tasks are available.

Risk event See **Employer risk event** and **Contractor risk event**.

Schedule Another name for the programme.

Slack Another name for total float.

Sub-network A group of activities or durations, logically linked. In the protocol it is to be used to illustrate the work flowing directly from an employer risk event.

Substantial completion See **Practical completion**.

Time impact analysis Method of delay analysis where the impacts of particular delays are mapped out at the point in time at which they occur, allowing the discrete effect of individual events to be determined.

Total float The amount of time that an activity may be delayed beyond its early start/early finish dates without delaying the contract completion date.

Updated programme In the protocol the updated programme is the accepted programme updated with all progress achieved. The final updated programme should depict the as-built programme.

Works What the contractor is obliged to construct is referred to as the works.

Variation See **Change**.

Appendix 2
Levels of programmes

Contents

1 Client's or owner's programme/schedule

The purpose of the client's or owner's programme/schedule is to set out the client's/owner's desired overall time requirements for the project.

A number of different types of organisation might produce this programme or schedule, including the client/owner themselves, their project manager, an architect, engineer or quantity surveyor. This will vary from industry to industry and will be largely dependent upon the structure and contractual arrangements of the individual project.

The purpose of this programme/schedule is to inform the project participants as to what the client/owner wants to be achieved. This programme/schedule is sometimes used as the basis for obtaining tenders for the work that follows. It also sometimes serves to describe the client's vision or aspirations, in terms of time, appointments, phasing, handovers and the like.

Rarely is this programme/schedule based on a critical path analysis. Sometimes it is not presented as a programme or schedule at all, instead being described by a set of dates in a contract, enquiry document, or as a set of milestone target dates to be achieved. This often lays out the major date time frames for design, procurement, assembly, production, construction, etc.

This programme/schedule has not been included within the standard levels as defined in this volume; it invariably is not part of the main planning/scheduling undertaken on the project – it defines the key stages and dates of all of the work that follows.

2 Proposed levels of programme/schedule for a single project

Appendix 1 at the end of this document presents the proposed standardised levels of programme/schedule for a single project. Later in this document the levels for an entire range of projects, or programme of projects, are described.

The various programmes or schedules produced for a single project are generally produced using five levels, and each is discussed within this volume.

The basic premise of this volume is that programmes/schedules should be produced using a standard set of levels.

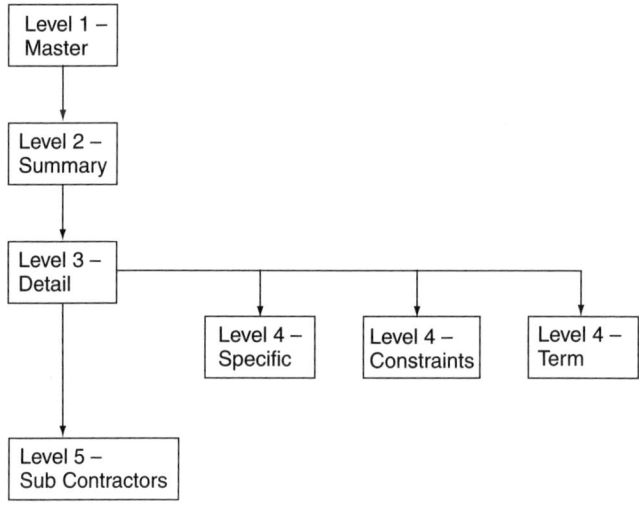

Level 1 The overall master programme/schedule for the project

The purpose of this level 1 programme/schedule is to show the overall co-ordinated timing of all aspects of the project. This will include topics such as feasibility, design, procurement, manufacture, assembly, production, construction, installation and commissioning.

Sometimes, this level 1 programme/schedule is used during the initiation or feasibility stage of a project and may form part of an overall business plan.

This is the high-level programme/schedule against which the overall timing of the project is set out and communicated against which the overall progress is reported to the client/owner. Often, it is presented not only as a barchart, but also with a set of milestone dates against which the project is monitored.

Ideally, this programme/schedule should be no more than a single sheet, containing perhaps 30 to 100 activities (depending upon the complexity of the project). The target milestone dates defined by the client/owner are often also included.

This programme/schedule will normally illustrate the critical path of the project.

The important point here is to consider who will receive and review this level 1 programme/schedule, which can often include people who do not readily understand such matters, meaning that the level of complexity should reflect this. There is little point in producing something that cannot be understood by those who need to access it.

Level 2 *The summary level programmes/schedules for the project*

The main purpose of these programmes/schedules at level 2 is to set out when each of the key elements will take place. For example, they should detail when each part of the design will be undertaken, or each part of the procurement/assembly, or each part of the installation, production or construction. These programmes/schedules are to illustrate a summary of the more detailed levels that follow.

They will often comprise a suite of linked individual programmes for each key element of the project, such as design, procurement and production or construction. Alternatively this could be one programme that includes the work of all key elements of the project, with the programmes of individual elements, such as design, procurement, production or construction, being created by using filters to select which activities are to be represented on individual programmes/schedules.

Ideally, these various programmes/schedules will all be produced or coordinated by a single party, although this will depend on the contractual arrangements for the project.

The entire scope of the project should be covered at this and subsequent levels. These summary programmes will show the critical path for the project. Another main purpose may be the control of the project by EVA, CPA, etc. They should involve sufficient detail to do three things.

First, they should enable all involved in that element to fully understand what needs to be done when and by whom.

Second, they should enable those involved in a particular element to fully understand how their own work interfaces with that work in another element (or within the same element). For the purposes of this volume, different elements might be design, procurement, installation, production or construction. A good example of this is the design of the project. The level 2 summary design programme will be used by, say, the procurement or construction team to understand how the timing of the design will affect the procurement or installation/construction activities that follow.

Third, they should facilitate the monitoring and reporting of progress on the project.

The number of activities on these level 2 programmes will obviously depend on the complexity of the project. As a suggestion, individual activities should take no longer than four to six weeks each, as longer periods make it difficult to assess progress.

In most cases, it will be essential for each of the level 2 programmes to be logically linked together, in order that the implications of progress achieved on one element can be seen on another element.

On smaller projects, these summary programmes/schedules may not be needed.

Level 3 The detailed level

The purpose of detailed level 3 programmes/schedules is to show the detailed timing of all of the activities on the project. They should definitely show the critical path, and will often include details of the resources needed to undertake that element or stage of the work.

Sometimes, depending on the contractual arrangements for the project, one party will be responsible for producing all of these level 3 programmes/schedules and for coordination between them. For example, on a project being undertaken on a design and build contractual arrangement, this will almost certainly be the case.

In other instances, say where the design is undertaken by one party and the installation/production/construction by a different separate party (for example, in UK traditional, fixed-price construction contracts) these various level 3 programmes/schedules might be produced by different organisations.

Examples of the different types of level 3 programme/schedule include the following:

- The detailed design programme, showing every drawing to be produced.
- The detailed authorities' approvals and statutory processes programme.
- The detailed procurement programme, outlining the timing of subcontract tenders to be obtained, placing of orders, manufacture times, lead times, delivery dates and the like.
- The detailed production, construction, installation or assembly programmes/schedules, including the timing of all physical works on site, for each part of the project.

Additionally, each of the programmes/schedules could be further broken down into off-site and on-site works.

Often, these detailed programmes are produced in advance of appointing the various specialists (designers and subcontractors) in order to set out the overall detailed timing of activities and interfaces on the project. This is often difficult to achieve as the input from those specialists is required to fully test the detail. Also, some degree of replacing the original detail will be required once the various specialists' own programmes/schedules are received.

Depending upon the contractual arrangements for the project, these programmes/schedules might or might not be shared with the client. Whether they are or not, the purpose of them is to clearly set out when each individual detailed part of the project is to be undertaken and by whom.

Level 4 The specific, term and constraints level

The main purpose of this level is to extract material from the level 3 key detailed information that is then used to create further programmes/schedules at level 4. These are a group of programmes/schedules often produced by filtering the detail of the level 3 programmes although sometimes these level 4 programmes are stand-alone programmes not linked electronically to other levels.

These cover a wide range of uses, these typically being:

- programmes/schedules produced to cover specific areas or aspects of the project;
- short-term and medium-term look-ahead programmes/schedules covering the detailed activities for the next few days, weeks or months, sometimes referred to as look-ahead programmes/schedules;
- programmes/schedules specifically produced to give guidance to individual subcontractors on when their work will need to be carried out, sometimes called constraints programmes.

Often these specific level programmes/schedules are derivatives of the detailed level 3 ones and are created by applying a number of different filters based on the coding structure and capabilities of the software used. For example, these filters/coding structures can be used to produce programmes/schedules of work for each manager, each subcontractor, or for different areas of work or location, or by floor level, etc.

Level 5 The subcontractors' programmes/schedules

These level 5 programmes/schedules allow the subcontractors to set out the detailed timing of their own work. They are often produced by subcontractors to further define their work if the detail contained at level 3 is insufficient for their purposes. No matter what system the subcontractors adopted, the overall time frame for their work must conform to the time frames set out in the level 3 programme/schedule.

The subcontractors uses these programmes/schedules to monitor and report progress of their own works. Most often, they are held in different software databases to the level 1, 2, 3 and 4 programmes/schedules.

The particular contractual arrangements and processes involved might determine that the level 5 programmes are not electronically linked to the levels above. They might be regarded as stand-alone in their own right. However, whether electronically linked to the levels above or not, it is essential that the critical path for each individual subcontractor's work is shown on their own programme. Later, if there is a claim from a subcontractor, it is crucial that the originally anticipated subcontractor's critical path was shown in order to assess the validity of that claim.

There are essentially two approaches to the subcontractors' programmes/schedules. The subcontractors could either produce these as stand-alone programmes/schedules, or the subcontractors could assist in the development of the level 3 programmes/schedules, with their own specific activities being included within the main level 3 programme/schedule.

3 Proposed levels for smaller projects

On some smaller projects, different arrangements may be used for the various levels of programming/scheduling.

Depending upon the size of the project, levels 3, 4 and 5 are sometimes combined together into one single level. This can incorporate the work of all parties into one detailed programme, with one party retaining responsibility for that detailed programme.

Additionally, on some smaller projects, the level 2 summary programmes/schedules may not be necessary.

4 Proposed levels of programme/schedule for a group or programme of projects

The proposed standardised levels of programme/schedule for a group or programme of projects are almost exactly the same as described for an individual project in section 4 above, in that the levels of programme/schedule for each project within a group of projects will be the same as that described in section 2.

The main difference with a group of projects is that an additional level of programme/schedule, called level 0, is introduced to show the summary of all projects within the group.

The level of detail in this level 0 programme/schedule depends on how many projects make up that group or programme. If it is a small number, say three or four, then each of the individual projects could be represented by, say ten activities each. If a large number of individual projects make up the group, then each project might be represented by only one activity.

5 Important associated considerations

When reviewing the various programmes/schedules defined in this volume, one also has to consider how they will be created. While this is not the purpose of this volume, it is worth mentioning here that there could be two approaches to this.

The first is whether all of the various levels are created as one integrated programme/schedule. One can see that the various levels could be produced working towards what will eventually be a single, totally integrated, fully logic-linked programme/schedule that is divided into the various levels. This can be achieved by the creation of the level 1 programme/schedule first, with level 2 being a detailed expansion of level 1, the level 2 programme/schedule is then in turn further detailed to create level 3, and so on.

This approach ensures that all activities are fully integrated with all other activities at every level. This is without a doubt the most suitable option as it aids simplicity – having all of the programme/schedule information in one place maintains control and limits the chance of confusion, or even worse, unco-ordinated programmes/schedules with the inevitable problems that will arise.

The second approach is potentially more difficult, in that the various levels are produced as separate individual programmes/schedules that are not integrated, but maintained as stand-alone. This approach is sometimes practically easier to achieve, in that the various parties responsible for certain aspects of the scheduling – say a design firm, a manufacturing firm, a construction contractor and subcontractors – will find it easier to produce their own programmes/schedules. However, this approach can lead to the content being held in different locations on different databases and can lead to confusion and out-of-date information being used.

It can be argued that one approach is more valid than the other but, as stated above, this is not the purpose of this volume.

Whichever approach is adopted, what is important is that, once the various levels of programme/schedule have been completed and approved by all, they become the as-planned programme/schedule against which all subsequent programmes/schedules are measured.

Occasionally, one hears of projects that run two sets of programmes/schedules – the master set and what is commonly known as a target programme or schedule. The latter is often used in an attempt to shorten the overall duration of the project but employing this method is fraught with difficulties due to the potential for confusion as to which programme/schedule different organisations, designers, contractors and subcontractors are working to. Extreme caution must be exercised if this approach is adopted.

Additionally, when creating the various levels of a programme/schedule, one often also has to consider the impact of the work breakdown structure

(WBS) of the project. From a programming/scheduling point of view, there is often no real requirement to take the WBS into consideration, but practical application shows that this can be helpful on complex projects in finding common ground between cost/budget and programming/scheduling.

The various programmes produced at prequalification and tender stage have been deliberately excluded here. This is due to the fact that most often, these are separate programmes/schedules that are not linked to the main project programmes/schedules.

What is not covered here is *how* the various levels of programme/schedule are produced. In some organisations, the level 1 programme is produced first, with all subsequent levels being created as a derivative of that. In other words, the various levels are created in sequence level 1, level 2, level 3, and so on. In researching for this volume, it has become apparent that in other organisations the detailed levels of programme/schedule may be created first and then generate the master level.

Appendix 3
Model specification for a 'windows' analysis

The starting point, as with any method of delay analysis, is the contract. This should be reviewed, together with contractual/legal advisers if appropriate, to find out if there are any specific or implied clauses which determine the methodology or type of analysis.

Introduction

A windows analysis focuses on the impact of delays in specific periods of time, identifying gains or losses (delays and recovery) to the actual critical and sub-critical paths as they occur within each period of time.

The project life is divided into a series of consecutive time 'windows'. Each 'window' is analysed to identify the activities that were impacted, i.e. delay or recovery, and the results are investigated to identify the events that caused the deviation in progress.

This form of analysis identifies concurrent delays, through the examination of progress within a defined and short period of the project's life. The length and impact of concurrent delays on the project is established by applying the same approach in consecutive windows.

It must be emphasised that the results of the analysis will not identify the causes of delays, but only quantify the effect, or time impact, of such causes. However, the linkage to a cause, or causes, should be able to be established by using the analysis results to research and locate the necessary contemporaneous factual information. This approach verifies the cause-and-effect relationship.

Further, as windows analysis is based on actual delay that has occurred, the results are more easily linked to quantum.

Methodology

General

1 The programme(s) used for analysis should be in the form of a network (CPM format). This format enables the impact of a delay on

the project completion date, or other contractual milestones, to be established. However, for some projects the 'baseline programme' is only in the form of a barchart with no logic relationships between activities. In these cases, a network should be created from the barchart by the analyst, using his construction experience and technical knowledge to introduce logic links between related work activities. The activity durations should remain the same. When 'time-analysed', the planned start and finish dates for activities should mirror those as shown on the 'baseline programme' barchart.

2　The use of specialist in-house software should be avoided.
3　It is recommended that a transparent approach in carrying out a windows analysis be adopted, and that an audit trail of the project's contemporaneous information reviewed and used for the analysis be maintained and made available to support the analysis results. It is advisable to provide reasoning for the selection of important information and for any amendments to progress data, etc.

Preparation

1　Define the baseline programme, or programmes, to serve as a basis for the analysis.

　　a　It is recommended that the 'baseline programme' established at the start of the project be used for analysis of the first window. However, the programme should be subject to a rigorous 'reliability exercise', and any necessary modifications made, before being used for analysis.

　　b　If the baseline programme underwent a complete revision, was issued to the contract administrator, and subsequent progress reports were related to the 'revised programme', then this revised programme should replace the original baseline programme for the windows analysis, as and when it became the working programme.

　　c　If further revised programmes were issued during the life of the project, and became the working programme, then these should also be incorporated into the analysis, replacing the previous programme, again, as and when they became the working programme.

2　Establish the length of each window, and the number of windows.

　　a　The windows can be weekly, fortnightly or monthly and will generally be defined by the frequency of reports of actual site progress. For example, if progress on a project was recorded monthly as of the last day of each month, then a 'window' would cover the period between 1 January and 31 January, and the next window would cover the period between 1 February and 28 February, and so on up to project completion.

　　b　Unless there are specific reasons, the first window should start on the project commencement date and the last window should end on the project completion date, i.e. certified date of handover or practical completion. This gives a series of consecutive windows covering the life of the project.

3   Collect the progress data and review apparent anomalies.
   a   *It is recommended that the project's contemporaneous progress reports should be used, where possible, as the basis for the 'progress data' in the analysis.*
   b   *Progress data consists of actual start and finish dates and, where an activity's actual duration spans more than a single window, the percentage progress achieved as at the end of a window.*
   c   *The collected progress data should be reviewed for apparent anomalies, e.g. an activity's reported actual progress achieved reduces in the subsequent window(s); an activity's actual start and finish dates are not consistent with the progress being reported.*

Performing the analysis

Step 1 For the first window, the programme defined as the baseline programme, having undergone the reliability exercise (see item 1a above), is used. This is now known as the 'start of window programme' as at the window start.

Step 2 Review and verify that the 'start of window programme' represents the planned intent as known at the time. This is done by reviewing the available contemporaneous project documentation, e.g. correspondence, meeting minutes, change orders/variations, etc.

Step 3 Input into the 'start of window programme' the 'progress data' for the end of the first window, and carry out a time analysis as at the end of the window (the data date being the first working day of the second window).

Step 4 Review the results of the time analysis; and carry out a further review, or 'reality check', of remaining work activities to ensure that the time-analysed programme represents the planned intent as known at the time. If necessary, amend activity logic and/or durations to comply with the planned intent, and carry out a second time analysis. This programme is now the 'end of window programme' as at the window end.

Step 5 The 'end of window programme' at the end of window 1, now becomes the 'start of window programme' for the start of window 2. Having carried out a 'reality check' on this programme, no further review or amendment should be necessary.

Step 6 For window 2, input into this 'start of window programme' the 'progress data' for the end of the second window, and carry out a 'time analysis' as at the end of the window. Then repeat steps 4 and 5.

Step 7 For subsequent windows, follow the procedure outlined in step 6.

On completion of the analysis of the final window, the full 'windows' analysis is complete.

Glossary and explanatory notes

Baseline programme The programme covering the totality of the works which has been submitted to the CA for acceptance.

End of window programme The programme as at the end of the window, showing the as-built situation up to the end of the window and the planned intent for the remaining works to project completion.

Reality check A review of the programme's future activities to ensure that they represent the planned intent as known at the time. This is done by reviewing the available contemporaneous project documentation, e.g. correspondence, meeting minutes, change orders/variations, etc.

Reliability exercise A rigorous review of the programme, activity durations and logic relationships.

Revised programme Once a revised programme is accepted by the contract administrator, it replaces the 'baseline' programme.

Start of window programme The programme as at the start of the window, showing the planned intent for works both in the window and the remaining works after the window up to project completion.

Appendix 4

Charts for worked example: time impact analysis

Activity ID	Activity Description	Orig Dur	Rem Dur	Early Start	Early Finish	Total Float
Appointment / Mobilisation						
9760	Appoint Main Contractor	0	0	06AUG02		0
9770	Overall Site Possession	0	0	06AUG02		0
9780	Mobilisation	9	9	06AUG02	16AUG02	0
9790	Site Establishment	5	5	06AUG02	12AUG02	117
9800	Remove Ext Claddings/Windows	21	21	06NOV02	04DEC02	57
9810	Alteration/Form New Openings	16	16	05DEC02	09JAN03	57
Piling						
9850	Sheet Piling-Install	9	9	16AUG02	29AUG02	0
9860	Piling incl Temporary Support	25	25	20AUG02	24SEP02	0
9890	Remove Raking Props to Sheet Piling	8	8	18FEB03	27FEB03	25
Substructure						
9910	Excavate Basement	30	30	25SEP02	05NOV02	0
9920	Install Temporary Propping	10	10	16OCT02	29OCT02	0
9930	Excavate Pile Caps	15	15	23OCT02	12NOV02	0
9940	Under Slab Drainage	15	15	23OCT02	12NOV02	0
9950	Blinding	17	17	30OCT02	21NOV02	0
Basement						
9970	Construct Pile Caps/Ground Beams	15	15	06NOV02	26NOV02	5
9980	Cellcore	22	22	06NOV02	05DEC02	0
9990	DPM	22	22	13NOV02	12DEC02	0
10000	RC Conc Slab	22	22	20NOV02	19DEC02	0
10010	Drainage Layer	11	11	18MAR03	01APR03	25
10020	Structural Screed	10	10	26MAR03	08APR03	25
RC Retaining Walls						
10040	Formwork	33	33	27NOV02	24JAN03	0
10050	Reinf	24	24	04DEC02	20JAN03	0
10060	Concrete	27	27	11DEC02	30JAN03	0
10090	Tanking	34	34	20DEC02	19FEB03	69
10100	Blockwork Inner Skin	25	25	03APR03	14MAY03	25
Frame/Upper Flrs: Level 0 - Level 1						
10130	RC Cols Level 0(Basmt) - Level 1	24	24	18DEC02	03FEB03	0

New Science Block

AS PLANNED
Programme MP01
Sorted by Work Area

APPENDIX 4A a

Start Date   06AUG02
Finish Date 07APR04
Data Date   06AUG02
Run Date   04SEP07 16:25

Activity ID	Activity Description	Orig Dur	Rem Dur	Early Start	Early Finish	Total Float	Schedule (2002–2004)
10140	RC Walls Level 0 - Level 1	24	24	18DEC02	03FEB03	0	RC Walls Level 0 - Level 1
10150	RC Slab at Level 1	17	17	17JAN03	10FEB03	0	RC Slab at Level 1
10170	Make Good Basmt Slab/Ret Walls/waterproof	20	20	28FEB03	27MAR03	25	Make Good Basmt Slab/Ret Walls/waterproof
10180	Backfill around Retaining Walls	15	15	18MAR03	07APR03	33	Backfill around Retaining Walls
Frame/Upper Firs: Level 1 - Level 2							
10200	RC Cols Level 1 - Level 2	17	17	28JAN03	19FEB03	0	RC Cols Level 1 - Level 2
10210	RC Walls Level 1 - Level 2	25	25	28JAN03	03MAR03	0	RC Walls Level 1 - Level 2
10220	RC Slab at Level 2	17	17	14FEB03	10MAR03	0	RC Slab at Level 2
Frame/Upper Firs: Level 2 - Level 3							
10250	2RC Cols Level 2 - Level 3	17	17	26FEB03	20MAR03	0	2RC Cols Level 2 - Level 3
10260	RC Walls Level 2 - Level 3	25	25	26FEB03	01APR03	0	RC Walls Level 2 - Level 3
10270	RC Slab at Level 3	17	17	14MAR03	07APR03	0	RC Slab at Level 3
Frame/Upper Firs: Level 3 - Level 4							
10300	RC Cols Level 3 - Level 4	17	17	26MAR03	17APR03	0	RC Cols Level 3 - Level 4
10310	RC Walls Level 3 - Level 4	25	25	26MAR03	06MAY03	0	RC Walls Level 3 - Level 4
10320	RC Slab at Level 4	16	16	14APR03	12MAY03	0	RC Slab at Level 4
Roof Slab							
10340	RC Roof Slabs/Conc Beams	13	13	13MAY03	29MAY03	0	RC Roof Slabs/Conc Beams
10350	RC Upstands	16	16	30MAY03	20JUN03	21	RC Upstands
Stairs							
10370	RC Staircase(No 2)/PC Staircases(Nos 1&3)	67	67	09APR03	17JUL03	29	RC Staircase(No 2)/PC Staircases(Nos 1&3)
Roof							
10390	Steel Structure Above Level 4	8	8	30MAY03	10JUN03	0	Steel Structure Above Level 4
10400	Steel Flue Support Frames	12	12	11JUN03	26JUN03	0	Steel Flue Support Frames
10410	Surface Treatment to Steel	9	9	27JUN03	09JUL03	0	Surface Treatment to Steel
10420	Galv Decking to Plantroom	12	12	10JUL03	25JUL03	6	Galv Decking to Plantroom
10430	Wall Cladding/Rainscreens-PRoom & Flues	35	35	28JUL03	12SEP03	6	Wall Cladding/Rainscreens-PRoom & Flues
10440	Fire Protection to Steel Structure	15	15	24JUL03	13AUG03	24	Fire Protection to Steel Structure
10450	Metal Balconies/Balcony Ladders	13	13	23JUN03	09JUL03	35	Metal Balconies/Balcony Ladders
10460	Cast Stainless Steel Roof Prong/Truss	20	20	11JUN03	08JUL03	1	Cast Stainless Steel Roof Prong/Truss
10470	Timber Roof Structures/Liners	20	20	10JUL03	06AUG03	0	Timber Roof Structures/Liners
10480	Slate Roofing	16	16	24JUL03	14AUG03	27	Slate Roofing

Start Date 06AUG02
Finish Date 07APR04
Data Date 06AUG02
Run Date 04SEP07 16:25

New Science Block

AS PLANNED
Programme MP01
Sorted by Work Area

APPENDIX 4A a

Activity ID	Activity Description	Orig Dur	Rem Dur	Early Start	Early Finish	Total Float
10490	Stainless Steel Gutters & Verges	25	25	18JUL03	21AUG03	23
10500	Stainless Steel Roofing	29	29	01AUG03	10SEP03	23
10510	Felt Roofing to Extg Roof	25	25	27JUN03	31JUL03	4
10520	Felt Roofing	21	21	24JUL03	21AUG03	14
10530	Ally Rooflights	9	9	04SEP03	16SEP03	41
10540	Cable Arrest System	17	17	04SEP03	26SEP03	118
	Disposal Instns					
10560	Rainwater Pipework	49	49	06APR03	20JUN03	8
10570	Foul Drainage	49	49	06APR03	20JUN03	71
10580	Laboratory Drainage	75	75	19MAY03	29AUG03	71
	External Walls/Glazing					
10600	Steel Windposts/Framing	24	24	06MAY03	06JUN03	0
	Brick/Blockwork					
10620	Facing Brickwork	35	35	01APR03	26MAY03	0
10630	Blockwalls	35	35	01APR03	26MAY03	5
10640	Composite Block/Brickwalls	35	35	01APR03	26MAY03	0
	Stonework					
10660	Stone Bands	48	48	29APR03	03JUL03	0
10670	Stone Cills/Beams etc	43	43	29APR03	26JUN03	0
10680	Stone Lintols	33	33	06MAY03	19JUN03	0
10690	New Stone Cladding	38	38	06MAY03	26JUN03	0
10700	Refix Set Aside Stone Cladding	25	25	19MAY03	20JUN03	13
	Glazing/Louvres/Ext Doors					
10720	Curtain Walling	27	27	13JUN03	21JUL03	0
10730	Velfac Windows	29	29	13JUN03	23JUL03	0
10740	Louvres & Frames	20	20	13JUN03	10JUL03	10
10750	Entrance Canopy	16	16	04JUL03	25JUL03	135
10760	Ext Doors	17	17	22JUL03	13AUG03	134
10770	Roller Shutter Doors	13	13	22JUL03	07AUG03	134
10780	Building Substantial Watertight	0	0		24JUL03	0
10790	Power/Water/Gas Supplies Required	0	0		24JUL03	81

New Science Block

AS PLANNED
Programme MP01
Sorted by Work Area

APPENDIX 4A a

Sheet 3 of 8

Start Date   06AUG02
Finish Date 07APR04
Data Date   06AUG02
Run Date   04SEP07 16:25

Activity ID	Activity Description	Orig Dur	Rem Dur	Early Start	Early Finish	Total Float	Gantt
Internal Walls							
10810	Blockwork	63	63	15APR03	17JUL03	15	Blockwork
10820	Stud Partitions	60	60	26JUN03	17SEP03	0	Stud Partitions
10830	Joinery 1st Fix & Door Frames	51	51	17JUL03	25SEP03	31	Joinery 1st Fix & Door Frames
10840	WC Cubicles	16	16	12DEC03*	02JAN04	38	WC Cubicles
Metalwork							
10860	Balustrades & Handrails	50	50	18JUL03	25SEP03	75	Balustrades & Handrails
10870	Access Ladders to Plant/LM Rooms	42	42	22AUG03	20OCT03	68	Access Ladders to Plant/LM Rooms
10880	Plantroom Handrails	34	34	22AUG03	06OCT03	68	Plantroom Handrails
Mech/Elec Services Instns							
Level '0'. Plant Room							
2	AHU 6/7 Installation deliver & move	5	5	09APR03*	14APR03	102	AHU 6/7 Installation deliver & move
3	AHU 6 Build	2	2	02MAY03	05MAY03	102	AHU 6 Build
4	AHU 7Build & Lift	3	3	15APR03	17APR03	102	AHU 7Build & Lift
5	Build AHU Support gantry	5	5	18APR03	01MAY03	102	Build AHU Support gantry
6	Ductwork Installation	15	15	20MAY03	09JUN03	127	Ductwork Installation
7	Booster/Tanks etc - Deliv/Position	5	5	13MAY03	19MAY03	102	Booster/Tanks etc - Deliv/Position
8	Build Steam Support Gantry	5	5	06MAY03	12MAY03	102	Build Steam Support Gantry
9	Steam Plant - Deliver & position	5	5	13MAY03	19MAY03	102	Steam Plant - Deliver & position
10	Plantroom Pipework Installation	40	40	20MAY03*	14JUL03	102	Plantroom Pipework Installation
11	Deliver / Position Control Panel	2	2	20MAY03*	21MAY03	156	Deliver / Position Control Panel
12	Controls wiring	15	15	25JUL03	14AUG03	94	Controls wiring
13	Commission Steam system	15	15	15AUG03	04SEP03	94	Commission Steam system
14	Specialist Commission Autoclave	15	15	05SEP03	25SEP03	94	Specialist Commission Autoclave
15	RMU Installation	5	5	20MAY03*	26MAY03	179	RMU Installation
16	LV Panel/Transformer Delivery	3	3	27MAY03	29MAY03	179	LV Panel/Transformer Delivery
17	Power On to Building	0	0		25SEP03*	94	Power On to Building
Level '0'. High Level							
20	Ductwork Large Mains	20	20	06MAY03*	02JUN03	107	Ductwork Large Mains
22	Pipework & Ductwork 1st Fix	30	30	04JUL03	14AUG03	84	Pipework & Ductwork 1st Fix
23	Test	10	10	13AUG03	26AUG03	91	Test
24	Insulation	25	25	27AUG03	30SEP03	91	Insulation
25	Electrical Containment	20	20	25JUL03	21AUG03	84	Electrical Containment
26	1st Fix Lighting & Power	10	10	22AUG03	04SEP03	84	1st Fix Lighting & Power
28	2nd Fix Lighting & Power	15	15	05SEP03	25SEP03	84	2nd Fix Lighting & Power
29	2nd Fix Fire Alarm	15	15	05SEP03	25SEP03	84	2nd Fix Fire Alarm

Start Date	06AUG02
Finish Date	07APR04
Data Date	06AUG02
Run Date	04SEP07 16:25

New Science Block

AS PLANNED
Programme MP01
Sorted by Work Area

APPENDIX 4A a

Activity ID	Activity Description	Orig Dur	Rem Dur	Early Start	Early Finish	Total Float	Timeline (2002 – 2004)
30	2nd Fix Security	5	5	05SEP03	11SEP03	84	2nd Fix Security
31	2nd Fix Data	10	10	12SEP03	25SEP03	84	2nd Fix Data
32	3rd Fix Electrical	10	10	26SEP03	09OCT03	84	3rd Fix Electrical
Level 'O', Low Level							
34	Ductwork 2nd fix	15	15	04JUL03	24JUL03	79	Ductwork 2nd fix
35	Carcass for San ware	10	10	24JUL03*	06AUG03	60	Carcass for San ware
36	Pipework 2nd fix	20	20	07AUG03	03SEP03	60	Pipework 2nd fix
37	San ware installation	10	10	04SEP03	17SEP03	100	San ware installation
38	Insulation	15	15	27AUG03	16SEP03	101	Insulation
39	Electrical Containment	20	20	03JUN03	30JUN03	112	Electrical Containment
40	1st Fix Lighting & Power	10	10	01JUL03	14JUL03	112	1st Fix Lighting & Power
41	2nd Fix Lighting & Power	15	15	15JUL03	04AUG03	112	2nd Fix Lighting & Power
42	2nd Fix Fire Alarm	15	15	15JUL03	04AUG03	112	2nd Fix Fire Alarm
43	2nd Fix Security	5	5	15JUL03	21JUL03	112	2nd Fix Security
44	2nd Fix Data	10	10	22JUL03	04AUG03	112	2nd Fix Data
45	3rd Fix Electrical	20	20	23SEP03	20OCT03	77	3rd Fix Electrical
46	Installation Complete	0	0		20OCT03	77	◆Installation Complete
Level '1'							
48	Pipework & Ductwork 1st Fix	35	35	03JUN03*	21JUL03	22	Pipework & Ductwork 1st Fix
50	Ductwork 2nd fix	20	20	25JUL03*	21AUG03	98	Ductwork 2nd fix
52	Pipework 2nd fix	30	30	04AUG03	12SEP03	53	Pipework 2nd fix
53	San ware	20	20	27OCT03	21NOV03	53	San ware
54	Test	10	10	15SEP03	26SEP03	53	Test
55	Insulate	20	20	29SEP03	24OCT03	53	Insulate
56	Electrical Containment	20	20	17JUN03	14JUL03	92	Electrical Containment
57	1st Fix Lighting & Power	15	15	15JUL03	04AUG03	92	1st Fix Lighting & Power
58	2nd Fix Lighting & Power	15	15	18AUG03	05SEP03	83	2nd Fix Lighting & Power
59	2nd Fix Fire Alarm	15	15	18AUG03	05SEP03	83	2nd Fix Fire Alarm
60	2nd Fix Security	5	5	18AUG03	22AUG03	83	2nd Fix Security
61	2nd Fix Data	10	10	25AUG03	05SEP03	83	2nd Fix Data
62	3rd Fix Electrical	25	25	23SEP03	27OCT03	72	3rd Fix Electrical
63	Floor installation complete	0	0		21NOV03	53	◆Floor installation complete
Level '2'							
65	Pipework & Ductwork 1st Fix	35	35	04JUL03*	21AUG03	19	Pipework & Ductwork 1st Fix
67	Ductwork 2nd fix	21	21	22AUG03	19SEP03	98	Ductwork 2nd fix
69	Pipework 2nd fix	30	30	01SEP03	10OCT03	32	Pipework 2nd fix
70	San ware	21	21	24NOV03	22DEC03	32	San ware
71	Test	10	10	13OCT03	24OCT03	32	Test

Start Date 06AUG02
Finish Date 07APR04
Data Date 06AUG02
Run Date 04SEP01 16:25

New Science Block

AS PLANNED
Programme MP01
Sorted by Work Area

APPENDIX 4A a

Activity ID	Activity Description	Orig Dur	Rem Dur	Early Start	Early Finish	Total Float
72	Insulate	20	20	27OCT03	21NOV03	32
73	Electrical Containment	20	20	16JUL03	12AUG03	71
74	1st Fix Lighting & Power	15	15	13AUG03	02SEP03	71
75	2nd Fix Lighting & Power	15	15	08SEP03	26SEP03	68
76	2nd Fix Fire Alarm	15	15	08SEP03	26SEP03	68
77	2nd Fix Security	5	5	08SEP03	12SEP03	68
78	2nd Fix Data	5	5	08SEP03	12SEP03	68
79	3rd Fix Electrical	10	10	15SEP03	26SEP03	68
80	Floor installation complete	25	25	29SEP03	31OCT03	68
		0	0		22DEC03	32
Level '3'						
82	Pipework & Ductwork 1st Fix	35	35	01AUG03*	18SEP03	19
84	Ductwork 2nd fix	20	20	19SEP03	16OCT03	79
86	Pipework 2nd fix	30	30	22SEP03	31OCT03	18
87	San ware	20	20	15DEC03	09JAN04	18
88	Test	10	10	03NOV03	14NOV03	18
89	Insulate	20	20	17NOV03	12DEC03	18
90	Electrical Containment	20	20	13AUG03	09SEP03	51
91	1st Fix Lighting & Power	15	15	10SEP03	30SEP03	51
92	2nd Fix Lighting & Power	15	15	20OCT03	07NOV03	38
93	2nd Fix Fire Alarm	15	15	20OCT03	07NOV03	38
94	2nd Fix Security	5	5	20OCT03	24OCT03	38
95	2nd Fix Data	10	10	27OCT03	07NOV03	38
96	3rd Fix Electrical	25	25	10NOV03	12DEC03	38
97	Floor installation complete	0	0		09JAN04	18
Level '4'						
99	Lift AHU's etc into roof plantroom	3	3	27JUN03	01JUL03	19
100	Pipework in Plantroom	87	87	04AUG03	02DEC03	6
101	Lift chillers onto roof	3	3	11JUL03*	15JUL03	19
102	Pipework/ductwork on roof	53	53	04AUG03	15OCT03	40
103	Test	15	15	08DEC03	23DEC03	6
104	Insulate	25	25	24DEC03	27JAN04	6
106	Plantroom small power/lighting	25	25	13OCT03	14NOV03	58
Non Haden Young Activities						
10910	Client Autoclave Delivery	0	0	05AUG02*	05AUG02*	224
10980	Cold Rooms	83	83	06JUN03	30SEP03	74
10990	Fume Cupboards	43	43	30JUN03	27AUG03	90
11030	Lift Instns	58	58	25JUL03	14OCT03	81

Start Date 05AUG02
Finish Date U/FRFA
Data Date 26MAR02
Run Date 04SEP02 16:25

New Science Block
AS PLANNED
Programme MP01
Sorted by Work Area

APPENDIX 4A a

Activity ID	Activity Description	Orig Dur	Rem Dur	Early Start	Early Finish	Total Float
Wall Finishes						
11050	Plaster to Walls/Columns	62	62	27JUN03	22SEP03	0
11070	PVC Wall Linings	30	30	30JUL03	09SEP03	81
11080	Trenco Spray	85	85	12SEP03	08JAN04	24
11090	Ceramic Tiling	40	40	14OCT03	08DEC03	11
11100	Painting to Plaster	41	41	28NOV03	23JAN04	11
Services Equipment						
11120	Fly/Frog/Worm Rooms	100	100	06JUN03	23OCT03	74
11130	Extract Flue	45	45	24JUL03	24SEP03	95
Floor Screed/Grano						
11150	Grano Screed	9	9	21JUL03	31JUL03	47
11160	Screed	50	50	21JUL03	26SEP03	13
Ceiling Finishes						
11180	Walk-on Ceilings; level 0: Frame	20	20	06MAY03	02JUN03	22
11190	Walk-on Ceilings; Level 0: Timber joists	20	20	13MAY03	09JUN03	82
11200	Walk-on Ceilings; Level 0: Plasterboard	10	10	10JUN03	23JUN03	82
11210	Suspended Plasterbd & Skim	17	17	21JUL03	12AUG03	24
11220	Plasterbd Bulkhead	17	17	21JUL03	12AUG03	84
11230	Suspended Ceiling: Grid	59	59	21JUL03	09OCT03	17
11240	Suspended Ceiling: Tiles	17	17	15JAN04	06FEB04	13
11250	Plaster	12	12	13AUG03	28AUG03	84
11260	Painting to Plaster/Concrete	25	25	14OCT03	17NOV03	52
Internal Doors						
11280	Hardwood Screens	25	25	14OCT03	17NOV03	0
11290	Internal Doors/Architraves etc	35	35	30OCT03	17DEC03	0
11300	Reception Desk / Kitchen Shutter	9	9	18DEC03	30DEC03	0
Sanitary Appliances						
11320	Laminated Panelling & Framework	34	34	22SEP03	06NOV03	38
11330	San Ware	42	42	15OCT03	11DEC03	38
Fittings/Furniture						
11350	Laboratory Fittings	120	120	25AUG03	06FEB04	13
11360	Shelving Level 0	12	12	24JUN03*	09JUL03	152

Start Date 06AUG02
Finish Date 07APR04
Data Date 06AUG02
Run Date 04SEP07 16:25

New Science Block

AS PLANNED
Programme MP01
Sorted by Work Area

APPENDIX 4A a

Activity ID	Activity Description	Orig Dur	Rem Dur	Early Start	Early Finish	Total Float
11370	Reception Desk	16	16	24JUN03	15JUL03	152
11380	Tea/Seminar Room Fittings	16	16	24JUN03	15JUL03	152
11390	24 hour Kitchen Fittings	16	16	24JUN03	15JUL03	152
11400	Equipment	15	15	01JUL03	21JUL03	152
11410	Vanitory Units to WC's	20	20	24JUN03	21JUL03	152
11420	Boards/Lockers/Signage etc	20	20	24JUN03	21JUL03	152
11430	Shower Doors/Tracks	20	20	24JUN03	21JUL03	152
Floor Finishes						
11450	Resin Flooring	29	29	19AUG03	26SEP03	93
11460	Vinyl	30	30	25AUG03	03OCT03	45
11470	Carpet	18	18	06JAN04	29JAN04	0
11480	Terrazzo	22	22	06JAN04	04FEB04	0
11490	Timber Flooring	22	22	06JAN04	04FEB04	0
Final Testing/Commission/Clean						
11510	Precommissioning	15	15	05FEB04	25FEB04	0
11520	Final Testing & Commissioning	30	30	26FEB04	07APR04	0
11530	Biological Medical Clean	10	10	25MAR04	07APR04	0
11540	HANDOVER	0	0		07APR04	0
External Areas						
11560	External Works	87	87	01SEP03*	30DEC03	71

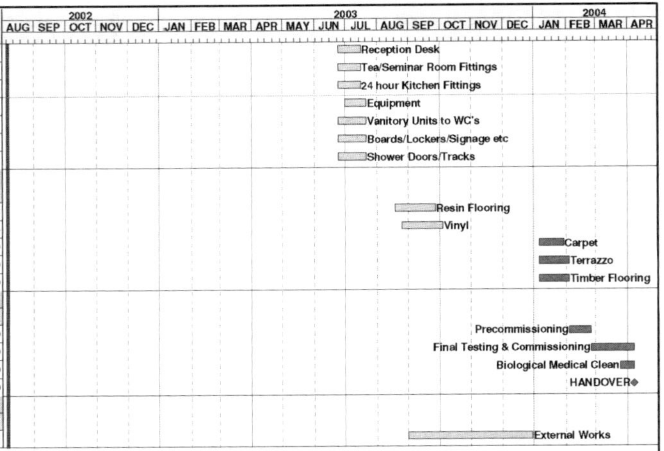

Gantt chart columns: 2002 (AUG SEP OCT NOV DEC) — 2003 (JAN FEB MAR APR MAY JUN JUL AUG SEP OCT NOV DEC) — 2004 (JAN FEB MAR APR)

Bar chart labels (right of grid):
- Reception Desk
- Tea/Seminar Room Fittings
- 24 hour Kitchen Fittings
- Equipment
- Vanitory Units to WC's
- Boards/Lockers/Signage etc
- Shower Doors/Tracks
- Resin Flooring
- Vinyl
- Carpet
- Terrazzo
- Timber Flooring
- Precommissioning
- Final Testing & Commissioning
- Biological Medical Clean
- HANDOVER◆
- External Works

Start Date	06AUG02
Finish Date	07APR04
Data Date	06AUG02
Run Date	04SEP07 16:25

New Science Block

AS PLANNED
Programme MP01
Sorted by Work Area

APPENDIX 4A a

Activity ID	Activity Description	Orig Dur	Rem Dur	Early Start	Early Finish	Total Float	2002 / 2003 / 2004
Appointment / Mobilisation							
9760	Appoint Main Contractor	0	0	06AUG02		0	Appoint Main Contractor
9770	Overall Site Possession	0	0	06AUG02		0	Overall Site Possession
9780	Mobilisation	9	9	06AUG02	16AUG02	0	Mobilisation
Piling							
9850	Sheet Piling-Install	9	9	16AUG02	29AUG02	0	Sheet Piling-Install
9860	Piling incl Temporary Support	25	25	20AUG02	24SEP02	0	Piling incl Temporary Support
Substructure							
9910	Excavate Basement	30	30	25SEP02	05NOV02	0	Excavate Basement
9920	Install Temporary Propping	10	10	16OCT02	29OCT02	0	Install Temporary Propping
9930	Excavate Pile Caps	15	15	23OCT02	12NOV02	0	Excavate Pile Caps
9940	Under Slab Drainage	15	15	23OCT02	12NOV02	0	Under Slab Drainage
9950	Blinding	17	17	30OCT02	21NOV02	0	Blinding
Basement							
9980	Cellcore	22	22	06NOV02	05DEC02	0	Cellcore
9990	DPM	22	22	13NOV02	12DEC02	0	DPM
10000	RC Conc Slab	22	22	20NOV02	19DEC02	0	RC Conc Slab
RC Retaining Walls							
10040	Formwork	33	33	27NOV02	24JAN03	0	Formwork
10050	Reinft	24	24	04DEC02	20JAN03	0	Reinft
10060	Concrete	27	27	11DEC02	30JAN03	0	Concrete
Frame/Upper Flrs: Level 0 - Level 1							
10130	RC Cols Level 0(Basmt) - Level 1	24	24	18DEC02	03FEB03	0	RC Cols Level 0(Basmt) - Level 1
10140	RC Walls Level 0 - Level 1	24	24	18DEC02	03FEB03	0	RC Walls Level 0 - Level 1
10150	RC Slab at Level 1	17	17	17JAN03	10FEB03	0	RC Slab at Level 1
Frame/Upper Flrs: Level 1 - Level 2							
10200	RC Cols Level 1 - Level 2	17	17	28JAN03	19FEB03	0	RC Cols Level 1 - Level 2
10210	RC Walls Level 1 - Level 2	25	25	28JAN03	03MAR03	0	RC Walls Level 1 - Level 2
10220	RC Slab at Level 2	17	17	14FEB03	10MAR03	0	RC Slab at Level 2
Frame/Upper Flrs: Level 2 - Level 3							
10250	2RC Cols Level 2 - Level 3	17	17	26FEB03	20MAR03	0	2RC Cols Level 2 - Level 3

Start Date	06AUG02	**New Science Block**
Finish Date	07APR04	
Data Date	06AUG02	**AS PLANNED**
Run Date	04SEP07 16:30	Programme MP01
		The Critical Path

Sheet 1 of 3

APPENDIX 4A b

Activity ID	Activity Description	Orig Dur	Rem Dur	Early Start	Early Finish	Total Float
10260	RC Walls Level 2 - Level 3	25	25	26FEB03	01APR03	0
10270	RC Slab at Level 3	17	17	14MAR03	07APR03	0
Frame/Upper Flrs: Level 3 - Level 4						
10300	RC Cols Level 3 - Level 4	17	17	26MAR03	17APR03	0
10310	RC Walls Level 3 - Level 4	25	25	26MAR03	06MAY03	0
10320	RC Slab at Level 4	16	16	14APR03	12MAY03	0
Roof Slab						
10340	RC Roof Slabs/Conc Beams	13	13	13MAY03	29MAY03	0
Roof						
10390	Steel Structure Above Level 4	8	8	30MAY03	10JUN03	0
10400	Steel Flue Support Frames	12	12	11JUN03	26JUN03	0
10410	Surface Treatment to Steel	9	9	27JUN03	09JUL03	0
10470	Timber Roof Structures/Liners	20	20	10JUL03	06AUG03	0
External Walls/Glazing						
10600	Steel Windposts/Framing	24	24	06MAY03	06JUN03	0
Brick/Blockwork						
10620	Facing Brickwork	35	35	01APR03	26MAY03	0
10640	Composite Block/Brickwalls	35	35	01APR03	26MAY03	0
Stonework						
10660	Stone Bands	48	48	29APR03	03JUL03	0
10670	Stone Cills/Beams etc	43	43	29APR03	26JUN03	0
10680	Stone Lintols	33	33	06MAY03	19JUN03	0
10690	New Stone Cladding	38	38	06MAY03	26JUN03	0
Glazing/Louvres/Ext.Doors						
10720	Curtain Walling	27	27	13JUN03	21JUL03	0
10730	Velfac Windows	29	29	13JUN03	23JUL03	0
10780	Building Substantial Watertight	0	0		24JUL03	0
Internal Walls						
10820	Stud Partitions	60	60	26JUN03	17SEP03	0

Start Date 06AUG02
Finish Date 07APR04
Data Date 06AUG02
Run Date 04SEP07 16:30

New Science Block

AS PLANNED
Programme MP01
The Critical Path

APPENDIX 4A b

Activity ID	Activity Description	Orig Dur	Rem Dur	Early Start	Early Finish	Total Float	
Wall Finishes							
11050	Plaster to Walls/Columns	62	62	27JUN03	22SEP03	0	Plaster to Walls/Columns
Internal Doors							
11280	Hardwood Screens	25	25	14OCT03	17NOV03	0	Hardwood Screens
11290	Internal Doors/Architraves etc	35	35	30OCT03	17DEC03	0	Internal Doors/Architraves etc
11300	Reception Desk / Kitchen Shutter	9	9	18DEC03	30DEC03	0	Reception Desk / Kitchen Shutter
Floor Finishes							
11470	Carpet	18	18	06JAN04	29JAN04	0	Carpet
11480	Terrazzo	22	22	06JAN04	04FEB04	0	Terrazzo
11490	Timber Flooring	22	22	06JAN04	04FEB04	0	Timber Flooring
Final Testing/Commission/Clean							
11510	Precommissioning	15	15	05FEB04	25FEB04	0	Precommissioning
11520	Final Testing & Commissioning	30	30	26FEB04	07APR04	0	Final Testing & Commissioning
11530	Biological Medical Clean	10	10	25MAR04	07APR04	0	Biological Medical Clean
11540	HANDOVER	0	0		07APR04	0	HANDOVER

Timeline header: 2002 AUG SEP OCT NOV DEC | 2003 JAN FEB MAR APR MAY JUN JUL AUG SEP OCT NOV DEC | 2004 JAN FEB MAR APR

Start Date	06AUG02
Finish Date	07APR04
Data Date	06AUG02
Run Date	04SEP07 16:30

New Science Block

AS PLANNED
Programme MP01
The Critical Path

APPENDIX 4A b

Sheet 3 of 3

New Science Block

Progress Data: relating to Programme MP01

No	Activity	Actual Start	Actual Finish	20-Oct	24-Nov	17-Dec	26-Jan	22-Feb	23-Mar	20-Apr	15-May	21-Jun	27-Jul	06-Aug
							2002							2003
9760	Appoint Main Contractor	06-Aug-01	---											
9770	Overall Site Possession	06-Aug-01	---											
9780	Mobilisation	06-Aug-01	16-Aug-01											
9790	Site Establishment	06-Aug-01	13-Aug-01											
9800	Remove Ext Claddings/Windows	05-Nov-01	03-Dec-01		0	100								
9810	Alteration/Form New Openings	04-Dec-01	09-Jan-02		0	55	100							
	Piling													
9850	Sheet Piling Install	16-Aug-01	08-Sep-01											
9860	Piling incl Temporary Support	16-Aug-01	24-Sep-01	100										
9890	Sheet Piling Withdraw	30-Mar-02	11-Apr-02						0	100				
	Substructure													
9910	Excavate Basement	24-Sep-01	12-Nov-01	44	100									
9920	Install Temporary Propping	16-Oct-01	23-Oct-01	33	100									
9930	Excavate Pile Caps	31-Oct-01	23-Feb-02	0	63	86	94	34	100					
9940	Under Slab Drainage	31-Oct-01	16-Feb-02	0	15	44	80	100	100					
9950	Blinding	12-Nov-01	01-Mar-02	0	55	60	65	95	100					
	Basement													
9970	Construct Pile Caps/Ground Beams	12-Nov-01	06-Mar-02	0	11	80	86	86	100	96	100			
9980	Cellcore	04-Dec-01	04-May-02		0	19	65	64	91	96	100			
9990	DPM	05-Dec-01	14-May-02		0	20	65	64	90	94	100			
10000	RC Conc Slab	21-Dec-01	07-Jun-02		0	0	44	80	86	90	96	100		
10010	Drainage Layer	29-Apr-02	23-May-02							0	50	100		
10020	Structural Screed	01-May-02	25-May-02						0	0	33	100		
	RC Retaining Walls													
10040	Formwork	09-Jan-02	23-Feb-02			0	0	68	100					
10050	Rebar	07-Jan-02	09-Feb-02			0	0	100	100					
10060	Concrete	11-Jan-02	12-Mar-02			0	0	58	100					
10090	Tanking	14-Jan-02	23-Mar-02			0	0	1+	88	100				
10100	Blockwork Inner Skin	28-May-02	26-Jun-02								0	81	100	
	Frame/Upper Flrs: Level 0 - Level 1													
10130	RC Cols Level 0(Bsemt) - Level 1	24-Jan-02	27-Feb-02			0	5	70	100					
10140	RC Walls Level 0 - Level 1	16-Feb-02	12-Mar-02				0	42	100					
10150	RC Slab at Level 1	13-Mar-02	16-Jul-02						0	48	83	96	98	99
10170	Make Good Basmt Slab/Ret Walls/waterproof	28-Feb-02	27-Apr-02					0	83	96	100			
10180	Backfill around Retaining Walls	19-Jan-02	13-Apr-02			0	3	13	27	100				
	Frame/Upper Flrs: Level 1 - Level 2													
10200	RC Cols Level 1 - Level 2	26-Mar-02	29-Apr-02					0	0	95	100			
10210	RC Walls Level 1 - Level 2	26-Mar-02	07-May-02					0	0	54	100			
10220	RC Slab at Level 2	19-Apr-02	13-May-02					0	0	59	100			
	Frame/Upper Flrs: Level 2 - Level 3													
10250	2RC Cols Level 2 - Level 3	26-Apr-02	20-May-02							0	98	100		
10260	RC Walls Level 2 - Level 3	26-Apr-02	01-Jun-02							0	50	100		
10270	RC Slab at Level 3	14-May-02	06-Jun-02							0	65	100		

New Science Block

Progress Data: relating to Programme MP01

Code	Description	Actual Start	Actual Finish	20-Oct (02)	24-Nov	17-Dec	26-Jan	22-Feb	23-Mar	20-Apr	15-May	21-Jun (03)	27-Jul	06-Aug	15-Oct	27-Nov	18-Dec	26-Jan
	Frame/Upper Flrs: Level 3 - Level 4																	
10300	RC Cols Level 3 - Level 4	20-May-02	19-Jun-02								0	100						
10310	RC Walls Level 3 - Level 4	20-May-02	19-Jun-02								0	100						
10320	RC Slab at Level 4	14-Jun-02	21-Jun-02								0	84	100					
	Roof Slab																	
10340	RC Roof Slabs/Conc Beams	14-Jun-02	21-Jun-02								0	84	100					
10350	RC Upstands	13-Jun-02	21-Jun-02								0	90	100					
	Stairs																	
10370	RC Staircase(No 2)/PC Staircases(Nos 1&3)	06-Jun-02	22-Jul-02								0	71	100					
	Roof																	
10390	Steel Structure Above Level 4	02-Jul-02	11-Dec-02									0	70	80	90	95	100	
10400	Steel Flue Support Frames	16-Sep-02	09-Dec-02									0		0	20	80	100	
10410	Surface Treatment to Steel	01-Jul-02	11-Jul-02									0	100					
10420	Galv Decking to Platfroom	07-Jul-02	08-Aug-02									0	65	96	100			
10430	Wall Cladding/Rainscreens;P-Room & Flues	20-Jun-03	01-Sep-03													0	0	4
10440	Fire Protection to Steel Structure	02-Dec-02	19-Feb-03													0		38
10450	Metal Balconies/Balcony Ladders	16-Jun-02	16-Aug-02								0	11	67	87	100			
10460	Cast Stainless Steel Roof Prong/Truss	22-Oct-02	17-Dec-02												0	50	100	
10470	Timber Roof Structures/Liners	28-Aug-02	10-Feb-03											0	50	65	75	85
10480	Slate Roofing	11-Nov-02	01-Feb-03											0	5	20	95
10490	Stainless Steel Gutters & Verges	02-Dec-02	01-Feb-03												0	0	80	90
10500	Stainless Steel Roofing	27-Aug-02	06-Mar-03											0	30	60	89	89
10510	Felt Roofing to Extg Roof	23-Oct-02	12-Apr-03											0	80	85	90
10520	Felt Roofing	18-Nov-02	12-Apr-03											0	62	66	80
10530	Ally Rooflights	09-Sep-02	19-Sep-02											0	100			
10540	Cable Arrest System	29-Oct-02	08-Jul-03												0	40	60	80
	Disposal Instns																	
10560	Rainwater Pipework	17-Jun-03	14-Jun-03								0	4	20	25	40	55	70	85
10570	Foul Drainage	17-Jun-02	06-Oct-02								0	4	36	47	100			
10580	Laboratory Drainage	17-Jun-02	20-Dec-02								0	4	24	31	69	94	98	100
	External Walls/Glazing																	
10600	Steel Windposts/Framing	30-Apr-02	28-Nov-02							0	10	76	76	76	85	95	100
	Brick/Blockwork																	
10620	Facing Brickwork	01-May-02	09-Nov-02							0	1	4	50	61	95	100	
10630	Blockwalls	01-May-02	09-Nov-02							0	1	4	59	61	95	100	
10640	Composite Block/Brickwalls	01-May-02	08-Nov-02							0	1	4	50	61	95	100	
	Stonework																	
10660	Stone Bands	29-May-02	14-Nov-02								0	9	65	68	90	100	
10670	Stone Cills/Beams etc	29-May-02	14-Nov-02								0	9	65	67	91	100	
10680	Stone Lintols	07-Jun-02	13-Nov-02								0	5	65	67	90	100	
10690	New Stone Cladding	07-Jun-02	14-Nov-02								0	5	65	67	92	100	
10700	Refix Set Aside Stone Cladding	07-Jun-02	12-Jul-02								0	40	100				

New Science Block

Progress Data: relating to Programme MP01

Code	Item	Actual Start	Actual Finish	2002 20-Oct	24-Nov	17-Dec	2003 26-Jan	22-Feb	23-Mar	20-Apr	15-May	21-Jun	27-Jul	06-Aug	15-Oct	27-Nov	18-Dec	26-Jan
Glazing/Louvres/Ext.Doors																		
10720	Curtain Walling	19-Aug-02	25-Jan-03											0	45	80	87	100
10730	Vitrac Windows	19-Aug-02	01-Feb-03											0	54	90	95	95
10740	Louvres & Frames	27-Jan-03	19-Feb-03											0	100			100
10750	Entrance Canopy	22-Sep-02	06-Oct-02															
10760	Ext Doors	07-Jul-03	01-Aug-03															
10770	Roller Shutter Doors	07-Jul-03	25-Aug-03															
10780	Building Substantial Watertight	03-Feb-03	03-Feb-03															
10790	Power/Water/Gas Supplies Required	26-Jul-02	26-Jul-02									0	100					0
Internal Walls																		
10810	Blockwork	13-May-02	30-Jan-03							0	1	20	65	70	92	96	96	100
10820	Stud Partitions	27-Aug-02	16-Aug-03									0		0	9	40	45	47
10830	Joinery 1st Fix & Door Frames	17-Mar-03	21-Nov-03															
10840	WC Cubicles	06-Oct-03	10-Jan-04															
Metalwork																		
10860	Balustrades & Handrails	31-Mar-03	19-Feb-04															
10870	Access Ladders to Plant/LM Rooms	30-Aug-03	19-Feb-04															
10880	Plantroom Handrails	30-Aug-03	08-Jan-04															
Mech/Elec Services Instns																		
Level 0 Plantroom																		
2	AHU 6/7 Installation deliver & move	22-Apr-02	26-Apr-02															
3	AHU 6 Build	19-Aug-02	20-Aug-02								100							
4	AHU 7 Build & Lift	19-Aug-02	21-Aug-02												100	100		
5	Build AHU Support gantry (by others)	24-Jun-02	28-Jun-02									0	100					
6	Ductwork Installation	16-Sep-02	11-Dec-02									0	20	0	60	80	80	100
7	Booster Tanks etc - Deliv/Position	10-Jul-02	12-Dec-02									0	20	20	25	25	25	100
8	Build Steam Support Gantry (by others)	21-Aug-02	11-Dec-02										0	0	50	50	50	100
9	Steam Plant - Deliver & position	17-May-02	21-Aug-02								0	0	50	50	100			
10	Plantroom Pipework Installation	24-Jan-03	05-Aug-03									50	50	50	100			0
11	Deliver/Position Control Panel	09-Dec-02	10-Dec-02															100
12	Controls wiring	31-Mar-03	13-May-03															
13	Commission Steam system	25-Feb-04	02-Apr-04															
14	Specialist Commission Autoclave	05-Apr-04	27-Apr-04															
15	RMU Installation	19-Aug-02	18-Sep-02											0	100			100
16	LV Panel/Transformer Delivery	19-Sep-02	23-Sep-02											0	100			100
17	Power On to Building	19-Sep-02	15-Sep-03															

New Science Block

Progress Data: relating to Programme MP01

No	Task	Actual Start	Actual Finish	2002 20-Oct	24-Nov	17-Dec	26-Jan	22-Feb	23-Mar	20-Apr	15-May	2003 21-Jun	27-Jul	08-Aug	15-Oct	27-Nov	18-Dec	26-Jan
	Level 0 High Level																	
20	Ductwork Large Mains	19-Aug-02	25-Feb-03											0	45	45	45	45
22	Pipework & Ductwork 1st Fix	11-Sep-02	04-Aug-03											0	25	30	45	55
23	Test	07-Jul-03	22-Sep-03															
24	Insulation	12-Sep-02	02-Dec-03											0	5	5	5	5
25	Electrical Containment	11-Sep-02	04-Aug-03											0	15	60	60	65
26	1st Fix Lighting & Power	04-Feb-03	04-Aug-03											0				0
28	2nd Fix Lighting & Power	07-May-03	29-Oct-03															
29	2nd Fix Fire Alarm	07-May-03	29-Oct-03															
30	2nd Fix Security	29-Oct-03	28-Jan-04															
31	2nd Fix Data	07-Mar-03	26-Nov-03															
32	3rd Fix Electrical	02-Jul-03	26-Nov-03															
	Level 0 Low Level																	
34	Ductwork 2nd fix	24-Feb-03	28-Jan-04															
35	Carcass for San ware (by others)	09-Dec-02	24-Feb-03															
36	Pipework 2nd fix	26-Nov-03	02-Feb-04														0	45
37	San ware installation	01-Jul-03	26-Nov-03															
38	Insulation	26-Nov-03	06-Feb-04															
39	Electrical Containment	19-Jun-02	28-Apr-03									0	25	50	75	75	80	85
40	1st Fix Lighting & Power	02-Sep-02	04-Aug-03											0	50	60	70	75
41	2nd Fix Lighting & Power	18-Nov-02	29-Oct-03												0	0	10	20
42	2nd Fix Fire Alarm	28-Apr-03	30-Oct-03															
43	2nd Fix Security	11-Jun-03	29-Oct-03															
44	2nd Fix Data	26-Feb-03	29-Oct-03															
45	3rd Fix Electrical	21-May-03	24-Mar-04															
46	Installation Complete		02-Apr-04															
	Level 1																	
48	Pipework & Ductwork 1st Fix	19-Jun-02	20-Feb-03									0	35	45	75	80	80	90
50	Ductwork 2nd fix	03-Oct-03	29-Mar-04															
52	Pipework 2nd fix	23-Jul-03	25-Mar-04															
53	San ware	12-Jun-03	27-Nov-03															
54	Test	04-Jun-03	27-Nov-03															
55	Insulate	05-Sep-02	27-Nov-03															
56	Electrical Containment	03-Jul-02	28-Apr-03											0	35	35	35	40
57	1st Fix Lighting & Power	02-Sep-02	04-Aug-03									0	25	50	75	75	80	85
58	2nd Fix Lighting & Power	16-Jan-03	26-Nov-03											0	50	60	70	75
59	2nd Fix Fire Alarm	22-Jan-03	26-Nov-03															
60	2nd Fix Security	11-Jun-03	26-Nov-03														0	50
61	2nd Fix Data	26-Feb-03	26-Nov-03															
62	3rd Fix Electrical	10-Jul-03	24-Mar-04														0	10
63	Floor installation complete		29-Mar-04															

New Science Block

Progress Data: relating to Programme MP01

No	Task	Actual Start	Actual Finish	2002 20-Oct	24-Nov	17-Dec	2003 26-Jan	22-Feb	23-Mar	20-Apr	15-May	21-Jun	27-Jul	06-Aug	15-Oct	27-Nov	18-Dec	26-Jan
Level 2																		
65	Pipework & Ductwork 1st Fix	17-Jul-02	20-Mar-03									0	20	35	65	70	70	80
67	Ductwork 2nd fix	14-Nov-03	31-Mar-04															
69	Pipework 2nd fix	14-Jul-03	29-Mar-04															
70	San ware	17-Jul-03	02-Dec-03															
71	Test	06-Jun-03	28-Jan-04															
72	Insulate	13-Sep-02	29-Jan-04											0	2	2	2	10
73	Electrical Containment	12-Nov-02	04-Aug-03											0	2	0	40	40
74	1st Fix Lighting & Power	05-Mar-03	04-Aug-03															
75	2nd Fix Lighting & Power	28-May-03	27-Nov-03															
76	2nd Fix Fire Alarm	20-Mar-03	27-Nov-03															
77	2nd Fix Security	28-May-03	26-Nov-03															
78	2nd Fix Data	05-Jun-03	26-Nov-03															
79	3rd Fix Electrical	14-Jul-03	26-Mar-04															
80	Floor installation complete		31-Mar-04															
Level 3																		
82	Pipework & Ductwork 1st Fix	10-Sep-02	25-Apr-03									0		0	12	20	35	60
84	Ductwork 2nd fix	11-Dec-03	02-Apr-04															
86	Pipework 2nd fix	24-Sep-03	25-Mar-04															
87	San ware	23-Jul-03	02-Dec-03															
88	Test	27-Jun-03	28-Jan-04															
89	Insulate	13-Sep-02	29-Jan-04											0	2	2	2	10
90	Electrical Containment	12-Nov-02	04-Aug-03											0	2	0	40	40
91	1st Fix Lighting & Power	05-Mar-03	04-Aug-03															
92	2nd Fix Lighting & Power	30-May-03	04-Aug-03															
93	2nd Fix Fire Alarm	29-May-03	27-Nov-03															
94	2nd Fix Security	09-Jun-03	26-Nov-03															
95	2nd Fix Data	16-Jun-03	27-Nov-03															
96	3rd Fix Electrical	24-Sep-03	26-Mar-04															
97	Floor installation complete		02-Apr-04															
Level 4																		
99	Lift AHU's etc into roof plantroom	19-Jun-02	14-Oct-02									0	80	80	80	100		
100	Pipework in Plantroom	12-Nov-02	03-Nov-03													0	40	60
101	Lift chillers onto roof	01-Aug-02	05-Aug-02										0	100				
102	Pipework/ductwork on roof	13-Sep-02	04-Nov-03											0	2	50	90	90
103	Test	23-Jun-03	03-Nov-03															
104	Insulate	01-Apr-03	03-Dec-03															
106	Plantroom small power/lighting	05-Dec-02	11-Nov-03													0	10	20
107	Commissioning	08-Nov-03	18-Jun-04															
108	Handover		18-Jun-04															

New Science Block

Progress Data: relating to Programme MP01

Code	Activity	Actual Start	Finish	20-Oct-02	24-Nov-02	17-Dec-02	26-Jan-03	22-Feb-03	23-Mar-03	20-Apr-03	15-May-03	21-Jun-03	27-Jul-03	06-Aug-03	15-Oct-03	27-Nov-03	18-Dec-03	26-Jan-04
Non-Subcontractor Activities																		
10910	Client Autoclave Delivery	05-Aug-02	05-Aug-02										0	100				
10980	Cold Rooms	13-Jan-03	21-Feb-04														0	5
10990	Fume Cupboards	11-Nov-03	10-Jan-04															
11030	Lift Installation	09-Sep-02	20-Feb-04											0	10	15	25	40
Wall Finishes																		
11050	Plaster to Walls/Columns	29-Jan-03	15-Aug-03															0
11070	PVC Wall Linings	01-Oct-03	09-Jan-04															
11060	Tremco Spray	21-Jul-03	27-Sep-03															
11090	Ceramic Tiling	15-Sep-03	22-Nov-03															
11100	Painting to Plaster	14-May-03	06-May-04															
Services Equipment																		
11120	Fly-Frog/Warm Rooms	26-Jun-03	10-Jan-04														0	10
11130	Extract Flue	13-Dec-02	23-Aug-03													0	10	20
Floor Screed/Grano																		
11150	Grano Screed	18-Jul-02	31-May-03									0	10	20	30	40	50	60
11160	Screed	18-Jul-02	31-May-03									0	50	75	80	83	86	89
Ceiling Finishes																		
11180	Frame	03-Jul-02	31-Jan-03									0	50	75	95	96	98	99
11190	Walk on Ceilings Level 0	10-Jul-02	05-Feb-03									0	8	19	62	75	85	95
11200	Walk on Ceilings Level 0	17-Jul-02	05-Feb-03									0	8	19	62	75	85	95
11210	Suspended Plasterbd & Skim	13-Jan-03	28-Mar-03										0					10
11220	Plasterbd Bulkhead	10-Jul-02	28-Aug-03															
11230	Suspended Grid & Tiles	25-Aug-03	23-Jan-04															
11240	Suspended Grid & Tiles	25-Aug-03	23-Jan-04															
11250	Plaster	13-Jan-03	28-Mar-03														0	25
11260	Painting to Plaster/Concrete	23-May-03	07-May-04															
Internal Doors																		
11280	Hardwood Screens	19-May-03	21-Jun-04															
11290	Internal Doors/Architraves etc	02-May-03	16-Aug-03															
11300	Reception Desk / Kitchen Shutter	08-Dec-03	21-Feb-04															
Sanitary Appliances																		
11320	Lamination/Panelling & Framework	01-Jul-03	10-Jan-04															
11330	San Ware	01-Jul-03	10-Jan-04															
Fittings / Furniture																		
11360	Shelving Level 0	10-Nov-03	24-Apr-04															
11370	Reception Desk	22-Nov-03	21-Feb-04															
11380	Tea/Seminar Room Fittings	15-Sep-03	10-Oct-03															
11390	24 hour Kitchen Fittings	31-Jan-04	21-Feb-04															
11400	Equipment	17-Feb-03	17-Feb-03															
11410	Vanitory Units to WC's	01-Jul-03	18-Sep-03															
11420	Boards/Lockers/Signage etc	01-Nov-03	12-Jun-04															
11430	Shower Doors/Tracks	15-Sep-03	10-Jan-04															

New Science Block

Progress Data: relating to Programme MP01

		Progress as of		2002									2003							
		Actual		20-Oct	24-Nov	17-Dec	26-Jan	22-Feb	23-Mar	20-Apr	15-May	21-Jun	27-Jul	08-Aug	15-Oct	27-Nov	18-Dec	26-Jan		
		Start	Finish																		
	Floor Finishes																				
11450	Resin Flooring	03-May-03	09-May-03																		
11460	Vinyl	02-Jun-03	20-Dec-03																		
11470	Carpet	21-Jul-03	09-Oct-03																		
11480	Terrazzo	11-Aug-03	22-Nov-03																		
11490	Timber Flooring	15-Jan-03	15-Feb-03															0			33
	Final Testing/Commission/Clean																				
11510	Precommissioning	17-Oct-03	12-Jun-04																		
11520	Final Testing & Commissioning	08-Nov-03	18-Jun-04																		
11530	Biological Medical Clean	14-Apr-03	14-Apr-03																		
	External Areas																				
11560	External Works	29-Jul-02	09-Apr-04									0		15	15	20	23			
	HANDOVER																				
11540	HANDOVER	12-Jun-04	12-Jun-04															26		

New Science Block

'Time Impact Analysis' Results

cat. 1:	Likely delay to contract completion date, and, likely delay to current forecast completion date for the project.
cat. 2:	Likely delay to current contract completion date for the project.
cat. 3:	Likely delay to activity(s) not started
cat. 4:	Likely delay to activity(s) in progress
cat. 5:	No likely delay

Tranche 1: Start on Site (6 Aug. 2002) to Start of Superstructure Work on 24 January 2003

column 1	col. 2	col. 3	col. 4	col. 5	col. 6	col. 7	col. 8	col. 9	col. 10	col. 11	col. 12	col. 13
Event		Description	Programme MP01 activity number affected	Forecast Completion Date PRIOR to Subnet	Forecast Completion Date AFTER Subnet	Extension of time Entitlement	Adjusted completion date	No delay	Likely delay to progress		Likely delay to proj.compl.	
ref nr.	date							5	4	3	2	1
T1-001	09-Aug-02	Ground beams added	9970									
T1-002	14-Aug-02	Additional works to Roof steelwork	10390							yes		
T1-003	14-Aug-02	Additional Louvres	10740							yes		
T1-004	15-Aug-02	Additional work to timber Roof structure.	10470							yes		
T1-005	17-Aug-02	RFI response with setting out info on pile C44	9860					no				
T1-006	22-Aug-02	Additional piles & pile caps	9860, 9970							yes		
T1-007	22-Aug-02	Substructure changes	9970, 10810							yes		
T1-008	24-Aug-02	Revisions to stairs 1, 2 & 3	10000, 10140, 10620, 10810, 10820, 10830	23-Apr-04	04-May-04	6 workdays	04-May-04				yes	
T1-009	29-Aug-02	Revisions to Curtain Walling	10720, 10730									
T1-010	29-Aug-02	Additional Brickwork and Stonework	10660, 10670, 10680	23-Apr-04	26-Apr-04	1 workday				yes		
T1-011	29-Aug-02	Riser 6 shaftwall changes	10820	27-Apr-04	12-May-04	10 workdays	12-May-04				yes	
T1-012	29-Aug-02	Changes to Roof	10390, 10440, 10470, 10480, 10490, 10500, 10510, 10520							yes		

New Science Block

'Time Impact Analysis' Results

cat. 1:	Likely delay to contract completion date, and, likely delay to current forecast completion date for the project.
cat. 2:	Likely delay to current contract completion date for the project.
cat. 3:	Likely delay to activity(s) not started
cat. 4:	Likely delay to activity(s) in progress
cat. 5:	No likely delay

column 1	col. 2	col. 3	col. 4	col. 5	col. 6	col. 7	col. 8	col. 9	col. 10	col. 11	col. 12	col. 13
Event								No delay	Likely delay to progress		Likely delay to proj.compl.	
ref nr.	date	Description	Programme MP01 activity number affected	Forecast Completion Date PRIOR to Subnet	Forecast Completion Date AFTER Subnet	Extension of time Entitlement	Adjusted completion date	5	4	3	2	1
T1-013	29-Aug-02	Details of screeds/toppings	10020	27-Apr-04	28-Apr-04	1 workday					yes	
T1-014	03-Sep-02	Details of Aquatic Room finishes	10810, 10820, 11080, 11460					no				
T1-015	04-Sep-02	Additional finishing work to riser 6 & phase 1 interface	10820, 11050, 11210					no				
T1-016	04-Sep-02	Revisions to screens in WC's	11410					no				
T1-017	04-Sep-02	Interface details, junctions of phases 1 & 2	10720, 10730, 10820, 11290	29-Apr-04	17-May-04	11 workdays	17-May-04					yes
T1-018	04-Sep-02	Additional fire-rated shaftwall	10820					no				
T1-019	06-Sep-02	Scope changes to External Works	11560							yes		
T1-020	06-Sep-02	Additional blockwork to level 4	10810							yes		
T1-021	10-Sep-02	Anti-vibration mounts for the roof chillers	10390					no				
T1-022	11-Sep-02	Revisions to Front Podium; changes to Basement, etc	9910, 9970, 10000, 10140							yes		
T1-023	11-Sep-02	Changes to Level 1 slab & External Works	10150, 11560							yes		
T1-024	11-Sep-02	Changes to Level 3 structural works	10140, 10210, 10260, 10310, 10390	05-May-04	14-May-04	7 workdays					yes	
T1-025	19-Sep-02	Changes to pile locations	9860					no				
T1-026	20-Sep-02	Revisions to Underslab Drainage manholes	9940					no				
T1-027	21-Sep-02	Reinforcement revisions to Basement	9970									

New Science Block

'Time Impact Analysis' Results

	cat. 1:	Likely delay to contract completion date, and, likely delay to current forecast completion date for the project.
	cat. 2:	Likely delay to current forecast completion date for the project.
	cat. 3:	Likely delay to activity(s) not started
	cat. 4:	Likely delay to activity(s) in progress
	cat. 5:	No likely delay

column 1	col. 2	col. 3	col. 4	col. 5	col. 6	col. 7	col. 8	col. 9	col. 10	col. 11	col. 12	col. 13
Event												
ref nr.	date	Description	Programme MP01 activity number affected	Forecast Completion Date PRIOR to Subnet	Forecast Completion Date AFTER Subnet	Extension of time Entitlement	Adjusted completion date	No delay	Likely delay to progress	Likely delay to progress	Likely delay to proj.compl.	Likely delay to proj.compl.
								5	4	3	2	1
T1-028	24-Sep-02	Reinforcement drawings & rebar schedules.	9970, 10000, 10130, 10140					no				
T1-029	26-Sep-02	Piling; steelwork to stairs	9860, 9940, 10370					no				
T1-030	26-Sep-02	Changes to External Works	11560					no				
T1-031	26-Sep-02	Changes to partitions at roof level	10820	10-May-04	24-May-04	10 workdays	24-May-04					yes
T1-032	26-Sep-02	Changes to roof details	10470, 10600					no				
T1-033	27-Sep-02	Changes to windows, etc	10730							yes		
T1-034	28-Sep-02	Reinforcement details for Basement slab	10000					no				
T1-035	28-Sep-02	Responses to RFI's re underslab drainage & structural details	9910, 9940, 9970, 9990, 10000, 10050							yes		
T1-036	01-Oct-02	Foul sump chamber changes	9940							yes		
T1-037	02-Oct-02	Response to RFI on autoclave pit reinforcement details	10000					no				
T1-038	02-Oct-02	Steelwork to plant room & water tank support	10000, 10810	13-May-04	01-Jun-04	12 workdays	01-Jun-04				yes	
T1-039	03-Oct-02	Structural details for Basement slab	10000, 10050					no				
T1-040	04-Oct-02	Stair 2 smoke vent details	10810							yes		
T1-041	04-Oct-02	Brickblock details, Level O	10620, 10630, 10640	14-May-04	04-Jun-04	15 workdays	04-Jun-04				yes	
T1-042	05-Oct-02	Brick/block details, Level O	10810	14-May-04	07-Jun-04	16 workdays	07-Jun-04				yes	

New Science Block

'Time Impact Analysis' Results

cat. 1:	Likely delay to contract completion date, and, likely delay to current forecast completion date for the project.
cat. 2:	Likely delay to current contract completion date for the project.
cat. 3:	Likely delay to activity(s) not started
cat. 4:	Likely delay to activity(s) in progress
cat. 5:	No likely delay

column 1	col. 2	col. 3	col. 4	col. 5	col. 6	col. 7	col. 8	col. 9	col. 10	col. 11	col. 12	col. 13
Event		Description	Programme MP01 activity number affected	Forecast Completion Date PRIOR to Subnet	Forecast Completion Date AFTER Subnet	Extension of time Entitlement	Adjusted' completion date	No delay	Likely delay to progress		Likely delay to proj.compl.	
ref nr.	date							5	4	3	2	1
T1-043	05-Oct-02	Builders work details, level 0	10620, 10630, 10640									
T1-044	09-Oct-02	Information for foul sump chamber	9910, 9940					no				
T1-045	11-Oct-02	Resp. to RFI's on sub-slab drainage & pump discharge pipe details	9940, 10000					no				
T1-046	12-Oct-02	Response to RFI on reinforcement for additional pile cap	9930, 9970					no				
T1-047	12-Oct-02	Ground beam details	9970, 10000							yes		
T1-048	15-Oct-02	Response to RFI on reinforcement drawings for level 0	10000							yes		
T1-049	15-Oct-02	Level 0 slab r.c. details and bar bending schedules	10000					no				
T1-050	18-Oct-02	Sections & details of level 0 slab & retaining wall	10040, 10050					no				
T1-051	18-Oct-02	Revised Basement foundation drawing	9970					no				
T1-052	18-Oct-02	Revised level 0 drawing	10000					no				
T1-053	18-Oct-02	Revised drawing for level 0 to level 1	10130, 10140							yes		
T1-054	18-Oct-02	Revised r.c. details for level 0	10000							yes		
T1-055	22-Oct-02	Reconstituted stone information for external works	11560									
T1-056	24-Oct-02	Revisions to pile caps	9970, 10000	17-May-04	27-May-04	8 workdays					yes	
T1-057	24-Oct-02	R.c. details of level 0 slab	10000, 10050	17-May-04	19-May-04	2 workdays					yes	

New Science Block

'Time Impact Analysis' Results

cat. 1:	Likely delay to contract completion date, and, likely delay to current forecast completion date for the project.
cat. 2:	Likely delay to current forecast completion date for the project.
cat. 3:	Likely delay to activity(s) not started
cat. 4:	Likely delay to activity(s) in progress
cat. 5:	No likely delay

column 1	col. 2	col. 3	col. 4	col. 5	col. 6	col. 7	col. 8	col. 9	col. 10	col. 11	col. 12	col. 13
Event		Description	Programme MP01 activity number affected	Forecast Completion Date PRIOR to Subnet	Forecast Completion Date AFTER Subnet	Extension of time Entitlement	Adjusted completion date	No delay	Likely delay to progress		Likely delay to proj.compl.	
ref nr.	date							5	4	3	2	1
T1-058	26-Oct-02	Revised details of pile caps	9970, 10000	17-May-04	28-May-04	9 workdays					yes	
T1-059	31-Oct-02	Change to floor slab, level 0	10000									
T1-060										yes		
T1-061	02-Nov-02	Waterproofing details	9990							yes		
T1-062	05-Nov-02	Waterproofing details	9990					no				
T1-063	05-Nov-02	Reinforcement detailing	10000, 10050, 10140, 10150					no				
T1-064												
T1-065	06-Nov-02	R.c. details to level 0 slab	10000	18-May-04	02-Jun-04	10 workdays					yes	
T1-066	06-Nov-02	R.c. details to lift shaft 1	10140, 10210, 10260, 10310	18-May-04	20-May-04	2 workdays					yes	
T1-067	08-Nov-02	Request for info on windows / cladding	10720, 10730									
T1-068	08-Nov-02	Response to RFI on waterproofing details.	10040, 10060					no				
T1-069								no				
T1-070	09-Nov-02	Doors & hatches	10000					no				
T1-071	09-Nov-02	Internal walls	10820					no				

Activity ID	Activity Description	Orig Dur	% Comp.	Rem Dur	Early Start	Early Finish	Total Float
Piling							
9650	Sheet Piling-Install	9	41	5	16AUG02A	02SEP02	-6
9660	Piling incl Temporary Support	25	25	19	16AUG02A	20SEP02	-6
9690	Remove Raking Props to Sheet Piling	8	0	8	20FEB03	03MAR03	-6
Substructure							
9910	Excavate Basement	30	0	30	23SEP02	01NOV02	-6
9920	Install Temporary Propping	10	0	10	14OCT02	25OCT02	-6
9930	Excavate Pile Caps	15	0	15	21OCT02	08NOV02	-6
9940	Under Slab Drainage	15	0	15	21OCT02	08NOV02	-6
9950	Blinding	17	0	17	28OCT02	19NOV02	-6
Basement							
9980	Cellcore	22	0	22	04NOV02	03DEC02	-6
9990	DPM	22	0	22	11NOV02	10DEC02	-6
10000	RC Conc Slab	22	0	22	18NOV02	17DEC02	-6
10010	Drainage Layer	11	0	11	20MAR03	03APR03	-6
10020	Structural Screed	10	0	10	28MAR03	10APR03	-6
RC Retaining Walls							
10040	Formwork	33	0	33	25NOV02	22JAN03	-6
10050	Reinft	24	0	24	02DEC02	16JAN03	-6
10060	Concrete	27	0	27	09DEC02	28JAN03	-6
Frame/Upper Flrs: Level 0 - Level 1							
10130	RC Cols Level 0(Basmt) - Level 1	24	0	24	16DEC02	30JAN03	-6
10140	RC Walls Level 0 - Level 1	24	0	24	16DEC02	30JAN03	-6
10150	RC Slab at Level 1	17	0	17	15JAN03	06FEB03	-6
10170	Make Good Basmt Slab/Ret Walls/waterproof	20	0	20	04MAR03	31MAR03	-6
Frame/Upper Flrs: Level 1 - Level 2							
10200	RC Cols Level 1 - Level 2	17	0	17	24JAN03	17FEB03	-6
10210	RC Walls Level 1 - Level 2	25	0	25	24JAN03	27FEB03	-6
10220	RC Slab at Level 2	17	0	17	12FEB03	06MAR03	-6
Frame/Upper Flrs: Level 2 - Level 3							
10250	2RC Cols Level 2 - Level 3	17	0	17	24FEB03	18MAR03	-6
10260	RC Walls Level 2 - Level 3	25	0	25	24FEB03	28MAR03	-6

Start Date 06AUG02
Finish Date 23APR04
Data Date 24AUG02
Run Date 05OCT07 09:05

New Science Block

EVENT T1-008
Chart A
The Critical Path; Prior to Event

APPENDIX 4D a

Activity ID	Activity Description	Orig Dur	% Comp	Rem Dur	Early Start	Early Finish	Total Float	
10270	RC Slab at Level 3	17	0	17	12MAR03	03APR03	-6	RC Slab at Level 3
Frame/Upper Flrs: Level 3 - Level 4								
10300	RC Cols Level 3 - Level 4	17	0	17	24MAR03	15APR03	-6	RC Cols Level 3 - Level 4
10310	RC Walls Level 3 - Level 4	25	0	25	24MAR03	02MAY03	-6	RC Walls Level 3 - Level 4
10320	RC Slab at Level 4	16	0	16	10APR03	08MAY03	-6	RC Slab at Level 4
Roof Slab								
10340	RC Roof Slabs/Conc Beams	13	0	13	09MAY03	28MAY03	-6	RC Roof Slabs/Conc Beams
Roof								
10390	Steel Structure Above Level 4	8	0	8	29MAY03	09JUN03	-6	Steel Structure Above Level 4
10400	Steel Flue Support Frames	12	0	12	10JUN03	25JUN03	-6	Steel Flue Support Frames
10410	Surface Treatment to Steel	9	0	9	26JUN03	08JUL03	-6	Surface Treatment to Steel
10470	Timber Roof Structures/Liners	20	0	20	09JUL03	05AUG03	-6	Timber Roof Structures/Liners
External Walls/Glazing								
10600	Steel Windposts/Framing	24	0	24	02MAY03	05JUN03	-6	Steel Windposts/Framing
Brick/Blockwork								
10620	Facing Brickwork	35	0	35	28MAR03	22MAY03	-6	Facing Brickwork
10640	Composite Block/Brickwalls	35	0	35	28MAR03	22MAY03	-6	Composite Block/Brickwalls
Stonework								
10660	Stone Bands	48	0	48	18APR03	02JUL03	-6	Stone Bands
10670	Stone Cills/Beams etc	43	0	43	18APR03	25JUN03	-6	Stone Cills/Beams etc
10680	Stone Lintals	33	0	33	02MAY03	18JUN03	-6	Stone Lintols
10690	New Stone Cladding	38	0	38	02MAY03	25JUN03	-6	New Stone Cladding
Glazing/Louvres/Ext.Doors								
10720	Curtain Walling	27	0	27	12JUN03	18JUL03	-6	Curtain Walling
10730	Velfac Windows	29	0	29	12JUN03	22JUL03	-6	Velfac Windows
10780	Building Substantial Watertight	0	0	0		23JUL03	-6	Building Substantial Watertight
Internal Walls								
10810	Blockwork	63	0	63	11APR03	16JUL03	-6	Blockwork
10820	Stud Partitions	60	0	60	25JUN03	17SEP03	-6	Stud Partitions

Start Date   06AUG02
Finish Date   23APR04
Data Date   24AUG02
Run Date   05OCT07 09:05

New Science Block

EVENT T1-008
Chart A
The Critical Path; Prior to Event

APPENDIX 4D a

Activity ID	Activity Description	Orig Dur	% Comp	Rem Dur	Early Start	Early Finish	Total Float	
Mech/Elec Services Instns								
Level '0', High Level								
20	Ductwork Large Mains	20	0	20	09JUL03*	05AUG03	-6	Ductwork Large Mains
22	Pipework & Ductwork 1st Fix	30	0	30	06AUG03	17SEP03	-6	Pipework & Ductwork 1st Fix
25	Electrical Containment	20	0	20	28AUG03	24SEP03	-6	Electrical Containment
Level '0', Low Level								
39	Electrical Containment	20	0	20	11SEP03	08OCT03	-6	Electrical Containment
40	1st Fix Lighting & Power	10	0	10	09OCT03	22OCT03	-6	1st Fix Lighting & Power
Level '1'								
53	San ware	20	0	20	16JAN04	12FEB04	-6	San ware
54	Test	10	0	10	27NOV03	10DEC03	-6	Test
55	Insulate	20	0	20	11DEC03	15JAN04	-6	Insulate
57	1st Fix Lighting & Power	15	0	15	16OCT03	05NOV03	-6	1st Fix Lighting & Power
58	2nd Fix Lighting & Power	15	0	15	06NOV03	26NOV03	-6	2nd Fix Lighting & Power
63	Floor installation complete	0	0	0		12FEB04	-6	Floor installation complete
Wall Finishes								
11050	Plaster to Walls/Columns	62	0	62	26JUN03	22SEP03	-6	Plaster to Walls/Columns
Ceiling Finishes								
11180	Walk-on Ceiling, Steelwork	10	0	10	12MAY03	23MAY03	-6	Walk-on Ceiling, Steelwork
11190	Walk-on Ceilings; Timber joists, flooring etc	36	0	36	19MAY03	08JUL03	-6	Walk-on Ceilings; Timber joists, flooring, etc
Internal Doors								
11280	Hardwood Screens	25	0	25	14OCT03	17NOV03	-6	Hardwood Screens
11290	Internal Doors/Architraves etc	35	0	35	30OCT03	17DEC03	-6	Internal Doors/Architraves etc
11300	Reception Desk / Kitchen Shutter	9	0	9	18DEC03	07JAN04	-6	Reception Desk / Kitchen Shutter
Floor Finishes								
11470	Carpet	18	0	18	14JAN04	06FEB04	-6	Carpet
11480	Terrazzo	22	0	22	14JAN04	12FEB04	-6	Terrazzo
11490	Timber Flooring	22	0	22	14JAN04	12FEB04	-6	Timber Flooring
Laboratory Fit-Out								
L01	Partitions: studs & board 1 side	70	0	70	25JUN03	01OCT03	-6	Partitions: studs & board 1 side
L02	Mechanical & Electrical 1st Fix	70	0	70	07JUL03	13OCT03	-6	Mechanical & Electrical 1st Fix
L03	Partitions: board 2nd Side	70	0	70	14JUL03	20OCT03	-6	Partitions: board 2nd Side
L04	Skim Coat	53	0	53	18JUL03	01OCT03	-6	Skim Coat
L05	Mist & 1 coat paint	70	0	70	01AUG03	07NOV03	-6	Mist & 1 coat paint

Start Date — 06AUG02
Finish Date — 23APR04
Data Date — 24AUG02
Run Date — 05OCT07 09:05

Sheet 3 of 4

New Science Block

EVENT T1-008
Chart A
The Critical Path; Prior to Event

APPENDIX 4D a

Activity ID	Activity Description	Orig Dur	% Comp	Rem Dur	Early Start	Early Finish	Total Float
L06	Vinyl flooring	70	0	70	06AUG03	12NOV03	-6
L07	Lab Furniture: benching	70	0	70	20AUG03	26NOV03	-6
L08	Lab Furniture: bench droppers & top spine	70	0	70	02SEP03	08DEC03	-6
L09	Lab Furniture: shelving	105	0	105	06AUG03	08JAN04	-6
L11	Ceiling to dropper M&E connections	70	0	70	23OCT03	05FEB04	-6
L13	Bench M&E terminations & 3rd fix to partitions	97	0	97	09SEP03	29JAN04	-6
L17	Top coat paint	70	0	70	30OCT03	12FEB04	-6
Final Testing/Commission/Clean							
11510	Precommissioning	15	0	15	13FEB04	04MAR04	-6
11520	Final Testing & Commissioning	30	0	30	05MAR04	23APR04	-6
11530	Biological Medical Clean	10	0	10	02APR04	23APR04	-6
11540	HANDOVER	0	0	0		23APR04	-6

Timeline bars (2002–2004):
Vinyl flooring
Lab Furniture: benching
Lab Furniture: bench droppers & top spine
Lab Furniture: shelving
Ceiling to dropper M&E connections
Bench M&E terminations & 3rd fix to partitions
Top coat paint
Precommissioning
Final Testing & Commissioning
Biological Medical Clean
HANDOVER

Start Date	06AUG02
Finish Date	23APR04
Data Date	24AUG02
Run Date	05OCT07 09:05

New Science Block

EVENT T1-008
Chart A
The Critical Path; Prior to Event

APPENDIX 4D a

Activity ID	Activity Description	Orig Dur	% Comp	Rem Dur	Early Start	Early Finish	Total Float
Subnet T1-008							
T1-008.01	Receipt of RHP dwgs. WP2500 to '05 /C01	0	0	0	27AUG02*		47
T1-008.02	SRM review of new information	5	0	5	27AUG02	02SEP02	47
T1-008.03	New duration for 'basement: rc conc slab' (22	23	0	23	18NOV02*	18DEC02	-7
T1-008.04	New duration for 'frame, lev 0 to lev1: rc wall	25	0	25	16DEC02*	31JAN03	-7
T1-008.05	New duration for 'facing brickwork' (35 wd +	37	0	37	28MAR03*	27MAY03	-8
T1-008.06	New duration for 'int. walls: blockwork' (63 wd	69	0	69	11APR03*	24JUL03	-12
T1-008.07	New duration for 'internal walls: stud partition	63	0	63	25JUN03*	22SEP03	-9
T1-008.08	New duration for 'internal walls: joinery 1st fi	54	0	54	16JUL03*	30SEP03	22
Internal Walls							
10810	Blockwork	63	0	63	28APR03	24JUL03	-12
Mech/Elec Services Instms							
Level '0', High Level							
20	Ductwork Large Mains	20	0	20	17JUL03*	13AUG03	-12
22	Pipework & Ductwork 1st Fix	30	0	30	14AUG03	25SEP03	-12
25	Electrical Containment	20	0	20	06SEP03	02OCT03	-12
Level '0', Low Level							
39	Electrical Containment	20	0	20	19SEP03	16OCT03	-12
40	1st Fix Lighting & Power	10	0	10	17OCT03	30OCT03	-12
Level '1'							
53	San ware	20	0	20	26JAN04	20FEB04	-12
54	Test	10	0	10	05DEC03	18DEC03	-12
55	Insulate	20	0	20	19DEC03	23JAN04	-12
57	1st Fix Lighting & Power	15	0	15	24OCT03	13NOV03	-12
58	2nd Fix Lighting & Power	15	0	15	14NOV03	04DEC03	-12
63	Floor installation complete	0	0	0		20FEB04	-12
Ceiling Finishes							
11180	Walk-on Ceiling, Steelwork	10	0	10	20MAY03	03JUN03	-12
11190	Walk-on Ceilings, Timber joists, flooring, etc	36	0	36	28MAY03	16JUL03	-12
Final Testing/Commissioning/Clean							
11510	Precommissioning	15	0	15	23FEB04	12MAR04	-12
11520	Final Testing & Commissioning	30	0	30	15MAR04	04MAY04	-12
11530	Biological Medical Clean	10	0	10	20APR04	04MAY04	-12
11540	HANDOVER	0	0	0		04MAY04	-12

New Science Block

EVENT T1-008

Chart B

Subnet and New Critical Path

APPENDIX 4 b

Sheet 1 of 1

Start Date 06AUG02
Finish Date 04MAY04
Data Date 24AUG02
Run Date 05OCT07 09:03

Activity ID	Activity Description	Orig Dur	% Comp	Rem Dur	Early Start	Early Finish	Total Float
Piling							
9850	Sheet Piling-Install	9	59	4	16AUG02A	04SEP02	-8
9890	Remove Raking Props to Sheet Piling	8	0	8	24FEB03	05MAR03	-8
Basement							
10010	Drainage Layer	11	0	11	24MAR03	07APR03	-8
10020	Structural Screed	10	0	10	01APR03	14APR03	-8
Frame/Upper Flrs : Level 0 - Level 1							
10170	Make Good Basmt Slab/Ret Walls/waterproof	20	0	20	06MAR03	02APR03	-8
Internal Walls							
10810	Blockwork	63	0	63	15APR03	18JUL03	-8
Mech/Elec Services Instns							
Level '0' High Level							
20	Ductwork Large Mains	20	0	20	11JUL03*	07AUG03	-8
22	Pipework & Ductwork 1st Fix	30	0	30	06AUG03	19SEP03	-8
25	Electrical Containment	20	0	20	01SEP03	26SEP03	-8
Level '0' Low Level							
39	Electrical Containment	20	0	20	15SEP03	10OCT03	-8
40	1st Fix Lighting & Power	10	0	10	13OCT03	24OCT03	-8
Level '1'							
53	San ware	20	0	20	20JAN04	16FEB04	-8
54	Test	10	0	10	01DEC03	12DEC03	-8
55	Insulate	20	0	20	15DEC03	19JAN04	-8
57	1st Fix Lighting & Power	15	0	15	20OCT03	07NOV03	-8
58	2nd Fix Lighting & Power	15	0	15	10NOV03	28NOV03	-8
63	Floor installation complete	0	0	0		16FEB04	-8
Ceiling Finishes							
11180	Walk-on Ceiling: Steelwork	10	0	10	14MAY03	28MAY03	-8
11190	Walk-on Ceilings; Timber joists, flooring, etc	36	0	36	21MAY03	10JUL03	-8
Final Testing/Commission/Clean							
11510	Precommissioning	15	0	15	17FEB04	08MAR04	-8
11520	Final Testing & Commissioning	30	0	30	09MAR04	27APR04	-8
11530	Biological Medical Clean	10	0	10	06APR04	27APR04	-8
11540	HANDOVER	0	0	0		27APR04	

Start Date 06AUG02
Finish Date 27APR04
Data Date 30AUG02
Run Date 05OCT07 09:59

New Science Block

EVENT T1-011
Chart A
The Critical Path; Prior to Event

APPENDIX 4D c

Sheet 1 of 1

Activity ID	Activity Description	Orig Dur	% Comp	Rem Dur	Early Start	Early Finish	Total Float
Subnet T1-011							
T1-011.01	Receipt of RHP dwg. WP710/C02	0	0	0	30AUG02*		166
T1-011.02	SRM review of new information	5	0	5	30AUG02	05SEP02	166
T1-011.03	New duration for 'int. walls: stud partitions' (	71	0	71	26JUN03*	03OCT03	-18
Internal Walls							
10820	Stud Partitions	60	0	60	11JUL03	03OCT03	-18
Wall Finishes							
11050	Plaster to Walls/Columns	62	0	62	14JUL03	08OCT03	-18
Internal Doors							
11280	Hardwood Screens	25	0	25	30OCT03	03DEC03	-18
11290	Internal Doors/Architraves etc	35	0	35	17NOV03	12JAN04	-18
11300	Reception Desk / Kitchen Shutter	9	0	9	13JAN04	23JAN04	-18
Floor Finishes							
11470	Carpet	18	0	18	30JAN04	24FEB04	-18
11480	Terrazzo	22	0	22	30JAN04	01MAR04	-18
11490	Timber Flooring	22	0	22	30JAN04	01MAR04	-18
Final Testing/Commissioning/Clean							
11510	Precommissioning	15	0	15	02MAR04	22MAR04	-18
11520	Final Testing & Commissioning	30	0	30	23MAR04	12MAY04	-18
11530	Biological Medical Clean	10	0	10	28APR04	12MAY04	-18
11540	HANDOVER	0	0	0		12MAY04	-18

Timeline annotations:
- Receipt of RHP dwg. WP710/C02
- SRM review of new information
- New duration for 'int. walls: stud partitions' (
- Stud Partitions
- Plaster to Walls/Columns
- Hardwood Screens
- Internal Doors/Architraves etc
- Reception Desk / Kitchen Shutter
- Carpet
- Terrazzo
- Timber Flooring
- Precommissioning
- Final Testing & Commissioning
- Biological Medical Clean
- HANDOVER

Start Date 06AUG02
Finish Date 12MAY04
Data Date 30AUG02
Run Date 09OCT07 10:07

New Science Block

EVENT T1-011
Chart B
Subnet and New Critical Path

APPENDIX 4D d

Activity ID	Activity Description	Orig Dur	% Comp	Rem Dur	Early Start	Early Finish	Total Float
Basement							
9980	Cellcore	22	0	22	27NOV02	09JAN03	-23
9990	DPM	22	0	22	04DEC02	16JAN03	-23
10000	RC Conc Slab	22	0	22	11DEC02	23JAN03	-23
RC Retaining Walls							
10040	Formwork	33	0	33	18DEC02	14FEB03	-23
10050	Reinft	24	0	24	09JAN03	10FEB03	-23
10060	Concrete	27	0	27	15JAN03	20FEB03	-23
Frame/Upper Flrs: Level 0 - Level 1							
10130	RC Cols Level 0(Basmt) - Level 1	24	0	24	22JAN03	24FEB03	-23
10140	RC Walls Level 0 - Level 1	24	0	24	22JAN03	24FEB03	-23
10150	RC Slab at Level 1	17	0	17	07FEB03	03MAR03	-23
Frame/Upper Flrs: Level 1 - Level 2							
10200	RC Cols Level 1 - Level 2	17	0	17	18FEB03	12MAR03	-23
10210	RC Walls Level 1 - Level 2	25	0	25	18FEB03	24MAR03	-23
10220	RC Slab at Level 2	17	0	17	07MAR03	31MAR03	-23
Frame/Upper Flrs: Level 2 - Level 3							
10250	2RC Cols Level 2 - Level 3	17	0	17	19MAR03	10APR03	-23
10260	RC Walls Level 2 - Level 3	25	0	25	19MAR03	29APR03	-23
10270	RC Slab at Level 3	17	0	17	04APR03	05MAY03	-23
Frame/Upper Flrs: Level 3 - Level 4							
10300	RC Cols Level 3 - Level 4	17	0	17	16APR03	15MAY03	-23
10310	RC Walls Level 3 - Level 4	25	0	25	16APR03	28MAY03	-23
10320	RC Slab at Level 4	16	0	16	12MAY03	03JUN03	-23
Roof Slab							
10340	RC Roof Slabs/Conc Beams	13	0	13	04JUN03	20JUN03	-23
Roof							
10390	Steel Structure Above Level 4	8	0	8	23JUN03	02JUL03	-23
10400	Steel Flue Support Frames	12	0	12	03JUL03	18JUL03	-23
10410	Surface Treatment to Steel	9	0	9	21JUL03	31JUL03	-23
10470	Timber Roof Structures/Liners	20	0	20	01AUG03	29AUG03	-23

Start Date	06AUG02
Finish Date	19MAY04
Data Date	27NOV02
Run Date	05OCT07 10:26

New Science Block

EVENT T1-102
Chart A
Progress Update; at date of Event

APPENDIX 4D e

Sheet 1 of 3

Activity ID	Activity Description	Orig Dur	% Comp	Rem Dur	Early Start	Early Finish	Total Float	2002 / 2003 / 2004 Schedule
External Walls/Glazing								
10600	Steel Windposts/Framing	24	0	24	28MAY03	30JUN03	-23	Steel Windposts/Framing
Brick/Blockwork								
10620	Facing Brickwork	35	0	35	29APR03	17JUN03	-23	Facing Brickwork
10640	Composite Block/Brickwalls	35	0	35	29APR03	17JUN03	-23	Composite Block/Brickwalls
Stonework								
10660	Stone Bands	48	0	48	20MAY03	25JUL03	-23	Stone Bands
10670	Stone Cills/Beams etc	43	0	43	20MAY03	18JUL03	-23	Stone Cills/Beams etc
10680	Stone Lintols	33	0	33	28MAY03	11JUL03	-23	Stone Lintols
10690	New Stone Cladding	38	0	38	28MAY03	18JUL03	-23	New Stone Cladding
Glazing/Louvres/Ext.Doors								
10720	Curtain Walling	27	0	27	07JUL03	12AUG03	-23	Curtain Walling
10730	Velfac Windows	29	0	29	07JUL03	14AUG03	-23	Velfac Windows
10780	Building Substantial Watertight	0	0	0		15AUG03	-23	◆Building Substantial Watertight
Internal Walls								
10810	Blockwork	63	0	63	13MAY03	08AUG03	-23	Blockwork
10820	Stud Partitions	60	0	60	18JUL03	10OCT03	-23	Stud Partitions
Mech/Elec Services Instns								
Level '0' High Level								
20	Ductwork Large Mains	20	0	20	01AUG03*	29AUG03	-23	Ductwork Large Mains
22	Pipework & Ductwork 1st Fix	30	0	30	01SEP03	10OCT03	-23	Pipework & Ductwork 1st Fix
25	Electrical Containment	20	0	20	22SEP03	17OCT03	-23	Electrical Containment
Level '0' Low Level								
39	Electrical Containment	20	0	20	06OCT03	31OCT03	-23	Electrical Containment
40	1st Fix Lighting & Power	10	0	10	03NOV03	14NOV03	-23	1st Fix Lighting & Power
Level '1'								
53	San ware	20	0	20	10FEB04	08MAR04	-23	San ware
54	Test	10	0	10	22DEC03	12JAN04	-23	Test
55	Insulate	20	0	20	13JAN04	09FEB04	-23	Insulate
57	1st Fix Lighting & Power	15	0	15	10NOV03	28NOV03	-23	1st Fix Lighting & Power
58	2nd Fix Lighting & Power	15	0	15	01DEC03	19DEC03	-23	2nd Fix Lighting & Power
63	Floor installation complete	0	0	0		08MAR04	-23	Floor installation complete◆

Start Date 06AUG02
Finish Date 19MAY04
Data Date 27NOV02
Run Date 05OCT07 10:26

New Science Block

EVENT T1-102
Chart A
Progress Update; at date of Event

APPENDIX 4D e

Activity ID	Activity Description	Orig Dur	% Comp	Rem Dur	Early Start	Early Finish	Total Float
Wall Finishes							
11050	Plaster to Walls/Columns	62	0	62	21JUL03	15OCT03	-23
Ceiling Finishes							
11180	Walk-on Ceiling; Steelwork	10	0	10	05JUN03	18JUN03	-23
11190	Walk-on Ceilings; Timber joists, flooring, etc	36	0	36	12JUN03	31JUL03	-23
Internal Doors							
11280	Hardwood Screens	25	0	25	06NOV03	10DEC03	-23
11290	Internal Doors/Architraves etc	35	0	35	24NOV03	19JAN04	-23
11300	Reception Desk / Kitchen Shutter	9	0	9	20JAN04	30JAN04	-23
Floor Finishes							
11470	Carpet	18	0	18	06FEB04	02MAR04	-23
11480	Terrazzo	22	0	22	06FEB04	08MAR04	-23
11490	Timber Flooring	22	0	22	06FEB04	08MAR04	-23
Laboratory Fit-Out							
L01	Partitions: studs & board 1 side	70	0	70	18JUL03	24OCT03	-23
L02	Mechanical & Electrical 1st Fix	70	0	70	30JUL03	05NOV03	-23
L03	Partitions: board 2nd Side	70	0	70	06AUG03	12NOV03	-23
L04	Skim Coat	53	0	53	12AUG03	24OCT03	-23
L05	Mst & 1 coat paint	70	0	70	27AUG03	02DEC03	-23
L06	Vinyl flooring	70	0	70	01SEP03	05DEC03	-23
L07	Lab Furniture: benching	70	0	70	01SEP03	19DEC03	-23
L08	Lab Furniture: bench droppers & top spine	70	0	70	25SEP03	08JAN04	-23
L09	Lab Furniture: shelving	105	0	105	01SEP03	02FEB04	-23
L11	Ceiling to dropper M&E connections	70	0	70	17NOV03	01MAR04	-23
L13	Bench M&E terminations & 3rd fix to partitions	97	0	97	02OCT03	23FEB04	-23
L17	Top coat paint	70	0	70	24NOV03	08MAR04	-23
Final Testing/Commission/Clean							
11510	Precommissioning	15	0	15	09MAR04	29MAR04	-23
11520	Final Testing & Commissioning	30	0	30	30MAR04	19MAY04	-23
11530	Biological Medical Clean	10	0	10	06MAY04	19MAY04	-23
11540	HANDOVER	0	0	0		19MAY04	

Gantt bar labels (timeline 2002–2004):
- Plaster to Walls/Columns
- Walk-on Ceiling; Steelwork
- Walk-on Ceilings; Timber joists, flooring, etc
- Hardwood Screens
- Internal Doors/Architraves etc
- Reception Desk / Kitchen Shutter
- Carpet
- Terrazzo
- Timber Flooring
- Partitions: studs & board 1 side
- Mechanical & Electrical 1st Fix
- Partitions: board 2nd Side
- Skim Coat
- Mst & 1 coat paint
- Vinyl flooring
- Lab Furniture: benching
- Lab Furniture: bench droppers & top spine
- Lab Furniture: shelving
- Ceiling to dropper M&E connections
- Bench M&E terminations & 3rd fix to partitions
- Top coat paint
- Precommissioning
- Final Testing & Commissioning
- Biological Medical Clean
- HANDOVER♦

Start Date 06JAN02
Finish Date 19MAY04
Data Date 27NOV02
Run Date 05OCT07 10:26

New Science Block
EVENT T1-102
Chart A
Progress Update; at date of Event

APPENDIX 4D e
Sheet 3 of 3

Activity ID	Activity Description	Orig Dur	Rem Dur	% Comp	Early Start	Early Finish	Total Float	Likely Delay due to Event
Subnet T1-102								
T1-102.01	Receipt of WBP fax: drainage query sheet	0	0	0	27NOV02*	27NOV02*	-46	0
T1-102.02	SRM review of new information	5	5	0	27NOV02	03DEC02	-46	0
T1-102.03	Procurement of new materials	15	15	0	04DEC02	07JAN03	-46	0
Substructure								
9940	Under Slab Drainage	15	11	28	31OCT02A	21JAN03	-46	-19
9950	Blinding	17	14	16	12NOV02A	30JAN03	-46	-19
Basement								
9970	Construct Pile Caps/Ground Beams	15	13	15	12NOV02A	30JAN03	-40	-19
9980	Cellcore	22	22	0	20DEC02	03FEB03	-40	-17
9990	DPM	22	22	0	10JAN03	10FEB03	-40	-17
10000	RC Conc Slab	22	22	0	17JAN03	17FEB03	-40	-17
RC Retaining Walls								
10040	Formwork	33	33	0	24JAN03	11MAR03	-40	-17
10050	Reinf	24	24	0	31JAN03	06MAR03	-40	-17
10060	Concrete	27	27	0	07FEB03	17MAR03	-40	-17
Frame/Upper Flrs: Level 0 - Level 1								
10130	RC Cols Level 0(Basmt) - Level 1	24	24	0	14FEB03	19MAR03	-40	-17
10140	RC Walls Level 0 - Level 1	24	24	0	14FEB03	19MAR03	-40	-17
10150	RC Slab at Level 1	17	17	0	04MAR03	26MAR03	-40	-17
Frame/Upper Flrs: Level 1 - Level 2								
10200	RC Cols Level 1 - Level 2	17	17	0	13MAR03	04APR03	-40	-17
10210	RC Walls Level 1 - Level 2	25	25	0	13MAR03	16APR03	-40	-17
10220	RC Slab at Level 2	17	17	0	01APR03	30APR03	-40	-17
Frame/Upper Flrs: Level 2 - Level 3								
10250	2RC Cols Level 2 - Level 3	17	17	0	11APR03	12MAY03	-40	-17
10260	RC Walls Level 2 - Level 3	25	25	0	11APR03	22MAY03	-40	-17
10270	RC Slab at Level 3	17	17	0	06MAY03	29MAY03	-40	-17

Timeline: 2002 (A S O N D) — 2003 (J F M A M J J A S O N D) — 2004 (J F M A M)

Gantt bar labels:
- Receipt of WBP fax: drainage query sheet nr 003
- SRM review of new information
- Procurement of new materials
- Under Slab Drainage
- Blinding
- Construct Pile Caps/Ground Beams
- Cellcore
- DPM
- RC Conc Slab
- Formwork
- Reinf
- Concrete
- RC Cols Level 0(Basmt) - Level 1
- RC Walls Level 0 - Level 1
- RC Slab at Level 1
- RC Cols Level 1 - Level 2
- RC Walls Level 1 - Level 2
- RC Slab at Level 2
- 2RC Cols Level 2 - Level 3
- RC Walls Level 2 - Level 3
- RC Slab at Level 3

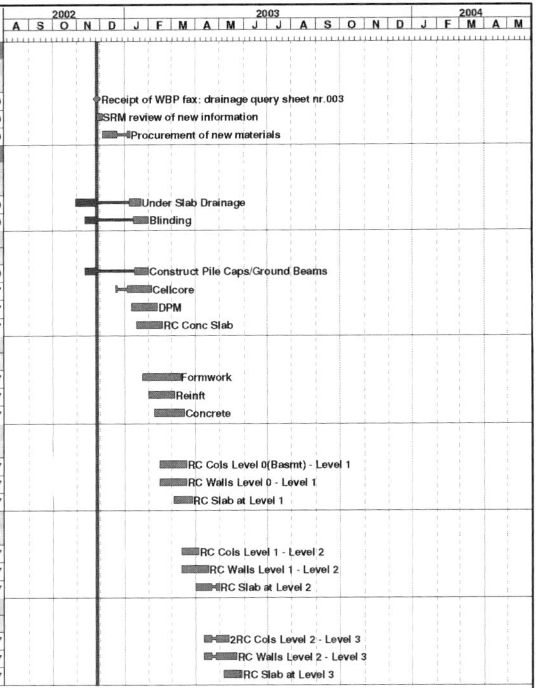

Start Date 06AUG02
Finish Date 14JUN04
Data Date 27NOV02
Run Date 05OCT07 10:32

New Science Block
EVENT T1-102
Chart B
Progress Update with Subnet

APPENDIX 4D f

Activity ID	Activity Description	Orig Dur	% Comp	Rem Dur	Early Start	Early Finish	Total Float	Likely Delay due to Event
	Frame/Upper Flrs: Level 3 - Level 4							
10300	RC Cols Level 3 - Level 4	17	0	17	16MAY03	10JUN03	-40	-17
10310	RC Walls Level 3 - Level 4	25	0	25	16MAY03	20JUN03	-40	-17
10320	RC Slab at Level 4	16	0	16	05JUN03	26JUN03	-40	-17
	Roof Slab							
10340	RC Roof Slabs/Conc Beams	13	0	13	27JUN03	15JUL03	-40	-17
	Roof							
10390	Steel Structure Above Level 4	8	0	8	16JUL03	25JUL03	-40	-17
10400	Steel Flue Support Frames	12	0	12	28JUL03	12AUG03	-40	-17
10410	Surface Treatment to Steel	9	0	9	13AUG03	26AUG03	-40	-17
10470	Timber Roof Structures/Liners	20	0	20	27AUG03	23SEP03	-40	-17
	External Walls/Glazing							
10600	Steel Windposts/Framing	24	0	24	20JUN03	23JUL03	-40	-17
	Brick/Blockwork							
10620	Facing Brickwork	35	0	35	22MAY03	10JUL03	-40	-17
10640	Composite Block/Brickwalls	35	0	35	22MAY03	10JUL03	-40	-17
	Stonework							
10660	Stone Bands	48	0	48	13JUN03	19AUG03	-40	-17
10670	Stone Cills/Beams etc	43	0	43	13JUN03	12AUG03	-40	-17
10680	Stone Lintols	33	0	33	20JUN03	05AUG03	-40	-17
10690	New Stone Cladding	38	0	38	20JUN03	12AUG03	-40	-17
	Glazing/Louvres/Ext.Doors							
10720	Curtain Walling	27	0	27	30JUL03	05SEP03	-40	-17
10730	Velfac Windows	29	0	29	30JUL03	09SEP03	-40	-17
10780	Building Substantial Watertight	0	0	0		10SEP03	-40	-17
	Internal Walls							
10810	Blockwork	63	0	63	06JUN03	03SEP03	-40	-17
10820	Stud Partitions	60	0	60	12AUG03	04NOV03	-40	-17
	Mech/Elec Services Instns							
	Level '0' High Level							
20	Ductwork Large Mains	20	0	20	27AUG03*	23SEP03	-40	-17

Start Date 06AUG02
Finish Date 14JUN04
Data Date 27NOV02
Run Date 05OCT07 10:32

New Science Block
EVENT T1-102
Chart B
Progress Update with Subnet

APPENDIX 4D f

Activity ID	Activity Description	Orig Dur	% Comp	Rem Dur	Early Start	Early Finish	Total Float	Likely Delay due to Event	Gantt
22	Pipework & Ductwork 1st Fix	30	0	30	24SEP03	04NOV03	-40	-17	Pipework & Ductwork 1st Fix
25	Electrical Containment	20	0	20	15OCT03	11NOV03	-40	-17	Electrical Containment
Level '0', Low Level									
39	Electrical Containment	20	0	20	29OCT03	25NOV03	-40	-17	Electrical Containment
40	1st Fix Lighting & Power	10	0	10	26NOV03	09DEC03	-40	-17	1st Fix Lighting & Power
Level '1'									
53	San ware	20	0	20	04MAR04	31MAR04	-40	-17	San ware
54	Test	10	0	10	22JAN04	04FEB04	-40	-17	Test
55	Insulate	20	0	20	05FEB04	03MAR04	-40	-17	Insulate
57	1st Fix Lighting & Power	15	0	15	03DEC03	23DEC03	-40	-17	1st Fix Lighting & Power
58	2nd Fix Lighting & Power	15	0	15	24DEC03	21JAN04	-40	-17	2nd Fix Lighting & P
63	Floor installation complete	0	0	0		31MAR04	-40	-17	Floor ins
Wall Finishes									
11050	Plaster to Walls/Columns	62	0	62	13AUG03	07NOV03	-40	-17	Plaster to Walls/Columns
Ceiling Finishes									
11180	Walk-on Ceiling; Steelwork	10	0	10	30JUN03	11JUL03	-40	-17	Walk-on Ceiling; Steelwork
11190	Walk-on Ceilngs; Timber joists, flooring, etc	36	0	36	07JUL03	26AUG03	-40	-17	Walk-on Ceilngs; Timber joists, flooring, etc
Internal Doors									
11280	Hardwood Screens	25	0	25	01DEC03	12JAN04	-40	-17	Hardwood Screens
11290	Internal Doors/Architraves etc	35	0	35	17DEC03	11FEB04	-40	-17	Internal Doors/Ar
11300	Reception Desk / Kitchen Shutter	9	0	9	12FEB04	24FEB04	-40	-17	Reception Des
Floor Finishes									
11470	Carpet	18	0	18	02MAR04	25MAR04	-40	-17	Carpet
11480	Terrazzo	22	0	22	02MAR04	31MAR04	-40	-17	Terrazzo
11490	Timber Flooring	22	0	22	02MAR04	31MAR04	-40	-17	Timber Fl
Laboratory Fit-out									
L01	Partitions: studs & board 1 side	70	0	70	12AUG03	18NOV03	-40	-17	Partitions: studs & board 1 sid
L02	Mechanical & Electrical 1st Fix	70	0	70	22AUG03	28NOV03	-40	-17	Mechanical & Electrical 1st F
L03	Partitions: board 2nd Side	70	0	70	01SEP03	05DEC03	-40	-17	Partitions: board 2nd Side
L04	Skim Coat	53	0	53	05SEP03	18NOV03	-40	-17	Skim Coat
L05	Mist & 1 coat paint	70	0	70	19SEP03	02JAN04	-40	-17	Mist & 1 coat paint
L06	Vinyl flooring	70	0	70	24SEP03	07JAN04	-40	-17	Vinyl flooring
L07	Lab Furniture: benching	70	0	70	08OCT03	21JAN04	-40	-17	Lab Furniture: bench

Start Date	06AUG02	Sheet 3 of 4
Finish Date	14JUN04	
Data Date	27NOV02	
Run Date	05OCT07 10:32	

New Science Block

EVENT T1-102
Chart B
Progress Update with Subnet

APPENDIX 4D f

Activity ID	Activity Description	Orig Dur	% Comp	Rem Dur	Early Start	Early Finish	Total Float	Likely Delay due to Event	2002	2003	2004
L08	Lab Furniture: bench droppers & top spine	70	0	70	20OCT03	02FEB04	-40	-17			Lab Furniture: ben
L09	Lab Furniture: shelving	105	0	105	24SEP03	25FEB04	-40	-17			Lab Furniture:
L11	Ceiling to dropper M&E connections	70	0	70	10DEC03	24MAR04	-40	-17			Ceiling to
L13	Bench M&E terminations & 3rd fix to partitions	97	0	97	27OCT03	17MAR04	-40	-17			Bench M&E
L17	Top coat paint	70	0	70	17DEC03	31MAR04	-40	-17			Top coat
Final Testing/Commissioning/Clean											
11510	Precommissioning	15	0	15	01APR04	29APR04	-40	-17			Prec
11520	Final Testing & Commissioning	30	0	30	30APR04	14JUN04	-40	-17			
11530	Biological Medical Clean	10	0	10	01JUN04	14JUN04	-40	-17			
11540	HANDOVER	0	0	0		14JUN04	-40	-17			

Start Date	06AUG02	**New Science Block**
Finish Date	14JUN04	
Data Date	27NOV02	
Run Date	05OCT07 10:32	**EVENT T1-102** **Chart B** **Progress Update with Subnet**

APPENDIX 4D f

Sheet 4 of 4

New Science Block — EVENT T1-108 — Chart A — Progress Update; at date of Event — APPENDIX 4D g

Activity ID	Activity Description	Orig Dur	% Comp	Rem Dur	Early Start	Early Finish	Total Float
Basement							
9980	Cellcore	22	0	22	04DEC02	16JAN03	-28
9990	DPM	22	0	22	11DEC02	23JAN03	-28
10000	RC Conc Slab	22	0	22	18DEC02	30JAN03	-28
RC Retaining Walls							
10040	Formwork	33	0	33	08JAN03	21FEB03	-28
10050	Reinft	24	0	24	15JAN03	17FEB03	-28
10060	Concrete	27	0	27	22JAN03	27FEB03	-28
Frame/Upper Flrs: Level 0 - Level 1							
10130	RC Cols Level 0(Basmt) - Level 1	24	0	24	29JAN03	03MAR03	-28
10140	RC Walls Level 0 - Level 1	24	0	24	29JAN03	03MAR03	-28
10150	RC Slab at Level 1	17	0	17	14FEB03	10MAR03	-28
Frame/Upper Flrs: Level 1 - Level 2							
10200	RC Cols Level 1 - Level 2	17	0	17	25FEB03	19MAR03	-28
10210	RC Walls Level 1 - Level 2	25	0	25	25FEB03	31MAR03	-28
10220	RC Slab at Level 2	17	0	17	14MAR03	07APR03	-28
Frame/Upper Flrs: Level 2 - Level 3							
10250	2RC Cols Level 2 - Level 3	17	0	17	26MAR03	17APR03	-28
10260	RC Walls Level 2 - Level 3	25	0	25	26MAR03	06MAY03	-28
10270	RC Slab at Level 3	17	0	17	11APR03	12MAY03	-28
Frame/Upper Flrs: Level 3 - Level 4							
10300	RC Cols Level 3 - Level 4	17	0	17	30APR03	22MAY03	-28
10310	RC Walls Level 3 - Level 4	25	0	25	30APR03	04JUN03	-28
10320	RC Slab at Level 4	16	0	16	19MAY03	10JUN03	-28
Roof Slab							
10340	RC Roof Slabs/Conc Beams	13	0	13	11JUN03	27JUN03	-28
Roof							
10390	Steel Structure Above Level 4	8	0	8	30JUN03	08JUL03	-28
10400	Steel Flue Support Frames	12	0	12	10JUL03	25JUL03	-28
10410	Surface Treatment to Steel	9	0	9	28JUL03	07AUG03	-28
10470	Timber Roof Structures/Liners	20	0	20	08AUG03	05SEP03	-28

Start Date 06JAN02
Finish Date 29MAY04
Data Date 04DEC02
Run Date 05OCT07 11:18

Activity ID	Activity Description	Orig Dur	% Comp	Rem Dur	Early Start	Early Finish	Total Float
External Walls/Glazing							
10600	Steel Windposts/Framing	24	0	24	04JUN03	07JUL03	-28
Brick/Blockwork							
10620	Facing Brickwork	35	0	35	06MAY03	24JUN03	-28
10640	Composite Block/Brickwalls	35	0	35	06MAY03	24JUN03	-28
Stonework							
10660	Stone Bands	48	0	48	28MAY03	01AUG03	-28
10670	Stone Cills/Beams etc	43	0	43	28MAY03	25JUL03	-28
10680	Stone Lintols	33	0	33	04JUN03	18JUL03	-28
10690	New Stone Cladding	38	0	38	04JUN03	25JUL03	-28
Glazing/Louvres/Ext.Doors							
10720	Curtain Walling	27	0	27	14JUL03	19AUG03	-28
10730	Velfac Windows	29	0	29	14JUL03	21AUG03	-28
10780	Building Substantial Watertight	0	0	0		22AUG03	-28
Internal Walls							
10810	Blockwork	63	0	63	20MAY03	15AUG03	-28
10820	Stud Partitions	60	0	60	25JUL03	17OCT03	-28
Mech/Elec Services Instns							
Level '0' High Level							
20	Ductwork Large Mains	20	0	20	08AUG03*	05SEP03	-28
22	Pipework & Ductwork 1st Fix	30	0	30	08SEP03	17OCT03	-28
25	Electrical Containment	20	0	20	29SEP03	24OCT03	-28
Level '0' Low Level							
39	Electrical Containment	20	0	20	13OCT03	07NOV03	-28
40	1st Fix Lighting & Power	10	0	10	10NOV03	21NOV03	-28
Level '1'							
53	San ware	20	0	20	17FEB04	15MAR04	-28
54	Test	10	0	10	06JAN04	19JAN04	-28
55	Insulate	20	0	20	20JAN04	16FEB04	-28
57	1st Fix Lighting & Power	15	0	15	17NOV03	05DEC03	-28
58	2nd Fix Lighting & Power	15	0	15	08DEC03	05JAN04	-28
63	Floor installation complete	0	0	0		15MAR04	-28

Start Date 06AUG02
Finish Date 29MAY04
Data Date 04DEC02
Run Date 05OCT07 11:16

New Science Block
EVENT T1-108
Chart A
Progress Update; at date of Event

APPENDIX 4D g

Activity ID	Activity Description	Orig Dur	% Comp	Rem Dur	Early Start	Early Finish	Total Float
Wall Finishes							
11050	Plaster to Walls/Columns	62	0	62	28JUL03	22OCT03	-28
Ceiling Finishes							
11180	Walk-on Ceiling: Steelwork	10	0	10	12JUN03	25JUN03	-28
11190	Walk-on Ceilings; Timber joists, flooring, etc	36	0	36	19JUN03	07AUG03	-28
Internal Doors							
11280	Hardwood Screens	25	0	25	13NOV03	17DEC03	-28
11290	Internal Doors/Architraves etc	35	0	35	01DEC03	26JAN04	-28
11300	Reception Desk / Kitchen Shutter	9	0	9	27JAN04	06FEB04	-28
Floor Finishes							
11470	Carpet	18	0	18	13FEB04	09MAR04	-28
11480	Terrazzo	22	0	22	13FEB04	15MAR04	-28
11490	Timber Flooring	22	0	22	13FEB04	15MAR04	-28
Laboratory Fit-Out							
L01	Partitions: studs & board 1 side	70	0	70	25JUL03	31OCT03	-28
L02	Mechanical & Electrical 1st Fix	70	0	70	06AUG03	12NOV03	-28
L03	Partitions: board 2nd Side	70	0	70	13AUG03	19NOV03	-28
L04	Skim Coat	53	0	53	19AUG03	31OCT03	-28
L05	Mist & 1 coat paint	70	0	70	03SEP03	09DEC03	-28
L06	Vinyl flooring	70	0	70	08SEP03	12DEC03	-28
L07	Lab Furniture: benching	70	0	70	22SEP03	05JAN04	-28
L08	Lab Furniture: bench droppers & top spine	70	0	70	02OCT03	15JAN04	-28
L09	Lab Furniture: shelving	105	0	105	08SEP03	09FEB04	-28
L11	Ceiling to dropper M&E connections	70	0	70	24NOV03	08MAR04	-28
L13	Bench M&E terminations & 3rd fix to partitions	97	0	97	09OCT03	01MAR04	-28
L17	Top coat paint	70	0	70	01DEC03	15MAR04	-28
Final Testing/Commission/Clean							
11510	Precommissioning	15	0	15	16MAR04	05APR04	-28
11520	Final Testing & Commissioning	30	0	30	06APR04	26MAY04	-28
11530	Biological Medical Clean	10	0	10	13MAY04	26MAY04	-28
11540	HANDOVER	0	0	0		26MAY04	-28

Start Date 06AUG02
Finish Date 26MAY04
Data Date 04DEC02
Run Date 05OCT07 11:16

New Science Block

EVENT T1-108
Chart A
Progress Update; at date of Event

APPENDIX 4D g

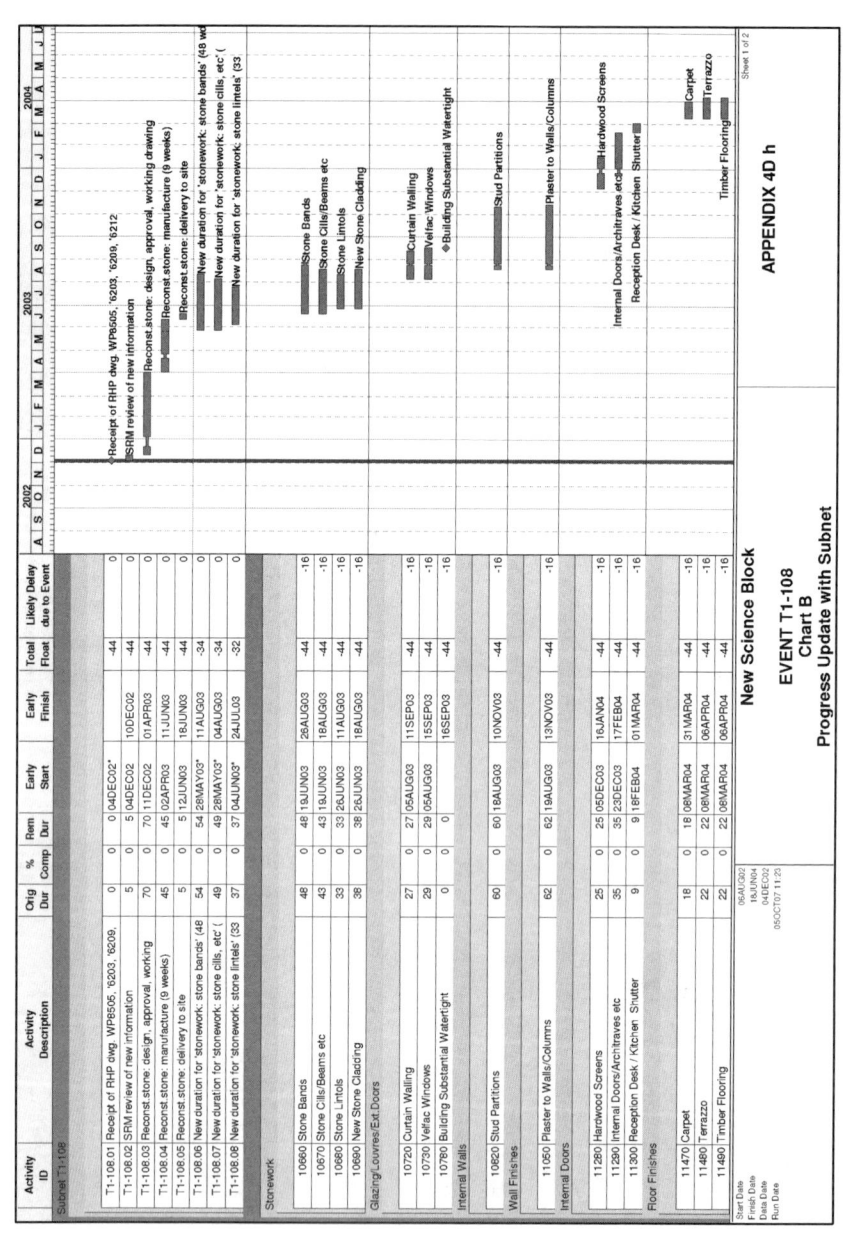

Activity ID	Activity Description	Orig Dur	% Comp	Rem Dur	Early Start	Early Finish	Total Float	Likely Delay due to Event
Subnet T1-108								
T1-108.01	Receipt of RHP dwg. WP8505, '6203, '6209,	0	0	0	04DEC02*		-44	0
T1-108.02	SRM review of new information	5	0	5	04DEC02	10DEC02	-44	0
T1-108.03	Reconst.stone: design, approval, working	70	0	70	11DEC02	01APR03	-44	0
T1-108.04	Reconst.stone: manufacture (9 weeks)	45	0	45	02APR03	11JUN03	-44	0
T1-108.05	Reconst.stone: delivery to site	5	0	5	12JUN03	18JUN03	-44	0
T1-108.06	New duration for 'stonework: stone bands' (48	54	0	54	28MAY03*	11AUG03	-34	0
T1-108.07	New duration for 'stonework: stone cills, etc' (	49	0	49	28MAY03*	04AUG03	-34	0
T1-108.08	New duration for 'stonework: stone lintels' (33	37	0	37	04JUN03*	24JUL03	-32	0
Stonework								
10660	Stone Bands	48	0	48	19JUN03	26AUG03	-44	-16
10670	Stone Cills/Beams etc	43	0	43	19JUN03	18AUG03	-44	-16
10680	Stone Lintols	33	0	33	26JUN03	11AUG03	-44	-16
10690	New Stone Cladding	38	0	38	26JUN03	18AUG03	-44	-16
Glazing/Louvres/Ext.Doors								
10720	Curtain Walling	27	0	27	05AUG03	11SEP03	-44	-16
10730	Velfac Windows	29	0	29	05AUG03	15SEP03	-44	-16
10780	Building Substantial Watertight	0	0	0		16SEP03	-44	-16
Internal Walls								
10820	Stud Partitions	60	0	60	18AUG03	10NOV03	-44	-16
Wall Finishes								
11050	Plaster to Walls/Columns	62	0	62	19AUG03	13NOV03	-44	-16
Internal Doors								
11280	Hardwood Screens	25	0	25	05DEC03	16JAN04	-44	-16
11290	Internal Doors/Architraves etc	35	0	35	23DEC03	17FEB04	-44	-16
11300	Reception Desk / Kitchen Shutter	9	0	9	18FEB04	01MAR04	-44	-16
Floor Finishes								
11470	Carpet	18	0	18	08MAR04	31MAR04	-44	-16
11480	Terrazzo	22	0	22	08MAR04	06APR04	-44	-16
11490	Timber Flooring	22	0	22	08MAR04	06APR04	-44	-16

Start Date   06AUG02
Finish Date   18JUN04
Data Date   04DEC02
Run Date   05OCT07 11:20

New Science Block
EVENT T1-108
Chart B
Progress Update with Subnet

APPENDIX 4D h

Activity ID	Activity Description	Orig Dur	% Comp	Rem Dur	Early Start	Early Finish	Total Float	Likely Delay due to Event
Laboratory Fit-out								
L01	Partitions: studs & board 1 side	70	0	70	18AUG03	24NOV03	-44	-16
L02	Mechanical & Electrical 1st Fix	70	0	70	29AUG03	04DEC03	-44	-16
L03	Partitions: board 2nd Side	70	0	70	06SEP03	11DEC03	-44	-16
L04	Skim Coat	53	0	53	11SEP03	24NOV03	-44	-16
L05	Mist & 1 coat paint	70	0	70	25SEP03	06JAN04	-44	-16
L06	Vinyl flooring	70	0	70	30SEP03	13JAN04	-44	-16
L07	Lab Furniture: benching	70	0	70	14OCT03	27JAN04	-44	-16
L08	Lab Furniture: bench droppers & top spine	70	0	70	24OCT03	06FEB04	-44	-16
L09	Lab Furniture: shelving	105	0	105	30SEP03	02MAR04	-44	-16
L11	Ceiling to dropper M&E connections	70	0	70	16DEC03	30MAR04	-44	-16
L13	Bench M&E terminations & 3rd fix to partitions	97	0	97	31OCT03	23MAR04	-44	-16
L17	Top coat paint	70	0	70	23DEC03	06APR04	-44	-16
Final Testing/Commissioning/Clean								
11510	Precommissioning	15	0	15	07APR04	06MAY04	-44	-16
11520	Final Testing & Commissioning	30	0	30	07MAY04	18JUN04	-44	-16
11530	Biological Medical Clean	10	0	10	07JUN04	18JUN04	-44	-16
11540	HANDOVER	0	0	0		18JUN04	-44	-16

Gantt chart timeline (2002, 2003, 2004) with bars:
- Partitions: studs & board 1 side
- Mechanical & Electrical 1st Fix
- Partitions: board 2nd Side
- Skim Coat
- Mist & 1 coat paint
- Vinyl flooring
- Lab Furniture: benching
- Lab Furniture: bench droppers & top spine
- Lab Furniture: shelving
- Ceiling to dropper M&E connections
- Bench M&E terminations & 3rd fix to partitions
- Top coat paint
- Precommissioning
- Final Testing & Commissioning
- Biological Medical Clean
- HANDOVER◆

Start Date 06AUG02
Finish Date 18JUN04
Data Date 04DEC02
Run Date 05OCT07 11:23

New Science Block
EVENT T1-108
Chart B
Progress Update with Subnet

APPENDIX 4D h

Appendix 5

Charts for worked example: windows analysis

Activity ID	Activity Description	Early Start	Early Finish	Orig Dur	% Comp	Rem Dur	TF
PRELIMINARY WORKS							
0010	Commence Preparatory Activity	05NOV02*		0	0	0	0
0020	Commence On Site	05NOV02*		0	0	0	20
0030	General Site Mobilisation	05NOV02	02DEC02	20	0	20	0
0040	Commerce Main Works	03DEC02	03DEC02	1	0	1	0
0050	Site Establishment	12NOV02	06JAN03	30	0	30	0
0060	Pile Probing	19NOV02	06JAN03	25	0	25	0
0070	Guide Walls	26NOV02	20JAN03	30	0	30	0
0080	Install Secant Piles	10DEC02	24FEB03	45	0	45	0
0090	Cut Down Piles	14JAN03	03MAR03	35	0	35	0
0100	Preliminary Works Complete	04MAR03	04MAR03	1	0	1	0
APARTMENT BLOCK							
SUBSTRUCTURE							
0110	FRC CAPPING BEAM	21JAN03	10MAR03	35	0	35	0
0120	BULK DIG LEAVING SUPPORTING BERMS	23JAN03	15MAY03	74	0	74	0
0130	FRC SECTION OF AREA 3 SLAB FOR TOWER CRANE 1	04MAR03	10MAR03	5	0	5	5
0140	ERECT TOWER CRANE	18MAR03		0	0	0	0
0150	FRC BASEMENT SLAB AREA 1	18MAR03	28MAR03	9	0	9	0
0160	INSTALL TEMPORARY WORKS JIGS 1 & 2	31MAR03	02APR03	3	0	3	0
0170	REMOVE SIDE BERMS AREA 1	02APR03	07APR03	4	0	4	0
0180	FRC CLOSING SECTIONS OF BASEMENT SLABS AREA 1	07APR03	15APR03	7	0	7	0
0190	FRC WALLS AND COLUMNS LOWER - UPPER BASEMENT	31MAR03	29APR03	16	0	16	0
0210	FRC UPPER BASEMENT SLAB AREA 1	04APR03	01MAY03	14	0	14	0
0220	FRC BASEMENT SLAB AREA 2	26MAR03	08APR03	10	0	10	0
0230	INSTALL TEMPORARY WORKS JIGS 3 & 4	10APR03	14APR03	3	0	3	0
0240	REMOVE SIDE BERMS AREA 2	15APR03	28APR03	4	0	4	0
0250	FRC CLOSING SECTIONS OF BASEMENT SLABS AREA 2	28APR03	06MAY03	6	0	6	0
0260	FRC WALLS & COLUMNS LOWER -UPPER BAS'NT AREA 2	10APR03	12MAY03	16	0	16	0
0280	FRC UPPER BASEMENT SLAB AREA 2	16APR03	15MAY03	15	0	15	0
0290	RELOCATE TEMPORARY WORKS JIGS 1 & 2	12MAY03	14MAY03	3	0	3	0
0300	INSTALL TEMP SUPPORT PROPS GL 1/A-J	04APR03	14MAY03	22	0	22	0
0370	REMOVE BERM	15MAY03	21MAY03	5	0	5	0
0380	BREAK BACK FEMALE PILES	20MAY03	23MAY03	4	0	4	0
0390	FRC CLOSING SECTION OF BASEMENT SLAB GL 1/A-J	22MAY03	30MAY03	6	0	6	0
0400	FRC WALLS & COLUMNS BASEMENT - UPPER BASEMENT	02JUN03	06JUN03	5	0	5	0
0410	FRC UPPER BASEMENT SLAB GL 1/A-J	05JUN03	13JUN03	7	0	7	0
0420	INSTALL TEMP SUPPORT PROPS GL 1/M-R	01APR03*	28APR03	14	0	14	0
0470	REMOVE BERM	29APR03	02MAY03	4	0	4	0
0480	BREAK BACK FEMALE PILES	02MAY03	07MAY03	3	0	3	0
0490	FRC CLOSING SECTION OF BASEMENT SLAB GL 1/M-R	07MAY03	13MAY03	5	0	5	0

Start Date 05NOV02
Finish Date 20DEC04
Data Date 05NOV02

MIXED-USE DEVELOPMENT
AS PLANNED
(Programme '01')
All Activities

APPENDIX 5A a

Activity ID	Activity Description	Early Start	Early Finish	Orig Dur	% Comp	Rem Dur	TF
0500	FRC WALLS & COLUMNS BASEMENT - UPPER BASEMENT	14MAY03	19MAY03	4	0	4	0
0510	FRC UPPER BASEMENT SLAB GL 1/M-R	19MAY03	27MAY03	6	0	6	0
0520	INSTALL TEMP SUPPORT PROPS GL 1/J-M	09APR03*	13MAY03	18	0	18	0
0580	REMOVE BERM	14MAY03	19MAY03	4	0	4	0
0590	FRC CLOSING SECTION OF BASEMENT SLAB GL 1/J-M	15MAY03	21MAY03	5	0	5	0
0600	FRC WALLS & COLUMNS BASEMENT - UPPER BASEMENT	22MAY03	30MAY03	6	0	6	0
0610	FRC UPPER BASEMENT SLAB GL 1/J-M	30MAY03	06JUN03	6	0	6	0
0620	FRC Walls/Columns Upper Basement- Ground Floor	13MAY03*	08JUL03	40	0	40	0
0630	Substructure Residential Complete	08JUL03		0	0	0	0

ARTS CENTRE

SUBSTRUCTURE

Activity ID	Activity Description	Early Start	Early Finish	Orig Dur	% Comp	Rem Dur	TF
0640	Crane Base	01JUL03	07JUL03	5	0	5	0
0650	Tower Crane 2	08JUL03*	08JUL03*	0	0	0	11
0660	FRC BASEMENT SLAB AREA 3	01MAY03	15MAY03	10	0	10	0
0670	RELOCATE TEMPORARY WORKS JIGS 1 & 2	18MAY03*	20MAY03	3	0	3	13
0680	FRC LOW LEVEL BASEMENT SLAB AREA 4	14MAY03	21MAY03	6	0	6	1
0690	FRC WALLS LOW - HIGH LEVEL AREA 4 GL 8-9/P-M	22MAY03	28MAY03	4	0	4	1
0700	FRC BASEMENT SLAB AREA 4	13MAY03	02JUN03	14	0	14	0
0720	FRC CLOSING SECTIONS OF BASEMENT SLABS AREA 3	03JUN03*	10JUN03	6	0	6	2
0730	FRC LIFT PITS IN CLOSING SECT. OF B3 GL Q-P/7-8	04JUN03*	12JUN03	7	0	7	4
0740	FRC WALLS & COLUMNS LOWER -UPPER BAS'NT AREA 3	16MAY03	23JUN03	26	0	26	0
0760	FRC UPPER BASEMENT SLAB AREA 3	21MAY03	26JUN03	26	0	26	0
0770	RELOCATE TEMPORARY WORKS JIGS 3 & 4	06JUN03	10JUN03	3	0	3	0
0780	REMOVE SIDE BERMS AREA 4	10JUN03	16JUN03	5	0	5	0
0790	FRC RAMP & WALLS BASEMT SLAB AREA 5 GL 9-10/H-E	13MAY03*	16MAY03	4	0	4	8
0800	FRC BASEMENT SLAB AREA 5	22MAY03	06JUN03	11	0	11	1
0810	FRC CLOSING SECTIONS OF BASEMENT SLABS AREA 4	16JUN03	20JUN03	5	0	5	0
0820	FRC WALLS & COLUMNS LOWER -UPPER BAS'NT AREA 4	29MAY03	26JUN03	21	0	21	0
0840	FRC UPPER BASEMENT SLAB 4	04JUN03	01JUL03	20	0	20	0
0850	RELOCATE TEMPORARY WORKS JIGS 1 & 2	27JUN03	01JUL03	3	0	3	0
0860	REMOVE SIDE BERMS AREA 5	01JUL03	07JUL03	5	0	5	0
0870	FRC LOW SECTION OF BASEMT SLAB AREA 6	04JUN03	13JUN03	8	0	8	0
0880	FRC WALLS LOW - HIGH BASEMENT SLAB AREA 6	16JUN03	20JUN03	5	0	5	0
0890	FRC INTERMEDIATE SLAB AREA 6	23JUN03	26JUN03	4	0	4	0
0900	FRC WALLS FROM INTERMEDIATE TO HIGH LVL. SLAB A6	27JUN03	01JUL03	3	0	3	0
0910	FRC HIGH LEVEL BASEMENT SLAB AREA 6	23JUN03	04JUL03	10	0	10	0
0920	FRC CLOSING SECTIONS OF BASEMENT SLABS AREA 5	07JUL03	14JUL03	6	0	6	1
0930	FRC WALLS & COLUMNS LOWER -UPPER BAS'NT AREA 5	06JUN03	18JUL03	31	0	31	1
0950	FRC UPPER BASEMENT SLAB 5	12JUN03	29JUL03	34	0	34	1
0960	RELOCATE TEMPORARY WORKS JIGS 3 & 4	07JUL03	09JUL03	3	0	3	0
0970	REMOVE SIDE BERMS AREA 6	09JUL03	15JUL03	5	0	5	0
0980	FRC BASEMENT SLAB SECTION 7	03JUL03	16JUL03	10	0	10	0

Start Date	05NOV02
Finish Date	20DEC04
Data Date	05NOV02

MIXED-USE DEVELOPMENT

AS PLANNED
(Programme '01')
All Activities

APPENDIX 5A a

Sheet 2 of 8

Activity ID	Activity Description	Early Start	Early Finish	Orig Dur	% Comp	Rem Dur	TF
0990	FRC CLOSING SECTIONS OF BASEMENT SLABS AREA 6	15JUL03	18JUL03	4	0	4	0
1000	FRC WALLS & COLUMNS LOWER -UPPER BAS'NT AREA 6	07JUL03	23JUL03	13	0	13	0
1010	FRC UPPER BASEMENT SLAB 6	11JUL03	31JUL03	15	0	15	0
1020	RELOCATE TEMPORARY WORKS JIGS 1 & 2	29JUL03	01AUG03	4	0	4	2
1030	REMOVE SIDE BERMS AREA 7	01AUG03	08AUG03	6	0	6	2
1040	FRC BASEMENT SLAB SECTION 8	15JUL03	28JUL03	10	0	10	0
1050	FRC CLOSING SECTIONS OF BASEMENT SLABS AREA 7	07AUG03	15AUG03	7	0	7	2
1060	FRC WALLS & COLUMNS LOWER -UPPER BAS'NT AREA 7	17JUL03	21AUG03	26	0	26	0
1080	FRC UPPER BASEMENT SLAB 7	23JUL03	08SEP03	33	0	33	0
1090	RELOCATE TEMPORARY WORKS JIGS 3 & 4	01AUG03	05AUG03	3	0	3	0
1100	REMOVE SIDE BERMS AREA 8	05AUG03	11AUG03	5	0	5	0
1110	FRC CLOSING SECTIONS OF BASEMENT SLABS AREA 8	11AUG03	18AUG03	6	0	6	0
1120	FRC WALLS & COLUMNS LOWER -UPPER BAS'NT AREA 8	29JUL03	22AUG03	19	0	19	0
1140	FRC UPPER BASEMENT SLAB AREA 8	04AUG03	08SEP03	25	0	25	0
1150	INSTALL SUPPORTING PROPS TO PILES ADJ. TO GL 17	29JUL03	06AUG03	7	0	7	0
1160	REMOVE SUPPORTING BERM	05AUG03	18AUG03	10	0	10	0
1170	FRC CLOSING SECTION OF BASEMENT SLAB	13AUG03	29AUG03	12	0	12	0
1180	FRC WALLS / COLUMNS LOWER - UPPER BASEMENT	21AUG03	05SEP03	11	0	11	0
1190	FRC CLOSING SECTION OF UPPER BASEMENT SLAB	01SEP03	15SEP03	11	0	11	0
1200	2 Week Allowance For Breaking Back Female Piles	30JUN03	11JUL03	10	0	10	0
1210	FRC Columns / Walls Upper Basement - Ground	14JUL03	06OCT03	60	0	60	0
1220	Substructure Arts Centre Complete	07OCT03	07OCT03	1	0	1	0

APARTMENT BLOCK

SUPERSTRUCTURE

Activity ID	Activity Description	Early Start	Early Finish	Orig Dur	% Comp	Rem Dur	TF
1230	Substructure Residential Complete	09JUL03		0	0	0	0
1240	FRC GF Slab Incl Part Sect. Of Area 3 GL 1-7/A-H	25JUN03	11JUL03	13	0	13	0
1250	FRC Ground Floor Slab Low Level GL 1-7/M-R	23JUN03	04JUL03	10	0	10	0
1260	FRC Remaining High Level Section Of GF SLAB	03JUL03	17JUL03	11	0	11	0
1270	FRC Walls / Columns Ground - Mezz	07JUL03	21JUL03	11	0	11	0
1280	FRC Mezz Floor Grid Lines 1-7/A-D	16JUL03	24JUL03	7	0	7	0
1290	FRC Mezz Floor Grid Lines 1-7/M-R	11JUL03	28JUL03	12	0	12	4
1300	FRC Walls / Columns Mezz- 2nd Floor	25JUL03	07AUG03	10	0	10	0
1310	FRC Walls / Columns Ground - 2nd Floor	14JUL03	30JUL03	13	0	13	1
1320	FRC 2nd Floor Slab GL 1-7/F-M	22JUL03	06AUG03	12	0	12	1
1330	FRC 2nd Floor Slab GL 1-7/M-R	01AUG03	12AUG03	8	0	8	0
1340	FRC 2nd Floor Slab 1-7/A-F	04AUG03	15AUG03	10	0	10	0
1350	FRC Walls/Columns 2nd - 3rd/4th Floor	08AUG03	29AUG03	15	0	15	0
1360	FRC 3rd Floor Slab GL 1-7/F-M	14AUG03	29AUG03	11	0	11	0
1370	FRC 3rd Floor Slab GL 1-7/M-R	22AUG03	02SEP03	7	0	7	6
1380	FRC 3rd Floor Slab GL 1-7/A-F	26AUG03	08SEP03	10	0	10	4
1390	FRC Walls / Columns 3rd - 4th Floor	01SEP03	17SEP03	13	0	13	0
1400	FRC 4th Foor Slab GL 4-7/A-L	22AUG03	12SEP03	15	0	15	1

Start Date	05NOV02
Finish Date	20DEC04
Data Date	05NOV02

MIXED-USE DEVELOPMENT

AS PLANNED
(Programme '01')
All Activities

APPENDIX 5A a

Activity ID	Activity Description	Early Start	Early Finish	Orig Dur	% Comp	Rem Dur	TF
1410	FRC Walls 4th Floor Low - 4th Floor High Level	15SEP03	18SEP03	4	0	4	5
1420	FRC 4th Floor Slab GL 1-3/J-R/ + 4-7/L-P	04SEP03	22SEP03	13	0	13	0
1430	FRC 4th Floor Slab GL A-J/1-3	11SEP03	24SEP03	10	0	10	4
1440	FRC 4th Floor Slab GL 6-7/M-R	16SEP03	29SEP03	10	0	10	0
1450	FRC Walls / Columns 4th - 5th Floor	16SEP03	03OCT03	14	0	14	0
1460	FRC 5th Floor Slab GL 1-6/K-R	17SEP03	01OCT03	11	0	11	0
1470	FRC 5th Floor Slab GL 1-6/A-K	23SEP03	08OCT03	12	0	12	0
1480	FRC Walls / Columns 5th - 6th Floor	02OCT03	17OCT03	12	0	12	0
1490	FRC 6th Floor Slab GL 1-6/K-R	07OCT03	21OCT03	11	0	11	0
1500	FRC 6th Floor Slab GL 1-6/A-K	09OCT03	23OCT03	11	0	11	0
1510	FRC Walls / Columns 6th - 7th Floor	22OCT03	04NOV03	10	0	10	0
1520	FRC 7th Floor Slab GL 1-6/K-R	27OCT03	10NOV03	11	0	11	0
1530	FRC 7th Floor Slab GL 1-6/A-K	30OCT03	13NOV03	11	0	11	0
1540	FRC Walls / Columns 7th - 8th Floor	11NOV03	24NOV03	10	0	10	0
1550	FRC 8th Floor Slab GL 1-6/K-R	17NOV03	28NOV03	10	0	10	0
1560	FRC 8th Floor Slab GL 1-6/A-K	24NOV03	08DEC03	11	0	11	0
1570	FRC Walls / Column 8th - 9th Floor	01DEC03	16DEC03	12	0	12	0
1580	FRC 9th Floor Slab GL 1-6/K-R	05DEC03	18DEC03	10	0	10	0
1590	FRC 9th Floor Slab GL 1-6/A-K	16DEC03	13JAN04	11	0	11	0
1600	FRC Walls / Columns 9th - 10th Floor	19DEC03	19JAN04	12	0	12	0
1610	FRC 10th Floor Slab GL 1-6/K-R	06JAN04	22JAN04	11	0	11	0
1620	FRC 10th Floor SlabGL 1-6/A-K	19JAN04	02FEB04	11	0	11	0
1630	FRC Walls / Columns 10th - 11th Floor	23JAN04	09FEB04	12	0	12	0
1640	FRC 11th Floor Slab GL 1-6/K-R	29JAN04	12FEB04	11	0	11	0
1650	FRC 11th Floor Slab GL 1-6/A-K	03FEB04	18FEB04	12	0	12	0
1660	FRC Walls / Columns 11th - 12th Floor	13FEB04	01MAR04	12	0	12	0
1670	FRC 12th Floor Slab GL 1-6/K-R	19FEB04	04MAR04	11	0	11	0
1680	FRC 12th Floor Slab GL 1-6/A-K	26FEB04	11MAR04	11	0	11	0
1690	FRC Walls / Columns 12th - 13th Floor	05MAR04	19MAR04	11	0	11	0
1700	FRC 13th Floor Slab GL 1-6/K-R	11MAR04	23MAR04	9	0	9	0
1710	FRC 13th Floor Slab GL 1-6/A-K	16MAR04	25MAR04	8	0	8	0
1720	FRC Walls / Columns 13th - 14th Floor	24MAR04	01APR04	7	0	7	0
1730	FRC 14th Floor Slab GL 1-6/K-R	29MAR04	06APR04	7	0	7	0
1740	FRC 14th Floor Slab GL 1-6/A-K	31MAR04	08APR04	7	0	7	0
1750	FRC Walls / Columns 14th - 15th Floor	07APR04	27APR04	9	0	9	0
1760	FRC 15th Floor Slab GL 1-6/K-R	20APR04	05MAY04	11	0	11	0
1770	FRC 15th Floor Slab GL 1-6/A-K	23APR04	07MAY04	10	0	10	1
1780	FRC Core Walls Level 15-16 GL A-B/2-5	06MAY04	13MAY04	6	0	6	0
1790	FRC Core Walls Level 16-Roof GL A-B/2-5	14MAY04	26MAY04	9	0	9	0
1800	FRC Cover Slab To Core	27MAY04	06JUN04	9	0	9	0
1810	Progressive Erection of Precast Stairs	18SEP03	17JUN04	177	0	177	0
1820	Main Concrete Frame Complete	06JUN04*		0	0	0	5

Start Date	05NOV02
Finish Date	20DEC04
Data Date	05NOV02

MIXED-USE DEVELOPMENT

AS PLANNED
(Programme '01')
All Activities

APPENDIX 5A a

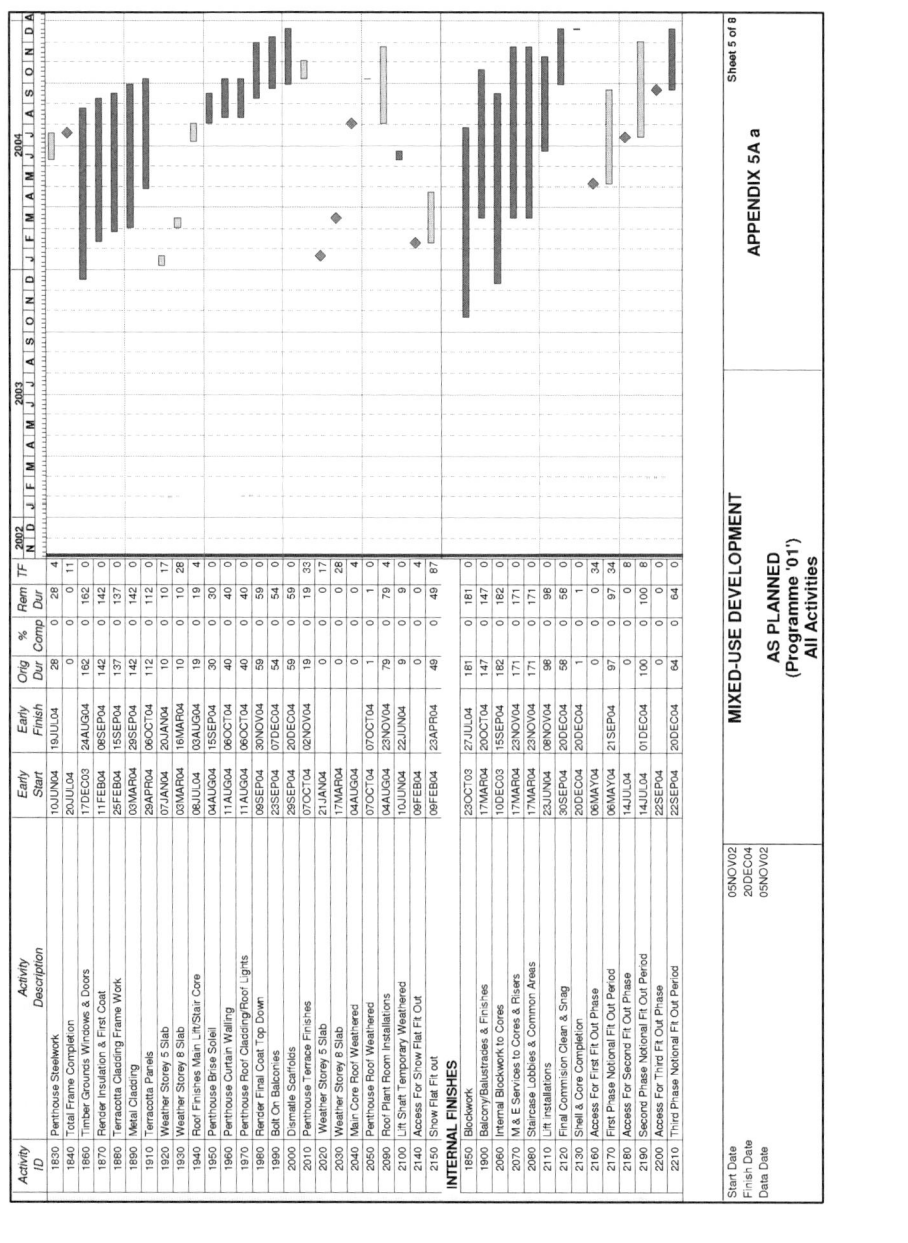

Activity ID	Activity Description	Early Start	Early Finish	Orig Dur	% Comp	Rem Dur	TF
1830	Penthouse Steelwork	10JUN04	19JUL04	28	0	28	4
1840	Total Frame Completion	20JUL04		0	0	0	11
1860	Timber Grounds Windows & Doors	17DEC03	24AUG04	162	0	162	0
1870	Render Insulation & First Coat	11FEB04	08SEP04	142	0	142	0
1880	Terracotta Cladding Frame Work.	25FEB04	15SEP04	137	0	137	0
1890	Metal Cladding	03MAR04	29SEP04	142	0	142	0
1910	Terracotta Panels	29APR04	06OCT04	112	0	112	0
1920	Weather Storey 5 Slab	07JAN04	20JAN04	10	0	10	17
1930	Weather Storey 8 Slab	03MAR04	16MAR04	10	0	10	28
1940	Roof Finishes Main Lift/Stair Core	08JUL04	03AUG04	19	0	19	4
1950	Penthouse Brise Soleil	04AUG04	15SEP04	30	0	30	0
1960	Penthouse Curtain Walling	11AUG04	06OCT04	40	0	40	0
1970	Penthouse Roof Cladding/Roof Lights	11AUG04	06OCT04	40	0	40	0
1980	Render Final Coat Top Down	09SEP04	30NOV04	59	0	59	0
1990	Bolt On Balconies	23SEP04	07DEC04	54	0	54	0
2000	Dismatle Scaffolds	29SEP04	20DEC04	59	0	59	0
2010	Penthouse Terrace Finishes	07OCT04	02NOV04	19	0	19	33
2020	Weather Storey 5 Slab	21JAN04		0	0	0	17
2030	Weather Storey 8 Slab	17MAR04		0	0	0	28
2040	Main Core Roof Weathered	04AUG04		0	0	0	4
2050	Penthouse Roof Weathered	07OCT04	07OCT04	1	0	1	0
2090	Roof Plant Room Installations	04AUG04	23NOV04	79	0	79	4
2100	Lift Shaft Temporary Weathered	10JUN04	22JUN04	9	0	9	9
2140	Access For Show Flat Fit Out	09FEB04		0	0	0	4
2150	Show Flat Fit out	09FEB04	23APR04	49	0	49	87
INTERNAL FINISHES							
1850	Blockwork	23OCT03	27JUL04	161	0	181	0
1900	Balcony/Balustrades & Finishes	17MAR04	20OCT04	147	0	147	0
2060	Internal Blockwork to Cores	10DEC03	15SEP04	182	0	182	0
2070	M & E Services to Cores & Risers	17MAR04	23NOV04	171	0	171	0
2080	Staircase Lobbies & Common Areas	17MAR04	23NOV04	171	0	171	0
2110	Lift Installations	23JUN04	08NOV04	98	0	98	0
2120	Final Commision Clean & Snag	30SEP04	20DEC04	58	0	58	0
2130	Shell & Core Completion	20DEC04	20DEC04	1	0	1	0
2160	Access For First Fit Out Phase	06MAY04		0	0	0	34
2170	First Phase Notional Fit Out Period	06MAY04	21SEP04	97	0	97	34
2180	Access For Second Fit Out Phase	14JUL04		0	0	0	8
2190	Second Phase Notional Fit Out Period	14JUL04	01DEC04	100	0	100	8
2200	Access For Third Fit Out Phase	22SEP04		0	0	0	0
2210	Third Phase Notional Fit Out Period	22SEP04	20DEC04	64	0	64	0

Start Date	05NOV02
Finish Date	20DEC04
Data Date	05NOV02

MIXED-USE DEVELOPMENT

AS PLANNED
(Programme '01')
All Activities

APPENDIX 5A a

ARTS CENTRE

SUPERSTRUCTURE

Activity ID	Activity Description	Early Start	Early Finish	Orig Dur	% Comp	Rem Dur	TF
2220	FRC Ground Floor Slab Low Level GL 7-9/A-J	23JUL03	07AUG03	12	0	12	0
2230	FRC Ground Floor Slab Low Level GL 7-9/M-R	28JUL03	08AUG03	10	0	10	0
2240	FRC Walls From Low - High Lvl GF Slab GL 7-9/M&J	08AUG03	18AUG03	7	0	7	0
2250	FRC Ground Floor Slab High Level GL 7-9/J-M	13AUG03	26AUG03	9	0	9	0
2260	FRC Ground Floor Slab Low Level GL 9-11/A-K	20AUG03	09SEP03	14	0	14	0
2270	FRC Grond Floor Slab Low Level GL 9-11/M-R	26AUG03	08SEP03	10	0	10	0
2280	FRC Walls From Low - High Lvl GF Slab GL 7-9/M&K	09SEP03	16SEP03	6	0	6	0
2290	FRC Ground Floor Sab High Level GL 9-11/K-M	08SEP03	19SEP03	10	0	10	0
2300	FRC Ground Floor Slab Low Level GL 12-15/A-L	22SEP03	10OCT03	15	0	15	0
2310	FRC Ground Floor Slab Low Level GL 12-15/L-R	22SEP03	09OCT03	14	0	14	0
2320	FRC Walls From Low - High Lvl GF Slab GL 12,14&K	10OCT03	17OCT03	6	0	6	0
2330	FRC High Level Slab GL 11-14/A-K	13OCT03	22OCT03	8	0	8	0
2340	FRC High Level Slab GL 11-12/K-M	22OCT03	28OCT03	5	0	5	0
2350	FRC Ground Floor Slab GL 15-17/F-R	06OCT03	27OCT03	14	0	14	0
2360	FRC Walls / Columns Ground - 2nd Floor	12AUG03	30OCT03	57	0	57	1
2370	FRC Mezzanine Slab GL 8-12/K-R	23SEP03	06OCT03	10	0	10	1
2380	FRC Mezzanine Slab GL 13-17/C-R	31OCT03	14NOV03	11	0	11	0
2390	FRC 2nd Floor Slab GL 7-9/A-J	21AUG03	08SEP03	12	0	12	0
2400	FRC 2nd Floor Sla Gbl 7-9/J-R	08SEP03	06OCT03	21	0	21	1
2410	FRC 2nd Floor Transfer Slab GL 9-15/H-R	25SEP03	20NOV03	41	0	41	1
2420	FRC Remainder Of 2nd Floor Slab	17NOV03	02DEC03	12	0	12	0
2430	FRC Walls / Columns 2nd - 3rd Floor	09SEP03	16DEC03	71	0	71	0
2440	FRC 3rd Floor Slab GL 7-9/L-R	17OCT03	13NOV03	20	0	20	0
2450	FRC 3rd Floor Slab GL 9-14/H-R	13NOV03	05DEC03	17	0	17	0
2460	FRC 3rd Floor Slab GL 14-17/F-R	26NOV03	14JAN04	24	0	24	0
2470	FRC Walls / Columns 3rd - 4th Floor	14NOV03	23JAN04	41	0	41	19
2480	FRC 4th FLoor Slab GL 7-9/A-L	15SEP03	10NOV03	41	0	41	4
2490	FRC 4th Floor Slab GL 7-9/L-M	10OCT03	14NOV03	26	0	26	4
2500	FRC 4th Floor Slab GL 7-9/M-R	11NOV03	24NOV03	10	0	10	4
2510	FRC 4th Floor Slab GL 9-15/F-R	12DEC03	20JAN04	18	0	18	0
2520	FRC 4th Floor Slab GL 15-17/G-R	20JAN04	10FEB04	16	0	16	23
2530	FRC Walls/ Columns 4th -5th Floor	12NOV03	17FEB04	60	0	60	19
2540	FRC 5th Floor Slab GL 7-9/A-N	19NOV03	12DEC03	18	0	18	4
2550	FRC 5th Floor E-N/12-17	26JAN04	02MAR04	27	0	27	19
2560	FRC Walls 5th - 6th Floor	18FEB04	10FEB04	17	0	17	75
2570	Concrete Studio Theater Roof	04FEB04	10FEB04	5	0	5	0
2580	Conc.Decks - Art Centre Lvl 5 & Lvl 7	01MAR04	12MAR04	10	0	10	62
2590	Concrete - Escape Stairs & Fly Tower	11MAR04	17MAR04	5	0	5	68
2600	Steelwork Level 2	21NOV03	05DEC03	11	0	11	11
2610	Steelwork Level 3	08DEC03	05JAN04	11	0	11	11

Start Date   05NOV02
Finish Date   20DEC04
Data Date   05NOV02

MIXED-USE DEVELOPMENT

AS PLANNED
(Programme '01')
All Activities

APPENDIX 5A a

Activity ID	Activity Description	Early Start	Early Finish	Orig Dur	% Comp	Rem Dur	TF
2620	Steelwork & Decking Level 4	21JAN04	03FEB04	10	0	10	0
2630	Steelwork - Theatre balcony	21JAN04	10FEB04	15	0	15	63
2640	Steelwork & Decking Level 5 - Arts Centre	12FEB04	27FEB04	12	0	12	62
2650	Secondary Steel - Level 5	12FEB04	18FEB04	5	0	5	62
2660	Steelwork & Decking - Level 7	19FEB04	03MAR04	10	0	10	62
2670	Steelwork & Decking - Level 8	04MAR04*	10MAR04	5	0	5	68
2680	Roof Slab to Escape Staircores 04 to 02	12MAR04	19MAR04	6	0	6	78
2690	Frame Complete	18MAR04	18MAR04	1	0	1	68
2700	Granite Panels Ground/Mezzanine Level	11DEC03	04FEB04	30	0	30	79
2710	Office Elev	04FEB04	17FEB04	10	0	10	79
2720	Stair Tower	24FEB04	08MAR04	10	0	10	75
2750	Other	17FEB04	22MAR04	25	0	25	91
2760	Theatre Ent	18FEB04	09JUN04	73	0	73	61
2770	Curtain Wal	18FEB04	06MAY04	50	0	50	63
2780	Stair Tower	16MAR04	20APR04	20	0	20	62
2790	Offices	18FEB04	30MAR04	30	0	30	98
2800	Metal Cladding Storey 3 to 5	17FEB04	29MAR04	30	0	30	99
2810	Theatre	02MAR04	19MAY04	50	0	50	62
2820	Render	31MAR04	18JUN04	50	0	50	62
2830	Roofing Roof Finishes Lvl 4 & 5	20JUN04	21APR04	61	0	61	0
2840	Stairs	21APR04	10MAY04	13	0	13	62
2850	Main Levels 4 & 5 Roof Areas Weathered	04MAR04	06MAY04	39	0	39	74
2860	Auditorium	04MAR04	02APR04	20	0	20	63
2870	Theatre Roof	08MAR04	02APR04	20	0	20	70
2880	Rooflights Fitness Centre	11FEB04	02MAR04	15	0	15	0
2890	Art Centre Lvl 5	09MAR04	20APR04	25	0	25	75
2910	Smoke Vents Fly Tower	05APR04	26APR04	10	0	10	70
2920	Arts Centre Roofs Weathered	07MAY04		0	0	0	63
2930	Dismantle External Scaffolds	11MAY04	22JUL04	52	0	52	61
3030	Car Park (Early Handovers) Walls/Finishes & Serv	17MAR04	18JUN04	60	0	60	64
3040	Barriers/Markings & Commission	20MAY04	09AUG04	57	0	57	64
3060	Barriers/Markings	26OCT04	20DEC04	40	0	40	0
3110	Barriers & Marking	23NOV04	20DEC04	20	0	20	0
INTERNAL FINISHES							
2730	Blockwork	19NOV03	30MAR04	85	0	85	62
2740	Curtain Walling Shop Fronts	29JAN04	07APR04	50	0	50	95
2900	Theatre	26MAR04	22APR04	14	0	14	78
2940	Blockwork Partitions/Builders Work	28JAN04	25JUN04	100	0	100	0
2950	Lift In Special Plant/Equipment Prior to Roof	11FEB04	24FEB04	10	0	10	19
2960	Service Installations/Commission	23MAR04	20DEC04	186	0	186	0
2970	Lifts & Escalator Installations	20MAY04	19OCT04	107	0	107	43
2980	Specialist Fit Out Works	18MAY04	20DEC04	153	0	153	0

Start Date	05NOV02
Finish Date	20DEC04
Data Date	05NOV02

MIXED-USE DEVELOPMENT

AS PLANNED
(Programme '01')
All Activities

APPENDIX 5A a

Activity ID	Activity Description	Early Start	Early Finish	Orig Dur	% Comp	Rem Dur	TF	2002	2003	2004
2990	Fitness Centre Shell Only Finishes	18NOV03	08MAR04	70	0	70	4			
3000	Specialist Fit Out	09MAR04	09AUG04	102	0	102	64			
3010	Shops Shell Only Finishes	28JAN04	12MAY04	69	0	69	3			
3020	Specialist Fit Out	11MAY04	12AUG04	67	0	67	61			
3050	Walls/Finishes & S	15SEP04	22NOV04	49	0	49	0			
3070	Office Area Fit Out	03AUG04	20DEC04	99	0	99	0			
3080	Remaining Retail Areas	20DEC04	20DEC04	1	0	1	0			
3100	Finishes & Service	03AUG04	22NOV04	79	0	79	0			

EXTERNAL WORKS

Activity ID	Activity Description	Early Start	Early Finish	Orig Dur	% Comp	Rem Dur	TF
3120	Statutory Service Connections	11FEB04	06APR04	40	0	40	62
3130	External Pavings Early Handovers (By Others)	08APR04	04AUG04	77	0	77	61
3140	External Pavings Remainder (By Others)	09NOV04	20DEC04	30	0	30	0

SECTIONAL COMPLETIONS

Activity ID	Activity Description	Early Start	Early Finish	Orig Dur	% Comp	Rem Dur	TF
SECT01	Show Flat (floor 03)		09FEB04	0	0	0	4
SECT02	Arts Complex (partial)		08MAR04	0	0	0	4
SECT03	Residential Floors 04 to 07(incl.)		04MAY04	0	0	0	0
SECT04	Shops		04MAY04	0	0	0	3
SECT07	Remaining Residential		20SEP04	0	0	0	0
SECT08	All Others Areas		20DEC04	0	0	0	0

Start Date	05NOV02
Finish Date	20DEC04
Data Date	05NOV02

MIXED-USE DEVELOPMENT

AS PLANNED
(Programme '01')
All Activities

APPENDIX 5A a

Activity ID	Activity Description	Orig Dur	% Comp	Rem Dur	Early Start	Early Finish	Total Float	
PRELIMINARY WORKS								
0010	Commence Preparatory Activity	0	0	0	05.NOV.02*		0	
0030	General Site Mobilisation	20	0	20	05.NOV.02	02.DEC.02	0	
0040	Commerce Main Works	1	0	1	03.DEC.02	03.DEC.02	0	
0050	Site Establishment	30	0	30	12.NOV.02	06.JAN.03	0	
0060	Pile Probing	25	0	25	19.NOV.02	06.JAN.03	0	
0070	Guide Walls	30	0	30	26.NOV.02	20.JAN.03	0	
0080	Install Secant Piles	45	0	45	10.DEC.02	24.FEB.03	0	
0090	Cut Down Piles	35	0	35	14.JAN.03	03.MAR.03	0	
0100	Preliminary Works Complete	1	0	1	04.MAR.03	04.MAR.03	0	
APARTMENT BLOCK								
SUBSTRUCTURE								
0110	FRC CAPPING BEAM	35	0	35	21.JAN.03	10.MAR.03	0	
0120	BULK DIG LEAVING SUPPORTING BERMS	74	0	74	23.JAN.03	15.MAY.03	0	
0140	ERECT TOWER CRANE	0	0	0	18.MAR.03		0	
0150	FRC BASEMENT SLAB AREA 1	9	0	9	18.MAR.03	28.MAR.03	0	
0160	INSTALL TEMPORARY WORKS JIGS 1 & 2	3	0	3	31.MAR.03	02.APR.03	0	
0170	REMOVE SIDE BERMS AREA 1	4	0	4	02.APR.03	07.APR.03	0	
0180	FRC CLOSING SECTIONS OF BASEMENT SLABS AREA 1	7	0	7	07.APR.03	15.APR.03	0	
0190	FRC WALLS AND COLUMNS LOWER - UPPER BASEMENT	16	0	16	31.MAR.03	29.APR.03	0	
0210	FRC UPPER BASEMENT SLAB AREA 1	14	0	14	04.APR.03	01.MAY.03	0	
0220	FRC BASEMENT SLAB AREA 2	10	0	10	26.MAR.03	08.APR.03	0	
0230	INSTALL TEMPORARY WORKS JIGS 3 & 4	3	0	3	10.APR.03	14.APR.03	0	
0240	REMOVE SIDE BERMS AREA 2	4	0	4	15.APR.03	28.APR.03	0	
0250	FRC CLOSING SECTIONS OF BASEMENT SLABS AREA 2	6	0	6	28.APR.03	06.MAY.03	0	
0260	FRC WALLS & COLUMNS LOWER -UPPER BAS'NT AREA 2	16	0	16	16.APR.03	12.MAY.03	0	
0280	FRC UPPER BASEMENT SLAB AREA 2	15	0	15	16.APR.03	15.MAY.03	0	
0290	RELOCATE TEMPORARY WORKS JIGS 1 & 2	3	0	3	12.MAY.03	14.MAY.03	0	
0300	INSTALL TEMP SUPPORT PROPS GL 1/A-J	22	0	22	04.APR.03	14.MAY.03	0	
0370	REMOVE BERM	5	0	5	15.MAY.03	21.MAY.03	0	
0380	BREAK BACK FEMALE PILES	4	0	4	20.MAY.03	23.MAY.03	0	
0390	FRC CLOSING SECTION OF BASEMENT SLAB GL 1/A-J	6	0	6	22.MAY.03	30.MAY.03	0	

Legend:
- The critical path
- Progress Bar
- Critical Activity

MIXED-USE DEVELOPMENT

AS PLANNED
TheCritical Path

APPENDIX 5A b

Activity ID	Activity Description	Orig Dur	% Comp	Rem Dur	Early Start	Early Finish	Total Float
0400	FRC WALLS & COLUMNS BASEMENT - UPPER BASEMENT	5	0	5	02.JUN.03	06.JUN.03	0
0410	FRC UPPER BASEMENT SLAB 1/A-J	7	0	7	05.JUN.03	13.JUN.03	0
0420	INSTALL TEMP SUPPORT PROPS GL 1/M-R	14	0	14	01.APR.03*	28.APR.03	0
0470	REMOVE BERM	4	0	4	29.APR.03	02.MAY.03	0
0480	BREAK BACK FEMALE PILES	3	0	3	02.MAY.03	07.MAY.03	0
0490	FRC CLOSING SECTION OF BASEMENT SLAB GL 1/M-R	5	0	5	07.MAY.03	13.MAY.03	0
0500	FRC WALLS & COLUMNS BASEMENT - UPPER BASEMENT	4	0	4	14.MAY.03	19.MAY.03	0
0510	FRC UPPER BASEMENT SLAB GL 1/M-R	6	0	6	19.MAY.03	27.MAY.03	0
0520	INSTALL TEMP SUPPORT PROPS GL 1/J-M	18	0	18	09.APR.03*	13.MAY.03	0
0580	REMOVE BERM	4	0	4	14.MAY.03	19.MAY.03	0
0590	FRC CLOSING SECTION OF BASEMENT SLAB GL 1/J-M	5	0	5	15.MAY.03	21.MAY.03	0
0600	FRC WALLS & COLUMNS BASEMENT - UPPER BASEMENT	6	0	6	22.MAY.03	30.MAY.03	0
0610	FRC UPPER BASEMENT SLAB GL 1/J-M	6	0	6	30.MAY.03	06.JUN.03	0
0620	FRC Walls/Columns Upper Basement- Ground Floor	40	0	40	13.MAY.03	08.JUL.03	0
0630	Substructure Residential Complete	0	0	0	09.JUL.03		0

ARTS CENTRE
SUBSTRUCTURE

Activity ID	Activity Description	Orig Dur	% Comp	Rem Dur	Early Start	Early Finish	Total Float
0640	Crane Base	5	0	5	01.JUL.03	07.JUL.03	0
0660	FRC BASEMENT SLAB AREA 3	10	0	10	01.MAY.03	15.MAY.03	0
0700	FRC BASEMENT SLAB AREA 4	14	0	14	13.MAY.03	02.JUN.03	0
0740	FRC WALLS & COLUMNS LOWER -UPPER BAS'NT AREA 3	26	0	26	16.MAY.03	23.JUN.03	0
0760	FRC UPPER BASEMENT SLAB AREA 3	26	0	26	21.MAY.03	26.JUN.03	0
0770	RELOCATE TEMPORARY WORKS JIGS 3 & 4	3	0	3	06.JUN.03	10.JUN.03	0
0780	REMOVE SIDE BERMS AREA 4	5	0	5	10.JUN.03	16.JUN.03	0
0810	FRC CLOSING SECTIONS OF BASEMENT SLABS AREA 4	5	0	5	16.JUN.03	20.JUN.03	0
0820	FRC WALLS & COLUMNS LOWER -UPPER BAS'NT AREA 4	21	0	21	29.MAY.03	26.JUN.03	0
0840	FRC UPPER BASEMENT SLAB 4	20	0	20	04.JUN.03	01.JUL.03	0
0850	RELOCATE TEMPORARY WORKS JIGS 1 & 2	3	0	3	27.JUN.03	01.JUL.03	0
0860	REMOVE SIDE BERMS AREA 5	5	0	5	01.JUL.03	07.JUL.03	0
0870	FRC LOW SECTION OF BASEM'T SLAB AREA 6	8	0	8	04.JUN.03	13.JUN.03	0
0880	FRC WALLS LOW - HIGH BASEMENT SLAB AREA 6	5	0	5	16.JUN.03	20.JUN.03	0
0890	FRC INTERMEDIATE SLAB AREA 6	4	0	4	23.JUN.03	26.JUN.03	0
0900	FRC WALLS FROM INTERMEDIATE TO HIGH LVL SLAB A6	3	0	3	27.JUN.03	01.JUL.03	0

▬▬▬ The critical path
▬▬▬ Progress Bar
▬▬▬ Critical Activity

MIXED-USE DEVELOPMENT

AS PLANNED
TheCritical Path

Sheet 2 of 7

APPENDIX 5A b

Activity ID	Activity Description	Orig Dur	% Comp	Rem Dur	Early Start	Early Finish	Total Float
0910	FRC HIGH LEVEL BASEMENT SLAB AREA 6	10	0	10	23.JUN.03	04.JUL.03	0
0960	RELOCATE TEMPORARY WORKS JIGS 3 & 4	3	0	3	07.JUL.03	09.JUL.03	0
0970	REMOVE SIDE BERMS AREA 6	5	0	5	09.JUL.03	15.JUL.03	0
0980	FRC BASEMENT SLAB SECTION 7	10	0	10	03.JUL.03	16.JUL.03	■
0990	FRC CLOSING SECTIONS OF BASEMENT SLABS AREA 6	4	0	4	15.JUL.03	18.JUL.03	0
1000	FRC WALLS & COLUMNS LOWER -UPPER BAS'NT AREA 6	13	0	13	07.JUL.03	23.JUL.03	0
1010	FRC UPPER BASEMENT SLAB 6	15	0	15	11.JUL.03	31.JUL.03	0
1040	FRC BASEMENT SLAB SECTION 8	10	0	10	15.JUL.03	28.JUL.03	0
1060	FRC WALLS & COLUMNS LOWER -UPPER BAS'NT AREA 7	26	0	26	17.JUL.03	21.AUG.03	0
1080	FRC UPPER BASEMENT SLAB 7	33	0	33	23.JUL.03	08.SEP.03	0
1090	RELOCATE TEMPORARY WORKS JIGS 3 & 4	3	0	3	01.AUG.03	05.AUG.03	0
1100	REMOVE SIDE BERMS AREA 8	5	0	5	05.AUG.03	11.AUG.03	0
1110	FRC CLOSING SECTIONS OF BASEMENT SLABS AREA 8	6	0	6	11.AUG.03	18.AUG.03	0
1120	FRC WALLS & COLUMNS LOWER -UPPER BAS'NT AREA 8	19	0	19	29.JUL.03	22.AUG.03	0
1140	FRC UPPER BASEMENT SLAB AREA 8	25	0	25	04.AUG.03	08.SEP.03	0
1150	INSTALL SUPPORTING PROPS TO PILES ADJ. TO GL 17	7	0	7	29.JUL.03	06.AUG.03	0
1160	REMOVE SUPPORTING BERM	10	0	10	05.AUG.03	18.AUG.03	0
1170	FRC CLOSING SECTION OF BASEMENT SLAB	12	0	12	13.AUG.03	29.AUG.03	0
1180	FRC WALLS / COLUMNS LOWER - UPPER BASEMENT	11	0	11	21.AUG.03	05.SEP.03	0
1190	FRC CLOSING SECTION OF UPPER BASEMENT SLAB	11	0	11	01.SEP.03	15.SEP.03	0
1200	2 Week Allowance For Breaking Back Female Piles	10	0	10	30.JUN.03	11.JUL.03	0
1210	FRC Columns / Walls Upper Basement - Ground	60	0	60	14.JUL.03	06.OCT.03	0
1220	Substructure Arts Centre Complete	1	0	1	07.OCT.03	07.OCT.03	0

APARTMENT BLOCK
SUPERSTRUCTURE

Activity ID	Activity Description	Orig Dur	% Comp	Rem Dur	Early Start	Early Finish	Total Float
1230	Substructure Residential Complete	0	0	0	09.JUL.03		0
1240	FRC GF Slab Incl Part Sect. Of Area 3 GL 1-7/A-H	13	0	13	25.JUN.03	11.JUL.03	0
1250	FRC Ground Floor Slab Low Level GL 1-7/M-R	10	0	10	23.JUN.03	04.JUL.03	0
1260	FRC Remaining High Level Section Of GF SLAB	11	0	11	03.JUL.03	17.JUL.03	0
1270	FRC Walls / Columns Ground - Mezz	11	0	11	07.JUL.03	21.JUL.03	0
1280	FRC Mezz Floor Grid Lines 1-7/A-D	7	0	7	16.JUL.03	24.JUL.03	0
1300	FRC Walls / Columns Mezz- 2nd Floor	10	0	10	25.JUL.03	07.AUG.03	0
1330	FRC 2nd Floor Slab GL 1-7/M-R	8	0	8	01.AUG.03	12.AUG.03	0

The critical path
Progress Bar
Critical Activity

MIXED-USE DEVELOPMENT

AS PLANNED
TheCritical Path

APPENDIX 5A b

Sheet 3 of 7

Activity ID	Activity Description	Orig Dur	Rem Dur	% Comp	Early Start	Early Finish	Total Float
1340	FRC 2nd Floor Slab 1-7/A-F	10	10	0	04 AUG 03	15 AUG 03	0
1350	FRC Walls/Columns 2nd - 3rd/4th Floor	15	15	0	08 AUG 03	29 AUG 03	0
1360	FRC 3rd Floor Slab GL 1-7/F-M	11	11	0	14 AUG 03	29 AUG 03	0
1390	FRC Walls / Columns 3rd - 4th Floor	13	13	0	01 SEP 03	17 SEP 03	0
1420	FRC 4th Floor Slab GL 1-3/J-R/ + 4-7/L-P	13	13	0	04 SEP 03	22 SEP 03	0
1440	FRC 4th Floor Slab GL 6-7/M-R	10	10	0	16 SEP 03	29 SEP 03	0
1450	FRC Walls / Columns 4th - 5th Floor	14	14	0	16 SEP 03	03 OCT 03	0
1460	FRC 5th Floor Slab GL 1-6/K-R	11	11	0	17 SEP 03	01 OCT 03	0
1470	FRC 5th Floor Slab GL 1-6/A-K	12	12	0	23 SEP 03	08 OCT 03	0
1480	FRC Walls/Columns 5th - 6th Floor	12	12	0	02 OCT 03	17 OCT 03	0
1490	FRC 6th Floor Slab GL 1-6/K-R	11	11	0	07 OCT 03	21 OCT 03	0
1500	FRC 6th Floor Slab GL 1-6/A-K	11	11	0	09 OCT 03	23 OCT 03	0
1510	FRC Walls / Columns 6th - 7th Floor	10	10	0	22 OCT 03	04 NOV 03	0
1520	FRC 7th Floor Slab GL 1-6/K-R	11	11	0	27 OCT 03	10 NOV 03	0
1530	FRC 7th Floor Slab GL 1-6/A-K	11	11	0	30 OCT 03	13 NOV 03	0
1540	FRC Walls/Columns 7th - 8th Floor	10	10	0	11 NOV 03	24 NOV 03	0
1550	FRC 8th Floor Slab GL 1-6/K-R	10	10	0	17 NOV 03	28 NOV 03	0
1560	FRC 8th Floor Slab GL 1-6/A-K	11	11	0	24 NOV 03	08 DEC 03	0
1570	FRC Walls / Column 8th - 9th Floor	12	12	0	01 DEC 03	16 DEC 03	0
1580	FRC 9th Floor Slab GL 1-6/K-R	10	10	0	05 DEC 03	18 DEC 03	0
1590	FRC 9th Floor Slab GL 1-6/A-K	11	11	0	16 DEC 03	13 JAN 04	0
1600	FRC Walls / Columns 9th - 10th Floor	12	12	0	19 DEC 03	19 JAN 04	0
1610	FRC 10th Floor SlabGL 1-6/K-R	11	11	0	08 JAN 04	22 JAN 04	0
1620	FRC 10th Floor SlabGL 1-6/A-K	11	11	0	19 JAN 04	02 FEB 04	0
1630	FRC Walls / Columns 10th - 11th Floor	12	12	0	23 JAN 04	09 FEB 04	0
1640	FRC 11th Floor Slab GL 1-6/K-R	11	11	0	29 JAN 04	12 FEB 04	0
1650	FRC 11th Floor Slab GL 1-6/A-K	12	12	0	03 FEB 04	18 FEB 04	0
1660	FRC Walls / Columns 11th - 12th Floor	12	12	0	13 FEB 04	01 MAR 04	0
1670	FRC 12th Floor Slab GL 1-6/K-R	11	11	0	19 FEB 04	04 MAR 04	0
1680	FRC 12th Floor Slab GL 1-6/A-K	11	11	0	26 FEB 04	11 MAR 04	0
1690	FRC Walls / Columns 12th - 13th Floor	11	11	0	05 MAR 04	19 MAR 04	0
1700	FRC 13th Floor Slab GL 1-6/K-R	9	9	0	11 MAR 04	23 MAR 04	0
1710	FRC 13th Floor Slab GL 1-6/A-K	8	8	0	16 MAR 04	25 MAR 04	0
1720	FRC Walls / Columns 13th - 14th Floor	7	7	0	24 MAR 04	01 APR 04	0

MIXED-USE DEVELOPMENT

AS PLANNED
The Critical Path

APPENDIX 5A b

The critical path
Progress Bar
Critical Activity

Activity ID	Activity Description	Orig Dur	% Comp	Rem Dur	Early Start	Early Finish	Total Float
1730	FRC 14th Floor Slab GL 1-6/K-R	7	0	7	29 MAR 04	06 APR 04	0
1740	FRC 14th Floor Slab GL 1-6/A-K	7	0	7	31 MAR 04	08 APR 04	0
1750	FRC Walls/ Columns 14th - 15th Floor	9	0	9	07 APR 04	27 APR 04	0
1760	FRC 15th Floor Slab GL 1-6/K-R	11	0	11	20 APR 04	05 MAY 04	0
1780	FRC Core Walls Level 15-16 GL A-B/2-5	6	0	6	06 MAY 04	13 MAY 04	0
1790	FRC Core Walls Level 16-Roof GL A-B/2-5	9	0	9	14 MAY 04	26 MAY 04	0
1800	FRC Cover Slab To Core	9	0	9	27 MAY 04	09 JUN 04	0
1810	Progressive Erection of Precast Stairs	177	0	177	19 SEP 03	17 JUN 04	0
1860	Timber Grounds Windows & Doors	162	0	162	17 DEC 03	24 AUG 04	0
1870	Render Insulation & First Coat	142	0	142	11 FEB 04	08 SEP 04	0
1880	Terracotta Cladding Frame Work	137	0	137	25 FEB 04	15 SEP 04	0
1890	Metal Cladding	142	0	142	03 MAR 04	29 SEP 04	0
1910	Terracotta Panels	112	0	112	29 APR 04	06 OCT 04	0
1950	Penthouse Brise Soleil	30	0	30	04 AUG 04	15 SEP 04	0
1960	Penthouse Curtain Walling	40	0	40	11 AUG 04	06 OCT 04	0
1970	Penthouse Roof Cladding/Roof Lights	40	0	40	11 AUG 04	06 OCT 04	0
1980	Render Final Coat Top Down	59	0	59	09 SEP 04	30 NOV 04	0
1990	Bolt On Balconies	54	0	54	23 SEP 04	07 DEC 04	0
2000	Dismatle Scaffolds	59	0	59	29 SEP 04	20 DEC 04	0
2050	Penthouse Roof Weathered	1	0	1	07 OCT 04	07 OCT 04	0
2100	Lift Shaft Temporary Weathered	9	0	9	10 JUN 04	22 JUN 04	0
INTERNAL FINISHES							
1850	Blockwork	181	0	181	23 OCT 03	27 JUL 04	0
1900	Balcony/Balustrades & Finishes	147	0	147	17 MAR 04	20 OCT 04	0
2060	Internal Blockwork to Cores	182	0	182	10 DEC 03	15 SEP 04	0
2070	M & E Services to Cores & Risers	171	0	171	17 MAR 04	23 NOV 04	0
2080	Staircase Lobbies & Common Areas	171	0	171	17 MAR 04	23 NOV 04	0
2110	Lift installations	98	0	98	23 JUN 04	08 NOV 04	0
2120	Final Commision Clean & Snag	58	0	58	30 SEP 04	20 DEC 04	0
2130	Shell & Core Completion	1	0	1	20 DEC 04	20 DEC 04	0
2200	Access For Third Fit Out Phase	0	0	0	22 SEP 04		0
2210	Third Phase Notional Fit Out Period	64	0	64	22 SEP 04	20 DEC 04	0

▬▬▬	The critical path
▬▬▬	Progress Bar
▬▬▬	Critical Activity

MIXED-USE DEVELOPMENT

AS PLANNED
TheCritical Path

APPENDIX 5A b

Sheet 5 of 7

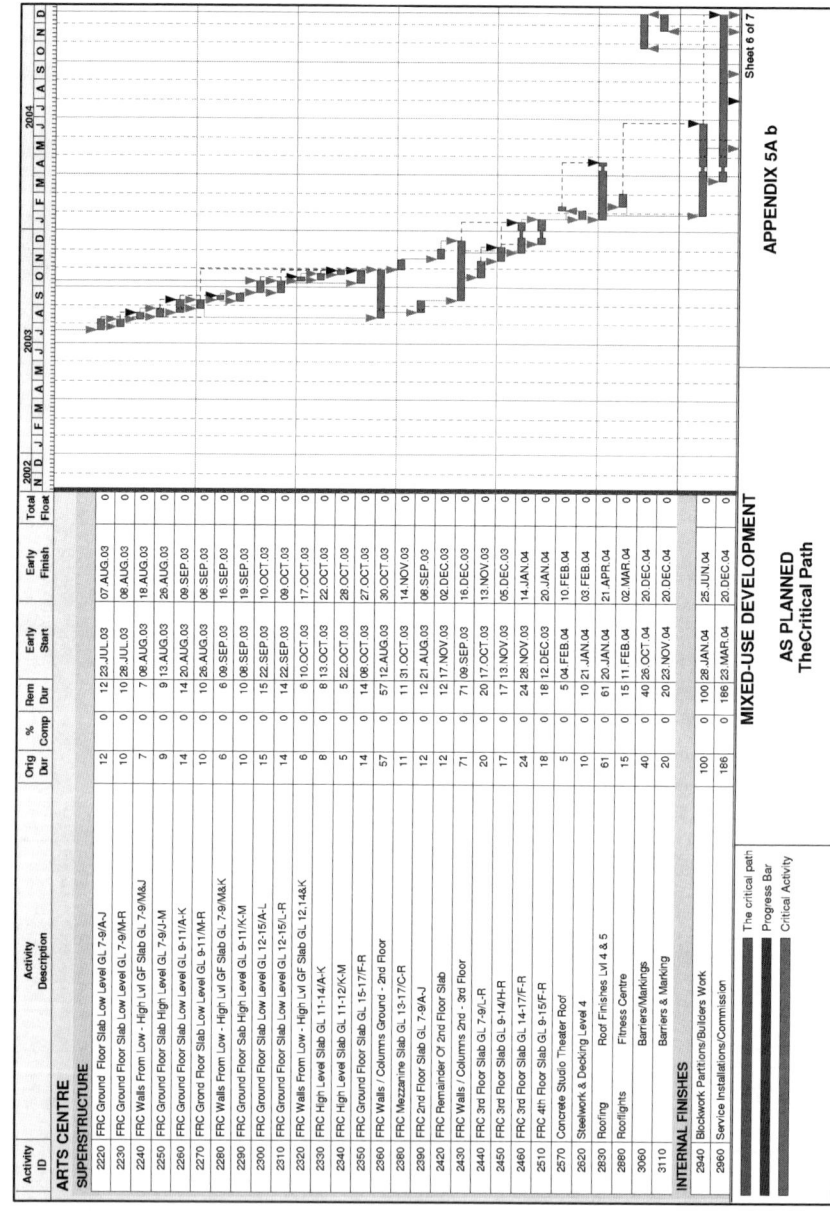

Activity ID	Activity Description	Orig Dur	% Comp	Rem Dur	Early Start	Early Finish	Total Float
ARTS CENTRE							
SUPERSTRUCTURE							
2220	FRC Ground Floor Slab Low Level GL 7-9/A-J	12	0	12	23 JUL 03	07 AUG 03	0
2230	FRC Ground Floor Slab Low Level GL 7-9/M-R	10	0	10	28 JUL 03	08 AUG 03	0
2240	FRC Walls From Low - High Lvl GF Slab GL 7-9/M&J	7	0	7	08 AUG 03	18 AUG 03	0
2250	FRC Ground Floor Slab High Level GL 7-9/J-M	9	0	9	13 AUG 03	26 AUG 03	0
2260	FRC Ground Floor Slab Low Level GL 9-11/A-K	14	0	14	20 AUG 03	09 SEP 03	0
2270	FRC Grond Floor Slab Low Level GL 9-11/M-R	10	0	10	26 AUG 03	08 SEP 03	0
2280	FRC Walls From Low - High Lvl GF Slab GL 7-9/M&K	6	0	6	09 SEP 03	16 SEP 03	0
2290	FRC Ground Floor Sab High Level GL 9-11/K-M	10	0	10	08 SEP 03	19 SEP 03	0
2300	FRC Ground Floor Slab Low Level GL 12-15/A-L	15	0	15	22 SEP 03	10 OCT 03	0
2310	FRC Ground Floor Slab Low Level GL 12-15/L-R	14	0	14	22 SEP 03	09 OCT 03	0
2320	FRC Walls From Low - High Lvl GF Slab GL 12,14&K	6	0	6	10 OCT 03	17 OCT 03	0
2330	FRC High Level Slab GL 11-14/A-K	8	0	8	13 OCT 03	22 OCT 03	0
2340	FRC High Level Slab GL 11-12/K-M	5	0	5	22 OCT 03	28 OCT 03	0
2350	FRC Ground Floor Slab GL 15-17/F-R	14	0	14	08 OCT 03	27 OCT 03	0
2360	FRC Walls / Columns Ground - 2nd Floor	57	0	57	12 AUG 03	30 OCT 03	0
2380	FRC Mezzanine Slab GL 13-17/C-R	11	0	11	31 OCT 03	14 NOV 03	0
2390	FRC 2nd Floor Slab GL 7-9/A-J	12	0	12	21 AUG 03	08 SEP 03	0
2420	FRC Remainder Of 2nd Floor Slab	12	0	12	17 NOV 03	02 DEC 03	0
2430	FRC Walls / Columns 2nd - 3rd Floor	71	0	71	09 SEP 03	16 DEC 03	0
2440	FRC 3rd Floor Slab GL 7-9/..-R	20	0	20	17 OCT 03	13 NOV 03	0
2450	FRC 3rd Floor Slab GL 9-14/H-R	17	0	17	13 NOV 03	05 DEC 03	0
2460	FRC 3rd Floor Slab GL 14-17/F-R	24	0	24	28 NOV 03	14 JAN 04	0
2510	FRC 4th Floor Slab GL 9-15/F-R	18	0	18	12 DEC 03	20 JAN 04	0
2570	Concrete Studio Theater Roof	5	0	5	04 FEB 04	10 FEB 04	0
2620	Steelwork & Decking Level 4	10	0	10	21 JAN 04	03 FEB 04	0
2830	Roofing Roof Finishes Lvl 4 & 5	61	0	61	20 JAN 04	21 APR 04	0
2880	Rooflights Fitness Centre	15	0	15	11 FEB 04	02 MAR 04	0
3060	Barriers/Markings	40	0	40	26 OCT 04	20 DEC 04	0
3110	Barriers & Marking	20	0	20	23 NOV 04	20 DEC 04	0
INTERNAL FINISHES							
2940	Blockwork Partitions/Builders Work	100	0	100	28 JAN 04	25 JUN 04	0
2960	Service Installations/Commission	186	0	186	23 MAR 04	20 DEC 04	0

MIXED-USE DEVELOPMENT

AS PLANNED
The Critical Path

The critical path
Progress Bar
Critical Activity

APPENDIX 5A b

Sheet 6 of 7

Activity ID	Activity Description	Orig Dur	% Comp	Rem Dur	Early Start	Early Finish	Total Float
2980	Specialist Fit Out Works	153	0	153	18 MAY 04	20 DEC 04	0
3050	Walls/Finishes & S	49	0	49	15 SEP 04	22 NOV 04	0
3070	Office Area Fit Out	99	0	99	03 AUG 04	20 DEC 04	0
3080	Remaining Retail Areas	1	0	1	20 DEC 04	20 DEC 04	0
3100	Finishes & Service	79	0	79	03 AUG 04	22 NOV 04	0

EXTERNAL WORKS

| 3140 | External Pavings Remainder (By Others) | 30 | 0 | 30 | 09 NOV 04 | 20 DEC 04 | 0 |

SECTIONAL COMPLETIONS

| SECT08 | All Others Areas | 0 | 0 | 0 | | 20 DEC 04 | 0 |

The critical path
Progress Bar
Critical Activity

MIXED-USE DEVELOPMENT

AS PLANNED
TheCritical Path

APPENDIX 5A b

Mixed-use Development
Progress Schedule

Activ. ID	Activity Description	Actual Start	Actual Finish	05-Jan End Wk 5 Wind.1	02-Feb End Wk 9 Wind.2	02-Mar End Wk 13 Wind.3	30-Mar End Wk 17 Wind.4	04-May End Wk 22 Wind.5	08-Jun End Wk 27 Wind.6	29-Jun End Wk 30 Wind.7	03-Aug End Wk 35 Wind.8	05-Oct End Wk 44 Wind.9	02-Nov End Wk 48 Wind.10
10	Commence Preparatory Activity	05-Nov-02	----	100									
20	Commence On Site	03-Dec-02	----	100									
PRELIMINARY WORKS													
30	General Site Mobilisation	06-Nov-02	04-Dec-02	100									
40	Commence Main Works	05-Dec-02	05-Dec-02	100									
50	Site Establishment	06-Nov-02	29-Nov-02	100									
60	Pile Probing	13-Nov-02	14-Feb-03	70	90	100							
70	Guide Walls	05-Dec-02	01-Mar-03	50	90	100							
80	Install Secant Piles	11-Dec-02	20-Mar-03	14	60	85	100						
90	Cut Down Piles	16-Dec-02	17-May-03	10	18	25	70	88	100				
100	Preliminary Works Complete	----	17-May-03					0	100				
APARTMENT BLOCK													
Substructure													
110	FRC CAPPING BEAM (ALL AREAS)	18-Feb-03	14-Jun-03		0	15	40	40	85	100			
120	BULK DIG LEAVING SUPPORTING BERMS	20-Feb-03	16-May-03		0	10	30	70	100				
130	FRC SECTION OF AREA 3 SLAB FOR TOWER CRANE 1	06-Mar-03	05-Apr-03			0	25	100					
140	ERECT TOWER CRANE	15-Apr-03	15-Apr-03				0	100					
150	FRC BASEMENT SLAB AREA 1	10-Apr-03	29-Apr-03				0	100					
160	INSTALL TEMPORARY WORKS JIGS 1 & 2	08-Apr-03	01-May-03				0	100					
170	REMOVE SIDE BERMS AREA 1	02-Jun-03	19-Jun-03					0	50	100			
180	FRC CLOSING SECTIONS OF BASEMENT SLABS AREA 1	12-Jun-03	10-Jul-03						0	70	100		
190	FRC WALLS AND COLUMNS LOWER - UPPER BASEMENT	01-May-03	15-May-03					0	10	100			
210	FRC UPPER BASEMENT SLAB AREA 1	08-May-03	28-May-03					0	100				
220	FRC BASEMENT SLAB AREA 2	03-Apr-03	03-May-03				0	100					
230	INSTALL TEMPORARY WORKS JIGS 3 & 4	06-May-03	15-May-03					0	100				
240	REMOVE SIDE BERMS AREA 2	19-May-03	26-Jun-03					0	50	100			
250	FRC CLOSING SECTIONS OF BASEMENT SLABS AREA 2	16-Jun-03	17-Jul-03						0	75	100		
260	FRC WALLS & COLUMNS LOWER -UPPER BASNT AREA 2	08-May-03	22-May-03					0	100				
280	FRC UPPER BASEMENT SLAB AREA 2	08-May-03	22-May-03					0	100				
290	RELOCATE TEMPORARY WORKS JIGS 1 & 2	23-Jun-03	25-Sep-03						0	50	68	100	
300	INSTALL TEMP SUPPORT PROPS GL 1/A-J	23-Jun-03	24-Jul-03						0	27	100		
370	REMOVE BERM	21-May-03	23-Jun-03					0	50	100			
380	BREAK BACK FEMALE PILES	10-Jun-03	14-Jun-03						0	100			
390	FRC CLOSING SECTION OF BASEMENT SLAB GL 1/A-J	12-Jun-03	26-Jun-03						0	100			
400	FRC WALLS & COLUMNS BASEMENT - UPPER BASEMENT	03-Jul-03	17-Jul-03							0	100		
410	FRC UPPER BASEMENT SLAB GL 1/A-J	03-Jul-03	31-Jul-03							0	100		
420	INSTALL TEMP SUPPORT PROPS GL 1/M-R	10-Jul-03	24-Jul-03							0	100		
470	REMOVE BERM	12-Jun-03	18-Jun-03						0	100			
480	BREAK BACK FEMALE PILES	12-Jun-03	26-Jun-03						0	100			
490	FRC CLOSING SECTION OF BASEMENT SLAB GL 1/M-R	01-Jul-03	05-Jul-03							0	100		
500	FRC WALLS & COLUMNS BASEMENT - UPPER BASEMENT	01-Jul-03	24-Jul-03							0	100		
510	FRC UPPER BASEMENT SLAB GL 1/M-R	01-Jul-03	31-Jul-03							0	100		
520	INSTALL TEMP SUPPORT PROPS GL 1/U-M	17-Jul-03	31-Jul-03							0	100		
580	REMOVE BERM	12-Jun-03	26-Jun-03						0	100			
590	FRC CLOSING SECTION OF BASEMENT SLAB GL 1/U-M	01-Jul-03	10-Jul-03							0	100		
600	FRC WALLS & COLUMNS BASEMENT - UPPER BASEMENT	01-Jul-03	27-Jul-03							0	100		
610	FRC UPPER BASEMENT SLAB GL 1/U-M	01-Jul-03	05-Aug-03							0	83	100	
620	FRC Walls/Columns Upper Basement- Ground Floor	05-Jun-03	04-Oct-03							0	23	62	100
Superstructure													
1240	FRC GF Slab Incl Part Section Of Area 3 GL 1-7/A-H	03-Jul-02	24-Jul-02							0	100		
1250	FRC Ground Floor Slab Low Level GL 1-7/M-R	29-May-02	19-Jun-02					0	60	100			
1260	FRC Remaining High Level Section Of GF SLAB	14-Aug-02	11-Sep-02							0	100		
1270	FRC Walls / Columns Ground - Mezz	21-Aug-02	04-Sep-02							0	100		
1280	FRC Mezz Floor Grid Lines 1-7/A-D	03-Sep-02	24-Oct-03								0	79	100
1290	FRC Mezz Floor Grid Lines 1-7/M-R	03-Sep-02	02-Oct-02								0	100	
1300	FRC Walls / Columns Mezz- 2nd Floor	11-Sep-02	11-Oct-02								0	75	100
1310	FRC Walls / Columns Ground - 2nd Floor	31-Jul-02	30-Oct-02							0	62	77	100
1320	FRC 2nd Floor Slab GL 1-7/F-M	06-Sep-02	25-Oct-02								0	25	100
1330	FRC 2nd Floor Slab GL 1-7/M-R	06-Sep-02	25-Oct-02								0	69	100
1340	FRC 2nd Floor Slab 1-7/A-F	06-Sep-02	25-Oct-02								0	100	
1350	FRC Walls/Columns 2nd - 3rd/4th Floor	02-Oct-02									0	7	97
1360	FRC 3rd Floor Slab GL 1-7/F-M	21-Oct-02									0	1	100
1370	FRC 3rd Floor Slab GL 1-7/M-R	21-Oct-02									0	23	
1380	FRC 3rd Floor Slab GL 1-7/A-F	21-Oct-02									0	5	

No other Apartment Block activities progressed in 'Time Period One'

ARTS CENTRE

Substructure

Activ ID	Activity Description	Actual Start	Actual Finish	05-Jan End Wk 5 Wind.1	02-Feb End Wk 9 Wind.2	02-Mar End Wk 13 Wind.3	30-Mar End Wk 17 Wind.4	04-May End Wk 22 Wind.5	08-Jun End Wk 27 Wind.6	29-Jun End Wk 30 Wind.7	03-Aug End Wk 35 Wind.8	05-Oct End Wk 44 Wind.9	02-Nov End Wk 48 Wind.10
660	FRC BASEMENT SLAB AREA 3	28-Apr-03	15-May-02				0	60	100				
670	RELOCATE TEMPORARY WORKS JIGS 1 & 2	02-May-03	22-May-02				0	70	100				
680	FRC LOW LEVEL BASEMENT SLAB AREA 4	29-May-02	05-Jun-02					0	100				
690	FRC WALLS LOW - HIGH LEVEL AREA 4 GL 8-9/P-M	12-Jun-02	26-Jun-02						0	100			
700	FRC BASEMENT SLAB AREA 4	02-May-02	22-May-02				0	40	100				
720	FRC CLOSING SECTIONS OF BASEMENT SLABS AREA 3	12-Jun-02	24-Jul-02						0	50	100		
730	FRC LIFT PITS IN CLOSING SECTION OF B3 GL Q-P/7-8	29-May-02	05-Jun-02					0	100				
740	FRC WALLS & COLUMNS LOWER -UPPER BAS'NT AREA 3	05-Jun-02	30-Jul-02					0	25	80	100		
760	FRC UPPER BASEMENT SLAB AREA 3	22-May-02	26-Jun-02					0	70	100			
770	RELOCATE TEMPORARY WORKS JIGS 3 & 4	03-Jul-02	31-Jul-02							0	100		
780	REMOVE SIDE BERMS AREA 4	12-Jun-02	26-Jun-02						0	100			
790	FRC RAMP AND WALLS BASEM'T SLAB AREA 5 GL 9-10/H-E	12-Jun-02	04-Sep-02						0	60	88	100	
800	FRC BASEMENT SLAB AREA 5	05-Jun-02	12-Jun-02					0	50	100			
810	FRC CLOSING SECTIONS OF BASEMENT SLABS AREA 4	07-Aug-02	01-Oct-02								0	100	
820	FRC WALLS & COLUMNS LOWER -UPPER BAS'NT AREA 4	29-May-02	26-Jun-02					0	40	100			
840	FRC UPPER BASEMENT SLAB 4	19-Jun-02	03-Jul-02						0	80	100		
850	RELOCATE TEMPORARY WORKS JIGS 1 & 2	03-Jul-02	31-Jul-02							0	100		
860	REMOVE SIDE BERMS AREA 5	22-May-02	05-Jun-02					0	100				
870	FRC LOW SECTION OF BASEM'T SLAB AREA 6	26-Jun-02	03-Jul-02						0	80	100		
880	FRC WALLS LOW - HIGH BASEMENT SLAB AREA 6	03-Jun-02	07-Jun-02					0	100				
890	FRC INTERMEDIATE SLAB AREA 6	03-Jul-02	17-Jul-02							0	100		
900	FRC WALLS FROM INTERMEDIATE TO HIGH LEVEL SLAB A6	03-Jul-02	02-Oct-02							0	36	100	
910	FRC HIGH LEVEL BASEMENT SLAB AREA 6	19-Jun-02	26-Jun-02						0	100			
920	FRC CLOSING SECTIONS OF BASEMENT SLABS AREA 5	12-Jun-02	17-Jul-02						0	50	100		
930	FRC WALLS & COLUMNS LOWER -UPPER BAS'NT AREA 5	24-Jul-02	07-Aug-02							0	50	100	
950	FRC UPPER BASEMENT SLAB 5	07-Aug-02	14-Aug-02								0	100	
960	RELOCATE TEMPORARY WORKS JIGS 3 & 4	29-Jul-02	02-Aug-02							0	100		
970	REMOVE SIDE BERMS AREA 6	03-Jul-02	31-Jul-02							0	100		
980	FRC BASEMENT SLAB SECTION 7	31-Jul-02	14-Aug-02							0	30	100	
990	FRC CLOSING SECTIONS OF BASEMENT SLABS AREA 6	31-Jul-02	14-Aug-02							0	30	100	
1000	FRC WALLS & COLUMNS LOWER -UPPER BAS'NT AREA 6	14-Aug-02	21-Aug-02								0	100	
1010	FRC UPPER BASEMENT SLAB 6	27-Aug-02	04-Sep-02								0	100	
1020	RELOCATE TEMPORARY WORKS JIGS 1 & 2	27-Jul-02	02-Aug-02							0	100		
1030	REMOVE SIDE BERMS AREA 7	17-Jul-02	31-Jul-02							0	100		
1040	FRC BASEMENT SLAB SECTION 8	07-Aug-02	21-Aug-02								0	100	
1050	FRC CLOSING SECTIONS OF BASEMENT SLABS AREA 7	31-Jul-02	14-Aug-02							0	30	100	
1060	FRC WALLS & COLUMNS LOWER -UPPER BAS'NT AREA 7	21-Aug-02	04-Sep-02								0	100	
1080	FRC UPPER BASEMENT SLAB 7	07-Aug-02	18-Sep-02								0	100	
1090	RELOCATE TEMPORARY WORKS JIGS 3 & 4	29-Jul-02	02-Aug-02							0	100		
1100	REMOVE SIDE BERMS AREA 8	24-Jul-02	07-Aug-02							0	70	100	
1110	FRC CLOSING SECTIONS OF BASEMENT SLABS AREA 8	07-Aug-02	21-Aug-02								0	100	
1120	FRC WALLS & COLUMNS LOWER -UPPER BAS'NT AREA 8	27-Aug-02	11-Sep-02								0	100	
1140	FRC UPPER BASEMENT SLAB AREA 8	04-Sep-02	25-Sep-02								0	100	
1150	INSTALL SUPPORTING PROPS TO PILES ADJACENT TO GL 17	29-Jul-02	02-Aug-02							0	100		
1160	REMOVE SUPPORTING BERM	05-Aug-02	09-Aug-02								0	100	
1170	FRC CLOSING SECTION OF BASEMENT SLAB	05-Aug-02	28-Aug-02								0	100	
1180	FRC WALLS / COLUMNS LOWER - UPPER BASEMENT	05-Aug-02	11-Sep-02								0	100	
1190	FRC CLOSING SECTION OF UPPER BASEMENT SLAB	05-Aug-02	25-Sep-02								0	100	
1200	2 Week Allowance For Breaking Back Female Piles	03-Jul-02	31-Jul-02							0	100		
1210	FRC Columns / Walls Upper Basement - Ground	31-Jul-02	02-Oct-02							0	35	100	
1220	Substructure Arts & Leisure Centre Complete	02-Oct-02	02-Oct-02								0	100	

Superstructure

Activ ID	Activity Description	Actual Start	Actual Finish	Wk5	Wk9	Wk13	Wk17	Wk22	Wk27	Wk30	Wk35	Wk44	Wk48
2220	FRC Ground Floor Slab Low Level GL 7-9/A-J	12-Jun-02	10-Jul-02						0	70	100		
2230	FRC Ground Floor Slab Low Level GL 7-9/M-R	18-Sep-02	02-Oct-02								0	100	
2240	FRC Walls From Low - High Level GF Slab GL 7-9/M & J	30-Sep-02	04-Oct-02								0	100	
2250	FRC Ground Floor Slab High Level GL 7-9/J-M	26-Jun-02	17-Jul-02						0	20	100		
2260	FRC Ground Floor Slab Low Level GL 9-11/A-K	25-Sep-02	02-Oct-02								0	100	
2270	FRC Grond Floor Slab Low Level GL 9-11/M-R	14-Aug-02	11-Sep-02								0	100	
2280	FRC Walls From Low - High Level GF Slab GL 7-9/M & K	30-Sep-02	04-Oct-02								0	100	
2290	FRC Ground Floor Sab High Level GL 9-11/K-M	17-Jul-02	31-Jul-02							0	100		
2300	FRC Ground Floor Slab Low Level GL 12-15/A-L	30-Sep-02	04-Oct-02								0	100	
2310	FRC Ground Floor Slab Low Level GL 12-15/L-R	14-Aug-02	25-Sep-02								0	100	
2320	FRC Walls From Low - High Level GF Slab GL 12,14 & K	30-Sep-02	04-Oct-02								0	100	
2330	FRC High Level Slab GL 11-14/A-K	03-Jul-02	31-Jul-02							0	100		
2340	FRC High Level Slab GL 11-12/K-M	14-Aug-02	04-Sep-02								0	100	
2350	FRC Ground Floor Slab GL 15-17/F-R	28-Aug-02	11-Sep-02								0	100	
2360	FRC Walls / Columns Ground - 2nd Floor	02-Oct-02									0	85	87
2370	FRC Mezzanine Slab GL 8-12/K-R	25-Sep-02	18-Sep-02								0	100	
2380	FRC Mezzanine Slab GL 13-17/C-R	25-Sep-02									0	12	59
2390	FRC 2nd Floor Slab GL 7-9/A-J	09-Oct-02	30-Oct-02									0	100
2400	FRC 2nd Floor Sla GbL 7-9/J-R	25-Sep-02									0	19	36
2410	FRC 2nd Floor Transfer Slab GL 9-15/H-R	25-Sep-02	30-Oct-02								0	20	100
2420	FRC Remainder Of 2nd Floor Slab	09-Oct-02											0	8
2430	FRC Walls / Columns 2nd - 3rd Floor	09-Oct-02											0	15

No other Arts Centre activities progressed in 'Time Period One'

PRELIMINARY WORKS

Activity ID	Activity Description	Orig Dur	% Comp	Rem Dur	Early Start	Early Finish	Total Float	Variance 2 Early Finish
PRELIMINARY WORKS								
0010	Commence Preparatory Activity	0	100	0	05.NOV.02A			0
0020	Commence On Site	0	100	0	03.DEC.02A			-20
0030	General Site Mobilisation	20	100	0	06.NOV.02A	04.DEC.02A		-2
0040	Commence Main Works	1	100	0	05.DEC.02A	05.DEC.02A		-2
0050	Site Establishment	30	100	0	06.NOV.02A	29.NOV.02A		16
0060	Pile Probing	25	70	8	13.NOV.02A	15.JAN.03	-7	-7
0070	Guide Walls	30	50	15	05.DEC.02A	29.JAN.03	-7	-7
0080	Install Secant Piles	45	14	39	11.DEC.02A	05.MAR.03	-7	-7
0090	Cut Down Piles	35	10	32	16.DEC.02A	12.MAR.03	-7	-7
0100	Preliminary Works Complete	1	0	1	13.MAR.03	13.MAR.03	-7	-7
APARTMENT BLOCK								
SUBSTRUCTURE								
0110	FRC CAPPING BEAM	35	0	35	30.JAN.03	19.MAR.03	-7	-7
0120	BULK DIG LEAVING SUPPORTING BERMS	74	0	74	03.FEB.03	27.MAY.03	-7	-7
0130	FRC SECTION OF AREA 3 SLAB FOR TOWER CRANE 1	5	0	5	13.MAR.03	19.MAR.03	-2	-7
0140	ERECT TOWER CRANE	0	0	0	27.MAR.03		-7	-7
0150	FRC BASEMENT SLAB AREA 1	9	0	9	27.MAR.03	08.APR.03	-7	-7
SECTIONAL COMPLETIONS								
SECT01	Show Flat (floor 03)	0	0	0		18.FEB.04	-3	-7
SECT02	Arts Complex (partial)	0	0	0		17.MAR.04	-3	-7
SECT03	Residential Floors 04 to 07(incl.)	0	0	0		13.MAY.04	-7	-7
SECT04	Shops	0	0	0		13.MAY.04	-4	-7
SECT07	Remaining Residential	0	0	0		29.SEP.04	-7	-7

Original plan
Current forecast at end of window
Progress Bar
Critical Activity

MIXED-USE DEVELOPMENT

As Built: as of 5 Jan..2003
end of WINDOW 1
Progress Comparison Chart

APPENDIX 5C a

Sheet 1 of 2

Activity ID	Activity Description	Orig Dur	% Comp	Rem Dur	Early Start	Early Finish	Total Float	Variance 2 Early Finish	2002 N D	2003 J F M A M J J A S O N D	2004 J F M A M J J A S O N D J F M A M J J A S O N D J
SECT08	All Others Areas	0	0	0		12.JAN.05	-7	-7			●

MIXED-USE DEVELOPMENT

As Built: as of 5 Jan..2003
end of WINDOW 1
Progress Comparison Chart

Original plan
Current forecast at end of window
Progress Bar
Critical Activity

APPENDIX 5C a

Sheet 2 of 2

Activity ID	Activity Description	Orig Dur	% Comp	Rem Dur	Early Start	Early Finish	Total Float	Variance 2 Early Finish
PRELIMINARY WORKS								
0060	Pile Probing	25	90	3	13.NOV.02A	05.FEB.03	-23	-15
0070	Guide Walls	30	90	3	05.DEC.02A	19.FEB.03	-23	-15
0080	Install Secant Piles	45	60	18	11.DEC.02A	26.MAR.03	-23	-15
0090	Cut Down Piles	35	18	29	16.DEC.02A	02.APR.03	-23	-15
0100	Preliminary Works Complete	1	0	1	03.APR.03	03.APR.03	-22	-15
APARTMENT BLOCK								
SUBSTRUCTURE								
0110	FRC CAPPING BEAM	35	0	35	20.FEB.03	09.APR.03	-22	-15
0120	BULK DIG LEAVING SUPPORTING BERMS	74	0	74	24.FEB.03	17.JUN.03	-22	-15
0130	FRC SECTION OF AREA 3 SLAB FOR TOWER CRANE 1	5	0	5	03.APR.03	09.APR.03	-17	-15
0140	ERECT TOWER CRANE	0	0	0	17.APR.03		-22	-15
0150	FRC BASEMENT SLAB AREA 1	9	0	9	17.APR.03	08.MAY.03	-22	-15
SECTIONAL COMPLETIONS								
SECT01	Show Flat (floor 03)	0	0	0		10.MAR.04	-18	-15
SECT02	Arts Complex (partial)	0	0	0		07.APR.04	-18	-15
SECT03	Residential Floors 04 to 07(incl.)	0	0	0		04.JUN.04	-22	-15
SECT04	Shops	0	0	0		04.JUN.04	-19	-15
SECT07	Remaining Residential	0	0	0		20.OCT.04	-22	-15
SECT08	All Others Areas	0	0	0		02.FEB.05	-22	-15

Legend:
- Original plan
- Current forecast at end of window
- Progress Bar
- Critical Activity

MIXED-USE DEVELOPMENT

As Built: as of 2 Feb.2003
end of WINDOW 2
Progress Comparison Chart

Activity ID	Activity Description	Orig Dur	% Comp	Rem Dur	Early Start	Early Finish	Total Float	
PRELIMINARY WORKS								
0060	Pile Probing	25	90	3	13 NOV 02A	05 FEB 03	-23	
0070	Guide Walls	30	90	3	05 DEC 02A	19 FEB 03	-23	
0080	Install Secant Piles	45	60	18	11 DEC 02A	26 MAR 03	-23	
0090	Cut Down Piles	35	18	29	16 DEC 02A	02 APR 03	-23	
0100	Preliminary Works Complete	1	0	1	03 APR 03	03 APR 03	-22	
APARTMENT BLOCK								
SUBSTRUCTURE								
0110	FRC CAPPING BEAM	35	0	35	20 FEB 03	09 APR 03	-22	
0120	BULK DIG LEAVING SUPPORTING BERMS	74	0	74	24 FEB 03	17 JUN 03	-22	
0140	ERECT TOWER CRANE	0	0	0	17 APR 03		-22	
0150	FRC BASEMENT SLAB AREA 1	9	0	9	17 APR 03	08 MAY 03	-22	
0160	INSTALL TEMPORARY WORKS JIGS 1 & 2	3	0	3	09 MAY 03	13 MAY 03	-22	
0170	REMOVE SIDE BERMS AREA 1	4	0	4	13 MAY 03	16 MAY 03	-22	
0180	FRC CLOSING SECTIONS OF BASEMENT SLABS AREA 1	7	0	7	16 MAY 03	27 MAY 03	-22	
0190	FRC WALLS AND COLUMNS LOWER - UPPER BASEMENT	16	0	16	09 MAY 03	02 JUN 03	-22	
0210	FRC UPPER BASEMENT SLAB AREA 1	14	0	14	15 MAY 03	04 JUN 03	-22	
0220	FRC BASEMENT SLAB AREA 2	10	0	10	06 MAY 03	19 MAY 03	-22	
0230	INSTALL TEMPORARY WORKS JIGS 3 & 4	3	0	3	21 MAY 03	23 MAY 03	-22	
0240	REMOVE SIDE BERMS AREA 2	4	0	4	27 MAY 03	30 MAY 03	-22	
0250	FRC CLOSING SECTIONS OF BASEMENT SLABS AREA 2	6	0	6	30 MAY 03	06 JUN 03	-22	
0260	FRC WALLS & COLUMNS LOWER -UPPER BAS'NT AREA 2	16	0	16	21 MAY 03	12 JUN 03	-22	
0280	FRC UPPER BASEMENT SLAB AREA 2	15	0	15	28 MAY 03	17 JUN 03	-22	
0290	RELOCATE TEMPORARY WORKS JIGS 1 & 2	3	0	3	12 JUN 03	16 JUN 03	-22	
0300	INSTALL TEMP SUPPORT PROPS GL 1/A-J	22	0	22	15 MAY 03	16 JUN 03	-22	
0370	REMOVE BERM	5	0	5	17 JUN 03	23 JUN 03	-22	
0380	BREAK BACK FEMALE PILES	4	0	4	20 JUN 03	25 JUN 03	-22	
0390	FRC CLOSING SECTION OF BASEMENT SLAB GL 1/A-J	6	0	6	24 JUN 03	01 JUL 03	-22	
0400	FRC WALLS & COLUMNS BASEMENT - UPPER BASEMENT	5	0	5	02 JUL 03	08 JUL 03	-22	
0410	FRC UPPER BASEMENT SLAB GL 1/A-J	7	0	7	07 JUL 03	15 JUL 03	-22	
0420	INSTALL TEMP SUPPORT PROPS GL 1/M-R	14	0	14	12 MAY 03*	30 MAY 03	-22	
0470	REMOVE BERM	4	0	4	02 JUN 03	05 JUN 03	-22	

Timeline columns: 2002 (N D) | 2003 (J F M A M J J A S O N D) | 2004 (J F M A M J J A S O N D) | 2005 (J F)

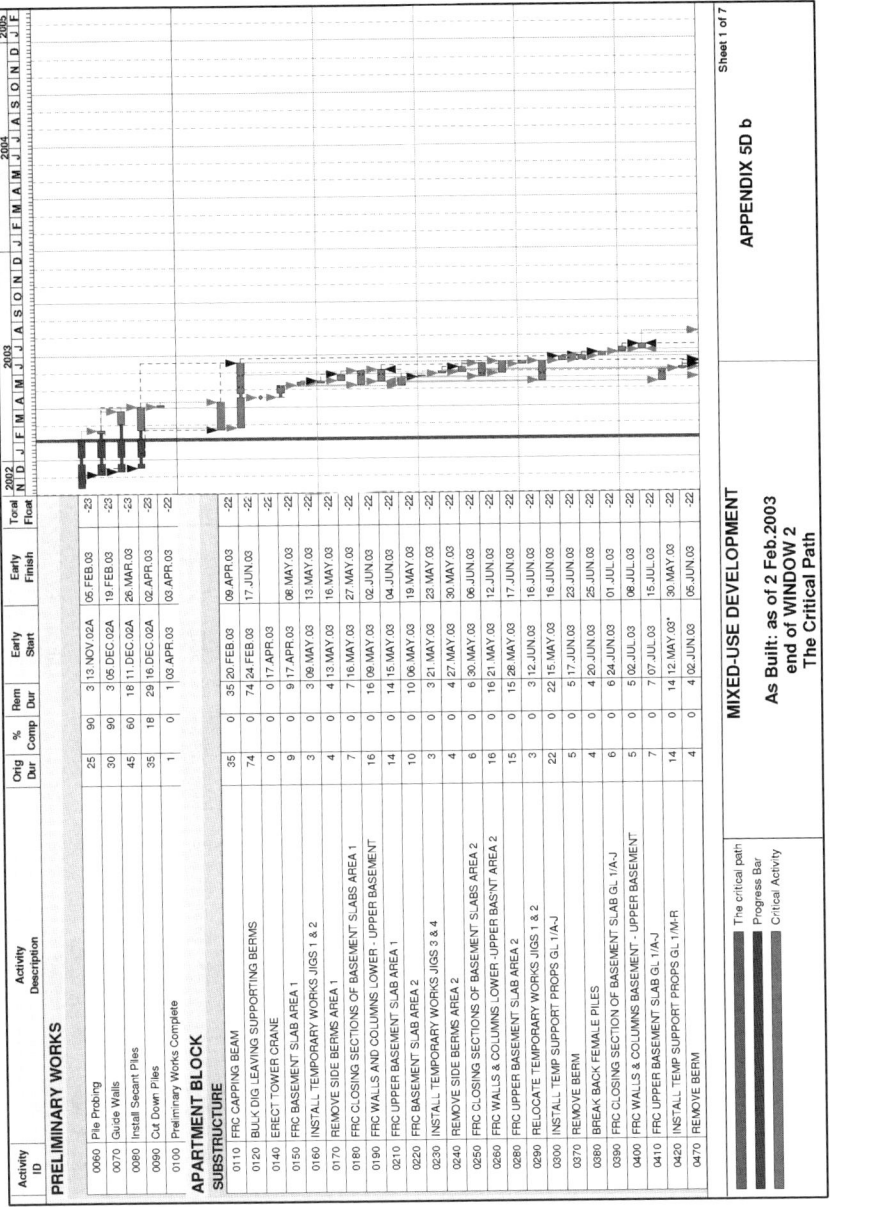

The critical path
Progress Bar
Critical Activity

MIXED-USE DEVELOPMENT

As Built: as of 2 Feb.2003
end of WINDOW 2
The Critical Path

APPENDIX 5D b

Activity ID	Activity Description	Orig Dur	% Comp	Rem Dur	Early Start	Early Finish	Total Float
0480	BREAK BACK FEMALE PILES	3	0	3	05.JUN.03	09.JUN.03	-22
0490	FRC CLOSING SECTION OF BASEMENT SLAB GL 1/M-R	5	0	5	09.JUN.03	13.JUN.03	-22
0500	FRC WALLS & COLUMNS BASEMENT - UPPER BASEMENT	4	0	4	16.JUN.03	19.JUN.03	-22
0510	FRC UPPER BASEMENT SLAB GL 1/M-R	6	0	6	19.JUN.03	26.JUN.03	-22
0520	INSTALL TEMP SUPPORT PROPS GL 1/J-M	18	0	18	20.MAY.03*	13.JUN.03	-22
0580	REMOVE BERM	4	0	4	16.JUN.03	19.JUN.03	-22
0590	FRC CLOSING SECTION OF BASEMENT SLAB GL 1/J-M	5	0	5	17.JUN.03	23.JUN.03	-22
0600	FRC WALLS & COLUMNS BASEMENT - UPPER BASEMENT	6	0	6	24.JUN.03	01.JUL.03	-22
0610	FRC UPPER BASEMENT SLAB GL 1/J-M	6	0	6	01.JUL.03	08.JUL.03	-22
0620	FRC Walls/Columns Upper Basement- Ground Floor	40	0	40	13.JUN.03	07.AUG.03	-22
0630	Substructure Residential Complete	0	0	0	08.AUG.03		-22
1230	Substructure Residential Complete	0	0	0	08.AUG.03		

ARTS CENTRE
SUBSTRUCTURE

Activity ID	Activity Description	Orig Dur	% Comp	Rem Dur	Early Start	Early Finish	Total Float
0640	Crane Base	5	0	5	31.JUL.03	06.AUG.03	-22
0660	FRC BASEMENT SLAB AREA 3	10	0	10	04.JUN.03	17.JUN.03	-22
0700	FRC BASEMENT SLAB AREA 4	14	0	14	13.JUN.03	02.JUL.03	-22
0740	FRC WALLS & COLUMNS LOWER -UPPER BAS'NT AREA 3	26	0	26	18.JUN.03	23.JUL.03	-22
0760	FRC UPPER BASEMENT SLAB AREA 3	26	0	26	23.JUN.03	28.JUL.03	-22
0770	RELOCATE TEMPORARY WORKS JIGS 3 & 4	3	0	3	08.JUL.03	10.JUL.03	-22
0780	REMOVE SIDE BERMS AREA 4	5	0	5	10.JUL.03	16.JUL.03	-22
0810	FRC CLOSING SECTIONS OF BASEMENT SLABS AREA 4	5	0	5	16.JUL.03	22.JUL.03	-22
0820	FRC WALLS & COLUMNS LOWER -UPPER BAS'NT AREA 4	21	0	21	30.JUN.03	28.JUL.03	-22
0840	FRC UPPER BASEMENT SLAB 4	20	0	20	04.JUL.03	31.JUL.03	-22
0850	RELOCATE TEMPORARY WORKS JIGS 1 & 2	3	0	3	29.JUL.03	31.JUL.03	-22
0860	REMOVE SIDE BERMS AREA 5	5	0	5	31.JUL.03	06.AUG.03	-22
0870	FRC LOW SECTION OF BASEM'T SLAB AREA 6	8	0	8	04.JUL.03	15.JUL.03	-22
0880	FRC WALLS LOW - HIGH BASEMENT SLAB AREA 6	5	0	5	16.JUL.03	22.JUL.03	-22
0890	FRC INTERMEDIATE SLAB AREA 6	4	0	4	23.JUL.03	28.JUL.03	-22
0900	FRC WALLS FROM INTERMEDIATE TO HIGH LVL. SLAB A6	3	0	3	29.JUL.03	31.JUL.03	-22
0910	FRC HIGH LEVEL BASEMENT SLAB AREA 6	10	0	10	23.JUL.03	05.AUG.03	-22
0960	RELOCATE TEMPORARY WORKS JIGS 3 & 4	3	0	3	06.AUG.03	08.AUG.03	-22
0970	REMOVE SIDE BERMS AREA 6	5	0	5	08.AUG.03	14.AUG.03	-22

Timeline columns: 2002 (N D J), 2003 (F M A M J J A S O N D), 2004 (J F M A M J J A S O N D), 2005 (J F)

The critical path
Progress Bar
Critical Activity

MIXED-USE DEVELOPMENT

As Built: as of 2 Feb.2003
end of WINDOW 2
The Critical Path

APPENDIX 5D b

Sheet 2 of 7

Activity ID	Activity Description	Orig Dur	% Comp	Rem Dur	Early Start	Early Finish	Total Float
0980	FRC BASEMENT SLAB SECTION 7	10	0	10	04 AUG 03	15 AUG 03	-22
0990	FRC CLOSING SECTIONS OF BASEMENT SLABS AREA 6	4	0	4	14 AUG 03	19 AUG 03	-22
1000	FRC WALLS & COLUMNS LOWER -UPPER BAS'NT AREA 6	13	0	13	06 AUG 03	22 AUG 03	-22
1010	FRC UPPER BASEMENT SLAB 6	15	0	15	12 AUG 03	02 SEP 03	-22
1040	FRC BASEMENT SLAB SECTION 8	10	0	10	14 AUG 03	28 AUG 03	-22
1060	FRC WALLS & COLUMNS LOWER -UPPER BAS'NT AREA 7	26	0	26	18 AUG 03	23 SEP 03	-22
1080	FRC UPPER BASEMENT SLAB 7	33	0	33	22 AUG 03	08 OCT 03	-22
1090	RELOCATE TEMPORARY WORKS JIGS 3 & 4	3	0	3	03 SEP 03	05 SEP 03	-22
1100	REMOVE SIDE BERMS AREA 8	5	0	5	05 SEP 03	11 SEP 03	-22
1110	FRC CLOSING SECTIONS OF BASEMENT SLABS AREA 8	6	0	6	11 SEP 03	18 SEP 03	-22
1120	FRC WALLS & COLUMNS LOWER -UPPER BAS'NT AREA 8	19	0	19	29 AUG 03	24 SEP 03	-22
1140	FRC UPPER BASEMENT SLAB AREA 8	25	0	25	04 SEP 03	08 OCT 03	-22
1150	INSTALL SUPPORTING PROPS TO PILES ADJ : TO GL 17	7	0	7	29 AUG 03	08 SEP 03	-22
1160	REMOVE SUPPORTING BERM	10	0	10	05 SEP 03	18 SEP 03	-22
1170	FRC CLOSING SECTION OF BASEMENT SLAB	12	0	12	15 SEP 03	30 SEP 03	-22
1180	FRC WALLS / COLUMNS LOWER - UPPER BASEMENT	11	0	11	23 SEP 03	07 OCT 03	-22
1190	FRC CLOSING SECTION OF UPPER BASEMENT SLAB	11	0	11	01 OCT 03	15 OCT 03	-22
1200	2 Week Allowance For Breaking Back Female Piles	10	0	10	30 JUL 03	12 AUG 03	-22
1210	FRC Columns / Walls Upper Basement - Ground	60	0	60	13 AUG 03	05 NOV 03	-22
1220	Substructure Arts Centre Complete	1	0	1	06 NOV 03	06 NOV 03	-22

APARTMENT BLOCK

SUPERSTRUCTURE

Activity ID	Activity Description	Orig Dur	% Comp	Rem Dur	Early Start	Early Finish	Total Float
1240	FRC GF Slab Incl Part Sect. Of Area 3 GL 1-7/A-H	13	0	13	25 JUL 03	12 AUG 03	-22
1250	FRC Ground Floor Slab Low Level GL 1-7/M-R	10	0	10	23 JUL 03	05 AUG 03	-22
1260	FRC Remaining High Level Section Of GF SLAB	11	0	11	04 AUG 03	18 AUG 03	-22
1270	FRC Walls / Columns Ground - Mezz	11	0	11	06 AUG 03	20 AUG 03	-22
1280	FRC Mezz Floor Grid Lines 1-7/A-D	7	0	7	15 AUG 03	26 AUG 03	-22
1300	FRC Walls / Columns Mezz- 2nd Floor	10	0	10	27 AUG 03	09 SEP 03	-22
1330	FRC 2nd Floor Slab GL 1-7/M-R	8	0	8	03 SEP 03	12 SEP 03	-22
1340	FRC 2nd Floor Slab 1-7/A-F	10	0	10	04 SEP 03	17 SEP 03	-22
1350	FRC Walls/Columns 2nd - 3rd/4th Floor	15	0	15	10 SEP 03	30 SEP 03	-22
1360	FRC 3rd Floor Slab GL 1-7/F-M	11	0	11	16 SEP 03	30 SEP 03	-22
1390	FRC Walls / Columns 3rd - 4th Floor	13	0	13	01 OCT 03	17 OCT 03	-22

Legend:
- The critical path
- Progress Bar
- Critical Activity

MIXED-USE DEVELOPMENT

As Built: as of 2 Feb.2003
end of WINDOW 2
The Critical Path

APPENDIX 5D b

Activity ID	Activity Description	Orig Dur	Rem Dur	% Comp	Early Start	Early Finish	Total Float
1420	FRC 4th Floor Slab GL 1-3/J-R/ + 4-7/L-P	13	13	0	06.OCT.03	22.OCT.03	-22
1440	FRC 4th Floor Slab GL. 6-7/M-R	10	10	0	16.OCT.03	29.OCT.03	-22
1450	FRC Walls / Columns 4th - 5th Floor	14	14	0	16.OCT.03	04.NOV.03	-22
1460	FRC 5th Floor Slab GL 1-6/K-R	11	11	0	17.OCT.03	31.OCT.03	-22
1470	FRC 5th Floor Slab GL 1-6/A-K	12	12	0	23.OCT.03	07.NOV.03	-22
1480	FRC Walls/ Columns 5th - 6th Floor	12	12	0	03.NOV.03	18.NOV.03	-22
1490	FRC 6th Floor Slab GL 1-6/K-R	11	11	0	06.NOV.03	20.NOV.03	-22
1500	FRC 6th Floor Slab GL 1-6/A-K	11	11	0	10.NOV.03	24.NOV.03	-22
1510	FRC Walls / Columns 6th - 7th Floor	10	10	0	21.NOV.03	04.DEC.03	-22
1520	FRC 7th Floor Slab GL 1-6/K-R	11	11	0	26.NOV.03	10.DEC.03	-22
1530	FRC 7th Floor Slab GL 1-6/A-K	11	11	0	01.DEC.03	15.DEC.03	-22
1540	FRC Walls/ Columns 7th - 8th Floor	10	10	0	11.DEC.03	07.JAN.04	-22
1550	FRC 8th Floor Slab GL 1-6/K-R	10	10	0	17.DEC.03	13.JAN.04	-22
1560	FRC 8th Floor Slab GL 1-6/A-K	11	11	0	07.JAN.04	21.JAN.04	-22
1570	FRC Walls / Column 8th - 9th Floor	12	12	0	14.JAN.04	29.JAN.04	-22
1580	FRC 9th Floor Slab GL 1-6/K-R	10	10	0	20.JAN.04	02.FEB.04	-22
1590	FRC 9th Floor Slab GL 1-6/A-K	11	11	0	29.JAN.04	12.FEB.04	-22
1600	FRC Walls / Columns 9th - 10th Floor	12	12	0	03.FEB.04	18.FEB.04	-22
1610	FRC 10th Floor Slab GL 1-6/K-R	11	11	0	09.FEB.04	23.FEB.04	-22
1620	FRC 10th Floor SlabGL 1-6/A-K	11	11	0	18.FEB.04	03.MAR.04	-22
1630	FRC Walls / Columns 10th - 11th Floor	12	12	0	24.FEB.04	10.MAR.04	-22
1640	FRC 11th Floor Slab GL 1-6/K-R	11	11	0	01.MAR.04	15.MAR.04	-22
1650	FRC 11th Floor Slab GL 1-6/A-K	12	12	0	04.MAR.04	19.MAR.04	-22
1660	FRC Walls / Columns 11th - 12th Floor	12	12	0	16.MAR.04	31.MAR.04	-22
1670	FRC 12th Floor Slab GL 1-6/K-R	11	11	0	22.MAR.04	05.APR.04	-22
1680	FRC 12th Floor Slab GL 1-6/A-K	11	11	0	29.MAR.04	20.APR.04	-22
1690	FRC Walls / Columns 12th - 13th Floor	11	11	0	06.APR.04	28.APR.04	-22
1700	FRC 13th Floor Slab GL 1-6/K-R	9	9	0	20.APR.04	30.APR.04	-22
1710	FRC 13th Floor Slab GL 1-6/A-K	8	8	0	23.APR.04	06.MAY.04	-22
1720	FRC Walls / Columns 13th - 14th Floor	7	7	0	04.MAY.04	12.MAY.04	-22
1730	FRC 14th Floor Slab GL 1-6/K-R	7	7	0	07.MAY.04	17.MAY.04	-22
1740	FRC 14th Floor Slab GL 1-6/A-K	7	7	0	11.MAY.04	19.MAY.04	-22
1750	FRC Walls/ Columns 14th - 15th Floor	9	9	0	18.MAY.04	28.MAY.04	-22
1760	FRC 15th Floor Slab GL 1-6/K-R	11	11	0	21.MAY.04	07.JUN.04	-22

Legend:
- The critical path
- Progress Bar
- Critical Activity

MIXED-USE DEVELOPMENT

As Built: as of 2 Feb.2003
end of WINDOW 2
The Critical Path

APPENDIX 5D b

Activity ID	Activity Description	Orig Dur	% Comp	Rem Dur	Early Start	Early Finish	Total Float
1780	FRC Core Walls Level 15-16 GL A-B/2-5	6	0	6	08-JUN-04	15-JUN-04	-22
1790	FRC Core Walls Level 16-Roof GL A-B/2-5	9	0	9	16-JUN-04	28-JUN-04	-22
1800	FRC Cover Slab To Core	9	0	9	29-JUN-04	09-JUL-04	-22
1810	Progressive Erection of Precast Stairs	177	0	177	21-OCT-03	19-JUL-04	-22
1860	Timber Grounds Windows & Doors	162	0	162	30-JAN-04	24-SEP-04	-22
1870	Render Insulation & First Coat	142	0	142	12-MAR-04	06-OCT-04	-22
1880	Terracotta Cladding Frame Work	137	0	137	26-MAR-04	15-OCT-04	-22
1890	Metal Cladding	142	0	142	02-APR-04	29-OCT-04	-22
1910	Terracotta Panels	112	0	112	02-JUN-04	15-OCT-04	-22
1950	Penthouse Brise Soleil	30	0	30	06-SEP-04	15-OCT-04	-22
1960	Penthouse Curtain Walling	40	0	40	13-SEP-04	05-NOV-04	-22
1970	Penthouse Roof Cladding/Roof Lights	40	0	40	13-SEP-04	05-NOV-04	-22
1980	Render Final Coat Top Down	59	0	59	11-OCT-04	13-JAN-05	-22
1990	Bolt On Balconies	54	0	54	25-OCT-04	20-JAN-05	-22
2000	Dismatle Scaffolds	59	0	59	29-OCT-04	02-FEB-05	-22
2050	Penthouse Roof Weathered	1	0	1	08-NOV-04	08-NOV-04	-22
2100	Lift Shaft Temporary Weathered	9	0	9	12-JUL-04	22-JUL-04	-22
INTERNAL FINISHES							
1850	Blockwork	181	0	181	24-NOV-03	26-AUG-04	-22
1900	Balcony/Balustrades & Finishes	147	0	147	26-APR-04	19-NOV-04	-22
2060	Internal Blockwork to Cores	182	0	182	23-JAN-04	15-OCT-04	-22
2070	M & E Services to Cores & Risers	171	0	171	26-APR-04	23-DEC-04	-22
2080	Staircase Lobbies & Common Areas	171	0	171	26-APR-04	23-DEC-04	-22
2110	Lift installations	98	0	98	23-JUL-04	08-DEC-04	-22
2120	Final Commission Clean & Snag	58	0	58	01-NOV-04	02-FEB-05	-22
2130	Shell & Core Completion	1	0	1	02-FEB-05	02-FEB-05	-22
2200	Access For Third Fit Out Phase	0	0	0	22-OCT-04		-22
2210	Third Phase National Fit Out Period	64	0	64	22-OCT-04	02-FEB-05	-22
ARTS CENTRE							
SUPERSTRUCTURE							
2220	FRC Ground Floor Slab Low Level GL 7-9/A-J	12	0	12	22-AUG-03	09-SEP-03	-22
2230	FRC Ground Floor Slab Low Level GL 7-9/M-R	10	0	10	28-AUG-03	10-SEP-03	-22
2240	FRC Walls From Low - High Lvl GF Slab GL 7-9/M&J	7	0	7	10-SEP-03	18-SEP-03	-22
2250	FRC Ground Floor Slab High Level GL 7-9/J-M	9	0	9	15-SEP-03	25-SEP-03	-22

Legend:
— The critical path
— Progress Bar
— Critical Activity

MIXED-USE DEVELOPMENT

As Built: as of 2 Feb.2003
end of WINDOW 2
The Critical Path

APPENDIX 5D b

Activity ID	Activity Description	Orig Dur	% Comp	Rem Dur	Early Start	Early Finish	Total Float
2260	FRC Ground Floor Slab Low Level GL 9-11/A-K	14	0	14	22.SEP.03	09.OCT.03	-22
2270	FRC Ground Floor Slab Low Level GL 9-11/M-R	10	0	10	25.SEP.03	08.OCT.03	-22
2280	FRC Walls From Low - High Lvl GF Slab GL 7-9/M&K	6	0	6	09.OCT.03	16.OCT.03	-22
2290	FRC Ground Floor Slab High Level GL 9-11/K-M	10	0	10	06.OCT.03	21.OCT.03	-22
2300	FRC Ground Floor Slab Low Level GL 12-15/A-L	15	0	15	22.OCT.03	11.NOV.03	-22
2310	FRC Ground Floor Slab Low Level GL 12-15/L-R	14	0	14	22.OCT.03	10.NOV.03	-22
2320	FRC Walls From Low - High Lvl GF Slab GL 12,14&K	6	0	6	11.NOV.03	18.NOV.03	-22
2330	FRC High Level Slab GL 11-14/A-K	8	0	8	12.NOV.03	21.NOV.03	-22
2340	FRC High Level Slab GL 11-12/K-M	5	0	5	21.NOV.03	27.NOV.03	-22
2350	FRC Ground Floor Slab GL 15-17/F-R	14	0	14	07.NOV.03	26.NOV.03	-22
2360	FRC Walls / Columns Ground - 2nd Floor	57	0	57	12.SEP.03	01.DEC.03	-22
2380	FRC Mezzanine Slab GL 13-17/C-R	11	0	11	02.DEC.03	16.DEC.03	-22
2390	FRC 2nd Floor Slab GL 7-9/A-J	12	0	12	23.SEP.03	08.OCT.03	-22
2420	FRC Remainder Of 2nd Floor Slab	12	0	12	17.DEC.03	15.JAN.04	-22
2430	FRC Walls / Columns 2nd - 3rd Floor	71	0	71	09.OCT.03	29.JAN.04	-22
2440	FRC 3rd Floor Slab GL 7-9/L-R	20	0	20	18.NOV.03	15.DEC.03	-22
2450	FRC 3rd Floor Slab GL 9-14/H-R	17	0	17	15.DEC.03	20.JAN.04	-22
2460	FRC 3rd Floor Slab GL 14-17/F-R	24	0	24	13.JAN.04	13.FEB.04	-22
2510	FRC 4th Floor Slab GL 9-15/F-R	18	0	18	27.JAN.04	19.FEB.04	-22
2570	Concrete Studio Theater Roof	5	0	5	05.MAR.04	11.MAR.04	-22
2620	Steelwork & Decking Level 4	10	0	10	20.FEB.04	04.MAR.04	-22
2830	Roofing Roof Finishes Lvl 4 & 5	61	0	61	19.FEB.04	24.MAY.04	-22
2880	Rooflights Fitness Centre	15	0	15	12.MAR.04	01.APR.04	-22
3060	Barriers/Markings	40	0	40	25.NOV.04	02.FEB.05	-22
3110	Barriers & Marking	20	0	20	23.DEC.04	02.FEB.05	-22
INTERNAL FINISHES							
2940	Blockwork Partitions/Builders Work	100	0	100	27.FEB.04	27.JUL.04	-22
2960	Service Installations/Commission	186	0	186	30.APR.04	02.FEB.05	-22
2980	Specialist Fit Out Works	153	0	153	18.JUN.04	02.FEB.05	-22
3050	Walls/Finishes & S	49	0	49	15.OCT.04	22.DEC.04	-22
3070	Office Area Fit Out	99	0	99	03.SEP.04	02.FEB.05	-22
3080	Remaining Retail Areas	1	0	1	02.FEB.05	02.FEB.05	-22
3100	Finishes & Service	79	0	79	03.SEP.04	22.DEC.04	-22

Legend:
- The critical path
- Progress Bar
- Critical Activity

MIXED-USE DEVELOPMENT

As Built: as of 2 Feb.2003
end of WINDOW 2
The Critical Path

APPENDIX 5D b

Sheet 6 of 7

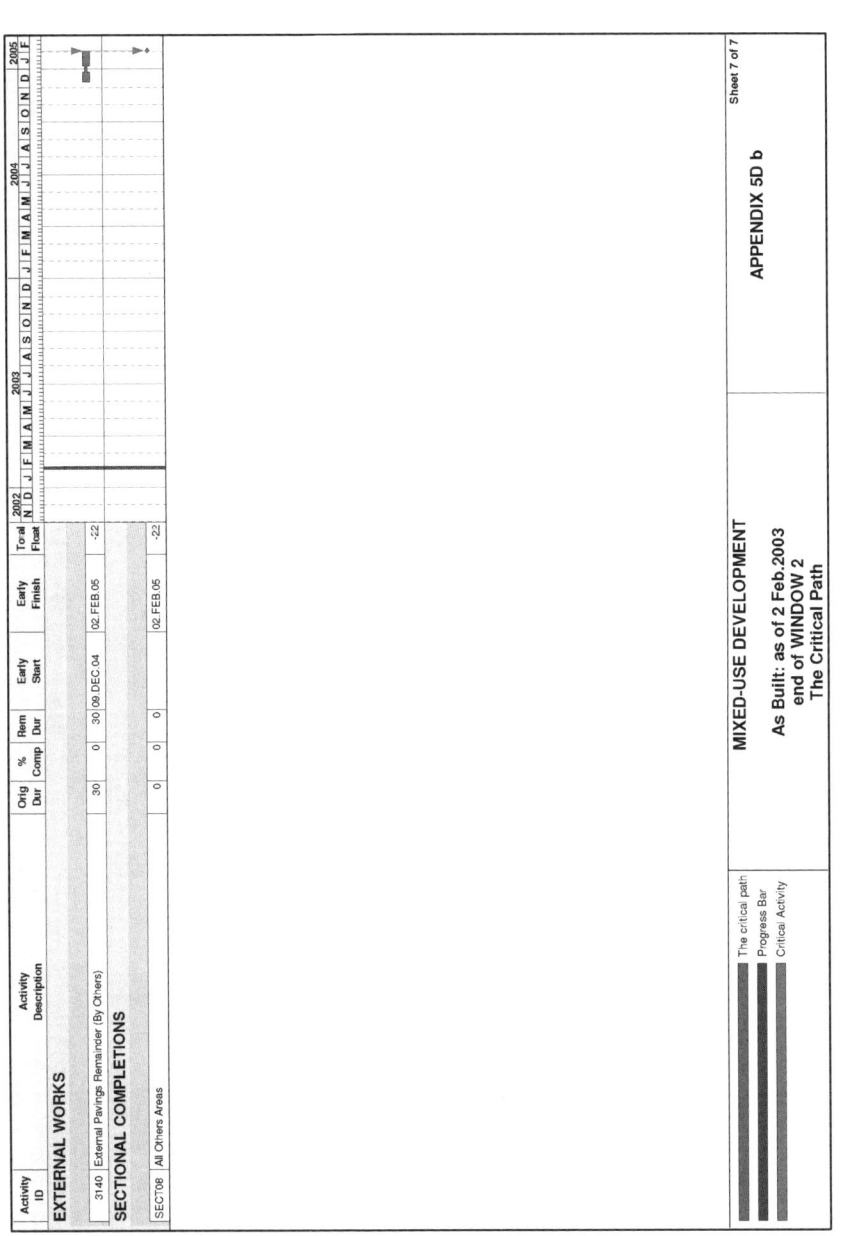

Activity ID	Activity Description	Orig Dur	% Comp	Rem Dur	Early Start	Early Finish	Total Float	2002 N D	2003 J F M A M J J A S O N D	2004 J F M A M J J A S O N D	2005 J F
EXTERNAL WORKS											
3140	External Pavings Remainder (By Others)	30	0	30	09.DEC.04	02.FEB.05	-22				
SECTIONAL COMPLETIONS											
SECT08	All Others Areas	0	0	0		02.FEB.05	-22				

		MIXED-USE DEVELOPMENT	Sheet 7 of 7
▬▬▬	The critical path	As Built: as of 2 Feb.2003	APPENDIX 5D b
▬▬▬	Progress Bar	end of WINDOW 2	
▬▬▬	Critical Activity	The Critical Path	

PRELIMINARY WORKS

Activity ID	Activity Description	Orig Dur	% Comp	Rem Dur	Early Start	Early Finish	Total Float	Variance 2 Early Finish
0060	Pile Probing	25	100	0	13.NOV.02A	14.FEB.03A		-7
0070	Guide Walls	30	100	0	05.DEC.02A	01.MAR.03A		-7
0080	Install Secant Piles	45	85	7	11.DEC.02A	04.APR.03	-8	-7
0090	Cut Down Piles	35	25	26	16.DEC.02A	11.APR.03	-8	-7
0100	Preliminary Works Complete	1	0	1	14.APR.03	14.APR.03	-8	-7

APARTMENT BLOCK
SUBSTRUCTURE

Activity ID	Activity Description	Orig Dur	% Comp	Rem Dur	Early Start	Early Finish	Total Float	Variance 2 Early Finish
0110	FRC CAPPING BEAM	35	15	30	18.FEB.03A	28.APR.03	-8	-7
0120	BULK DIG LEAVING SUPPORTING BERMS	74	10	67	20.FEB.03A	13.JUN.03	-20	2
0130	FRC SECTION OF AREA 3 SLAB FOR TOWER CRANE 1	5	0	5	01.APR.03	07.APR.03	-15	2
0140	ERECT TOWER CRANE	0	0	0	15.APR.03		-20	2
0150	FRC BASEMENT SLAB AREA 1	9	0	9	15.APR.03	06.MAY.03	-20	2
0160	INSTALL TEMPORARY WORKS JIGS 1 & 2	3	0	3	07.MAY.03	09.MAY.03	-20	2
0170	REMOVE SIDE BERMS AREA 1	4	0	4	09.MAY.03	14.MAY.03	-20	2
0180	FRC CLOSING SECTIONS OF BASEMENT SLABS AREA 1	7	0	7	14.MAY.03	22.MAY.03	-20	2
0190	FRC WALLS AND COLUMNS LOWER - UPPER BASEMENT	16	0	16	07.MAY.03	29.MAY.03	-20	2
0210	FRC UPPER BASEMENT SLAB AREA 1	14	0	14	13.MAY.03	02.JUN.03	-20	2
0220	FRC BASEMENT SLAB AREA 2	10	0	10	01.MAY.03	15.MAY.03	-20	2
0230	INSTALL TEMPORARY WORKS JIGS 3 & 4	3	0	3	19.MAY.03	21.MAY.03	-20	2
0240	REMOVE SIDE BERMS AREA 2	4	0	4	22.MAY.03	28.MAY.03	-20	2
0250	FRC CLOSING SECTIONS OF BASEMENT SLABS AREA 2	6	0	6	28.MAY.03	04.JUN.03	-20	2
0260	FRC WALLS & COLUMNS LOWER -UPPER BAS'NT AREA 2	16	0	16	19.MAY.03	10.JUN.03	-20	2
0280	FRC UPPER BASEMENT SLAB AREA 2	15	0	15	23.MAY.03	13.JUN.03	-20	2

Legend:
- Original plan
- Current forecast at end of window
- Progress Bar
- Critical Activity

MIXED-USE DEVELOPMENT

As Built: as of 2 Mar.2003
end of WINDOW 3
Progress Comparison Chart

APPENDIX 5E a

Activity ID	Activity Description	Orig Dur	% Comp	Rem Dur	Early Start	Early Finish	Total Float	Variance 2 Early Finish
0300	INSTALL TEMP SUPPORT PROPS GL 1/A-J	22	0	22	13 MAY 03	12 JUN 03	-20	2
0420	INSTALL TEMP SUPPORT PROPS GL 1/M-R	14	0	14	08 MAY 03*	29 MAY 03	-20	2
0470	REMOVE BERM	4	0	4	29 MAY 03	03 JUN 03	-20	2
0480	BREAK BACK FEMALE PILES	3	0	3	03 JUN 03	06 JUN 03	-20	2
0490	FRC CLOSING SECTION OF BASEMENT SLAB GL 1/M-R	5	0	5	05 JUN 03	11 JUN 03	-20	2
0520	INSTALL TEMP SUPPORT PROPS GL 1/J-M	18	0	18	16 MAY 03*	11 JUN 03	-20	2

ARTS CENTRE
SUBSTRUCTURE

0660	FRC BASEMENT SLAB AREA 3	10	0	10	02 JUN 03	13 JUN 03	-20	2

SECTIONAL COMPLETIONS

SECT01	Show Flat (floor 03)	0	0	0		08 MAR 04	-16	2
SECT02	Arts Complex (partial)	0	0	0		05 APR 04	-16	2
SECT03	Residential Floors 04 to 07(incl.)	0	0	0		02 JUN 04	-20	2
SECT04	Shops	0	0	0		02 JUN 04	-17	2
SECT07	Remaining Residential	0	0	0		18 OCT 04	-20	2
SECT08	All Others Areas	0	0	0		31 JAN 05	-20	2

Original plan
Current forecast at end of window
Progress Bar
Critical Activity

MIXED-USE DEVELOPMENT
As Built: as of 2 Mar.2003
end of WINDOW 3
Progress Comparison Chart

APPENDIX 5E a

Sheet 2 of 2

APARTMENT BLOCK
SUBSTRUCTURE

Activity ID	Activity Description	Orig Dur	% Comp	Rem Dur	Early Start	Early Finish	Total Float
0120	BULK DIG LEAVING SUPPORTING BERMS	74	10	67	20.FEB.03A	13.JUN.03	-20
0140	ERECT TOWER CRANE	0	0	0	15.APR.03		-20
0150	FRC BASEMENT SLAB AREA 1	9	0	9	15.APR.03	06.MAY.03	-20
0160	INSTALL TEMPORARY WORKS JIGS 1 & 2	3	0	3	07.MAY.03	09.MAY.03	-20
0170	REMOVE SIDE BERMS AREA 1	4	0	4	09.MAY.03	14.MAY.03	-20
0180	FRC CLOSING SECTIONS OF BASEMENT SLABS AREA 1	7	0	7	14.MAY.03	22.MAY.03	-20
0190	FRC WALLS AND COLUMNS LOWER - UPPER BASEMENT	16	0	16	07.MAY.03	29.MAY.03	-20
0210	FRC UPPER BASEMENT SLAB AREA 1	14	0	14	13.MAY.03	02.JUN.03	-20
0220	FRC BASEMENT SLAB AREA 2	10	0	10	01.MAY.03	15.MAY.03	-20
0230	INSTALL TEMPORARY WORKS JIGS 3 & 4	3	0	3	19.MAY.03	21.MAY.03	-20
0240	REMOVE SIDE BERMS AREA 2	4	0	4	22.MAY.03	28.MAY.03	-20
0250	FRC CLOSING SECTIONS OF BASEMENT SLABS AREA 2	6	0	6	28.MAY.03	04.JUN.03	-20
0260	FRC WALLS & COLUMNS LOWER -UPPER BAS'NT AREA 2	16	0	16	19.MAY.03	10.JUN.03	-20
0280	FRC UPPER BASEMENT SLAB AREA 2	15	0	15	23.MAY.03	13.JUN.03	-20
0290	RELOCATE TEMPORARY WORKS JIGS 1 & 2	3	0	3	10.JUN.03	12.JUN.03	-20
0300	INSTALL TEMP SUPPORT PROPS GL 1/A-J	22	0	22	13.MAY.03	12.JUN.03	-20
0370	REMOVE BERM	5	0	5	13.JUN.03	19.JUN.03	-20
0380	BREAK BACK FEMALE PILES	4	0	4	18.JUN.03	23.JUN.03	-20
0390	FRC CLOSING SECTION OF BASEMENT SLAB GL 1/A-J	6	0	6	20.JUN.03	27.JUN.03	-20
0400	FRC WALLS & COLUMNS BASEMENT - UPPER BASEMENT	5	0	5	30.JUN.03	04.JUL.03	-20
0410	FRC UPPER BASEMENT SLAB GL 1/A-J	7	0	7	03.JUL.03	11.JUL.03	-20
0420	INSTALL TEMP SUPPORT PROPS GL 1/M-R	14	0	14	08.MAY.03*	28.MAY.03	-20
0470	REMOVE BERM	4	0	4	29.MAY.03	03.JUN.03	-20
0480	BREAK BACK FEMALE PILES	3	0	3	03.JUN.03	05.JUN.03	-20
0490	FRC CLOSING SECTION OF BASEMENT SLAB GL 1/M-R	5	0	5	05.JUN.03	11.JUN.03	-20
0500	FRC WALLS & COLUMNS BASEMENT - UPPER BASEMENT	4	0	4	12.JUN.03	17.JUN.03	-20
0510	FRC UPPER BASEMENT SLAB GL 1/M-R	6	0	6	17.JUN.03	24.JUN.03	-20
0520	INSTALL TEMP SUPPORT PROPS GL 1/J-M	18	0	18	16.MAY.03*	11.JUN.03	-20
0580	REMOVE BERM	4	0	4	12.JUN.03	17.JUN.03	-20
0590	FRC CLOSING SECTION OF BASEMENT SLAB GL 1/J-M	5	0	5	13.JUN.03	19.JUN.03	-20
0600	FRC WALLS & COLUMNS BASEMENT - UPPER BASEMENT	6	0	6	20.JUN.03	27.JUN.03	-20

Timeline: 2002 N D | 2003 J F M A M J J A S O N D | 2004 J F M A M J J A S O N D | 2005 J F

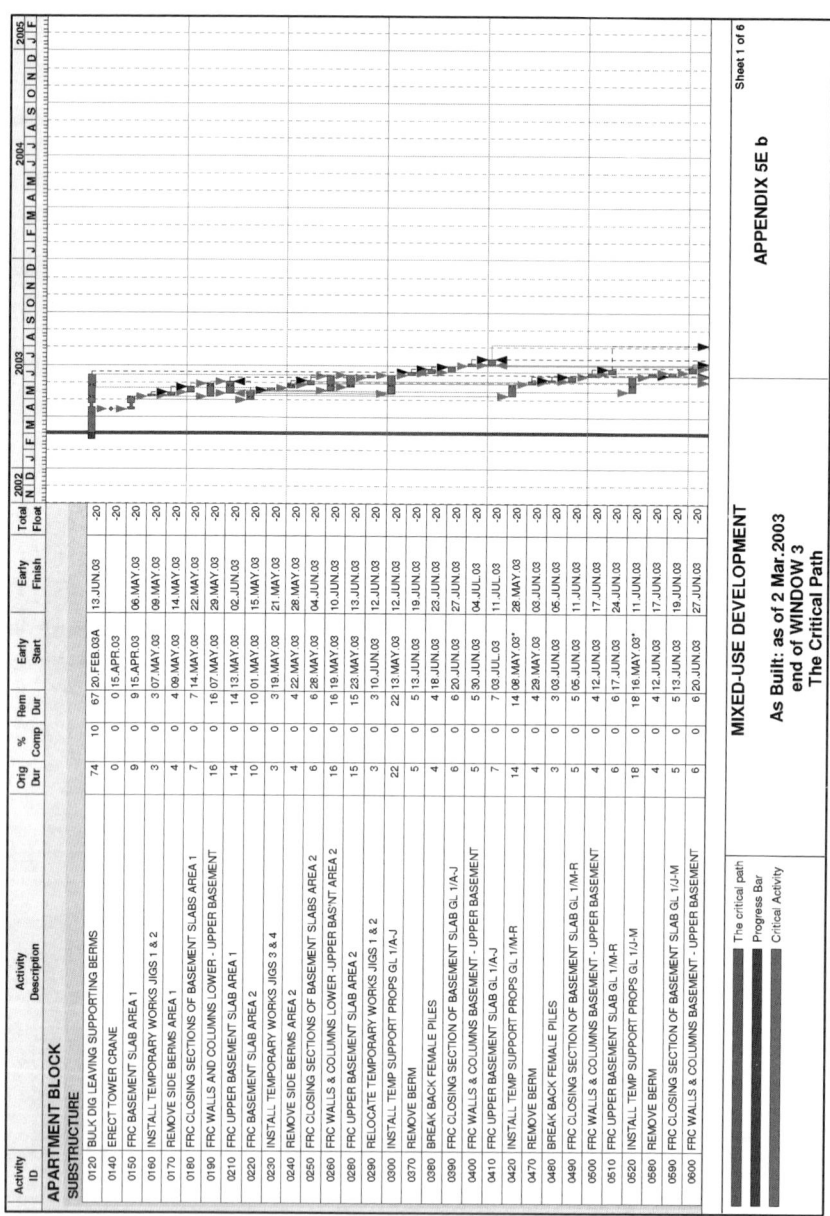

Legend:
— The critical path
— Progress Bar
— Critical Activity

MIXED-USE DEVELOPMENT

As Built: as of 2 Mar.2003
end of WINDOW 3
The Critical Path

APPENDIX 5E b

Sheet 1 of 6

Activity ID	Activity Description	Orig Dur	% Comp	Rem Dur	Early Start	Early Finish	Total Float	2002 N D	2003 J F M A M J J A S O N D	2004 J F M A M J J A S O N D	2005 J F
0610	FRC UPPER BASEMENT SLAB GL 1/J-M	6	0	6	27.JUN.03	04.JUL.03	-20				
0620	FRC Walls/Columns Upper Basement- Ground Floor	40	0	40	11.JUN.03	05.AUG.03	-20				
0630	Substructure Residential Complete	0	0	0	06.AUG.03		20				
1230	Substructure Residential Complete	0	0	0	06.AUG.03		-20				

ARTS CENTRE

SUBSTRUCTURE

Activity ID	Activity Description	Orig Dur	% Comp	Rem Dur	Early Start	Early Finish	Total Float	2002 N D	2003 J F M A M J J A S O N D	2004 J F M A M J J A S O N D	2005 J F
0640	Crane Base	5	0	5	29.JUL.03	04.AUG.03	-20				
0660	FRC BASEMENT SLAB AREA 3	10	0	10	02.JUN.03	13.JUN.03	-20				
0700	FRC BASEMENT SLAB AREA 4	14	0	14	11.JUN.03	30.JUN.03	-20				
0740	FRC WALLS & COLUMNS LOWER -UPPER BAS'NT AREA 3	26	0	26	16.JUN.03	21.JUL.03	-20				
0760	FRC UPPER BASEMENT SLAB AREA 3	26	0	26	19.JUN.03	24.JUL.03	-20				
0770	RELOCATE TEMPORARY WORKS JIGS 3 & 4	3	0	3	04.JUL.03	08.JUL.03	-20				
0780	REMOVE SIDE BERMS AREA 4	5	0	5	08.JUL.03	14.JUL.03	-20				
0810	FRC CLOSING SECTIONS OF BASEMENT SLABS AREA 4	5	0	5	14.JUL.03	18.JUL.03	-20				
0820	FRC WALLS & COLUMNS LOWER -UPPER BAS'NT AREA 4	21	0	21	26.JUN.03	24.JUL.03	-20				
0840	FRC UPPER BASEMENT SLAB 4	20	0	20	02.JUL.03	29.JUL.03	-20				
0850	RELOCATE TEMPORARY WORKS JIGS 1 & 2	3	0	3	25.JUL.03	29.JUL.03	-20				
0860	REMOVE SIDE BERMS AREA 5	5	0	5	29.JUL.03	04.AUG.03	-20				
0870	FRC LOW SECTION OF BASEM'T SLAB AREA 6	8	0	8	02.JUL.03	11.JUL.03	-20				
0880	FRC WALLS LOW - HIGH BASEMENT SLAB AREA 6	5	0	5	14.JUL.03	18.JUL.03	-20				
0890	FRC INTERMEDIATE SLAB AREA 6	4	0	4	21.JUL.03	24.JUL.03	-20				
0900	FRC WALLS FROM INTERMEDIATE TO HIGH LVL SLAB A6	3	0	3	25.JUL.03	29.JUL.03	-20				
0910	FRC HIGH LEVEL BASEMENT SLAB AREA 6	10	0	10	21.JUL.03	01.AUG.03	-20				
0960	RELOCATE TEMPORARY WORKS JIGS 3 & 4	3	0	3	04.AUG.03	06.AUG.03	-20				
0970	REMOVE SIDE BERMS AREA 6	5	0	5	06.AUG.03	12.AUG.03	-20				
0980	FRC BASEMENT SLAB SECTION 7	10	0	10	31.JUL.03	13.AUG.03	-20				
0990	FRC CLOSING SECTIONS OF BASEMENT SLABS AREA 6	4	0	4	12.AUG.03	15.AUG.03	-20				
1000	FRC WALLS & COLUMNS LOWER -UPPER BAS'NT AREA 6	13	0	13	04.AUG.03	20.AUG.03	-20				
1010	FRC UPPER BASEMENT SLAB 6	15	0	15	08.AUG.03	29.AUG.03	-20				
1040	FRC BASEMENT SLAB SECTION 8	10	0	10	12.AUG.03	26.AUG.03	-20				
1060	FRC WALLS & COLUMNS LOWER -UPPER BAS'NT AREA 7	26	0	26	14.AUG.03	19.SEP.03	-20				
1080	FRC UPPER BASEMENT SLAB 7	33	0	33	20.AUG.03	06.OCT.03	-20				
1090	RELOCATE TEMPORARY WORKS JIGS 3 & 4	3	0	3	01.SEP.03	03.SEP.03	-20				

▬▬▬ The critical path	**MIXED-USE DEVELOPMENT**	Sheet 2 of 6
▬▬▬ Progress Bar		**APPENDIX 5E b**
▬▬▬ Critical Activity	As Built: as of 2 Mar.2003 end of WINDOW 3 The Critical Path	

Activity ID	Activity Description	Orig Dur	% Comp	Rem Dur	Early Start	Early Finish	Total Float
1100	REMOVE SIDE BERMS AREA 8	5	0	5	03 SEP 03	09 SEP 03	-20
1110	FRC CLOSING SECTIONS OF BASEMENT SLABS AREA 8	6	0	6	09 SEP 03	16 SEP 03	-20
1120	FRC WALLS & COLUMNS LOWER -UPPER BAS'NT AREA 8	19	0	19	27 AUG 03	22 SEP 03	-20
1140	FRC UPPER BASEMENT SLAB AREA 8	25	0	25	02 SEP 03	06 OCT 03	-20
1150	INSTALL SUPPORTING PROPS TO PILES ADJ. TO GL. 17	7	0	7	27 AUG 03	04 SEP 03	-20
1160	REMOVE SUPPORTING BERM	10	0	10	03 SEP 03	16 SEP 03	-20
1170	FRC CLOSING SECTION OF BASEMENT SLAB	12	0	12	11 SEP 03	26 SEP 03	-20
1180	FRC WALLS / COLUMNS LOWER - UPPER BASEMENT	11	0	11	19 SEP 03	03 OCT 03	-20
1190	FRC CLOSING SECTION OF UPPER BASEMENT SLAB	11	0	11	29 SEP 03	13 OCT 03	-20
1200	2 Week Allowance For Breaking Back Female Piles	10	0	10	28 JUL 03	08 AUG 03	-20
1210	FRC Columns / Walls Upper Basement - Ground	60	0	60	11 AUG 03	03 NOV 03	-20
1220	Substructure Arts Centre Complete	1	0	1	04 NOV 03	04 NOV 03	-20

APARTMENT BLOCK
SUPERSTRUCTURE

Activity ID	Activity Description	Orig Dur	% Comp	Rem Dur	Early Start	Early Finish	Total Float
1240	FRC GF Slab Incl Part Sect. Of Area 3 GL 1-7/A-H	13	0	13	23 JUL 03	08 AUG 03	-20
1250	FRC Ground Floor Slab Low Level GL 1-7/M-R	10	0	10	21 JUL 03	01 AUG 03	-20
1260	FRC Remaining High Level Section Of GF SLAB	11	0	11	31 JUL 03	14 AUG 03	-20
1270	FRC Walls / Columns Ground - Mezz	11	0	11	04 AUG 03	18 AUG 03	-20
1280	FRC Mezz Floor Grid Lines 1-7/A-D	7	0	7	13 AUG 03	21 AUG 03	-20
1300	FRC Walls / Columns Mezz- 2nd Floor	10	0	10	22 AUG 03	05 SEP 03	-20
1330	FRC 2nd Floor Slab GL 1-7/M-R	8	0	8	01 SEP 03	10 SEP 03	-20
1340	FRC 2nd Floor Slab 1-7/A-F	10	0	10	02 SEP 03	15 SEP 03	-20
1350	FRC Walls/Columns 2nd - 3rd/4th Floor	15	0	15	08 SEP 03	26 SEP 03	-20
1360	FRC 3rd Floor Slab GL 1-7/F-M	11	0	11	12 SEP 03	26 SEP 03	-20
1390	FRC Walls / Columns 3rd - 4th Floor	13	0	13	29 SEP 03	15 OCT 03	-20
1420	FRC 4th Floor Slab GL 1-3/U-R/ + 4-7/L-P	13	0	13	02 OCT 03	20 OCT 03	-20
1440	FRC 4th Floor Slab GL 6-7/M-R	10	0	10	14 OCT 03	27 OCT 03	-20
1450	FRC Walls / Columns 4th - 5th Floor	14	0	14	14 OCT 03	31 OCT 03	-20
1460	FRC 5th Floor Slab GL 1-6/K-R	11	0	11	15 OCT 03	29 OCT 03	-20
1470	FRC 5th Floor Slab GL 1-6/A-K	12	0	12	21 OCT 03	06 NOV 03	-20
1480	FRC Walls/ Columns 5th - 6th Floor	12	0	12	30 OCT 03	14 NOV 03	-20
1490	FRC 6th Floor Slab GL 1-6/K-R	11	0	11	04 NOV 03	18 NOV 03	-20
1500	FRC 6th Floor Slab GL 1-6/A-K	11	0	11	06 NOV 03	20 NOV 03	-20

Legend:
- The critical path
- Progress Bar
- Critical Activity

MIXED-USE DEVELOPMENT

As Built: as of 2 Mar.2003
end of WINDOW 3
The Critical Path

APPENDIX 5E b

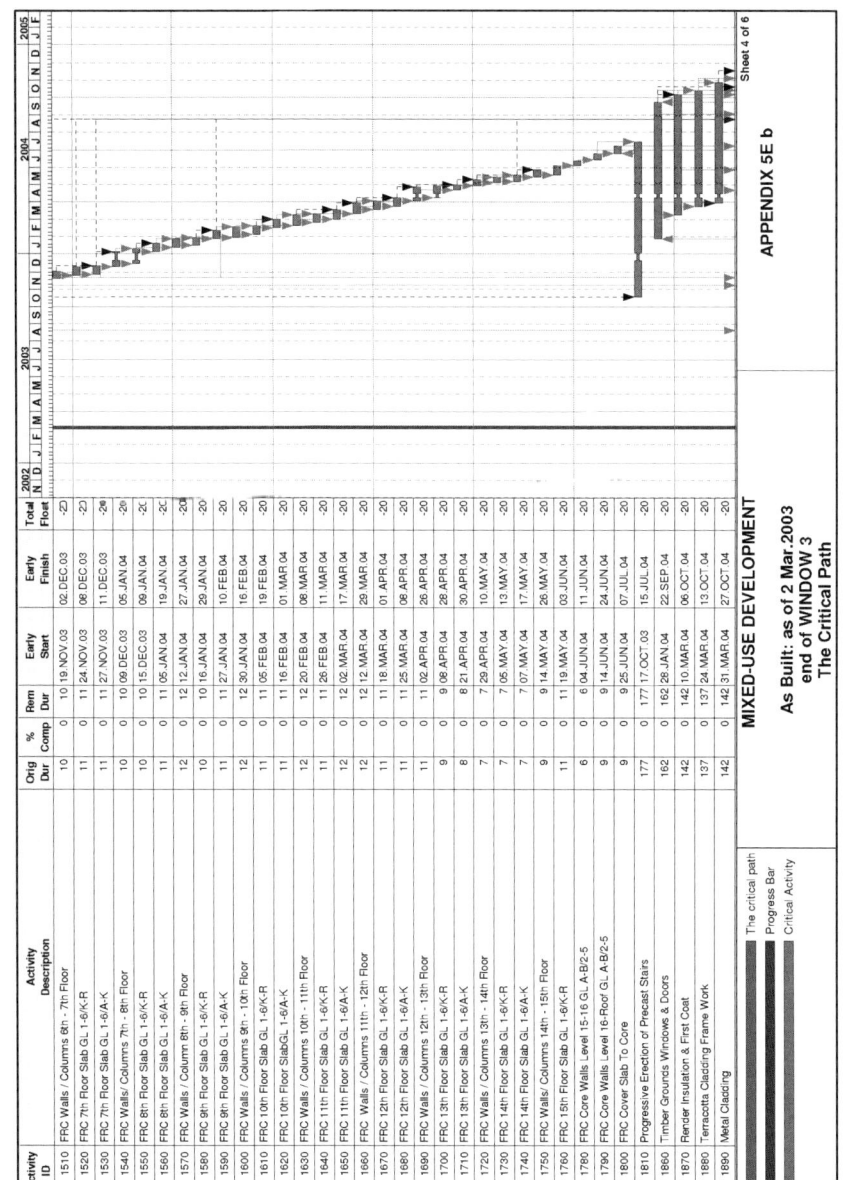

Activity ID	Activity Description	Orig Dur	% Comp	Rem Dur	Early Start	Early Finish	Total Float
1510	FRC Walls / Columns 6th - 7th Floor	10	0	10	19 NOV 03	02 DEC 03	-20
1520	FRC 7th Floor Slab GL 1-6/K-R	11	0	11	24 NOV 03	08 DEC 03	-20
1530	FRC 7th Floor Slab GL 1-6/A-K	11	0	11	27 NOV 03	11 DEC 03	-20
1540	FRC Walls/ Columns 7th - 8th Floor	10	0	10	09 DEC 03	05 JAN 04	-20
1550	FRC 8th Floor Slab GL 1-6/K-R	10	0	10	15 DEC 03	09 JAN 04	-20
1560	FRC 8th Floor Slab GL 1-6/A-K	11	0	11	05 JAN 04	19 JAN 04	-20
1570	FRC Walls / Column 8th - 9th Floor	12	0	12	12 JAN 04	27 JAN 04	-20
1580	FRC 9th Floor Slab GL 1-6/K-R	10	0	10	16 JAN 04	29 JAN 04	-20
1590	FRC 9th Floor Slab GL 1-6/A-K	11	0	11	27 JAN 04	10 FEB 04	-20
1600	FRC Walls / Columns 9th - 10th Floor	12	0	12	30 JAN 04	16 FEB 04	-20
1610	FRC 10th Floor Slab GL 1-6/K-R	11	0	11	05 FEB 04	19 FEB 04	-20
1620	FRC 10th Floor SlabGL 1-6/A-K	11	0	11	16 FEB 04	01 MAR 04	-20
1630	FRC Walls / Columns 10th - 11th Floor	12	0	12	20 FEB 04	08 MAR 04	-20
1640	FRC 11th Floor Slab GL 1-6/K-R	11	0	11	26 FEB 04	11 MAR 04	-20
1650	FRC 11th Floor Slab GL 1-6/A-K	12	0	12	02 MAR 04	17 MAR 04	-20
1660	FRC Walls / Columns 11th - 12th Floor	12	0	12	12 MAR 04	29 MAR 04	-20
1670	FRC 12th Floor Slab GL 1-6/K-R	11	0	11	18 MAR 04	01 APR 04	-20
1680	FRC 12th Floor Slab GL 1-6/A-K	11	0	11	25 MAR 04	08 APR 04	-20
1690	FRC Walls / Columns 12th - 13th Floor	11	0	11	02 APR 04	26 APR 04	-20
1700	FRC 13th Floor Slab GL 1-6/K-R	9	0	9	08 APR 04	28 APR 04	-20
1710	FRC 13th Floor Slab GL 1-6/A-K	8	0	8	21 APR 04	30 APR 04	-20
1720	FRC Walls / Columns 13th - 14th Floor	7	0	7	29 APR 04	10 MAY 04	-20
1730	FRC 14th Floor Slab GL 1-6/K-R	7	0	7	05 MAY 04	13 MAY 04	-20
1740	FRC 14th Floor Slab GL 1-6/A-K	7	0	7	07 MAY 04	17 MAY 04	-20
1750	FRC Walls/ Columns 14th - 15th Floor	9	0	9	14 MAY 04	26 MAY 04	-20
1760	FRC 15th Floor Slab GL 1-6/K-R	11	0	11	19 MAY 04	03 JUN 04	-20
1780	FRC Core Walls Level 15-16 GL-A-B/2-5	6	0	6	04 JUN 04	11 JUN 04	-20
1790	FRC Core Walls Level 16-Roof GL-A-B/2-5	9	0	9	14 JUN 04	24 JUN 04	-20
1800	FRC Cover Slab To Core	9	0	9	25 JUN 04	07 JUL 04	-20
1810	Progressive Erection of Precast Stairs	177	0	177	17 OCT 03	15 JUL 04	-20
1860	Timber Grounds Windows & Doors	162	0	162	28 JAN 04	22 SEP 04	-20
1870	Render Insulation & First Coat	142	0	142	10 MAR 04	06 OCT 04	-20
1880	Terracotta Cladding Frame Work	137	0	137	24 MAR 04	13 OCT 04	-20
1890	Metal Cladding	142	0	142	31 MAR 04	27 OCT 04	-20

The critical path
Progress Bar
Critical Activity

MIXED-USE DEVELOPMENT

As Built: as of 2 Mar.2003
end of WINDOW 3
The Critical Path

APPENDIX 5E b

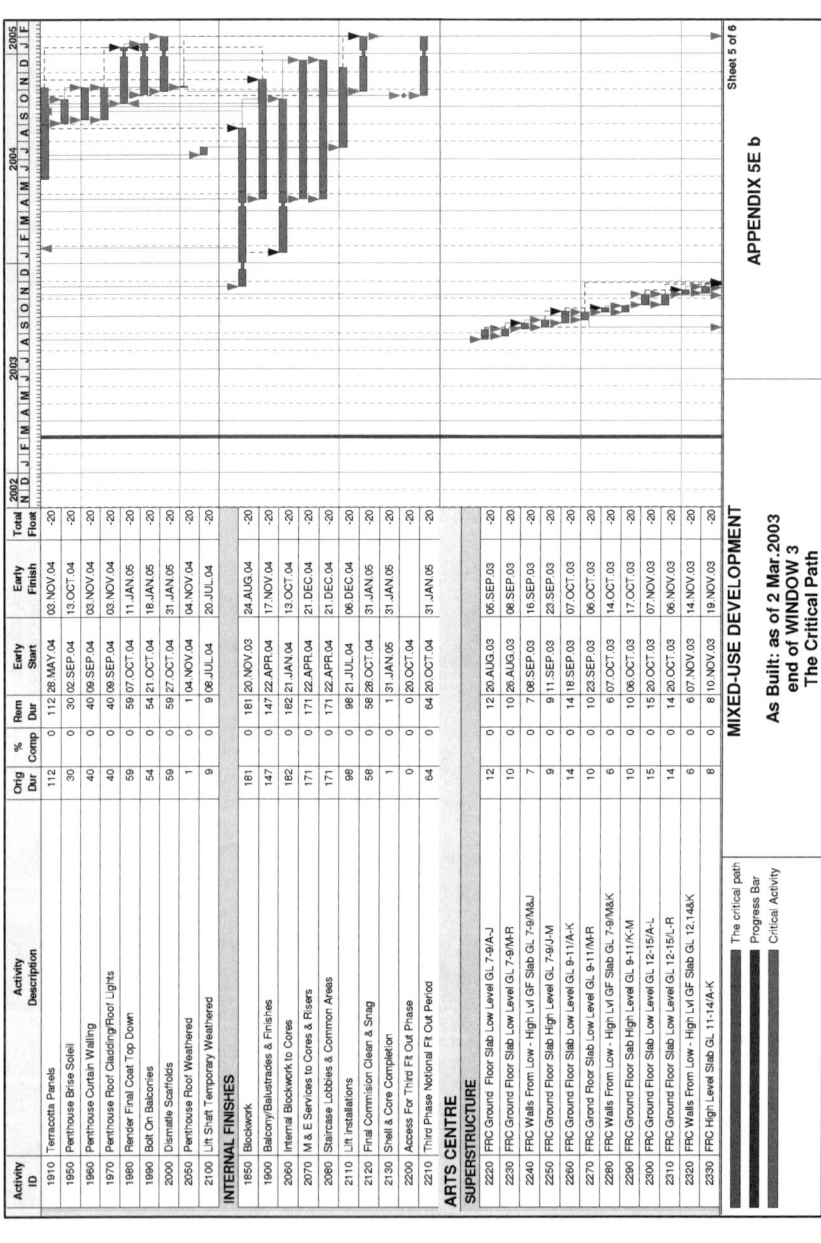

Activity ID	Activity Description	Orig Dur	% Comp	Rem Dur	Early Start	Early Finish	Total Float
1910	Terracotta Panels	112	0	112	28 MAY.04	03.NOV.04	-20
1950	Penthouse Brise Soleil	30	0	30	02.SEP.04	13.OCT.04	-20
1960	Penthouse Curtain Walling	40	0	40	09.SEP.04	03.NOV.04	-20
1970	Penthouse Roof Cladding/Roof Lights	40	0	40	09.SEP.04	03.NOV.04	-20
1980	Render Final Coat Top Down	59	0	59	07.OCT.04	11.JAN.05	-20
1990	Bolt On Balconies	54	0	54	21.OCT.04	18.JAN.05	-20
2000	Dismatle Scaffolds	59	0	59	27.OCT.04	31.JAN.05	-20
2050	Penthouse Roof Weathered	1	0	1	04.NOV.04	04.NOV.04	-20
2100	Lift Shaft Temporary Weathered	9	0	9	08.JUL.04	20.JUL.04	-20
INTERNAL FINISHES							
1850	Blockwork	181	0	181	20.NOV.03	24.AUG.04	-20
1900	Balcony/Balustrades & Finishes	147	0	147	22.APR.04	17.NOV.04	-20
2060	Internal Blockwork to Cores	182	0	182	21.JAN.04	13.OCT.04	-20
2070	M & E Services to Cores & Risers	171	0	171	22.APR.04	21.DEC.04	-20
2080	Staircase Lobbies & Common Areas	171	0	171	22.APR.04	21.DEC.04	-20
2110	Lift Installations	98	0	98	21.JUL.04	06.DEC.04	-20
2120	Final Commision Clean & Snag	58	0	58	28.OCT.04	31.JAN.05	-20
2130	Shell & Core Completion	1	0	1	31.JAN.05	31.JAN.05	-20
2200	Access For Third Fit Out Phase	0	0	0	20.OCT.04		-20
2210	Third Phase National Fit Out Period	64	0	64	20.OCT.04	31.JAN.05	-20
ARTS CENTRE							
SUPERSTRUCTURE							
2220	FRC Ground Floor Slab Low Level GL 7-9/A-J	12	0	12	20.AUG.03	05.SEP.03	-20
2230	FRC Ground Floor Slab Low Level GL 7-9/M-R	10	0	10	26.AUG.03	08.SEP.03	-20
2240	FRC Walls From Low - High Lvl GF Slab GL 7-9/M&J	7	0	7	08.SEP.03	16.SEP.03	-20
2250	FRC Ground Floor Slab High Level GL 7-9/J-M	9	0	9	11.SEP.03	23.SEP.03	-20
2260	FRC Ground Floor Slab Low Level GL 9-11/A-K	14	0	14	18.SEP.03	07.OCT.03	-20
2270	FRC Ground Floor Slab Low Level GL 9-11/M-R	10	0	10	23.SEP.03	06.OCT.03	-20
2280	FRC Walls From Low - High Lvl GF Slab GL 7-9/M&K	6	0	6	07.OCT.03	14.OCT.03	-20
2290	FRC Ground Floor Sab High Level GL 9-11/K-M	10	0	10	06.OCT.03	17.OCT.03	-20
2300	FRC Ground Floor Slab Low Level GL 12-15/A-L	15	0	15	20.OCT.03	07.NOV.03	-20
2310	FRC Ground Floor Slab Low Level GL 12-15/L-R	14	0	14	20.OCT.03	06.NOV.03	-20
2320	FRC Walls From Low - High Lvl GF Slab GL 12,14&K	6	0	6	07.NOV.03	14.NOV.03	-20
2330	FRC High Level Slab GL 11-14/A-K	8	0	8	10.NOV.03	19.NOV.03	-20

The critical path
Progress Bar
Critical Activity

MIXED-USE DEVELOPMENT

As Built: as of 2 Mar.2003
end of WINDOW 3
The Critical Path

APPENDIX 5E b

Sheet 5 of 6

Activity ID	Activity Description		Orig Dur	% Comp	Rem Dur	Early Start	Early Finish	Total Float	2002 N D	2003 J F M A M J J A S O N D	2004 J F M A M J J A S O N D	2005 J F
2340	FRC High Level Slab GL 11-12/K-M		5	0	5	19.NOV.03	25.NOV.03	-20				
2350	FRC Ground Floor Slab GL 15-17/F-R		14	0	14	05.NOV.03	24.NOV.03	-20				
2360	FRC Walls / Columns Ground - 2nd Floor		57	0	57	10.SEP.03	27.NOV.03	-20				
2380	FRC Mezzanine Slab GL 13-17/C-R		11	0	11	28.NOV.03	12.DEC.03	-20				
2390	FRC 2nd Floor Slab GL 7-9/A-J		12	0	12	19.SEP.03	06.OCT.03	-20				
2420	FRC Remainder Of 2nd Floor Slab		12	0	12	15.DEC.03	13.JAN.04	-20				
2430	FRC Walls / Columns 2nd - 3rd Floor		71	0	71	07.OCT.03	27.JAN.04	-20				
2440	FRC 3rd Floor Slab GL 7-9/L-R		20	0	20	14.NOV.03	11.DEC.03	-20				
2450	FRC 3rd Floor Slab GL 9-14/H-R		17	0	17	11.DEC.03	16.JAN.04	-20				
2460	FRC 3rd Floor Slab GL 14-17/F-R		24	0	24	09.JAN.04	11.FEB.04	-20				
2510	FRC 4th Floor Slab GL 9-15/F-R		18	0	18	23.JAN.04	17.FEB.04	-20				
2570	Concrete Studio Theater Roof		5	0	5	03.MAR.04	09.MAR.04	-20				
2620	Steelwork & Decking Level 4		10	0	10	18.FEB.04	02.MAR.04	-20				
2830	Roofing	Roof Finishes Lvl 4 & 5	61	0	61	17.FEB.04	20.MAY.04	-20				
2880	Rooflights	Fitness Centre	15	0	15	10.MAR.04	30.MAR.04	-20				
3060		Barriers/Markings	40	0	40	23.NOV.04	31.JAN.05	-20				
3110		Barriers & Marking	20	0	20	21.DEC.04	31.JAN.05	-20				
INTERNAL FINISHES												
2940	Blockwork Partitions/Builders Work		100	0	100	25.FEB.04	23.JUL.04	-20				
2960	Service Installations/Commission		186	0	186	28.APR.04	31.JAN.05	-20				
2980	Specialist Fit Out Works		153	0	153	16.JUN.04	31.JAN.05	-20				
3050		Walls/Finishes & S	49	0	49	13.OCT.04	20.DEC.04	-20				
3070	Office Area	Fit Out	99	0	99	01.SEP.04	31.JAN.05	-20				
3080	Remaining Retail Areas		1	0	1	31.JAN.05	31.JAN.05	-20				
3100		Finishes & Service	79	0	79	01.SEP.04	20.DEC.04	-20				
EXTERNAL WORKS												
3140	External Pavings Remainder (By Others)		30	0	30	07.DEC.04	31.JAN.05	-20				
SECTIONAL COMPLETIONS												
SECT08	All Others Areas		0	0	0		31.JAN.05	-20				

▬▬▬ The critical path	**MIXED-USE DEVELOPMENT**	Sheet 6 of 6
▬▬▬ Progress Bar		**APPENDIX 5E b**
▬▬▬ Critical Activity	As Built: as of 2 Mar.2003 end of WINDOW 3 The Critical Path	

Activity ID	Activity Description	Orig Dur	% Comp	Rem Dur	Early Start	Early Finish	Total Float	Variance 2 Early Finish
PRELIMINARY WORKS								
0080	Install Secant Piles	45	100	0	11.DEC.02A	20.MAR.03A		11
0090	Cut Down Piles	35	70	11	16.DEC.02A	14.APR.03	-9	-1
0100	Preliminary Works Complete	1	0	1	15.APR.03	15.APR.03	-9	-1
APARTMENT BLOCK								
SUBSTRUCTURE								
0110	FRC CAPPING BEAM	35	40	21	18.FEB.03A	07.MAY.03	-14	-6
0120	BULK DIG LEAVING SUPPORTING BERMS	74	25	56	25.FEB.03A	26.JUN.03	-29	-9
0130	FRC SECTION OF AREA 3 SLAB FOR TOWER CRANE 1	5	85	1	06.MAR.03A	31.MAR.03	-10	5
0140	ERECT TOWER CRANE	0	0	0	28.APR.03		-23	-3
0150	FRC BASEMENT SLAB AREA 1	9	0	9	28.APR.03	09.MAY.03	-23	-3
0160	INSTALL TEMPORARY WORKS JIGS 1 & 2	3	0	3	12.MAY.03	14.MAY.03	-23	-3
0170	REMOVE SIDE BERMS AREA 1	4	0	4	14.MAY.03	19.MAY.03	-23	-3
0180	FRC CLOSING SECTIONS OF BASEMENT SLABS AREA 1	7	0	7	19.MAY.03	28.MAY.03	-23	-3
0190	FRC WALLS AND COLUMNS LOWER - UPPER BASEMENT	16	0	16	12.MAY.03	03.JUN.03	-23	-3
0210	FRC UPPER BASEMENT SLAB AREA 1	14	0	14	16.MAY.03	05.JUN.03	-23	-3
0220	FRC BASEMENT SLAB AREA 2	10	0	10	07.MAY.03	20.MAY.03	-23	-3
0230	INSTALL TEMPORARY WORKS JIGS 3 & 4	3	0	3	22.MAY.03	27.MAY.03	-23	-3
0240	REMOVE SIDE BERMS AREA 2	4	0	4	05.JUN.03	10.JUN.03	-29	-9
0260	FRC WALLS & COLUMNS LOWER -UPPER BAS'NT AREA 2	16	0	16	02.JUN.03	23.JUN.03	-29	-9
0280	FRC UPPER BASEMENT SLAB AREA 2	15	0	15	06.JUN.03	26.JUN.03	-29	-9
0300	INSTALL TEMP SUPPORT PROPS GL 1/A-J	22	0	22	27.MAY.03	25.JUN.03	-29	-9
0420	INSTALL TEMP SUPPORT PROPS GL 1/M-R	14	0	14	13.MAY.03*	02.JUN.03	-23	-3
0520	INSTALL TEMP SUPPORT PROPS GL 1/J-M	18	0	18	21.MAY.03*	16.JUN.03	-23	-3

Original plan
Current forecast at end of window
Progress Bar
Critical Activity

MIXED-USE DEVELOPMENT

**As Built: as of 30 Mar.2003
end of WINDOW 4
Progress Comparison Chart**

APPENDIX 5F a

Sheet 1 of 2

Activity ID	Activity Description	Orig Dur	% Comp	Rem Dur	Early Start	Early Finish	Total Float	Variance 2 Early Finish	2002 N D	2003 J F M A M J J A S O N D	2004 J F M A M J J A S O N D	2005 J F M A M J J F M A
SECTIONAL COMPLETIONS												
SECT01	Show Flat (floor 03)	0	0	0		19.MAR.04	-25	-9				
SECT02	Arts Complex (partial)	0	0	0		26.APR.04	-25	-9				
SECT03	Residential Floors 04 to 07(incl.)	0	0	0		15.JUN.04	-25	-9				
SECT04	Shops	0	0	0		15.JUN.04	-26	-9				
SECT07	Remaining Residential	0	0	0		29.OCT.04	-29	-9				
SECT08	All Others Areas	0	0	0		11.FEB.05	-29	-9				

MIXED-USE DEVELOPMENT

As Built: as of 30.Mar.2003
end of WINDOW 4
Progress Comparison Chart

APPENDIX 5F a

APARTMENT BLOCK
SUBSTRUCTURE

Activity ID	Activity Description	Orig Dur	% Comp	Rem Dur	Early Start	Early Finish	Total Float
0120	BULK DIG LEAVING SUPPORTING BERMS	74	25	56	25 FEB 03A	26 JUN 03	-29
0240	REMOVE SIDE BERMS AREA 2	4	0	4	05 JUN 03	10 JUN 03	-29
0250	FRC CLOSING SECTIONS OF BASEMENT SLABS AREA 2	6	0	6	10 JUN 03	17 JUN 03	-29
0260	FRC WALLS & COLUMNS LOWER -UPPER BAS'NT AREA 2	16	0	16	02 JUN 03	23 JUN 03	-29
0280	FRC UPPER BASEMENT SLAB AREA 2	15	0	15	06 JUN 03	26 JUN 03	-29
0290	RELOCATE TEMPORARY WORKS JIGS 1 & 2	3	0	3	23 JUN 03	25 JUN 03	-29
0300	INSTALL TEMP SUPPORT PROPS GL 1/A-J	22	0	22	27 MAY 03	25 JUN 03	-29
0370	REMOVE BERM	5	0	5	26 JUN 03	02 JUL 03	-29
0380	BREAK BACK FEMALE PILES	4	0	4	01 JUL 03	04 JUL 03	-29
0390	FRC CLOSING SECTION OF BASEMENT SLAB GL 1/A-J	6	0	6	03 JUL 03	10 JUL 03	-29
0400	FRC WALLS & COLUMNS BASEMENT - UPPER BASEMENT	5	0	5	11 JUL 03	17 JUL 03	-29
0410	FRC UPPER BASEMENT SLAB GL 1/A-J	7	0	7	16 JUL 03	24 JUL 03	-29
0470	REMOVE BERM	4	0	4	11 JUN 03	16 JUN 03	-29
0480	BREAK BACK FEMALE PILES	3	0	3	16 JUN 03	18 JUN 03	-29
0490	FRC CLOSING SECTION OF BASEMENT SLAB GL 1/M-R	5	0	5	18 JUN 03	24 JUN 03	-29
0500	FRC WALLS & COLUMNS BASEMENT - UPPER BASEMENT	4	0	4	25 JUN 03	30 JUN 03	-29
0510	FRC UPPER BASEMENT SLAB GL 1/M-R	6	0	6	30 JUN 03	07 JUL 03	-29
0620	FRC Walls/Columns Upper Basement- Ground Floor	40	0	40	24 JUN 03	18 AUG 03	-29
0630	Substructure Residential Complete	0	0	0	19 AUG 03		-29
1230	Substructure Residential Complete	0	0	0	19 AUG 03		-29

ARTS CENTRE
SUBSTRUCTURE

Activity ID	Activity Description	Orig Dur	% Comp	Rem Dur	Early Start	Early Finish	Total Float
0640	Crane Base	5	0	5	11 AUG 03	15 AUG 03	-29
0660	FRC BASEMENT SLAB AREA 3	10	0	10	13 JUN 03	26 JUN 03	-29
0700	FRC BASEMENT SLAB AREA 4	14	0	14	24 JUN 03	11 JUL 03	-29
0740	FRC WALLS & COLUMNS LOWER -UPPER BAS'NT AREA 3	26	0	26	27 JUN 03	01 AUG 03	-29
0760	FRC UPPER BASEMENT SLAB AREA 3	26	0	26	02 JUL 03	06 AUG 03	-29
0770	RELOCATE TEMPORARY WORKS JIGS 3 & 4	3	0	3	17 JUL 03	21 JUL 03	-29
0780	REMOVE SIDE BERMS AREA 4	5	0	5	21 JUL 03	25 JUL 03	-29
0810	FRC CLOSING SECTIONS OF BASEMENT SLABS AREA 4	5	0	5	25 JUL 03	31 JUL 03	-29
0820	FRC WALLS & COLUMNS LOWER -UPPER BAS'NT AREA 4	21	0	21	09 AUG 03	06 AUG 03	-29

Legend:
- The critical path
- Progress Bar
- Critical Activity

MIXED-USE DEVELOPMENT

As Built: as of 30 Mar.2003 end of WINDOW 4 The Critical Path

APPENDIX 5F b

Sheet 1 of 6

Activity ID	Activity Description	Orig Dur	% Comp	Rem Dur	Early Start	Early Finish	Total Float	Timeline
0840	FRC UPPER BASEMENT SLAB 4	20	0	20	15 JUL 03	11 AUG 03	-29	
0850	RELOCATE TEMPORARY WORKS JIGS 1 & 2	3	0	3	07 AUG 03	11 AUG 03	-29	
0860	REMOVE SIDE BERMS AREA 5	5	0	5	11 AUG 03	15 AUG 03	-29	
0870	FRC LOW SECTION OF BASEM'T SLAB AREA 6	8	0	8	15 JUL 03	24 JUL 03	-23	
0880	FRC WALLS LOW - HIGH BASEMENT SLAB AREA 6	5	0	5	25 JUL 03	31 JUL 03	-29	
0890	FRC INTERMEDIATE SLAB AREA 6	4	0	4	01 AUG 03	06 AUG 03	-29	
0900	FRC WALLS FROM INTERMEDIATE TO HIGH LVL. SLAB A6	3	0	3	07 AUG 03	11 AUG 03	-29	
0910	FRC HIGH LEVEL BASEMENT SLAB AREA 6	10	0	10	01 AUG 03	14 AUG 03	-25	
0960	RELOCATE TEMPORARY WORKS JIGS 3 & 4	3	0	3	15 AUG 03	19 AUG 03	-29	
0970	REMOVE SIDE BERMS AREA 6	5	0	5	19 AUG 03	26 AUG 03	-29	
0980	FRC BASEMENT SLAB SECTION 7	10	0	10	13 AUG 03	27 AUG 03	-29	
0990	FRC CLOSING SECTIONS OF BASEMENT SLABS AREA 6	4	0	4	26 AUG 03	29 AUG 03	-29	
1000	FRC WALLS & COLUMNS LOWER -UPPER BAS'NT AREA 6	13	0	13	15 AUG 03	03 SEP 03	-29	
1010	FRC UPPER BASEMENT SLAB 6	15	0	15	21 AUG 03	11 SEP 03	-29	
1040	FRC BASEMENT SLAB SECTION 8	10	0	10	26 AUG 03	08 SEP 03	-29	
1060	FRC WALLS & COLUMNS LOWER -UPPER BAS'NT AREA 7	26	0	26	28 AUG 03	02 OCT 03	-29	
1080	FRC UPPER BASEMENT SLAB 7	33	0	33	03 SEP 03	17 OCT 03	-29	
1090	RELOCATE TEMPORARY WORKS JIGS 3 & 4	3	0	3	12 SEP 03	16 SEP 03	-29	
1100	REMOVE SIDE BERMS AREA 8	5	0	5	16 SEP 03	22 SEP 03	-29	
1110	FRC CLOSING SECTIONS OF BASEMENT SLABS AREA 8	6	0	6	22 SEP 03	29 SEP 03	-29	
1120	FRC WALLS & COLUMNS LOWER -UPPER BAS'NT AREA 8	19	0	19	09 SEP 03	03 OCT 03	-29	
1140	FRC UPPER BASEMENT SLAB AREA 8	25	0	25	15 SEP 03	17 OCT 03	-29	
1150	INSTALL SUPPORTING PROPS TO PILES ADJ. TO GL 17	7	0	7	09 SEP 03	17 SEP 03	-29	
1160	REMOVE SUPPORTING BERM	10	0	10	16 SEP 03	29 SEP 03	-29	
1170	FRC CLOSING SECTION OF BASEMENT SLAB	12	0	12	24 SEP 03	09 OCT 03	-29	
1180	FRC WALLS / COLUMNS LOWER - UPPER BASEMENT	11	0	11	02 OCT 03	16 OCT 03	-29	
1190	FRC CLOSING SECTION OF UPPER BASEMENT SLAB	11	0	11	10 OCT 03	24 OCT 03	-29	
1200	2 Week Allowance For Breaking Back Female Piles	10	0	10	08 AUG 03	21 AUG 03	-29	
1210	FRC Columns / Walls Upper Basement - Ground	60	0	60	22 AUG 03	14 NOV 03	-29	
1220	Substructure Arts Centre Complete	1	0	1	17 NOV 03	17 NOV 03	-29	

APARTMENT BLOCK
SUPERSTRUCTURE

Activity ID	Activity Description	Orig Dur	% Comp	Rem Dur	Early Start	Early Finish	Total Float	Timeline
1240	FRC GF Slab Incl Part Sect. Of Area 3 GL 1-7/A-H	13	0	13	05 AUG 03	21 AUG 03	-29	

MIXED-USE DEVELOPMENT

As Built: as of 30 Mar.2003
end of WINDOW 4
The Critical Path

APPENDIX 5F b

▬▬	The critical path
▬▬	Progress Bar
▬▬	Critical Activity

Activity ID	Activity Description	Orig Dur	% Comp	Rem Dur	Early Start	Early Finish	Total Float
1250	FRC Ground Floor Slab Low Level GL 1-7/M-R	10	0	10	01 AUG 03	14 AUG 03	-29
1260	FRC Remaining High Level Section Of GF SLAB	11	0	11	13 AUG 03	28 AUG 03	-29
1270	FRC Walls / Columns Ground - Mezz	11	0	11	15 AUG 03	01 SEP 03	-29
1280	FRC Mezz Floor Grid Lines 1-7/A-D	7	0	7	27 AUG 03	04 SEP 03	-29
1300	FRC Walls / Columns Mezz- 2nd Floor	10	0	10	05 SEP 03	18 SEP 03	-29
1330	FRC 2nd Floor Slab GL 1-7/M-R	8	0	8	12 SEP 03	23 SEP 03	-29
1340	FRC 2nd Floor Slab 1-7/A-F	10	0	10	15 SEP 03	26 SEP 03	-29
1350	FRC Walls/Columns 2nd - 3rd/4th Floor	15	0	15	19 SEP 03	09 OCT 03	-29
1360	FRC 3rd Floor Slab GL 1-7/F-M	11	0	11	25 SEP 03	09 OCT 03	-29
1390	FRC Walls / Columns 3rd - 4th Floor	13	0	13	10 OCT 03	28 OCT 03	-29
1420	FRC 4th Floor Slab GL 1-3/J-R/ + 4-7/L-P	13	0	13	15 OCT 03	31 OCT 03	-29
1440	FRC 4th Floor Slab GL 6-7/M-R	10	0	10	27 OCT 03	07 NOV 03	-29
1450	FRC Walls / Columns 4th - 5th Floor	14	0	14	27 OCT 03	13 NOV 03	-29
1460	FRC 5th Floor Slab GL 1-6/K-R	11	0	11	28 OCT 03	11 NOV 03	-29
1470	FRC 5th Floor Slab GL 1-6/A-K	12	0	12	03 NOV 03	18 NOV 03	-29
1480	FRC Walls/ Columns 5th - 6th Floor	12	0	12	12 NOV 03	27 NOV 03	-29
1490	FRC 6th Floor Slab GL 1-6/K-R	11	0	11	17 NOV 03	01 DEC 03	-29
1500	FRC 6th Floor Slab GL 1-6/A-K	11	0	11	19 NOV 03	03 DEC 03	-29
1510	FRC Walls / Columns 6th - 7th Floor	10	0	10	02 DEC 03	15 DEC 03	-29
1520	FRC 7th Floor Slab GL 1-6/K-R	11	0	11	05 DEC 03	19 DEC 03	-29
1530	FRC 7th Floor Slab GL 1-6/A-K	11	0	11	10 DEC 03	07 JAN 04	-29
1540	FRC Walls/ Columns 7th - 8th Floor	10	0	10	05 JAN 04	16 JAN 04	-29
1550	FRC 8th Floor Slab GL 1-6/K-R	10	0	10	09 JAN 04	22 JAN 04	-29
1560	FRC 8th Floor Slab GL 1-6/A-K	11	0	11	16 JAN 04	30 JAN 04	-29
1570	FRC Walls / Column 8th - 9th Floor	12	0	12	23 JAN 04	09 FEB 04	-29
1580	FRC 9th Floor Slab GL 1-6/K-R	10	0	10	29 JAN 04	11 FEB 04	-29
1590	FRC 9th Floor Slab GL 1-6/A-K	11	0	11	09 FEB 04	23 FEB 04	-29
1600	FRC Walls / Columns 9th - 10th Floor	12	0	12	12 FEB 04	27 FEB 04	-29
1610	FRC 10th Floor Slab GL 1-6/K-R	11	0	11	18 FEB 04	03 MAR 04	-29
1620	FRC 10th Floor SlabGL 1-6/A-K	11	0	11	27 FEB 04	12 MAR 04	-29
1630	FRC Walls / Columns 10th - 11th Floor	12	0	12	04 MAR 04	19 MAR 04	-29
1640	FRC 11th Floor Slab GL 1-6/K-R	11	0	11	10 MAR 04	24 MAR 04	-29
1650	FRC 11th Floor Slab GL 1-6/A-K	12	0	12	15 MAR 04	30 MAR 04	-29
1660	FRC Walls / Columns 11th - 12th Floor	12	0	12	25 MAR 04	19 APR 04	-29

The critical path
Progress Bar
Critical Activity

MIXED-USE DEVELOPMENT

As Built: as of 30 Mar.2003
end of WINDOW 4
The Critical Path

APPENDIX 5F b

Sheet 3 of 6

Activity ID	Activity Description	Orig Dur	% Comp	Rem Dur	Early Start	Early Finish	Total Float
1670	FRC 12th Floor Slab GL 1-6/K-R	11	0	11	31.MAR.04	22.APR.04	-29
1680	FRC 12th Floor Slab GL 1-6/A-K	11	0	11	07.APR.04	29.APR.04	-29
1690	FRC Walls / Columns 12th - 13th Floor	11	0	11	23.APR.04	10.MAY.04	-29
1700	FRC 13th Floor Slab GL 1-6/K-R	9	0	9	29.APR.04	12.MAY.04	-29
1710	FRC 13th Floor Slab GL 1-6/A-K	8	0	8	05.MAY.04	14.MAY.04	-29
1720	FRC Walls / Columns 13th - 14th Floor	7	0	7	13.MAY.04	21.MAY.04	-29
1730	FRC 14th Floor Slab GL 1-6/K-R	7	0	7	18.MAY.04	26.MAY.04	-29
1740	FRC 14th Floor Slab GL 1-6/A-K	7	0	7	20.MAY.04	28.MAY.04	-29
1750	FRC Walls/ Columns 14th - 15th Floor	9	0	9	27.MAY.04	09.JUN.04	-29
1760	FRC 15th Floor Slab GL 1-6/K-R	11	0	11	02.JUN.04	16.JUN.04	-29
1780	FRC Core Walls Level 15-16 GL A-B/2-5	6	0	6	17.JUN.04	24.JUN.04	-25
1790	FRC Core Walls Level 16-Roof GL A-B/2-5	9	0	9	25.JUN.04	07.JUL.04	-25
1800	FRC Cover Slab To Core	9	0	9	08.JUL.04	20.JUL.04	-29
1810	Progressive Erection of Precast Stairs	177	0	177	30.OCT.03	28.JUL.04	-29
1860	Timber Grounds Windows & Doors	162	0	162	10.FEB.04	05.OCT.04	-29
1870	Render Insulation & First Coat	142	0	142	23.MAR.04	19.OCT.04	-29
1880	Terracotta Cladding Frame Work	137	0	137	06.APR.04	26.OCT.04	-29
1890	Metal Cladding	142	0	142	21.APR.04	09.NOV.04	-29
1910	Terracotta Panels	112	0	112	11.JUN.04	16.NOV.04	-29
1950	Penthouse Brise Soleil	30	0	30	15.SEP.04	26.OCT.04	-29
1960	Penthouse Curtain Walling	40	0	40	22.SEP.04	16.NOV.04	-29
1970	Penthouse Roof Cladding/Roof Lights	40	0	40	22.SEP.04	16.NOV.04	-29
1980	Render Final Coat Top Down	59	0	59	20.OCT.04	24.JAN.05	-29
1990	Bolt On Balconies	54	0	54	03.NOV.04	31.JAN.05	-29
2000	Dismantle Scaffolds	59	0	59	09.NOV.04	11.FEB.05	-29
2050	Penthouse Roof Weathered	1	0	1	17.NOV.04	17.NOV.04	-29
2100	Lift Shaft Temporary Weathered	9	0	9	21.JUL.04	02.AUG.04	-29
INTERNAL FINISHES							
1850	Blockwork	181	0	181	03.DEC.03	07.SEP.04	-29
1900	Balcony/Balustrades & Finishes	147	0	147	06.MAY.04	30.NOV.04	-29
2060	Internal Blockwork to Cores	182	0	182	03.FEB.04	26.OCT.04	-29
2070	M & E Services to Cores & Risers	171	0	171	06.MAY.04	17.JAN.05	-29
2080	Staircase Lobbies & Common Areas	171	0	171	06.MAY.04	17.JAN.05	-29
2110	Lift installations	98	0	98	03.AUG.04	17.DEC.04	-29

Legend:
- The critical path
- Progress Bar
- Critical Activity

MIXED-USE DEVELOPMENT

As Built: as of 30 Mar.2003
end of WINDOW 4
The Critical Path

APPENDIX 5F b

Activity ID	Activity Description	Orig Dur	% Comp	Rem Dur	Early Start	Early Finish	Total Float	2002	2003	2004	2005
2120	Final Commision Clean & Snag	58	0	58	10.NOV.04	11.FEB.05	-29				
2130	Shell & Core Completion	1	0	1	11.FEB.05	11.FEB.05	-29				
2200	Access For Third Fit Out Phase	0	0	0	02.NOV.04		-29				
2210	Third Phase Notional Fit Out Period	64	0	64	02.NOV.04	11.FEB.05	-29				

ARTS CENTRE
SUPERSTRUCTURE

Activity ID	Activity Description	Orig Dur	% Comp	Rem Dur	Early Start	Early Finish	Total Float	2002	2003	2004	2005
2220	FRC Ground Floor Slab Low Level GL 7-9/A-J	12	0	12	03.SEP.03	18.SEP.03	-29				
2230	FRC Ground Floor Slab Low Level GL 7-9/M-R	10	0	10	08.SEP.03	19.SEP.03	-29				
2240	FRC Walls From Low - High Lvl GF Slab GL 7-9/M&J	7	0	7	19.SEP.03	29.SEP.03	-29				
2250	FRC Ground Floor Slab High Level GL 7-9/J-M	9	0	9	24.SEP.03	06.OCT.03	-29				
2260	FRC Ground Floor Slab Low Level GL 9-11/A-K	14	0	14	01.OCT.03	20.OCT.03	-29				
2270	FRC Grond Floor Slab Low Level GL 9-11/M-R	10	0	10	06.OCT.03	17.OCT.03	-29				
2280	FRC Walls From Low - High Lvl GF Slab GL 7-9/M&K	6	0	6	20.OCT.03	27.OCT.03	-29				
2290	FRC Ground Floor Sab High Level GL 9-11/K-M	10	0	10	17.OCT.03	30.OCT.03	-29				
2300	FRC Ground Floor Slab Low Level GL 12-15/A-L	15	0	15	31.OCT.03	20.NOV.03	-29				
2310	FRC Ground Floor Slab Low Level GL 12-15/L-R	14	0	14	31.OCT.03	19.NOV.03	-29				
2320	FRC Walls From Low - High Lvl GF Slab GL 12,14&K	6	0	6	20.NOV.03	27.NOV.03	-29				
2330	FRC High Level Slab 11-14/A-K	8	0	8	21.NOV.03	02.DEC.03	-29				
2340	FRC High Level Slab GL 11-12/K-M	5	0	5	02.DEC.03	08.DEC.03	-29				
2350	FRC Ground Floor Slab GL 15-17/F-R	14	0	14	18.NOV.03	05.DEC.03	-29				
2360	FRC Walls / Columns Ground - 2nd Floor	57	0	57	23.SEP.03	10.DEC.03	-29				
2380	FRC Mezzanine Slab GL 13-17/C-R	11	0	11	11.DEC.03	08.JAN.04	-29				
2390	FRC 2nd Floor Slab GL 7-9/A-J	12	0	12	02.OCT.03	17.OCT.03	-29				
2420	FRC Remainder Of 2nd Floor Slab	12	0	12	09.JAN.04	26.JAN.04	-29				
2430	FRC Walls / Columns 2nd - 3rd Floor	71	0	71	20.OCT.03	09.FEB.04	-29				
2440	FRC 3rd Floor Slab GL 7-9/L-R	20	0	20	27.NOV.03	07.JAN.04	-29				
2450	FRC 3rd Floor Slab GL 9-14/H-R	17	0	17	07.JAN.04	29.JAN.04	-29				
2460	FRC 3rd Floor Slab GL 14-17/F-R	24	0	24	22.JAN.04	24.FEB.04	-29				
2510	FRC 4th Floor Slab GL 9-15/F-R	18	0	18	05.FEB.04	01.MAR.04	-29				
2570	Concrete Studio Theater Roof	5	0	5	16.MAR.04	22.MAR.04	-29				
2620	Steelwork & Decking Level 4	10	0	10	02.MAR.04	15.MAR.04	-29				
2830	Roofing Roof Finishes Lvl 4 & 5	61	0	61	01.MAR.04	03.JUN.04	-29				
2880	Rooflights Fitness Centre	15	0	15	23.MAR.04	20.APR.04	-29				

████ The critical path	**MIXED-USE DEVELOPMENT**		Sheet 5 of 6
████ Progress Bar		**APPENDIX 5F b**	
████ Critical Activity	**As Built: as of 30 Mar.2003** **end of WINDOW 4** **The Critical Path**		

Activity ID	Activity Description	Orig Dur	% Comp	Rem Dur	Early Start	Early Finish	Total Float
3060	Barriers/Markings	40	0	40	06.DEC.04	11.FEB.05	-29
3110	Barriers & Marking	20	0	20	17.JAN.05	11.FEB.05	-29
INTERNAL FINISHES							
2940	Blockwork Partitions/Builders Work	100	0	100	09.MAR.04	05.AUG.04	-29
2960	Service Installations/Commission	186	0	186	12.MAY.04	11.FEB.05	-29
2980	Specialist Fit Out Works	153	0	153	29.JUN.04	11.FEB.05	-29
3050	Walls/Finishes & S	49	0	49	26.OCT.04	14.JAN.05	-29
3070	Office Area Fit Out	99	0	99	14.SEP.04	11.FEB.05	-29
3080	Remaining Retail Areas	1	0	1	11.FEB.05	11.FEB.05	-29
3100	Finishes & Service	79	0	79	14.SEP.04	14.JAN.05	-29
EXTERNAL WORKS							
3140	External Pavings Remainder (By Others)	30	0	30	20.DEC.04	11.FEB.05	-29
SECTIONAL COMPLETIONS							
SECT08	All Others Areas	0	0	0		11.FEB.05	-29

Legend:
- The critical path
- Progress Bar
- Critical Activity

MIXED-USE DEVELOPMENT

As Built: as of 30.Mar.2003
end of WINDOW 4
The Critical Path

APPENDIX 5F b

Sheet 6 of 6

PRELIMINARY WORKS

Activity ID	Activity Description	Orig Dur	% Comp	Rem Dur	Early Start	Early Finish	Total Float	Variance 2 Early Finish	2002 N.D.J.F.M.A.M.J.J.A.S.O.N.D	2003 J.F.M.A.M.J.J.A.S.O.N.D	2004 J.F.M.A.M.J.J.A.S.O.N.D	2005 J.F
0090	Cut Down Piles	35	88	4	16.DEC.02A	09.MAY.03	-21	-12				
0100	Preliminary Works Complete	1	0	1	12.MAY.03	12.MAY.03	-21	-12				

APARTMENT BLOCK
SUBSTRUCTURE

Activity ID	Activity Description	Orig Dur	% Comp	Rem Dur	Early Start	Early Finish	Total Float	Variance 2 Early Finish
0110	FRC CAPPING BEAM	35	40	21	18.FEB.03A	04.JUN.03	-33	-19
0120	BULK DIG LEAVING SUPPORTING BERMS	74	70	22	25.FEB.03A	02.JUL.03	-33	-4
0130	FRC SECTION OF AREA 3 SLAB FOR TOWER CRANE 1	5	100	0	06.MAR.03A	05.APR.03A		-4
0140	ERECT TOWER CRANE	0	100	0	15.APR.03A			3
0150	FRC BASEMENT SLAB AREA 1	9	100	0	10.APR.03A	29.APR.03A		7
0160	INSTALL TEMPORARY WORKS JIGS 1 & 2	3	100	0	08.APR.03A	01.MAY.03A		8
0170	REMOVE SIDE BERMS AREA 1	4	0	4	06.MAY.03	09.MAY.03	-17	6
0180	FRC CLOSING SECTIONS OF BASEMENT SLABS AREA 1	7	0	7	09.MAY.03	19.MAY.03	-17	6
0190	FRC WALLS AND COLUMNS LOWER - UPPER BASEMENT	16	10	14	01.MAY.03A	23.MAY.03	-17	6
0210	FRC UPPER BASEMENT SLAB AREA 1	14	0	14	08.MAY.03	28.MAY.03	-17	6
0220	FRC BASEMENT SLAB AREA 2	10	100	0	03.APR.03A	03.MAY.03A		11
0230	INSTALL TEMPORARY WORKS JIGS 3 & 4	3	0	3	14.MAY.03	16.MAY.03	-17	6
0240	REMOVE SIDE BERMS AREA 2	4	0	4	11.JUN.03	16.JUN.03	-33	-4
0250	FRC CLOSING SECTIONS OF BASEMENT SLABS AREA 2	6	0	6	16.JUN.03	23.JUN.03	-33	-4
0260	FRC WALLS & COLUMNS LOWER -UPPER BASNT AREA 2	16	0	16	06.JUN.03	27.JUN.03	-33	-4
0280	FRC UPPER BASEMENT SLAB AREA 2	15	0	15	12.JUN.03	02.JUL.03	-33	-4
0290	RELOCATE TEMPORARY WORKS JIGS 1 & 2	3	0	3	27.JUN.03	01.JUL.03	-33	-4
0300	INSTALL TEMP SUPPORT PROPS GL 1/A-J	22	0	22	02.JUN.03	01.JUL.03	-33	-4
0370	REMOVE BERM	5	0	5	02.JUL.03	08.JUL.03	-33	-4

Legend:
- Original plan
- Current forecast at end of window
- Progress Bar
- Critical Activity

MIXED-USE DEVELOPMENT

As Built: as of 4 May.2003
end of WINDOW 5
Progress Comparison Chart

APPENDIX 5G a

Activity ID	Activity Description	Orig Dur	% Comp	Rem Dur	Early Start	Early Finish	Total Float	Variance 2 Early Finish	2002 N D	2003 J F M A M J J A S O N D	2004 J F M A M J J A S O N D	2005 J F M
0380	BREAK BACK FEMALE PILES	4	0	4	07.JUL.03	10.JUL.03	-33	-4				
0390	FRC CLOSING SECTION OF BASEMENT SLAB GL 1/A-J	6	0	6	09.JUL.03	16.JUL.03	-33	-4				
0400	FRC WALLS & COLUMNS BASEMENT - UPPER BASEMENT	5	0	5	17.JUL.03	23.JUL.03	-33	-4				
0410	FRC UPPER BASEMENT SLAB GL 1/A-J	7	0	7	22.JUL.03	30.JUL.03	-33	-4				
0420	INSTALL TEMP SUPPORT PROPS GL 1/M-R	14	0	14	06 MAY.03*	23.MAY.03	-18	5				
0470	REMOVE BERM	4	0	4	17.JUN.03	20.JUN.03	-33	-4				
0480	BREAK BACK FEMALE PILES	3	0	3	20.JUN.03	24.JUN.03	-33	-4				
0490	FRC CLOSING SECTION OF BASEMENT SLAB GL 1/M-R	5	0	5	24.JUN.03	30.JUN.03	-33	-4				
0500	FRC WALLS & COLUMNS BASEMENT - UPPER BASEMENT	4	0	4	01.JUL.03	04.JUL.03	-33	-4				
0510	FRC UPPER BASEMENT SLAB GL 1/M-R	6	0	6	04.JUL.03	11.JUL.03	-33	-4				
0520	INSTALL TEMP SUPPORT PROPS GL 1/J-M	18	0	18	06 MAY.03*	30.MAY.03	-12	11				
0680	REMOVE BERM	4	0	4	23.JUN.03	26.JUN.03	-27	-4				
0590	FRC CLOSING SECTION OF BASEMENT SLAB GL 1/J-M	5	0	5	01.JUL.03	07.JUL.03	-32	-4				
0600	FRC WALLS & COLUMNS BASEMENT - UPPER BASEMENT	6	0	6	08.JUL.03	15.JUL.03	-32	-4				
0610	FRC UPPER BASEMENT SLAB GL 1/J-M	6	0	6	15.JUL.03	22.JUL.03	-32	-4				
0620	FRC Walls/Columns Upper Basement - Ground Floor	40	0	40	30.JUN.03	22.AUG.03	-33	-4				

ARTS CENTRE
SUBSTRUCTURE

Activity ID	Activity Description	Orig Dur	% Comp	Rem Dur	Early Start	Early Finish	Total Float	Variance 2 Early Finish				
0660	FRC BASEMENT SLAB AREA 3	10	60	4	28.APR.03A	26.JUN.03	-29	0				
0670	RELOCATE TEMPORARY WORKS JIGS 1 & 2	3	70	1	02.MAY.03A	06.MAY.03	23	39				
0680	FRC LOW LEVEL BASEMENT SLAB AREA 4	6	0	6	25.JUN.03	02.JUL.03	-28	0				
0690	FRC WALLS LOW - HIGH LEVEL AREA 4 GL 8-9/P-M	4	0	4	03.JUL.03	08.JUL.03	-28	0				
0700	FRC BASEMENT SLAB AREA 4	14	40	8	02.MAY.03A	10.JUL.03	-28	1				
0720	FRC CLOSING SECTIONS OF BASEMENT SLABS AREA 3	6	0	6	11.JUL.03*	18.JUL.03	-26	1				
0730	FRC LIFT PITS IN CLOSING SECT. OF B3 GL Q-P/7-8	7	0	7	14.JUL.03*	22.JUL.03	-24	1				

Legend:
- Original plan
- Current forecast at end of window
- Progress Bar
- Critical Activity

MIXED-USE DEVELOPMENT

As Built: as of 4 May.2003
end of WINDOW 5
Progress Comparison Chart

APPENDIX 5G a

Sheet 2 of 3

Activity ID	Activity Description	Orig Dur	% Comp	Rem Dur	Early Start	Early Finish	Total Float	Variance 2 Early Finish
0740	FRC WALLS & COLUMNS LOWER -UPPER BAS'NT AREA 3	26	0	26	27.JUN.03	01.AUG.03	-29	0
0760	FRC UPPER BASEMENT SLAB AREA 3	26	0	26	02.JUL.03	06.AUG.03	-29	0
0770	RELOCATE TEMPORARY WORKS JIGS 3 & 4	3	0	3	17.JUL.03	21.JUL.03	-29	0
0780	REMOVE SIDE BERMS AREA 4	5	0	5	21.JUL.03	25.JUL.03	-29	0
0790	FRC RAMP & WALLS BASEM'T SLAB AREA 5 GL 9-10/H-E	4	0	4	06.MAY.03*	09.MAY.03	13	34
0800	FRC BASEMENT SLAB AREA 5	11	0	11	02.JUL.03	16.JUL.03	-27	1
0810	FRC CLOSING SECTIONS OF BASEMENT SLABS AREA 4	5	0	5	25.JUL.03	31.JUL.03	-29	0
0820	FRC WALLS & COLUMNS LOWER -UPPER BAS'NT AREA 4	21	0	21	09.JUL.03	06.AUG.03	-29	0
0840	FRC UPPER BASEMENT SLAB 4	20	0	20	15.JUL.03	11.AUG.03	-29	0
0870	FRC LOW SECTION OF BASEM'T SLAB AREA 6	8	0	8	15.JUL.03	24.JUL.03	-29	0
0880	FRC WALLS LOW - HIGH BASEMENT SLAB AREA 6	5	0	5	25.JUL.03	31.JUL.03	-29	0
0890	FRC INTERMEDIATE SLAB AREA 6	4	0	4	01.AUG.03	06.AUG.03	-29	0
0910	FRC HIGH LEVEL BASEMENT SLAB AREA 6	10	0	10	01.AUG.03	14.AUG.03	-29	0
0930	FRC WALLS & COLUMNS LOWER -UPPER BAS'NT AREA 5	31	0	31	17.JUL.03	29.AUG.03	-28	0
0950	FRC UPPER BASEMENT SLAB 5	34	0	34	23.JUL.03	09.SEP.03	-28	0

SECTIONAL COMPLETIONS

Activity ID	Activity Description	Orig Dur	% Comp	Rem Dur	Early Start	Early Finish	Total Float	Variance 2 Early Finish
SECT01	Show Flat (floor 03)	0	0	0		25.MAR.04	-29	-4
SECT02	Arts Complex (partial)	0	0	0		30.APR.04	-29	-4
SECT03	Residential Floors 04 to 07(incl.)	0	0	0		21.JUN.04	-33	-4
SECT04	Shops	0	0	0		21.JUN.04	-30	-4
SECT07	Remaining Residential	0	0	0		04.NOV.04	-33	-4
SECT08	All Others Areas	0	0	0		17.FEB.05	-33	-4

Original plan
Current forecast at end of window
Progress Bar
Critical Activity

MIXED-USE DEVELOPMENT

As Built: as of 4 May.2003
end of WINDOW 5
Progress Comparison Chart

Sheet 3 of 3

APPENDIX 5G a

APARTMENT BLOCK

SUBSTRUCTURE

Activity ID	Activity Description	Orig Dur	% Comp	Rem Dur	Early Start	Early Finish	Total Float
0110	FRC CAPPING BEAM	35	40	21	18 FEB 03A	04 JUN 03	-33
0120	BULK DIG LEAVING SUPPORTING BERMS	74	70	22	25 FEB 03A	02 JUL 03	-33
0240	REMOVE SIDE BERMS AREA 2	4	0	4	11 JUN 03	16 JUN 03	-33
0250	FRC CLOSING SECTIONS OF BASEMENT SLABS AREA 2	6	0	6	16 JUN 03	23 JUN 03	-33
0260	FRC WALLS & COLUMNS LOWER -UPPER BAS'NT AREA 2	16	0	16	06 JUN 03	27 JUN 03	-33
0280	FRC UPPER BASEMENT SLAB AREA 2	15	0	15	12 JUN 03	02 JUL 03	-33
0290	RELOCATE TEMPORARY WORKS JIGS 1 & 2	3	0	3	27 JUN 03	01 JUL 03	-33
0300	INSTALL TEMP SUPPORT PROPS GL 1/A-J	22	0	22	02 JUN 03	01 JUL 03	-33
0370	REMOVE BERM	5	0	5	02 JUL 03	08 JUL 03	-33
0380	BREAK BACK FEMALE PILES	4	0	4	07 JUL 03	10 JUL 03	-33
0390	FRC CLOSING SECTION OF BASEMENT SLAB GL 1/A-J	6	0	6	09 JUL 03	16 JUL 03	-33
0400	FRC WALLS & COLUMNS BASEMENT - UPPER BASEMENT	5	0	5	17 JUL 03	23 JUL 03	-33
0410	FRC UPPER BASEMENT SLAB GL 1/A-J	7	0	7	22 JUL 03	30 JUL 03	-33
0470	REMOVE BERM	4	0	4	17 JUN 03	20 JUN 03	-33
0480	BREAK BACK FEMALE PILES	3	0	3	20 JUN 03	24 JUN 03	-33
0490	FRC CLOSING SECTION OF BASEMENT SLAB GL 1/M-R	5	0	5	24 JUN 03	30 JUN 03	-32
0500	FRC WALLS & COLUMNS BASEMENT - UPPER BASEMENT	4	0	4	01 JUL 03	04 JUL 03	-33
0510	FRC UPPER BASEMENT SLAB GL 1/M-R	6	0	6	04 JUL 03	11 JUL 03	-33
0620	FRC Walls/Columns Upper Basement- Ground Floor	40	0	40	30 JUN 03	22 AUG 03	-33
0630	Substructure Residential Complete	0	0	0	26 AUG 03		-33
1230	Substructure Residential Complete	0	0	0	26 AUG 03		-33

ARTS CENTRE

SUBSTRUCTURE

Activity ID	Activity Description	Orig Dur	% Comp	Rem Dur	Early Start	Early Finish	Total Float
0640	Crane Base	5	0	5	15 AUG 03	21 AUG 03	-33
0980	FRC BASEMENT SLAB SECTION 7	10	0	10	19 AUG 03	02 SEP 03	-33
1040	FRC BASEMENT SLAB SECTION 8	10	0	10	01 SEP 03	12 SEP 03	-33
1060	FRC WALLS & COLUMNS LOWER -UPPER BAS'NT AREA 7	26	0	26	03 SEP 03	08 OCT 03	-33
1080	FRC UPPER BASEMENT SLAB 7	33	0	33	09 SEP 03	23 OCT 03	-33
1120	FRC WALLS & COLUMNS LOWER -UPPER BAS'NT AREA 8	19	0	19	15 SEP 03	09 OCT 03	-33
1140	FRC UPPER BASEMENT SLAB AREA 8	25	0	25	19 SEP 03	23 OCT 03	-33
1150	INSTALL SUPPORTING PROPS TO PILES ADJ TO GL 17	7	0	7	15 SEP 03	23 SEP 03	-33

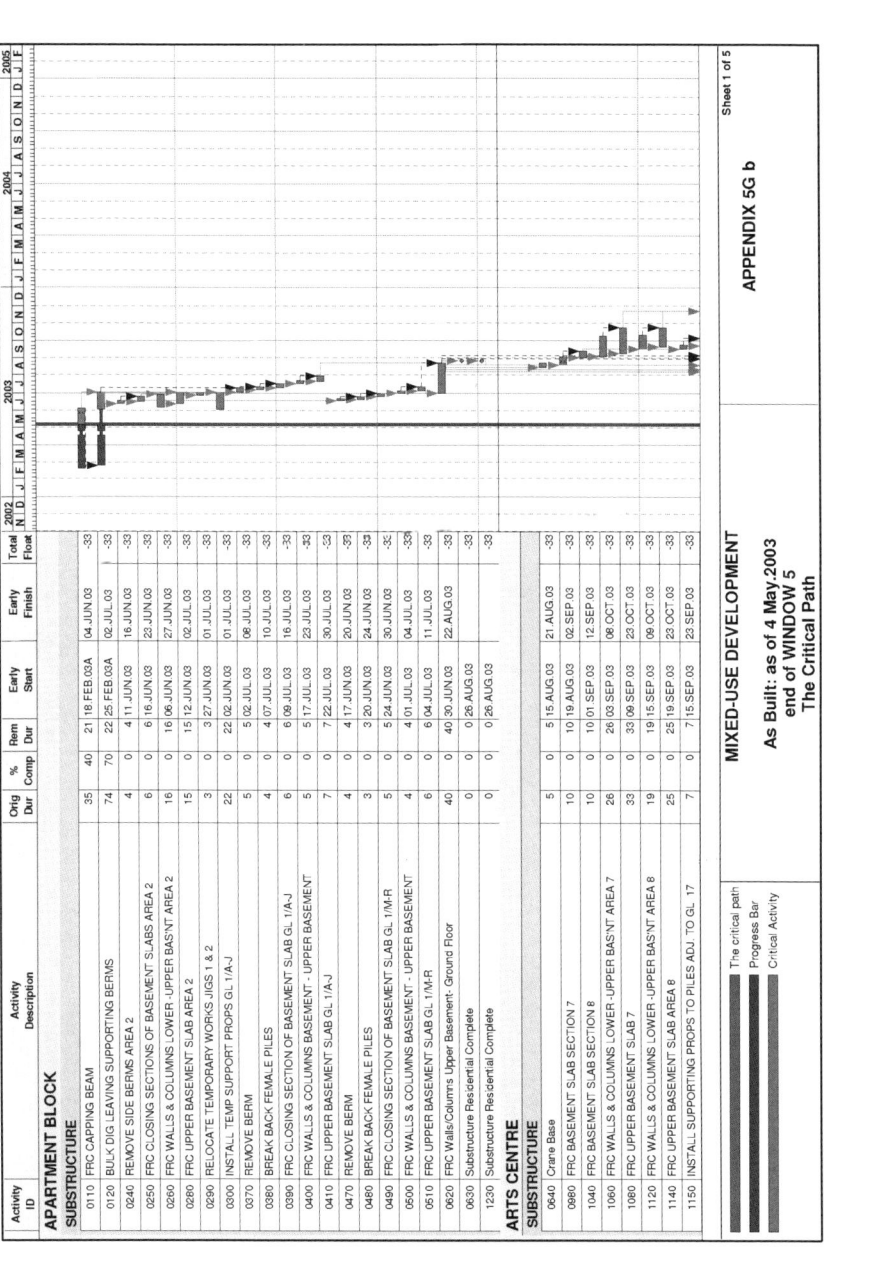

Legend:
- The critical path
- Progress Bar
- Critical Activity

MIXED-USE DEVELOPMENT

As Built: as of 4 May.2003
end of WINDOW 5
The Critical Path

APPENDIX 5G b

Sheet 1 of 5

Activity ID	Activity Description	Orig Dur	% Comp	Rem Dur	Early Start	Early Finish	Total Float	2002 N D	2003 J F M A M J J A S O N D	2004 J F M A M J J A S O N D	2005 J F
1160	REMOVE SUPPORTING BERM	10	0	10	22.SEP.03	03.OCT.03	-33				
1170	FRC CLOSING SECTION OF BASEMENT SLAB	12	0	12	30.SEP.03	15.OCT.03	-33				
1180	FRC WALLS / COLUMNS LOWER - UPPER BASEMENT	11	0	11	08.OCT.03	22.OCT.03	-33				
1190	FRC CLOSING SECTION OF UPPER BASEMENT SLAB	11	0	11	16.OCT.03	30.OCT.03	-33				
1210	FRC Columns / Walls Upper Basement - Ground	60	0	60	29.AUG.03	20.NOV.03	-33				
1220	Substructure Arts Centre Complete	1	0	1	21.NOV.03	21.NOV.03	-33				

APARTMENT BLOCK
SUPERSTRUCTURE

Activity ID	Activity Description	Orig Dur	% Comp	Rem Dur	Early Start	Early Finish	Total Float				
1240	FRC GF Slab Incl Part Sect. Of Area 3 GL 1-7/A-H	13	0	13	11.AUG.03	28.AUG.03	-33				
1250	FRC Ground Floor Slab Low Level GL 1-7/M-R	10	0	10	07.AUG.03	20.AUG.03	-33				
1260	FRC Remaining High Level Section Of GF SLAB	11	0	11	19.AUG.03	03.SEP.03	-33				
1270	FRC Walls / Columns Ground - Mezz	11	0	11	21.AUG.03	05.SEP.03	-33				
1280	FRC Mezz Floor Grid Lines 1-7/A-D	7	0	7	02.SEP.03	10.SEP.03	-33				
1300	FRC Walls / Columns Mezz- 2nd Floor	10	0	10	11.SEP.03	24.SEP.03	-33				
1330	FRC 2nd Floor Slab GL 1-7/M-R	8	0	8	18.SEP.03	29.SEP.03	-33				
1340	FRC 2nd Floor Slab 1-7/A-F	10	0	10	19.SEP.03	02.OCT.03	-33				
1350	FRC Walls/Columns 2nd - 3rd/4th Floor	15	0	15	25.SEP.03	15.OCT.03	-33				
1360	FRC 3rd Floor Slab GL 1-7/F-M	11	0	11	01.OCT.03	15.OCT.03	-33				
1390	FRC Walls / Columns 3rd - 4th Floor	13	0	13	16.OCT.03	03.NOV.03	-33				
1420	FRC 4th Floor Slab GL 1-3/J-R/ + 4-7/L-P	13	0	13	21.OCT.03	06.NOV.03	-33				
1440	FRC 4th Floor Slab GL 6-7/M-R	10	0	10	31.OCT.03	13.NOV.03	-33				
1450	FRC Walls / Columns 4th - 5th Floor	14	0	14	31.OCT.03	19.NOV.03	-33				
1460	FRC 5th Floor Slab GL 1-6/K-R	11	0	11	03.NOV.03	17.NOV.03	-33				
1470	FRC 5th Floor Slab GL 1-6/A-K	12	0	12	07.NOV.03	24.NOV.03	-33				
1480	FRC Walls/ Columns 5th - 6th Floor	12	0	12	18.NOV.03	03.DEC.03	-33				
1490	FRC 6th Floor Slab GL 1-6/K-R	11	0	11	21.NOV.03	05.DEC.03	-33				
1500	FRC 6th Floor Slab GL 1-6/A-K	11	0	11	25.NOV.03	09.DEC.03	-33				
1510	FRC Walls / Columns 6th - 7th Floor	10	0	10	08.DEC.03	19.DEC.03	-33				
1520	FRC 7th Floor Slab GL 1-6/K-R	11	0	11	11.DEC.03	08.JAN.04	-33				
1530	FRC 7th Floor Slab GL 1-6/A-K	11	0	11	16.DEC.03	13.JAN.04	-33				
1540	FRC Walls/ Columns 7th - 8th Floor	10	0	10	09.JAN.04	22.JAN.04	-33				
1550	FRC 8th Floor Slab GL 1-6/K-R	10	0	10	15.JAN.04	28.JAN.04	-33				
1560	FRC 8th Floor Slab GL 1-6/A-K	11	0	11	22.JAN.04	05.FEB.04	-33				

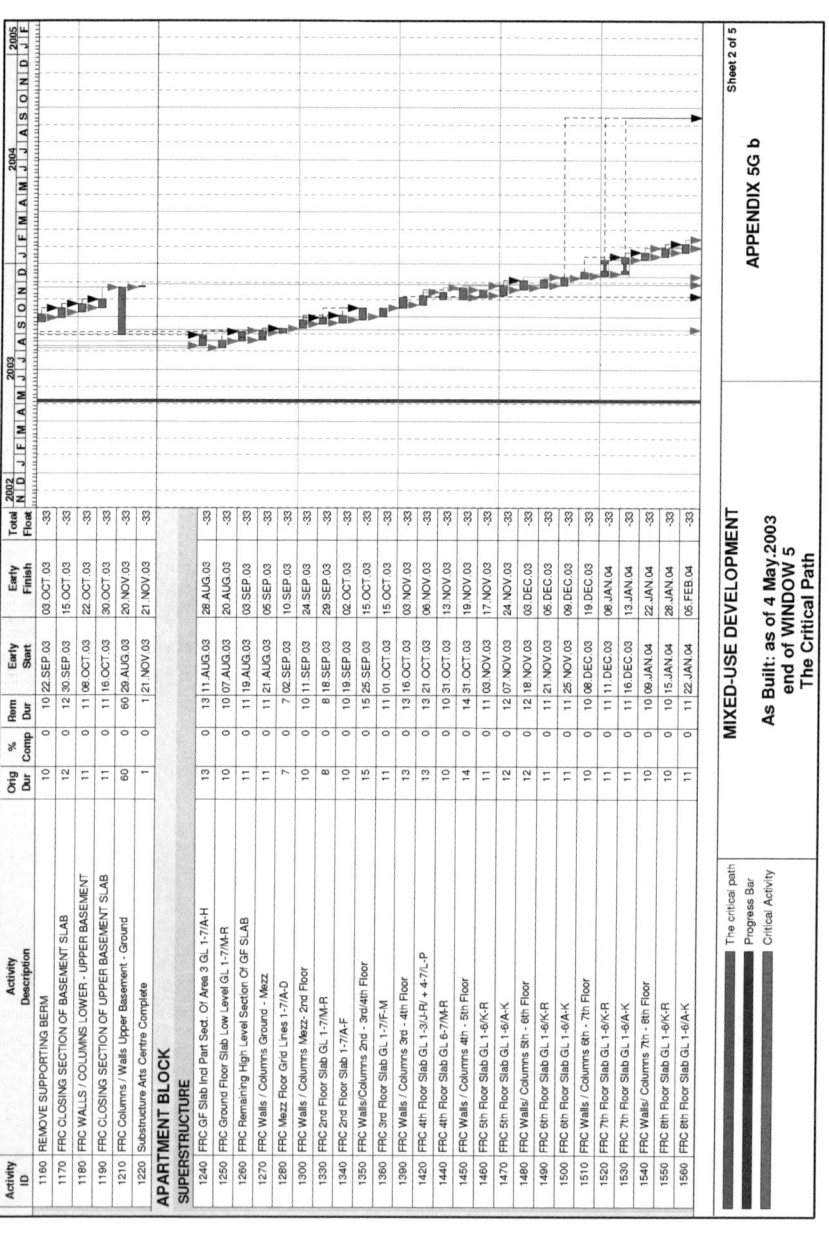

The critical path
Progress Bar
Critical Activity

MIXED-USE DEVELOPMENT

**As Built: as of 4 May.2003
end of WINDOW 5
The Critical Path**

APPENDIX 5G b

Activity ID	Activity Description	Orig Dur	% Comp	Rem Dur	Early Start	Early Finish	Total Float
1570	FRC Walls / Column 8th - 9th Floor	12	0	12	29.JAN.04	13.FEB.04	-33
1580	FRC 9th Floor Slab GL 1-6/K-R	10	0	10	04.FEB.04	17.FEB.04	-33
1590	FRC 9th Floor Slab GL 1-6/A-K	11	0	11	13.FEB.04	27.FEB.04	-33
1600	FRC Walls / Columns 9th - 10th Floor	12	0	12	18.FEB.04	04.MAR.04	-33
1610	FRC 10th Floor Slab GL 1-6/K-R	11	0	11	24.FEB.04	09.MAR.04	-33
1620	FRC 10th Floor SlabGL 1-6/A-K	11	0	11	04.MAR.04	18.MAR.04	-33
1630	FRC Walls / Columns 10th - 11th Floor	12	0	12	10.MAR.04	25.MAR.04	-33
1640	FRC 11th Floor Slab GL 1-6/K-R	11	0	11	16.MAR.04	30.MAR.04	-33
1650	FRC 11th Floor Slab GL 1-6/A-K	12	0	12	19.MAR.04	05.APR.04	-33
1660	FRC Walls / Columns 11th - 12th Floor	12	0	12	31.MAR.04	23.APR.04	-33
1670	FRC 12th Floor Slab GL 1-6/K-R	11	0	11	06.APR.04	28.APR.04	-33
1680	FRC 12th Floor Slab GL 1-6/A-K	11	0	11	21.APR.04	06.MAY.04	-33
1690	FRC Walls / Columns 12th - 13th Floor	11	0	11	29.APR.04	14.MAY.04	-33
1700	FRC 13th Floor Slab GL 1-6/K-R	9	0	9	06.MAY.04	18.MAY.04	-33
1710	FRC 13th Floor Slab GL 1-6/A-K	8	0	8	11.MAY.04	20.MAY.04	-33
1720	FRC Walls / Columns 13th - 14th Floor	7	0	7	19.MAY.04	27.MAY.04	-33
1730	FRC 14th Floor Slab GL 1-6/K-R	7	0	7	24.MAY.04	02.JUN.04	-33
1740	FRC 14th Floor Slab GL 1-6/A-K	7	0	7	26.MAY.04	04.JUN.04	-33
1750	FRC Walls/ Columns 14th - 15th Floor	9	0	9	03.JUN.04	15.JUN.04	-33
1760	FRC 15th Floor Slab GL 1-6/K-R	11	0	11	08.JUN.04	22.JUN.04	-33
1780	FRC Core Walls Level 15-16 GL A-B/2-5	6	0	6	23.JUN.04	30.JUN.04	-33
1790	FRC Core Walls Level 16-Roof GL A-B/2-5	9	0	9	01.JUL.04	13.JUL.04	-33
1800	FRC Cover Slab To Core	9	0	9	14.JUL.04	26.JUL.04	-33
1810	Progressive Erection of Precast Stairs	177	0	177	05.NOV.03	03.AUG.04	-33
1860	Timber Grounds Windows & Doors	162	0	162	16.FEB.04	11.OCT.04	-33
1870	Render Insulation & First Coat	142	0	142	29.MAR.04	25.OCT.04	-33
1880	Terracotta Cladding Frame Work	137	0	137	20.APR.04	01.NOV.04	-33
1890	Metal Cladding	142	0	142	27.APR.04	15.NOV.04	-33
1910	Terracotta Panels	112	0	112	17.JUN.04	22.NOV.04	-33
1950	Penthouse Brise Soleil	30	0	30	21.SEP.04	01.NOV.04	-33
1960	Penthouse Curtain Walling	40	0	40	28.SEP.04	22.NOV.04	-33
1970	Penthouse Roof Cladding/Roof Lights	40	0	40	28.SEP.04	22.NOV.04	-33
1980	Render Final Coat Top Down	59	0	59	26.OCT.04	28.JAN.05	-33
1990	Bolt On Balconies	54	0	54	09.NOV.04	04.FEB.05	-33

Sheet 3 of 5

		2002	2003	2004	2005
		N D	J F M A M J J A S O N D	J F M A M J J A S O N D	J F

The critical path
Progress Bar
Critical Activity

MIXED-USE DEVELOPMENT

As Built: as of 4 May.2003
end of WINDOW 5
The Critical Path

APPENDIX 5G b

Activity ID	Activity Description	Orig Dur	% Comp	Rem Dur	Early Start	Early Finish	Total Float	
2000	Dismantle Scaffolds	59	0	59	15.NOV.04	17.FEB.05	-33	
2050	Penthouse Roof Weathered	1	0	1	23.NOV.04	23.NOV.04	-33	
2100	Lift Shaft Temporary Weathered	9	0	9	27.JUL.04	06.AUG.04	-33	
INTERNAL FINISHES								
1850	Blockwork	181	0	181	09.DEC.03	13.SEP.04	-33	
1900	Balcony/Balustrades & Finishes	147	0	147	12.MAY.04	06.DEC.04	-33	
2060	Internal Blockwork to Cores	182	0	182	09.FEB.04	01.NOV.04	-33	
2070	M & E Services to Cores & Risers	171	0	171	12.MAY.04	21.JAN.05	-33	
2080	Staircase Lobbies & Common Areas	171	0	171	12.MAY.04	21.JAN.05	-33	
2110	Lift installations	98	0	98	09.AUG.04	23.DEC.04	-33	
2120	Final Commision Clean & Snag	58	0	58	16.NOV.04	17.FEB.05	-33	
2130	Shell & Core Completion	1	0	1	17.FEB.05	17.FEB.05	-33	
2200	Access For Third Ft Out Phase	0	0	0	08.NOV.04		-33	
2210	Third Phase Notional Fit Out Period	64	0	64	08.NOV.04	17.FEB.05	-33	
ARTS CENTRE								
SUPERSTRUCTURE								
2220	FRC Ground Floor Slab Low Level GL 7-9/A-J	12	0	12	09.SEP.03	24.SEP.03	-33	
2230	FRC Ground Floor Slab Low Level GL 7-9/M-R	10	0	10	12.SEP.03	25.SEP.03	-33	
2240	FRC Walls From Low - High Lvl GF Slab GL 7-9/M&J	7	0	7	25.SEP.03	03.OCT.03	-33	
2250	FRC Ground Floor Slab High Level GL 7-9/J-M	9	0	9	30.SEP.03	10.OCT.03	-33	
2260	FRC Ground Floor Slab Low Level GL 9-11/A-K	14	0	14	07.OCT.03	24.OCT.03	-33	
2270	FRC Ground Floor Slab Low Level GL 9-11/M-R	10	0	10	10.OCT.03	23.OCT.03	-33	
2280	FRC Walls From Low - High Lvl GF Slab GL 7-9/M&K	6	0	6	24.OCT.03	31.OCT.03	-33	
2290	FRC Ground Floor Sab High Level GL 9-11/K-M	10	0	10	23.OCT.03	05.NOV.03	-33	
2300	FRC Ground Floor Slab Low Level GL 12-15/A-L	15	0	15	06.NOV.03	26.NOV.03	-33	
2310	FRC Ground Floor Slab Low Level GL 12-15/L-R	14	0	14	06.NOV.03	25.NOV.03	-33	
2320	FRC Walls From Low - High Lvl GF Slab GL 12,14&K	6	0	6	26.NOV.03	03.DEC.03	-33	
2330	FRC High Level Slab GL 11-14/A-K	8	0	8	27.NOV.03	08.DEC.03	-33	
2340	FRC High Level Slab GL 11-12/K-M	5	0	5	08.DEC.03	12.DEC.03	-33	
2350	FRC Ground Floor Slab GL 15-17/F-R	14	0	14	24.NOV.03	11.DEC.03	-33	
2360	FRC Walls / Columns Ground - 2nd Floor	57	0	57	29.SEP.03	16.DEC.03	-33	
2380	FRC Mezzanine Slab GL 13-17/C-R	11	0	11	17.DEC.03	14.JAN.04	-33	
2390	FRC 2nd Floor Slab GL 7-9/A-J	12	0	12	06.DEC.03	23.OCT.03	-33	
2420	FRC Remainder Of 2nd Floor Slab	12	0	12	15.JAN.04	30.JAN.04	-33	

The critical path
Progress Bar
Critical Activity

MIXED-USE DEVELOPMENT

As Built: as of 4 May.2003
end of WINDOW 5
The Critical Path

APPENDIX 5G b

Activity ID	Activity Description		Orig Dur	% Comp	Rem Dur	Early Start	Early Finish	Total Float	2002 – 2005
2430	FRC Walls / Columns 2nd - 3rd Floor		71	0	71	24.OCT.03	13.FEB.04	-33	
2440	FRC 3rd Floor Slab GL 7-9/L-R		20	0	20	03.DEC.03	13.JAN.04	-33	
2450	FRC 3rd Floor Slab GL 9-14/H-R		17	0	17	13.JAN.04	04.FEB.04	-33	
2460	FRC 3rd Floor Slab GL 14-17/F-R		24	0	24	28.JAN.04	01.MAR.04	-33	
2510	FRC 4th Floor Slab GL 9-15/F-R		18	0	18	11.FEB.04	05.MAR.04	-33	
2570	Concrete Studio Theater Roof		5	0	5	22.MAR.04	26.MAR.04	-33	
2620	Steelwork & Decking Level 4		10	0	10	08.MAR.04	19.MAR.04	-33	
2830	Roofing	Roof Finishes Lvl 4 & 5	61	0	61	05.MAR.04	09.JUN.04	33	
2880	Rooflights	Fitness Centre	15	0	15	29.MAR.04	26.APR.04	-33	
3060		Barriers/Markings	40	0	40	10.DEC.04	17.FEB.05	-33	
3110		Barriers & Marking	20	0	20	21.JAN.05	17.FEB.05	-33	

INTERNAL FINISHES

Activity ID	Activity Description		Orig Dur	% Comp	Rem Dur	Early Start	Early Finish	Total Float	2002 – 2005
2940	Blockwork Partitions/Builders Work		100	0	100	15.MAR.04	11.AUG.04	-33	
2960	Service Installations/Commission		186	0	186	18.MAY.04	17.FEB.05	-33	
2980	Specialist Fit Out Works		153	0	153	05.JUL.04	17.FEB.05	-33	
3050		Walls/Finishes & S	49	0	49	01.NOV.04	20.JAN.05	-33	
3070	Office Area	Fit Out	99	0	99	20.SEP.04	17.FEB.05	-33	
3080	Remaining Retail Areas		1	0	1	17.FEB.05	17.FEB.05	-33	
3100		Finishes & Service	79	0	79	20.SEP.04	20.JAN.05	-33	

EXTERNAL WORKS

Activity ID	Activity Description	Orig Dur	% Comp	Rem Dur	Early Start	Early Finish	Total Float	2002 – 2005
3140	External Pavings Remainder (By Others)	30	0	30	24.DEC.04	17.FEB.05	-33	

SECTIONAL COMPLETIONS

Activity ID	Activity Description	Orig Dur	% Comp	Rem Dur	Early Start	Early Finish	Total Float	2002 – 2005
SECT08	All Others Areas	0	0	0		17.FEB.05	-33	

The critical path
Progress Bar
Critical Activity

MIXED-USE DEVELOPMENT

As Built: as of 4 May.2003
end of WINDOW 5
The Critical Path

APPENDIX 5G b

Sheet 5 of 5

Index